SOCIAL
PSYCHOLOGY
AND
CONTEMPORARY SOCIETY

SOCIAL PSYCHOLOGY AND CONTEMPORARY SOCIETY

Edward E. Sampson

Illustrations by Penelope G. Williams

JOHN WILEY & SONS, INC.

New York   London   Sydney   Toronto

Library of Congress Catalogue Card Number: 76-138918

ISBN 0-471-75117-0

Printed in the United States of America

10 9 8 7 6 5 4 3 2 1

To my mother and father
       who gave me birth and let me grow

To my friends and students
       who gave me cause to try

To my co-conspirators
       who gave me hope that we might make it

PREFACE

The following is an edited transcript of an interview held with the author.

Interviewer: What is this?
Author: A text in social psychology.

I: Another text?

A: Well yes; but this one is different.

I: Sure it is. But why write a textbook?

A: Many's the time I've asked myself that very question.

I: You ever answer it?

A: No, not really.

I: You said that this text is different.

A: That's right. You see, it's not written in the same style as most texts. It's less formal, if you know what I mean. More first person; more anecdotal; more chatty asides—personal comments, analyses, and opinions. I attempt to discuss topics of general social and personal relevance, like population, groups, technology, the media, morality, protest, person perception, ideology.

I: That doesn't sound either like a textbook or like social psychology.

A: In a sense you may be right. That is, if we must stick only to our old categories. But, personally, I think this book represents a transition, encompassing what social psychology is traditionally and pointing to a future direction for the field. It's my version of social.

I: I note that you use some examples from your own experiences, including those at Berkeley.

A: Yes, that's right.

I: Everyone knows that Berkeley is sort of an oddball in an otherwise prosaic universe. Why should we believe that your examples are relevant, say, to a student at Iowa or Mississippi?

A: Good question, and difficult to answer. In the first place, I really don't know if by choosing many of my own experiences, especially around Berkeley, I have gotten too far out and idiosyncratic. On the other hand, I've proceeded on the faith that my experiences and the Berkeley scene are really not that different; perhaps they just highlight problems and themes that exist everywhere today—or if not today, then possibly tomorrow.

I: I also note that you frequently use contemporary incidents. Aren't you afraid that what seems so hot and newsworthy today will simply fade into nothingness by the time people read your book?

A: Another good question. I thought about this carefully. I tried to select contemporary incidents that could have lasting import. Of course, I might have guessed badly. But even more importantly, I noted what passes for examples in other books. For instance, the Ghost Dance of the late 1800's is often cited as an example of a social movement. I asked myself why *that* had lasting value, and decided it was because someone writing a textbook included it in his discussion. Now, why should I talk about Ghost Dances when there is so much happening of immediate relevance? And even if these immediate incidents fade from history books, their life in this text will still serve the purpose of highlighting the processes or theories I am discussing. Do you follow what I'm trying to say?

I: Yes, pretty much. I hadn't thought of it that way before.

A: I know. Neither had I. But when you do, contemporary events, even if not mellowed with age, become every bit as useful for examples as something out of the pages of history.

I: Could we return to an earlier question? Just why did you write this book?

A: I guess I never answered that one, did I?

I: No, not really.

A: Well, it's difficult to say. I think that everyone who has been teaching a course feels he knows best how it should be organized and what it should cover. So you finally almost write your own text just in preparing for your course. Also, I think that I have something to say, and writing a text is one way of getting it out and said. Maybe we're all preachers of sorts; writing a textbook conveys our message.

I: I hear that there's often good money in it for a successful textbook writer.

A: I've heard those stories. I'm certain I won't mind if they're true.

I: Was it difficult to write the book?

A: Unequivocally, yes! What I really mean is that there was so much material to cover, including journals in psychology and sociology and occasionally other disciplines, other textbooks, books of general interest, specific monographs. Even more importantly for me than for most, I monitored weekly magazines and daily newspapers to keep up with current issues. Finally, all of this diverse material had to be put together in some manner. As you must know, a text often makes more sense out of a field than there really is. We're supposed to give order to what often is chaos. Also, I felt it important to take a stand and present a position while writing this book, rather than simply to summarize and report things—though this of course has to be done as well.

I: That's an interesting point. You say you felt you had to take a stand?

A: That's right. I felt that in this text I should raise questions more often than provide simple answers as though I or my field knew these answers. So if you read through it you'll notice that I ask questions and introduce some doubt. Some would say that this shouldn't be done in a textbook, but I feel that the introduction of doubt is an important step to gaining knowledge.

I: Would you say, then, that you hope students come away from this text with some answers but many questions?

A: Yes, I think that's a fair summary of my position.

I: In spite of all this, you still spend considerable time going over research and reports of data. Isn't that too traditional for this type of book?

A: Remember that I don't want to throw out the baby with the bathwater. Some of the traditional material is useful and good; other material highlights a problem or points to a direction for further study. I think that disciplined thinking and careful documentation, though anathema to many modern experiential sorts, are nevertheless essential to any knowledgeable person.

I: For whom did you write this book?

A: Ah, if I understand your question, you want to know if I wrote with a particular audience in mind.

I: That's right.

A: Well, in a sense, I wrote to myself and a handful of students I know. I sort of talked to them through the typewriter. I included material that I find interesting and useful in understanding people. I know that it must sound selfish, but in the end you have yourself and your interests, your views, your peculiar way of thinking about your field; and that's what you have as your guide.

I: Does that mean you never paid attention to others' conceptions of the field?

A: Oh, of course not! That would be absurd. An author is sort of like a politician. He must follow the dictates of his own conscience but at the same time he wants to be effective in reaching others. So you compromise here and there just in order to be heard.

I: Is there anything in particular that you hope students get out of this book?

A: Sure. I hope they get interested in social psychology, excited by its possibilities, not discouraged by its failures or its weaknesses. I hope they begin thinking about themselves and about others; that they try to apply whatever knowledge exists in this book to situations they are familiar with. I guess, deep down, I hope that they get involved in their world and work toward making it a better, more humane place for everyone. Oh, I know, you're going to ask me if I really think that this book can do all of that.

I: Well, I was getting somewhat doubtful.

A: You're absolutely right, of course. A book, like a teacher, in fact, can only open small doors. Neither can force learning; that's up to the student. I guess what I'm really saying is that I hope the student takes this material and does something good with it.

I: What I hear you saying is that you'd be disappointed if the student just read this book, memorized parts of it, fed it back on an examination, and then forgot everything.

A: That's partly right. Not just forgot everything, but *did* nothing. And I know that neither this book nor I can work miracles; but sometimes I feel that miracles are needed. I just hope that some student, somewhere, someday, will do more than simply let his eyes pass over the print and his mind passively vomit up meaningless material. I would like the student to work over the material, bring it to himself and to his situation, and maybe then it will seem less distant and abstract, and maybe then he'll act on his knowledge in some personally and socially beneficial way.

I: Well, our time is just about up. Thank you very much for the interview, Dr. Sampson.

A: You're most welcome, Ed.

Acknowledgments

Although one person, the author, bears the responsibility for writing a book, it never appears in print without the help of many others, including those who have kept the author alive and well and willing to continue during those dark moments when the end, in sight just yesterday, is lost in the rewrites of today and the expected modifications of tomorrow. Sue Fox of the Wiley editorial staff was extraordinarily helpful both as an editor of great merit and, more importantly, as a person I could easily talk with about many things, including the manuscript. All too rapidly I found that my words were being cut (Freud was right), my paragraphs shredded, my neat manuscript (which I thought to be final) marked over in red, blue, and green. I paled and fought off both nausea and a deep sense of outrage. Then I met Sue: a real person, not a machine tooled up to edit. And I knew that the book was in good hands. I sincerely hope that this briefly written public thanks captures the real spirit and full sense of my appreciation for all that Sue has done to help me get this book into print.

Of those who reviewed the manuscript in its initial stages, Dan Katz was especially helpful and kind. He balanced sharp criticism with sufficient positive support to keep me moving along.

I should also like to express my appreciation to those persons who helped type parts of the manuscript—Danielle Rosenman and Denise Oyama—and especially to Pamela Anikeeff for her considerable assistance in getting the references organized and properly checked out. To Marya, I give a special kind of thanks; her patience, help, and love made the final efforts possible.

To be complete, I would also like to acknowledge those music stations that kept pace with my own keyboard antics and those beverages and other types of mind-bender that helped to expunge my academic journal writing style and to free me to write as I more normally think and speak.

Edward E. Sampson

January, 1971

CONTENTS

SOCIAL
PSYCHOLOGY
AND
CONTEMPORARY SOCIETY

Part One

THE KNOWLEDGE PROCESSES: INTRODUCTION AND GENERAL BACKGROUND

It is almost 7 P.M. I luck out and find that last-minute, nearby parking place right across the street from the old Victorian mansion that will serve as our group's meeting place each Monday night. I wonder how many will show up. Who will they be? What will this group be like?

The door is unlocked, swinging open. I pause, toss aside those careful years of training—knock before entering—and plunge inside. People are milling about. Some sit in the corner, burning incense, and chant. One stares at the ceiling. Marvelous world, I think. Where will our group meet? It would be awkward in this public living room. I look about for someone in charge and spot a young woman moving among the assorted people with apparent ease and authority. I introduce myself. She smiles. We chat amiably for a bit, and then she guides me and several others upstairs into our meeting room. No furniture. One bright overhead light and a worn table lamp on the floor. Pillows scattered comfortably around a tattered rug. I grab a spot for myself near the window; they'll be smoking tonight.

Others begin to drift in. Most arrive alone, silently. Heads peer in: "Is this the encounter group?" "Yes." They enter, seeking pillows. Several head toward corners, others move into the more visible middle-room positions. One plops himself in the center of the room and lies prone so that others must step over him. I look around the room and count: including me, twelve; jury size. I get up and close the door. We're ready to begin.

I clear my throat a little awkwardly. It's time for my speech. "Good evening." It comes out nervously, slightly off normal pitch. "This is a self-analytic group. We are all here to learn about ourselves, about others, and about groups in general. We can do whatever we want to while we meet here. It's up to us to decide. Our only goal is to understand ourselves and others."

I sit back quietly. Now it's in their hands; I've done my bit for the time being. I wonder who'll take the lead. Silence. Laughter, the nervous, little-girl giggly kind. Two-by-two small chat, always an easy substitute for addressing the entire group. More silence. Will anyone take the lead? It's not easy. Unstructured situation. Does anything go? They wait and wonder. Silence. Laughter. Two-chat. And then someone begins to speak. You can almost feel the tension of the group recede—the personal burden of responsibility is removed; someone else has taken that first step. . . .

He introduces himself: first name . . . last name . . . "I'm a student . . . a junior . . . major . . . sociology." Silence again. I wonder: Will this be the way it is tonight? They too must wonder. How do you get it going with twelve people? Across the room a girl, fidgeting nervously in her chair, looks up and breaks this silence. She offers only her first name, but she smiles, looks friendly. Others relax. Then one by one, around the room, first names are cast out.

The introductions have been made. Silence again takes over. I speak: "I wonder what's happening? That is, I wonder what we are all thinking and *feeling* right now?" Several heads suddenly jerk upward; eyes eagerly search for the one who will answer me. The bold one— he broke that first silence—answers:

"I'm feeling sort of anxious . . . you know what I mean? Well . . . because, I guess I don't know what I'm suppposed to do . . . here. I mean that . . . well . . . I just don't know if we're supposed to talk, or just what." He addresses all of his remarks to me. "And . . . if it's talk, then, about what?" He pauses and looks around the room. Several others nod in agreement. A few agree, "uh-huh." No one volunteers to follow up. He continues, apparently speaking for many of the others in the group, expressing feelings they have but cannot as easily express.

"I guess that I'm feeling sort of scared, you know, of the rest of you." He pauses again, waiting for some reaction to that comment. Someone across the room repeats, "scared?" "Well, yes . . . but . . . it's not a fear that you'll get up and punch me or something foolish like that." They all laugh nervously. "No, not that, really . . . it's more of a worry . . . yeah, that's it, more of a worry than scared. A worry about not knowing what to expect from him [he points to me] and from the rest of you. Yeah, that's it . . . I guess I just don't know what to make of this entire situation . . . here we all are . . . a bunch of unknowns in an unknown situation. And that scares . . . I mean . . . it worries me."

Strangers have come together in a situation that they see as relatively ambiguous, confusing,

and replete with several unknowns. They are trying to make some sense out of this situation, give it some meaning, some order, some sense of predictability. They are trying to understand this single slice of time in their lives. How do they proceed? There are twelve people, perhaps from diverse backgrounds. Many unknowns are built into the situation. Strangers: What are they like? What will they do? What do they think? How will they respond to me? How will I respond to them? What are the guidelines, the rules, the norms that govern this group in this encounter?

To come to some understanding of this often madly complex event called man: that is our goal as social psychologists, and clearly that is the goal of the members of that group, even in their very first encounter. But by what means shall we approach this goal? In the first part of this book we focus our attention on what is perhaps best called the *knowledge processes*, the means whereby each of us comes to know, define, order, construct, or transform his physical and social environments. In that group of twelve persons each may be seen as seeking to come to know the situation; to define it in such a way that he may act in it; to give some order and meaning to it; to construct it in ways that for him are understandable and follow at least his own logic of thinking and knowing.

IMPLICIT PERSONALITY THEORY

Throughout this section we are interested in the actual contents of an individual's knowledge system. What are the assumptions he makes about himself and others? What are the beliefs he holds? His opinions? His attitudes? What concepts does he employ to define situations? We are thus concerned with *what* he knows. In addition, we are concerned with *how* he knows. By what techniques or rules does a person process the material of his knowledge system? How are the contents transformed, interrelated, modified, operated on by the individual?

Let us return briefly to the group and see this *what* and *how* of the knowledge system in operation. We have one member's direct statement about the content of his knowledge system concerning this group encounter. For him it is a frightening situation. Had we listened to more of the group's early interaction, we would have noted that each member eventually offered his own preliminary assessment of the situation. We would have seen, for example, that one of the girls viewed the entire situation as sexually threatening; one of the other males saw it primarily in terms of competition for leadership; another female saw it as an opportunity to be with friendly people. Of course, even if an individual had not told us how he saw the situation, we might very well have inferred his perceptions from his actions. For example, we might assume that an individual who cuts in when others are speaking, who takes every opportunity to be in the spotlight, and who continually seeks to push the group in directions he finds pleasing defines the situation primarily in terms of aggressive competition.

With increasing contact with this group we soon would be interested in enumerating the particular *concepts* or *constructs* each one uses in defining the situation, himself, and the other group members. We would note, for example, that for some members the other people are either "good" or "bad," whereas other members employ a more highly differentiated set of person-defining concepts; the emotions of some members are either happiness or extreme sorrow, whereas for others a wider range of emotions exists; for some, the relationships they have with others may be defined in terms of "winner-loser" or "man with power and control" versus "weakling"; others may have a more variable repertoire of concepts for defining relationships.

We would note, in addition, that some constructs used for defining the situation are specific to a given individual, whereas others, like cultural stereotypes, are shared by many. For example, one group member may look at a neatly dressed, well-coiffured, blond young lady across the room and see a sorority-girl stereotype. He may expect her, according to the stereotype, to be a rather shallow, superficial person with somewhat conventional values and sense of morality. Of course he may be entirely mistaken. Nevertheless, he may proceed for some time to relate to her in terms of that

stereotypic definition. Another member, by contrast, may see the same girl as just the type he'd like to marry—someone neat, smiling, and friendly—a conception perhaps unique to his own world view.

It seems out of vogue nowadays to speak of culturally shared stereotypes or, for that matter, to admit that any sophisticated person even possesses stereotypic concepts of others. Alas, although we would like to treat each person as a completely unique entity, most of us tend to build conceptual models of the world that hold a great deal of shared meaning; we use the shorthand of stereotypes, at least until we get to know another person in a more highly differentiated way.

In 1933 Katz and Braly provided us with a study of racial stereotypes in college students. They asked Princeton undergraduates to select traits from a prepared list to characterize 10 racial and national groups, and found extensive use of classic stereotypes. For example, the students rated Germans as scientifically minded, industrious, stolid; Italians as artistic, impulsive, passionate, quick-tempered; Negroes as superstitious, lazy, happy-go-lucky; Jews as shrewd, mercenary, industrious, grasping; the list of stereotypes goes on and on. A replication of the Katz and Braly work (Gilbert, 1951), again with Princeton college students, showed both a general stability of the stereotypes over time (between 1933 and 1951) and an increasing unwillingness of the subjects to admit to any such thing as a stereotype.

In addition to the concepts they employ, we are interested in examining the *assumptions* or *hypotheses* individuals make about themselves, about the situation, and about others in their group. For example, some person in the encounter group may assume (or hypothesize) that anyone who disagrees with majority opinion will be subjected to painful ostracism. At this point we are less concerned with the truth or falsity of this assumption than we are interested in its actual content. As another example, we may find that some group members hold the hypothesis (or guess, or hunch) that people who speak precisely, loudly, and with reasonably good grammar are strong, calm persons, generally lacking any problems. Again, this hunch may be incorrect; nevertheless, to understand their behavior in this situation we find it helpful to know about it.

After careful analysis, we would note that each member of the group appears to possess what has been referred to as an *implicit theory of personality*. Each has concepts or constructs that define other people; assumptions about psychology and human nature; hypotheses that link one set of concepts with another. Each person, it seems, is a common-sense psychologist complete with his own theory of human behavior and his own empirical data, based on his experiences, to support this theory. And he uses this personality theory in his encounters with others.

Several interesting efforts have been undertaken by social psychologists to uncover and examine our implicit personality theories (see, e.g., Asch, 1952; Cronbach, 1958; Crockett, 1965; Heider, 1958). Much of this work is derived from a context not unlike that provided by our small-group example. How are first impressions of others formed? We meet a group of strangers. After even a brief moment's encounter we come away with an impression of those persons. To be sure, some of them leave fleeting impressions; we may not even recall meeting them. Some exist in our memory only as stereotypes. Others offer us, somehow, a fairly lasting, detailed first impression.

If a psychologist asks us to describe the people we just met we may very well resist, arguing that it is impossible to describe persons met for so brief a time. What we are probably saying is that, rather than being impossible, it is not desirable; as men of good reason we do not want to be held *that* accountable for the first impressions we have of others and they have of us. We do not want to think of ourselves as users of stereotypes. Once we come to realize, however, that each of us *is* a first-impression former, and that indeed it is no sin to be so, we may find it profitable to examine the nature of those impressions.

How is it that we take one or two small bits of information from a person and from those infer what is often a full story about him or her? It is an amazing feat of human thought; apparently such feats are commonplace and are to

be understood best from the perspective of an implicit personality theory. A rough analogy may make aspects of this matter clearer. Recall your visits to your family doctor. You enter with some vague upset or complaint. He sits you down and begins his inquiry. "Does it hurt when I push in here?" "How about here?" From this and possibly one or two other pieces of information he makes a diagnosis, writes a prescription, and sends you on your way. Essentially, he has employed a theory of illness to give meaning to the few *cues* (symptoms) you present.

The process, although we hope of finer precision than our own first-impression formation, is based on a similar type of thinking mechanism. A theory exists (later we shall be concerned with how it comes to be); specific cues, symptoms, or bits of information are noted. The theory orders these bits of information and allows a diagnosis or interpretation to be made. The propositions that form an essential base of the theory provide building blocks that permit us to infer a more complete diagnosis or interpretation from one or a few bits of information. Propositions, which formally stated might read, "If A, then B," allow us, therefore, to infer that given the presence of A (e.g., a pain in the side of the neck), it is likely that B (e.g., some swelling in the lymph nodes), will also occur. These separate propositions and inferences in turn build into more complex sequences, resulting finally in a diagnosis: Mumps!

In the interpersonal arena our implicit personality theory provides propositions that order the bits of data we receive from or about another person and out of which an impression emerges. Someone you meet for the very first time shakes your hand with great force and vigor and looks you straight in the eye. These few bits of information might very well lead you to rate him as honest, strong, forthright, confident, friendly. Another stranger, who greets you with eyes downcast, seemingly searching for meaning in his shoelaces, and who has a handshake reminiscent of warmed-over oatmeal, might be rated as lacking self-confidence, weak, shifty, unfriendly, shy. Of course you might be incorrect in your first impressions, or at best only partially correct. Nevertheless, note how two pieces of information, strength of handshake and direction of eyes, are often used in a particular implicit personality theory to reach fairly extensive conclusions about another person.

Research on implicit personality theory

Efforts by social psychologists to study implicit personality theories in the controlled setting of the laboratory occurred rather late in the history of systematic research in person perception. For the most part, early investigations of how we perceive others were concerned primarily with the *accuracy* of our perceptions (see Bruner & Tagiuri, 1954, for a summary of this early work). Were some persons better perceivers than others? Did we perceive others as they "really" were? What they "really" were was usually defined in terms of consensual criteria; at other times they were "really" what they described themselves to be. Think for a moment of the complexity of seemingly simple statements concerning what a person "really is."

Without getting into the details of philosophical speculation, the assessment of the accuracy of our perception of another person requires some specification of the criteria for accuracy, some details concerning his "real" qualities. This is no easy matter, although it is usually solved by comparing our judgment of his traits with his own judgment or the judgment of some experts or some averaged group of raters.

Although I shall not review the research literature, it is relevant to note that as long as *accuracy* of perception remained the major concern, notions of implicit personality theory were shunted aside. A personal, common-sense theory of personality might be accurate or inaccurate in perceiving others; if *accuracy* is the thing to be studied, the *process* whereby one makes inferences and forms impressions of others only gets in the way.

In a highly valuable critique of much of this earlier work on person perception, Cronbach (1958; Gage & Cronbach, 1955) suggested that one of the major areas in need of detailed study involved the determination of each individual's *personal map* of the world of other people: his implicit personality theory. The early work, of which Cronbach was so appropriately critical,

asked a person (called a *judge*) to make judgements about another *(target)* person on a rating checklist of descriptive adjectives. A *discrepancy score* was computed between the judge's rating of that target person and the ratings given by other judges. From this an accuracy score could be obtained; did this judge rate the target person in ways similar to others' ratings of the target?

The discrepancy score, as Cronbach suggested, conceals several separable factors within it. For example, this particular judge may have a tendency—which we refer to as his implicit personality theory—to rate *all* target persons in a certain manner. Let us assume that the rating scales include the terms INTELLIGENT, BRAVE, HONEST, REASONABLE, SINCERE, GOOD. This judge may have a tendency to see the traits INTELLIGENT and GOOD correlated in all persons; that is, one aspect of his own mapping of others is to group together certain traits, so that whenever he decides someone is INTELLIGENT he also decides that person is GOOD. Such an intertwining of his ratings reflects more about him and the way he thinks about people than it necessarily reveals anything about the target person. If our interest were only in his accuracy of person perception, we would undoubtedly overlook this correlation and rate him as sometimes accurate, sometimes inaccurate, depending on how the two traits, INTELLIGENT–GOOD, varied within the target population. We would have ignored a highly significant aspect of psychological data: the judge's own knowledge processes.

Passini and Norman (1966) offer us some interesting insights into this matter of implicit personality theory. Suppose you have several groups of persons who have interacted with each other for different periods of time; some groups have been together in close association for a period of three days, others for periods as long as three years. You present these individuals with a set of rating scales that includes pairs of opposite descriptive adjectives: TALKATIVE–SILENT; GOOD-NATURED–IRRITABLE; RESPONSIBLE–UNDEPENDABLE; POISED–NERVOUS; POLISHED, REFINED–CRUDE, BOORISH. You ask each person to use a peer-nomination technique to "nominate" a certain number of persons from his group he feels are described by one pole of each descriptive pair and a certain number who are described by the other pole of the pair. For example, say each member nominates three persons in his group whom he would describe as TALKATIVE and another three whom he would describe as SILENT. After all members complete this peer-nomination task, you—the psychological researcher—conduct what is known as a *factor analysis* of the resulting rating data.

Essentially, factor analysis is a statistical data-reduction and analysis technique that seeks to "explain" an array of data by discovering major *factors* that will account for the actual distribution of data. Let us say that you have obtained 75 separate measurements on a given individual, among them height, weight, age, place of birth, father's occupation and education, mother's occupation and education, year in school, parent's income, and religion. You wonder if these 75 separate measures group themselves together into any particular pattern. Is there some correspondence or correlation between certain items to form subsets of the total set of 75 measurements? Through factor analysis you can get an empirical answer to this question. You intercorrelate each of the 75 separate measures with every other measure, and by one of several different methods of factor analysis, extract factors that will group these 75 separate measures into clusters. You might find, for example, that all the *physical* measures cluster together in one factor (e.g., height, weight, age), and that another cluster or factor is *socioeconomic status* (relating to parents' occupation, education, and income).

If you wish to go into the method in more detail you will find texts by Fruchter (1954) and Harman (1967) useful. For our purposes, however, it is important only that you gain an intuitive appreciation of the aim of the method: to reduce a large set of data into interrelated subsets, which are variously referred to as clusters or factors.

Passini and Norman subjected the ratings each group completed to a factor analysis. In several different studies the results of this analysis revealed a stable pattern in which *five* major factors emerge. These factors are pre-

sented in Table 1 by name and sample item content; a glance through the table will add to the understanding of factor analysis. As can be readily seen, the ratings can be reduced to five major clusters. This suggests, for example, that when persons rate others as TALKATIVE they are also *likely* to rate them as OPEN and SOCIABLE, or that when someone is rated as GOOD-NATURED he is also *likely* to be rated as COOPERATIVE and MILD. Furthermore, the correspondences *within* clusters are greater than the correspondences *between* clusters. Thus TALKATIVE-OPEN-SOCIABLE correspond more closely to one another than they do to GOOD-NATURED-MILD-COOPERATIVE.

Table 1 Factor structure of peer-nomination rating studies

Factor I	Extroversion or surgency:	e.g., TALKATIVE-SILENT OPEN-SECRETIVE ADVENTUROUS-CAUTIOUS SOCIABLE-RECLUSIVE
Factor II	Agreeableness:	e.g., GOOD-NATURED-IRRITABLE NOT JEALOUS-JEALOUS MILD, GENTLE-HEADSTRONG COOPERATIVE-NEGATIVISTIC
Factor III	Conscientiousness:	e.g., FUSSY, TIDY-CARELESS RESPONSIBLE-UNDEPENDABLE SCRUPULOUS-UNSCRUPULOUS-PERSEVERING-QUITTING
Factor IV	Emotional stability:	e.g., POISED-NERVOUS, TENSE CALM-ANXIOUS COMPOSED-EXCITABLE
Factor V	Culture:	e.g., ARTISTICALLY SENSI-TIVE-NOT ARTISTI-CALLY SENSITIVE INTELLECTUAL-UNREFLECTIVE, NARROW POLISHED, REFINED-CRUDE, BOORISH IMAGINATIVE-SIMPLE, DIRECT

Of particular interest to us is the finding that these *same* five factors have emerged in several different studies using different populations of subjects with different amounts of personal contact (from three days to three years—Norman, 1963; Tupes & Christal, 1961). Of even greater interest (and puzzlement) is that longer periods of contact apparently produce hardly any difference in the stability of these factors when compared with relatively brief contacts. The question, then, is whether these ratings reflect some quality of the persons being rated —as we initially assume they do—or whether, perhaps, the factors primarily reflect the judges' own implicit personality theory. Have we uncovered five factors on which a person's behavior may be rated, or have we uncovered five factors that most judges use when rating others?

To seek an answer to this question, Passini and Norman (1966) replicated some of this earlier work. The basic design and format of the Passini and Norman study followed in most of its essentials the procedures of other work in this area. One major difference was that they used persons who had been in contact with one another for less than 15 minutes. At the first regular class meeting of each introductory experimental psychology course they asked students to nominate others in that class for the several descriptive ratings. They sought rather successfully to ensure that there had been no prior contact between members of these classes and that, in fact, they had not even interacted verbally in class. Picture yourself, if you will, faced with this task. You arrive alone for the very first meeting of your psychology class. The instructor almost immediately asks you to complete ratings of others in your class along dimensions like those in Table 1. "But," you complain, if only to yourself, "I don't know any of them and they don't know me." The instructor says, "We need these data from strangers to use as a baseline against which to compare data from better-acquainted samples of students." So you and the others complete the ratings, which are then subjected to a factor analysis.

If the results from this factor analysis are very similar to the results obtained from the earlier studies, what then would be a reasonable answer to our initial inquiry? If total strangers produce the same kinds of rating of each other as do long-term acquaintances, might we not appropriately conclude that we have obtained data more relevant to the psychological structure of the raters than to the characteristics of the ratees? This result and this conclusion are, in fact, Passini and Norman's. They report a high degree of similarity between the factor structure produced by total strangers and that produced by longer-term acquaintances. To account for these results, they turn to the Cronbach concept of implicit personality theory. They suggest, and I agree, that each judge brings with him to the classroom an implicit personality theory that (1) "tells" him what traits go together with what other traits in people in general; and that (2) he apparently shares roughly with others of his group. Both notions aid our understanding of the Passini and Norman results. We assume it is the individual's implicit personality theory that produces the same five-factor structure whether strangers or friends are rated; and we assume further that *interrater agreement* (agreement among judges) stems from the sharing within a given group and perhaps within a given culture of a relatively common framework of such implicit theories. These shared factors are not necessarily correlated with racial or group stereotypes, but they function in a similar manner. Each allows us to work from a small base of data about another to an impression of that other person. Each, so to speak, sets the limits within which our interpersonal inference process works.

Dornbusch, Hastorf, Richardson, Muzzy, & Vreeland (1965), using a free-response method for obtaining person descriptions, came up with a similar conclusion. In a free-response method, unlike the Passini and Norman studies, the investigator asks *P* (the perceiver) to describe *O* (the other person), using whatever terms he wishes (see Beach & Wertheimer, 1961, for another example of this method). Dornbusch and his associates conducted their research at several summer camps, asking each child at the camps to describe selected target children: "Tell me about Johnny Doe." Their answers to this interview question were tape-recorded and later analyzed for content. Of special interest to implicit personality theory is the analysis of descriptive categories employed when two different Ps describe the same O. By comparing the amount of overlap in such descriptions with responses when one P describes two different Os or two Ps describe two different Os, it is possible to uncover the relative importance of the perceiver and the perceived in determining the kind of impression that is formed. Dornbusch's results led him to conclude, ". . . our findings indicate that the most powerful influence on interpersonal description is the manner in which the perceiver structures his interpersonal world" (p. 440). Clearly this conclusion, consistent with the Passini and Norman findings, argues that implicit personality theory is an important determinant of the manner by which we structure and organize our perceptions of other persons. It is the perceiver more than the perceived that affects the kinds of perception we have of others.

By way of summary

Up to this point we have seen that to gain an understanding of human social behavior—as, for example, in the encounter group at the beginning of the chapter—it is helpful to understand how people subjectively know or define the situations and persons they encounter. Each of us carries around a set of constructs or concepts and a series of operations by which we utilize these concepts—a common-sense, implicit personality theory. Together the concepts and the operations are employed in our process of coming to know our world. This implicit theory guides our dealings with other persons, especially in coming to form impressions of them. The concepts of our implicit theory employ trait names or descriptive adjectives to characterize others; the theory's assumptions, propositions, and general modes of operation permit us to group traits, impute motives, interpret causes of behavior, and so on.

THE GESTALT FORMULATION OF IMPRESSION FORMATION

We are now ready to consider one major view concerning the mode of operation of the implicit personality theory; we turn to the pioneering conceptions and research of Asch. To help us gain a fuller understanding of Asch's orientation —with which I am also attuned—it will be helpful to place his ideas briefly in a larger historical context. Asch is associated with the *Gestalt* approach to psychology. We shall find that much of the contemporary work in cognition (the knowledge processes) owes its heritage to this Gestalt school. A brief summary of anything so complex as an entire school or approach to psychology is of necessity incomplete; nevertheless, a grasp of the distinction between the Gestalt approach and the Associationist approach with which it is contrasted will be useful to an understanding both of Asch's work and of other work discussed throughout this part of the book.

The early British Associationists—among them Locke, Hume, Berkeley—were philosophers interested in understanding how people come to learn about their world. They offered a doctrine, particularly in the form espoused by Locke, that man at birth has a mind like an empty slate (a blank tablet or *tabula rasa*); sensory experience "writes" on it, leaving behind messages in the form of simple ideas.

Gestalt psychology emerged from a different philosophical tradition; it was especially influenced by doctrines (e.g., those of Kant and Leibniz) that emphasized innate ideas as the initial state of man's mind. Rather than being born a total blank to be written on by sensory experiences, man came prepackaged within certain ideas, that is, with certain *categories* or *schemata*. These pre-experiential categories gave a structure to incoming sensory experience; they reshaped or transformed the sensory event to varying degrees.

In addition, the Gestaltists emphasized the *Gestalt qualities* that complex wholes possess. Sometimes this point has been stated—overstated at that—as, "The whole is greater than the sum of its parts." It is not possible to reduce the whole to its parts and still retain the meaning that the whole as an entity possesses; a new property emerges that is not the same as the elemental ingredients. To study complex forms of behavior, then, we are compelled to study the *emergent whole* with its unique properties. A triangle, for example, is said to have the emergent property of triangularity. According to the Gestaltists we should study the property of triangularity apart from the separate lines that are its elements. In the area of group dynamics, of which more will be said later (Chapters 19 & 20), the Gestalt argument is that a group has emergent properties that must be understood apart from the properties that any of its constituent parts—its individual members—possesses.

The Asch formulation

In a manner guaranteed not to endear him to the loyal opposition, but that helped to highlight the Gestalt approach to impression formation, Asch (1952) erected a straw-man associationistic-type theory, which he then proceeded to destroy. If asked how we form an impression of another person, Asch's straw man would answer: "Well, we note certain traits that they possess and then we just add them together. And that's our impression. We note, for example, that Andrew is TRUSTWORTHY; he is also HELPFUL; and finally, he is very NEAT. And so our impression of Andrew is HELPFUL + TRUSTWORTHY + NEAT."

By contrast, Asch's Gestalt formulation suggests that the impression we have of another is a *dynamic whole*, in which the several trait elements interact to create a new emergent: our impression. By examining several of the studies Asch conducted we can gain further knowledge of the manner by which each of our implicit theories of personality operates.

You are given a set of terms said to describe a person and are asked to write a sketch of that person. You are told that he is INTELLIGENT, SKILLFUL, INDUSTRIOUS, WARM, DETERMINED, PRACTICAL, CAUTIOUS. Now, form an impression of this person and write your sketch.

What, however, if you are given a list that reads INTELLIGENT, SKILLFUL, INDUSTRIOUS, COLD, DETERMINED, PRACTICAL, CAUTIOUS? Form an impression of this person and write your sketch.

This describes perhaps the most classic of all of Asch's impression-formation studies. He presented one group of students with the first list and another group with the second list. Note that the lists differ only in one element: WARM

versus COLD. On completion of their written sketches Asch had the students select, from a checklist of pairs of traits, those that best fitted the impression they had formed. An examination of the traits selected by the two different groups revealed some striking differences. For example, the WARM group more frequently saw the person as generous, good-natured, humorous, and popular than did the COLD group. In general, Asch reports, the WARM group saw the person in a more favorable light than did the COLD group.

An important point in the Gestalt argument is that certain personal traits, such as the WARM–COLD dimension, are *central* to the process of impression formation. Being central, in the Gestalt formulation, means that such traits provide a key theme around which other characteristics are built. Central traits have a drawing and a shaping power, effectively transforming the meaning of other subsidiary traits with which they interact. For example, the trait DETERMINED in combination with WARM is said to have a different meaning than in combination with COLD. It is not the same DETERMINED. When DETERMINED is keyed around the central trait COLD, for example, the impression that emerges is harsh and negative—a driving, perhaps ruthless person. By contrast a WARM and DETERMINED person might be seen as highly motivated, enthusiastic, a doer. This is the essence of the Gestalt interpretation of most psychological phenomena; because of the interaction that occurs when certain traits are combined, it is inappropriate simply to add a single trait willy-nilly to other single traits in an effort to form a complex impression.

Asch is not the only one who obtained such results using the WARM–COLD dimension. Kelley (1950) attempted to test the formulation in a "live" situation, and provided substantial support for the differential impact of WARM and COLD as central traits. He provided two descriptions of a visiting lecturer to his class; these were identical except that as part of the description one group of students received the passage, "people who know him consider him to be a rather cold person . . .," whereas the other group received the same passage with "warm" inserted. All were asked to write free descriptions of the speaker and to use a check-list, as with the original Asch study. Kelley reports findings much like those reported by Asch.

In an effort to demonstrate that central traits provide the Gestalt interaction effect, whereas peripheral traits do not, Asch replicated his original study, but this time he used what he felt were more peripheral traits in the list: POLITE versus BLUNT. With these traits he reports only slight differences between his two groups of students; those in the POLITE group described a person much like the person described by the BLUNT group.

Before we move on, one further impression-formation study by Asch deserves mention. This study is concerned primarily with the impact of first impressions on later ones, in terms of Asch's Gestalt formulation.

One manner of studying first-impression formation is to view the process in terms of the *order* in which impression data are received. Suppose, for example, that you present a list of descriptive terms to two separate groups; each list contains precisely the same terms, differing only in their order. Would the different order of presentation produce two entirely distinct impressions? Asch presented one group with the following list: INTELLIGENT, INDUSTRIOUS, IMPULSIVE, CRITICAL, STUBBORN, ENVIOUS. Another group received the same list in reverse order, starting with ENVIOUS and ending with INTELLIGENT. Asch reports differences between the two groups in the impressions formed: "In general, the impression from Series A [INTEL-LIGENT first] is that of an able person who possesses certain shortcomings. . . . On the other hand, B [ENVIOUS first] impresses the majority as a problem whose abilities are hampered by his serious difficulties" (1952, p. 212).

As with the WARM–COLD study, the Gestalt interpretation of these findings emphasizes how first information induces a direction that shapes the second bit of information, and so on. To begin with INTELLIGENT sets a direction that gives the second term, INDUSTRIOUS, a meaning that it does not possess when it appears toward the end of a list begun with ENVIOUS.

In one reanalysis of the Asch work, Wishner (1960) sought to replicate aspects of the pre-ceding study. He had a list of traits read to his subjects (e.g., SKILLFUL, INDUSTRIOUS, DE-TERMINED, PRACTICAL, CAUTIOUS), with INTELLIGENT inserted into the list in the first, third, and sixth positions respectively for three different groups. Three entirely different groups received UNINTELLIGENT in those same posi-tions. His first results indicated that, regardless of where in the list INTELLIGENT, or UNINTEL-LIGENT appeared, the effect on the descrip-tions was the same. There was no difference as a function of order of presentation, a result in apparent conflict with Asch's original finding.

The present state of the art of the social sciences is such that we should not be surprised or terribly distraught when we encounter results from attempted replications that fail to repli-cate. Unfortunately, it is rarely, if ever, known, just why one researcher gets positive results when another does not. Although we shall have more to say about this at other points in the book, it is important for you to have a sense now of the kinds of factor that make replications difficult; to mention but a few: subjects differ; experimenters differ; procedures differ; cultures and subcultures differ. Perhaps, after all, we should be more surprised to find two different experimenters, using two different groups of subjects and slightly different procedures at two different periods in history (e.g., Asch did his work in the 1940's; Wishner, in the 1960's) ever getting roughly similar results!

Another point that by now must have irked several of you concerns the experimental approaches taken to uncover the dynamics of impression formation. "What the hell," you might ask, "does forming an impression on the basis of a list of words have to do with real impression formation, *out there* [pointing with vigor] in the real world?" To tell the truth, we really do not have a very good answer to this query. Most clearly, however, if we are inter-ested in isolating the effects of order on the nature of the impression formed, we must create an artificial situation in which order can be experimentally manipulated. Although the real world may never provide as neatly packaged an arrangement as we study in the laboratory, at least we have some intuitive reason to believe that order affects impressions in reality as well as in the lab. It is our hope, of course, that what we learn in the laboratory will *generalize* to the kinds of process that occur as we form impressions of others in the more complex context of our daily lives.

It is a somewhat unfortunate truth that some psychologists of all persuasions become enraptured by the games of laboratory research to such an extent that they cease being concerned with whether their findings apply to any world other than that of college sophomores seeking course credit by serving as subjects in experiments. Nevertheless, I personally feel that Asch's efforts, although clearly removed from real-life encounters, offer us a most useful examination of what that complex process of impression formation must be like. To be sure, it is undoubtedly more complex and detailed than his work reveals; yet there is good reason to believe that it proceeds according to the kinds of principle Asch has outlined.

Lest you worry that we have deserted our self-analytic group meeting in that old Victorian house, let us reflect on it briefly before moving ahead. We have argued to this point that each member of that group has an implicit personality theory, his own hard-won, do-it-yourself psychology kit. And as each sits there on Monday night, seeking to know the situation in which he finds himself, he is undoubtedly giving a good workout to that implicit theory. He has already formed first impressions of the others; they have formed impressions of him. These impressions may be based partly on what he looks like, what he says (or does not say), and what he does; and they will be based partly on each "judge's" own theory, each person's own particular set of concepts and procedures for processing interpersonal information.

FROM KNOWLEDGE TO BEHAVIOR

By now you may be wondering why we have been so interested in the individual's perceptual-cognitive knowledge processes. *Why do we care* how he knows that group, forms impressions of others, or uses his implicit theory to assess and define the situation? Much of our interest, and that of a long line of philosophers, psychologists, and social psychologists, hinges on a single, seemingly self-evident, and essentially simple assumption: If we know how a person perceives his world, we shall understand both how he will behave in that world and the reasons why. We shall see this proposition in action throughout much of this book. Lewin (1951), whose work is central to our later concerns with group processes (see Chapter 19), put it as follows:

"The food that lies behind doors at the end of a maze so that neither smell nor sight can reach it is not a part of the life space of the animal. If the individual knows that food lies there this *knowledge*, of course, has to be represented in his life space, because this knowledge affects behavior. . . . Indeed, the individual will start his journey if he thinks the food is there even if it is actually not there, and he will not move toward the food which actually is at the end of the maze if he does not know it is there" (pp. 57–58).

To understand the *why* of behavior, then, we must understand the *what* of the psychological environment or life space; and this holds whether we are talking about rats or men.

Kelly's approach

The work and writings of G. A. Kelly (1955; 1963), although centered primarily in the area of personality theory, are nevertheless relevant to our concern with the knowledge processes. Kelly's approach to the study of personality emphasizes what he refers to as the individual's *personal constructs*. A *personal construct* is a model, format, or schema that provides a psychological representation of the environment; the environment, represented to the individual through his system of personal constructs, becomes a world of alternative pathways for action. From Kelly's perspective, the issue to which psychologists who seek to explain human behavior should address themselves is the manner by which an individual's action is directed by the constructs he employs to anticipate events in the physical and social world; Kelly sees man as actively engaged in *construing* his environment rather than (as in more mechanistic approaches to psychology such as a stimulus-response approach) merely reacting to an already presented world. Having construed an aspect of the environment in a particular fashion, the individual defines the nature of the situation in which he is located, the available routes for his action within that situation, and the rules of psycho-logic by which his behavior in that situation is to be guided.

An analyst using this perspective would argue that if one has construed the situation in a particular fashion, his consequent behavior makes good sense. It is understandable and it is logical: it follows *his* rules for coping with *his* environment. Rather than seeing a person as driven by total illogic, blind passion, madness, or whatever other such point of view one might take, a personal-construct analyst would look for the underlying system of construed logic that exists in even the most bizzare (by our definition) behavior. He would argue that behavior that to us is bizarre is actually intelligible if we know the way the person has construed his world.

An example might help at this point to clarify matters. Two people are conversing; we shall call them Reginald and Margaret.

R: Margaret? Hi! Say, what may I call you for short?
M: I beg your pardon?
R: I asked what your nickname was.
M: People rarely use my nickname.
R: Nice day isn't it?
M: Yes, it is.
R: Have you been waiting here very long?
M: Not very.
R: Neither have I.
M: That's nice.
R: Seen any good movies lately?
M: No.
R: There's a good picture playing tonight.
M: That's nice
R: Really top stars, top story, top director. I'm going to see it.
M: That's nice
R: You really ought to see it, you know. I bet you'd like it.
M: I probably would, but I'm so busy.
R: Oh, that's too bad.
M: Not really.
R: Well, I've got to be going now. See you.

How can we understand the manner by which they have construed this situation? Let us suppose that we have gotten inside their heads and are now looking over that same dialogue, but this time with the construal process pushed to the surface.

R: *(I've seen that girl in class. She sits off there in the corner most of the time by herself. I don't think I've ever seen anyone walking with her. Not even talking to her. I bet she's lonely. Possibly even frightened. I think her name's Margaret. Maybe I'll stop and chat with her a bit before my next class.)* Margaret? Hi! Say, what may I call you for short?
M: *(Oh, that boy is trying to pick me up. I just wish people would leave me alone.)* I beg your pardon?
R: *(Strikes me that she's lonely because she's sort of a cold fish. Well, maybe I shouldn't think of it that way. Sure, she's probably scared of me.)* I asked what your nickname was.
M: *(Why does he want to know my name? I wish he'd buzz off. I can't stand boys with acne anyway. Looks like a slob to me. Such a crude technique. I'll cool him off before he gets started.)* People rarely use my nickname.
R: *(Boy, is that the old freeze! Such sarcasm. You'd almost think that she thought I was going to rape her right here. I only wanted to be friendly and strike up a conversation. Well, I'll give it one more try.)* Nice day isn't it?
M: *(Nice day isn't it? Boy, does he want to make conversation with me! I wonder why? I just don't trust him. Why does he want to talk with me? I'm not attractive, not at all. Boys never like me. I think he's got something on his mind. I just don't trust him; not at all.)* Yes, it is.
R: Have you been waiting here very long?
M: Not very.
R: Neither have I.
M: That's nice.
R: *(That's it! Sure. She's not really scared of me, she's just being coy. I should have known. She just looks like a naive innocent. She's waiting for me to take the first step. Well, I'll test this one out and see.)* Seen any good movies lately?
M: *(I knew it! That's what he wants to do, get me in the dark movie theater. I don't trust him. I wish he'd just leave me alone. I hate to be rude, but I can't believe that he really wants to take me out to a movie. He just wants to fool around. That's it. I'm certain of it. It's not me he wants. No one wants me.)* No.
R: *(Well, perhaps she'd like to go to a show tonight.)* There's a good picture playing tonight.
M: That's nice.
R: Really top stars, top story, top director. I'm going to see it.
M: That's nice.

R: (*Well, I'm not sure anymore. She's not picking up on any of these chances I've given her. She's not interested in me. That must be it. My acne. I've got to work on that soon, no more chocolates. Maybe I'm just too crude in my approach.*) You really ought to see it, you know. I bet you'd like it.

M: (*Well! now he's begging off. Finally. Now maybe he'll just let me be by myself.*) I probably would, but I'm so busy.

R: (*Busy! Hah! She just doesn't want to go out with me. I thought she was so lonely and scared. That's a joke. Probably got hundreds of boyfriends. What's wrong with me?*) Oh, that's too bad.

M: (*Bad! I'm happy I'm busy. Then I won't have to worry about boys like him bothering me. I've got to keep myself busy all the time.*) Not really.

R: (*That does it! I'll try to remain polite, but that just does it. She dropped me like I was some clod.*) Well, I've got to be going now. See you.

In our expanded example, of course, we included much more cognitive detail than may actually occur in any such situation. Nevertheless, excusing if you will whatever exaggeration may result, it should be clear that both persons were actively involved in the process of construing this brief encounter, and that in addition both employed personal constructs throughout the entire process; for example, lonely-girl-needs-friends-so-I'll-stop-and-chat; forward-boy-trying-to-pick-me-up-so-I'll-brush-him-off. Furthermore, it is clear that the manner by which each construed the encounter changed over time. For example, Reggie changed his construction of Maggie from a lonely girl needing a friend to a cold fish, to a coy tease, and so on; on her part, Maggie changed her view of Reginald from fresh flirt to untrustworthy sexual threat. Note how knowing each person's personal constructs helped us gain an added understanding of their behavior. What they said had a logic provided through an understanding of the manner by which they construed the situation.

Finally, it is important to note how they construed the situation in somewhat different, even contradictory terms. They were not talking *with* each other; rather each appeared to be holding a conversation between himself and the construed image of the other. And to the extent to which the construed image differed from the image each had of himself, they were hardly engaged in a very meaningful exchange. Yet their exchange is not unlike many we all have every day. If they, along with us, could have access to one another's constructions of their encounter, perhaps they, too, would gain a better understanding of what was going on. By extension, perhaps Margaret and Reginald would be sitting happily together in the movie: a happy ending to what is otherwise a tragic saga of everyday life.

It might be inferred incorrectly from the preceding example that the entire focus of Kelly's theory is on *consciously* held constructs. Kelly suggests, however, that personal constructs, although guiding behavior, may be at a relatively low level of conscious awareness. Therefore, if we ask someone directly how he construes a given situation, we may not hear the actual constructs he is using or the actual psycho-logic he is employing. Although our choices and actions may follow a certain logic, it is not necessary to assume that we are fully aware of that logic.

The Case of Larry. Consider a self-analytic training group that has been meeting for about 10 sessions. One member of that group draws some special attention to himself; let's call him Larry. He is somewhat older than the other members of the group, in his middle fifties while the others are in their mid-twenties. On first encounter he comes across as a skid-row drifter, a wino. Whenever he speaks the mind boggles in trying to discover the meaning of his stream of clearly enunciated English words. You listen to him attentively; you know he's speaking the same language you speak; yet when he's finished talking you puzzle: what did he say? Larry speaks a great deal, but rather more to himself, and somewhat vaguely about himself, than to anyone else. Everyone remains polite, few daring to cut in even with an inquiry. He knows this is a self-analytic group. In fact, he keeps repeating *that* over and over again, prefacing all his remarks with the statement, "Well, so when are we going to get self-analytic?" People occasionally ask him what he'd like us to do. His answer is interesting, and I think revealing. If I may paraphrase, yet use quotation marks:

"If we are to be a self-analytic discussion group, we've got to begin to look into each other . . . we've got to analyze each of us. We must take that big crowbar and pry into each and every one of us. Who wants to take the spear first and skewer someone and then pass him around for all of us to analyze? If we are to be self-analytic, then we've got to open everyone up wide. We've got to begin to peel away the layers, piece by piece until we finally get down into that inner core—if there is one. To be self-analytic in our discussion, we've got to breach the walls of each person's fortress; break through the barriers, cut down his defenses, and get deep inside."

The group meets every week. Whenever anyone asks Larry a direct question—which by the tenth week they have begun to do—he shies away from answering. He comes on with rough time as a kid." He continues relating some some distant, vague reply. For example, Betty will ask Larry how he feels about something Bill has just said to him. Larry replies: "This reminds me of the time back in Boston when I was a kid. It wasn't easy living then. I had a distant experience, which perhaps he, but no one else, can see as relevant to Betty's question. Finally, people get mad at Larry. They accuse him of avoiding doing exactly what he says a self-analytic group should be doing, of knowing what such a group is about but refusing to play the game that way. Several full meetings are spent in detailed argument *with, to,* and *about* Larry. Much heat but little light is generated. People yell at him. Someone even goes so far as to lunge angrily at him. He is most frustrating to everyone in the group. They try to reach him, but get only this protective shield of evasive and vague response. Their anger increases; they near a breaking point.

What understanding can we get of this situation if rather than jumping on Larry we seek to look at that group through his eyes? As we do this, primarily using the quoted passage in which he offers us his description of what the group is about, we shall gain an insight into the reason for his refusal to participate except evasively. What does the group's task look like to Larry? Just examine his descriptions to gain a sense of how threatening and fearful a group this must be to him: the group is supposed to use a *crowbar* to pry into people. Each person is to be *skewered on a spear* and passed around for all to examine. People must

be *opened up wide*; layers are to be *peeled away*; barriers are to be *broken.* If this is how the group's task appears to him, is it so surprising that his participation is evasive, vague, and thereby frustrating to everyone else? How much courage it must take for him to arrive at each meeting, given that he thinks the goal of those meetings is to cut people up, tear them apart, pry them apart, skewer them!

Yet Larry's view and system of personal constructs exists for him at only a very low level of awareness. I would go so far as to suggest that Larry is not even aware of the ways by which he construes this situation; his constructs are unconscious. In effect, Larry is viewing this group through dark-tinted, frighteningly evil glasses; through them he sees the world as a dark and dangerous place; certainly he sees danger out there with his fellow group members. But if he is not aware that he is wearing dark glasses with distortive lenses, he cannot easily know that it is also possible to wear other kinds of glasses.

In this regard Kelly uses a phenomenological framework in which personal constructs need not always be well-stated principles or rules of logic. Similarly, Piaget's experiments with children—some of which we examine on pp. 177–179 —demonstrate the logic of a child's world that orders his experiences for him, just as personal constructs do so for the adult. The child's rules of logic, the grammar of his mind, is something Piaget discovers; it is as yet unavailable to the child's own verbal report or conscious awareness. He acts according to a logic of which he does not have much conscious grasp. Larry, too, acts according to his logic, although he does not have a conscious grasp of that logic. This should not be surprising. We all read and speak the English language, yet most of us are unaware of the principles of grammar and logic that underlie this behavior.

The Reptest. Kelly's approach to the study of personality by means of personal constructs was aided considerably by his development of a measuring instrument to assess a person's constructs: the *Reptest* (Role Construct Repertory Test). In the test an individual is presented with a list of roles such as father, mother, brother, person you like, friend, boss, work partner. He is asked to indicate the names of persons he knows who fit each role category. The experimenter selects three persons from the subject's list and asks him to indicate which two are alike in one important quality while differing from the third. For example, the individual may be presented with BROTHER, FRIEND, BOSS. He indicates which two of these are alike in an important quality while differing from the third in that same quality.

Suppose he says that brother and boss are alike in that they are both excessively domineering. The personal construct that emerges from this description is then written down in its bipolar form: DOMINEERING at one end, NOT DOMINEERING at the other. A similar procedure is conducted a number of times, with 20 to 30 different trios of roles from the original list. Each trio yields a personal construct that the individual uses in describing significant others in his life. The total procedure produces a mapping of his system of personal constructs. Variations of the Reptest have been employed, but the general idea in each instance is the same: the subject defines his interpersonal world view.

Several successful efforts to determine the test-retest reliability of the Reptest have been reported in the literature of the field (see Bonarius, 1965, for a review). Reliability is expressed in terms of a *correlation coefficient*, a statistic that indicates the degree of correspondence between a person's score on one set of measures with his score on another set of measures. In test-retest reliability we are concerned with correlation of the score achieved on the same test on occasion 1 with the score achieved on occasion 2. A study reported by Fjeld and Landfield (1961), as one example, indicates a coefficient of .79 over a period of two weeks between the first and second administration of the Reptest. Since the highest correlation coefficient possible is 1.00, meaning perfect correspondence, a coefficient of .79 indicates very good though not perfect test-retest reliability. Given the variety of factors that could intervene to alter a subject's score over that two-week period, a coefficient of .79 must be taken as substantial and strongly suggesting a reasonably reliable measuring instrument. Added evidence for the reliability of the Reptest comes from similar results from other studies.

Reliability of a test, although essential, is not sufficient. We are always left with the question about its *validity*: does it measure what it's supposed to measure? This question is not simple to answer.

It would be plausible to expect that if personal constructs are related to actual social behavior (as Kelly's theory suggests they should be), judges watching a group of persons in actual social interaction should be able to identify which of several Reptest protocols belongs to which person. Essentially, if the test measures X, and if X is manifested in observable behavior, then judges who observe subject behavior should be able to identify those who possess X in the test. This procedure is applied frequently in the validation of psychological instruments. Studies by Shoemaker (in Bonarius, 1965) used it with the Reptest, reporting in one case significant matching between observed behavior and Reptest protocols and in another case, with a different group of subjects, nonsignificant results.

Another expectation from the theory, not unlike the preceding, is that knowledge of a person's personal constructs would permit better understanding of that individual than would purely descriptive information about him; to understand another person is to understand how he construes his world. Thus with access to his Reptest scores we should understand him better than with access only to others' descriptions about him. Payne (in Bonarius, 1965) sought to examine this derivation of the theory, comparing accuracy of prediction about the target person, based on the target's own Reptest, with accuracy based on peers' descriptions of the target. He found significantly greater accuracy of prediction from a knowledge of the target's own constructs.

Although there have been many further, more finely differentiated efforts at assessing the usefulness of the Reptest and of Kelly's entire approach in understanding and predicting P's behavior, we shall forego any further discussion at this time (Bonarius, 1965, reviews much of this work). This approach, along with other similar approaches, will appear again throughout the text.

TOWARD A NEW PSYCHOLOGY: CENTER STAGE FOR THE KNOWLEDGE PROCESSES

As we examine developments in any field of human knowledge and inquiry, we cannot help realizing that a certain mainstream of legitimate ideas and approaches, a *Zeitgeist*, characterizes each era. This *Zeitgeist* (literally, "spirit of the times") sets the tone for the kinds of work that actually get done and outlines areas of thought and of method that are to be ignored or in some instances to be labeled as illegitimate for the science to examine.

A *Zeitgeist* does not exist in isolation either from the larger society or from other scientific and philosophical thought. Each knowledge seeker finds himself working within the *Zeitgeist* of his era; this is as true for workers in psychology as for those in the physical sciences. Advances in one science often have a significant impact on other sciences. Changes in the structure of a society itself, in turn, may bring to the surface new problems or new ways of thinking that become a part of the mainstream of a given discipline. Therefore in examining the *Zeitgeist* of one field we must of necessity pay attention to developments in other fields and in the larger society.

In an especially brilliant and insightful essay Kuhn (1962) explores this issue in the physical sciences. He argues that there exist *paradigms* (patterns or models) in a science that form the rules of the game for that science. A paradigm defines the legitimate objects and methods of study; it provides an established mode of conceptualization. For example, the paradigm in physical optics of the eighteenth century argued that light consisted of material particles or corpuscles. In the early nineteenth century, however, it was argued that light consisted of transverse wave motion. Today we read in physics texts that light consists of photons that exhibit some properties of waves and some properties of particles.

Kuhn argues through careful documentation that the transitions in these conceptions of physical optics came about by a revolutionary movement in which one paradigm replaced another. While a given paradigm dominated the field, normal science proceeded with its usual examination of the phenomena that were de-

clared legitimate objects of study according to that particular paradigm. Kuhn argues that just as political revolutions develop out of a growing sense that the existing institutions of a society fail adequately to meet the needs of the people in solving their problems of living,

"Scientific revolutions are inaugurated by a growing sense . . . that an existing paradigm has ceased to function adequately in the exploration of an aspect of nature to which that paradigm itself had previously led the way. In both political and scientific development the sense of malfunction that can lead to crisis is prerequisite to revolution" (1962, p. 91).

Eighteenth-century man was considered a highly rational being; but the impact of Darwinism reshaped the views of man in the next century. As an evolutionary derivative of animals, man could be studied in roughly the same terms as all living things; since animals had instincts that guided their behavior, why shouldn't man be similarly guided? Since animals did not appear to engage in rational, thoughtful, or planful activity, was it not reasonable to suggest that man was likewise driven by nonrational, even unconscious instincts? To be sure, a shift in paradigm is not a smooth or an overnight process. As Kuhn suggests, it is more a revolution than a transition. The acceptance of a view of man as animal, man as instinctually driven, man as irrational, did not replace the rational-man theories of the eighteenth century without a battle.

Freud and McDougall

Both Freud's view (see 1951; 1954 editions) in individual psychology and McDougall's (1908) emphasis in social psychology can be viewed against this background of a paradigm shifting from rational man to instinctual man. In Freud's view man was a biological creature driven by instincts of libido and aggression. The story of man's life was a story of the development of his instincts through the oral, anal, phallic, and genital-psychosexual stages. In the new field of social psychology McDougall posited the existence of five basic instincts: flight, repulsion, curiosity, self-abasement–self-assertion, and the parental instinct. Each of these instincts was defined as an innate disposition that led its possessor to perceive and attend to objects of a certain class, to experience a particular kind of emotion in response to these objects, and finally, to act in a particular manner in regard to these objects. McDougall's version of social psychology, then, was also founded on an instinct doctrine.

Decline of the instinct theories and the rise of behaviorism

Although the *Zeitgeist* had shifted, providing a background supportive of the instinct-rooted approaches of Freud and McDougall, criticisms from within the field, developments in other fields, and events in the larger society in which American psychology and social psychology flowered led to radical modifications of both of these perspectives.

Instincts Overused. One key reason for the decline of instinct theories of human behavior was simply their overuse and misuse. In 1924 Bernard examined books in biology, psychology, education, sociology, and other similar disciplines, and uncovered more than 15,000 separate instincts listed. Apparently whenever anyone encountered a new behavior in need of explanation he reached into his back pocket, withdrew the day's newest list of instincts, and searched for the appropriate one. Some days the list worked well; every behavior had its appropriate instinct. But there were days when the list did not suffice. Where to turn? To another instinct, of course! The game became instinct-naming. Anyone could play it. All you needed was a versatile mind, a large vocabulary, and perhaps a faulty view of social science.

The Growth of Sociology and Cultural Anthropology. A second, more important factor in the transition away from instinct doctrines came through developments in sociology and cultural anthropology. These fields informed us that man was influenced by his society and his culture; if this were so, then man must be more plastic and malleable than the universalistic instinct notions would have led us to believe. Freud's own theory came in for some extreme cultural criticism. It was pointed out that his ideas of human behavior had evolved within a particular period in a particular culture. His critics argued that although sexually repressed Viennese women might indeed possess the characteristics he discussed, it would be a grave

error to posit this culturally restricted view as universal. Anthropologists jumped on this anti-Freudian bandwagon, examining in particular the Oedipal situation that was so central a part of the Freudian doctrine. Malinowski's (1922) careful examination of the Trobriand Islanders indicated how faulty he felt Freud's analysis of the universality of the Oedipal situation was.

Unlike the Western society of which Freud primarily wrote, the Trobriand Islanders are matrilineal rather than patrilineal; that is, children are members of their mother's clan. Much of a child's support and education come from his mother's brother (the child's material uncle) rather than from his father. Malinowski reports that there is no horror among the Trobrianders over the idea of infantile sexuality. Furthermore, the attitude of the father toward his child is that of a near friend and helper. By contrast with Western society, it is the child's uncle who seems to serve the kinds of function we of the West associate with "father." Any sense of rivalry or jealousy develops toward the uncle rather than the father. To further highlight the differences, Malinowski reports that the important taboo in the society concerns brother-sister incest; this taboo makes even accidental contact with one's sister in sexual matters a crime. Here, then, repressed aggressive-ambivalent attitudes are directed toward the maternal uncle (not the father) and presumably repressed sexual wishes are directed toward the sister (not the mother). Malinowski concludes that in a matrilineal society such as that of the Trobriand Islanders, one finds a *matrilineal complex*, which is unlike the Freudian notion of an Oedipal complex.

But those hardy Freudian analysts (myself included) are hard to put down. Jones (1925), for example, while accepting Malinowski's description of the family situation among the Trobrianders, argued that the forbidden sister was in reality only a substitute for the mother, just as the uncle was merely a substitute for the father. Naturally, if you begin with the assumption that the Oedipal complex is a universal instinct, anything that does not perfectly match must be reshaped somewhat to fit the initial assumption. It's not good science, but imaginative and resourceful (and perhaps correct).

Later efforts to curtail the rampaging generality of Freudianism are exemplified by Benedict's study (1934) of the matrilineal Zuñi culture. Contrary to both Malinowski's analysis and Freud's original thesis, Benedict suggests that Zuñi children grow up without any form of resentment toward the father or sexual longings after the mother. Another such argument is provided by Eggan's (1953) analysis of another matrilineal culture, the Hopi. Eggan felt that if there were an Oedipus complex in Hopi families, it must of necessity have been built around a "composite" mother and a "composite" father, because each child, given the Hopi's extended family organization, has several of both. She concluded that there was really only a very weak case for the existence of an Oedipal "instinct" that centers around the mother and father.

Most anthropological efforts to debunk the universality of Freud's notion of the Oedipal complex tended to use relatively superficial criteria for determining its existence. Roheim (1950) by contrast, sought the Oedipal complex in its more disguised forms, particularly as expressed in fantasy behavior. Roheim argues that the Marquesans, a culture that both Seward (1946) and Kardiner (1939) had pointed out as having no Oedipal complex, in reality have a major myth about the hero-god Tobe-Tika that contains several "classical" Oedipal elements. For instance, the god commits incest with his daughter and becomes the prototype of criminals; there are efforts to castrate the Primal Father by cutting off his feet and arms. For Roheim this provides evidence for the existence of an Oedipal complex among the Marquesans.

As we have seen, the problem of determining the universality, or lack thereof, of an Oedipal complex provides a number of important subproblems. What criteria are to be used in judging whether a given culture "has" an Oedipal complex? Shall we focus on consciously reported relationships between children and their parents? Shall we turn to myths? No matter what the arguments on each side, the cross-cultural evidence fit into the developing anti-instinct, social-man *Zeitgeist* better than did evidence of universality. Thus further doubts were cast on biologically rooted instinct theories.

The picture was beginning to shift from the immutable *instinct man* to the highly variable and modifiable *cultural man*.

The Growth of Scientific Psychology. The physical sciences created a model of proper science; to emulate good science, psychology had to become experimental and operational. Concepts had to be carefully defined and operationally measured; that is, the operations or procedures by which the concepts could be measured empirically had to be specified. Causal variables had to be created experimentally and their effects systematically studied. Most of Freud's concepts seemed to defy such strict experimental test; McDougall's instinct notions did not lend themselves to experimental manipulation in the scientific laboratory. On the other hand, Pavlov's (1960; 1963) work in Russia on conditioning, and the inspiration it gave to Watson (1925) in the United States, provided an outline for a scientific program in psychology. Watson called his brand of psychology *behaviorism*, and showed how he could shape responses in people—much as Pavlov had done in conditioning animals—through the controlled presentation of stimuli.

Allport (1924) adopted some of these ideas and brought them into the social-psychological laboratory. There he demonstrated that well-defined behavioristic principles could explain social behavior that formerly had been explained by reference to imprecise mentalistic concepts that were difficult if not impossible to put to the experimental test. While Watson was creating and later reducing a fear response in Little Albert and Little Peter through the use of conditioning techniques (1925), Allport was studying social facilitation in the laboratory. Building on the observation of some European researchers (e.g., Meumann, in Zajonc, 1966) that student assistants' work improved under scrutiny by their major professor, Allport (1920; 1924) demonstrated this facilitative effect in his laboratory. He showed how subjects' performance *quantity* rose under conditions in which they saw and heard others working on similar tasks; the *quality* of their performance, however, declined under these "social" conditions.

Allport suggested that this increment in performance quantity and decrement in quality could explain crowd behavior without calling on such vague concepts as the "group mind," which Le Bon (1896) had posited to explain collective behavior. Le Bon's man-in-the-crowd was indeed less intellectually critical than a man alone (a qualitative decrement), and was more agitated and active (a quantitative increment), but this was not because he had submitted himself to the mysterious "group mind." Rather, his individual behavior was facilitated under social conditions. Allport argued that simple conditioning could explain the entire effect.

U.S. Pioneers and Pragmatists. I think a fourth reason for the decline in instinct notions lies in the pioneer spirit and ideology of the United States. The United States was a nation built on pragmatism and a doctrine of individualism. It was said that any man could become anything he wanted; he only needed to work hard. A boy from the slums could become President. Given this cultural ethos, it would truly be surprising to find a psychological theory of man that argued that inborn instincts fixed us at birth and that their development outlined our personal life histories. Scientific behaviorism, on the other hand, offered a psychological theory and method that seemed to embody American values. Anyone could become President; we are not fixed biologically at birth. It was an approach that stressed the study of man with the same vigor as was employed in studying and modifying nature. Psychology could be a can-do discipline; psychologists could be men who took charge in their laboratories, who manipulated independent variables. It offered an optimistic view of psychology and of man in a nation of optimists.

Decline of behaviorism

Even behaviorism, flowering in the decades following the 1920's, was to see its own bloom begin to fade. In 1959 White, a distinguished Harvard psychologist, wrote an article that ostensibly dealt with a new conception of motivation. He entitled this article "Motivation Reconsidered: The Concept of Competence." In what can only be taken as a masterwork of synthesis, White pieced together the basic similarities that existed between the behavioristic and the Freudian doctrines of man and contrasted them with newly developing notions embodied within the neo-Freudian emphasis on ego functions and *mastery* and the neo-behavioristic emphasis on *novelty seeking*. His article provides an essential documentation of a further shift in the *Zeitgeist*.

The point so far is that the *Zeitgeist* in the early twentieth century began to shift away from a strictly instinctual model of man toward a greater emphasis on man's social and cultural capabilities. I have attributed this change to the misuse of the instinct doctrines, the growing body of material from sociology and cultural anthropology, the push toward rigorous scientism that engulfed the relatively young discipline of psychology, and the pragmatic spirit of the times. White took this outline one step further; he pointed out a change within behaviorism that parallels a change within Freudian psychology.

One of the basic concepts of early behaviorism, especially as it was developed within learning theory (e.g., Hull, 1943), had been that man, like the animals studied (usually rats), was a tension-reducing, equilibrium-seeking organism. Disequilibrium was produced by a state of tissue deprivation, as, for example, a condition of physiological deficit or need. A hungry person, a thirsty person, a person without sexual gratification, for example, was a person in need. According to this view learning occurred when a response was made and reinforced, that is, when that response led to the reduction of the tension produced by the state of biological need. A long and glorious line of research seemed to demonstrate that animals would learn to run into the left arm of a T-maze when hungry in order to be fed there and thereby have their state of tension reduced. Similar research on other needs and in other contexts appeared amply to support the contention that animals and, by extension, man as well, were tension-reducing beings.

But then, White noted, some embarrassing empirical data began to come in. Highlights will indicate the kind of impact it had. First, several researchers showed that animals were capable of learning a new response with no other reinforcement than to satisfy what might be termed a need or demand for novelty. For example, an animal would learn a response just to be allowed to take a quick peek from his enclosed cage into the laboratory room (Berlyne, 1950, 1955, 1958; Butler, 1958; Butler & Harlow, 1957). Other animals learned responses for no better reward than to play with and manipulate complex objects (Harlow, Harlow, & Meyer, 1950). Either novelty and manipulation were new drives, and should be added to the list of hunger, thirst, and sex—fearful shades of that instinct-naming era!—or possibly the entire notion of tension reduction should be cast aside or, at minimum, radically altered.

Second, some fascinating studies suggested that animals would work themselves to near exhaustion in a Skinner box, pushing a lever not for food but for a jolt of electricity to a specified area of the cortex (Olds & Milner, 1954). That did shake up those who maintained that learning would occur only in order to reduce physiological need. It would be possible to extend this listing much further; in sum, however, the data suggested that the behavioristic model of the organism (man and animal) as a tension reducer did not stand up well. A new model that stressed curiosity, novelty, mastery, manipulation, or, in White's term, *competence*, was needed. Rather than being driven solely by physiological drives, men and animals seemed to be driven by more *cognitive* conditions: to know, to find meaning, to play, to enjoy, to manipulate, to explore, to experience novelty, to master, and so on.

It was White's argument that anyone who spent time examining a young child's behavior would soon see how much of what the child did, especially by way of his playful and exploratory activities, was not to be understood simply by reference to a physiological model of tension reduction. Much of his activity allows a child to learn to become competent in his encounters with his environment. Although he is not driven to play with objects just to learn more about them so that in 25 years he will be a better engineer, a young child's exploration of his world of objects is a natural, fun-filled activity that provides the basis for his later competence in dealing effectively with his world.

The rule-following model of man

It is helpful to our discussion to introduce at this point a particular conception of human motivation that fits in well with the cognitive orientation so far. I base this discussion on the work of Peters (1958), a British philosopher interested in some of the basic issues, problems, and theories with which psychologists have dealt. Peters examines the meaning of *explanation* in the realm of the psychological. What do we mean when we try to *explain* someone's actions or behavior? In the tradition of McDougall we would explain *P*'s action by reference to certain innate instincts that motivated it. Or, if we were more classically Freudian, we would refer to the interaction of the dynamic psychic institutions of id, ego, and superego. On the behavioristic side, we would use some version of a stimulus-response learning theory and seek the drive state or physiological need that "caused" the behavior.

Peters argues that explanations of this sort are contrasted with what he terms the *rule-following, purposive* model of explanation. Let us paraphrase Peters' own example to clarify this matter. The human behavior we seek to explain is given by a person (*P*) who performs some action that brings about some effect or outcome. Our interest is in explaining "why" *P* did what he did. Let us say *P* crosses the street. We ask, "Why did he do that?" or "What was his reason for crossing the street?" "In order to purchase some tobacco" presumably would satisfy us as an answer; it gives the *end* or *goal* toward which *P*'s action was directed. We feel pleased in actually understanding *P*'s behavior, because, given the logic of the situation, his reason—to purchase tobacco—makes sense.

Peters takes us a step further. As a rule-following animal, man not only directs his actions toward goals, as in the example, but in addition adheres to certain rules or norms. That is, there are certain standards and conventions of conduct; we act out of a knowledge of these rules. There are few, if any, human actions that do not come under some kind of normative direction; even the most biologically rooted needs are eventually brought under the guidance of cultural or societal norms. Eating, definitely of biological origin, quickly develops into a normatively regulated pattern in which legitimate food objects and legitimate times and locales are culturally defined. We find grubworms repulsive and are not likely to eat them; the Aruntas of Australia, on the other hand, define grubworms as reasonable food. Even sexual behavior, rooted deeply in man's biological makeup, is guided by cultural norms as to objects and age-appropriate sexual behavior.

These ideas suggest that even so simple an action as *P*'s crossing the road to purchase some tobacco is itself a complex behavior rooted in a particular normative system of which *P* is knowledgeable. He walks across the road rather than runs. He enters a store in which he has learned tobacco may be purchased. We would find it puzzling—that is, not fitting the rule-following explanation of his behavior—if he hopped on one foot while crossing the street and then entered a ladies' lingerie store to purchase his tobacco. His actions would not fit the rule-following model and in effect would demand that we look elsewhere for an explanation of his behavior.

For the most part, however, if we assume that man is a rule-following, purposive animal, we shall find satisfactory explanations for his behavior when the goals and the rules are made explicit. Recall that *rule-following* refers to the normative regulation of actions, while *purposive* refers to the goals or end-seeking nature of man's action. His actions are explained to the extent to which they follow rules and are appropriate to the goals he is seeking.

A *causal* explanation for *P*'s action, as contrasted with the rule-following explanation, is usually offered when *P*'s actions deviate from the appropriate situational norms. When his behavior does not fit the rule-following model we look for some kind of causal disruption, say, of his nervous system or of his perceptual apparatus. An explanation of *P*'s behavior in terms of a physiological state (for instance, *P* hops on one foot because his other is broken, or is stricken with the gout, or has a muscle spasm) would be an effort to offer a causal analysis. A knowledge of *P*'s physiology might provide several necessary elements to explain his action, but without the rule-following perspective no physiological explanation could be *sufficient*. Peters argues that only a rule-following, purposive perspective can offer us sufficient explanation of human behavior.

Freud's theory enters this picture, according to Peters, in a positive light. In that Freud attempted to explain behaviors that deviated from the rule-following model—such as breakdowns in the normal routines of action because of anxiety or intrapsychic conflict—he sought to discover the conditions necessary to understanding why *P* did not act in accordance with the appropriate rule-following logic. Actions that *happen* to a person or actions that do not appear to have any conscious goal (e.g., forgetting someone's name) are of the sort that the rule-following model does not handle. In these instances a causal model, perhaps of the Freudian sort, is a useful device.

According to Peters, causal explanations should serve three major functions in psychological theory.

1. They can provide an outline of the necessary conditions to human action. A theory of physiological activation based on man's biological needs, for example, points out certain organismic need states necessary to an understanding of his behavior.

2. They can point to individual differences in performance as a function of variations in these necessary organismic states. In a physiological theory such causal explanations could offer clues as to why *P responds*, say, more quickly in a given situation than *O*.

3. Finally, causal explanations can explain actions that involve an extreme breakdown in performance. For example, a physiological deficit such as a vitamin deficiency might be both necessary and sufficient as an explanation for certain kinds of behavior by *P*. Usually, however, such causal explanations are not themselves sufficient explanation.

Peters' approach to explanation is a useful bridge between psychology and the disciplines of sociology and anthropology; as social psychologists, this is the kind of bridge on which we should be wandering. On one hand we are interested in the knowledge processes from a strictly psychological perspective. Here we focus on the mechanisms by which individuals come to define their world. If we know both *how* they know and *what* they know, we shall be able to understand and, in Peters' sense, explain their behavior. Likewise, we are intersted in the structure of situations, especially the normative structure, within which human actions occur. If we know the norms governing action in a given social situation, we can fairly well explain, via the rule-following, purposive model, the behavior we observe in that situation.

Taken together, as should be the case in social psychology, the psychological and the sociological perspectives can provide us with a very powerful explanatory tool. With the perceptive use of both orientations we should be able to note both the situational rules and the manner by which they are transformed by an individual entering the situation. So armed, we should find ourselves capable of anticipating the *idiosyncracies* as well as the *communalities* of human behavior. Ideally—although ideals are damned difficult to attain, as we shall continually see—we should gain an understanding of man as individual and man as member of society, of man as transformer of society and man as transformed by society. As Kluckhohn and Murray (1956) state it,

"Every man is in certain respects a. like all other men, b. like some other men, c. like no other man" (p. 53). By this they mean that fundamental biological makeup is shared with all other persons, and that in addition we all live in a physical environment to which we must adapt, so we face a common set of problems that compel a certain communality among all human beings. Yet, as members of cultures and groupings in those cultures (age, sex, and occupational groups, social classes, etc.), we are similar to others of the same groups. For example, we can suppose that all small businessmen share a degree of similarity with other small businessmen, both in their own society and in other societies. Thus we are in some ways similar to some other men. Finally, each of us is a unique individual who has grown up in a particular context with configurations of persons, experiences, and events

not shared with any other person. Thus each of us is in some ways like no other.

THE SOCIOLOGICAL TRADITION: DEFINITION OF THE SITUATION

To this point we have focused primarily on psychologists who expressed a concern with the cognitive (i.e., knowledge) processes. This should in no way imply, however, that the discipline of sociology ignored this cognitive emphasis. Nothing could be further from the truth. There exists a long and well-represented tradition in the mainstream of sociology that has concerned itself with the *subjective* bases of human behavior, and to this tradition we shall briefly turn our attention.

Within the Germanic philosophical tradition, including the writings of Hegel and Dilthey, a distinction is made between *verstehen* (to understand) and *erklären* (to explain) (see Mann & Kreyche, 1966, pp. 52ff.; and Tymieniecka, 1962, for a discussion). This roughly parallels Peters' distinction between causal explanations of psychological events and rule-following, purposive explanations. According to the philosophical distinction, *verstehen* operates in our knowledge of persons; to understand human behavior we need to grasp the network of goals, rules, and choices that are involved in the individual's activity. *Erklären* is involved in our knowledge of the material or nonhuman world of objects; to explain the behavior of physical objects we must turn to causal laws, the laws of nature. For example, a student understands *(verstehen)* the behavior of his professor because he has come to know something about the situational role requirements of a professor. As long as the professor's behavior fits the network of expectations the student has learned, his behavior is understood and need not come into further question. One would explain *(erklären)* human behavior only when it deviated from the understood logic of the situation. To gain understanding of the *verstehen* sort requires a kind of quasi-intuition; the behavioral analyst stands in the place of those he is investigating and sees the situation through their eyes or through their perspective. Note how similar this point of view is to the psychological views on cognition: if we know *P*'s personal constructs (a knowledge on our part, however, that is gained more through systematic examination than through intuition), we may see the situation as he sees it; thus his behavior becomes understandable to us.

The subjectivist approach in the cultural sciences

The *verstehen-erklären* distinction directs those involved in the social and cultural sciences toward principles of behavior and a logic of methodology separable from, although complementary to, the principles and methods used by those involved in the natural or physical sciences. Man as an object of study operates by principles unlike those by which physical objects function because his consciousness of self and world creates for him a collectivity of mental products whose reality is not of the same order as the reality of purely physical objects. To study this order of consciously produced objects requires a methodology that leads an investigator to seek out his subject's perspective and view the world through his eyes. It was within this tradition that much of Weber's work evolved.

The *verstehen* approach in strictly sociological thought found an early home of sorts in the Department of Sociology at the University of Chicago. The subjective orientation that this perspective demands was an intimate part of sociological thought at Chicago in the 1920's and 1930's, and other sociologists, then and now, adopted aspects of it. Several ingredients of this perspective are to be found in the writings of Hinkle (1963) and Tiryakian (1965). We shall consider them before looking a bit further into the Chicago-type work, especially that of Mead (1934) and Thomas (in Volkart, 1951).

In its basics the subjective or cognitive orientation in sociology involves the following propositions.

1. Human action or behavior arises from a symbolic (i.e., meaningful) representation of the self, as subject, and of the situation, including other persons, nonpersons, and cultural entities as objects. The point is that "the world is *sym-bolically perceived* and not simply responded to physically*" (Tiryakian, 1965, p. 684). We impute meanings to ourselves and to situations; these meanings *transform* the physical properties of objects into psychological terms for us. A rock, for example, is not always simply to be understood in terms of its physical properties but rather may have the psychological meaning of a physical barrier blocking individual movement, or even of a weapon to be thrown.

2. To explain human behavior we must refer to the subjective meaning or definition of the situations in which action occurs. As I have previously indicated, this understanding calls for a rule-following model rather than a causal model of action.

3. Human behavior or action is purposive. Men act within a normative structure to attain their subjectively defined purposes, intentions, objectives, goals. Human behavior is thus seen as involving *choices* among alternatives, *decisions* about appropriate courses of action, *evaluations* of opportunities and obstacles, and so on.

4. Given the assumptions concerning man's active participation in and negotiation with his world, his perspective is one of *becoming* rather than of *being;* becoming emphasizes potential, activity, selection, choice, and future-directedness, whereas being indicates a more mechanistic, static, fixed determination.

Weber

From this tradition of *verstehen* Weber, one of the significant historical figures of sociology, emerged; and in the Weberian tradition a substantial amount of contemporary sociology has its historical roots. Weber's contributions to the field of sociology covered such varied areas as organizational behavior, social stratification, and types of societal authority (1946; 1947), and, in his classic work (1930), linked the Protestant Ethic to the economic system of capitalism. In this section, however, we are concerned with Weber's emphasis on the subjective in the approach to sociology.

In its subjective emphasis Weber's approach sharply contrasts with the alternative sociological approach of *objectivism*, especially as exemplified in the works of Durkheim (e.g., 1933; 1938; 1951). Durkheim's approach to sociology was to deal out individual personality, psychological processes, and motivation, while dealing in objectively measurable *societal-level* variables. In his classic work, *Suicide* (1951; original French edition, 1897), Durkheim sought to demonstrate how what appears at first to be a very individualistic act—suicide—is in fact a social act with societal origins. Each society, according to Durkheim, possesses, as one of its characteristics, a particular suicide rate. By intentionally ignoring individual motives, Durkheim was able to demonstrate how suicide *rates*, a social fact, varied systematically according to certain parameters of the society. He differentiated major types of suicide, linking each type to a particular set of qualities of a society rather than to the motivational or psychological structure of the society's individual members.

Weber's theory, then, should be viewed against this objectifying background in which individual motives and subjective definitions of the situation are eliminated from the concern of the sociologist. The turn to the subjective in Weber's approach is paralleled by the psychological concern with cognition; both are contrasted to the respective objectifying views: behaviorism in psychology and social-rate analysis in sociology.

For Weber the discipline of sociology was intended to deal with all human action to which an actor attaches a *subjective meaning*. Action is *social* to the extent to which an individual actor takes into account the behavior of others and is thereby influenced. In setting forth his directive for the science of sociology Weber urged that we be concerned with how each actor *subjectively defines* the situations in which he is located, rather than being concerned with whether the definitions are in some sense true or correct or valid; we understand the "why" of *P*'s behavior when we gain access to the subjective meaning he utilizes.

Weber also makes a distinction between the subjective and what he terms the *reactive*, a distinction not easy to make in any given instance. It rests primarily on the degree of active engagement of an actor in constructing a situation rather than more passively reacting to it. In subjective action *P* has defined (construed) the situation and his place in it; reactive action is not preceded by an act of definition or meaning-giving. Reflexive behavior, for example your knee jerking upward when the patella is struck sharply, is a good example of reactive rather than subjective action. In Weber's use of the term, most psychophysical processes involving the mechanics of pure visual perception and neural reaction are not at all subjective, although he freely admits that many actions, such as highly routinized, traditional behavior patterns, are somewhat marginal between the subjective and the reactive.

Like most theoreticians who take this subjective tack, Weber must cope with the problem that arises when actions appear to us to be unintelligible or irrational. How can we understand *P*'s behavior when he seems to be acting in a peculiar manner? Peters, as we have noted, suggested that at this point we might have to call on causal rather than rule-following explanations. Weber, on the other hand, would employ an *ideal-typical analysis*. One of Weber's contributions to contemporary sociology was his development and use of the concept of the ideal type, a theoretically constructed model productive both in the formulation of hypotheses about reality and in the actual understanding of reality. We may formulate ideal types of societies without ever encountering our formulations in actuality. Or, as did Weber, we may refer to an ideal type of bureaucratic organization, detailing a set of highly specific qualities that it ideally should have. We would not really expect to encounter this ideal in an actual bureaucracy, but the typology is a useful conceptual tool for understanding the real world.

In the case of seemingly irrational human behavior Weber suggests that we work from an ideal, conceptually pure view of rational, reasonable, or logical action. As behavioral analysts we first ask ourselves what the usual ideal-typical action would be in a given situation, noting how deviant from this ideal the actual observed behavior is. We may then introduce other factors—perhaps even those Peters sees as causal—to aid our full understanding of the behavior.

Mead

Mead (1934) is usually thought of as the founder of an approach called *symbolic interaction*. He begins his analysis by focusing on the basic situation of interaction. The stimulus unit involved as the interactive encounter begins is called the *gesture*. The gesture, like the stimulus in psychological work, serves to bring out reactions or responses in the other person involved in the social act. An example on a very simple level is Mead's description of a dogfight; the act of each dog is the stimulus or gesture that evokes a response by the other. Fido comes on with teeth bared, snarling. Rover responds to these gestures by hunching up, tensing his body, preparing to do battle. Fido in turn responds to Rover's gestures with intensified preparatory activity. As Mead puts it, the dogs are engaged in a *conversation of gestures.* (Allport's conception of crowd behavior as social facilitation involves this same reflexive "conversation." See pp. 18–19.)

At this point we have what is basically a simple stimulus-response theory; gestures do not yet contain symbolic meaning. We do not assume that Rover "reads" Fido's intent and says to himself, "Well, I guess now is the time for a showdown." Rather, Mead assumes that each gesture from one is the *unmediated* stimulus for the response in the other; each animal or person adjusts his own actions in accordance with the pattern of gestural stimulation provided by the other.

At some point in the social act, however, we move from gesture to symbol. In Mead's terms, gestures become *significant symbol*s when each actor has in his mind a representation of the meanings of the gesture in the mind of the other; *intersubjective meaning* has thus been added to the situation. My gesture, say a tightly held fist raised in the air as though ready to strike a blow, is a significant symbol when the meaning embodied in it is understood by me and by the person toward whom it is directed. At that moment we share an intersubjective definition of the situation. In human encounters language is perhaps the widest and most clearly noted use of significant symbols. As Mead puts it, "The vocal gesture becomes a significant symbol . . . when it has the same

effect on the individual making it that it has on the individual to whom it is addressed or who explicitly responds to it . . ." (p. 172). When gestures have become significant symbols the course of interaction flows more smoothly; each person may make adjustments to what he understands of the meanings the other gives to their mutual encounter. When I can "read" you —or at least assume that I am doing so with some accuracy—and you can "read" me, we share anticipations that allow us to behave jointly in a relatively smooth manner.

An important concept that Mead introduces at this point in his theoretical discussion is *taking the role or the attitude of the other* through the use of significant symbols, and becoming capable of adjusting behavior accordingly. If I know what my gestures mean to you (because they are significant symbols), I can see the situation through your eyes, through your role. The reverse holds true as well; you, in turn, can see through my eyes.

In a detailed explication of several parts of his theory Mead discusses the distinction between *play* and *the game*. A brief examination of this discussion will help clarify certain confusing aspects of his theory of symbolic interaction. In *the game*, for example baseball (in contrast to a simple *play* situation such as two kids in a sandbox, each working on his own sand castle), each player is involved in the process of taking the other's attitude and modifying or adjusting his own performance. A baseball team—at least one that hopes to win— involves nine players, each of whom possesses in himself the repertoire of relevant actions he assumes each of his teammates possesses. The catcher is not only the catcher, but is also the pitcher, the first baseman, the center fielder, and so on. Each player *is* (in this role-playing sense) everyone on the team; it becomes possible for the team to operate with organization and finesse. A group of individuals brought together for the very first time and asked to play baseball, of course, can do so—assuming that each is aware of the nature of the game. However, as long as each defines the others only in terms of vague role assignments such as "you're the first baseman, you cover first base," the team will not perform as an organization.

When each comes to know the others in ways relevant to the game—knowing, for instance, that the first baseman is slow on his feet and disinclined to move far back in the infield to cover balls hit between first and second—each may adjust his own actions accordingly; the second baseman may try to cover parts of the field normally included within the first baseman's domain.

Thomas and Znaniecki

Thomas and Znaniecki, who produced an early classic empirical investigation, *The Polish Peasant* (1918–1920), round out this brief overview of sociological contributions to the subjective-cognitive tradition. Theirs was a transitional work; it stood between the speculative sociology of armchair philosophy and the empiricist tradition. Thomas and Znaniecki sought to provide a new methodology for sociology. In their examination of the transition of the Polish peasant from Europe to the United States they took two relatively innovative approaches. First, they concentrated on a small *total* society in order to understand the operation of social process. In this regard their sociological approach was much like that employed by anthropologists and even by the Gestalt tradition in psychology; the emphasis was on unified wholes or total social systems as entities rather than on parts of the whole. To understand social process, one must understand it in its own social context, not on display in the laboratory.

Second, Thomas and Znaniecki employed personal documents such as diaries to trace the life histories of their subject population. They did this for a reason basic to the perspective we have been developing throughout this section: the use of personal documents gets at the inner, mental life of individuals, and it was subjective phenomena rather than objective events that were essential, according to Thomas and Znaniecki, to any sociological investigation. In this aspect of their methodology they were very much akin to clinical psychologists, who use a life-history approach to understand a patient's world, and even akin to folklorists, who use the folktales of a culture as the documents that give access to the world view of members of that culture.

Thomas (in Volkhart, 1951) maintained that before any intentional act of behavior a person engages in a process of deliberation and assessment. He called this the *definition of the situation*. As a sociologist, he stressed the culturally shared modes of defining that characterize a group of people rather than the more idiosyncratic modes of special interest to a cognitive psychologist.

Thomas developed a theory of *the four wishes*; these wishes, he said, formed the basic subjective components of an individual's definition of the situation. They are: desire for new experience and fresh stimulation; desire for recognition; desire for mastery; desire for security. Without an understanding of these subjective components, Thomas argued, one could never hope to gain a complete explanation of human behavior. In his deliberations before action each individual must make a decision about the situation. In this decision there is always a rivalry between his own spontaneously generated definition and the ready-made societal definition. To choose the ready-made definition, Thomas said, involves conforming, because the individual uses existing rules to define his situation; to use his own definition involves deviation. Thomas sees this choice as based on the balance in the individual's personality between the wish for security and the wish for new experience. Regardless of which tack he takes, he will have to reconcile the often competing, even contradictory, demands of the situation.

The methodological picture: Briefly noted

While Thomas and Znaniecki used highly subjective personal documents to gain entry into the mental life of their subjects, others involved in sociological inquiry were beginning to turn their attention toward the growing developments in statistics. Some (e.g., Lundberg, 1929; Ogburn, 1922) strongly maintained that the only manner by which sociology could become a respectable science was through a quantitative—that is, statistical—approach. As occurs all too often in all areas of life, including the world of the intellectual-academician, sides quickly became polarized. On one side stood those in the subjectivist camp, urging their associates to employ all techniques that would allow them to understand the individual's definition of the situation. On the other side were those who strongly rejected anything that smacked of subjectivism and urged their colleagues to utilize the tools of statistics and controlled research design to understand the principles of human social behavior. For this latter group, unless behavior could be quantified it could not fit into the social scientist's research interests. As a citizen one might indeed be interested in problems of the "mind"; as a social *scientist* he should be interested in studying only those observable things and processes that could be quantified and subjected to careful statistical analysis.

Psychology itself, of course, went through the same polarizing battles. On one shore stood the behaviorists and the practitioners of many related approaches, waving spears and hurling invectives at the other shore, on which were camped the surviving members of the introspectionist or subjectivist groups. The impact of operationalism (the defining of concepts in terms of specific, observable procedure for their measurement), which was emerging from the joint efforts of philosophers and physical scientists (the Vienna Circle Group) fed this growing controversy, giving weight to the non- (or anti-) subjectivist groups. Only behavior that was open and observable seemed to fit the operational scheme. Meanings, inner mental processes, consciousness, Freudian conceptions, and so on, were outside the realm of the reasonable when it came to measurement operations. And so they were cast aside, read out of the establishment of social-scientific inquiry.

Another theme of the Vienna Circle was a general unity of all sciences; there exist universal principles with which all sciences deal. This theme had its impact on all scientific disciplines from physics to the social sciences. It was clearly antithetical to the subjectivist tradition, which stressed the uniqueness of human action. According to the *verstehen* mode, which most subjectivist approaches emphasized either explicitly or implicitly, the rule-following, purposive quality of human behavior was removed from the realm of the causal, mechanistic principles applicable to nonhuman objects. Those who sought unity in all sciences

tended to turn away from this seemingly disunifying perspective.

Change fortunately did occur, leading eventually to the present situation in which lines between camps are blurred, and in which the so-called subjective can be and is examined systematically and objectively and can be subjected to refined statistical analysis. In social psychology, for example, the development of paper-and-pencil self-report tests to measure individual or group attitudes and values (e.g., Thurstone & Chave, 1929) provided demonstration that man's values, beliefs, opinions, and attitudes, *could* be measured and subjected to careful statistical analysis. The requirement of operationalism was thus realized; a person's checkmark on an attitude scale became the concrete operation that defined the internal concept of "value" or "attitude." Certain assumptions about the metric properties of those checkmarks, in turn, allowed investigators to make statistical analyses. As we saw on pp. 14–15, the development of tests to measure cognition, personal constructs for example, provides another instance of the now-blurred distinction between the once finely differentiated definitions of "legitimate" science.

INTRODUCTION TO FIVE PROPOSITIONS

Two transformations, *of* man and *by* man, have appeared in this review. They form our view of social psychology. Transformations *by man* center on the cognitive or knowledge processes, the means whereby man comes to construct the environment of people, relationships, processes, institutions, and objects, with which he lives. The transformation *of man*, on the other hand, is concerned with the structures, norms, and rules, the values and ideologies, and the practices of the society into which a man is born and of the groups and organizations in which he spends his life.

This dual-transformation perspective produces a social psychology that has a great deal in common with its codisciplines psychology, sociology, and anthropology. I personally am disinclined toward neat packaging and labeling of fields and subfields, especially given our shared goal of understanding human behavior.

Without hesitation, therefore, I shall call on all sorts and varieties of thinking, crossing departmental lines and historical periods whenever possible, in order better to achieve the goal of understanding.

In the pages that follow I build on the introductory remarks about the knowledge processes —the transformation *by* man—and offer five relevant propositions with supporting data; in the second part of the book I deal with transformations *of* man. The five propositions are intended to be heuristic rather than neatly derivable from some more general theory. Several share much with Krech and Crutchfield's early effort (1948) to organize social psychology in terms of a set of propositions. These propositions or statements provide one useful manner of organizing and focusing what is a vast amount of data and thinking about man's perceptual-cognitive processes. They are best seen as tools for viewing the field and grasping its essentials. They are interdependent in nature and overlapping in content rather than mutually exclusive statements; each, however, does bring a slightly different perspective to the entire picture.

The propositions about the perceptual-cognitive processes are not to be taken as isolated events having little relevance to man's personal or social life. In fact, they are the building blocks, the fertile soil out of which our lives are formed, our choices made, our actions taken. To understand the operation of such processes, therefore, brings us just that much closer to an understanding of ourselves and our world.

And finally, an extensive variety of topics usually treated by social psychologists are treated here primarily as they may be conceptualized in perceptual-cognitive terms. The five propositions offer us an approach to understanding such matters as attitude formation and change, person perception and interaction, conformity and deviation or independence, choice and decision making, language behavior, communication, distortion, defense, illness, and so on. Several of these topics are dealt with in some detail. For the most part, to study the perceptual-cognitive processes by which man comes to transform and know his social world is to study one of the most significant aspects of man's social-psychological existence.

The five propositions we shall examine argue that our encounter with the world is: I, mediated; II, meaning-giving; III, relative and comparative; IV, selective; V, sociohistorical.

Section I

On mediation

Proposition I
Man's encounter with the world is mediated through and
transformed by perceptual-cognitive processing

Chapter 1

The inference process
in person perception

You see a chair over there across the room. Beside the chair stands a person. On a nearby table you see an ashtray. These things hit you with a sense of their immediacy. You feel definitely about the matter: "I have direct contact with my world!" Just open your eyes and look about. It is as though the objects and persons are somehow touched by our eyes; much as we may pass our hand over the contours of a rock, sensing its shape directly, we feel that we may likewise pass our eyes over that rock, that chair, that person, and thereby directly, visually, grasp their form.

THE COGNITIVE MODEL

To put this phenomenal experience into other terms, we might say that we feel that we are in direct—that is, *unmediated*—contact with the stimuli of our environment. As Gestalt psychologist Koffka put it, however, "if things look as they do because they are what they are, then perception would not contain in its very makeup a cognitive problem" (quoted in Scheerer, 1954, p. 97). The absence of any simple correspondence between our percept of an object and the stimulus deriving from that object suggests that we do have, in Koffka's terms, "a cognitive problem." The Gestalt school of psychology forced such matters to our attention. A dotted figure, say Figure 1.1*a,* has a perceptual unity to it—a complete rectangle—

that exists apart from the stimuli that such an arrangement of dots presents. We perceive an arrangement such as Figure 1.1*b* as a complete circle, whereas the stimulus patterning is an incomplete form. There is a correspondence, a fortunate one, to be sure, between our percept of the forms and the actual stimulus pattern they present; but it seems we must speak of certain principles of cognitive organization that are not to be found in the stimulus array.

To Gestalt psychologists, especially Wertheimer and his associates Köhler and Koffka, the complete circle, the configuration of the square, and innumerable other cases suggested that our perception is not direct but rather is *mediated* by internal organizational structures that transform an object-out-there into an organized perceptual field (see Peters, 1962). As Scheerer (1954), a more contemporary cogni-

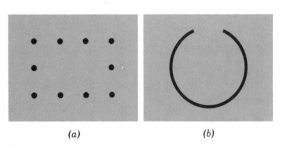

(a)   (b)

Figure 1.1 Gestalt qualities in simple visual perception

tive theorist, puts it, "... we do not see stimuli but see *because* of stimuli" (p. 97). Our contact is not directly with the stimulus, but with the *consequences* of the stimuli that are out there in our environment.

It is useful at this point to call on a relatively common conceptual model based on the writing of Heider (1958) and of Scheerer (1954). This model, presented as a diagram in Figure 1.2, provides a way to illuminate the mediated nature of our perceptual-cognitive processes.

On the far left side of the diagram is the actual *physical world*, the geographic environment. Physical objects and persons are *distal stimulus sources*. At the far right of the diagram is the individual's perceived world, his *psychological field*. Here is the world as transformed by the individual, his *representation* of the distal objects. This is the world of the *phenomenal object*, the *percept*; that is, the world of his experience.

Between the two worlds we find several stages of mediation. The distal source does not operate directly on an individual, but rather stimulates his sensory receptors *via some medium*. For example, a distal stimulus source, say a chair, reaches our visual sensory receptors at the retina of the eye by the medium of patterns of light waves. Sound waves are another medium that transmits a distal stimulus to our sensory receptors. In the realm of person perception, our primary interest as social psychologists, the distal stimulus object is another person and the medium consists of all manifestations of that person that serve as *cues* to our perception of him. This medium therefore includes the words he utters, the intonations of his speech, nonverbal material such as fidgeting, smiling, frowning, his physical appearance, his actual behavior in a given setting, and so on.

The medium, including such things as light and sound as well as the complex person-perception cues, impinges on our sense receptors, setting up a *proximal* (nearby) *stimulus array*. This is a second step removed from the actual physical object; for example, the light from a chair provides a proximal stimulus pattern on the retina; we respond to this latter pattern or array. *Sensory organization* in Figure 1.2 includes a variety of organizational proper-

ties or groupings of the proximal array. It is out of this last step in the mediation chain that the percept emerges.

Objective and subjective determinants of perception

The Gestalt psychologists disagreed among themselves about the nature of the sensory organizational processes, although they were in basic agreement about the mediated nature of the perceptual-cognitive process itself. It is possible, in theory at least, to distinguish two kinds of organizational processing of the proximal stimulus array. Krech and Crutchfield (1948) refer to these as *structural* in contrast to *functional* determinants; they may also be termed *objective* versus *subjective* determinants. The objective or structural organizational principles that were of major interest to such Gestaltists as Wertheimer and his associates at the Berlin School of Gestalt Psychology include such major principles of organization as: (1) *nearness*—the grouping into one unified whole of several parts or events that are close together in space or in time; (2) *quality*—the grouping together of objects sharing similar qualities or characteristics; (3) *common destiny* —the grouping together of things that are moving together; (4) *membership character*— the impact on the part that derives from its immersion in the context of the whole; (5) *Pragnänz*—the grouping that evolves in terms of goodness, orderliness, simplicity, or stability of form.

The Gestalt approach argues that we are always confronted with a phenomenal world that we organize, by these principles, into some kind of unity or whole. We do not experience disarray, isolated bits of random objects or events, chaos, discrete, unbounded things. *Our experienced world is an organized world* (Krech & Crutchfield, 1948, p. 84); the structural or objective principles form the basis for that organization. An additional example or two will be helpful before we turn our attention briefly to the subjective or functional principles of organization.

Let us take two key Gestalt principles, membership character and *Pragnänz*. The principle of membership character states that the context in which an event is encountered colors the

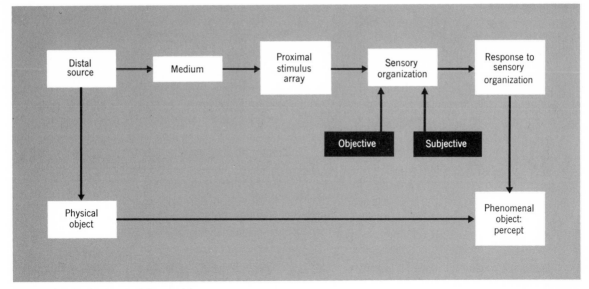

Figure 1.2 The basic cognitive model

perception of that event. We have already seen this notion in Asch's approach to impression formation (see p. 9–10); the context in which a descriptive adjective is located changes the perceived meaning of the word. "INTELLIGENT" is said not to be the same when it appears in the surrounding context of "COLD" as when it appears in the context of "WARM." The *membership character* derived from location in the "COLD" context provides a different meaning for the member "INTELLIGENT."

In what is presumed to be a similar fashion, a musical note—the member or part—has different perceived qualities when it is a member of an arrangement of notes that forms a melody. The parts are defined in terms of their membership in the totality. They have perceived properties in one totality that are unlike their perceived properties in another totality—another melodic passage.

Persons likewise are seen to be different as members of different totalities. A man at work has membership character in his office; the same man at home has membership character at home. Many of his qualities may shift, and usually do, in fact, as he moves from one context to another.

The interesting structural principle of *Pragnänz* or good form states that all wholes have a dynamic tendency toward simplicity, precision,

stability, goodness, or fulfillment. Essentially, if we encounter an unstable system, this system should tend toward stability and simple good form. When we examine the issue in some greater depth (see Chapters 7 and 8) we will note how the very important theories of cognitive consistency are founded on a notion similar to *Pragnänz*. If we take *Pragnänz* as a given quality of human perceptual-cognitive functioning, we would maintain that people seek to make simple order out of more complex chaos. They attempt to reduce confusion to a minimum; they try to complete the incomplete; they seek to make stable the unstable. In broader terms, they seek to develop *simplifying strategies* to deal with their world.

It has been argued that the objective, structural principles are only one part of the total picture of perceptual-cognitive mediation, and that past experience, mental set, attitudes, expectations, beliefs, hypotheses, personality, need, and so on, also play an important role as functional factors. In the organization of the proximal array, therefore, we find both the individual's history and his momentary set playing an important role in the entire mediation process. These subjective factors will form a significant basis of our discussion of the several other propositions, especially in Section IV on selectivity.

Summary and preview

The phenomenal world, our world of percepts, is, then, the end product of an often rather complex mediation. Between the distal object and our response to it lies a series of transformations. Our contact with the world, which we feel to be direct, is in fact mediated by objective and subjective factors. Although the mediation is instantaneous, through it we conduct our initial transformation of the distal environment into our phenomenal field. It is important to note that this point of view in no way denies the reality of the physical world, nor does it see the physical world as unimportant. Rather, it argues for a transformational process by which the distal world becomes known to us through its translation into our terms.

Our primary interest as social psychologists is person perception and interaction rather than object perception; we turn now to the mediated nature of our perceptions of others. For the sake of simplicity, we will select a situation that rarely, if ever, actually occurs: a static, one-way encounter. Imagine yourself as the perceiver (P) and another person (O) as the person-object of your perception. The distal object, in this case, is the person "out there," a physical reality in the environment. He is the object you are attending to, the object of your perceptual-cognitive processing. You are not directly in touch with O's inner psychological life, but rather with the manifestation of the person. The mediation you receive and act on through your principles of organization to yield your percept of O includes his style of dress, his manner of walking, his speech, his actions in and on the environment, and any other of an extensive variety of ways through which he manifests himself.

As in object perception, many of the cues that mediate our perception of another person are not very consciously available to us. Because we are often unaware of the mediation, we may experience the world out there as though it were direct rather than a mediated construction. It is, of course, possible to attend to the mediation itself, seeking to become aware of the cues on which our perception is based. In the case of an object, for example, we may try to attend consciously to its contours or to its texture, its shading, its blending of colors. An artist, in fact, often takes this as his point of departure in viewing a scene to be painted; his view becomes more analytic than that of a nonartist. Essentially, he sees the object through a conscious mediation; we see the object without such awareness. Anyone who has sought to take the perspective of artist, photographer, movie maker—anyone who seeks the mediation cues that "give" the object to him—will be able to appreciate this distinctly different encountering of the world.

In person perception, then, especially when it comes to "seeing" another's moods and emotions, we may be unaware of the mediation cues that lead us to read O as angry or O as depressed. We sense that O feels angry but cannot enumerate the ingredients of that sense. Our phenomenal experience, however, is anger, directly perceived. A trained psychologist, in a manner similar to that of a trained artist, attempts to attune himself to cues that yield the perception of anger, joy, fear, and other such emotional states. That is, he attempts to become consciously aware of the cues that mediate his impressions of others. Naturally, when we look at a person whose fist is tightly clenched, his arm raised high and moving rapidly downward in a striking motion, most of us are quite aware of both his mood *and* the mediating cues that yield our impression of his mood.

THE INFERENCE MODEL

In an effort to provide both theoretical clarification and empirical examination of the perceptual-cognitive inference process, two psychologists, Jones and Davis (1965), offer us a useful approach. Figure 1.3 provides a diagrammatic summary of their position. They assume that the perceiver begins with an observation of some action by O that produces one or more effects in the environment. For example, O reaches across a table and picks up a butter dish. This single action can have a variety of effects, including the most direct one of moving the butter dish from one side of the table to the other and such others as making it difficult for someone else to get the butter dish, using

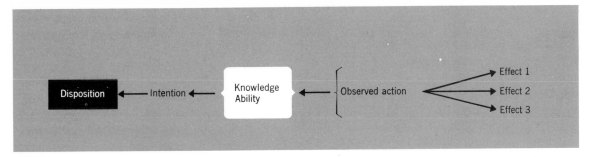

Figure 1.3 A model of the inference process in person perception (adapted from Jones & Davis, 1965, p. 222)

up the last pat of butter, blocking, by *O*'s reach, someone's eating, and so on. According to Jones and Davis, the cognitive problem for the perceiver is to decide first of all whether the action was *intentional* or *accidental*. Did *O* act intentionally? If so, we will understand his behavior in one way. Did *O* act accidentally? If so, our understanding will be different.

To gauge *O*'s intention, we must assess or at least make some assumptions about his *knowledge* of the consequences of his actions and his *abilities* to engage in such actions intentionally. When we feel that *O* has no knowledge of the consequences of his actions, we usually do not blame him for the effects produced. On the other hand, when we assume that he knows we place him at the root cause of the action. As Heider (1958) suggests in his analysis of *phenomenal causality*, we tend to form a single gestalt or unit made up of an action that produces change in the environment and the origin of that action, perhaps an individual. Persons are usually seen as the causes of actions; thus we tend to attribute to them the responsibility for their actions and the effects. In criminal law a man who is under the influence of alcohol or drugs, or one who is deemed legally insane, is said not to know at the time of his action the consequences of that action; thus he is not held responsible. A person who is presumed to be entirely in touch with reality and is assumed to have good knowledge of the consequences of his actions, on the other hand, is considered to be responsible.

Knowledge alone is not sufficient, however, when it comes to inferring intentionality on *O*'s part. Does he possess the skills or abilities requisite to performing the act? Does he possess the ability to regulate the consequences of

his actions? When we view the situation as involving great difficulty, for example, we are inclined to attribute *O*'s failures to the environmental difficulty rather than to any attribute in him. On the other hand, when we assume that the level of environmental difficulty is low, failure on *O*'s part leads us to a conclusion about him rather than about the environment. The same is true of our inferences when we note *O*'s *successful* actions on the environment; if he succeeds when everyone else succeeds, we presumably have less information about him than if he succeeds when others fail or if he fails when everyone else succeeds.

Intentionality: Origin or pawn?

Although knowledge and ability are of primary concern to Heider, and to Jones and Davis in their analysis of the intentionality of actions, other workers in the field have broadened their focus to include what has been called the *origin-pawn* dimension (e.g., deCharms, Carpenter, & Kuperman, 1965). At issue is the degree to which an individual, although he may be fully aware of the consequences of his actions, is enacting them by his own intent or in response to external force or pressure. Is he the origin of his acts or a pawn in the hands of others? If our view of the individual suggests to us that he is the origin, our inferences about him and how we perceive him will be different than if we read him as a pawn. For example, an individual who is the origin of a socially disapproved act will be held responsible and receive generally negative evaluations. An individual who does the same act but is forced by external agents to do it may not be held comparably responsible or evaluated as negatively. As with most human endeavors, such a distinction is not always simple.

A highly salient situation provides an interesting case in point. In the Nuremburg War Crimes Tribunal held at the conclusion of World War II a decision was reached that although one was a pawn in the hands of the state, the responsibility for heinous acts was still one's own. Denial of being the origin of the killing of Jews —"I was only following orders," the pawn response—did not affect the judges' decision of individual responsibility. During this country's involvement in Vietnam, similar interpretations were made by some individuals. They declared that one must violate the draft laws and refuse to serve in what many felt to be an immoral war. They argued that although one might at first glance appear to be a pawn in the hands of the Selective Service system, one would still be responsible for any killings done. Those who take this point of view see all military men as origins rather than as pawns in war.

Efforts to study systematically the impact of the origin-pawn dimension on perceptual inferences have been undertaken in the social psychological laboratory. For example, deCharms, Carpenter, and Kuperman (1965) examined a variety of conditions involving a "hero" who was being persuaded to do something. They presented a group of college-student subjects with a series of short vignettes in which they varied (1) the nature of the hero; (2) his relationship and attitude toward the agent who was influencing him; (3) the nature of the act asked of him; and (4) the extra reward that would be given for excellent performance. They developed stories about seven different heroes: an army private, a political precinct worker, a salesman, an embassy clerk, a medical intern, a union member, and a university professor. The influencing agent was another individual, a small group, or a large institution; the hero either liked or disliked the agent. In the case of the college professor the only reward was the intrinsic one of benefiting mankind through his actions. Subjects read through 42 vignettes and responded on an agree-disagree scale to six items about the origin-pawn feeling that the hero would experience. For example, they were asked to agree or disagree with "[The hero]

will feel that all decisions are being made for him by [X]" (the hero's name and the agent were filled in). Two additional items asked the subjects to indicate the extent to which they felt the hero would find the action or task a pleasant one.

Note how the use of a paper-and-pencil test in this instance, although admittedly artificial, permits the systematic variation of several kinds of variable that otherwise would be very difficult to study in any given situation. In this case it strikes me that the knowledge gained from the study warrants the costs of its rather artificial and hypothetical method of data collection.

What are those results? In the first place, subjects reported seeing the hero as more of a pawn when the persuasive agent was unattractive to him. Second, they saw him as more of a pawn when he was reacting to a large organization and more as the origin when he acted in response to the request of a small group.

DeCharms and his colleagues also utilized a measure of a general tendency to view one's self as an origin or as a pawn. This is a test developed primarily by Rotter and his associates and is referred to as the *I-E Scale* (Lefcourt, 1966; Rotter, Seeman, & Liverant, 1962). *I (internal)* refers to those who see the locus of control over events in their lives as lying within themselves; *E* refers to a general tendency to view the *external* world as having control. In origin-pawn terms, the high-internal individual tends to see himself as an origin of events in this world: "I can do it"; "I can make things happen"; "I am responsible." The high-external, on the other hand, tends to view himself as more of a pawn: "Things happen to me"; "I have little control over my fate"; "What can you expect me to do about it?"

A third major finding of the deCharms et al. study relates the subject's *I-E* score to his perception of the hero in the stories: high-externals tend to perceive the hero as more of a pawn under *all* conditions (in all 42 stories). It is as though they generalize to the hero their own world-view: "I cannot control my own fate; I don't feel he can control his own fate either." A fourth result of the study indicates that the hero is seen to enjoy the task much more when the agent is attractive to him. The professor, the only intrinsically motivated hero, was seen as far more of an origin than any of the others. This finding, like the others, makes good sense. One who is seen as self-motivated is essentially the definition of an "origin."

In summary, the study indicated that the perceptual-cognitive inference is itself a function of the perceiver's own personality, the situation or agency that induces the action, and the nature or role of O. The major implication of this study, which we shall shortly follow up, is that P is likely to attribute enduring personality dispositions or traits to an O who is held responsible for his actions.

Another study, performed by Hastorf, Kite, Gross, and Wolfe (1965), extends the origin-pawn theme one step further in the direction we are walking. Hastorf and his co-workers sought to examine the manner in which we as perceivers handle the *change* in another's behavior. If John is different today from the way he was last week, do we attribute that difference in him *to him* or to external causes? If we attribute the source of his changed behavior to personal, internal causes, presumably we will change our impression of him to incorporate his "new behavior." On the other hand, if we attribute his changed behavior to a changed environment or to social pressure, for example, our impression of him may retain some constancy: "It's the same old John, just acting a little funny from drinking too much." This inference is very unlike one in which we attribute John's funny—or strange—behavior to an actual change in him: "He's crazy, off his bloomin' nut!"

Hastorf et al. set up two separate experiments to study the nature of this attribution and its effect on the impression formed about another. In the first study subjects were asked to make judgments and evaluations of taped group discussions. Each subject heard two taped discussions by a group of three men talking for about 10 minutes on a human-relations problem. Script-following accomplices systematically varied the discussions, so that on one tape an accomplice did a lot of talking and on the other he was the quiet one. Clearly, this was a noticeable change in behavior.

In one condition of the study the experimenter told the subjects how he had tried to manipulate the behavior of the discussants for the second discussion session. Several details about the procedure were given to indicate that the behavior change was of the pawn variety rather than the origin sort; if behavior was being systematically manipulated by E, presumably its change could be attributed to external rather than to personal causes. Thus, presumably, the impressions the subjects formed about the target persons would not be altered. In another condition no such information was given. Subjects filled out a rating form about the target persons after the first discussion and then after the second. The expectation was that their impressions of the target persons should change minimally under pawn-type conditions and much more so under origin conditions.

As a part of the second study, which used the same procedures, Hastorf included among the questions an item specifically asking the subjects to indicate in general how much they felt the target person *usually* participates in group discussions, and how confident they were of this judgment. The expectation was that when change was attributed to external causes (as in the experimental condition) the subjects should confidently rate the target person in terms of his first-discussion behavior rather than his changed behavior. That is, if the target person talked very little during the first discussion but increased considerably during the second discussion when the experimenter had actively manipulated his participation rate, the perceptual-cognitive inference would be that he usually talks little. He is not held responsible for the shift in his behavior. In the origin condition, by contrast, when the change could easily be attributed to personal causes, the expectation was that the subjects would be somewhat more confused and less confident about their ratings.

The combined results of both experiments by the Hastorf group supported the predictions. Behavior that was perceived as externally caused was not weighted as heavily in evaluations about O as behavior seen as internal. The authors conclude that when we "read" the locus of causality for a change in another's behavior, the nature of this reading influences the inference we make about that person. Even if the change was in a positive direction but he was not responsible, we are less likely to alter our impression of him than when we can impute the motivation for the change to internal causes.

You Deserve What You Get. That we seem to prefer living in an orderly world, one that makes sense, is a matter that will be of considerable concern to us as we consider several of the later propositions (see especially Sections II and III). It will nevertheless be helpful to introduce a bit of cognitive consistency theory here while we are dealing with the inference process as it relates to the matter of the causality or responsibility for one's acts.

There are many kinds and degrees of orderliness that we could imagine as "oughts"—as things we feel *should* exist for us in our world. For example, in our society at least, effort and hard work *ought* to be rewarded. "Neither is there work without reward, nor reward without work being expended." We may feel that the world is a just place if people get by way of outcomes what they deserve; or, as it is also phrased, people deserve what they get.

For the moment, let us assume that within each of us there exist certain rules of psycho- or socio-logic that associate particular behaviors with certain kinds of outcome. Further, let us assume that these rules govern our inference process, leading us to complete the inference, "If action *A* occurs, then *B* will appear as an outcome," or the converse, "if *B*, then *A*." This suggests that whenever we encounter a situation with half of the inference present we complete it according to our rules. Thus, for example, if we encounter a man who is receiving a reward, we tend to infer that he must have worked hard or contributed something in order to get that reward. Likewise, if we encounter a man who is suffering, we may assume that he deserves this suffering, or we may assume, on seeing someone in a relatively severe accident, that he has caused this by his own actions.

Clearly, what we are talking about in these examples is another series of cases in which we tend to perceive *O* as being a responsible

origin or a victimized pawn. In each case the inference of origin-pawn is made on the basis of a complex *inferential set* (if *A*, then *B*) that we have assumed each of us maintains. Given one part of that complex set, we are led to complete it with the "logical" remaining part. Several laboratory investigations have been undertaken in an effort to study this matter. We shall briefly examine a few of these studies, in particular those performed under the direction of Lerner.

In one of his series of investigations Lerner (1965) studied observers' reactions to a situation involving the relationship between effort and desirable outcomes. He assumed that one of our rules of psycho-logic is a tendency to view the world as orderly if effort produces positive outcomes. He reasoned that if observers witnessed one of two persons working on a task rewarded, *strictly by chance*, while the other received nothing, they would be likely to view the rewarded worker as contributing more to the task than the unrewarded worker. Subjects listened to the same tape-recorded interaction between two persons who presumably were "over in that other room working." The experimenter then had the subjects rate each of the target persons in terms of his contribution to the team's task. Results support the expectation; *even knowing the reward was by chance drawing*, subjects rated the worker who was paid for his work as contributing significantly more to the team's task than the unpaid worker. The same act, therefore, is perceived differently according to the perceiver's inferential rules of psycho-logic.

In a somewhat more complex study on a related point Lerner and Simmons (1966) investigated observers' reactions to what they called the "innocent victim." They created an experimental situation in which subjects viewed a victim (actually an accomplice, presented on videotape) undergoing electric shock as part of an experiment. Some of the subjects were told the victim could not avoid the shocks; other subjects were allowed to intervene to prevent the shocks; for still other subjects the victim volunteered, martyr-like, to undergo further shocks just to help them gain lab credit for observing the entire experiment. Subjects were all told that the study was concerned with emotional cues. They made ratings of the victim's attractiveness.

The interesting results indicated that (1) the suffering victim who was shocked without any hope of subjects' intervention was perceived relatively negatively and as being unattractive; (2) the least rejection of the victim occurred when the subjects' actions could alleviate the shock situation; (3) the greatest rejection occurred when she was a willing martyr. In the main, therefore, results suggest that when there was little to be done to aid the innocent victim the reaction was to devalue her, as though to maintain the inferential psycho-logic that "she must deserve the shock she's getting."

In another study Lerner and Matthews (1967) found that when P felt indirectly responsible for O's suffering, P tended to devalue O, as in the preceding studies. They found, however, in contrast to Lerner and Simmons, that O's self-inflicted negative fate did not produce a devaluative description of her.

In one further study in this vein Walster (1966) found that the more serious the consequences of an accident by O, the more observers saw O as being responsible. That is, the more severe the consequences, the more observers tended to feel, "He got what he deserved." Other studies have shown that we often tend to *devalue* the victim of our own misdeeds. When students were killed on several college campuses in the early 1970's, much public sentiment repeated: "They got just what they deserved."

Assigning dispositions

In our efforts to make inferences about our interpersonal environment, then, we seek to distinguish between *intentional, accidental*, and *externally constrained* determinants of O's actions. Through our assessment of his knowledge, his ability, and the nature of the situation in which his action occurs, we reach a conclusion: "YES, his actions are intentional and primarily self-determined; he is the origin of his acts"; or "NO, his actions are accidental and primarily externally caused; he is a pawn in the hands of others' demands."

Once intentionality has been assigned by P to O's actions, P is able to infer certain stable *dispositional characteristics* that give meaning and coherence to O's behavior. Heider's discussion (1958) of dispositional properties in social perception is instructive. He maintains that although actual mediation may vary considerably, the phenomenal or experienced constancy of our impressions derives in great measure from the invariant properties of the distal, object world. Extending the notion of object constancy from physical objects to person objects, Heider's position is that our impressions of other persons maintain a constancy even though they are mediated by a variety of different cues; just as size or shape constancy is found, so too is human constancy. For example, different *proximal patterns* (different cues) still yield an impression of the same underlying mood or emotion. To use an example cited by Heider, a wish for something may be conveyed to the perceiver by a variety of different mediations. A person might proclaim, "I want that"; or he might convey the same impression by means of a long, tortured dialogue, the summary of which would lead the perceiver to say, "You want that?" Or his actions might convey his wish; a child may go into a tantrum when he sees another child licking the red lollypop he himself wants. In spite of these changing conditions of mediation, we are still able to read the wish.

Dispositional properties in person perception, then, are O's underlying personality characteristics that appear to be relatively invariant across a variety of mediations and that give a coherence to the impression we form of him. To the extent to which we are able to pin a dispositional quality onto O, we are able to retain a relatively enduring impression under varying conditions; the personality disposition allows a variety of separate mediations to occur without a change in the phenomenal impression. Let us say that we attribute the dispositional personality characteristic of *friendly* to O. This single property serves a dual function for us. First, a variety of separate mediational cues become organized under that heading and permit us thereby to maintain a constancy of impression. He may smile, approach us, speak softly, shake hands, show a twinkle in his eyes, say, "Hi, can I help?" and in any number of ways give us the cues of friendliness. Although these cues are different, they gain the property of *synonyms* in that they all come to mean to us that *O* is friendly.

A second function of constancy is that, having attributed to *O* a dispositional property *friendly*, we may make predictions about *O* and our relationship with him. As Heider puts it:

"Just as one can predict the rolling behavior of the ball because its spherical shape is a persisting property, so one can predict (albeit with less confidence) that *O* will help *P* because of his friendly nature, an enduring personality trait" (1958, p. 30).

Heider's thesis, which forms the basis for the empirical work by Jones and Davis (see pp. 40–44), maintains that the essential orderliness and intelligibility of our interpersonal environment derives from this attribution of dispositional characteristics to other persons. Without such attribution, Heider suggests, the behavior of others as mediated through proximal stimulus arrays would be an unintelligible series of momentary, chaotic events.

Heider and Simmel examined certain facets of this matter in early research (1944). They showed a group of subjects a movie that involved a fixed-position rectangle with a small, movable section in its upper right-hand corner, and three solid, moving geometrical forms: a large triangle (*T*), a small triangle *(t)* and a small circle (*c*). At first the subjects saw the film only in terms of movement of separate items; Heider reports that as long as they did so the film had little meaning to them. However, when they began to attribute motives and sentiments (that is, psychological dispositions) to the moving objects, the entire film acquired a meaningful organization. As soon as the subjects saw the movements in terms of acts by persons, they could talk about one object *following* another (*t follows T*), or *pursuing* another (*T chases t*), and so on. The enclosure with the movable part was most often seen as a house with a door. The objects in the film came in contact with the door; subjects usually viewed this in terms of persons opening or pushing on the door. *T, t,* and *c* were seen as persons with motives and intentions. When *T* moved behind *t* and *c* around the house, subjects reported that *T* was chasing *t* and *c*; they attributed greater strength to *T* and an antagonism between *T* and the other two.

In other words, sense rather than nonsense occurred when subjects anthropomorphized the situation. Don't we, in fact, do much the same in seeking to understand the behavior of animals? If we attribute to them the same kinds of psychological trait as persons possess, their actions often take on a new kind of intelligibility. We may be in error in this anthropomorphism; yet in our pursuit of an understandable world such attributions often are helpful tools in producing order and meaning.

Situational roles and psychological dispositions

Referring back to Figure 1.3, we can now see what is meant when Jones and Davis say that once *P* has assessed *O*'s knowledge and abilities and determined whether *O*'s actions were intentional or accidental, he refers intentional acts and effects to a basic, underlying dispositional property that he attributes to *O*. *O*'s acts and their effects, therefore, provide the mediational cues that form *P*'s organization of his impression into the language of psychological disposition.

Let us assume we are dealing with events that are intentional rather than accidental or of a chance nature. In inferring enduring psychological dispositions from *O*'s actions and their effects we make several additional assumptions. First, given that most acts produce a variety of effects, we assume that certain ones were more likely than others to be the effects *O* intended. Second, if we assume that *O* freely chose an act from several alternatives, we will know more about his psychological disposition than we would if he had been constrained by the situation to do this particular act. Essentially, Jones and Davis suggest that clearly defined role requirements that limit *O*'s freedom of choice in any given situation can prove relatively *uninformative* as to *O*'s personal characteristics. In other words, pawns are less informative about dispositions than origins are.

Jones, Davis, and Gergen (1961) sought to

provide an empirical test for several theoretical notions about the inference process in person perception. Subjects were presented a tape-recorded job interview in which the interviewee was presumably being interviewed either for the job of astronaut or submariner. All subjects who heard the astronaut interview session heard the interviewer describe the ideal astronaut as a self-sufficient, inner-directed person. Those who heard the submariner interview heard the interviewer describe a more gregarious, other-directed person as the ideal. The role-playing accomplice had been trained to follow a pre-pared script during his taped interviews. In half of the sessions for each job the recording portrayed him as *fitting* the job requirements; that is, as the astronaut interviewee he was inner-directed, as the submariner he was other-directed. In the other half of the sessions his behavior *deviated* from the role prescription; in the astronaut interview he was other-directed and in the submariner interview he was inner-directed.

At the conclusion of the tapes all subjects were asked to rate the interviewee as they thought him to be *really*. The theory, of course, predicted that in-role performances would pro-vide relatively uninformative cues for inferring psychological dispositions, whereas role-de-viant behavior would provide good cues for such inferences. The results strongly supported this prediction. The in-role interviewee was rated as only moderately inner-directed or moderately outer-directed, and the ratings were made with little confidence. The out-of-role interviewee, on the other hand, was rated more extremely and with greater confidence by the subjects. The role-deviant astronaut, for ex-ample, was seen as *very* conforming, affiliative, and other-directed. Because the role called for an inner-directed manner, while his actual behavior on tape was other-directed, the sub-jects could infer that therefore he *really* was other directed. If he had behaved as the role required they could not have been sure whether his real disposition or the situation had prompted his behavior. The role-deviant sub-mariner, behaving inner-directedly when the role called for outer-direction, likewise was confidently rated by the subjects as independent

and nonaffiliative; in other words, as inner-directed.

This study provides interesting support for the argument made earlier by Peters in his discus-sion of the rule-following, purposive model (see pp. 20–22). As you will recall, when we seek to explain human behavior we turn to an analy-sis of the norms of the situation in which the behavior occurs. Actions that conform to the requirements of a situation are intelligible to us. We need go no further. The man who crosses the street to buy some tobacco is acting in a way that we may explain fairly easily. However, when action deviates from the normative rules defining behavior in a given situation, Peters suggests we must turn our attention more toward a causal explanation than to the rule-following model. The behavior of a man who hops across the street cannot readily be ex-plained by, "to get some tobacco": "But why did he hop?" Jones and Davis argue that in this context of *role-violation* or *deviation* the ob-server learns more about the dispositional properties of O than in the rule-following con-text. If everyone does it that way, we need not refer to some property of O to make the situation intelligible. If everyone does it that way, but O does it in another manner, however, we will be inclined to turn to an examination of O to understand what is happening and why.

The Jones et al. study took place in a non-face-to-face situation; subjects only heard a tape-recorded interview. Several studies in face-to-face encounters both substantiate and extend their findings. In one study (Steiner & Field, 1960), for example, groups of subjects met to discuss desegregation of public schools. One of the subjects was an accomplice instructed to play the role of a segregationist. In half of the groups the experimenter publicly as-signed him this role; in the other half no roles were assigned, although the subjects were en-couraged to take into consideration a wide variety of viewpoints on the issue, including those of a segregationist, a member of the NAACP, and a northern clergyman. The re-search question concerns the subjects' impres-sion of the accomplice. In the free-choice condition, it was assumed, they should form a stronger impression of his psychological disposition. Furthermore, given their own integrationist beliefs, they should evaluate him more negatively than in the role-playing condition. Results from the study generally supported his expectation.

In terms of the mediation of the perceptual-cognitive process, the preceding discussion argues for two classes of functional factor: *situationally defined rules or norms* that give meaning, coherence, or intelligibility to an interpersonal event; and *psychological dispositions* that serve the same function. It is likely that both situational rules or norms and psychological dispositions operate in nearly every live human interaction, although one or the other may predominate. The actions of persons in our environment have the quality of *meaningfulness*, either because we attribute psychological motives and traits to them, or because we see them as governed by a rule-following model, or both. Although Heider and Jones and Davis placed their greatest emphasis on the psychological-disposition side of the picture, it seems reasonable to argue that situational rules operate in much the same manner and to the same ends: to provide coherence and intelligibility to what would otherwise be a series of unrelated, discrete, ever-changing, disturbing, and difficult-to-deal-with collages of persons, objects, and events.

INGRATIATION

Imagine yourself as a college professor holding office hours. A student knocks on your door and enters, somewhat hesitantly. You sense her nervousness, so to make her feel more comfortable you put on a great big fatherly grin, and with soft sincerity politely ask her to have a seat. You cannot help noting that she's a rather attractive young thing. She's in your social psychology class. After her initial nervousness has passed, she comes on as a rather self-confident and noticeably very friendly young woman. She pointedly and repeatedly compliments you on your lectures: "They're so interesting. You've really got a brilliant mastery of your field. This must be the best psych course I've ever had. I hope that someday I

can do just half that well, that is, if I ever get to teach like you; I bet you could make the dullest subject a living, exciting field." On and on she continues. Just before she gets up to leave, she quietly asks if you would really mind if she turns her paper in a week late. "What, me mind! Of course, my dear, of course you may."

The old maxim warns against looking a gift horse in the mouth. Yet, as we all well know, it does not imply paranoia if you pause a bit and wonder about the intentions of that young lady. In the Jones and Davis inference-process model, we have a situation in which the girl, O, acts verbally and produces certain effects. Based on your assessment of her intention, you, P, are likely to arrive at one of two kinds of inference about her personality dispositions. On one hand, you might infer that she is basically a very friendly, warm, sincere, and honest person. After all, she behaved in such a complimentary manner, made you feel just great; your ego was desperately in need of inflation that particular morning. On the other hand, you might infer *ingratiation*: you might infer that you really cannot judge her to be sincere and honest because the context of the encounter was one in which ulterior, manipulative motivations might well have prompted her complimentary behavior. Essentially, therefore, her positive behavior *in this context* provides an ambiguous source of mediating cues with which to make inferences. In a manner very much akin to the Gestalt notion of membership character and its effect on the stimulus event, the contextual surround within which the behavior takes place changes the inferential meaning of that behavior. Behavior therefore has different meaning for our perceptual inferences *as a function of the context in which it occurs.*

The example involves a particular kind of role relationship between the two protagonists. Professor and student occupy positions that differ in their power to determine effects. The student is in an inferior power position in terms of controlling the professor's behavior (ha!); he, on the other hand, has a greater degree of control in determining what we assume to be important consequences for her. Jones (1964), who has extensively studied ingratiation, suggests that under the conditions in which *P* controls resources important to *O*, *P*'s inferences about *O*'s intentions will be ambiguous because he can infer either sincerity or ingratiation. On the other hand, Jones suggests, in a situation of greater equality of power, positive behavior on the part of *O* provides a less ambiguous inference for *P*; *P* is more likely to attribute to *O* the disposition of sincerity or friendliness. He is more likely to read *O*'s compliments as honest rather than as ingratiating and manipulative.

Jones' efforts to provide experimental support for the ingratiation effect reveal general but not always unequivocal empirical validation. In the standard experimental design for testing these ideas subjects who differ in status or in their degree of dependence on one another are placed together in a situation at the conclusion of which each evaluates the sincerity of the other. For example, Jones, Gergen, and Jones (1963) used as subjects upperclassmen and freshmen in a campus ROTC unit; this clearly involved a real status difference. In the experimental or *ingratiation* condition of the study subjects were told that the experimenter was attempting to find compatible leader-follower pairs for a later important study of leadership. In the control condition subjects were simply told that they were involved in a study of first impressions in which it was important not to mislead one's partner.

Subjects sent messages to one another concerning their views on a variety of issues. All messages were intercepted by the experimenter, who substituted controlled messages for all subjects; differences in postexperiment ratings of partners were therefore unlikely to be attributable to differential message content. At the conclusion of the study subjects rated their partners on several traits, all of which indicated sincerity and trustworthiness or insincerity and unreliability. Of particular interest for the ingratiation model is a comparison of the sincerity ratings by high-status as opposed to low-status subjects. Under control conditions, as we might expect, this comparison revealed no difference in ratings; high-status subjects perceived the lows as being as sincere as the lows perceived the highs. Under ingratiation conditions, how-

ever, the high-status subjects, as predicted, perceived the lows as being less sincere and the lows perceived the highs as being more sincere.

Recall that the high-status person is the one who must decide whether *O*'s positive comments reflect sincerity or ingratiation. As this study suggests, the high-status subjects are inclined to view the low-status subjects' messages as relatively insincere.

Further ingratiation studies conducted by Jones and his co-workers offer additional support for this facet of the inference process. Subjects in one study (Jones, Jones, & Gergen, 1964) served as bystanders asked to evaluate an individual who either agreed very closely with the opinions of a third person or did not. Under one condition this individual was obviously in a power-inferior position needing approval from the other person; in the second condition their relationship lacked this kind of dependency. In the power-inferior condition the individual's behavior was evaluated by subjects as more positive and he was better liked when he disagreed than when he agreed. Apparently, even for bystanders not directly involved in the situation, close agreement on the part of a power-inferior or approval-seeking individual is taken to mean ingratiation.

Experimental research validates our own impressions of this phenomena. How often have students who do in fact *really* value their instructor found themselves in the position of having to proclaim, "I'm *not* saying this for a grade, but because I really mean it"? This proclamation to the instructor and to all bystanders is intended to remove the ingratiation interpretation that we all sense is a potential one under these circumstances. In essence the student is saying, "infer sincerity, not ingratiation." Jones would argue that we would be less inclined to make that proclamation with peers. How does this jibe with your own experience?

Criticism

Jones' work on ingratiation emphasizes the perceptual-cognitive inferences that may be made from *positive* actions on the part of *O*, given his status relative to *P*. It is also possible to examine the negative side of this picture.

You, as the college professor, meet with your small seminar in social psychology. A student is presenting his term paper to the entire seminar. You sit back and listen. "Not at all bad," you think to yourself. "Of course, there are a few things that could be improved." You tell the student about them. After you finish your appraisal, another student in the seminar decides to pitch in with his own critical comments. You listen to his criticisms of his fellow student and find them rather reasonable, well thought out, pleasantly (i.e., diplomatically) delivered. But what impressions of you and of the student-critic have the others formed?

Results of two methodologically different studies provide suggestive answers (Deutsch, 1961; Iverson, 1964). Basically, if I may dare to generalize these findings, you, the professor, will be perceived in more positive terms than the student critic; the same act of criticism performed by persons of different status means different things and produces different impressions of the criticizer. The criticizer of high status in relation to the one criticized is "good"; the low- or equal-status criticizer is "bad."

In one effort to study this phenomenon Iverson (1964) had a group of subjects listen to the same taped talk and then make ratings of the speaker. Subjects used adjectives descriptive of personality to make these ratings: quick-witted, intelligent, considerate of others, friendly, obstinate, vengeful, and so on. They first heard a relatively neutral passage and recorded their impressions. The experimenter then introduced the taped speaker as a well-known authority in the field of mental deficiency, presumably recorded in a professional colloquium address, or as a high-school student whose talk was recorded as an entry in a high-school speaking contest. The subjects for the experiment were all college students, so this introduction produced a speaker of either higher or lower status than their own. In his talk the speaker made several asides in which he tended to be critical of his audience. After hearing the talk the subjects recorded their impressions once again. In evaluating his results Iverson found that the high-status speaker who was critical of his audience was rated as having more positive personality traits than the low-status speaker. Of course the remarks were all precisely the same, yet one context produced different impressions about the speaker than another context. When the speaker had high status he could be critical of his audience and yet be read as a good person who was concerned and trying to be helpful. When he was of low status the very same remarks led subjects to read him as impudent and generally unpleasant.

In another relevant study Deutsch (1961) used a paper-and-pencil test to examine the effects of social context on the interpretation of praise and criticism. Briefly, the subjects in this study were in the position of observers viewing a *particular act* performed by a *particular O* on a *particular P* in a *certain context*. Deutsch presented his subjects several evaluative statements about an action: "you did that extremely well; you did that well; you did that poorly; "you did that extremely poorly."

He placed the evaluations in a variety of institutional contexts, including, for example, family, school, the military, and work. Within each context, finally, he defined three kinds of role relation between P and O: O as P's superior; O as subordinate to P; O and P as peers. For example, "You did that extremely well," Mr. Pitman, a student, told his teacher, Mr. Anderson; "You did that poorly," Bob Simon said to his father. The subjects were asked to answer several questions, but the key was: What did P (the recipient of the act) think O's (the actor's) purpose was? Essentially, therefore, the subjects were to indicate what they felt the P in the statement would see as O's intention.

Analyses of the data from this study provide general support for the kind of conclusion reached by Iverson in his research. That is, criticism by superiors is typically seen as intended to be helpful. Criticism by peers in all but the work setting is also seen as trying to be helpful; in the work setting their criticism is perceived as designed to make P feel bad. In general, criticism by subordinates is seen as negative in purpose in the military and school contexts, but not in the family. Over all, praise more often than criticism is seen as motivated by positive "trying-to-be-helpful" intentions. Furthermore, in general all evaluations made by superiors are more likely to be perceived as motivated by

Table 1.1 Conclusions of perceptual-cognitive studies of the inference process

O's Acts	P's Perception	O's Acts	P's Perception
1. O praises P ⟶	P perceives ingratiation . . . (a) when O's status is lower than P's. (b) when O is dependent on P.	6. O's actions are constrained or restricted by external conditions ⟶	P perceives O as the pawn and as not being responsible for his behavior . . . No inference is made from O's acts to O's personality.
2. O criticizes P ⟶	P Forms (+) impression of O . . . (a) when O is P's superior. (b) when O and P are peers. (c) in less formal social contexts. P forms (−) impression of O . . . (a) when O's status is lower than P's. (b) in formal social contexts.	7. O's actions lead to relatively severe negative consequences in the environment ⟶	P perceives O as being responsible for his acts.
		8. O's actions are rewarded, even though by chance factors ⟶	P perceives O as being responsible for the actions that get rewarded.
		9. O martyrs himself for P ⟶	P forms (−) impression of O.
3. O has the knowledge to judge the consequences of his actions ⟶	P perceives O as being responsible for his intended acts, as an origin . . . P infers from the acts to O's personality dispositions.	10. O is responsible for his own negative outcomes ⟶	P forms (+) impression of O.

	P's acts on O	P's perception
4. O does not have the knowledge to judge the consequences of his actions ⟶ P perceives O as the victim or the pawn and as not being responsible for his behavior . . . No inference is made from O's acts to O's personality.	1. P is responsible for O's negative fate ⟶	P forms (−) impression of O.
	2. P's actions cannot prevent O's suffering ⟶	P forms (−) impression of O.
5. O's actions are relatively free from external constraints ⟶ P perceives O as being responsible for his intended acts, as an origin . . . P infers from the acts to O's personality dispositions.	3. P's acts remove O from a negative situation ⟶	P forms (+) impression of O.

good intentions than are evaluations by peers or subordinates. Criticism by O is thought to lead to the affective response of contempt, pity, or anger when O is subordinate to P. Resentment is expected as P's reaction to criticism only when O is of higher status and then only in the military and work contexts. The feeling that P will attempt to improve his performance after evaluation is expected most often after a superior offers criticism and least often after a subordinate's criticism. As for the effects of praise, we will let Deutsch report for himself:

"Praise by a peer is most frequently perceived as motivated by a desire to make ego 'feel good' or 'happy,' praise by a superordinate is most frequently seen as having the intention of 'helping' ego (e.g., 'letting him know that he is right,' 'encouraging him,' 'teaching him'), while praise from a subordinate is most commonly interpreted as being motivated by the subordinate's own needs (e.g., to ingratiate himself with his superior, to get the boss to do something, to be a big shot)" (p. 398).

CONCLUSION

Clearly, the program of research conducted under the direction of Jones plus the work of Iverson and of Deutsch all lend substantial support to the same general conclusion concerning the nature of the perceptual-cognitive inference process in the realm of person perception: the same behavior does not lead one to make the same inference about the behaver in different social contexts. Although the subjects on whom much of the validating research has been conducted were college students, it seems reasonable to suggest that the manner by which their perceptual-cognitive inferences are drawn are shared to a large extent with other members of the U.S. society. It is likely that each of us comes to learn what meaning to give to contextual mediators as we form our impressions of others; these learnings exist in the form of shared expectations that occur within a common cultural context.

The specific *content* of inferences might vary in another cultural milieu; the *process*, however, is assumed to be general across the entire human species. Thus, for example, there may be certain cultures in which an insult from a superior might lead P to infer that the superior is not acting with good intent, for in such cultures only equals offer insults with good intentions. This would be an example of the same process of drawing the perceptual-cognitive inference; that is, the inference varies as a function of the status relationship between P and O, but in this example the content of the inference produces a different impression of O. A nod of the head means "yes" to most Americans; in the Middle East, however, a very similar single nod means "no." Argyle (1967) reports that a gesture such as sticking out the tongue leads to rather different meanings in different cultures: "Sticking out the tongue means an apology in parts of China, the evil eye in parts of India, deference in Tibet, and simple negation in the Marquesans" (pp. 80–81).

For convenience I have summarized the conclusions of several perceptual-cognitive studies of the inference process in Table 1.1.

In Chapters 2 and 3 we shall examine some of these matters in more detail. Clearly, however, the same act will have a different meaning—and therefore produce a different impression as the outcome of the inference process—as a function of the context within which it occurs.

Chapter 2

Language and mediation

"**I ain't** gonna do it nohow." "Everyone here cool to a joint?" "My son, she play good tennis, no?" "Please do sit down for tea." "Mommie, I gotta go weewee." "That which we call a rose by any other name would smell as sweet." Or would it? "Like man, he got busted pushing grass." "There's just no word to describe how much I love you, Betty." "Clearly it's only a matter of semantics." "Now, remember Margaret, he's daddy's boss, so call him '*Mister*' Drubble." "Say, kid, where can a guy find a john around here?" "Head's over there."

Words, sentences, paragraphs, pages. Exclamations, questions, requests, demands, information. Objects and ideas come brightly packaged in linguistic bundles. Language offers us new views and perspectives; it offers possibilities unavailable to the preverbal infant (Church, 1961). It transforms us and our experience. With language we can create worlds that may have little or no objective reality: dreams; fantasies; ghosts; monsters; fears; loves; hates; hopes. We can manipulate in thought rather than in deed; we can bend symbols to our whim. We can reach out and touch another who is not present; we can convey complex information; we can request, deny, order; change behavior; shape the nature of reality.

Words and language form a basic part of every man's everyday common-sense social psychology. Not only every man, but every politician and every international diplomat as well, lives, breathes, gets re-elected, or enters the realm of oblivion on the shirttails of words and language. Kremlinologists spend endless hours poring over pronouncements from the U.S.S.R., hoping to find a shade of difference in a word or a phrase on the basis of which U.S. national policy and response can be formed. The change of a single word in a statement during late 1967 by the government in North Vietnam brought about a re-evaluation of the appropriate U.S. response. In one speech a North Vietnamese official indicated that if the United States stopped bombing, peace talks *might* be held. In a later statement the wording shifted perceptibly to, "If the bombing stops, talks *will* be held." All the difference in the world was embodied in that one-word change. Wars have been fought over languages; nations are still split over what the sanctioned speech of the country is to be.

The relationships that exist between language and mankind are relationships that have been recognized for several thousand years. Yet it is only recently that the systematic study of language has entered the social-psychological scene.

A DIFFERENTIATED FIELD

Initially the study of language focused primarily on *structural linguistics*. Efforts were directed at delineating the formal, structural properties of all languages. The limited collection of sounds within a given language, the manner by which these sounds are formed into larger units such as words, the arrangement of words into larger grammatical units, and so on, were of primary interest to linguistic analysts. For the most part psychologists were interested in applying methods of learning theory to the understanding of language acquisition. At what age did what sound emerge? Are nouns learned before verbs? More recently, the convergence of several language disciplines has provided an exciting new perspective on language and thought and on language and social behavior.

For the sake of simplicity in thinking about these newer developments, it is convenient to organize the approaches in three basically interdependent groups. In the first, *developmental psycholinguistics*, language use and development are viewed as an important specific instance of more general cognitive functioning (see Chomsky, 1965; 1969; Fodor, 1966; McNeill, 1966). Through an analysis of the underlying principles of grammatical organization and transformation, workers in this field hope to gain access to the nature of the human thinking process. The second grouping, dealing with *linguistic relativity*, emphasizes the role of language as a mediator and shaper of the environment. The world out there is differently processed by users of different linguistic codes; our own world is mediated by the particular linguistic code we are using. Finally, the third area, usually termed *sociolinguistics*, focuses on the manner by which our relationships with others in both face-to-face and larger, institutional encounters are affected by the formal structure and properties of language. Linguistic analysis in this case can reveal both the way in which language structures our relationships and the way in which our relationships are reflected through the linguistic forms we employ. The second and third groupings overlap substantially, and are of primary relevance to our interest in language as a mediator of the cognitive-perceptual pro-

cess. Both examine the relationship between two systems: linguistic and social. I have separated them for convenience and, as importantly, to highlight the fact that the third focus, sociolinguistics, has recently taken a radical upswing in significance as its methods for analysis have become increasingly refined.

DEVELOPMENTAL PSYCHOLINGUISTICS

It is most instructive to examine developmental psycholinguistics, if only briefly, as a case example of cognitive theory. The puzzle is simple; its solution is complex, difficult, and to a large extent still speculative. Human infants acquire language in a relatively short period of time. Between the ages of 24 and 42 months, a truly brief period of time, the basic processes of language acquisition have taken place. Lenneberg (1966) reports a study of 500 middle- and lower-class children in the Boston area in which trained social workers made field observations of children's verbal behavior. He finds that nine out of 10 children, by their thirty-ninth month, were able to name any object in their home, were able to understand verbal instructions, and were able spontaneously to utter syntactically complex sentences; that is, they had acquired most of the basic essentials of language.

During this period of language acquisition a child is exposed to a body of linguistic utterances from the fluent speakers who surround him. The sampling he receives is likely to be biased both in its breadth of coverage and its actual formal properties; a developing infant is not likely to encounter all the instances of language usage—both vocabulary and grammar—that he will shortly be able to handle. In addition, during this brief period he undoubtedly is exposed to adult constructions that are childlike in themselves—that is, adults may talk babytalk to him—yet somehow he comes to know the proper adult forms. Somehow, or so it appears, the infant works on the language data he receives and derives the regularities and the principles of his language.

Chomsky (1965; 1968) and others following his general orientation have suggested that any explanation of this apparent puzzle of language acquisition must consider an interaction between intrinsic organizational structures and the empirical language data presented to the child. As with cognitive theory in general, they assume that each of us possesses certain intrinsic structures of organization that transform the distal input to yield our percept. As Fodor (1966) put it, we can picture a child as a "black box" that receives certain kinds of input and emits certain kinds of output. By comparing the linguistic inputs with the nature of the child's outputs, we can gain a good sense of the transformational properties of the intrinsic structures within the "black box" (pp. 107–108). It sounds much simpler than it actually is, of course, but the design for gaining understanding of the process is clear.

Linguists who have adopted this developmental approach to the study of language acquisition concern themselves with the nature of the intrinsic transformational system. As a first approximation to the nature of this mechanism, it has been suggested that each actual complex verbal utterance (e.g., a sentence) may be reduced to a *base* or *deep syntactic structure* that contains, in highly abstract form, the components of the structure (e.g., verb, subject, object) and the rules for putting them together. A frequent example involves the distinction in the English language between active and passive sentences. To most active sentences there is a corresponding passive form: I hit the ball/The ball is hit by me; The dog eats the meat/The meat is eaten by the dog. An adult speaker, given a novel active form of a sentence, can convert it into its corresponding passive form without any further information. For example, if I presented you with an active form, *The zilch toves the mulk*, you would find it very easy to make that into its passive, *The mulk is toved by the zilch*, and you would not require any further information. What the developmental psycholinguists assume is that both the active and the passive surface structure may be reduced to a common underlying base or deep structure, which includes rules for constructing actives and for converting them into passives. It is assumed that these deep structures are sufficiently abstract and underground that only

a linguistic analyst can identify them; no speaker of a given language would know or recognize the base structures because they are not themselves possible utterances in the language.

Chomsky's argument is that, although they may correlate sound and meaning units in different ways, all languages are built on the same base structures or general principles of percept formation. He calls such linguistic principles of organization and transformation the *generative grammar*, which includes the rules that generate the specific surface structures characteristic of any language. As Chomsky sees it, the generative grammar is analogous to our "theory of language." It is roughly similar to the implicit personality theory, but this time it is our *implicit language theory*. If we needed actually to experience a specific sentence in order to use it, our speech would indeed be highly restricted and the rapid acquisition of language by children would not be possible. However, the rules of generative grammar are said to permit us to create an infinite variety of new sentences out of minimal actual experience of language data. A child, then, has a set of implicit rules (his implicit language theory) by which he can generate fluent speech from small amounts of linguistic data.

Computer simulation of human cognition

This manner of conceptualizing developmental psycholinguistics has led to the use of computer technology to *simulate* generative grammars; this amounts to computer simulation of human thought processes. The computer's programs are the rules of transformation, of logic, or of inference that the researcher assumes characterize human patterns of speech or thought. Data are fed into the computer and output is examined for accuracy of fit with actual known human output. To the extent to which the computer's output, given its *known* programmed rules, is able to approximate human output, given the as-yet *unknown* rules, we are able to gain an understanding of the human cognitive process.

In the use of computer simulation for social psychology the efforts of Abelson (1963; Abelson & Carroll, 1965) are especially noteworthy. Abelson and some of his associates have been interested in uncovering an individual's subjective logic by examining the manner by which he assesses the truth value of various assertions, especially those involved in persuasive communications. It can be argued that persons evaluate the credibility of a general statement by a process of induction from specific instances. This evaluation involves recruitment of evidence in order to test a specific statement (Gilson & Abelson, 1965). The computer enters the picture primarily as a tool to test cognitive hypotheses rapidly. In addition, before we can program a computer to simulate the human cognition involved in subjective logic, we must carefully specify a set of assumptions that we claim to be at work. Thus the computer forces a precision that is too often missing in psychological investigation.

Summary

It should by now be apparent, even with so brief an overview of this orientation, that we have been dealing with a highly sophisticated form of cognitive theory. Stripped down to its bare bones, this approach to language behavior is analogous to the several other approaches we have discussed in person perception: certain intrinsic structures are assumed to exist that organize and transform the distal input. The approach through language behavior focuses on what we have called structural properties rather than on the more functional determinants of percept formation (e.g., personality, past experience and history, expectancy), yet the argument is basically the same. The nature of human behavior (output) is such that a model based entirely on unmediated stimulus input is insufficient to account for it. Therefore one must posit certain internal mechanisms that transform the input to yield the kinds of behavioral outputs observed. And this holds for language behavior, person perception and impression formation, interpersonal interaction, and so on.

THE SAPIR-WHORF HYPOTHESIS OF LINGUISTIC RELATIVITY

Have you ever paused to wonder about the role that language plays in our conception of the world? Do *John, Juan*, and *Giovanni*, each knowing and speaking a different tongue, experience the same kinds of physical and social environment? Since antiquity man has felt some special quality about his own language. The ancient Greeks, justly proud of their language, may have been scornfully imitating the stammering "bar-bar" sounds of foreigners, when they referred to them as barbarians. The apparent appropriateness of a certain language to certain purposes is most aptly expressed in a statement attributed to Charles V of Spain: "If I were to speak to the ladies, I would speak Italian; to men, French; to my horse, High Dutch; to God, Spanish" (In Stevenson, 1948, p. 1345). Of course, not everyone views languages in precisely the same way. Another suggestion, for example, was "German for soldiers, French for women, Italian for princes, Spanish for God."

Wilhelm von Humboldt, to whom Chomsky (1968) refers in tracing the contributors to his own conception of generative grammar, is credited with pointing out the role language plays in presenting us a view of our world. But the more specific contributions of the anthropologist Sapir (1956) and the pioneering work of Whorf (1956) brought the principle of linguistic relativity into sharper focus. The hypothesis of linguistic relativity is deceptively simple in its statement and extraordinarily complex in its proof. The basic notion is that the kaleidoscopically maddening flux of sense impressions that exists out there in the world of distal stimuli is ordered and organized in terms of linguistic categories. Thus language mediates our world view. An implication of this hypothesis is that persons who speak different languages live in different worlds; their views of the world, mediated by linguistic categories, yield different ways of transforming and constructing their experience. Our world view, or *Weltanschauung,* as speakers of English is said to be different from that of speakers of the Hopi Indian language, for example.

This perspective is usually contrasted with a *neutral tag* view of language, according to which there is a common world of experience shared by all but simply labeled differently. A horse is a horse is a horse: in English we say *horse*, in Spanish, *caballo*, in German, *pferd*, and so on.

Whorfians, on the other hand, argue that our conceptions of "reality" are in their very essence relative to the language.

A systematic view

In a particularly helpful effort to provide some order and systematization to the Whorfian hyopthesis, Fishman (1960) has given us a four-fold analytic scheme. To understand the scheme (see Table 2.1) it is first necessary to distinguish

Table 2.1 A systematic version of the Whorfian hypothesis (from Fishman, 1960)

| | Data of Speaker's Behavior | |
Data about Language Characteristics	Language Data (Cultural Themes)	Nonlinguistic Data
Lexical characteristics	I	II
Grammatical characteristics	III	IV

between two levels of language: lexical and grammatical. The *lexical level* consists primarily of the meaningful units or words in any given language. One language may have a single term for referring to a phenomenon; another language may have no term for that phenomenon, or many terms, or may require some more complex phrase. *Codifiability* describes this lexical difference; if we can refer to a phenomenon by one term in English but require five terms in Hopi, we say that the phenomenon is more *easily codified* in English.

The *grammatical level* of language refers primarily to syntactical arrangements—the manner by which larger structural units are organized. At this level emphasis is on grammatical arrangements that native speakers of a language employ. For example, in English we say "the red house" rather than "the house red," as noun and adjective might be arranged in another language. Speakers of English use this arrangement and can quickly identify errors in its usage, often without being able to state the grammatical rule they are following.

In addition to language characteristics, it is possible to talk about social behavior of the speaker that is itself linguistic and social behavior that is nonlinguistic. A selection among objects or a particular manner of sorting things are examples of nonlinguistic behavior. This distinction will become clearer if we take an example or so for each of the four levels Fishman presents.

Level I involves a relationship between the lexical properties of a language and the speaker's linguistic behavior. For example, English has separate words for airplane-connected things, like fly, pilot, and airplane itself, whereas Hopi has only one. Eskimo has many individual words to indicate kinds of snow, whereas English has only one basic word. In any of numerous examples that could be cited the major issue is codifiability; what in one language is a highly differentiated phenomenon may be minimally differentiated in the lexicon of another. Ease of describing and discussing such differentiations, therefore, vary from one language to another. An Eskimo will generally find it easier to describe and discuss a wide variety of snows than will a typical speaker of English. (A skier will, of course, develop his own vocabulary to differentiate the kinds of snow that are important to him.) A speaker of English may report Fords, Chevrolets, Volkswagens, and so on, whizzing past on a freeway. A speaker of Hopi would report cars. (Both would share the choked-up feeling of smog sickness.)

Level II involves the relationship between lexical properties of a language and the nonlinguistic behavior of the speakers of the language. The classic study at this level was conducted by Brown and Lenneberg (1954). They presented subjects with a series of color discs and found that colors that were most highly codified in a language were responded to more quickly than those less highly codified. Further analyses demonstrated that recognition and recall were greater for the most highly codified colors. A highly codified color in a given language is one that can be described by a single word. For example, presented with red, white, blue, blue-gray, greenish-yellow, and brownish-black, most speakers of English will more readily respond to and recall the red-white-blue set than the set requiring longer descriptions. Additional work by Lenneberg (1957) demonstrated that the more easily codified colors were also more easily learned in a paired-associate learning task.

Level III, the relationship of grammatical characteristics and linguistic behavior, is more central to Whorf's original hypothesis than are Levels I and II. Whorf's primary concern was to relate the underlying grammatical structure of a language to the world view held by the speakers of the language. His analyses of Hopi (Whorf, 1956) and the anthropologist Hoijer's (1951) analyses of Navaho reflect this basic concern. Whorf selected Hopi to compare with what he called the Standard Average European (SAE) languages, of which English is one.

In one of his analyses Whorf distinguished between the manner by which Hopi treat plurality and numeration, in comparison with SAE languages. The basic SAE formula for plurality is NUMERATOR + NOUN FORM + S: TEN APPLES, SEVENTY-SIX TROMBONES. Whorf noted that the formula holds regardless of the nature ("real" or "imaginary") of the noun forms. He selected time references or *phases of cycle* (hour, day, week, year, summer, winter, afternoon) as examples of imaginary noun forms. Grammatically, he argues, we treat TEN DAYS in exactly the same manner by which we treat TEN APPLES, as countable and collectable realities possessing physical outlines and properties. Therefore, he continues, because of comparable grammatical treatment, we come to *think about* time in exactly the same way we think about real noun quantities: "I *give one day* each week to the Red Cross"; "If you continue doing it that way, you'll *lose too much time.*" Here, then, is Whorf's link between a linguistic occurrence (grammatical treatment) and a manner of thinking on the part of a speaker.

Whorf suggests that in Hopi real noun forms are treated differently from imaginary forms. The grammatical forms for real nouns are comparable to the SAE TEN APPLES formula. However, for time nouns the Hopi employ an entirely different form, a grammatical class referred to as *temporal adverbs*. Adverbs in English modify or qualify verbs or action forms; if time is treated as an adverb, then, it is seen not as a real entity but rather as *qualifying the action that is taking place*. Whereas in Spanish we say a man *tiene quarenta años*, "has" 40 years

or is 40 years old, in Hopi a man does not *have* 40 years; rather, he *is old fortyishly* or he *is acting fortyishly.*

Thus, whereas possession of an actual quantity of time marks SAE languages, Hopi centers on actions, *eventings* in Whorf's terms, that are qualified by a temporal adverb. The Hopi could not think about "saving" time, "spending" time, or "wasting" time, as speakers of English do. Time sequencing is less central to the Hopi grammar, and, Whorf would argue, the Hopi world view, than is action. Consider a footrace. In English we are grammatically set to be concerned with the time taken to run the race: one minute, five minutes, 10 minutes. The Hopi are grammatically attuned to experience how the race was run: rapidly, slowly, or just what.

Some interesting work on bilingualism by Ervin-Tripp (1967) is suggestive in this matter of the relation between language and world view. Ervin-Tripp was concerned with the content change that occurred as an individual shifted from one of his languages to another. She studied bilingual Japanese women who had married American servicemen during World War II. The women were given a variety of projective tests, including the Thematic Apperception Test (TAT) in which they were to make up stories to pictures, a word-association test, and a sentence-completion test. Ervin-Tripp computed the discrepancy between the content norms appropriate to a monolingual American or a monolingual Japanese group and the content of the material given by her bilinguals. Her results indicate that when asked to give word associations or make up stories or complete sentences in Japanese the subjects produced content more typical of women in Japan; when speaking English, by contrast, their material was closer to the monolingual American norm. These results held up particularly on the word-association and the sentence-completion tests. For example:

". . . Japanese women more often say 'what I want most in life . . . is peace.' Americans say '. . . happiness.' 'When I am with men . . .' Japanese women are uncomfortable, American women contented. 'When a husband finds fault with his wife, the wife . . .' in Japan, 'is defensive,' in America, 'tries to improve'" (p. 84).

Apparently, therefore, there were significant shifts in content with shifts in language. These data cannot be taken as a proof of the Sapir-Whorf hypothesis. However, they do indicate the important correlation that exists between language and thinking, including the kind of imaginative thought picked up by Ervin-Tripp's projective tests.

A *Level IV* analysis in Fishman's scheme relates the kinds of linguistic determinant presented in the preceding examples to some observable nonlinguistic behavior on the part of speakers of the language. Fishman reports one major study conducted by Carroll and Casagrande (1958), who presented groups of children with an object-classification task. They presented the children with a pair of objects that differed from each other in two qualities—for example, color and shape—and asked them to class a third object with one member of the pair. Subjects were Navaho-dominant Navaho children, English-speaking Navaho children, and a sample of white Bostonian middle-class children, about the same age. The grammatical feature of concern involved the nature of Navaho verb forms. In Navaho the verb form changes as a function of the nature of the object being dealt with. Long, flat objects for example, receive a verb form that is unlike the form required by objects with other qualities such as round and squat. The study was set up so that when a child's behavior was governed by the Navaho grammar he would select a specific one from the original pair of objects with which to match the third. For example, if Navaho grammar demanded the same verb form for all long flat objects, he would classify the long and flat *red* third object with the long and flat *green* original object rather than with the round and squat *red* object of the original pair.

Carroll and Casagrande's findings lend some slight support to the Whorfian hypothesis. They report that the Navaho-dominant Navahos made object choices as predicted by the grammatical verb form more frequently than did the English-dominant Navahos. The comparison with the Bostonian sample, however, lends another dimension of interest. The Bostonian school children made even more Navaho-like object-sorting responses than the Navaho-dominant sample! This finding suggests that the linguistic determinants of which Whorf spoke could be only one of several factors that mediate cognition and behavior. Nonlinguistic cultural factors such as experience in playing with particular kinds of objects may be as important in any given situation as the more purely linguistic factors.

So, then, what can we conclude about the Sapir-Whorf hypothesis? It does seem that linguistic factors, ranging from the most trivial and obvious lexical features to the more underground and complex grammatical features, have a degree of mediating influence over our perceptual-cognitive processes. "Having a word for it" speeds recognition, recall, and learning. A "grammatical imperative" influences the manner by which one comes to relate to certain parts of his world. However, the *Weltanschauung* or language-world-view contention of the Whorfian hypothesis, although remaining provocative and tantalizing, has not yet taken its place in the world of accepted facts. Language mediates our perceptual-cognitive processes; but whether it shapes our entire view of the world is still open to further exploration and research. When all the chips are in someday on this matter, it is likely that the answer will be a compromise between the Whorfian view and the neutral tag view. Language will then take its place as one important one among several mediators of our perceptual-cognitive transformational system.

SOCIOLINGUISTICS

At first we might think that the Sapir-Whorf hypothesis demands that we compare entirely different languages in order to test its validity; most of Whorf's examples were of this sort. On the other hand, *intralanguage* comparisons are also relevant in examining the relationship between language and social behavior. The study on codifiability of color words is one example of an intralinguistic approach. Perhaps this point will be clearer if we begin to talk in terms of linguistic *codes* rather than referring simply to "languages."

Although you and I speak the English language, each of us has the possibility of selecting among different linguistic forms and codes within that global category. Essentially, there is a variety of linguistic codes grouped under the common heading of English, or any other language. One of the major concerns of sociolinguistics is to examine the correspondences between linguistic codes and social behavior. Note that I have used the term *correspondence.* One reasonable assumption is that these linguistic codes both reflect a particular kind of social situation or social relationship and provide information that mediates our knowledge of that relationship. We are not necessarily talking about a causal bond, but rather a correspondence in which the linguistic code plays a significant role as mediator of the perceptual-cognitive processes employed in coming to define the social environment.

Bernstein's approach

One of the important contemporary contributors to the sociolinguistic examination of language and behavior is Bernstein (1958). Most of his work has been done in England and involves an analysis of the British middle-class and working-class modes of linguistic usage. Stripped bare of details, his thesis states that various socioeconomic levels have characteristically different linguistic codes, which in turn reflect different approaches to understanding social relationships. Bernstein goes so far as to suggest that the British middle class and working class have two distinct, entirely different modes of speech. These different modes orient speakers to different types of relationship with persons, events, and objects.

But what are these two class-linked linguistic codes? Bernstein views the language code of the middle class as involving complex syntactical properties that are used to clarify, expand, and make meaning explicit. This he calls a *formal* language. The working class, on the other hand, utilizes what he refers to as a *public* language, a relatively condensed speech in which the syntactical organizations are highly limited and restricted, reducing the possibilities for clarification and expansion.

". . . if the words used are part of a language which contains a high proportion of short commands, simple statements and questions where the symbolism is descriptive, tangible, concrete, visual and of a low order of generality, where the emphasis is on the emotive rather than the logical implications, it will be called a *public* language. . . . The language-use of the middle class is rich in personal, individual qualifications, and its form implies sets of advanced logical operations. . . . This mode of language-use will be termed *formal*" (1958, pp. 164–165).

Bernstein argues that a middle-class child acquires the use of *both* formal and public language, whereas the working-class child has access only to the public language code; further, that the middle-class child, unlike the working-class youngster, grows up in a highly rationalized, future-directed subsociety. Direct expression of feelings, especially hostility, is discouraged; the middle-class child learns to substitute words for deeds, to verbalize his feelings rather than express them more directly. The nuances of his mother's linguistic form convey clues about her mood, hence about the kind of response she is looking for from him. A subtle change in her sentence structure, intonation, or word placement will carry with it considerable meaning. Bernstein cites a mother's request to her child: "I'd rather you made less noise, darling." The words "less" and "rather" arouse in the child a fairly complete understanding of her intention and the consequences of his not obeying. In a working-class household, by contrast, "shut up" may be required to gain the same reduction in noise.

Bernstein's point is that a middle-class youngster also knows what to do when he hears "shut up," but a working-class child will respond only to the public language form and not to the formal linguistic expression. He is attuned to his parents' actions more than to anything in their language behavior. He is *not* attuned to picking up linguistically conveyed subtleties of mood, intention, or desire. His contacts are less verbally mediated and much more direct.

Given their importance and potential for expressing the nuances of mood and intent, verbal techniques become mechanisms for social control for the middle-class child. As he develops to adulthood, a child with formal language background retains an attentive set to the language forms and uses of others as cues to mediate his impression of them, their moods, desires, intents, and so on. He reads structural shifts in others' verbal behavior as cues to changes in the nature of his relationship with them.

In Bernstein's analysis of the working-class family desire for gratification in the present, rather than a future-orientation, and the generally more direct relationship with parents lead to a lesser emphasis on language cues as mediators. Furthermore, the lack of language emphasis in turn leads to minimization of the relationships between present and future, of the ability to deal with nonimmediately present abstract concepts, and of the ability to read subjective feeling and intention in one's own and another's actions. In public language, if a child's mother says "do it," and he asks why, her answer invokes the relationship: "Because I told you to, that's why." The paucity of complex structure makes it unlikely that he will be able to make the kind of differentiation and elaboration that permits an analysis or a challenge of "reasons" independent from the speaker; he is forced to view the reasons for acting in terms of his relationship to the authority making the demand rather than in terms of the validity of the reasons themselves.

Back in the United States. Although class structures in the United States are not so rigid as in Britain, it seems reasonable to expect that different family backgrounds will engender different code preferences. The kinds of formal linguistic organization that are requisite to more complex and fully elaborated abstract modes of thinking and relationship therefore may not be available to all persons who speak the general language, English. Some may have acquired a code of public language that orients them toward immediate, primarily nonverbal encounters with their physical and social environments rather than toward an interest in process, intent, or abstraction. One who speaks a formal language can play games with words and create new worlds far removed from the immediately given concretes of reality. A person whose language structure does not allow this,

however, is more restricted and finds it troublesome to imagine things "as if" or "as though." He cannot juxtapose in mind what does not present itself immediately. He cannot be concerned with the nuances of verbal representation.

An interview study conducted by Schatzman and Strauss (1955) sheds some empirical light on the issues raised by Bernstein. They interviewed 10 upper-middle-class (on education and income) and 10 lower-class individuals after a tornado disaster had hit their community. They report finding differences between the two social-class groups in terms of the number and kinds of perspective used to communicate; the ability to take the listener's role; the handling of classifications; and the devices used to order and implement their communications. More specifically, the lower-class subjects gave descriptions as seen entirely through their own eyes, whereas the upper-middle-class subjects' descriptions took a much broader perspective. The lower-class respondents rarely qualified anything they stated. The authors see this absence of qualifiers as suggesting that the lower-class subjects took it for granted that their views represented a reality shared with everyone else. By contrast, the upper-middle-class subjects expanded their responses, seeking to provide the context within which their observations were made, thus qualifying and enriching their descriptions. Furthermore, Schatzman and Strauss report the great difficulty that their lower-class respondents had in formulating a coherent, straight story. Their data, then, are substantially congruent with Bernstein's model.

In her review of some of the other literature relevant to this social class difference Ervin-Tripp (1969) discusses some additional supportive—but by no means unequivocal—evidence. For example, Lawton (in Ervin-Tripp, 1969) reported significant class differences in group-discussion sessions, but not in interviews calling for a description and interpretation of picture material. Cowan (1969) found that pairs of working-class children initially had greater difficulty than middle-class children in a two-person game situation in which one person communicates to another by describing an object he wants the other person to select from a larger array. Cowan's data indicate, however, that working-class children were able to become successful at the task when paired with middle-class partners.

Ervin-Tripp (1969) has complained that there have been too few studies of this sort in a natural situation. Reasoning that part of the apparent difficulty in working-class children's verbal behavior may stem from the unknown experimental situation, she urges that more research be conducted in natural interaction settings. She reports studies (Labov & Cohen; Mitchell & Mitchell) conducted in a naturalistic setting that found that lower-class Negro speakers are highly verbal and engage with great skill in a wide variety of verbal games. It may very well be, therefore, that all efforts to test a Bernstein-type notion in a strict lab setting only yield supportive evidence because the setting itself stifles the free verbal interchange of which the lower-class respondents are capable. Even in the Schatzman and Strauss interview survey, the middle-class status of the interviewer might have brought out the worst in the lower-class respondents. If it does exist, such confounding of course makes it difficult to offer any unequivocal interpretation of the laboratory studies. Class differences in language behavior undoubtedly do exist; that such differences produce the wide-ranging cognitive effects Bernstein proposes is doubtful, although this still remains to be seen.

Recent efforts in the United States have sought to relate measures of general social deprivation—rather than social class per se—to assessments of intellectual development and school performance, both of which are heavily dependent on verbal abilities. In one such effort Whiteman and Deutsch (1968) developed a cumulative *Deprivation Index* based on such background factors as housing dilapidation, parent's educational aspiration for the child, size of household, extent of dinner conversation, number of cultural experiences expected for a weekend (such as visits to relatives, the zoo, the library), attendance in kindergarten. A high score on this index indicated generally higher social deprivation or what might best be termed a low degree of social stimulation and variation.

Whiteman and Deutsch relate this Deprivation Index to a variety of verbal measurements; they report a correlation in which those who were more deprived socially manifested this deprivation in their poor performances on reading achievement, vocabulary development, and assessed IQ. One implication of this work is that any verbal differences found in a population can be related to environmental conditions that can be remedied. In other words, although there are language or conceptual barriers that develop within a given population, these are not immutable conditions but can be overcome by efforts to provide a more enriched, stimulating, and variable social environment.

Dialect and impression formation

Up to this point we have focused primarily on the manner by which *P*'s language mediates his own perceptual-cognitive processes. Now we can consider for a moment the effect that *O*'s language behavior has on *P*'s perception of *O*. Language behavior, like dress, manner of walking, actions, and so on, provides a system of cues that each of us uses in forming impressions of other people. As Rex Harrison intoned so delightfully in *My Fair Lady*,

"Why can't the English learn to speak? . . . Look at her, a prisoner of the gutters, condemned by every syllable she utters. By rights she should be taken out and hung for the cold-blooded murder of the English tongue. . . . It's 'aow' and 'garn' that keep her in her place, not her wretched clothes and dirty face. . . . If you spoke as she does, sir, instead of the way you do, why you might be selling flowers too . . ." (Loewe & Lerner, 1956).

Our common experiences provide one very strong basis of support for this thesis. Dialect differences, for example, are usually quickly picked up by the listener and provide a ready category into which the person-object gets placed. It is as though the dialect triggers in each listener a wide variety of associations, which then come to play a role in his impression formation.

Triandis, Loh, and Levin (1966), in one of a series of controlled laboratory studies, varied the race (white or Negro), status (working- or middle-class), quality of spoken English (excellent or grammatically poor English), and attitude toward integrated housing (pro or con) of an actor about whom their subjects were to form an impression. Their findings indicate that the quality of the actor's spoken English was one of the most important characteristics that influenced the subjects' attitudes toward him. Ungrammatical English produced a negative impression—at least among college-student subjects.

Distinct southern Negro dialect often provokes the same kind of impression in even the least prejudiced of white listeners. It has been argued that language factors, and especially dialect, provide one of the serious handicaps of Negro employment. Some white businessmen, for example, claim that they cannot possibly hire Negroes because the distinct dialect, when it exists, drives away too much business. They seek "neutral" Negro or "neutral" white speakers. How many big-time radio or television announcers offer anything but dialectal neutrality?

More systematic efforts to examine the effect of *O*'s language behavior on *P*'s impression formation are to be found especially in a series of studies undertaken by W. E. Lambert and his associates (1967). Lambert's procedure is to have judges react to taped passages read by perfectly bilingual speakers, first in one language and then in the other. He refers to these speakers as *matched guises*, and reports that no subjects have ever become aware that they were hearing the same speaker read two different passages.

Several of Lambert's studies were conducted in Montreal, where there has been a long history of rivalry and tension between the French-speaking and the English-speaking Canadians. In one such study a group of English-speaking Canadians (EC) was asked to evaluate the personalities of matched guises speaking French-Canadian (FC) and English. Results indicated that the EC judges rated the English-speaking matched guises more positively. They saw them as better looking, taller, more intelligent, kinder, more ambitious, and so forth; these are judgments based on *voice* cues alone. Lambert then presented the same tapes to a group of French Canadian judges. Surprisingly, they too found the English-speaking matched guises to

be more favorable in personality characteristics than the FC speakers. This is interesting as a finding in that even the French-Canadian speaker downgrades his own linguistic group.

In a follow-up study conducted by Preston and reported by Lambert (1967), 80 male and female EC and 92 male and female FC first-year college students served as judges. They heard male and female matched guises speaking French-Canadian and English and rated the personalities of the speakers on such dimensions as competence, integrity and attractiveness. Results indicated that EC judges rated FC female guises more favorably than EC female guises, and rated EC male guises more favorably than male FCs. Male EC judges saw female FC speakers as more intelligent, confident, dependable, sincere, and so on, than their English guises, and female EC judges produced similar, if less gracious, ratings. When the speaker is a woman, French certainly seems to be her language for good impressions. When the speaker is a man, however, at least in this sample from Montreal, English seems to give the better impression. FC judges also generally evaluated EC guises more favorably, thus replicating Lambert's original finding. In one pleasant contradiction, however, female FC judges saw the FC male guises as more competent and socially attractive than the EC male guises.

Ervin-Tripp reports several other relevant studies. One conducted by Lambert in Israel (reported in Ervin-Tripp, 1969) found mutually hostile impressions formed by Arabic-speaking judges' evaluations of Hebrew guises and Hebrew-speaking judges' evaluations of Arabic guises. In a study by Tucker and Lambert (in Ervin-Tripp, 1969) northern white college students judged southern Negro speech most negatively; southern Negro college students favored educated southern white speech. In yet another study Harms (in Ervin-Tripp, 1969) found that a 10- to 15-second sample of speech of members of different social classes could be differentiated by judges. In addition, the judges rated highly ranked speakers as more credible.

Language behavior, then, serves as a source of cues by which we form impressions of others and react toward them. One who speaks ungrammatically is likely to be rejected, thought poorly of, not believed; his message will not get across as well, he will be much less persuasive than one who, other things being equal, offers his listeners a grammatical presentation. As Lambert's work suggests, within a given community social conditions provide the breeding ground for a rich associative pool from which our impressions are drawn.

Sociolinguistic rules

Like most of our behavior, language behavior follows certain basic rules. One major effort by sociolinguists is to uncover the rules that govern our linguistically mediated encounters with others. In her excellent summary, Ervin-Tripp (1969) provides us with numerous examples of these sociolinguistic rules and their operation in actual interaction situations. Basically, persons interact in a variety of situational contexts for which there are many levels and kinds of rule. These are usually cataloged by sociologists who study norms and their influence on behavior. The sociolinguist, however, is primarily interested in rules that govern language behavior, including the choice of linguistic code, the organization of the sentence structure, rules of address, rules for initiating and for closing the interaction, rules for inclusion and exclusion of particular persons from the interaction, status rules, sex-role rules, and so on.

Rules of Address. You are invited to a party at the home of a friend's parents. Your friend answers the door: "Hi Bill," he says; "Hi Jerry," you reply. He moves you away from the door and into the living room. "I'd like you to meet my parents: Mother, here's my friend Bill Robinson." "Hello Bill." "How do you do, Mrs. Morgan." "And my father." "Hi Bill." "Hello Dr. Morgan." This small exchange of introductions contains within it several sociolinguistic rules of address that most of us use without much conscious concern. Substantial work, particularly by Brown and his associates (Brown & Ford, 1961; Brown & Gilman, 1960; see also, Slobin, 1963; Slobin, Miller, & Porter, 1968) has been done to uncover these underlying rules.

We learn to use one form of address with children, another with adults; one form with peers and intimates, another with superiors and strangers. The brief encounter in the example includes an instance of the address rule between friends, a mutual exchange of first names, and the address form employed by those older to those younger, a nonreciprocated use of first name: the older calls the younger by his first name (FN), and receives a last name (LN) or a title last name (TLN) in return. The use of LN or TLN is another aspect of the American address system. In formal settings such as business meetings, or in encounters in which impersonality governs, persons exchange LN or TLN: "How do you do, Mr. Jones." "Pleased to meet you Reverend Smith." In settings marked by greater closeness of relationship and informality, or when persons wish to create a sense of intimacy or equality, a first-name exchange is more common: "Hi John," "Hi Bill."

There is still another sociolinguistic address rule in the example: shortened greeting forms such as "hi" to communicate intimacy, informality, or friendship, and the use of more formal, standard greeting forms such as "How do you do" to indicate some distance or formality.

Once the sociolinguist has analyzed the address rules of a language he can use the rules to determine the pattern of social relationships that exist in a given situation. For example, if we happen on an entirely new situation and hear one person use TLN to another and receive FN in return, we assume that a subordinate—perhaps an employee—is addressing his superior in a formal setting.

As most speakers of English know when they begin to learn a foreign language, pronoun usage communicates status relationships and intimacy or friendship relationships. Many languages have a two-choice system. The *tu* or *vous* forms in French, for example, are used as a function of the speaker's relationship to the person addressed. One would not be likely to use the formal *vous* when addressing a child. Within the family, *tu* expresses intimacy; when meeting a stranger, however, it is inappropriate to address him as *tu*. Brown (1965, pp. 51–100) presents an excellent discussion of these forms and rules.

One sure way to know whether specific

address rules exist is to break them and note the effect produced. When such rules are broken, any one of several additional messages are communicated to the person addressed; the greeting becomes a vehicle conveying meanings beyond its greeting function. Take an example cited by Ervin-Tripp (1969, p. 4):

"What's your name, boy?" the policeman asked.
"Dr. Poussaint. I'm a physician."
"What's your first name, boy?"
"Alvin."

The policeman has communicated much more than a simple inquiry. In the first place, he has insulted Dr. Poussaint by using the address form *boy*, which commonly is employed only when addressing children or, in certain parts of the country, Negroes. We note that even after Dr. Poussaint has identified himself, offering TLN plus a further specification, "I'm a physician," the policeman continues the insulting address form: boy. He even goes one insult further, asking for first name, and clearly breaking address rules that indicate no conditions under which a stranger addresses a physician by his first name.

That address forms are important to others than social psychologists and sociolinguists can be attested to by several newsworthy developments. In one, the Australian government passed a law making it an offense for a white to refer to a native (i.e., an Australian aborigine) by his first name, unless the native explicitly gave him permission to do so. Natives were to be addressed by the same TLN (Mr.) as employed for all others. Clearly this legal action was taken in order to restore a sense of equality to the relationship between whites and the native residents.

A second example was cited in an issue of *Newsweek* that appeared in mid-1968, reporting an effort on the part of the Washington, D.C., police to involve themselves in what might best be called the semantics of human relations. As part of this effort they keep updated lists of insulting terms of address, so that they will not inadvertently refer to someone improperly and thereby provoke an incident. In addition to older terms—spic, wop, kike, chink, dago, nigger, polack, limey, frog—the updated list includes a ban on the use of the word boy. It should be added that Negro policemen are asked not to use the words whitey or honky when referring to the white community.

Address systems have been studied in a wide variety of languages (Ervin-Tripp, 1969, reviews several of these studies). In all cases the evidence is clear: address forms are one important system of sociolinguistic rules. They specify the terms to be used in addressing given types of persons in particular contexts. In addition, in all languages a change in social relationship between persons is reflected quickly by a change in the manner of address: "My boy, now that you've been made a partner of our firm, you can call me by my first name." "Oh, gee whiz, thanks a lot Mr. Dougherty . . . I mean . . . thanks a lot, Dad."

Other Sociolinguistic Rules. In addition to the extensive sociolinguistic analyses of address rules, some effort has been directed toward the examination of *rules of sequencing*, as in the initial and final phases of an encounter, as well as rules that Ervin-Tripp (1969) refers to as *invitation sets*, fairly detailed rules specifying entry into and exit from an interactive episode. To varying degrees we all function within this rule-following model. When taking leave, for example, we typically say something like, "Goodbye, happy to have seen you" (or "met you"); this brings a response such as "Thank you," rather than a silent departure.

Ervin-Tripp points to yet another class of sociolinguistic rules, which she calls *co-occurrence* rules. In all languages that have a variety of codes and styles of usage, rules exist for maintaining a co-occurrence of codes and styles within the same utterance. Hymes (1964) suggests that most languages seem to have three style levels: *formal, colloquial*, and *slang* or *vulgar*. In a large, formal gathering, for example a college graduation, it would violate the assumed co-occurrence rules if the speakers were to switch from formal speech to colloquial or slang. Your friend would be surprised if you suddenly began writing to him in formal prose.

Language switching, however, provides another class of linguistic features of substantial interest to the sociolinguist. Most of us carry about several varieties of linguistic code and style, which the more versatile may use with great control to important purpose. I am not speaking of bilinguals who switch from one linguistic system to another; I mean, rather, the variation of style and usage by an individual speaker as a function of such factors as audience, role relationship, and situation. Those who have observed Stokely Carmichael in speech-making action say that he possesses a great repertoire of linguistic styles, easing himself out of one and into another to match the background of his audience. When addressing his black brothers, his array of syntax, lexicon, and dialect perfectly matches that of his audience. In visiting a predominantly white college campus, on the other hand, he switches into an academic format. Most good politicians have this ability, and sense what style to utilize with what audience. Reporters following Lyndon Johnson around the campaign trails in the 1964 Presidential election reported that he had never sounded more "southern" in the south or more "northern" in the north. For those who play mainly to a narrowly circumscribed audience, however, the potential for switching may exist, but the lack of practice can make its usage more stilted and unnatural than helpful.

Situational norms, including role relationship between speaker and listener, also influence the possibilities for language switching. In lectures to an introductory class a professor may utilize language forms and style different from those he uses in his advanced graduate seminar. Naturally we are all too aware of the professor who seems unable to switch, who comes on in his introductory course with a style that befuddles 90 percent of those who continue to attend his lectures. Ervin-Tripp (1969) notes the example of a priest who delivers his formal sermon in one style and then at the end of the church service, meeting and talking with individuals of the congregation, turns to an entirely different, more casual, friendly style. In yet another example she reports an observation made by Blom and Gumperz in which the local residents of a Norwegian town use standard Norwegian when enacting their roles as buyer and seller, but change to the local dialect if they wish to initiate a private conversation on more personal matters. In this case the switching serves as a cue for a desire to change the nature of the role relationship. As in several earlier rules, switching carries with it additional information.

A fascinating example of code switching was reported to me by a white colleague. He lived in a black neighborhood, and his daughter played most of the time with the small Negro children in the area. He and his wife noticed one day that their daughter had begun to adopt all of the speaking habits of the other children; this, of course, is not surprising. Most of the children, however, spoke with a rural southern Negro dialect and syntax. The parents wanted their daughter to develop a middle-class language form without developing any sense of language or group prejudice. They decided that they would pretend not to understand her dialect speech, but would respond only when she spoke middle-class English. Eventually they noticed that she had developed two distinct language codes that she used differentially. With her friends she spoke in their code; with her parents she spoke in theirs. An incident that occurred at a Christmas party indicated the functional meaning of her language switching. While the girl was standing in line to visit Santa Claus, a Negro schoolteacher came up and casually asked her (in middle-class code) what she wanted Santa to bring her; the little girl replied entirely within her well-learned Negro dialect and syntax. The parents were embarrassed; they thought the teacher might feel their daughter was trying to ridicule her. Apparently, however, the girl had learned the kinds of cue that would evoke one or the other language code. Yet she did not report knowing what it meant to be a Negro; she could not report any specific difference between herself and the friends she played with.

Chapter 3

The nonverbal mediators

In our efforts to define the social situations in which we are engaged, we also turn to mediating cues of a primarily nonverbal sort. In Chapter 2 we noted that even a strictly verbal message carries more than one level of meaning with it. The address form, for example, can convey both a greeting message and a message about our social relationship with the other person. Likewise, a wide variety of nonverbal cues mediate the message-borne impressions we develop about persons with whom we are interacting. Such nonverbal mediators vary from voice qualities through more directly nonvocal, physical communication. Several different modes of nonverbal communication can be discussed: *tactile; proxemic; kinesic; paralinguistic.*

TACTILE COMMUNICATION

Whenever two persons come together and interact, they talk with more than words. As Hall (1959), describes it, we all also communicate through our *silent language*. Tactile communication involves touch. Among animals such acts are usually more prevalent than among humans. A great deal of animal tactile talk occurs, for example, around sexual activity and grooming behavior. Abrahamson (1966), a sociologist, reports an early observation in Carpenter's study of monkeys and apes: The mountain gorilla

who wishes to be groomed by another gorilla communicates this message most simply by reaching over and tapping the other animal on the arm.

There are numerous examples of tactile communication between human beings as well. The handshake is often used as a basis for reaching a definite impression about the other person. Tactile contact between mother and child conveys messages of definite importance; an inexperienced or anxious mother who feeds her young infant may very well convey anxiety to the child through tactile cues such as a rigid body and a cold skin temperature. Examples from the clinical literature that discuss the concept of *double-bind communication* frequently note a tactile message on top of a verbal message. A double-bind communication between two persons is a message that has two separable, usually contradictory meanings. For example, a person who intones "I love you" with words may be communicating "I hate you; I'm fearful of you," with his body. The recipient of this double-bind communiqué naturally ends up in a confused state, not knowing which message to accept. But, as Goffman (1959) points out, in our reading of another person we often adopt as the true message the one that is not under the direct management or control of the sender. Since verbal communication is under much greater conscious control, in the case of a double-bind message we might believe the nonverbal component.

A clinical example is a mother whose son is in an institution. She visits him every Sunday, professing love as she greets him but feeling anger at having to suffer the embarrassment and the nuisance of having him institutionalized; even less consciously she feels guilt at her contribution to his illness. As he rushes toward her, she holds out her arms for a warm embrace. He seeks to fold himself up into her body. He cries out, "Mommy, Mommy, I've missed you so much. . . ." She says softly, "Honey, you know Mommy loves you . . . she loves you very, very much." But at his touch, her body has become stiff. The arms that should be warmly enfolding are stretched out as though pushing him off. He withdraws quickly, begins to cry, and rushes out of the room. She is puzzled, not really understanding why her son has so suddenly rejected her. After all, she did show up; after all, she did tell him she loves him. After all. . . . Uptight is a good description of this physical manifestation of anxiety and fear.

In the United States tactile communication between adult strangers is usually frowned on. For that matter, even among good friends the degree of touch allowed seems to be guided by particular cultural norms. In a crowded elevator, for example, persons in the United States actively seek to avoid touching anyone else (sometimes this is a feat requiring rare skill). Under such circumstances touch conveys a degree of intimacy that is felt to be inappropriate. The Italian man's hobby of pinching attractive (even unattractive) women is less the norm in the United States. The physical embrace or *abrazzo* that characterizes contact between males in Latin American and other countries or the kiss on the cheeks that characterizes certain French and other Continental encounters between males, is a level of physical contact that is unusual among American males.

Jourard (1968) examined tactile contact areas for American students. His study shows differences in the body areas that are legitimate to contact as a function of the contactor and contactee. Figure 3.1 will quickly convey a sense of these tactile communication norms. What the diagram omits are the kinds of situational factor that play a role in human tactile communication. Football players, coaches, and trainers, for example, characteristically pat one another on the back and on the buttocks. After a hard-fought game, with victory won in the last seconds, warm embraces, hugs, and kisses are usual. Basketball players go through a particular hand contact after making an especially good shot; one player holds out his hands palms up, while the other rushes by and slaps or slides his fingers on the open palms. The message of camaraderie, "good job, well done," is thus tactilely communicated. A similar greeting (probably the original, occurring before the adoption of the gesture into basketball and other sports) occurs among musicians, especially Negro jazz musicians. "Give me some skin" reflects this form of tactile communication.

PROXEMICS

Hall (1963) coined the term proxemic communication. This type of nonverbal communication involves the use of spatial cues to convey the message. As with the other forms of both verbal and nonverbal communication, proxemic communication may be consciously manipulated by the actor or, usually more likely, may be a part of his unintended, unconscious repertoire of behaviors. Spatial cues have been extensively studied in animal social behavior. Under the heading of *territoriality*, ethologists have examined the manner by which animal species mark out their territory and define it, usually through noisy and colorfully symbolic displays of aggression, when another animal or another species "invades." A dog with a bone needs only to growl and show his teeth to another dog that is violating his "territory"; the other dog will generally retreat. See Brown (1965) for a summary of some of this work, and Ardrey (1961) for a provocative human application.

Human territoriality has come in for several systematic and several vastly speculative examinations. Some of these are discussed by the sociologist Sommer (1966). When two persons come together to interact, they arrange themselves spatially as a function of the kind of interaction taking place. Let us suppose that two persons reasonably well acquainted are simply

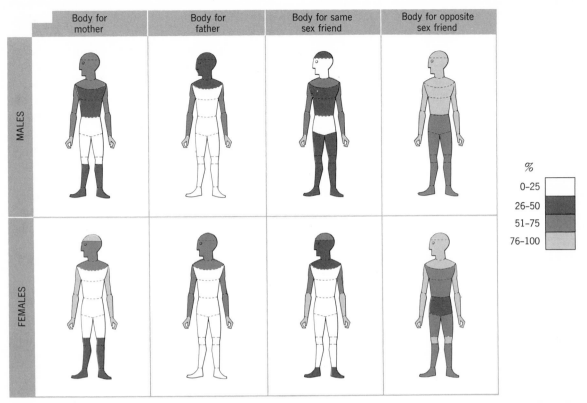

	Body for mother	Body for father	Body for same sex friend	Body for opposite sex friend
MALES				
FEMALES				

%
0–25
26–50
51–75
76–100

Figure 3.1 "Body-for-others" as experienced through amount of touching received from others (from Jourard, 1968, p. 148)

talking together. What distance will they establish between themselves? As Hall suggests, the distance for comfortable conversation in the United States is noticeably greater than in Latin American countries. Unless we wish to convey hostility or intimacy, we will "keep our distance" when conversing comfortably with someone in the United States. When Americans visit Latin American nations, by contrast, they are likely to be distressed by rather close conversational distances employed. As a demonstration of this human form of territoriality, or at least use of and communication through space, you might violate the American distance norms and take careful note of the reaction. Select a friend with whom to hold a conversation on some topic of more or less general interest. As your conversation begins, slowly move in closer, breaking the normative barrier. Will your friend retreat a bit to re-establish the initial distance? Will he interpret your movement as a message of intimacy, or, for that matter, of hostility on your part? And what if you move

out further than the normal distance? Will your friend move in to re-establish normalcy, or will he interpret your move outward as a cooling off or as a desire to end the conversation? Try it.

In his systematic efforts to study the distance for comfortable conversation Sommer usually selects pairs of subjects and asks them to enter a room and hold a conversation on a given topic (1962). The room is furnished with two couches arranged to give subjects a choice of either sitting side by side on the same couch or facing one another on the two separate couches. By systematically varying the distance between the couches from one to five feet, Sommer was able to determine how the distance affected seating arrangement. He found, for example that with the couches less than three and a half feet apart subjects sat facing each other. At greater distances comfortable conversation was best achieved by sitting on the same couch.

In another study Sommer (1965) furnished a room with four chairs so placed that both the distance across and the side-by-side distance could be systematically varied. Sometimes the chairs were placed facing across only one foot but five feet from the chair at the side; in other instances they were placed three feet across and four feet at the side. Data indicated that persons holding general conversations preferred to sit across rather than side by side. Think about your own living room. To converse with a person who is sitting beside you you must shift to a somewhat angled position to be able to look at each other. Facing one another, however, you can sit back comfortably and still gain all those direct facial cues that we usually seek in our conversations. Sommer found that this general preference for sitting across did not hold when the distance across violated the distance norm; when the distance across became too great subjects chose side-by-side arrangements.

As Hall notes, and as most of us are aware if we pause to think about it, the messages that are communicated by our spatial distancing vary with the kind of relationship sought or being expressed. To convey a secret we must violate the normal American distance of four to five feet. To express intimacy we likewise break the five-foot barrier. Psychological closeness is communicated by physical closeness; so is anger or hostility. Closeness less than five feet and a certain type of stance is the usual manner by which two people are depicted in an angry exchange.

Distance cues have been noted by most persons who have done work with sensitivity training groups. It is usual to seat such a group in a circle to facilitate communication. Note that this circular pattern in itself is intended to convey equality of participation rather than the spatial inequality conveyed by the leader-audience arrangement of a typical classroom. (For some workers in this area, it is also typical to remove all tables behind which people usually sit, forcing each to face each with full body, unshielded by the table. Often this becomes an issue, as persons seek to return themselves physically behind the shielding table rather than sitting somewhat nakedly out there.) It is often noticed that as a group develops over time and becomes more cohesive, expressing greater good will and mutual affection,

the circumference of the circle diminishes, sometimes reaching a knee-to-knee point. At times of distress, when hostility and ill will abound, the distance becomes greater. In any one meeting a member may be picked out for special scrutiny by the entire group. If such examination is of a hostile sort, that target person will almost invariably begin to move his chair further and further back until, in some cases I've seen, his back is literally up against the wall. His spatial relationship with the group expresses the conditions of his psychological relationship with them at that moment. In a very similar manner, persons who are low participators or who wish to make a display of their distrust of and alienation from the group move their chairs outside the circle; just a slight amount, but enough to be noted. This appears to be an intentional spatial message of their anger or alienation or boredom.

Systematic laboratory investigation generally supports these several field observations. Some small-group researchers maintain that the seating patterns within groups are the basis for *implicit* communication networks. Work by Sommer (1965) and by Strodtbeck and Hook (1961) demonstrated, for example, that formal group leaders were more likely than others to select a position at the end of a rectangular table, a spatial representation of their functional role in the group. Furthermore, persons who communicated least during group discussion seemed to occupy positions at the corners of the table.

A study of *sociofugal space* by Sommer (1967) is instructive in connection with this last point. Sociofugal space, a term coined by Osmond (1957), is an area or arrangement in which persons try to avoid interacting with one another. Sommer selected a library study hall as having sociofugal properties. In addition to making systematic observations of the actual seating arrangements people selected on arriving at the library, Sommer passed out a questionnaire and seating-arrangement diagram to a group of subjects in order to learn about what he called *territorial defense*. If study-hall space has a sociofugal quality about it, and you go there to avoid interaction and to get studying done (in *some* universities this is true) then you might employ tactics to discourage others from occupying space that would too easily facilitate the unwanted interaction. The diagram depicted a rectangular table with a varied number of chairs at it. Sommer asked one group of subjects where they would sit "If you wanted to be as far as possible from the distraction of other people," and another group, "If you wanted to have the table to yourself, where would you sit to discourage anyone else from occupying it?" Results indicated that those who wanted to sit by themselves chose the *end* chairs, while those who wished to discourage others from sitting at the same table overwhelmingly selected a *middle* chair.

To provide even more detailed experimental data relevant to these implicit spatial communication patterns, Hare and Bales (1963) analyzed a variety of five-man discussion groups seated around a rectangular table. One finding, substantiated by several other studies (e.g., Steinzor, 1950), indicated that persons who sat across from each other tended to speak most in the group. In correlating personality-test measures of dominance with high-participation seating location, Hare and Bales report a small but statistically significant positive correlation of .30. In general this analysis suggested that highly dominant subjects tended to select the high-participation spatial locations and to talk a great deal. As a follow-up, Hare and Bales (1963) examined data from actual discussion groups. The data generally support their expectation that an implicit communication network exists within small groups as a function of the seating arrangements.

From a knowledge of seating arrangements, then, we can make reasonable predictions about interaction; for example, that both central seats and opposites will be high participators. The relationship between personality variables and seating preferences reappears in the Hare and Bales follow-up. Although the correlations are in no case extremely high—we might in fact not expect a single personality variable to predict much about seating preference—they suggest an important research lead to pursue. In one important exception to the Hare and Bales data, they found that when group interaction focused more on social than on task matters, side-by-side participation increased noticeably over central or opposite seating patterns. In every sensitivity-training group I've been in or observed, precisely this same pattern emerges. When the group is doing its work, more communication occurs between persons oppositely arranged than side by side. But at the moment when the group flees its task and moves rapidly toward a more sociable or intimate mode, side-by-side, paired interactions take over. When the gears shift again into the work mode, the other spatial communication patterns again emerge.

KINESICS

In what strikes me as not too unlike the human pattern, the female howler monkey has a routine she uses to communicate her receptivity to approaching males. She opens her mouth, forms an oval through which she places her tongue, and waves it up and down, in and out (Abrahamson, 1966). This is a *kinesic* message. Kinesic communication refers primarily to the motion of body and limbs and involves the usually well-noticed language of gestures, including postural and facial gestural cues. If you are at some distance beyond earshot, you will often be able to get the gist of a conversation by noting the gestural language employed. Some people are better providers of gestural cues than others; the advice too often given by undoubtedly well-intentioned high-school speech teachers seems to have stifled the gesture language of many people. Other cultural factors have played an even greater part. Argyle (1967) reports work by Ruesch and Kees (1956) that suggests that American and British gestures are usually directed toward activities; Italian gestures are expansive expressions of emotion; Jewish gestures tend to emphasize and underscore a particular point.

The usual research model employed by psychological investigators of gestural cues uses the static presentation of photographed emotions; subjects are asked to identify the emotion expressed. Unfortunately, live human interaction involving gestural and facial cues rarely has that caught-in-an-instant quality of a photograph. Rather, it is part of an ongoing process occurring in a particular context. Such early efforts, however, offered some evidence that certain kinds of emotion could be identified from photographs. Thompson and Meltzer (1964), for example, showed subjects photographs of faces of persons caught in live emotive contexts. They found that their subjects were generally able to pick up the emotion just from the facial cues, being especially successful in noting happiness and fear.

Perhaps the finest recent efforts to study kinesic communication are to be found in the program of research conducted under the direction of Ekman and his associates (Ekman, 1962, 1964, 1965a and b; Ekman, Friesen, & Taussig, 1969). Ekman uses motion picture films or a series of sequenced still photographs of people in controlled interaction situations. For example, he photographs or films a subject during an interview with an interviewer who intentionally tries to bring out certain kinds of feeling. Judges then view the sequence of stills or the movies and make assessments of the meaning of the gestural language. Filmed interviews conducted with patients on admission and on discharge communicate a great deal about the psychological state of the person being interviewed even when viewed by relatively untrained observers.

The work on *micromomentary facial expressions* (MMEs) is an especially exciting development (Haggard & Isaacs, 1966). If an interview is filmed and then the film is run extremely slowly, certain components of the gestural act become visible. These components are MMEs. In some of his own studies of these phenomena Ekman (1968) has demonstrated a striking and informative discrepancy between the verbal message and the MME. For example, he asks a patient being filmed to state, several times in succession, "I don't hate him any more." The experimental subject then looks at the silent film of this enactment at the regular film speed of about 18 frames per second. To the average, untrained viewer, the film seems to add little information. The person in the film is seen to make gestures with her hands and her feet, moving them back slightly as she talks. Her head seems to be tilting to the side a little and her mouth almost has a tiny smile as the lips

appear to move upward slightly. But then the frame speed is slowed down considerably and the same scene shown over again. Accompanying the easily lip-read words, "I don't hate him anymore," are the now clearly visible gestural cues. The mouth comes up not in a smile, but rather in a strikingly anger-filled, one might even say hateful, sneer. And the hands that seemed at first simply to be sliding back along the arm of the chair can now be seen to move backward in an aggressively clawing manner, with the fingers digging into the arm of the chair. This gestural message if seen, would lead us to infer anger or hate.

Apparently a certain percentage of the population studied by Ekman was able to perceive these MMEs at the normal film speed; these people picked them up as they actually occurred. There also seemed to be some persons who could not see them even at the slow speed. This tantalizing bit of material, which needs further clarification and refinement, points out a possibly important difference between individuals in their sensitivity to others' feelings. A person who can perceive MMEs has access to a range of gestural communication from others that puts him in closer touch with their true feelings than even they are. Perhaps it is through some gestural means similar to MMEs that you come at certain times to experience that uncanny feeling that you are in deep communion with another person, usually one who is well known to you. You take one look at him, disregard what he says, and infer his psychological state from these subtle gestural cues.

A further question to which Ekman and his colleagues have directed their attention concerns *nonverbal leakage*. Recall that in any act of communication you are likely to use several different channels simultaneously, both verbal and nonverbal. Furthermore, as we have noted, the several cues that O gives off provide the mediators for the impression that P forms of O. Leakage, a concept introduced by Ekman (Ekman, 1965b; Ekman & Friesen, 1969), suggests that a given channel will give off or leak cues that inadvertently reveal O's real emotion or real intent. For example, a person who is telling a lie may have good control over his verbal message but leak the idea that he is lying through excessive foot shuffling, hand movements, and so on.

Ekman made the plausible working assumption that body channels are less under conscious control and thus will leak the true message or feeling to a greater extent than head channels. He set up an experimental situation in which *O* was instructed to withhold information about her emotional upset. Subjects were asked to rate *O*'s affective state. Some were shown motion picture films of *O*'s head; others saw films only of *O*'s body. The prediction was that subjects who had access only to head cues would not be able to pick up *O*'s actual affective state (i.e., emotional upset) as well as those who saw body cues only. Subjects made their ratings on an adjective checklist, and Ekman recorded the adjectives that each group checked. Those who saw the head only described *O* as SENSITIVE, FRIENDLY, COOPERATIVE, SELF-PUNISHING. By contrast, those who saw the body only described *O* more accurately as: TENSE, EXCITABLE, HIGH-STRUNG, FEARFUL, RESTLESS. It appears therefore that the language of the body *leaks* one's feelings and thereby provides the kinds of cue that *P* can use to mediate a more accurate impression of *O*.

Another substantial contribution to kinesic communication is to be found in the work of Birdwhistell (1952). Abrahamson (1966) reports an observation by Birdwhistell of a group of adolescent boys in which leadership was communicated kinesically rather than by means of any direct verbal indicators. The recognized leader of this small group was observed to initiate conversations and contribute verbally in about the same amount as the average group member; anyone using the usual verbal recording techniques would not identify him as the leader through his participation rate—a frequently employed index of leadership ability. As Birdwhistell suggests, however, this boy was "kinesically more 'mature' than the other boys." By this he meant that he engaged in less fidgeting, foot shuffling, extraneous movements, and so on. Postural examination indicated that he was an especially good and attentive listener. What direction he gave to the group seemed to be given through bodily gestural communication.

The eyes have it

In most human encounters the face is one of the most crucial senders of nonverbal kinesic cues. And on the face, the eyes seem to have it. As the sociologist Simmel (as quoted by Heider, 1958) stated,

"Of the special sense organs, the eye has a uniquely sociological function. The union and interaction of individuals is based upon mutual glances. . . . So tenacious and subtle is this union that . . . the smallest deviation from it, the slightest glance aside, completely destroys the unique character. . . . By the same act in which the observer seeks to know the observed, he surrenders himself to be understood by the observer. The eye cannot take unless at the same time it gives" (Simmel, 1921, p. 358).

You probe the eyes of another to gauge his mood. Downcast eyes tell you of shame or guilt; furtive, darting eyes reveal fear; bleary or foggy eyes tell of illness or drunkenness; bright eyes with enlarged pupils indicate an attentive or interested person. Through the mutual exchange of glances you make contact with another across a room. Barroom behavior of both a heterosexual and homosexual sort proceeds importantly on the basis of that first mutual glance preliminary to the actual verbal encounter.

Throughout history the eyes have been thought of as the windows of the soul, revealing a person's true sentiments, carrying messages beyond his control. They have been feared as agents of unnatural power—the "evil eye." It is said that ancient merchants would decide how best to bargain with a customer by reading the size of his pupils. If his eyes lit up—that is, the pupils enlarged—at the sight of an item, the merchant knew it was sold and could bargain accordingly.

Systematic social psychological investigation has concentrated primarily on eye contact during actual interaction. In some of the research an accomplice is instructed to gaze continuously at a naive subject while observers record the direction of the subject's gaze and the length of his glance. In another method films are made of interactions taking place between two "real" subjects. Results of a variety of such investigations conducted by such researchers as Argyle (1967), Kendon (1967), and Exline and his associates (Exline, 1963; Exline, Gray & Schuette, 1965; Exline & Winters, 1965) reveal several interesting eye-contact behaviors. For example, Argyle reports that each subject looks at the other on the average between 30 and 60 percent of the time during the interaction. Steady gazing, therefore is not the rule. Each glance varies from about one to seven seconds. Now, although seven seconds does not sound like a long time, compare it with the usual quarter-second fixation that occurs in general scanning. Argyle reports further that of all the facial features examined, the other's eyes seem to be the prime targets of the gaze. When a person is listening to another speak he tends to look more and longer than when speaking himself. This is something you can easily demonstrate to yourself. When you speak to another person, try to note how frequently you look at him as compared to when he is speaking to you. It has also been found that as the speaker comes to the conclusion of his utterance he is likely to look at the other person, as though signaling that he has finished and the other may now begin. Argyle (1967, p. 108) reports on the work of Kendon, who found that if O finishes his utterance but does not look up at P, giving him this signal of completion, in 71 percent of the cases P either does not speak or delays speaking for a substantial period of time.

In general, and fitting the proverbial advice, when someone is not telling the truth he tends to look less at the other person. As we might well expect, people look more and longer when they like the other person than when they do not. It was found that during a personal type of interview, individuals engaged in minimal eye contact with the interviewer (Exline, Gray, & Schuette, 1965). Several investigators, including Exline and his associates, report individual differences in gazing behavior. Women seem to engage in more eye contact than men (Argyle, 1967, pp. 115 ff). Under generally friendly conditions, persons high in the need for affiliation tend to look more at O (Exline & Winters, 1965) than do persons low in this need.

With regard to this matter of duration of the gaze, Goffman (1963a) makes an interesting point. Suppose you are walking down the street and rather than doing what is usual with respect to looking at others, you gaze for a substantial period of time at someone. In Goffman's analysis you have violated an interaction rule referred to as *civil inattention* and thus have conveyed, even if unwittingly, one of several messages to the other person. One message might be that there is something wrong or peculiar about the person you are gazing at. A man might check the zipper on his pants; a woman might become self-conscious about her makeup or the possibility that her slip is showing. Another message, of course, might be a more than routine interest in the other person. It could suggest that you are trying to flirt or establish a relationship, that you are attempting a pickup.

The eyes of the other as well as his general facial and head features are conveyers of the feedback that is so essential for coordinated interaction between two or more persons. The speaker seeks feedback from the other to guide his own behavior. Head nods, or the vocalization of "uh-huh," or appropriate movements of the eyes glancing at the person can provide him cues as to the way in which his message is being received. A demonstration that students in particular can try goes roughly as follows. First of all, select a large lecture class and take a seat somewhere within view of the professor. During the first 10 minutes of the lecture, keep a tally on the number of times the professor turns his gaze in your direction. During the next 10 minutes, every time he gazes your way, shake your head disapprovingly, and tally the number of times he looks your way. Then, if perchance he looks again, give him that good old positive feedback, the approving nod, "that's right, old bean." Tally how many times he glances in your direction. If all works as predicted, you should note how the negative feedback can cut down his use of you as a source of information. He should decrease his glances in your direction. But when you nod approvingly. . . . If you are the only one in the class who is playing this game, the only behavior modification on his part will probably be his use or rejection of you as a source of information. If many students are participating, however, he may change his presentation to adapt to the positive or negative feedback he is getting. In this way all of us pick up cues from visual and other such related material that are useful in evaluating our own performance in addition to mediating our impression of others.

With regard to self-feedback, there is a developing interest in the use of instant videotape playback to give a person an immediate sense of his body's message (e.g., Maccoby, Jecker, Brictrose, & Rose, 1964; Stoller, 1966, 1967a and b). Although my own work with such material has been minimal up to now, I have had one striking experience. I videotaped a two-hour meeting of a T-group and played it back several times for the members. One girl in the group had felt herself to be experiencing and openly expressing all the range of feelings brought forth in those two hours. However, when she viewed herself she was dumbstruck, for there on the tube was a stone-faced, immobile, inexpressive figure. She looked again. "Could that be me?" she cried. She thought her face had been vividly expressing her feelings, whereas in fact it had expressed only coldness, distance, and an almost total lack of emotion. Now she came slowly to understand the other group members' reactions to her.

Not all cultures put the same stress on eye contact or visual cues. In some countries of the Far East, for example, it is considered rude to gaze at another person while conversing with him (Argyle, 1967). An interesting related cultural practice has been discussed by anthropologist Murphy (1964), who examined the Tuareg tribes of the Sudan. Among the Tuareg, all males who have approached the state of manhood, around 17, outfit themselves with a face-covering veil as a crucial and basic part of their dress. The veil covers the entire face, revealing only a small area around the eyes, and at times not even the eyes are to be seen. As Murphy describes it, the veil is worn almost continually: at home, when traveling, day and night, while eating, and apparently, for some Tuaregs, even while asleep. Of course it conceals almost every facial feature that might provide cues essential to judging and forming an impression of another person; thus other cues become of greater importance.

Murphy describes a Tuareg male who left home as an unveiled boy and returned as a veiled man five years later. He was easily recognized by his sister, who "knew his feet." A Tuareg clearly cannot gain access to another's subjective state except by becoming an eye-watcher. During typical interaction one Tuareg will fix his gaze in a steady, unwavering stare on the eyes of the other. He looks for such eye cues as the position of the eyelids and the lines and wrinkles of the eyes and nose. To a foreigner, accustomed, albeit with minimal awareness, to picking up major facial cues, the material presented to him by a veiled Tuareg must pose a significant problem of interaction. Even in the United States, where literal veiling is rare, one who covers his face or blocks off his eyes with something like sunglasses makes interaction uncomfortable until we learn another cue system. Likewise, the blank-wall appearance of the non-reactive psychiatrist often adds to an already uncomfortable situation. Presumably this intentional absence of cues is thought to be an essential component of the therapeutic relationship.

The Tuareg, interestingly enough, actually use the veil as a communication medium in its own right. Most Tuareg males, for example, are continually adjusting and readjusting the veil in accordance with a pattern of rules; the adjustments communicate a change in relationship or in the quality of a relationship. When facing women or persons of very high prestige, a Tuareg will pull up his veil nearly to the bridge of his nose, while the higher person retains his own veil at a somewhat lower level. When a cohesive and friendly group of younger men congregate, the veil may be shifted considerably, down to or slightly below the tip of the nose. The mouth remains covered under all conditions, but that leaves a small range within which to convey respect or friendship.

PARALINGUISTICS

Paralinguistic or paraverbal communication cues especially involve the tonal qualities of speech. Recent development of voiceprint apparatus, used primarily in police work, suggests that each person has his own vocal patterning that is so unique that certain police officials, and in at least one instance a judge deciding a court case, see the voiceprint replacing the fingerprint in investigation. The legal case involved a young Negro who was being interviewed on television about his participation in the Watts upheaval in Los Angeles in 1965. During this interview, in which his face could not be identified, he admitted to having made and thrown a Molotov cocktail into a store. The police picked him up at a later time and were able to get a voiceprint match with his admission on the taped interview. This was accepted in a court case brought against him. The uniqueness of our vocal qualities marks both another advance in police investigation and a potential further puzzle for the citizen who would be entirely private in so intrusive a world.

For the psychologist, however, unique vocal qualities have been of interest in that such paralinguistic modes provide cues on which our impressions of others may be based. Most of us who remember the days of radio can recall the images we formed of the voice in the box, based on the qualities of his speech. Often we were shocked when with the advent of television we had the opportunity to match our voicebased impression with the real person. "Why, I thought he was much younger and more handsome than that!" "Why, she's fat and old and ugly and all these years I pictured her as a lovely young teenager!"

An early study of voice qualities analyzed the reports from radio listeners in England about certain characteristics of persons heard on radio (Pear, 1931). Results suggested that age and sex were easiest to guess correctly from voice alone, while such far-out things for the inexperienced listener as birthplace of the speaker were not guessed with any significant accuracy. Even that Hungarian linguist Karpathy was fooled into thinking that Eliza Doolittle, so carefully trained in voice and speech by Henry Higgins, was a Hungarian princess!

Apparently one can judge certain characteristics from voice qualities alone with success better than chance. The speaker's age, for example, is generally judged with a reasonable degree of accuracy (Allport & Cantril, 1934; Pear, 1931). In his review of the relevant literature Kramer (1963) suggests that there is both

positive and negative evidence that another physical quality, height, can be guessed from voice alone better than by chance by matching voice cues with photographs of the speakers. Judgments of intelligence from vocal cues alone were reported in one study discussed by Kramer; however the possibility that judgments were made primarily on the basis of vocal stereotypes, some of which hit on target and some of which missed, makes the interpretation of this finding less than satisfactory.

Efforts to detect emotion from vocal qualities alone are also of interest. As every good clinical psychologist knows, or for that matter, anyone who listens attentively to how moods and feelings influence the voice, nonverbal qualities of speech often provide key cues to the other person's emotional condition or psychological state. Some experimental studies have found that such nonverbal intrusions as "uh . . . uh . . . uh" or heavy sighs or sudden laughter occur during periods of anxiety (e.g., Kasl & Mahl, 1965). The cracking, squeaking voice of a nervous speaker; the dull monotone of a depressed, passive patient; the rapid rush of slurred sounds of an excited young child; the sighs of an anxiously guilt-ridden neurotic all suggest that we are indeed aware of and utilize nonverbal vocal cues in making inferences about others.

In one interesting and politically informative approach to this issue of paralinguistic communication, Starkweather (reported by Kramer, 1963) selected samples from the recordings of the hearings held by Senator Joseph McCarthy in 1954. The voices of both McCarthy and Robert Welch were included in the sampled excerpts. Starkweather filtered out the actual semantic content of the passages, leaving only the sound of the voices. Twelve clinical psychologists were asked to rate the passages for emotional content. Generally, there was rather high interjudge agreement on the ratings, although the judges did not feel confident in making their judgments. The raters were then presented with the normal passages in which full semantic content was present, and made their ratings again. By comparing the ratings made under the two conditions, and assuming that the ratings with *both* content and vocal cues provide the "true" picture of emotional expression, Starkweather reports that Welch's voice was judged appropriately on the filtered assessments but McCarthy's voice qualities were not related to the content of his speech. This could mean that the judges were at fault, in that they were unable to pick up the vocal cues in McCarthy's speech as easily as those offered by Welch. It could also mean, however, that there was an essential *mismatch* between the emotional tone of McCarthy's voice and the message he was trying to convey. Clinical psychologists, when well trained and experienced, attend closely to such discrepancies between the verbal content and the quality of the speech. A person who enters their office and describes some personal disaster in totally unemotional, passionless tones is someone whose message channels are not congruent; a sign of some underlying psychological conflict.

CONCLUSION

As a communicator both with and without awareness and controlled intent, man employs a variety of channels and media ranging from the verbal through nonverbal. As a receiver, likewise, man picks up this wide range and variety of cues, which he then uses as mediators of the impression he forms of others and of the definition he gives to his interactive encounters with them. As with sending, receiving is not invariably a well-controlled, conscious act; impressions and definitions are often conclusions we have reached without awareness of either the process or the cues we have used to get to that conclusion. Although for purposes of explanation I have tried to separate the variety of communications media and channels that are employed in the human interactive encounter, it should go without saying that in the *live* situation many channels are running simultaneously, at times with congruent messages, at times without. And it is from this multichanneled display that each of us manages to create an impression of the other. Even when the process is more completely understood by scientific investigators, this act of inference will still be appreciated as a truly amazing psychological feat.

Section II

On giving meaning:
man the problem solver

Proposition II

Knowing involves an active transformational or constructive
process by which one creates a world that is more meaningful than
meaningless, more ordered than chaotic

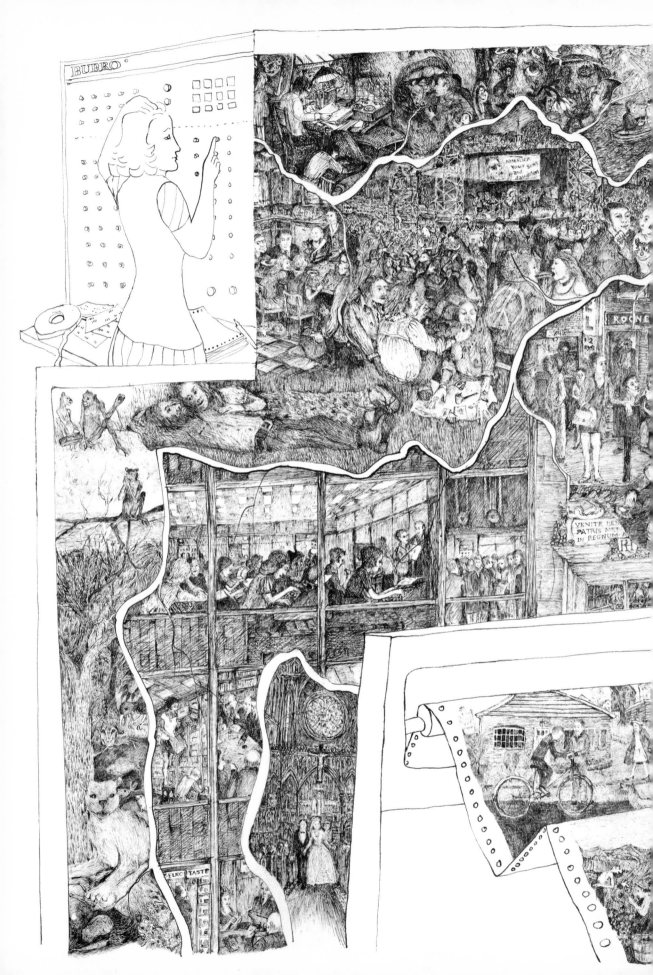

Chapter 4

The social psychology of the psychological experiment

By now it should be apparent that the cognitive approach to social psychology gives us a view of man as actor. Coming to *know* one's world involves an active process in which the person does not simply represent what is, but rather transforms what is into a percept, an image, an idea. By this view man is not merely reacting, machine-like, to stimuli out there, but rather is involved in a series of negotiations with the reality around him. This matter is already included in Proposition I and in the discussion of the mediation process. In this section, therefore, we shall explore several implications of this active perspective. As we examine these implications we move several steps further into social-psychological inquiry.

Perhaps one of the most surprising blind spots of psychological investigation, until the last several years at least, has been the absence of interest in the dynamics of the psychological experiment itself. Blithely, laboratory researchers conducting investigations of human behavior have attended to the variables they fed into the experiment—the independent variables—and the variables their subjects gave as outputs—the dependent variables—while ignoring the nature of their measuring instrument: the experimental situation itself. They took great pains to establish a well-controlled setting in which to conduct their research. They eliminated extrane-

ous variables—as those guidebooks to beautiful research tell us—through randomization, through measurement, through control groups, and so on. What they ignored, however, was the plain and all-too-obvious fact that the experimental situation itself was an interactive encounter between people. Unlike a measuring tape, which cares little about who or what uses it to measure a table edge, live human beings interacting in an experiment *do* care. And as we shall see, their caring makes a difference.

DEMAND CHARACTERISTICS

Let us assume that a subject in a psychological experiment is just like people everywhere, at least in his active efforts to define the situation he happens to be in. Basically, he seeks to pick up whatever cues the situation offers him. In a sense the situation of the psychological experiment is like a game or problem to be solved: What are its rules? What's that guy over there, the experimenter, up to? What's his role?

This subject is not a passive recipient of the independent variables the experimenter throws at him, but rather is actively engaged in a puzzle-solving activity. For him the situation is an interactive encounter with an interesting set of rules. Although, like every situation he faces, the experiment is one he seeks to define and give subjective meaning, it is also, unlike most others, part of the venture known as science. This interaction he is going through with the experimenter is for the purpose of gaining understanding of psychological phenomena. To be sure, he may have other, less noble perspectives; he may be a subject for money, for credit in his introductory psychology course, or for any number of other ends. Nevertheless, one of the key defining rules of the situation is its rootedness in the pursuit of scientific knowledge, which makes legitimate a wide variety of actions by him and by the experimenter that in other situations would seem absurd or inappropriate. For science, what may seem silly gains a new status of legitimacy: "After all, he must know what he's doing, even if I don't." He is willing to play the role of a good subject undergoing what he assumes to be meaningful scientific research.

In a somewhat anecdotal demonstration of this latter point, Orne (1962), who has contributed significantly to the examination of the psychological experiment, reports two interesting events. In one Orne asked some casual acquaintances if they would do some pushups for him as a favor. Their reply was a curt *"Why?"* He approached another group of individuals and got them to agree to participate in a psychological experiment; their response when asked to do some pushups was a revealing *"Where?"* In another demonstration Orne sought to devise an experimental task that was both meaningless and boring. He required subjects to add a series of numbers. They were given a stack of more than 2000 sheets of paper, each containing 224 separate additions. The experimenter simply told them to begin and to continue to work, that he would return eventually. As Orne reports it, "Five and one-half hours later, the experimenter gave up!" Apparently the rules that defined this as an experiment gave it considerable legitimacy for the subjects: "After all, he must know what he's doing, even if I don't."

However, it is not always only the foolish and seemingly meaningless that become legitimate under the guise of psychological experimentation. The dangerous, as well, is legitimized, as

Milgram (1963) most potently demonstrated. Milgram invited subjects to participate in what was presumably a study of learning. One subject was to be the teacher, asked to teach another subject (really a role-playing assistant) to perform a routine learning task. The teacher was told that the experimenter was interested in the relationship between punishment and learning. Therefore the teacher was to punish the pupil every time he made an error. For punishment Milgram provided his subjects with an elegant-looking electric-shock apparatus. The pupil was taken to an adjoining room and hooked up to this "electric chair." The experiment began. Every time the subject erred, the teacher was to give him a shock; furthermore, he was to keep increasing the intensity of the shock with each error, and the absence of a response was to be considered an error. The apparatus was clearly labeled as to magnitude of the shock and its potential to provide harm. Such labels as SEVERE SHOCK, or DANGER, VERY SEVERE SHOCK, were clearly evident. In truth, of course, no actual shocks were administered. As the experiment ran its course, the subject began to deliver what he thought were increasingly strong, dangerous shocks to the pupil. At around 300 volts the pupil no longer gave any responses on the learning task. The experimenter indicated that the shock level should be increased. Whenever the subject-teacher protested that the shock was too great—as when he heard the pupil cry out in pain and finally no longer cry out at all (perhaps he had passed out?)—the experimenter urged that he continue. And continue he did. For science, Milgram found his subjects willing to give shocks all the way to the uppermost level, which, by the way, was beyond EXTREME DANGER, and was simply labeled XXX.

When the results of Milgram's study hit the scientific world, and shortly thereafter the lay public, everyone shuddered, remembering the experiments that Nazi scientists had conducted during World War II—all in the name of legitimate science. Most of those who had heard of Milgram's study had predicted incorrectly that no subject would go through with it. Even Milgram was shocked by his findings. Milgram's report of his subjects' behavior during this experience leaves little doubt as to the intensity of the revulsion most of them felt; yet they were obedient to the experimenter's requests. For science they were willing to obey the experimenter and go all the way in shocking and, for all they knew, permanently damaging another human being. "After all, he must know what he's doing, even if I don't."

Two factors

Although the "true" meaning of the situation may not be fully known to the subject, in his own active manner he is trying to pick up cues that will facilitate his playing the role of good experimental subject and will give him a meaning for the experimental game he is playing. Essentially, there are two interrelated parts to this picture. First, he seeks cues to help him be a good experimental subject. If only he knew what to do, he could be more useful to science. Of course, he knows that telling him too directly what to do would violate the legitimate rules of scientific inquiry. Thus he seeks out, often with little conscious awareness, more subtle cues that will help him play his role better. These cues may range from campus rumors about the study to information he picks up from the experimental procedure itself and from the explicit and implicit messages the experimenter sends out. Orne refers to this entire array of cues as the *demand characteristics* of the experimental situation. They are the sources of information that help the subject figure out what the role of good subject—or, if he's especially rebellious, of bad subject—should be.

Second, the subject accepts the challenge that exists more or less implicitly in most psychological experiments: try to figure out the hypothesis. This has become quite a game. On one side is the wily psychologist with a bagful of tricks, trying to disguise the true purpose of his experiment; on the other side is the curious, problem-solving subject, trying to ascertain the true purpose. Who will win today's encounter? At the end, as we all know, the proud experimenter will announce, "Thanks for your help today, this really was a study of. . . ." The subject sitting across from him will then know whether his hypothesis was correct. If his guess is a hit, he will carefully disguise his victory smile so as not to destroy the validity of the

poor devil's research. If it's a miss, he turns out to be the "poor devil." He takes it like the good sport he really is and leaves, having served science but having lost the battle of wits.

As Orne says, demand characteristics can never be eliminated entirely from the experimental situation. One can only hope to measure their effect, an all-too-rare occurrence among investigators. Given the active problem-solving nature of subjects and the implicit demand characteristics that experimental procedures and experimenters communicate, an experimenter must inevitably wonder if his results are to be attributed to the variables he has manipulated or to those damned-nuisance demand characteristics. Several of Orne's own studies are perfect examples of the problem the psychological experimenter faces. One of special interest involves the study of antisocial behavior under hypnosis (Orne & Evans, 1965); another, of equal interest and importance, involves the study of sensory deprivation (Orne & Scheibe, 1964).

Hypnosis

It is often stated that you can get people under hypnosis to commit antisocial or dangerous acts. In some relatively early studies it was shown, for example, that hypnotized subjects were willing to reach into a cage containing a poisonous snake or throw acid into the face of another person (Rowland, 1939; Young, 1952). It almost goes without saying that a clear pane of glass prevented the subject from actually reaching into the snake's cage, and a harmless substance was substituted for the acid. The subjects, however, did not know this, and did tend to reach out to grab at the snake and actually threw the "acid." This seemed to be clear-cut evidence to support the contention that persons would act in antisocial and dangerous ways under hypnosis.

Orne's analysis of the experimental situation offers another interpretation. In the context of an experiment one of the implicit understandings is that we will not be placed in or place another in a definitely injurious situation. The rules of the experimental game that permit us to do things that on the outside would seem foolish or meaningless also let us assume that truly dangerous actions are illegitimate. Thus the demand characteristics are such that it is plausible that subjects will go through what appear to be dangerous and antisocial activities with the implicit understanding that harmful results will not actually occur. Although they may not know what means an experimenter will employ to prevent the disaster, they have implicit faith that he will do so. It should be noted that Milgram seems to have convinced the subjects fairly successfully that they were actually shocking the other person. Their own reactions indicate how deeply troubled they were at giving such severe shocks, especially when they heard the "pupil" cry out and plead for a cessation. Thus they apparently knew they were hurting the "pupil," even though they may have persisted with the belief (or hope) that the experimenter would not allow permanent damage to result.

In order to examine the role of demand characteristics in the hypnotic situation Orne employed a technique that he found useful in several of his studies. He instructed *simulators* to role-play hypnotized subjects. If the simulators performed in the same way as the actually hypnotized subjects, it would be more difficult to attribute the dangerous and antisocial actions to hypnosis; a simpler explanation would focus on the demand characteristics and implicit understandings that existed in the context of the experiment.

In just such an experiment (Orne & Evans, 1965) one group of subjects was hypnotized and put through a variety of procedures, including handling the poisonous snake and throwing the acid. Another group was instructed to try to fool an experienced hypnotist in an experimental setting by pretending to be deeply hypnotized. The experimenter who ran the subjects through the experiment was in fact not informed about the condition of any one subject; he did not know whether a person he was dealing with was really hypnotized or just simulating. In this manner Orne and Evans hoped to minimize any differential handling of the subjects. The results indicated that under real hypnosis five out of six grasped the snake and five out of six threw the acid; six out of six of the *simulators* did likewise. Because simulators acted every bit as dangerously and antisocially as did hypnotized subjects, hypnosis cannot unequivocally

be seen as the factor that caused the subjects to do so.

Postexperimental inquiry showed that most subjects felt they were relatively safe in carrying out the seemingly dangerous activities because they occurred in an experimental setting. They assumed, for example, that the snake had been defanged, that the solution was really not acid, that the assistant would be able to duck in time. So potent is the *legitimacy of the situation* that subjects are hard pressed to imagine that real harm could occur. For the purposes of psychological inquiry, the findings are annoying. They suggest that the legitimacy of the experimental situation precludes any simple attribution of the observed antisocial behavior to the process of hypnosis.

Sensory deprivation

In another study Orne and Scheibe (1964) sought to replicate the classical form of the sensory deprivation experiment, but this time removing the actual deprivation. We shall have more to say about sensory deprivation in Chapter 5; suffice it to indicate for now, however, that being greeted by a man in a white doctor's jacket with stethoscope hanging out, and being placed in a room with an obvious "panic button" or "emergency alarm," provides a host of procedural demand characteristics that convey, all too clearly, a message to an active, problem-solving subject. Ask yourself what hunches you'll have if you are told to enter that room and remain there for several hours, possibly an entire day. If you ever feel you have to get out, there's an emergency alarm; you need only push it and the entire experiment is over. Finally, you are to pay attention to any special visual or other sensations. One message you might easily get is, simply, "There must be something that's going to happen to me that will make me want to get out"; it should be enough of a demand characteristic to create some of the effects that have been observed in actual sensory deprivation. Another message you might get from the same procedural panic button is, "He's testing my courage; he wants to know how long I can hold out. I'll show him." This challenge has consequences for your behavior that may have little relationship at all to what the experimenter is studying. The problem for the experimenter is to differentiate between effects that are a function of the independent variables (in this case, sensory deprivation) and those that are a consequence of the disturbing intrusion of the demand characteristics. Orne and Scheibe's subjects demonstrated some of the typical effects of sensory deprivation—restlessness and task impairment—even though they were in a nondeprived setting.

The argument to this point has been simply that subjects in experiments are trying their best both to be good subjects and to figure out what the situation is really all about. They are active problem solvers. From the variety of demand-characteristic cues they pick up they form their own hunches, hypotheses, impressions, or what have you, about the experimental situation. It is always possible, of course, and often likely, that the hypothesis the subject acquires is *not* the hypothesis the experimenter is studying. The experimenter thinks he is studying the effects of X on subject behavior, while the subject thinks that the experimenter is interested in studying the effects of Y. During a lengthy series of pretests for a complicated experimental study, I realized this with a light-bulb-above-the-head flash. My associates and I had created a situation in which we thought we had manipulated the status relationships in a group of three people. Our theory suggested that one of the subjects, occupying what we felt to be a low-status position, would feel anxious or tense and would have to act in some way to deal with this tension. We observed the interactions from behind one-way mirrors. We noticed that one of the subjects chattered almost incessantly. A symptom of his tension, we thought. I felt terribly proud: I was right; he was talking to reduce the tension he felt because of the status variables we had manipulated. What a self-inflating feeling it is to see your hypothesis supported, if even in a pretest conducted months before the actual experiment!

It was my fate to have this feeling shattered. Because we are sensitive to demand characteristics, we routinely conduct lengthy, open-ended interviews with all of our subjects at the conclusion of the experiment. We want to find out what they thought we were really trying to investigate. When asked for his hypothesis, the talkative subject said, "Oh, I thought you were studying dominance as a personality trait . . . you wanted to know which of us was the most dominant person . . . I like to think of myself as being very dominant . . . so I talked a great deal so you'd note how dominant I was." When pressed for details, he really could not verbalize the covert cues that had given him that hypothesis. Nevertheless, it struck me at that moment that *his* explanation for *his* behavior, based on *his* hypothesis about what we were studying, was a much better explanation for his observed behavior than the complicated theory I *thought* I was studying. There apparently is nothing better for a scientist's learning than such a humbling interview in which you discover that your subject is indeed an active, problem-solving human being who is going about his business of psyching out your study with a degree of success that may be embarrassingly greater than your own. The price of gaining knowledge is often at the cost of one's immediate pride.

EXPERIMENTER EFFECTS

Let us not forget the other member of a typical experimental situation, the experimenter himself. If we characterize our human subject as an active problem solver, we surely can do no wrong in characterizing our experimenter as ever hopeful. Rosenthal (1964a), a social psychologist who has devoted considerable attention to the systematic investigation of the experimenter effects in psychological research, describes the instructive case of Clever Hans.

Clever Hans was a horse, but not just any old horse. Hans apparently was an intelligent, mathematically inclined horse. Hans could figure out arithmetic problems, giving the answer by tapping his foot. Should one ask Hans, for example, to multiply two times three, he would tap out the answer, "six." After carefully examining the situation a group of experts decided that no explanation other than true mathematical ability could explain this phenomenon. Hans could perform his feats even when his owner was not present.

Hans truly was clever; it took an even more clever investigator, Pfungst, to find the gimmick.

It turned out that those who gave Hans the problems also inadvertently provided him with the answers. Picture what happens when you ask Hans to multiply two times three. Knowing that his answer will be communicated by his tapping foot, you tilt your head down to watch. This very slight cue is sufficient for Hans to begin tapping. When Hans has tapped six times you will very slightly raise your head, or an eyebrow, or in some similar manner communicate to the horse that he has arrived at the correct answer. He stops. Hans is clever, but not mathematical. Embodied in this interesting case are the ingredients of the experimenter effect: an expectant or hopeful experimenter may inadvertently communicate the correct response to his experimental subjects.

Merton, a sociologist, referred to a very similar effect as the *self-fulfilling prophecy* (1957). Consciously or not, people seem capable of creating conditions that increase the likelihood that their prophecies or expectancies concerning the future will actually occur. Take an example from clinical psychology for a starter. A person who believes himself to be incompetent in his social relationships with others is able, although usually not with conscious intent, to *set up* social situations in ways that will fulfill this belief or prophecy. When he enters a situation, for example, he may manage to engage in curt, even hostile attacks against others. They may be puzzled and move away from him. He is vindicated; his belief about himself has been fulfilled. Or he may enter a social situation and move forward hesitantly, head down, perhaps blushing, communicating extreme shyness. Others withdraw, fearing to offend one who seems so fragile. Again his prophecy has been fulfilled. But in each instance it has been fulfilled by means of *actions he has taken*; it is *self*-fulfilling.

The well-known *placebo effect*, seen primarily in medical research, provides still another related case of experimenter and subject effects (see Shapiro, 1960). Essentially, the term refers to the observation that a good percentage of persons given a placebo (e.g., a sugar pill) react as favorably as groups given real medication. As every good doctor knows and many patients suspect, a substantial part of medical practice

is faith healing. A patient down with a cold calls the doctor, who recommends two aspirins every four hours, rest, and plenty of fluids, "And call me at the end of the week." A few additional soothing words, and faith begins to work its miracle. It is likely that the placebo effect relies on faith: the patient's faith in the powers of the physician and the doctor's faith in the power of certain drugs to cure. In some medical research to test the efficacy of a new drug a doctor may subtly communicate his belief in the drug (which he may not know is a placebo) to his patient, thereby facilitating the patient's favorable response.

In psychological experiments, no less than in any other circumstance, the situation is ripe for experimenters to communicate to their subjects, covertly and inadvertently, the desired outcome. I am not discussing experimenters who may be more overt and intentional about pushing subjects into behaving in ways that confirm their experimental predictions; that is an entirely different matter. Here I wish only to talk about the experimenter striving for truth who inadvertently communicates his expectations to his subjects, thus increasing the likelihood of fulfilling his prophecies.

It is useful to think of two different kinds of situation in which experimenter effects occur. In the first the subject's response is sufficiently ambiguous that a person with a deeply held wish to see certain effects can *read* the response in a manner that confirms his expectations. In the second the subject's response is fairly clear, and the experimenter has communicated the desired outcome through some covert channels.

Ambiguous responses

As an example of the first type of experimenter effect, let us look at what is potentially an ambiguous response, the bunching-up of the body of a flatworm when a light flashes on. How bunched up must the body become before the experimenter says the response has occurred? Will a little bunching up count? Or must it go all the way? The decision has a certain degree of ambiguity built in. An experimenter conducting research on flatworms with the expectation that under condition *X* the worm will bunch up whereas under condition Y it will not may find his expectations influencing his observations of the rather ambiguous response. This in fact was shown in a study of such experimenter effects (Hartrey, 1966).

A similar experimenter effect, again usually unintended and likely to happen to even the most honest researcher, occurs with the interpretation of a subject's responses to an open-ended or projective interview question. An interviewer who expects a particular kind of response, because of his impression of the subject or his hypothesis about how the person should respond to a particular item, given his response to other items, has a certain degree of leeway in interpreting the meaning of the response. To complicate the matter even further, the interviewer's own personal views can interact with the situation to produce a biasing interpretation of the response. The outcome might very well be something like, "Someone like him must have meant. . . ."

Let us suppose, for example, that your experimental hypothesis predicts that males will present more achievement or competition themes whereas females will give more themes of affiliation in completing the sentence stem, "J. likes. . . ." One response might be, "J. likes to play games with others." It is possible to interpret this response as evidence of achievement if we read playing games in terms of competitive athletics, or in terms of affiliation if we concentrate on the phrase "with others." It is possible, then, that the interpretation will be a function of the hypothesis; if the completion is given by a male, the achievement interpretation may tempt the researcher; if the subject is female, the affiliation meaning may be read.

In his initial efforts to study experimenter effects Rosenthal (1964b, 1966, 1967) reversed the usual roles encountered in the experimental situation. He made his subjects into experimenters and gave them expectations concerning the kinds of experimental results they might find in their data. In one study (1966), for example, one group of subject-experimenters was told that they were studying rats that came from a maze-bright stock while another group was told that their animals were a maze-dull variety. All rats were actually from the same laboratory stock. This information led the former group to expect a good performance on the part of their rats and the latter group to expect a poor performance. The experimenters who expected good performances did find better performances than those expecting poor performances. As Rosenthal suggests, this type of experimenter expectation could explain some of the differences that were repeatedly found between the classic animal studies done at Berkeley under Tolman's direction and those done at Iowa under Hull. Each found rats performing in ways supportive of his own theory!

Covert communication

In another set of studies Rosenthal (1966) had his subject-experimenters run human subjects through a person-perception situation. Half were informed that their subjects were selected because they tended to view photographs of people in terms of "success"; the other half expected their subjects to see "failure" in photographs of faces. Subjects were randomly assigned to experimenter conditions; yet somehow the experimenters' expectations were sufficiently communicated to the subjects that those expecting success ratings of the photos found success ratings and those expecting failure ratings found failure ratings.

Rosenthal and his colleagues (Rosenthal, Persinger, Vikan-Kline, & Fode, 1963) demonstrated that when an experimenter got early positive or negative returns from his subjects the final outcome of the study was influenced. Again Rosenthal used the success-failure photo-rating task, but this time his subject-experimenters worked with stooges rather than real subjects. Each subject-experimenter ran six stooge-subjects. In one condition the first two of these stooges were instructed to give responses that were congruent with the experimenter's expectations. In a second condition the first two gave responses that did not fit the experimenter's expectations; in a third condition only naive, real subjects were used as a control. Again, somehow, the experimenter's expectations, influenced by preliminary subject behavior, were covertly communicated to subsequent subjects.

Having demonstrated that the experimenter's

expectations for particular results are somehow covertly communicated to the experimental subjects, Rosenthal turned his attention to the processes of such communication (1967). It is not surprising that his efforts took him into an examination of the variety of nonverbal mediators that we discussed earlier. As one approach to the study of covert experimenter communication Rosenthal and his colleagues secretly filmed experimenters during their encounters with subjects. Like Pfungst's approach to Clever Hans, they attempted to uncover subtle cues that the hopeful experimenter was probably communicating to his attentive subjects.

One finding of interest was the differential treatment given to male and female subjects by male and female experimenters. Even during the very early, preliminary parts of their encounters with all subjects, male experimenters interacted in a friendlier manner than female experimenters, as rated both by observers of the films and by the subjects themselves. The films revealed that female subjects brought out a greater amount of smiling by the experimenters than did male subjects. Further examinations of these films revealed what Rosenthal referred to as "interested" behavior on the part of male experimenters facing female subjects. Male experimenters appeared to take a longer time interacting with the female subjects than with the male subjects. Female experimenters seemed to be a bit more "modest," both in regard to the time spent interacting with male subjects and to the degree of physical closeness with male subjects. Male experimenters in general were observed to lean over toward both male and female subjects, whereas female experimenters maintained a distance from male subjects.

Now, a student of boy-girl relationships would not be surprised by these results. That they occur in an experimental situation as well as in real life may be somewhat surprising; one commonly thinks of the experimental setting as rather sexless and sterile. These sex differences in covert communication, however, suggest that even in the laboratory men and women behave like men and women. Just how these covert communiques systematically influence

the results of the experiment is not yet known. What is generally known, however, is that male and female experimenters do not always get the same experimental findings. Rosenthal's works on covert communication provides leads that would be valuable to follow up.

Other efforts have revealed the importance of paralinguistic cues as a source of information (Duncan, Rosenberg, & Finkelstein, 1969). You are sitting in an experimental room and listening to an experimenter tell you that some of the pictures he'll show you are designed to represent success while others represent failure. When he intones these words, is it not possible that by means of such paralinguistic cues as intonation, emphasis, or pause, he may communicate that you should see "success" or "failure"? The answer seems to be yes. The experimenter hoping to get ratings of "success" from you happens to place a stress on the word "success" while reading his instructions; or he happens to surround the word with two noticeable pauses. In each case you—an attuned subject—can pick up these cues and respond accordingly and dutifully.

As for other mechanisms, something such as the *Greenspoon effect* (Greenspoon, 1955) might be operative in any experimental context. Greenspoon asked his subjects to give as many different kinds of words as they could. Every time they gave a plural noun he responded with "uh huh." After a while he found the number of plural nouns considerably greater than during the prereinforcement period. Verplanck (1955) had students conduct a similar study in a field setting, and found similar results. Although there is some argument over just how *covert* such communications are—that is, do subjects respond with or without awareness of the experimenter's verbal reinforcer?—the responsiveness of the subjects to the very subtle cues sent out by the experimenter suggests a parallel to the kind of communication that Rosenthal is attempting to pinpoint in his film work.

Rosenthal and his colleagues have sought to examine other covert channels of communication, including the effects of the experimenter's inexperience, level of anxiety, and the nature of the setting in which the research is being conducted. In Rosenthal's work to date the manifold means of covert communication are still a puzzle, but if anything seems true it is that "... human beings can engage in highly effective and influential unprogrammed and unintended communication with one another" (1967, p. 365). And, as we already know, covert communication cues, as part of both the verbal and the nonverbal message, are important sources of perceptual-cognitive data that we employ in defining our interpersonal environment.

CONCLUSION

As an illustration of man's active nature, the study of the psychological experiment reveals the interesting combination of a problem-solving subject and an inadvertently communicating, hopeful experimenter. The methodological implications of this perspective are somewhat frightening. They suggest that only through careful controls, not usually a part of most social-psychological research, can we hope to use the experimental situation as a precise investigatory tool. Controls that seek to measure the demand characteristics of the setting and controls that keep the experimenter blind (without expectation or hypothesis) as to the nature of his experiment are needed if we want precision of measurement and clarity of inference.

Orne tells us that, given the active, problem-solving nature of experimental subjects, we can never eliminate demand characteristics but only attempt to measure their effects. Rosenthal tells us that given this active, probing nature of the subject and the unintended covert communication of the experimenter we can only hope to run studies in which experimenters are kept in the dark as to what to expect. With such restraints it is likely that there will be some limitation to the variety of social-psychological experiments that can be conducted.

But lest you imagine that these qualities of human nature that create methodological problems do so only in the social-psychological laboratory, let me remind you that most of the same issues prevail in most research, even of a field sort. It is difficult to imagine *any* situation into which a social-psychological investigator enters that would not involve some kind of demand characteristic or experimenter effect. These effects provide a kind of *indeterminacy principle*, which undoubtedly pertains to all varieties of social-psychological investigation and for that matter to work in other social sciences as well. That this is true, however, need not dissuade us from conducting systematic research on human phenomena.

Throughout this book I report research data from experiments, surveys, and observations, most of which did not attempt systematically to control for demand characteristic or experimenter effects. Although the findings from such studies may very well be confounded, and the conclusions thereby equivocal, they are the best we have to offer at this point. To do away with all data returns while waiting for the new ship to arrive someday is to act foolishly in the extreme. If anything, the methodological indeterminacy principle, founded on the very nature of the human organism, should lead us to more intelligent modes of investigation and fewer pretensions about the precision of our methods or the clarity of our inferences at this time. To know that our methods have built-in indeterminacies and difficulties is a greater advance of knowledge than to insist that such effects as Orne and Rosenthal have examined do not apply. As many have said, from Confucius through Plato to more contemporary thinkers, "To be conscious that you are ignorant is a great step to knowledge" (Disraeli, in Stevenson, 1948, p. 1324). I think we should approach the research reported in this book and in others as well with this in mind.

Chapter 5

Perceptual isolation

Imagine that you wake up one morning but you are not certain that you have actually awakened. You do not know for certain whether it is morning or evening. Your experiences could be a part of your dream or part of your waking reality; you simply are not certain. Your eyes are covered with translucent goggles that permit only a diffuse light, giving you an unpatterned world of haze. Your fingers, hands, and arms are wrapped in gloves and placed in cardboard cuffs that limit your sense of touch. You are told to remain perfectly still. You hear only a continuous dull noise, and eventually come to hear almost nothing at all. You are fed and you are taken to the toilet, but beyond that you have no contact with the world around you. As a subject in an experiment you have been asked to remain in that situation for as long as you can; a situation in which the usual channels of sensory input have been minimized.

During your stay in this sensory deprivation situation you are administered several types of psychological test. Some of them involve simple arithmetic operations; others demand some memory; still others involve anagram solutions. During part of your stay if you wish you may listen to a recorded message that argues for a belief in such things as telepathy, poltergeists, clairvoyance, and related parapsychological phenomena. At the conclusion of your stay you

complete several questionnaires and retake some of the psychological tests.

The researchers who originally conducted this program of research at McGill University in Canada between 1951 and 1954 were interested in comparing the test and questionnaire data obtained from subjects who had been through the sensory deprivation situation with those of subjects in a nondeprived, control condition (Bexton, Heron, & Scott, 1954; Heron, 1957, 1961; Heron, Doane, & Scott, 1956; Scott, Bexton, Heron, & Doane, 1959). Their results were startling. On nearly every psychological test the sensory-deprived group performed significantly *worse* than the control group; it was as though the deprivation experience had impaired their normal cognitive and intellectual abilities. Although both the experimental and the control subjects showed a greater belief in the existence of the parapsychological phenomena argued for in the recordings, the deprived group showed a significantly greater change toward belief in such phenomena.

The subjects' subjective reports indicated that after a while they let their minds drift, and finally ran into blank periods during which they could think of nothing. Some could not distinguish between sleep and waking states. Many reported feeling confused and unable to grasp any ordered thought. Perhaps most surprising of all were the several reports of hallucinatory experiences; 25 of 29 subjects reported some form of visual hallucination. In most cases these were relatively simple patterns of vision over which the subject reported little control. Dots and lines would appear, taking geometric forms. In some instances entire scenes were reported as though subjects had viewed a movie, again without being able to control the pictures.

IMPAIRMENT OR FACILITATION?

There are three major facets to the McGill research that have important implications. First, there is the finding of intellectual and cognitive impairment as a function of the deprivation experience. Is man the type of beast that requires a particular *level* of contact with his environment, suffering definite impairment when that level is either underachieved (as in the deprivation work) or overachieved (as with excessive sensory input)? Is it not correct, however, that learning occurs *best* under conditions of minimal interference from other sensory input; and thus that so-called deprivation conditions should *facilitate* rather than impair cognitive abilities? In addition, is it not correct that many Eastern religions are oriented around the practice of meditation, in which one seeks to achieve the "deprivation" condition for benefit, rather than impairment? We appear to encounter conflict between two seemingly opposing perspectives.

Although the original McGill work conceptualized the deprivation situation in terms of reduced sensory input, it is also possible to reconceptualize it in terms of a reduction in information input. The interesting argument and research of A. Jones (1966) adopts this model. Jones suggests, and his research generally demonstrates, that people have a need for information that will enable them to reduce uncertainty to a particular level in their physical and social environments. Information deprivation—a condition that can commonly occur during sensory deprivation—induces a person to seek out information that will reduce the uncertainty of the deprivation situation. Jones' research also suggests that, when deprived of informational input, subjects respond favorably to information stimuli; essentially, stimulus information serves as an incentive to an information-deprived person in much the same way as food is an incentive to a hungry or food-deprived person.

Jones' discussion of his subjects' reports at the conclusion of the studies sheds further light on the effect an information-deprived environment has on an information-seeking organism. He reports, for example, how minor variations in the feeding routine, small details to the experimenters, became a major event in the lives of the information-deprived subjects. Subjects could choose whether they wanted carrot or celery sticks with their meal. On one occasion, out of 26 meals served during a 96-hour deprivation period, the wrong item was included by mistake on one subject's meal tray. The subject reported feeling puzzled about this unexpected change in routine. He concluded finally that the experimenter had done this to communicate to him about his poor performance in the experimental situation! In another instance the carrots ordered by a subject were accidentally omitted from his tray. He got so upset that he declined to eat that entire meal. Because the subjects remained in darkness, the experimenter always opened their milk cartons for them. On one occasion he forgot to do this. The subject interpreted the omission as having great significance; he thought the experimenter was attempting to communicate with him. Jones reports numerous other instances of this sort.

All in all, these anecdotal reports, combined with the quantified measures obtained as the major part of his studies, reveal the information-seeking character of human behavior under deprivation conditions. That the feeding routine should become so critical and symbolic an issue would delight the Freudian analyst, especially given the nature of the adult subjects' infant-like dependence on the experimenter for need satisfaction in this deprivation environment. And just as a child presumably is satisfying more than hunger during his mealtime routines, the adult subjects satisfied an informational need by reading added meaning into slight discrepancies from the normal, expected pattern. Note, of course, that such discrepancies gained added significance against the background of a relatively homogenous deprivation field. As an active seeker of meaning in his environment, man, it seems, will read significance into what appears to the dispassionate observer as the most minor of occurrences.

A group of researchers at Princeton (Vernon & Hoffman, 1956; Vernon & McGill, 1957) studied the sensory-deprivation situation from a somewhat different perspective. Their concern was with the potentially facilitating consequences of a sensorily reduced environment. Their research, differing in several procedural details from the original McGill work, demonstrated in one study a facilitation of learning for the deprived experimental group as compared with the nondeprived control group. A second study, however, failed to produce any difference between the deprived and nondeprived groups. Another researcher, Brownfield (1964), essentially replicating the experimental learning task of the Princeton group and the deprivation procedure of the McGill group, reports neither deterioration nor facilitation. In his efforts to deal with what appears to be a possible contradiction as well as a nonreplication in findings, Brownfield turns to an argument much like that proposed by Jones.

Taken as a whole, even including the apparent contradictions, the experiments by the McGill group, the Princeton group, Brownfield, and Jones provide support for an activity or information-seeking model of human perceptual-cognitive functioning. That a reduction in sensory input will result either in detrimental or beneficial mental functioning cannot be unequivocally inferred from the studies to date. That man actively seeks to give meaning and order to events in his environment, and under deprivation conditions picks up seemingly minor cues, however, seems to be a well-warranted conclusion of most of the relevant studies.

Whether the deprivation state attained during meditation is beneficial is something psychological experimenters of the McGill and Princeton traditions have not yet answered. Anecdotal material obtained from those who block out extraneous input during peak periods of meditation suggests refreshing, positive benefits of such activity. But perhaps we are dealing with another side of the matter: just as living in a sensorily deprived world can heighten man's demand for new inputs, living in a world overabundant in its inputs can heighten man's demand for a reduced level. In either case we can infer efforts toward maintaining a beneficial level. For anyone who has lived amid the mad scramble of daily urban life, meditation or for that matter retreat into the silence of a country hillside can be seen as having clearly beneficial effects.

HALLUCINATIONS

A second facet of the original McGill work is the hallucinatory experiences their subjects reported. In a review of the relevant literature, Zuckerman and Cohen (1964) distinguish between two types of hallucinatory experience. The first type includes relatively meaningless, minimally structured light flashes, geometric forms, spots, and so on. The second involves more meaningful scenes including objects, people, and events. We commonly think of the second variety as being "true hallucinations," although the Zuckerman and Cohen distinction is helpful in pinning down the actual nature of the visual and auditory experience that subjects under deprivation conditions report.

Of all the studies examined, an extensive array, Zuckerman and Cohen report finding only three that failed to find either type of visual hallucination. The McGill group turned up a greater number of true, type-two hallucinations; Princeton research apparently produced only type one. Brownfield reported finding none of the hallucinatory experiences the McGill group reported. On the other hand, in perhaps one of the most extreme of the deprivation situations, Lilly and his colleagues (Lilly, 1956; Lilly & Shurley, 1958) reported hallucinations and disorganized thinking occurring almost immediately. In the Lilly research subjects were placed in a water tank heated to body temperature. Picturing oneself encased thus and dropped into a tank of water is enough to bring forth hallucinations! In addition to whatever other consequences such immersion produced, it is clear that the Lilly technique produced a truer condition of sensory deprivation than either the McGill work or the Princeton efforts. If anything, the McGill and Princeton subjects were subjected more to a reduction to a boring or monotonous level of stimulus input than to a cessation of all input; the latter condition, nearly impossible to achieve with a living human organism, was more closely approximated in the Lilly work. I must also add that giving subjects the suggestion of hallucinations—as some of the experimenters did—can and does increase the rapidity with which hallucinatory experiences are seen and reported. Whether this is merely a suggestion effect or a statement that legitimizes the reporting of unusual experiences is still not clear.

The ganzfeld

Several studies that are useful to look at briefly involve work on the ganzfeld, an entirely undifferentiated visual field. In 1930 Metzger (discussed in Avant, 1965) seated subjects about four feet from a carefully whitewashed panel with wings extended far enough to the sides to eliminate any peripheral vision. He asked them to verbalize their experiences as they viewed this field. Viewing in the ganzfeld duplicates the visual deprivation effect of goggles that homogenize the entire visual field. Research provides several interesting subjective reports (see Avant, 1965 for a review). Subjects, for example, feel themselves to be swimming in a fog, lost and confused. Some even report a complete cessation of visual experience. Reported aftereffects include fatigue, loss of coordination, disturbed time perception, and dizziness. Shortly after being exposed to the ganzfeld, subjects search for something on which to focus. The undifferentiated field yields nothing. Soon they report seeing retinal blood vessels and at times hallucinations. They quickly lose a sense of where they are looking; having no standard reference point they cannot be certain whether they have shifted their gaze from one fixation to another or have continued to look at exactly the same point. Confusion results. The actual loss of visual perception is an interesting consequence observed in some subjects; Cohen (1960) has

called this experience a *blankout*. Essentially, the experience is of *not* seeing, or at best seeing only a flash, but not enough for object identification, even when figures are presented.

It seems from the striking findings of *ganzfeld* research, and from the visual effects produced during most sensory-deprivation or perceptual-isolation studies, that the homogenization of the sense field (at least with respect to vision) produces strong negative effects on the individual, including disorientation in time and space and, in certain cases, type-one or type-two visual hallucinations. It is probable, in fact, that deprivation studies that report the greatest amount of visual hallucinations and psychological disorientation have managed to homogenize the visual field in a manner somewhat parallel to what occurs in the *ganzfeld*.

To psychological theoreticians the hallucinations originally reported in the McGill studies were support either for a Freudian model involving regression or for a cognitive model involving a search for meaning. The Freudian interpretation stresses the regression from secondary-process, reality-oriented thinking of the sort that occurs under normal waking commerce with the environment to a primary-process, dream-like thinking that occurs when such commerce is reduced. The cognitive model, especially as once proposed by Bruner (1961), argues that the hallucination is the person's effort to reconstitute a meaningful environment. When the external world is cut off, meaning becomes structured by internal organization and takes the form of hallucinations. In a sense the Freudian and the cognitive models argue from the same perspective; for each the removal of external stimulation sends the person back on a more internal mode, so that hallucinations are man's manner of coping with what would otherwise be meaningless. Other efforts to explain the visual effects produced by reduced sensory input or the homogeneous input created by the *ganzfeld* technique have turned to physiological processes (Avant, 1965).

Although no completely satisfactory explanation has yet emerged, evidence suggests the importance of variable contact with the surrounding physical—and social—environments for stable human functioning. The adult has developed strategies for dealing with his world and for giving meaning to objects, persons, and events he encounters. To a great extent these strategies depend on frequent checking with that world, a validation or reality-testing process (see Section III for a further discussion of this matter). Conditions that deprive an individual of the ability to test reality by directly examining external cues force him increasingly back on inner schemes of meaning and understanding. In a sense he maintains meaning and a degree of coherence by constructing a new world, which may be widely discrepant from the external world. In his newly constructed world a slight gradation of light can become a flash of lightning on a stormy sea; a celery stick can become a message from the missing experimenter; a dream may become his conscious waking state.

SUGGESTIBILITY

We come to the third effect observed by the McGill group: the apparent hyperinfluenceability of deprived subjects. Recall that the recordings heard by both deprived and control subjects advocated belief in a variety of parapsychological phenomena of dubious validity. Those who had completed the deprivation experience changed more toward the advocated position than the control group. We could hypothesize, as did Jones, that the deprivation experience increases a person's hunger for information. He becomes increasingly capable of "eating" almost anything, of accepting as correct material that in a more critical state of mind he might find objectionable or laughable. This argument is consistent with the several theses that seek to explain visual hallucinations as an effort to restore meaning to a confusing situation. Even in the psychoanalytic view a sensorily deprived person is seen as having regressed to a primitive level of functioning at which his critical, rational thinking is minimized, thus increasing the chances of his being influenced. Of course the dependency that the sensory deprivation procedure fosters should in itself increase the likelihood that one would be amenable to ac-

cepting influence, especially from those who are the need satisfiers. Thus there are several reasonable bases for expecting a person undergoing sensory deprivation or perceptual isolation to be more accepting of influence attempts.

The Korean War rattled the United States by surprises in several areas, but perhaps none so extreme as American soldiers giving in to the influence and propaganda techniques of Chinese and North Korean forces. To explain how otherwise good soldiers could be subverted to the point of aiding the Chinese against their fellow prisoners, Americans turned to thoughts of magical-scientific techniques of brainwashing. The image of the brain being washed, replanted with new thoughts, then hung out and dried, conveys the combination of science and mysticism that most Americans attributed to the apparently successful Chinese venture. An examination of the variety of techniques actually employed by the Chinese showed that they were neither mysterious nor newly discovered; they were classic modes of inducing conversion and attitude change (see Chapters 19, 20, and 21). Thought reform was achieved through the use of isolation and controlled communication. Lines of authority were undermined by segregating enlisted men from officers. In the U. S. Army, unlike some of the other United Nations forces that were captured, when men are trained to accept orders from above they have no one else to fall back on if those above are removed. Physical and social isolation were thus a basic ingredient in the Chinese techniques of brainwashing. While isolated, the men were given controlled doses of new attitudinal information. Lacking the usual sources for reality testing—that is, for checking with others on the validity of the new material—some came to accept the messages. Not unlike the subjects in the original McGill work, men in the prison camps, communicating only to and through their captors, often came to see the world through their eyes.

This technique, of course, is by no means original. As every good propagandist knows more or less intuitively, if you can isolate an individual from his normal contacts with others, remove him from the usual social supports for the attitudes he holds, you have him one step on the road toward adopting the position you advocate. Every dictator worth his salt quickly seeks to take absolute control of the communications media in his society; if he can isolate the entire society and feed his own message into it he has already won much of the battle over most of the people. Hitler did this well in Nazi Germany. In every totalitarian nation similar isolation techniques are employed at both the individual and the societal level, often with great success. It is no wonder that freedom of the press and other communications media is guarded so strongly in the so-called free nations.

An especially interesting laboratory example of the effects of deprivation on propaganda acceptance is a study by Suedfeld (1963). He selected subjects with generally neutral attitudes toward Turkey and the Turks from a larger pool who had completed an attitude inventory measuring pro- or anti-Turkish attitudes. The sensory-deprivation condition of his experiment was not so extreme as in the McGill work. Suedfeld confined subjects in a completely dark, relatively soundproof chamber for a period of 24 hours. All food and toileting were conducted within the chamber; tubes carried bland food from a food box to the subjects' bed, and a chemical toilet was used. All subjects were instructed to lie down and not move unnecessarily or even sit up on the bed.

Suedfeld told his control group, nonconfined subjects, that they were to spend half of the 24-hour period in the reading rooms of the university library, or, if they wished, to walk around the campus or even to attend a movie. For the remainder of the period they were asked to remain in the laboratory. Essentially, then, the two groups differed mainly in terms of over-all sensory input during a 24-hour period. Just before the end of the experiment subjects heard a tape-recorded message that sought to influence them in the direction of a pro-Turkish attitude. They were then retested and their attitudes remeasured.

Suedfeld's results are interesting; they demonstrate a significant attitude change toward the taped communication in the sensory-deprivation group but not in the nonconfined control group. Thus the results offer some laboratory confirmation for the more generally observed conse-

quences of isolation on attitude change. Clearly, of course, the issue selected for this study was not of very high relevance for the subjects; recall that they were selected for being neutral on the issue. In the Korean brainwashing cases we can assume that the attitudes to be changed were not so neutral and the change technique involved more than simple sensory deprivation. Although Suedfeld's research does not strictly parallel the brainwashing situation (it was not intended to), it does suggest the potential of sensory isolation to produce shifts in attitudes.

What I am suggesting, then, is that man's meaning- and information-seeking nature can lead him to accept various attitudes and beliefs that others package for him, in the absence of competing perspectives or after a period of isolation from his usual modes of reality testing. The sensory-deprivation situation provides only one small example of what is basically a much larger, often political matter.

SUMMARY

I shall return to this theme in Section III and in Part Two. For now let me merely reiterate. Man's perceptual-cognitive processes are active, leading him to create meanings in his world that often may be based on the barest of cues. When deprived of his usual externally based cue systems, he may turn inward toward more primitive, ideational systems (e.g., hallucinations) or pick up, with a heightened sensitivity, the most subtle cues on which to construct the meaning he gives even to a momentary slice of his experience. It appears that with reduced sensory input he is still capable of finding cues on which to build a story for that day. With more extensive deprivation, as seems to occur with the Lilly immersion technique, or for the visual sense with the *ganzfeld*, he is thrust increasingly inward, experiencing greater hallucinatory effects, greater confusion, and over-all disorientation. So-called sensory deprivation or isolation, although usually viewed in physical terms, refers as well, and perhaps even more importantly, to a deprivation and isolation from the inputs of other persons. When we realize this we have laid part of the groundwork for our discussion of social comparison processes (Section III).

Section III

The relative and comparative bases of cognition

PROPOSITION III

The perceptual-cognitive processes are relative and comparative

Chapter 6

Adaptation level and judgmental process theory

We live in a world of judged relationships. Take three buckets of water. Draw the first steaming from the hot water tap; let the second come to room temperature. Add ice to the third. Dip your right hand into the cold water, your left hand into the hot, and leave them there for a while; then plunge both into the room-temperature water. To your left hand, which has been in hot water, this water will feel cool, but to your right hand it will feel warm; the same water yields different experiences. It must be, then, that our perceptual judgment of warm or cool lies not in the water itself, but rather in the *relationship* between our state and that of the water. Usually, of course, this *relativity* of our perception is not self-consciously experienced. In the world of our immediate experience we believe that the temperature is out there, existing as an absolute. Only with such a demonstration as this do we gain an awareness of the relativity that governs such apparently absolute perceptions.

It may be useful to refer briefly to relativity theory. *The Newtonian absolute space principle,* against which relativity theory was posed, argued that there must exist an *absolute* spatial frame of reference relative to which all movements take place. Relativity theory, by contrast suggested that the observer is himself always involved in a particular referential system while making his observations of movement. The point is that no one referential frame should occupy privileged status in making judgments of motion. If I am in a car making observations of another person riding on a nearby train, my observations of his movement are relative to the movement of the car in which I am riding. For most earthly matters we would make minimal errors in using a Newtonian absolute referential system. However, in matters of human perception and cognition, I choose to become a relativity theorist, arguing that the observer's framework must be taken into consideration in evaluating his judgments of his world.

ADAPTATION LEVEL

The relative experience of warm and cool water in the same bucket communicates the flavor of the concept of adaptation level and the judgmental process model. The basic idea is to understand the judgments we make of physical stimuli in terms of their relationship to some standard, frame of reference, or anchor point. That we may experience that ashtray in the corner as heavy rather than light is a function of a comparative judgment by which we relate the ashtray to some standard.

Helson (1964) was instrumental in explicating

the judgmental process model. He introduced the concept of *adaptation level* (AL) to refer to a neutral or indifference point along a stimulus dimension that is used as the current standard for making judgments. Suppose we are speaking about weight. Suppose further that I present you with an object—an ashtray—to pick up and judge as heavy or light. You will judge the ashtray according to the location of your AL along the dimension of weight; for example, if you had recently been hefting very heavy weights, you would be likely to judge the ashtray as light. Baseball players usually swing several bats just before they take up their stance at the plate; this makes the bat they finally select seem lighter.

In these examples the AL is a function of a series of stimuli immediately preceding the introduction of a new object to be judged. According to Helson, however, there are actually three determinants of the AL; he refers to these as *focal, contextual*, and *residual stimuli*. Focal stimuli fall within the series actually being judged. In the weight example the preliminary series of heavy weights provides the focal stimulus against which the new object's weight is judged. Contextual stimuli are background stimuli that are present but are not directly being judged at the time; for example, lighting in a room, sound level, and so on. Residual stimuli are all residues of earlier experience, including such things as personality, attitudes, moods, and expectations, as well as prior dealings with the stimulus objects being judged. These stimuli interact to produce our AL for a given stimulus dimension, and our judgments about objects in the environment occur as a comparison with our AL. What is heavy or light, happy or sad, good or bad, is a *relative judgment* based on the comparison of what is now being attended to with our AL—"where we are at"— at the moment of judgment.

Assimilation and contrast

Two further concepts, derived primarily from work on judgments of physical stimuli, are important to consider before we examine the relevance of this approach to social psychology: these are *assimilation* and *contrast*, involving two points, the AL or *standard* and the incoming

stimulus. Assimilation is said to occur when we judge the incoming events as *closer* to our standard than it "actually is." Contrast occurs when we judge the incoming event as *farther* from our standard than it "actually is." In the usual terms of judgmental process theory, what something "actually is" is defined by observers who have not experienced the standard and who thereby are more objective in their judgments than the person under scrutiny.

Suppose that for some subjects in a weight-judging situation a new weight is relatively close to the standard of the weights they have been lifting, while for others it is more distant. The expectation is that the former group will tend to assimilate the new weight to the standard, reporting it to be more like the standard than it actually is, and the latter group will contrast it with the standard and report it as more distant than it actually is. P and O have just been lifting a series of weights varying between 25 and 30 pounds each. P is given a new weight to judge that weighs about 20 pounds. O's new weight is about 12 pounds. P reports his new weight to be about 22 pounds; O reports his is about 10 pounds. P has assimilated the new weight to the standard; O has contrasted it.

Applications to social psychology

How do these judgmental process notions apply to social psychology? One obvious problem is that in the arena of social judgments it becomes difficult, if not impossible, to speak about the implication of only a single stimulus dimension. Weights are one thing, social judgments a very different matter; when it comes to judging the attitude of another person, the meaning of his behavior, his degree of friendliness, and so on, we are working with multiple dimensions. What forms the AL for my attitude on an issue or toward another person? Although the neat elegance of the judgmental model breaks at this point, it remains useful as an analog to more complex judgments.

One interesting example of such a use of judgmental process notions is found in a study by Hovland, Harvey, and Sherif (1957), who were concerned with reactions to communications that advocated different positions about alcohol prohibition in a locale where this was a hot social issue. One communication advocated a strong "wet" position; a second advocated a "dry" position; the third was moderately "wet." We may consider these communications as analogous to the incoming stimulus event. A subject's standard, analogous to his adaptation level, was his own attitude toward prohibition. Note that this analogy is not really a precise translation of the AL notion; one's own attitude on such an issue is not likely to be a point of indifference as the AL is supposed to be. However, the manner by which one's own position functions in evaluating others' positions does appear to parallel the manner by which the AL functions as a standard or frame of reference.

Hovland and his associates found that subjects whose own attitude was closest to that of the communication reported a relatively true picture of the message. Those whose position was only moderately removed from the message tended to assimilate, reporting the message to be more like their own position than it actually was. Those whose position was farthest from the communication judged it to be more unlike theirs than it really was: a contrast effect.

In the person-perception literature the term *assimilative projection* has been used to describe the process whereby we tend to see others as being more like ourselves than they actually are (see Berkowitz, 1960). Presumably, from the perspective of a judgmental process model, we would also expect to find *contrastive projection*, in which we tend to see others as being more different from ourselves than they actually are. Here the standard against which we judge others is our own self-concept. In his efforts to apply judgmental process theory to the realm of social judgments Berkowitz reports several studies that support a contrastive projection notion. In one (Goldings, 1954), for example, judges rated their own degree of happiness or unhappiness and then rated the happiness of persons shown in a set of pictures. Berkowitz argues that, assuming that the average degree of happiness in the pictures was somewhere in the middle of a happy-unhappy continuum, Goldings' results parallel those of the Hovland, Harvey, and Sherif study. Goldings reports that subjects who rated themselves as

very unhappy rated the pictures as relatively happy, while those who rated themselves as very happy tended to attribute unhappiness to the pictures; in both cases, a contrast effect. Those who reported themselves to be around the midpoint on the happy-unhappy dimension tended to assimilate; they saw the pictures as being like themselves.

Although these experimental results seem to fit the assimilation-contrast interpretation, what are we to do about that all-too-common experience in which our own mood of deep depression tends to cast a dark pall over the entire world, or our moments of euphoria send bright rays of happiness to our environs? In such cases it seems that our extreme moods lead to assimilation rather than to the contrast effect reported in the study. Perhaps asking subjects to check-rate themselves and photographs brings about a kind of contrast effect that is more a function of the measurement procedure than it is a portrayal of the phenomenon itself.

THE McCLELLAND-ATKINSON APPROACH

The AL analogy in social psychology does provide a useful conceptual tool for understanding a variety of phenomena. For example, the social milieu within which we operate daily provides a background that determines our social adaptation level. The people we work with, live with, play with, meet every day, go to parties with, and so on, provide a sort of unseen body of furniture for our world. Like the AL, these social factors form an *indifference zone*, an area within which things and people evoke little beyond an automatic, even cursory response. Once we have adapted we become indifferent, unpuzzled, unconcerned about these background phenomena. When events fall outside this social AL, however, indifference gives way to surprise, wakefulness, conscious concern.

But how do we evaluate such events? In the first place, we clearly are not talking about evaluations along a single stimulus dimension; events that fall outside the daily social AL fall outside a multidimensional space. Our emotional reaction, however, may be discernible along a major dimension of pleasure-and-approach versus displeasure-and-avoid. McClelland and At-kinson propose a theory of motivation (Atkinson, 1964; McClelland, 1951; McClelland, Atkinson, Clark, & Lowell, 1953), according to which every person has a particular state of *activation* or *arousal* at any moment in time. This state is much like Helson's adaptation level; each person is presumed to be locatable at a given moment at a particular point along a dimension. For Helson the dimensions correspond to sense modalities; for McClelland and Atkinson the dimension is activation-arousal. In sleep the state of arousal is low; during periods of hyper-excitability—say with one minute to play, the score 17 to 14 against the home team, the home team's ball on the six-yard line—it is high. McClelland and Atkinson argue that incoming events at the existing arousal level are ex-perienced with indifference or neutrality; so far, their notion is similar to the AL. Incoming events that fall *near* the present level are ex-perienced as *affectively positive* (we like them and want more of the same), while incoming events that are *more widely discrepant* from the present level are experienced as affectively negative (we don't like them and wish to avoid them). This produces what is called a *butterfly curve*. A study by Haber (1958) lends support to this model. He had subjects adapt themselves to a water bath of a given temperature and then place their hands in water that varied in specific degrees from the temperature of the AL. He reports that small amounts of temperature de-viation produced positive feelings, whereas large discrepancies produced negative feelings.

Verinis, Brandsma, and Cofer (1968) sought to examine this hypothesis in a series of four separate experiments. In one they asked college students to read a booklet describing a situa-tion that was relevant to them. Each description established a level of expectancy; in one book-let, for instance, which described course exam-inations, subjects were led to expect a particular grade on the remaining quizzes given in the class. Once this expectancy was established subjects were given feedback about grades they received on the next test. Some were told they had done much better than expected; some much worse; some slightly better; slightly worse; or exactly as expected. All were asked to rate

the pleasantness of this situation. According to the McClelland-Atkinson model, those who re-ceived grades *either* slightly better *or* slightly worse than expected should feel more pleased than those who received grades that were much better or much worse. However, not sur-prisingly for anyone who has waited for quiz grades, Verinis' results indicated that subjects were most pleased with grades that were *most discrepant in a positive direction* from their expectancy. If they expected a C but got an A they were happier than if they received a B. This finding appears to contradict the McClelland-Atkinson hypothesis; it seems the disconfirma-tion of certain kinds of expectancy is met with joy rather than with sorrow.

Of the three additional experiments by Verinis and his colleagues, two were similar in method and in outcome to the first. The one that differed placed subjects in a task situation in which their performance on actual tasks of varying difficulty established their level of expectancy; some support was found for the McClelland-Atkinson model. Note that the difference in method—verbal instructions versus actual tasks —makes it difficult to interpret the Verinis et al. results as nonconfirmatory of the theoretical model; the one confirmatory study may reflect more accurately the conditions expressed by the model than the more hypothetical, nonconfirma-tory studies. *Imagining* an AL may not function in the same way as actually *having* an AL.

An interesting aspect of the McClelland-Atkinson approach is that it suggests a tie-in between motivational and emotional responses and adaptation-level theory. Essentially, it argues that not only are our judgments of the properties of stimuli assessed relative to a standard, but also that our emotional reactions and motiv-ations to approach and avoid are rooted in such judgments. Further, the kind of emotional response postulated by the McClelland-Atkinson model fits with notions of both novelty and stability in human behavior; the model suggests that slight variations from our present AL are positive and sought after, while larger discrep-ancies are negative, to be avoided. We might be titillated by roller-coaster rides but horrified by a too-fast bus ride down a mountain road. Given World War II crewcut standards, a little long hair is rated positively; too much is bad. A little casualness in dress is fine; too much is rejected. A little deviation from group norms is fine; too much is a threat. I am not necessarily agreeing with this position as desirable; I am indicating what seems to be a plausible representation of the human judgmental process seen in terms of our relative and comparative focus.

A personal example may be useful. Several years ago, when the "hippie" fashion was not a national happening, the Bay Area and the Berkeley campus had already begun to reflect the new directions in young American manner and dress. Residents became accustomed to seeing males with long hair, beards, boots, beads, and so on, and women without makeup, wearing jeans and sandals, their hair hanging long and straight to their waists. This became my background AL for daily living; the cosmopolitan atmosphere of the area admitted almost any form of dress and nearly any action. I spent 1965 at a small liberal arts college in southern California. Although southern California is hardly noted for Establishment manners or dress, this college had a reputation for being safe, straight, Establishment, and *appropriately* liberal. Occasionally, however, a Bay Area "deviant" would be passed through the admissions committee. Against the classic collegiate background, such students stood out on campus like a man in a tux at a nudists' Christmas dance. This type was part of my expected norm so I paid them little heed; however, I could not help noting the kind of attention they received from the other students and some of the faculty. What for me fell well within my indifference zone or AL, for most of the others fell into the range of novelty or beyond into the range of the rejected.

ADAPTATION LEVEL AND SOCIAL EXCHANGE: THIBAUT AND KELLEY

Perhaps the most direct extension of an adaptation-level concept into the realm of interpersonal relationships is to be found in the small-group theory proposed by Thibaut and Kelley (1959). (This type of model is discussed again in Chapters 9 and 21 in a different context.) Theirs is an *exchange model of social interaction*. When P and O come together in their interactive encounter, each possesses an entire repertoire of possible actions. P's repertoire can be represented along one axis of a two-dimensional matrix, O's along the other axis. The matrix itself is a series of cells that represent the action of P and the action of O (see Figure 6.1). Each action has a reward-cost value attached to it; a reward is anything that P or O feels is desirable, good, pleasant, enjoyable about the interaction; a cost is anything that P or O finds inhibiting to his performance of the action. For example, physical effort adds to the cost of an action; repeating an action over a period of time will induce fatigue, which adds to its cost. By subtracting the costs of an action from its reward value, we may obtain the outcome of the action for P. A similar computation produces the outcome of the action for O. In theory, and somewhat analogous to a Lewinian plot of life space, the Thibaut and Kelley scheme establishes a matrix of *interaction outcomes* indicating the reward-cost value for a given interaction between P and O. Each cell contains P's action, O's action, and the outcomes to P and to O for that interaction.

There are many important facets to the Thibaut and Kelley model, but for our present purposes we are primarily concerned with the manner by which P and O evaluate the outcomes of their interaction. What are the standards each uses to judge whether the outcome is a good one?

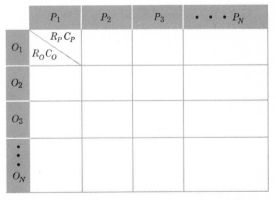

Figure 6.1 Reward-cost matrix of interactions between P and O

Thibaut and Kelley differentiate two kinds of standard, each of which deals with a different aspect of outcome evaluation. They introduce, first, the concept of *comparison level* (CL) to represent an individual's standards for evaluating the attractiveness of the outcomes he receives from his relationships. The CL as a standard for outcome evaluation is analogous to the AL as a standard for judgmental evaluation; it is an individual's sense of *what he deserves* in a relationship. Any outcome in *P*'s relationship with *O* (or *O*'s relationship with *P*) that falls above *P*'s CL will be experienced as positive or good, while outcomes that fall below his CL will be experienced as unsatisfactory. *P*'s comparison level is influenced by a host of factors, including all earlier relationships he has experienced, even in fantasy or imagination. For a person who has only had bad luck in his relationships, even a smile from another may be an outcome above his shattered CL; being accustomed to little, he evaluates outcomes differently than does a person with a history of long and happy relationships. Whereas a person with a low CL needs only small outcomes to feel satisfaction, a person with a high CL needs much more in a relationship in order to feel satisfaction.

Fantasy or fictional relationships also effect an individual's CL. A young person brought up on Hollywood movies and contemporary television, in which all is love and joy and heroism and happiness ever after, may feel cheated by most real human relationships, for they can rarely, if ever, contain outcomes that are superior to his fictionally based CL. He has come to expect so much from a relationship that anything real pales by comparison.

The second standard by which outcomes are evaluated is the *comparison level for alternatives* (CL-alt). Again we are dealing with an adaptation-level concept, an internalized standard by which a person evaluates the goodness or badness of outcomes. The CL-alt involves an evaluation of the outcomes in the relationship *P* now has with those available in alternative relationships. If *P*'s present relationship is with one other person, the alternatives range from other dyads through larger group relationships and back to being alone. Essentially, *P* evaluates the outcomes in his present relationship with outcomes he could obtain elsewhere, including the outcomes of being outside any relationship. By definition, any enduring relationship must provide outcomes that are superior to the CL-alt. At the moment the outcomes within a relationship fall below a person's CL-alt, he will leave the relationship and enter the alternative. To the extent that an individual is able to obtain highly rewarding outcomes by himself, he will find few relationships attractive. A person with a high CL-alt thus is one for whom there are few, if any, satisfactory alternative relationships. At the other extreme is an individual who has so low a CL-alt that almost anything else is attractive.

Thibaut and Kelley see the CL as influencing the *attractiveness* of a relationship to *P* and the CL-alt as influencing *P*'s *dependence* on the relationship. How satisfying or attractive it is is determined as *P* compares his outcomes in the relationship with those he expects to obtain as indicated by his CL; how dependent he is is a function of what alternative outcomes exist for him as compared to those he is obtaining within the relationship. The fewer the viable alternatives with better outcomes, the more he is dependent on the existing relationship.

To indicate a further aspect of the relationship between CL and CL-alt, Thibaut and Kelley suggest several possible arrangements of the elements.

1. OUTCOMES
CL-alt
CL

In this first example the outcomes in the relationship are slightly better than those *P* could obtain in an alternative relationship, but they are well above his CL. Thus he is more attracted to the relationship than he is dependent on it.

2. OUTCOMES
CL
CL-alt

In this case *P* is more dependent on the relationship than he is attracted to it because the outcomes within the relationship are well above his CL-alt but only slightly greater than his CL.

3. CL
OUTCOMES
CL-alt

This is an example of what may best be termed a nonvoluntary relationship. The outcomes fall below P's CL; thus the relationship is unattractive. On the other hand, the alternative outcomes are inferior to those within the relationship; that is, outcomes are above CL-alt. In an involuntary relationship such as a prisoner in jail, the outcome value is importantly determined by the costs incurred were he to try to escape; the outcomes of remaining in jail are better than those to be obtained elsewhere because of the costs that would be incurred in an effort to get out and obtain them elsewhere.

As even this relatively brief overview of the McClelland-Atkinson, Thibaut and Kelley, and other such schemes should indicate, it is possible to extend aspects of a judgmental process model into the arena of interpersonal relationships. Clearly, these schemes extend the issue well beyond the original boundaries set forth either by those who applied judgmental theory to the evaluation of physical stimuli or by those who sought to extend the model into the area of judgments of person perception. Thibaut and Kelley in particular have moved the basics of a judgmental model well into the realm of highly complex human relationships.

Chapter 7

Social comparison and general consistency theory

As we have seen, the relativity position states that we view the world against a background or frame of reference and thus *relatively* rather than *absolutely*. A closely related idea is *social comparison process* (see especially Festinger's theory and related research: e.g., Festinger, 1954a, 1954b). Background factors within which our perceptions occur include such things as the social situation; the state, condition, or personality of the person making the judgment; the nature of the thing perceived, especially its relationship to the perceiver; and, importantly, the surrounding state of *social reality* concerning the thing perceived, that is, our concern with "How do others see it?" "What do others think about it?"

Most of our judgments do not occur in a social vacuum, but involve a process in which we compare our view with that of relevant others. Through this comparison we note similarities and dissimilarities between us and them; we gain a foothold on social reality. Discrepancies between the way we see a situation and the way others see it usually produce a tension state that leads us to act to reduce the discrepancy. As we make our judgments, then, we are especially attuned to others' judgments about comparable persons, objects, and events. Their views provide the background within

which our own perceptual-cognitive definitions are made.

The question of major importance to social psychologists goes beyond object perception to the processes of person perception and interaction. Does a relative and comparative principle apply in this realm as well? Are our judgments of others, which we may experience as absolute, better understood as relative to a particular frame of reference or perspective we hold? The answer is *yes*.

BALANCE THEORY AND PERCEPTUAL-COGNITIVE FUNCTIONING

There are any number of ways of entering what in the last decade has become one of the most bountiful regions of social psychological inquiry. I choose to begin our initial foray into this world of consistency theory by placing it in the context of Proposition III: We shall consider consistency theory as one manifestation of the relative and comparative nature of our perceptual-cognitive processes.

Balance theory

Building many of his ideas on the fruitful foundation laid down in the 1940's by Heider (1958), Newcomb (1953), one of the significant figures in American social psychology, suggested that our perceptions of others take place in a process he called *co-orientation*. When we see another person we do not simply see an isolated chunk of flesh and bones. Rather, as with all of our perceptual processing, we view him as a figure against one of many kinds of background. Newcomb suggests that we see O against the background of his attitudes and values toward mutual objects of regard. For convenience, these objects are summarized by the term X. Thus P orients himself both to O and to the background of O's attitudes and values, and when he views X he sees it against the background of O. P also has his own attitudes and values. In fact, it is assumed that P must orient himself *both* to O-X and to P-X; that is, he *co*-orients himself in his encounters with O. Wayne meets Bob and they begin a brief conversation; soon it drifts around to the war and the draft. Wayne has his own attitudes on both issues, as does Bob. Shortly, Wayne begins to "see" Bob not as some isolated person, but rather as someone who holds attitudes on those very issues on which he too holds definite attitudes. Wayne has now co-oriented himself, viewing Bob relatively and from the frame of reference provided by his attitudes.

The triad P-O-X is a *cognitive system*. Systems are composed of elements and relationships, and function in such a way that a change in one element of the system has consequences for the other elements. In P-O-X the elements are P-X, P-O, and O-X. P-X is P's attitude toward whatever X stands for (say, the war in Southeast Asia, or the draft); P-O is his attraction to or repulsion from O (Does he like O? Dislike O? Feel indifferent?). O-X is O's attitudes toward X, as *P perceives them.*

A Complication. In human encounters the situation is usually much more complex than the P-O-X triad suggests. Although our major efforts in this book are directed at an examination of the more simply grasped situation, it is useful and humbling to introduce some of the complicating features that exist in even a dyadic encounter.

In his encounter with O, P has his own representation of the P-O-X triad, and usually realizes that O does too. As Asch (1952) pointed out years ago, P and O live in a *shared field*.

Human encounters are unlike meetings with inanimate objects or with objects to which we do not attribute consciousness; in the latter instances we do not feel that we share a conception of our mutual situation. Figure 7.1 represents a basic human encounter; it conveys the idea that P is orienting himself to the minimal cognitive system, P-O-X; that O is doing likewise; that P knows that O is seeing the same situation; and that O knows that P is seeing the situation: I know that you know that I know; you know that I know that you know; and so on. Although this is undoubtedly a reasonable representation of a two-person encounter, it is clearly unreasonable as a conceptual tool for empirical study. In the main, therefore, efforts to deal empirically, and theoretically as well, turn to the simpler, more useful three-element system P-O-X. It is true, however, that Newcomb's scheme adds a fourth element, O's orientation toward P.

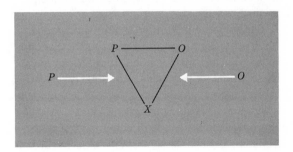

Figure 7.1 A basic human encounter

The Dynamics of Balance. Theories of cognitive balance or consistency, regarding the three-element cognitive system only and usually viewing the situation only through P's eyes, add a dynamic component to the entire system. The argument, deriving in part from a Gestalt framework of *Prägnanz* and in part from a social-learning point of view, is simply that cognitive systems *tend* toward a state of harmony (Heider, 1958), balance (Cartwright & Harary, 1956), consistency (Zajonc, 1960a), symmetry (Newcomb, 1953), congruity (Osgood & Tannenbaum, 1955), or consonance (Festinger, 1957), to use almost all of the terms employed in several different theories.

Heider suggests that we all intuitively sense

when a situation is disharmonious or imbalanced. He points out, for example, that we sense such imbalance in a person who avoids people he likes, or dislikes people with whom he agrees but likes persons with whom he disagrees. Other intuitive perceptions of disharmony or imbalance occur if the hero gets killed at the end of the movie or the man who puts in all the hard work and effort gets nothing while the lazy man gets fame, fortune, and a lovely starlet.

From the same common-sense, intuitive perspective Heider suggests that a balanced or harmonious *P-O-X* system exists whenever people we like agree with us and people we dislike disagree. When our world is in balance and harmonious—and Heider in no way argues that such a world is necessarily exciting, as we shall see later—good, positive elements fall on one side of our personal ledger and bad, negative elements fall on the other side. Similarly, Newcomb notes that if we begin by assuming that *P* and *O* like one another, the *P-O-X* system is imbalanced when they disagree in their evaluations of *X*.

Cartwright and Harary (1956), who have attempted to formalize the Heider and Newcomb models in the mathematical terms of graph theory, present useful ways of quickly assessing the balance or imbalance of a *P-O-X* cognitive system. Let the lines between *P* and *O* and *X* represent the presence of some kind of relationship. Let a plus sign stand for a positive or attractive relationship and a minus sign for a negative relationship. Let us call a system *balanced* if the algebraic multiplication of the signs is positive—for example, a *P-O-X* system with all positive or two negative relationships yields a positive or balanced system—and this is said to hold regardless of the relationships to which the signs refer. Figure 7.2 indicates the possibilities for the basic *P-O-X* situation.

The easiest way to read the eight systems is to say "likes" for the plus sign and "dislikes" for the minus; system 3 would read: *P* dislikes *O*; *P* dislikes *X* and perceives that *O* likes *X*"; or, more simply, *P* notes that he disagrees on a particular matter with someone he dislikes. This is said to be a balanced or harmonious state. System 6, by contrast, is imbalanced in that *P* notes that he disagrees with someone he

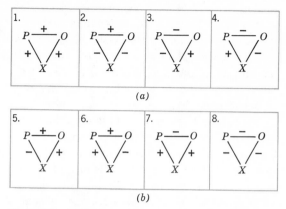

Figure 7.2 (a) Balanced and (b) imbalanced cognitive systems

likes. Situation 8 is regarded somewhat ambiguously by Heider and others working in this framework. Although the multiplication of signs produces a negative total, Heider suggests that in noting a shared dislike *P* may come to like *O*. Should he do so, of course, system 8 would change toward balance. We shall continue to refer to system 8 as imbalanced, although in our intuition it seems less strikingly so than the other situations.

Reducing Imbalance. Just what does this imbalance do to one who has it? All theories agree that cognitive systems tend toward balance and thus that an imbalanced system is unstable and likely to change. How then might the change occur? An extensive list of modes of imbalance reduction or consistency seeking can be culled from the various consistency theorists. Although systematic research has not examined these in equal depth, a preliminary examination of the list is nevertheless extremely useful for gaining still further insights into the perceptual-cognitive processes and their implications for interpersonal behavior.

1. A person who confronts a situation that induces imbalance may try to stop thinking about it, to put it out of mind and thereby get rid of it, if only for a brief time. The mechanism of *repression*, derived from psychoanalytic theory, may be viewed in these terms. Although an individual's conscious role in repressing conflictful material may be minimal, the material nevertheless is put out of mind, possibly later to roar back with a vengeance. Note at this point how the psychological state of *ambiva-*

lence meets the general definition of imbalance; an ambivalent orientation to another person involves both loving and hating him, a disharmonious state of affairs. Often such ambivalences are put out of thought through the active, unconscious intervention of repression.

2. As Newcomb emphasizes in his own theory, one may rid himself of an imbalanced interpersonal relationship by means of *influence-oriented communication*. Suppose, for example, *P* likes *O* but notes that they disagree about *X*. *P* may begin to talk a great deal to *O* in an effort to change *O*'s attitude toward *X*: "Why can't you see things my way?" Newcomb suggests that such an awareness of an imbalanced state is a primary instigation to communication. A discrepancy in attitude between two persons who like each other, for example, initiates communication between them oriented toward reducing the discrepancy.

3. If the situation permits, one may reduce imbalance by *distortions of perception*. For example, unless *P* is so blatantly presented with *O*'s real attitude that there is no room for distortion, he may be able to construe the situation so as to see *O* as "more similar" to *P* than he actually is—if *P* likes *O*—or "less similar"—if *P* dislikes *O*. This *assimilation* process, recall, is common for many kinds of perceptual judgment. We do see persons and objects as more like ourselves than they "really" are. The more ambiguous the thing being judged, the more alternative interpretations it permits, thus the greater possibility for distortions. As in most attitude and value issues, ambiguity and complexity are often sufficient to allow us to see unwarranted similarity and thus to gain balance. "I think what he really means to say . . . ," completed with a meaning *like P's own view,* reflects this mode of harmony making. Naturally when *P* dislikes *O* harmony can be achieved if *P* misperceives any actual similarity of attitude: "He really means something quite *different* from what I mean."

4. Of course it is possible to *change one's own attitude* toward *X*. Disagreement with a liked friend may provide *P* with the stimulus to change his attitude toward *X* so that it is more like *O*'s. In fact, we would expect that friends, over time, would end up with a greater *over-all*

similarity than dissimilarity in attitudes and values. This may derive from influence-oriented communications or self-initiated efforts to change their own attitude.

5. One may *change his attitude toward O*. "How could I ever have liked someone who thinks as you do!"

6. *Selective conversation* provides yet another manner of keeping harmony. Here we must think of balance in a relationship as extending over time rather than as a one-shot, one-encounter matter. Two persons deeply in love may come, perhaps through painful trial-and-error confrontations, to talk only about certain things and to leave other things unmentioned. For example, if religion is an especially abrasive point in their relationship they may choose, often by an implicit understanding, never to bring that topic up in their household. Over time they can maintain a relatively harmonious situation; the cost, of course, is the avoidance of whole areas of possible discussion.

7. A variant of selective conversation is to *leave the field*. This phrase coined by Lewin is a useful way of thinking about both actual physical departure and psychological withdrawal. *P* may be physically present in a discussion in which friends bring up bones of contention in the relationship—*X* objects around which there is disagreement—but may remain psychologically withdrawn or preoccupied in other matters. At the moment when the "danger" topic rears its ugly head, *P* may pick up a magazine and bury his head in it, or momentarily tune out the talk, or daydream, or in many similar ways leave the field.

8. As Newcomb once noted, persons may *agree to disagree*. This is an interesting manner of dealing with imbalances in an interpersonal encounter by encompassing them in a *normative* context. For example, two debators, each of whom likes the other, agree to accept the norms of a debate situation and therefore to disagree on *X*. Or two lawyers may accept the normative framework of the courtroom that minimizes the disharmonious impact of the disagreements that occur.

9. A variant of agreement to disagree *places the disagreement over X in a larger cognitive framework*; the disagreement pales when compared with the total picture. One swallow doesn't make a summer, and one disagreement needn't break a relationship. "Considering all that we mean to each other I think we can afford this one little disagreement." In dissonance theory this is referred to as *bolstering*: seeking a large body of consonant or balanced relationships with which to bolster the one or few dissonant or imbalanced structures.

10. *Cognitive differentiation*, by which X is broken into highly differentiated subparts, provides still another mode of reducing imbalance. If P likes O and they disagree about X, P can minimize imbalance by noting that X is a very complex affair and that he is talking about X_1 whereas O is referring to X_2. Unlike distortion as a means of reducing imbalance, cognitive differentiation need not involve any misperception. Persons and attitude issues are sufficiently complex that points can be found about which agreements occur and points can be found about which to disagree.

11. The brilliance and complexity of the human mind allows still another approach: one may reduce imbalance by a process that McGuire (1966) has called *transcendence*. Here P puts the conflicting elements into a super-system or overriding structure of beliefs. For example, he may maintain a Christlike philosophy of turning the other cheek and thus be able to minimize disagreements with friends. He assumes that what occurs has been divinely ordained.

12. One may *relish the imbalance*. Although strictly speaking this is not a mode of reducing imbalance or cognitive inconsistency, it exists both as a real possibility and as an entirely different, alternative theoretical framework. "What is the sound of one hand clapping?" Such paradoxes are food for thought in many Eastern systems of religion. They are appreciated for their very absence of the usual rationality and for the means they provide to enter new and higher realms of thinking.

Heider argued that most interesting people are disharmonious in certain respects. We come to appreciate, to relish, to enjoy the imbalanced configuration rather than to get rid of it; meeting a person who does not fit neatly together tempts us to look further, to explore, to know rather than to put out of mind or to withdraw in haste to avoid imbalance. How dull, in fact, as Heider states it, is a character whose entire life is balanced, compared to a mysterious person who "dislikes everything he produces, who hates to own what he likes, and who always tries to live with people he dislikes" (1958, p. 181). Heider also noted that much good drama builds on imbalance and disharmony. In contemporary theater the playwright Pinter is a virtual master at presenting characters with elusive backgrounds and contradictory actions. As Pinter himself (1963) stated when questioned about his characters and his play,

"A character on the stage who can present no convincing argument or information as to his past behavior, his present behavior, or his aspirations, nor give a comprehensive analysis of his motives is as legitimate and as worthy of attention as one who, alarmingly, can do all these things."

Studies on balance

In general and, for the moment at least, despite the last point, balance or consistency theory argues that one tries to keep harmonious, balanced cognitive configurations. Does research support this perspective? Indeed it does. In fact, a vast array of studies suggests that imbalanced situations are rated as unpleasant; persons complete P-O-X triads so as to achieve balance; friendships revolve around balanced rather than imbalanced configurations; persons change their behavior or outlook in order to achieve balance; persons seek to change others' behavior or outlook in order to achieve balance.

Let us first restate the general context of Proposition III within which we view this work on balance theory. Recall that the proposition states that our perceptual-cognitive processes are both relative and comparative; the balance model is founded on such principles. The act of co-orienting, as we have seen, leads P to view O against the background of attitudes he and O share. Co-orienting is a social-comparison process in which P *compares* his and O's attitudes on shared issues. The balance principle states that we tend to prefer harmonious outcomes; we wish to be similar to those we like and dissimilar to those we dislike. As we examine the literature on balance theory and other theories of cognitive consistency, all seen within this relative and comparative framework, we will note several important implications.

One of the earliest balance studies was conducted by Jordan (1953), who sought simply to demonstrate that persons would rate hypothetical instances of Heider's imbalanced configurations as more unpleasant than balanced configurations. They did. Morrissette (1958) presented subjects with a hypothetical social situation in which they were to imagine themselves becoming the roommate of two other persons who had been living together for some time. Morrissette varied the subjects' hypothetical relationship to one of the prospective roommates and that between the long-time roommates. Subjects were told that they knew one of the prospective roommates only slightly and were asked to predict how they would probably feel about the other. Findings generally supported balance-theory expectations. For example, knowing that someone you like likes his roommate leads you to predict that you'll like the roommate too: you like Jim, but you do not know Jim's roommate Bob; you do know that Jim likes Bob. Under these conditions, 91 percent of the subjects predicted that they too would like Bob. Similar support for the other configurations studied was apparent in Morrissette's data. In general, therefore, people complete cognitive triads so as to attain balance.

Reasoning that persons would have an easier time learning cognitively balanced than imbalanced configurations, Zajonc and Burnstein (1965) presented subjects with several hypothetical relationships to be learned. They uncovered two interesting findings: as expected, it was generally easier for subjects to learn a balanced social structure than an imbalanced one; and they found it easier to learn positive relationships (P likes O) than negative ones (P disapproves of O). This finding of a *positivity effect* suggests that the nature of the relationship involved in a cognitive structure plays a role at least in its learning and possibly more generally in the manner by which balance is restored. In other words, the balanced and imbalanced structures outlined in Figure 7.2 simplify a more complex picture. Structures involv-ing positive relationships do not appear to function in the same manner as structures containing negative relationships.

Perhaps the most extensive systematic test of balance-theory predictions is to be found in Newcomb's study of what he called the *acquaintance process* (1961). Newcomb acquired enough money to rent a house large enough for about 17 students. He sent letters to male students before the beginning of a new semester, offering them an interesting deal: they would be given free rooms for the semester in exchange for a few hours commitment to social psychological research. From a pool of interested subjects Newcomb and his co-workers were able to select a group who were total strangers, and invited them to arrive at the house at roughly the same time. These men had completed lengthy questionnaires concerning their attitudes and values on a wide variety of issues (X objects). On their arrival they were asked to make guesses about their new roommates' attitudes on the same issues. Of course they protested: "We're total strangers." Nevertheless, not wishing to look a gift house in the mouth, they completed the questionnaires. Further observations and measures were obtained on these 17 men throughout the semester. At the end Newcomb had collected fairly complete data on the acquaintance process: how a group of strangers weaves itself into a complex fabric of friendships. He found, not unexpectedly, that those early ratings that P made of O were generally *balanced* with regard to important kinds of X objects. For example, although O was a total stranger to P, P tended to see O as feeling "much the same as I do" on issues of importance.

This demonstrates what others as well have discovered (e.g., Tagiuri, Bruner, & Blake, 1958), that we tend to *assume similarity*—which makes for cognitively balanced situations—when guessing how others think about matters. If we dislike those others we are likely to assume *dissimilarity*. At this early point in relationships we are dealing with *perceived* balance but not necessarily with actual balance. Newcomb found that whereas P tended to perceive balance in his relationships with O in the new encounters, the degree of actual balance was low; O actually did not think as P thought. After they had been living together in the house for a substantial period of time, actual balance was achieved by changing friendships rather than attitudes or values. The balance model allows for persons who already are friends to try to influence one another toward attitudinal agreement. In the Newcomb situation, however, the formation of friendships in an initial group of strangers derived from shared attitudes and values; it was as though the students shopped around for friends and formed generally homogeneous subgroups in the house on the basis of similarity on important attitudes and values.

As another interesting analysis of his data Newcomb examined the evolution of subgroups when X was another person rather than an attitude or value. A *perceived perfect triad* exists when P likes O and X and perceives that O likes X and is liked by X in return. Newcomb found that such triads in both the perceived and the actual sense did occur, with perfect triads resulting after a few months of "assortive mating." When P liked O and X but discovered that in fact, O did not like X, one of several things happened: the initially attracted P-O combination split; O changed his mind about X and began to like him; P changed his mind about X and began to dislike him. In any case, balanced conditions were actually achieved as the strangers became acquainted, and in many cases triads of friends evolved from an initial mixture of separate individuals. In much the same fashion Newcomb noted how tetrads and larger groupings were formed within this house.

Of course these findings are not startling. We all know intuitively that many of our friendship cliques are based on shared attitudes toward persons, objects, events, and values. The importance of Newcomb's study was to demonstrate the direction of this evolution from strangership to friendship, the kinds of X object of major importance, the process by which group structure emerges out of an initial unstructured state, and finally, the mechanisms employed to achieve and maintain interpersonal balance in both perceived and actual relationships.

Traits and Attitudes. You will have noted that Newcomb's presentation of the P-O-X

scheme distinguishes between the perceived and the actual situation, maintaining that the balance principle applies to both. Others, too, have demonstrated actual balance existing within friendships in addition to *perceived* balance. Izard (1960a; 1960b), for example, has contributed a series of studies of similarity in personality profile between pairs of friends. Note at this point that X has become traits of personality, and that the model has been generalized to include *possession of traits* in addition to *attitude toward objects*. When we say, for example, that P is high in the trait *dominance*, we are making a statement about something P possesses in himself rather than something outside himself toward which he holds an attitude.

Balance in trait possession is thought to operate in the same manner as in attitudes. In this development of balance theory it is argued that persons who share similar personality traits will evolve into friends. Just as our attitudes are expressed as we relate to others, and thereby become a basis for their evaluations and ours, so too are personality traits expressed in our manner of behaving toward others, similarly forming a background against which others make their evaluations of us. For the most part, Izard's work demonstrates support for the thesis that personality similarity makes for friendship. By administering personality tests to groups of students Izard has frequently (although not always) found that mutual friends have a greater similarity in personality-test profiles than random pairings of persons.

Recently developed business firms that engage in computerized mate selection operate on much the same kind of principle. General attitudes and in several cases personality-test data are X. When they are programmed into a computer a perfectly matched couple should result. The state of our knowledge concerning the relevant X factors, however, is usually sufficiently poor that we are likely to get a matchmate who, although similar in X, still lacks that certain ingredient we have longed for but cannot even define to ourselves. Moreover, if Newcomb is correct in suggesting that communication between persons derives in great measure from imbalance, the perfectly matched computer pair might have little to talk about. Smoke? Yes, thanks, nice that you use my brand. Drink? Happy that we both drink only Scotch. Coffee? Pleasant that we both take it black. Eat? Good that we both love hamburgers and ketchup on our french fries. Ride? So happy that we both love riding to the seashore. Talk? Interesting that we have so much in common to talk about.

Similarity, complementarity, or what?

Perhaps by now you have turned up one important problem in the balance model, especially as it involves personality similarity and friendship. Most of us find it difficult to believe that a dominant P would like a dominant O. Our intuition tells us that theirs would be a life of incessant brawls, each trying to out-dominate the other. Yet it appears that they share the same X object, the personality trait of dominance. We can intuitively accept, with certain reservations to be sure, that some kinds of X object fit the balance model, whereas others do not. Attitudinal similarity seems intuitively acceptable, and as the research has shown, generally correct empirically. When X is another person, once again our intuition and the empirical data are generally harmonious. But is such the case with X as a personality trait? We would imagine, of course, that if X is the trait of affiliation, the similarity required by the balance model may be fine. But with dominance, power, perhaps aggression, and other traits, we intuit *complementarity* rather than similarity as the harmonious state.

As though anticipating this possibility, in his initial formulation of the balance paradigm Heider (1958) suggested that Xs that appear at first to be opposites, on closer examination may be similar on another level. This second level often involves the mutual *purpose* or *goals* for which P and O have come together. If X is one's sex, we might argue that balanced configurations exist only within but not between the sexes; this is patently absurd. The apparent dissimilarity obviously involves a similarity of purposes on another level that makes dissimilarity in sex a basis for attraction. The word *implies* is useful here. To the extent to which purposes implied by similarity in X characteris-

tics are at odds with one another, this similarity provides imbalance rather than balance. Say P and O are both in love and wish to marry the same girl, X. Does this similarity in their liking of X provide a basis for their mutual attraction? Hardly. "O likes X" *implies* for P that he will thereby lose X. He and O are at cross-purposes; the situation is imbalanced.

Perhaps a useful manner of looking at this complicating factor is to build on the distinction made by Secord and Backman (1964; 1965), who define the concept of *congruency* in interpersonal relationships. Congruency exists when P perceives that O will behave in such a manner as to confirm P's self-concept. Let us say that at some level of awareness P thinks of himself as a submissive individual. A congruency exists in his relationship with O if O behaves in a manner that confirms this submissiveness; that is, if O is generally dominant. This is akin to the old joke about the delightful pairing of a sadist with a masochist. They are perfectly congruent; each meets the needs of the other and each confirms the self-concept of the other.

Just as similarity can lead to attraction between persons, so too can congruency. The relationship between congruency and similarity is complicated. Certain traits, for example affiliation, are both similar and congruent. Other traits may be similar but incongruent: for example, dominance. Congruency appears closer in meaning to complementarity than to similarity. A series of marital studies conducted by Winch (1958), often cited in refutation of the balance model, demonstrates the importance of need complementarity (congruency in Secord and Backman's sense) in pair attraction and satisfaction.

If we argue that balance in interpersonal relationships generally occurs at the level of shared purposes, we can view similarity, congruency, and complementarity as being specific instances of a more general principle. This manner of viewing the P-O-X encounter shares much with the Jones and Thibaut interaction scheme (1958). As P relates to O, the particular purposes of their interaction provide the more general framework within which similarity or complementarity will emerge as the relevant determinant of P's attraction to O.

Mutual need satisfaction, which may be an important aspect of long-term, close relationships, including those between marriage partners and intimate friends, may require both similarity and complementarity in personality traits. We would expect that when needs expressed by one deflect the other's attainment of his own need satisfaction, and thus are detrimental to the pair's shared purpose, complementarity provides a balanced harmonious state of affairs, while similarity creates only conflict. On other needs, however, which are more *promotively interdependent* (imply opportunity for mutual satisfaction), to use Deutsch's term, similarity of need profile would offer a balanced harmonious state.

In an interesting examination of one aspect of this matter Secord and Backman (1964) had subjects characterize themselves and their best friends along several personality-need dimensions such as succorance, dominance, and nurturance. The data analysis sought to uncover the need-pair combinations that characterized the best-friend dyads. Secord and Backman examined similarity by noting how many dyads contained similarity between the subject's own need score and the rating he gave his best friend on that need; they examined congruency by noting the number and nature of dyads that were characterized by differential self- and friend-need ratings. Over all they found greater similarity than congruency of needs in best-friend dyads, although most of the need pairs examined required both similarity and congruence. Of course the use of perceived rather than actual scores, and the nature of the pairs examined, may have biased the results in this direction. They did find certain need pairs that were congruent rather than similar, particularly in needs for succorance and dominance; intuitively this makes good sense.

COGNITIVE DISSONANCE

I have introduced the model of cognitive balance as one example of the relative and comparative nature of man's perceptual-cognitive processes. In fact, however, in today's world of social psychology the balance model takes

second place in the consistency model derby to the principle of cognitive dissonance.

In 1957 Festinger first published his book on dissonance. Thunder rolled; lightning struck; and the floods came. Finally, when the storm settled and the sun shone again on American social psychology, came the golden age of dissonance. Nearly every issue of every reputable journal on social psychology carried several articles on some facet of Festinger's theory. This theory that created such a stir was dramatic and ingenious simplicity; a beautiful structure built on a foundation that was apparent parsimony; a delight to behold; for many, the foundation of their fame, as creative study after study flowed from production lines into the ripe academic marketplace. The dissonance idea, forerunners of which occur in Festinger's earlier comparison-process model (1950; 1954a; 1954b) and in Heider's balance conceptions (1958; originally published in the 1940's), posits three kinds of relationship that can exist between two cognitions: any two cognitions—which are simply beliefs or knowledges about anything—may be in a *consonant* relationship, a *dissonant* relationship, or an *irrelevant* relationship.

Cognitions are consonant to the extent to which one follows psycho-logically from the other. If, for example, cognition A is my belief that "It is raining outside," and cognition B is my belief that "While standing outside I am getting soaked to the skin," A and B are in a consonant relationship; getting wet while standing outside in the rain has a compelling harmony about it. It is also silly, but that's another story. It makes psychological sense; it fits; it is congruent, consonant, balanced.

A dissonant relationship exists if cognition A is "It is raining outside," and cognition B is "While standing outside, I am not getting at all wet." Although there is a more formal definition of dissonance, this example presents the essence of the notion: one cognition does not follow from the other, but from the other's *opposite*. "I am not getting wet" does not follow from cognition A, but rather from cognition *not-A* ("It is not raining outside").

An irrelevant relationship between two cognitions exists whenever there is neither a consonant nor a dissonant connection between them. My cognition A, "It rains very heavily in Brazil in June," and my cognition B, "I am not getting wet," undoubtedly are irrelevant to one another, neither consonant nor dissonant. This does not mean that through the complex machinations of one's mind they cannot somehow be related; a creative person could link almost anything. Rather, it is an *unlikely* pair of cognitions for any consonant or dissonant relationship.

The next step in the theory of cognitive dissonance (comparable to steps taken in all cognitive consistency theories) is to maintain that man abhors dissonance with as much passion as nature was said to abhor a vacuum. Thus whenever cognitive dissonance exists pressures are set up to reduce the dissonance and head toward consonance. The techniques whereby one reduces dissonance mimic our earlier listing (pp. 102–104 of techniques for establishing cognitive balance. But in dissonance theory, to a much greater degree than with the balance model, bolstering has become one of the primary points of concern. The notion is that one may reduce dissonance by changing the ratio of consonant-to-dissonant cognitions. If I believe that it is raining (cognition A) and that in addition I am not getting wet (cognition B), I may reduce the dissonance by finding other cognitions consonant with A or with B. For example, cognition C, "I am holding an umbrella over my head," is consonant with cognition B and thus changes the ratio of consonant-to-dissonant cognitions. Cognition D, "I am in possession of magical powers that keep me dry," is also consonant with B.

One beauty of the dissonance model, at least in the hands of ingenious experimenters, is its ability to make nonobvious predictions; and when psychology can come up with predictions that seem to deviate from our common-sense notions, excitement reigns. Let's look at several dissonance studies that serve to demonstrate both the bolstering technique and the apparently nonobvious predictions.

One body of work on dissonance theory examines a person in a free-choice situation who is about to make a decision. Imagine an individual making a decision about which of

several new cars he is going to purchase. He finally narrows his choices to a Volkswagen or a Saab, deciding at long last on the Saab. According to the dissonance model, all cognitions that indicate favorable aspects of the chosen alternative and negative aspects of the rejected alternatives are consonant with the choice; cognitions that play up positive features of the Volkswagen and negative features of the Saab are dissonant with the choice. Since the theoretical model argues that we reduce dissonance when it exists, and by extension try to avoid placing ourselves in a dissonant situation, we would expect the person in this example to seek out cognitions consonant with his choice; we would not expect him to examine ads for Volkswagens. A study conducted by Ehrlich and several associates (Ehrlich, Guttmann, Schönbach, & Mills, 1957) support these expectations. However, as we shall see later in our discussion on the selective qualities of our perceptual-cognitive processes (pp. 173–175), the data from the Ehrlich study has not consistently been replicated. This fact is in itself dissonant with our belief in the validity of the theory; as scientists we must be guided by such dissonant occurrences to develop more sophisticated models of human behavior.

In a similar vein, Brehm and Cohen (1959) asked a group of grade-school children how much they liked each of a large selection of toys. The children rated the desirability of each toy before and after they were allowed to choose one to play with. The dissonance prediction, which was substantiated by the data, was simply that the children would enhance their liking for the chosen toy and decrease their liking for the rejected one. One further aspect of dissonance theory in this study involved varying the number of alternative toys from which the children's choice was made, assuming it would be dissonant to value rejected alternatives highly or to value the chosen alternative minimally, and that this dissonance is greater when one chooses from a large array. To avoid such dissonance, a person overvalues the chosen and devalues the rejected. Brehm and Cohen found that children who had to choose one out of four possibilities enhanced their evaluation of the chosen toy (and decreased their liking of the rejected toys) to a greater degree than children who chose one toy out of a selection of two. (See Brehm & Cohen, 1962, for a review and an extension of the dissonance model.)

In search of bolsterers

One manner of finding information (i.e., cognitions) that bolsters what is otherwise a dissonant situation is to find others who agree with us or who are in the same boat as we are. In a sense, if I can maintain that "My beliefs cannot be that wrong; see how many feel as I do," or, "There is nothing wrong with me, see how many are just like me," I can provide support for what might otherwise be a dissonant experience. In a classic study Festinger and his co-workers (Festinger, Riecken, & Schachter, 1956) examined a religious group that predicted the world was going to end on a given day. Clearly, Festinger thought, here was a belief that was bound to be disconfirmed, a perfect instance of cognitive dissonance—"I believe that the world will end tomorrow; tomorrow has come and gone and the world is still here." What will be the response to such dissonance? (Note how safe this study was; if the group were correct and Festinger wrong, who'd ever know?)

Festinger argued that the true believers could do little other than bolster their convictions by providing a context of otherwise consonant information. If they could gather additional members to show them how desirable the group was, clearly this could restore faith in their leadership and in themselves and bury the one dissonant event amid otherwise self-confirmatory material. In support of this prediction Festinger and his staff noted an increase in proselytizing that occurred after the fateful day had come and passed.

In an effort to replicate this study Hardyck and Braden (1962) studied a group called the Church of the True Word. Anticipating a nuclear disaster, this group built and stocked underground shelters. On July 4 one of the prophets of the group got a command from God that led him and approximately 135 men, women, and children to flee into shelters where they remained for 42 days and nights. As Hardyck and Braden describe it, early on the morning of August 16 more than 100 faithful who had stayed in the shelters for the full 42 days emerged to hold a joyous reunion in which they celebrated their "victory." Although the group had experienced what one must suppose to be a grand dissonance, in that their strongly held beliefs were not validated by the nuclear disaster from which they had sought escape, their beliefs remained intact. What they did was *reinterpret the purpose* of their 42-day episode. Their action was newly interpreted as both a test of their faith and as a gesture designed to awaken an otherwise sleepy world to the fearful facts of the nuclear age. Unlike the group Festinger and his colleagues had studied, this group, while retaining its belief that destruction would soon occur, sought neither publicity nor to proselytize new members.

Hardyck and Braden interpreted this difference in findings between their study and the Festinger work by pointing out two important factors. The first involves the actual degree of additional social support needed by a group facing dissonance. If a group already has substantial support within itself, it has little need to prove itself to others. The True Word Church, in existence longer than the group studied by Festinger, needed little additional soul support. The second factor is the influence the amount of ridicule a group receives has on its need to prove itself. With more ridicule from outsiders it becomes increasingly important for the group to prove itself by making more converts. Apparently the True Word Church received little ridicule from townsfolk, as compared with the group studied by Festinger. These post hoc ideas, put forth to explain the failure of this study to confirm the findings of the original Festinger study, sound plausible but indeed are post hoc. Naturally, true believers are very capable of reinterpreting disconfirmations. And perhaps this is a principle with greater generality than even the dissonance theorists imagine.

Certain groups seem intuitively to operate according to a dissonance principle, especially when they permit members into their group only after a relatively severe initiation ceremony. The dissonance argument is simply that it would be dissonant to think poorly of a group one joined after a difficult initiation experience; a consonant state exists if P can say, "This group I have suffered so much to get into is really a great group." This might be seen as a technique of creating "true believers." Aronson and Mills (1959) tested this by inviting female students to join a sex discussion group. As their preparation for entry into this discussion group, the girls were to meet individually with a male experimenter. In the mild condition they read a list of sex-related words to the experimenter; in the high-severity condition they read a list of obscene words. Each girl then listened to what was supposedly an ongoing discussion by their group. In actuality, as we sophisticates of research method well know, what they heard was a taped session of a group discussing sex in a decidedly scientific, even dull and boring way. Each girl then rated the discussion and how much she thought she would like the members. Results showed that girls who had gone through the embarrassing severe initiation were more favorable toward the group and the discussion than either a control group (which heard and rated the discussions without the initiation rite) or the mild-initiation group.

Another manner of dealing with dissonance, a technique akin to bolstering, involves seeing others in the same boat as oneself. This approach is especially useful when the dissonance involves self-relevant material. For example, a state of cognitive dissonance exists whenever one gets feedback that is contrary to his own image of himself. A strong man who tries to ring the bell in a carnival game and receives information that he is very weak will experience dissonance between his cognition about himself as strong and the data he is receiving. One manner of dealing with his dissonance is to see others as suffering the same fate: "I am not weak; I'll bet that everyone does badly in this carnival situation." Such a response is very similar to, although not precisely the same as the defense mechanism of *projection*. In theory, with projection one may rid himself (unconsciously) of forbidden impulses, primarily sexual and aggressive, by attributing them to others: "They are dirty-minded people; I am pure." In dissonance theory, however, one minimizes

the dissonance by viewing others as being in the same bag; the unwanted evil need not be cast out but is merely put into a bolstered context: "I may be dirty-minded, but so is everyone else."

In an ethically questionable study Bramel (1963) sought to convince pairs of male subjects that each was sexually aroused by pictures of other males in various stages of undress. To do this he brought pairs of subjects to an experimental room where they were hooked up to what was purported to be a lie-detection machine registering changes in physiological arousal. Half of the subjects received prior information about themselves that was intended to lower their self-esteem; the other half received information designed to create a sense of high self-esteem. The task for each subject was to record the reading of his own metered recorder and to predict the meter reading of his partner. Of course the meters were controlled by the experimenter.

The prediction Bramel tested and for which he found supportive evidence was that subjects in the high-self-esteem conditions who read high levels of homosexual arousal on their own meters would project a greater amount of homosexual arousal to their partners than would subjects in the low-self-esteem conditions. The derivation from dissonance theory is straightforward: the feedback that one is homosexually inclined is more dissonant to those having high self-esteem than to those of low esteem. Those of low esteem figuratively can say to themselves: "I knew it. I just knew it. First I learn that my feet are flat; next that I am half blind; next that I am dumb, dirty, hostile, mean; so finally I learn that I'm homosexual. What else is new?" To handle the dissonance experienced, Bramel argues, the high-self-esteem subjects would see their partners as similar to themselves in their arousal. Generally this is what the data indicated; the high-esteem group rated themselves and their partners as more similarly aroused than the low-esteem groups.

In an article critical of dissonance theory Bem (1967) argues that we need not posit a dissonance interpretation to explain such results. He suggests that we view the situation simply as one in which subjects are asked to make estimates about others' meter readings. Having no standards of judgment on which to base their guesses, subjects use their own scores as a guideline. If a subject is told that he is "good" (high-self-esteem condition), he interprets his high meter reading as being a good score, and attributes a similar goodness to his partner. If a subject is told he is "bad," he interprets his high meter reading as indicating badness and does not attribute similar badness to his partner. Unfortunately, because cognitive dissonance is an internal state inferred from subjects' overt behavior and rarely checked by their own reports of the situation, it is difficult to choose between Bem's and Bramel's interpretations. As we shall soon see, this failure to check the subject's phenomenology provides a real problem for most of the dissonance work in which several often equally plausible alternative interpretations are possible.

Insufficient justification

I give a separate heading to this aspect of dissonance theory because, perhaps to a greater extent than any other part of the theory, it is responsible for the so-called *nonobvious predictions*. In the paradigm for the study of insufficient justification a subject is forced to comply with an activity that to him is aversive or contrary to his own attitudes, beliefs, or sense of morality. The greater the external force applied, the less the individual sees himself as responsible for his actions; the greater therefore is the justification for doing what he must do, and the less dissonance he experiences. A man with a gun in his back, threatened with death unless he performs some act he otherwise would not perform, will feel perfectly justified in having done it; and with the feeling of justification—"I had to do it or die"—comes a lesser degree of dissonance. On the other hand, if a man notes that he has more or less freely done something contrary to his own beliefs (i.e., with insufficient justification from external pressure), there exists a strong dissonance between his beliefs and his actions. As dissonance theory so aptly recognizes, once he has acted he cannot take it back. Thus he is likely to reduce dissonance by changing his attitudes to fit the action.

In what is clearly the winner for classics among dissonance studies, Festinger and Carlsmith (1959) paid subjects either $1 or $20 to tell a lie. When a subject showed up for his experimental hour he was asked to perform a rather long, boring, repetitive task. The experimenter then hired him as an assistant for either $1 or $20 to tell a subject in the waiting room (who was a stooge) how enjoyable, exciting, and interesting a task it was. Festinger and Carlsmith compared the $1 and $20 groups with a control group (which simply worked on the dull task) on their ratings of the enjoyableness of the task; the measures were obtained at a later time. Results show that the $1 group found the task to be much more exciting than the $20 group. These results apparently support the dissonance prediction, and are nonobvious in that common sense—so we are told—would indicate that the higher the reward, the greater the willingness to tell and believe a lie. The insufficient-justification argument is simply that $20 provided sufficient justification for the lie, so that there was little dissonance to be reduced. On the other hand, to have sold out for one lousy dollar creates the kind of dissonance that needs reduction. The subject has already lied, and cannot take that back. What he can do is say to himself, "The task must have been interesting after all."

In a replication of sorts of this famous $1-$20 study, A. R. Cohen (1962) paid subjects amounts varying from $.50 to $10 to write an essay taking a position counter to their own. The insufficient-justification concept would maintain that a man who sold out for $.50 would change his attitude more to fit the essay he had just written than a man paid $1.00, who in turn would change more than a man paid $5.00, and so on. Results show striking support for these predictions.

Another forced-compliance study based on a complex form of the insufficient-justification theme is the infamous grasshopper study (E. E. Smith, 1961). Army reservists were induced to eat grasshoppers by a leader who was either casual and likable or cooly official and distant. Those who ate the grasshoppers when induced by the "bad-guy" leader later rated grasshoppers more highly than those who were induced by the "good-guy" leader. A puzzlement you say? Not for dissonance theory, which predicts this kind of finding. If we assume that, comparable to the $1 bribe, the bad guy provides insufficient justification for the action, whereas the good guy, like the $20, provides sufficient justification, the entire explanation becomes apparent. Presumably a subject's conversation with himself runs, "I've eaten these hoppers because that bastard asked me to. He's still a bastard, but damn it, I've eaten them, so maybe they aren't so bad after all." A reservist with a nice-guy leader, on the other hand, might say to himself, "Hoppers . . . ugh. But that nice guy asked me to eat them and I suppose I should . . . he is a decent sort . . . but I still don't like the critters."

The Critics. Not everyone accepted the $1-$20 study with equanimity. In fact, a regular cadre of dissonance-theory debunkers developed, and each critic managed to show either a simpler alternative interpretation or that, in fact, the $1-$20 effect works in just the opposite manner or in no differential manner!

Rosenberg (1965) sought to replicate many aspects of the $1-$20 setting, using Cohen's variation of counterattitudinal essay writings. His results indicate that the *high*-payment group changed their attitude more to be consonant with their behavior than did the low-payment groups, just the opposite effect to that found in the original study. Rosenberg's thesis was that a condition he called *evaluation apprehension* had operated in the original $1-$20 study and that this factor accounted for the results. According to Rosenberg, evaluation apprehension describes a subject's feeling that he was being paid the $20 to test his honesty, and that to be rated highly he must not waver in his attitudes. To separate out this effect Rosenberg painstakingly divided his experiment into two distinct parts. In the first part subjects wrote counterattitudinal essays for varying amounts of payment. Later, in an *entirely different context*, he had subjects complete an attitude questionnaire that assessed their attitude on a variety of issues, including the one on which they had written the essay. Rosenberg's argument is that the subject's evaluation apprehension will not be aroused because he

doesn't associate this later measurement with his earlier expression on the essay. Results did not confirm the Festinger and Carlsmith $1-$20 effect. Another set of critics, Janis and Gilmore (1965), performed a complicated study in which they found no difference at all between the $1 and $20 groups.

Bem (1967) adopts a still different explanation. As in his previous critiques, he takes the stance of an outside observer looking in on subjects' behavior: if you see someone extolling the exciting virtues of an experimental task, and you know that he has been paid $20, you may suspect him of not being truthful, whereas if you know that he has only been paid $1 you may actually believe him. This is akin to the Jones and Davis argument on inferring dispositions from behavior: when the external context provides sufficient explanation, you need not turn to some unique internal personality state. Bem next argues that a subject uses the same framework for evaluating his own actions that an outside observer uses. Thus if he sees himself telling a lie for $1, he says to himself "Well, since I did it, I must have meant it." The distinction between the dissonance explanation and Bem's can get foggy; primarily, however, Bem maintains that the subject doesn't experience the internal state known as dissonance, but only interprets his actions in the same way he would interpret another's. To demonstrate this Bem asked a group of subjects to estimate how another person would feel about a dull task. He played a tape recording to them that essentially duplicated the $1-$20 study. Subjects then estimated how the character on the tape would rate the task. Not surprisingly, Bem's data parallel the original $1-$20 data, although his subjects did not go through the dissonance-inducing experience. It is not yet clear just what Bem's study adds to the dissonance literature other than showing that observers can predict others' reactions in a manner that parallels how those others have actually performed. This does not in itself disprove the dissonance interpretations; observers may in fact use a dissonance-type theory in making their prediction.

Unfortunately, if no one makes any substantial efforts to get more directly at subjects' phenomenology, it will continually be possible for imaginative investigators to come up with alternative interpretations to the dissonance work. That, of course, is the problem when we deal with unmeasured intervening mental states as explanatory devices. It is only a rare experiment that can provide the crucial differentiating proof that theory *A* works while theory *B* is incorrect.

One effort to get into a subject's skull was undertaken by Ellsworth (1966), who created a classic dissonance situation and then interviewed the subjects about their cognitions during the experimental manipulations. She reports five reasons offered by subjects for their behavior: 68 percent reported that they changed their attitudes from the predissonance to the postdissonance position because of *forgetting;* 25 percent attributed their behavior to *achievement motivation* (see p. 153 ff); 15 percent indicated some awareness of the experimenters' desires in the situation (*demand characteristics*); 37 percent suggested that their behavior was a *consciously undertaken strategy* to perform well in the situation; 28 percent attributed their actions to *dissonance reduction.* These data clearly indicate the wide variety of reasons a person may act as he does in an experimental situation that purports to test the principle of cognitive dissonance.

In the main the theory of cognitive dissonance has proved an extremely useful explanatory model and has stimulated prolific and ingenious research efforts. The bolstering strategy seems to operate here as well; the vast body of supportive data far overshadows the body of refutory material. So imaginative and productive a model as dissonance theory has much to commend it to our attention and intelligently informed use. Its existence marks a significant period in the history of American social psychology. Is it simply another fad in the social scientific fields? I think not. If anything, the faddish and too-frequent demonstration, through cutely ingenious experiments, that dissonance theory does this or that is now reaching its demise as researchers begin to examine the more basic questions concerning the conditions under which the dissonance principle holds. But more of this later.

ATTITUDINAL CONSISTENCY THEORIES

Historically, the study of attitudes has been a key foundation for the field of social psychology (Allport, 1954). An *attitude* is a presumed inner orientation of an individual that has several components to it, depending on one's particular persuasion. Based largely on the platonic trichotomy, an attitude is said to have *cognitive, affective*, and *conative* components. The cognitive component is the *object* of the attitude; just what is the referent? Negroes? Jews? Political candidates? Ice cream sundaes? The affective component is the *direction of feeling* about the object. Like it? Dislike it? Feel indifferent to it? The conative component, often omitted in attitude theories, is the action the attitude brings about. Does hate of Negroes lead one to act to exclude them from living in the same neighborhood? Does love of country lead one to kill all who dissent against it?

Given these several components, the study of attitudes becomes a natural for the examination of a consistency model. How are the components related? And, as importantly, can a change in one component produce a change in others? If a change is induced in your feelings (affective component) about some object, will this in turn produce a change in your beliefs (cognitive component) about that object? If the several parts of an attitude form an interdependent system analogous to a *P-O-X* cognitive system, a change in one element of that system should reverberate throughout the entire system, resulting eventually in a "new" attitude. This assumes, of course, that an attitude does form a system that, like other systems, seeks a harmonious, balanced, consistent state; a change in one element of the system would disrupt the harmonious state and lead to some alteration in the direction of consistency.

Rosenberg's classic study

In what is perhaps the most direct, systematic examination of this consistency notion Rosenberg (1960) used hypnosis to alter his subjects' affective state and studied the consequent cognitive changes that occurred. In one study he selected subjects who initially felt the United States should continue its economic aid to other nations. Rosenberg suggested to the subjects under hypnosis that when they awoke they would feel opposed to the present U. S. foreign aid policy, that the mere idea of such aid would make them feel displeased and disgusted. In addition, he suggested that on awakening they would have no memory of any suggestions. He made no other direct suggestion about the issue. Affect was measured before and after the manipulation by rating scales ranging from "extremely in favor" to "extremely opposed." One scale asked subjects to rate their *feeling* on the issue. Two additional scales involved issues about which no hypnotic manipulation had taken place; these served as control issues.

The cognitive component of the subjects' attitude was measured by a deck of 32 value cards, each listing some goal or end state that might be valued or desired: "All human beings have equal rights," "People being well educated," "Attaining economic security," and so on. Subjects were asked to rate both the importance of each value and the likelihood that it would be attained as a consequence of the issue under consideration. For example, each subject rated the importance of "All human beings have equal rights." Next, he indicated to what extent that value would come to be if the United States abandoned its economic aid to foreign governments. To test the hypothesis that affect changes produce cognitive changes, Rosenberg compared pre- and posthypnotic measures of both affect and cognition.

Results generally supported the hypothesis. The typical subject in Rosenberg's study changed his affect from negative (United States *should not* abandon aid) to positive (United States *should* abandon aid) as a function of the hypnotic suggestion. Subjects also—and this is the test of the hypothesis—changed many of the cognitive components of their attitude. Whereas they might have felt initially that giving up foreign aid would block the attainment of certain valued goals (e.g., preventing economic depression) or facilitate the occurrence of undesirable goals (e.g., open expression of disagreement), after the hypnotic manipulation they reported that giving up foreign aid would *help prevent* depression and *block* the open expres-

sion of disagreement. The psycho-logic can be diagrammed simply, as in Table 7.1. A new

Table 7.1 Change in affect and cognition on an issue as a result of hypnotic suggestion

Initial state	(1) *P* dislikes *abandoning* U.S. foreign aid policy (2) *P* likes the goal of avoiding economic depressions (3) *P* believes that giving up U.S. aid policy helps produce depressions

Hypnotic suggestion to dislike U.S. foreign aid policy

Posthypnotic state	(1) *P* dislikes U.S. foreign aid policy (2) *P* likes the goal of avoiding economic depressions (3) *P* believes that giving up U.S. aid policy helps *avoid* depressions

consistency is achieved in which the cognitive and affective components of the person's attitudes are harmonious.

This case shows a cognitive change; Rosenberg also reports actual value shifts whereby something that before hypnotic suggestion was seen as a positive value was seen as a negative value after the affect change. After a while Rosenberg removed his subjects' amnesia for the hypnotic episode; not surprisingly, with affect restored to its initial state the cognitive component of the attitude shifted back, restoring a balanced state.

Carlson's efforts

In a study in the same general framework Carlson (1956) showed how a change in the internal structure of an attitude leads to an overall shift in the attitude itself. His goal was to change subjects' attitudes on the issue of allowing Negroes to move into a white neighborhood. Carlson's idea was that if subjects could be made aware of the *perceived instrumentality* between this issue and the attainment of goals they valued, they would alter their attitudes on the issue itself to bring it to a consistency with their new awareness. If I believe that allowing Negroes to live in white neighborhoods is not desirable, but can be convinced that it is instrumental to attaining something I value very highly, such as American prestige in other countries, the psycho-logic of consistency theory indicates that I will change my attitude.

Carlson's technique was similar to Rosenberg's, but whereas Rosenberg used hypnotic suggestion to change one facet of attitude structure, Carlson employed what he termed a *test of objectivity*. He introduced his study as an exercise in the use of the scientific method. Subjects were first asked to rate a variety of 25 value statements including four key items: American prestige in other countries; protection of property values; equal opportunity for personal development; and being experienced, broad-minded, and so on. They were to indicate how much importance they attached to each. Next they were asked to rate the extent to which they felt Negroes moving into white neighborhoods would be instrumental to attaining these values. How probable was it, for example, that one who allowed Negroes to move into all-white neighborhoods would be demonstrating his own broad-mindedness? In the change procedure subjects were asked to write objective essays to support propositions linking the Negro move with the four key value items. Then they completed a questionnaire. Results clearly indicated that subjects who changed in their perceived instrumentality also showed a change in their attitude toward Negroes moving into white neighborhoods. Essentially, then, Carlson demonstrated a consistency principle: after writing arguments supporting the proposition that Negroes moving into white neighborhoods will attain for me those things I value most, I now act consistently to favor the move.

The general topic of change is of central interest in the second part of this text; clearly these consistency theories of attitudinal structure all deal with this important social-psychological matter. To be sure, a man who would produce an attitude change in another rarely has the luxury of a captive subject in a psychological experiment. Nor, for that matter, can he simply create a hypnotic trance, or even get people to write arguments in support of things they may not believe. The consistency principle, however, does argue that, given man's apparent passion for his own unique brand of psycho-logical consistency, one can effect some attitude change by inducing an alteration in one component of the over-all attitude system. Thus we would expect that propaganda directed toward and *only* toward the negative affective side of an attitude issue would increase the likelihood of negative cognitive elements appearing and the likelihood that subjects so propagandized would be ready to accept negative belief items. For example, if you grow up in a society in which negative affect is attached to the objects "black" and "Jew," you should develop supporting negative beliefs about blacks and Jews and should be more ready to accept the introduction of negative beliefs about each group. A white who has little or no contact with blacks but who has learned since childhood to fear them is likely either to have built up a set of beliefs about blacks that is consistent with the feeling of fear—for example, they are not to be trusted; they steal; they rape white women; they have fiery tempers; they fight a great deal—or to be more ready to accept such cognitive items than items inconsistent with the affective state of fear. Once the feeling toward Jews was carefully inculcated in most of the people in Nazi Germany, they were ready to believe all kinds of evil but few good things about Jews.

Socratic effect

In a fascinating, suggestive application of the attitudinal consistency perspective, McGuire (1960) used the Socratic method to demonstrate inconsistency. If you ask someone simply to state his attitudes on logically related issues, any inconsistencies uncovered should induce pressures in him to change toward consistency. This assumes that certain conditions, including something like wishful thinking, have initially allowed him to retain inconsistent attitudes. The Socratic method forces him to heed these inconsistencies and then lets nature (in this case, psycho-nature) take its course. McGuire tested the Socratic approach by having subjects respond to 48 opinion statements including the following.

(1) Students who violate any regulation which has been made to safeguard the lives and property of other students will be dismissed from the University.

(2) With respect to drafting college students, the Government will adopt whatever military service program is in the best interest of the nation as a whole.

(3) Any change in the curriculum that would result in a better education for the students would be adopted by the University administration.

(4) The Government will adopt the policy of deferring all college students at least until they have completed their education.

(5) Students who violate the regulations against smoking in the classrooms and buildings of the University will be dismissed from the University.

(6) Having more required courses results in a better education for students.

(7) The military service program with respect to college students which is in the best interest of the nation as a whole is to defer all students at least until they have completed their education.

(8) The University administration will change the curriculum to include more required courses.

(9) The regulations against smoking in the classrooms and buildings of the University have been made to safeguard the lives and property of the students.

McGuire's listing of 48 statements contains 16 sets of syllogisms, separated and appearing in different parts of the test; note how items 1-9-5; 2-7-4; 3-6-8 form syllogisms. When subjects were made aware of their logical inconsistencies within each three-statement syllogism, McGuire noted the predicted Socratic effect in which the subjects changed toward greater consistency.

Osgood's congruity principle

Although they apparently did not derive it by means of Socratic introspection, Osgood and his associates proposed a cognitive *principle of congruity* that has much in common with other consistency theories (Osgood & Tannenbaum, 1955; Osgood, Suci, & Tannenbaum, 1957). Osgood's work began with an interest in representing the "meaning" of particular concepts for the individual. To assess these meanings Osgood developed a measuring instrument called the *semantic differential*, on which

individuals are asked to rate concepts—for example, MOTHER—on a series of seven-point scales such as the following.

good	$+3:+2:+1:0:-1:-2:-3$	bad
weak	$-3:-2:-1:0:+1:+2:+3$	strong
active	$+3:+2:+1:0:-1:-2:-3$	passive

Factor analyses of longer lists of adjectives indicated three major factors, which were termed *evaluative* (e.g., good-bad), *potency* (weak-strong), and *activity* (active-passive). Most research has been on the evaluative scale. Given a variety of concepts to be rated and the use of *discrepancy scores*, it is possible to represent a given individual's meaning or *semantic space*. For example, you could rate the concepts MYSELF, MY MOTHER, MY FATHER, MY BROTHER, MY SISTER. Discrepancies computed between these several concepts as they exist for you can be used to obtain a spatial representation of the your family configuration. A representation of closeness between yourself and your father and distance between yourself and your mother and between your father and mother could be used by a clinician to infer tension within your family.

In his principle of congruity Osgood argues that the semantic spatial distance between two attitudinal concepts, rated, for instance, in terms of the good-bad evaluative factor, tends toward equilibrium whenever the concepts are joined by an *assertion*. McGuire's Socratic method appears on its surface simply to point out to a person that he believes *A* and *not-A* about the same object, or that if you believe *A* and you believe *B*, then logically you must believe *C* as well. Osgood joins the two beliefs by an assertion that can be *associative*—*A* likes *B*, advocates *B*, goes with *B*—or *dissociative*—*A* dislikes *B*, avoids *B*, disavows *B*. If RMN is said to like Scotch whiskey, RMN and Scotch are two concepts linked by an associative assertion. If RMN is said to dislike vodka, RMN and vodka are joined by a dissociative assertion. In either case the assertion brings the two concepts into that single cognitive breath. Each concept presumably exists within the individual's total meaning space; when they are joined by the assertion the process of cognitive interaction toward congruity occurs.

If I like RMN and I like Scotch and the associative assertion indicates that RMN likes Scotch, all is cognitively harmonious in my little world of presidents and alcohol. Or is it? Osgood's relatively refined measuring tool of the semantic differential permits him to argue that two concepts are not in a congruous relationship (not in equilibrium or harmonious) until *each changes* toward an equilibrium point, with the concept moving most that is least polarized; that is, least intense or extreme in its evaluation. If I like Scotch whiskey +3 on the semantic differential evaluative rating scale and I like RMN only +1, the situation is not congruous until I shift *each* concept toward an equilibrium point. In this case congruity would be achieved if my evaluation of Scotch shifts downward to +2.5 and my evaluation of RMN shifts upward to +2.5. This example demonstrates two things about Osgood's congruity principle: first, congruity is achieved when two concepts reach *equally* intense polarization; second, the concept that is least polarized changes most. RMN moves up 1.5 units, whereas Scotch whiskey, the concept that is initially more intensely held, moves only 0.5. The implication for a wily politician (in their wisdom most wily politicians have been using this technique since long before Osgood saw the light of day) is that he must associate himself believably with things persons value highly. Thus a barely known politico (rated +1 on the semantic differential) who loudly asserts, "I'm for MOTHERHOOD" (+3) manages to benefit considerably from the assertion. Of course motherhood, like Scotch, suffers slightly from the associative linking; but good Scotch, and for that matter motherhood, have managed to survive even the nastiest politicos' claims.

The congruity principle has something to say as well about two concepts that are rated on different sides of the center. For example, suppose we have the assertion that Hitler (−3) likes motherhood (+3). In this case the congruity principle argues that each will change toward an equilibrium point of 0, *assuming that we believe the assertion*. Osgood inserts a term called *correction for incredulity* into his com-

putations to deal with assertions that seem blatantly absurd and unbelievable.

One of the initial systematic studies of the congruity principle was a 1955 study by Osgood and Tannenbaum. Subjects were initially measured on the semantic differential for attitudes toward three sources (labor leaders, the *Chicago Tribune*, Robert Taft) and three concepts (legalized gambling, abstract art, accelerated college programs). At a later date they were presented with fake newspaper accounts in which the sources made favorable or unfavorable assertions about the concepts. Subjects read the story, briefly summarized its major features, and then filled out another semantic differential evaluation for the sources and concepts. Actual changes toward congruity were compared with the theoretically predicted changes; the data showed striking confirmation for the theory. In an interesting sidelight to their data Osgood and Tannenbaum discovered that changes toward congruity were greater for the concepts than for the sources. This finding fits with our common-sense expectations; if someone I like (the source) advocates the support of something that I feel slightly negative about, I am more likely to change my evaluation of the object than of the source. I may like the object more, but not like the person less, in contrast to the original prediction of congruity theory.

To conclude this necessarily brief glimpse into the workings of the congruity notion, let me indicate one critical distinction between this approach and several of the other consistency ideas we have been examining. Whereas most of the approaches allow for a wide variety of techniques to rid the mind of inconsistency, the congruity principle appears to allow only the route of attitude change along the evaluative factor of the semantic differential. That one is always driven to use the single method outlined in the congruity notion seems to be an unfortunate oversimplification of what is undoubtedly a very complicated matter.

As an effort to systematically depict one mode of cognitive interaction the congruity principle provides a helpful guideline to our further understanding of the perceptual-cognitive processes. In this case the background against which we make our judgments of a focal concept or person is provided by those other concepts with which the focal concept is related by an assertion. And as we have seen, it is a very *active* background, having the potential to change the meaning of the focal concept itself.

SUMMARY

In this chapter we have examined several key consistency theories, including balance, dis-sonance, and congruity. In each case we have noted a general tendency for persons to seek harmony in their cognitive world. In addition, we have seen the possibility of considering this tendency in a larger context, involving a social-comparison process. In the following chapters we dig more deeply into this process, seeking to uncover the bases both for social comparison and the tendencies toward balance, conso-nance, and congruity to which they give rise.

Chapter 8

Functional bases of consistency

Why in the world should consistency or balance matter? What is there about human beings that makes congruence or balance the harmonious, preferred state? If we recall the old Gestalt argument, man seems to have the kind of mind that goes for good figure, *Prägnanz*, completion of the incomplete. Somehow, then, imbalanced situations do not "ring true"; they are incomplete, badly composed, poor figure. We can even withdraw into nineteenth-century history and dredge up Herbart's (see 1950) notion of the *apperceptive mass*.

For Herbart the essence of man's consciousness was change. Ideas were in constant flux. The apperceptive mass is that mass of ideas that exist in consciousness at any one time. New ideas that fit into the equilibrium or balanced state of that mass gain entry with minimal conflict and strain; ideas that do not fit—are incongruent—have an uphill battle to gain entry.

But these notions about our mental processes, although they may be interesting and even of some value, do not operate on the level we are seeking. Some, in fact, just take us on a pleasant circular tour in which we ask why and are told because that's the way we think. For the most part, theorists who have sought to offer an answer to the questions about Why balance? have worked within a functional frame-

work. Doing so provides no magic; functionalism too has often been accused of routing us on a circular tour: Why does such and such take place? Because it's functional. But as the sociologist Merton (1957) pointed out in an excellent essay, the most useful approach to functionalism is to distinguish between *functional, nonfunctional*, and *dysfunctional* on one hand and *manifest* and *latent* functions on the other.

THE FUNCTIONAL VIEW

A functional analysis of some behavior, event, institution, or social practice seeks to relate the existence of the act or practice to a larger system of purposes within which it fits and that its occurrence serves. Funeral practices, for example, can be subjected to a functional analysis through which the functions these practices satisfy become apparent. In addition to the manifest function of dealing with a dead body, much of the ritual of the funeral ceremony serves important functions for the living, both immediate relatives and friends and the larger society that is concerned about this important point of transition. In a time of grief and mourning the funeral activities help alleviate some suffering as the mourners get caught up in busy routines. The living sense the tribute that awaits their own death, which may ease the fear of death that exists in each. Communal ceremonies, moreover, are integrating; they bring everyone together, and in the face of death, the act that threatens disintegration, all integrating activities serve a positive function.

Merton's analysis suggests that certain actions that are functional for one group in society may be dysfunctional or nonfunctional for another group. Likewise, the manifest functions of a practice are only one level for analysis; many latent functions or even dysfunctions may also be served by that particular practice. Here Merton approaches Freudian analysis of dreams, discussing the manifest content—what we report—and its underlying symbolic meaning or latent content.

Two examples, two themes

What functions are served by a balanced cognitive state? Let us picture two instructive interpersonal situations in which balance does not prevail.

1. John likes Mary and thinks she likes him, but she really hates him. This is imbalanced, to be sure. And undoubtedly it is an awkward situation for both John and Mary because their interaction is based on an erroneous assumption. Thus at least one virtue of cognitive balance is that it offers *shared assumptions* on which to base interactions with another. And shared assumptions—or shall we say shared definitions of the interactive encounter—can provide the oil that helps the encounter rumble along a bit more smoothly.

2. John likes Bill. Over time they have developed a good deal of mutual trust and respect. Being of draft age and without deferment, John is pondering what he will do if called up. He is not certain that he is generally opposed to all wars, but feels a deep revulsion about the particular war in which he will undoubtedly be asked to serve. He learns, quite to his surprise, that his friend Bill very strongly feels that every citizen in a democracy must support his nation's decisions, even if on specific occasions those decisions are contrary to his private view. He will serve willingly when called and cannot respect anyone who would do otherwise.

A discrepancy between John and Bill over X,

a discrepancy of which John was not aware, has built one aspect of their relationship on a somewhat false assumption. The revelation of the discrepancy throws the relationship into a confusing state. One can almost hear John mumbling to himself: "How could I have been so mistaken about you?" Imbalance here may cast doubts on other aspects of what John had not seen as a problematic relationship with his good friend. Furthermore, intertwined with everything else, the discovered imbalance puts a seed of doubt in John's mind about his own position on X. Perhaps he relied on the social support of his best friend's views to reinforce his own position on this issue of such importance to him; on learning that he and Bill disagree, he loses this support, opening to question the basis for his own view.

Although numerous other examples are available, these two offer glimpses of the functional significance a balanced interpersonal situation provides. Two related themes have emerged: the accuracy of the assumptions on which one's relationships are based, and the correctness of one's own conceptions of reality. Most of us, much of the time, proceed about our daily lives without any idea that the world as we see it may differ from the world as others see it. For the most part, in fact, we are likely to assume that "What I see as correct, others see as correct," and to assume it about both the nature of our relationship with others and our conception of reality. For example, we are likely to assume that persons we like also like us and that persons we dislike dislike us. Research on this matter generally substantiates this tendency to view relations between persons as symmetrical (e.g., Tagiuri, Bruner, & Blake, 1958).

An interesting aspect of this issue, which has broad relevance to balance theory and to its several applications, is the relation between self-esteem and this tendency to assume a congruence between our attitude toward others and their attitude toward us. In a situation in which P hates himself, or at best thinks badly of himself, the proper prediction from the balance model would be that P should *dislike* those who *like* him and like only those who share his own negative evaluation of himself. "How could I ever like anyone who liked someone so evil, worthless, and bad as I am?" If this aspect of the balance model is correct, congruence itself is based on the assumption that *P* likes himself; if we assume that people we like like us in return, this congruency requires that we have a fairly positive self-evaluation.

Wiest (1965) examined this point in his study of evaluations in elementary and junior-high classrooms. He employed self-descriptive statements and teacher ratings to assess each student's self-esteem. Analyses of the data indicated that in general the higher a person's self-esteem, the greater is the likelihood that he will perceive a congruence between his attitudes toward others and his perception of their attitudes toward him.

A SHARED SOCIAL REALITY

Not only do we perceive congruence in our interpersonal attitudes; we also generally assume that "we" and "they" all live in the same world of experience. The chair I see is the chair you see; the car I drive recklessly is the car you are trying to dodge; the suit I wear is the same suit you see; that person over there is also over there for you. This is not a simple principle, for at the same time we may also argue that our personal world is unique, peculiar to us, and is unshared by anyone. I can explicate my experiences to you only with great difficulty; even then I doubt that you can know them as I do. The taste of apple pie is an experience in my personal world that I can hardly share with you. Although you may empathize, my pains are part of an inner world open only to me. My life as a black man in the ghetto is a life filled with experiences that no white man can ever understand in the same terms I do.

Despite this admittedly complex relationship between the shared and the unique, which most of us intuitively understand, our daily lives are usually spent in a world we assume is more shared than unique. The picture fogs up somewhat, however, when we shift from the shared world of physical objects to the world of social reality. Years ago this distinction between

physical and social realities became a central part of Festinger's social comparison process theory (1950; 1954a; 1954b). Today it serves us well in providing a useful framework within which to understand the functional basis of the balance model.

Physical reality versus social reality

Let us assume along with Heider, Festinger, and Newcomb that in our quest for stability and order each of us wants to know something about the validity of the perspectives he maintains. Am I correct in my view of the world in which we live? Do I see what you see? Are my views accurate? Do I live in the *same* world as you? If the world about which we are asking questions is the world of physical reality, we can test the validity of our own view by direct or at least highly standardized means. If I wonder how many teeth there are in this donkey's mouth, I may put it to the direct test and count. Or, if I want to know if that piece of glass is clear enough to look through, again I can test it directly by looking through it. If I accept the words of experts, I may use indirect tests to check the validity of my own point of view. I can read in a textbook, for example, that the sun rises in the east and sets in the west, and "know" my direct observation is correct.

If the world about which we wonder is a world of social reality—of beliefs, opinions, values, ideologies, and so on—then not only are most direct tests beyond possibility, but in addition we find fewer experts on whom we can depend. Criteria for noting the scientific validity of an idea become clouded with arguments and opinions, putting even an expert adrift on a sea of confusion. Here we turn to others who think as we think in order to validate our own perspectives through consensus. We become correct in a sense because others we know think as we think.

This distinction between physical and social reality is a useful one and provides the basis for many specific empirical hypotheses and studies (see Festinger 1950; 1954a; 1954b for a summary). Note that in either case our own experiences, our own eyes and ears, and our own observations are never sufficiently complete to provide all the information we need.

Although direct tests of reality may be available, in most circumstances we have learned to depend on others as sources of information about the nature of our physical and social world. As children we learn how valuable our mothers and fathers are in providing for most of our basic physiological needs, and in addition, for offering wise counsel on the nature of the physical and social world. "Why, Daddy?" He may answer with fact or with "Shut up," but in any case a child gets much of his early knowledge through such adult sources of information. Later he turns to peers, to books, to education. And, of course, all along he tries things out on his own, learning by doing, through trial and error and oops-I-didn't-know-the-gun-was-loaded efforts.

As sources of information, other persons offer us a path through the myriad events that comprise our lives. What they think, what they know, what they say, what they believe, all become touchstones by which we judge our own knowledge. When we and they agree, we stand together in a common world, a reality on which there is consensual validation. When we and they disagree, however, the ever-present possibility creeps into our minds that somehow we have not been seeing what is to be seen; somehow we may be wrong. This seed of doubt may grow in some, may be dispelled in others by self-confidence, and in others ... well, we shall deal with everyone in due time.

If we like someone, trust him, value his opinion, we are especially thrown off when we find that we do not live in the same world. When we turn to him for validation and find that he disagrees, how disheartening it is, how potentially shattering, how doubt-inducing. With maturity we come to realize how few absolutes there are, and how many of our own views do not exist in isolation but rather are embedded within one or more sociohistorical contexts. And yet, for the most part, we forget this embeddedness as we engage in the routines of everyday living, recalling it with a start when we come up against a discrepancy between "where we are at" and where others are on some particular matter.

Invasion from Mars. The year was 1938, and radio was the "in" household machine. News broadcasts, comedy shows, soap operas, mysteries, and Orson Welles' "War of the Worlds." Widely advertised in advance as a dramatization, and even introduced as such on the night of its premiere presentation, the show brought many people out of their houses in panic; men from Mars had invaded the earth and were already gaining a foothold on the American countryside. To be sure, the show had a realistic sound; what was supposedly an evening of danceband music was interrupted with a news flash concerning the sighting of mysterious objects. As the show went on, the invasion became more threatening. To those listening today the dramatic devices used to create realism would sound phony, yet we can appreciate the feeling that must have overtaken the people who first heard the show. Those who tuned in late did not hear the dramatization disclaimer. For many it appeared that the world really was being invaded. Many listeners, initially taken aback by this news flash, sought actively to test reality by changing the radio dial: "Surely a real invasion would be carried by all the networks." Finding business as usual, they settled back to enjoy the dramatic treat. Out of ignorance or fear some did not test reality in this manner; or, having tested, did not accept the life-as-usual programming of the other stations, and ran out into the streets. Others saw people in the streets and also ran out. In fact, as one study of the event indicated, some persons, seeing no traffic on their block, assumed that traffic must be already jammed up elsewhere by escaping throngs (Cantril, Gaudet, & Hertzog, 1940). For those who sought to validate the reality of the impending doom by checking with their friends this social-comparison process often brought only further confirmation that indeed they had better pack and prepare to flee the invaders from outer space. For that one moment in time man's world view had been shaken by another perspective; for many the response was panic.

Summer Riot. The process of social comparison through which we gain a sense of the validity of our own conceptions, as we have seen, can lead people to the streets in panic. But we need not have lived in the gullible and unsophisticated thirties to respond in this manner. The time is now; the season, summer; the weather, oppressively hot and humid; the place, a ghetto. You feel trapped by the walls of your small room, choked by polluted city air and the smell of rotting garbage. People move into the streets seeking some relief. Crowds congregate. Kids play under open hydrants. The elderly swing lazily on porch rockers. Young adults wander aimlessly in small groups, joking, laughing, teasing. As they gather, they compare notes on their common plight, share thoughts on the misery of the heat without the white luxury of pools and air conditioning. The ghetto seems more like hell than ever. You sense all too deeply the feeling of being trapped. There is nowhere to go, nowhere to turn, no relief in sight.

This is the season for the ghetto revolt. White storekeepers look apprehensively down the street and see the black crowds milling about. They sense the trapped seeking to break out of a city grave. "More people are on the streets now than before," each storekeeper notes to himself. "Wonder if I should close up the store? Board up the windows? Don't want my big front windows broken." One especially anxious merchant does close. He puts on extra locks, begins to board up the windows. Across the street another merchant looks out. He too had noticed the crowd and felt its mood, and now he sees his friend closing and boarding up. "Perhaps he has heard something? A rumor? A riot?" He too closes his store to get out before the riot occurs. Merchants up and down the block begin to lock up, board up, flee. People on the street notice the merchants' frantic, fearful actions. "Maybe a riot," each thinks. Movements quicken. Parents rush children off the street and back into those sweltering rooms. Old people take one more weary rock and move upstairs into the safety of their rooms. A deathly quiet comes over the area; the young adults sense something amiss and gather together into tighter groups. A police patrol car, called to the scene by a nervous store owner, passes and stops. Words are exchanged, tempers flare, the inevitable explosion occurs.

It is during such periods that those knowledgeable about riot prevention attempt to con-

vince store owners to keep their stores open; business as usual is the watchword. In sensitive times a slight change in routine can so affect the social-comparison process that an already tense situation can be cued into an actual riot. As individuals look about for clues, the closed stores provide adequate information to guide behavior; they get out. Not only do other persons aid us in testing and validating our sense of reality, they often create the sense of reality we come to have.

Social comparison and emotion

In an interesting laboratory investigation Schachter and Singer (1962) provided a demonstration of the compelling influence another person can have on so personal and private an event as our labeling of an emotion we feel. Their ingenious experimental procedure placed a naive subject in an experimental situation with a stooge paid to enact certain detailed routines. Subjects were initially given an injection of a drug, epinephrine, that would produce a state of physiological arousal (in some conditions a placebo was injected). The drug increases blood pressure and heart rate and gives a subjective experience of rapid heartbeat, tremor, and sometimes a feeling of flushing.

In one condition of the experiment the stooge, presumed to have had the same injection, ran through a routine designed to convey the emotional experience of *euphoria*. He began to act playfully giddy, like a small child. Toward the end of his routine he played with a Hula-Hoop. In another condition the enactment was of *anger*. Here the stooge's routine took him through an increasingly growing rage against a questionnaire he and the subject were asked to complete. Toward the end of this routine he ripped up the questionnaire, hurled the bits of paper at the floor, and stamped out of the room. Of particular interest to our examination of the social-comparison process is the interesting finding that a naive subject, given a state of physiological arousal (the epinephrine rather than the placebo) and lacking a definite label for the experience, tends to label his state and describe his feelings in terms of the cues available to him, in this instance provided by the stooge. The subject felt himself to be euphoric when the model was euphoric; he felt anger when the stooge was angry.

So, for aid in clarifying or establishing the validity of our own judgments, we learn to turn to others as providers of information. Discrepancies that exist between our own judgments and theirs thus always have the potential to create doubt about the validity of our own perspective. Naturally, we do not go about comparing our views with those of everyone else; we tend to be somewhat selective. Those we like, trust, and respect become more important as validating agencies than those we dislike or distrust, or for whom we have little respect. Thus disagreements with liked others prove more shattering to our own perspective than disagreements with those we dislike, just as the balance model predicts.

Social comparison and the autokinetic effect

In 1935 Sherif utilized a perceptual phenomenon known as the *autokinetic effect* to study the development of social "norms" in a small group. A tiny pinpoint of light in an otherwise totally darkened room appears to be in motion, even though it is in fact stationary. This self-movement of the light is called *autokinesis*. The effect works even on those who are aware of the absence of movement; I used to enter our experimental room, flick out the overhead light, turn on the pinpoint of light, and watch it move up and down, in and out, around, and around, and around. The situation is extremely ambiguous. In a totally darkened room you cannot judge depth and distance. If you enter the room blindfolded, thus lacking cues even of room size, you can see that light move almost any number of inches.

Sherif had subjects estimate how far the light moved during a specific period of time. In some conditions subjects judged the light's movement for several trials alone before they were placed in a situation with other subjects. In the group condition subjects were asked to announce their judgments out loud. Sherif noted the development of convergences in judgment toward a common judgmental frame or, in his terms, a *norm of judgment*. Persons who might

initially have diverged in their judgments achieved a judgmental norm after a while in the group. This was especially true for subjects who experienced the group situation first. Those who had first established a judgmental norm alone, although affected by the group, were more resistant than those who came into the group without norms.

Sampson and Insko (1964) took advantage of the ambiguity and apparently easy influenceability of judgment on the autokinetic effect in a demonstration of how social comparison works with liked and disliked others. We used that famous fixture in social-psychological laboratory research, the ever-faithful stooge; in this case we established a complex (I might even say, immodestly, ingenious) series of subject-stooge interactions to create a condition in which half of the subjects disliked the stooge (*O*) and half liked him. During an early part of the experiment, ostensibly to help the experimenter check his equipment, subjects (*Ps*) made several judgments of autokinetic light movement. These served as a baseline that allowed us to manipulate systematically the similarity in judgment of *P* and *O*. In half of the cases in the main part of the experiment *O* gave judgments of light movement that were very similar to those initially given by *P*. In the other half *O*'s judgments were widely discrepant from those initially given by *P*. The question of interest was what *P* would do when he noted that the only other person making judgments in this highly ambiguous situation disagreed (or agreed) with his earlier judgments. How would the *P-O* relationship influence his use of *O* as a social comparison point for his own later judgments? According to a balance model, *P* should find the condition balanced and harmonious when his judgments are *similar* to those of the *liked O* or *dissimilar* to those of the *disliked O*, and should stick to his initial judgments. When *P*'s judgments are dissimilar to those of the liked *O* or similar to those of the disliked *O*, the imbalance of the situation should lead him to act; in this case we would predict that *P* would change his judgments of the light movement. Essentially, therefore, the balance model suggests that one will not compare himself with a disliked other, but will compare himself with a liked other. This comparison will lead *P* to change to be more similar to the *O* he likes and less similar to the *O* he dislikes. Convergence should characterize *P likes O*; divergence should characterize *P dislikes O*. In general, this is what we found, lending support both to the balance model and to the social-comparison process framework within which the model is to be understood. In addition, of course, the results add a further specification to Sherif's studies of the formation of social norms.

PRESSURES TOWARD UNIFORMITY

Up to this point I have indicated that one of the major functional bases for the balance or consistency model is to be found in each person's efforts to test his conceptions of reality by comparing them with others. In his formulation of the theory of social comparison Festinger (1954a and b) hypothesized that this comparison process formed one of the major bases for *uniformity pressures* within groups; that is, pressures toward attaining group consensus. The balance model makes much the same argument if we assume an initial attraction between members of the group.

A classic and, in my estimation, most instructive study was published by Schachter in 1951. For his study Schachter employed three stooges, each of whom was to play a particular role in a discussion group. The case history of a juvenile delinquent, Johnny Rocco, was presented to groups of subjects (each group included all the stooges) for discussion. They were given a seven-point rating scale to focus their discussion around a question: What should be done with Johnny Rocco? Point 1 on the scale urged extreme compassion and care; point 7 emphasized punishment as being the only way to treat Johnny. Being a wise social psychologist, Schachter could fairly well estimate in advance the position his population of college-educated, sophisticated subjects was likely to adopt: between 2 and 4 on the scale, balancing love with a little discipline. This permitted him to instruct each stooge to adopt a position that was in various ways related to

this dominant group opinion. The *deviate* was instructed to take position 7 (extreme punishment) and to stick with it throughout the entire group discussion. The *slider* was instructed to take position 7 at the beginning of the discussion and, about halfway through, to slide in toward the modal position. The third stooge, the *mode*, was to adopt the dominant group opinion and retain it throughout the discussion. Observers noted the nature of the interaction within the group and toward whom it was directed. In addition, all subjects completed several self-report questionnaires, some of which asked them to rank the attractiveness of group members and to nominate persons for membership on committees that had varying degrees of desirability.

Data from Schachter's study indicated that the deviate and slider received more communication than the mode, with the communication to the slider dropping off as he began to "see the light" and slide into harmonious consensus with the rest of the group. In general, communication to the deviate began to drop off slightly when it appeared that he could not be swayed by the group's efforts. Questionnaire data indicated clearly that the deviate was a sociometric reject.

Although few studies in psychological research seem to have been replicated successfully there have been some successful replications of Schachter's study. One, an experiment by Sampson and Brandon (1964), is of special interest, in that it both replicates Schachter's results for the deviate position and extends the theory one step further. We used only one stooge (it was a low-budget project) and four subjects for each group. All subjects were female. The groups were to discuss the case of James Johnson, a Negro juvenile delinquent; other than the change of name and racial identification the case was identical to Schachter's. As with Schachter's original investigation, we could assume the group would take a modal position of 2 to 4 on how to deal with James Johnson. The deviate was instructed to take position 7 and stick with it. Two trained observers watched from behind a one-way mirror and used the standardized interaction rating scale developed by Bales (1950a, b) to code the interaction that took place during each group's meeting. Analyses of these data showed clearly that the pattern of communication to the deviate increased rapidly and then decreased over time as it became certain that she was not going to change.

Unlike Schachter's study, in which the only dimension of deviation from the group norm or consensus involved an attitude issue, we also studied another kind of deviation. This we termed *role deviation*, a deviation in the total configuration of attitudes and beliefs of an individual; his personality or life style more than his attitude on a specific issue.

In order to create a role deviate, we carefully trained the stooge to portray a character "out of line with" what was assumed to be the generally expected character of a Berkeley student. By means of dress, mannerisms, and actual speech, the stooge sought to communicate a person who was either definitely anti-Negro (the deviate) or much involved in civil rights causes and activities (the norm). In our terms—but not communicated as such to subjects—the deviate was called a "Southern Bigot" and the norm-fitting character was termed "Northern Liberal."

Observers rated the communication directed at the stooge in these two roles. Unlike the pattern of communication directed at the attitude deviate, the role deviate received increasingly *less* amounts of communication; it was as though subjects were actively seeking to avoid any confrontation with the deviating character. Their reaction seemed analogous to one many of us have on seeing a badly crippled person walking on the street; we actively try to avoid looking at him. Physically, the group members turned their chairs at an angle to the role-deviate's, seeking to avoid contact with her. Careful analysis of the kinds of communication revealed only that what little there was did not fall into any one category more than any other. They were neither more hostile nor more aggressive. They tried only to push her out of sight and out of mind.

I might add that this was a difficult role to play. The rejection was keenly felt, despite the fact that the stooge was role-playing. The fact that it is a role usually provides sufficient justification for being rejected to carry most accomplices through without much personal pain; so intense, however, was the group's rejection of her as a bigot that awareness of role-playing did not adequately shield her from the *active* disinterest. Perhaps it is difficult to appreciate the position of deviate in either the Schachter study or ours. In the bare presentation of the data we see only a series of numbers lined up, suggesting more or less communication over time. To the person in that deviating position, however, the pressures toward uniformity can be overwhelming. I have used the Johnny Rocco case in numerous class discussions and before other large groups. In these cases instructions are handed out as part of the case-history form given to all subjects. The deviate's form states, NOTE, THIS IS A PSYCHOLOGICAL EXPERIMENT. PLEASE FOLLOW INSTRUCTIONS. AT THE END, EVERYONE WILL BE INFORMED ABOUT THIS STUDY. He is instructed to adopt position 7 and stick with it throughout the discussion, and he is given one or two points to use in arguing for his position. Almost every time I've done this as a demonstration the deviate actually changes his position from 7 toward 5 near the end of the discussion. When asked if he has understood the instructions, he answers, "Yes, of course." When asked why he has changed, he says, "Well, if you were out there under all that pressure...." Pressures toward uniformity are a very real thing, as any recipient can only too readily testify.

In terms of the social-comparison process model the argument is that a deviate threatens the consensual validation of social reality that exists within a group. Members attempt to influence him to adopt their position. They are correct—because others agree with them—and he is wrong; all wrongs must be eliminated. When it appears that he cannot be swayed the response is to stop comparing themselves with him; essentially, they redefine the boundaries of their group to exclude the one who threatens consensual validation. When the issue is not a specific one but rather an entire personality (as in the role-deviate study), it is a problem to induce character change by interacting with the person at all. The reaction is to define him out of the group early, to wall him off, to actively eliminate the problem.

Before we move to the next points it is useful to examine one further variation in Schachter's study. According to the *P-O-X* balance model, the stronger the bonds between *P* and *O* the greater should be the pressure to attain balance —agreement on *X*. Similarly, the more relevant the *X* issue is to *P* and *O*, the greater should be the pressures toward balance. This latter finding occurred in Newcomb's housing study in which agreement on important rather than trivial *X* issues served as the basis for clique formation. Schachter experimentally varied both the *P-O* relationship and the importance of the *X* issue to the goals of the group. Let us think of *P* as "the group" and *O* as the deviate member. *X* remains the case of Johnny Rocco. In half of his conditions Schachter created a condition of *high cohesiveness*, defined in terms of the expectation by the group of positive attraction between members and the group. In the other half he created *low cohesiveness*, the expectation of minimal positive attraction. Thus the deviate in half the groups was initially expected to be liked, whereas in the other half he was expected to be more neutral: that is, the *P-O* bond was high-positive for half of the groups and low-positive or zero for the other half. One would expect greater pressures on the deviate in the high-positive than in the low-positive groups. Generally this was what Schachter found.

In addition, Schachter so arranged his study that the case discussion was a relevant *X* issue for half the groups—that is, they had been formed to discuss just such material—and an irrelevant issue for the other half, which had other purposes for forming. Assuming there are greater pressures toward balance for important *X* issues than for unimportant ones, we would expect more pressure on the deviate under conditions of *X-is-important*. This is generally what Schachter discovered. Greatest pressure over-all on the deviate should be expected under the combination of high-positive attraction and high relevance. Least pressure should occur under the low-low condition. Again Schachter's data provide general support for

these further specifications of the balance and social comparison process models.

The pressures toward uniformity and the walling off or isolation responses, which the Schachter and Sampson and Brandon studies demonstrate in the laboratory in a systematic manner—in that they isolate the key ingredients that trigger the pressures—can be observed repeatedly in everyday life. Have you ever worn a beard? Grown ivy on a suburban lawn when all the neighbors have lush green grass? Carried a picket sign? If male, have you ever worn your hair long in straight society, or crew-cut in young hip society? Ever refused to stand up during the playing of the national anthem? If you're a girl, ever worn your Saks-Fifth-Avenue best to a guitar-playing folk concert?

Whatever the dominant norms are that define a given group, reactions to the deviate are not unlike those in the preceding studies. People may gang up on him and try to make another convert; they may ostracize him or try actively to ignore him, call him crazy, or in some way *devalue* him as an important person to them. The often extreme reactions elicited by certain kinds of deviation in the most trivial, superficial matters of coiffure and attire suggest that they have a meaning far beyond the surface. Long hair and hippie costume, for example, bring out in many persons a definite and extreme negative reaction, as if to a serious crime, far in excess of the reaction we normally would expect clothing or hair style to create. The comparison process model would argue that such deviations threaten the conception of social reality held by straight middle-class society. "Long hair means protest against my way of life, and protest against what I have struggled so long to achieve cannot be taken lightly." The ridicule directed at a besuited and crewcut man wandering through a young hip area suggests a parallel process. Although the rhetoric states, "Each can do his own thing and express himself as he wishes," actions often betray the same human tendency to reject a deviate.

When the coherence and continuity of a group depend on consensual validation of a particular conception of the nature of man and the universe, outsiders who deviate from such consensus are threats to the very existence of the group. The question that plagues a philosophically democratic society (or for that matter a philosophically democratic group) concerns the amount of *dissensus* that can be tolerated without splitting the entire society or group into multiple pieces. The democratic philosophy argues for dissensus and freedom of expression; yet coherence and continuity seem to require certain kinds of consensual agreement. When these are challenged—as perhaps they should be—the society or group itself may dissolve into isolated elements, each coherent in itself but barely united, if at all, into some larger unity.

FUNCTIONAL TO THE GROUP

Uniformity pressures lead to similarity in outlook among persons attracted to one another and thus provide a *reconfirmation* of the group's world view or perspective. Each such reconfirmation serves as an integrating force to maintain the group in a manner analogous to the function of formalized ritual in a society. By pressuring deviating members to conform, a group or society can reconfirm its existence, its importance, its relevance to the lives of all its members. How pleased the subjects must have felt when the slider slid, for his movement toward their position could only serve to validate their own sense of correctness. A deviating member thus is not only a problem for an individual who is seeking to validate his particular views (the initial functional focus of the model), but also is a problem to the very integrity of the group or society of which he is a member.

To more fully explicate the group level, let me call on several ideas that will take us beyond the functional value of balance to an individual into its value for the social order itself. To do this I shall make four plausible working assumptions (see Sampson, 1963, for a similar discussion).

Interdependence

Human beings, unlike so many other species inhabiting this planet, are ready at birth

to do little but make noises appropriate to drawing the attention of those who will listen and help. As the human infant grows up he manages, in most cases, to emerge from his initial state of utter dependency; yet he never achieves a condition of total independence. Most of us live our lives in a variety of dependencies on and interdependencies with others. Most of the time we pay little attention to this condition. We take much for granted. But our very survival depends on an endless stream of activities by others. Ask any New York City resident during the early 1968 garbage strike how much his daily life depends on the garbage collectors to rid the city of its daily tonnage of waste material.

For most of us in the midst of the highly civilized, technological United States, others' efforts provide the essentials of our personal survival. Without those who supply the markets with food, those who keep us warm with heat and electricity, with gas, with clothing, most of us would be lost. But we need not examine so complex a civilization as the United States to find testimony to the interdependencies that mark men's lives. I have heard of an anthropologist who devoted considerable time and energy to the study of ancients who were "great rock movers." His interest was not simply another of the array of esoterica that so fascinates academicians. Rather, he noted that to move big rocks required a cooperative system in a society. No one person alone could move big rocks; two or more could. Thus in studying societies that moved big rocks around this anthropologist was studying an early form of human cooperation. If human survival places man in an inevitable position of interdependence with other men, interaction that evolves out of such interdependencies must be coordinated in order to be effective. With Umweg pushing on one side and Glog pushing in the opposite direction on the other side, they could not move that rock.

I have used the term interdependence on several occasions. A simple example will illustrate just what I mean. Picture a game board with two players, each of whom has a control knob; a twist of the knob varies the position of the board. The board has a carpenter's level attached to it to show at a glance if it is level. Whenever P and O turn their knobs they tilt the board off level in one direction or another. To achieve a level state each must carefully coordinate his turning of the knob with the other's. Only some to-be-discovered combination will keep the board level. P and O are in an interdependent relationship.

Although in a game situation failure will not endanger survival, it is not difficult to picture a life situation in which faulty coordination under conditions of interdependence could be a life-and-death matter. Driving down a freeway often has this survival quality about it; unless you coordinate your actions with actions of others driving in the same situation, miserable accidents can and do occur. Not all interaction situations have as vital a quality; nevertheless it is helpful to assume that a *degree* of coordination is necessary between persons who are engaging in an interactive encounter. Furthermore, coordination requires communication between the interactants. This brings us around to our second assumption.

Roles: Bracketing expectations

We do not have sufficient knowledge at this time to detail the totality of factors that are necessary for coordinated human interaction. We shall focus, however, on the *anticipatory knowledge* each participant has about the behavior to be expected of the others in a situation. This knowledge exists in each of us as expectancies, hunches, hypotheses, or any similar concept that denotes anticipation. This notion is similar to one advanced years ago by Mead (1934), especially in his distinction between *play* and *the game*. Recall that in "the game" (e.g., baseball) each player moves about with a set of expectancies concerning the likely behavior of his teammates and his opponents in any given part of the game (see pp. 25–26). By knowing what to expect from others, each becomes capable of making appropriate adjustments in his own behavior, thus facilitating coordination. If Umweg expects Glog to push on the rock, he can try to coordinate their efforts by pushing in the same rather than in an opposing direction.

Many ideas incorporated into a body of knowledge referred to as *role theory* fit in with this second assumption (see Sarbin & Allen, 1968). Basically, we locate another person in our scheme of expectancies, and thus locate ourselves, once we can define a given situation in terms of the roles of the participants. In the usual approach to role theory a society or its subparts (an organization, a group, etc.) is viewed as a structural arrangement composed of positions and relationships between positions. For each position there is a set of actions defined for the occupant, even if the occupant changes. In an organization, for example, there may be the positions of secretary and boss; each position has a set of actions or behaviors that accrue to it and to the interactions between the two positions.

Roles vary in the explicitness of the actions that define them and in terms of the sanctions that occur for failure to enact them properly. As a class, boss-secretary interactions may be distinguishable from boss-wife interactions, even though there is a fair degree of leeway in defining the actions appropriate to each position. On the other hand, the role of undertaker may contain a much lesser degree of leeway in appropriate role performance. The roles of lecturer and student may be so strictly defined that deviation, as when a lecturer refuses to lecture or a student insists on taking over the class, brings about sanctions, if only of social approbation or rejection.

As role theory suggests, to define another's role in a given situation is both to place a bracket around the range of possible interactions likely with that other and to define one's own reciprocal role; that is, to define the kind of bracket that ought to be placed around one's own behavior in that situation. A friend of mine, at that time a college freshman, was fortunate enough to be traveling by ship from Europe to the United States at the end of a summer vacation. As is typical aboard ships, he was assigned to a table for meals. At first the others at the table were all strangers to him and he to them, so bracketing of behaviors was based on norms defining what was appropriate for strangers aboard ship at mealtime. My friend tended to be playfully gregarious with the others at his table, telling jokes, stealing the spotlight, and in general having a comedian's ball. By the time dessert came around after the first meal, he was somewhat like a master of ceremonies, directing the table's conversation.

About the second or third day out a fateful moment arrived: each revealed his identity; that is, each told his occupation. In the United States, at least, occupational role often defines an entire character—for better or worse—by which persons tend to relate with others. As it turned out, the major audience at my-friend-the-college-freshman's table was the president of Harvard University and his wife. My friend's entire demeanor altered, as though he had been struck by a thunderbolt. The situation's meaning shifted, given the new brackets the occupational roles had defined. My friend became a humble and quiet student playing a role reciprocal to the president of Harvard. We may all sorrow at the sudden quiet that came over that table for the rest of the voyage. Proclaiming bravely—since we weren't there—"Well, why didn't he just be himself?", we tend to forget how much each of us uses those brackets that are in fact a part of ourselves in any given situation.

Few, if any, situations involving humans in interaction occur without some form of the role-defining process. Of importance to this second assumption is the notion that role definitions, once proferred, establish the anticipatory knowledges each holds about the behavior to be expected of the other, and thus help facilitate coordinated human interaction. If I know your role, I generally know what to expect from you. If you know my role, you generally know what to expect from me. Given this, we two can interact somewhat more smoothly and in a more coordinated fashion than without such definitions.

Model of reality

I shall be a bit briefer on this third heuristic assumption. Over time we each develop a model or theory that contains our principles of human behavior. This model of physical and social reality is developed by intentional instruction, incidental learning, and trial-and-error learning. Our world view is composed from direct and, more often, indirect experiences, of various assumptions, hunches, hypotheses, and expectancies. On the level of the group this model exists as norms, values, rules, ideology, or even the group's culture. When we view the group's culture in terms of its *guidelines for action*, we are offering a conception analogous to implicit personality theory on the level of the individual.

Consistency

The final assumption is the point toward which we have been working in this effort to examine the functional bases of the consistency approaches: it is plausible to maintain that a model that is both *internally consistent* and *externally valid* is more useful to the individual and to the collectivity than one that is unreliable and invalid. An internally consistent model is one that offers *noncontradictory* guidelines to action, ways of organizing and defining physical and social environment that do not grossly conflict. For example, a model that contains two expectancies, "If I do *A* I'll be rewarded," and "If I do *not-A*, I'll be rewarded," gives contradictory guidelines to an individual's actions. Such models do exist; in some cultures (like our own) inconsistency in child-rearing may produce that very kind of inconsistency in guidelines. Nevertheless, consistency of expectancy is more helpful to individuals in organizing their physical and social environment than is inconsistency; thus any tendency toward consistency can be viewed as facilitating a coordinated intercourse with the environment.

Note that I have said that internal consistency is helpful both to individuals *and* to the collectivity. A society that is founded on a series of basic inconsistencies in norms or ideology thus should suffer the same fate of confusion and distress as an individual whose guidelines urge both *A* and not-*A*. Much of contemporary American society, in fact, seems to suffer from this kind of problem. One form of our ideology, for instance, calls for equal opportunity for all, while another form suggests that some are more equal than others (see p. 331 ff. for another discussion of this American dilemma). Guidelines within a society, especially during times of rapid change and transition, tend to be internally inconsistent, contributing thereby to feelings of restlessness, confusion, and even alienation. These terms have been used by many authors to characterize the state of contemporary Western civilization, where sets of values and action guidelines that were embedded in an agrarian economy clash with the evolving values of an urban, technological society. Not only do generational models differ under such conditions, but within any one generation we are likely to encounter contradictory sets of guidelines.

Fromm (1941) eloquently expressed many of these themes in his analysis of man's contemporary *escape from freedom*. His argument was that while man was rooted within the feudal system, with definite roles offering him unequivocal guidelines for action and aspirations for his future, he had few conflicts of value with which to cope. In our terms, his and the collectivity's models were internally consistent; they offered relatively consistent ways to organize the world. As the feudal system began its disintegration, releasing man from the shackles of his bondage, it gave him a new freedom with a wider variety of individual choice. The escape *from* freedom of which Fromm spoke involves man's efforts to deal with this newly won freedom, with its higher level of individual responsibility and its often conflicting guidelines for social belief and action.

For the individual this can mean confusion about appropriate behaviors and realistic aspirations. He may never be very certain about what role is appropriate in a given situation. On one hand he learns that "Children should be seen but not heard"; on the other he learns that in a democracy all should speak out and let their views be known. Which is the correct guideline for him to follow? Or he comes to the university, where he learns how to think critically. Then he begins to become critical of the university, and people tell him to hush up: "What does a dumb kid like you know?" Which guideline is he to follow? More on this later, especially in Chapters 23 and 25.

External validity forms the second part of the functional duo. One may have a perfectly consistent view of the world that is entirely or at least to a great extent incorrect; that is, your views of the world may not match the world itself or others' views of it. The delusional system of the paranoid, for example, has much of this quality about it. Note that there is a basic internal consistency about his delusional system; if you really believe that someone is continually following you and attempting to bug your conversations, it makes sense to keep your window shades drawn, to take a circuitous route to work and home again, and to keep the radio playing at full blast whenever holding a private conversation in your home. These actions all have a high degree of internal consistency, but we can question the degree to which they offer valid pictures of the world in which such an individual lives.

It is reasonable to state that the greater the match between an individual's world view and the actual inputs received from and about the world (i.e., the greater the model's validity), within a tolerable range of error, the more able he is to deal effectively with his physical and social environment.

A person whose world view always entails seeing others as a threat, for example, is likely to read an unnecessary degree of danger into situations that are otherwise innocuous; thus he is not likely to be able to function effectively in most situations. A society whose ideology embodies a similar view, for example that all other nations are threats to its own integrity, is a nation that likewise may not be able to deal effectively in its relations with other nations of the world. It may spend billions building up its armies while letting its domestic scene rot away; it may seek to engage other nations in open battle in order to conquer before being conquered. Needless to say, national paranoia is a much more complex pattern of behavior than individual paranoia. Nevertheless, national ideologies can and do have their own degree of invalidity. Admittedly, it usually takes a historian looking backward to determine the validity of a nation's world view, while a good psychiatrist may be more helpful in this regard when the point of concern is the individual.

Chapter 9

Two comparative functions: Mastery and justice

The four working assumptions offered in Chapter 8 provide a foundation from which to view the functional basis of the balance and consistency models as they operate on both the individual and the collective level. In systematic research, in addition to the work on cognitive balance that we have examined, there is a series of interrelated studies focusing on implications and aspects of these assumptions. One such body of work has its origins in studies conducted by De Soto and several associates (De Soto, 1960; 1961; De Soto & Bosley, 1962), who attempted to understand what De Soto calls man's *"predilection for single orderings."* Another such body of work involves the concept of *status consistency.*

SINGLE ORDERINGS

According to De Soto, it is possible to differentiate between single and multiple orderings (ways of organizing) of various phenomena. Let us say, for example, that you are dealing with the manner by which people order other people. You ask an individual to learn several orderings of the same group of Os, one ordering to be based on the Os' age, another to be based on their height. De Soto presented a group of subjects with a variety of such orderings of the same group of Os to note the ease or difficulty

with which they were able to perform this learning task. His data suggest that persons have great difficulty in learning two different orderings for the same set of material. The *halo effect*, a tendency to rate a person's characteristics in one area according to his characteristics in another or according to a general impression of him (e.g., to see the "most popular" person as "most intelligent" and "most sincere" as well) is another example of an apparent preference for single rather than multiple orderings. Presumably there is a social function or usefulness to such a predilection in that it offers the individual a convenient, noncontradictory manner of relating to the objects of his world. Single orderings or schema of organization are cognitively easier to handle than multiple orderings and, like cognitive balance, characterize an interesting quality of human thinking.

De Soto has suggested that if man generally has a predilection for single orderings, then that subgroup of man called *Homo social scientist* should also function in this manner; his theories should be characterized by an aversion to multiple orderings of objects, persons, and events, and a tendency toward simpler, perhaps incorrect versions. De Soto points to the theory of unilinear cultural evolution as one of several instances of this predilection. According to this theory all cultures can be placed along a single continuum extending from primitive to advanced. What this theory overlooks is the possibility of multiple orderings of the same data in such a way that, for example, one culture is advanced in industrialization but primitive in techniques of social cohesion and integration.

STATUS CONSISTENCY

Another area of social-scientific inquiry that seems to be marked by the predilection for single orderings is the literature on social class. For some time it has been recognized that any person in a given society can be ranked along a variety of dimensions such as education, occupational prestige, income, power. Acting somewhat as though this possibility of multiple orderings was to be avoided, many early sociologists sought to combine into a single index the various ranking patterns that emerged. This index, usually termed SES or socioeconomic status, ordered persons along a single dimension of social class. Some theorists, however, noted the possible importance of the multiple ordering itself as a social indicator (e.g., Benoit-Smullyan, 1944; Lenski, 1954; Weber, 1946). This material is instructive as an example of De Soto's point; more important, however, it provides another arena of social behavior that is illuminated by the balance or consistency framework. Furthermore, as we wander through this arena we shall gain added insights into the *relative* and *comparative* nature of man's perceptual-cognitive processes.

Recall that we are beginning with a social indicator, the multiple ways in which any given person—our friend *P*—may be ordered on the several status dimensions of his group or society. To the extent to which *P*'s positions along these dimensions are intercorrelated, we say that his statuses are *congruent* or *consistent;* by this we mean that if he ranks at a particular position along one of the status dimensions, given a high degree of intercorrelation, he ranks similarly on the other dimensions. For example, if *P* ranks high in education and if his statuses are consistent, he will also rank high in occupation and income; if he is low in education,

he will likewise be low in occupation and income. By contrast, a condition of *status inconsistency* occurs when the intercorrelation between the status dimensions is low; that is, *P* ranks high in education, but ranks middle or low in occupation and middle or low in income. In De Soto's terms, then, *P* is subjected to multiple orderings, in apparent defiance of his and our predilection for single orderings.

In the sociological literature dealing with status consistency the terms status congruence, status crystallization, and status consistency have been used in a generally interchangeable manner. For the most part, however, I refer to *status consistency* or *inconsistency*. Note before we proceed that status consistency can have as its referent either a person or a social system itself. We may speak of an *individual's* degree of status consistency, a class of individuals' degree of status consistency (e.g., school teachers), or, in more general terms, the degree of consistency that characterizes an *entire society*.

What happens to persons who are status inconsistent? Early work, primarily speculative, suggested that rankings within a society tend toward *equilibration* (movement toward balance) (Benoit-Smullyan, 1944). Thus a person whose status ranks were inconsistent would find himself feeling dissatisfied and could be expected to act to restore an equilibrium to his disarrayed status positions. Benoit-Smullyan, who initially proposed this notion, viewed disequilibration as the basis for social upheavals and revolution. As he put it, a condition in which a man's wealth and prestige are not in accord with his power to influence the political structure of the society—a condition of inconsistency —leads to such social upheaval.

Although he did not specify the mechanism precisely, two related matters appear relevant. One, which I term the *mastery* factor (Sampson, 1969), focuses on the degree to which status inconsistency, like most conditions of imbalance, provides a problem of interaction difficulty or conflict. Mastery of a situation involves coming to know it in a predictably consistent way.

Much of the material in Chapter 8 deals with this mastery function. If we picture status inconsistency as a situation in which there are multiple, often conflicting ways of relating to a person, we see that this factor is one with which we are familiar from our discussions of the functional basis of the consistency model. A man who ranks high on status dimension *A* should be treated thus and so; a person who ranks low on status dimension *B* should be treated in such and such a manner. If the same person is multiply ordered, so that he is high on *A* and low on *B*, we do not clearly know how to interact with him. In a sense he is sending out two discrepant messages to all who deal with him.

The second factor, also implied although not explicitly formulated in the Benoit-Smullyan conception of status equilibration, I term *justice*. Here the concern is not so much with mastery of a situation as it is with a sense of what is right and just in social relationships. The matter is one of *who gets what?* How are resources distributed? Keep this second factor stored for the moment while we examine some of the initial data relevant to the entire issue of status consistency.

General effects of status inconsistency

Several studies have followed up Benoit-Smullyan's contention that a status-incongruent person would seek to equilibrate his discrepant ranks by reordering the status arrangements of his society. Goffman (1957), for example, asked a national sample of the U.S. population to rank five groups (state government, big business, labor unions, small businesses, and national government), first, in terms of their present relative influence over national life and policy and, second, in terms of how the subjects *would like to* see the groups ordered in terms of influence. The discrepancy between the subjects' ratings of present and preferred arrangements was taken by Goffman as an indicator of their desire for a reordering of the social structure. This discrepancy score in turn was related to an index of a subject's own status inconsistency. Goffman defined a person as consistent if his income and education ranks were *both* consistent with his occupational rank, and and as inconsistent if *either* income or education were higher or lower than occupational

rank. In general, his findings indicated that persons with status inconsistency desired a greater change in the structure of their society than persons who were status-consistent.

Goffman's is not the only study to provide findings relating status inconsistency to desire for change in the structure of society. Edwards (1927) found that those most interested in social change in several actual revolutions were from groups with discrepancies between their political and economic power. The classic case is the French Revolution (see Brinton, 1957). A study of political activists in Iran (Ringer & Sills, 1952) found that extremists on both the political right and left were more inconsistent in their education, occupation, and income ranks than were the political moderates. The contemporary American sociologist who has contributed most substantially to this literature is Lenski (1954; 1956; 1967), who has demonstrated that individuals low in status consistency more frequently have liberal political orientations and tend to vote for the political party that favors the greatest amount of general social innovation and change. In a cross-national study in which the voting patterns in Australia, Britain, Canada, and the United States were related to an index of status inconsistency, Lenski (1967) again found that inconsistents tend toward greater liberalism in voting behavior.

It appears that one of the earlier voting studies in the United States can usefully be re-interpreted in terms of this same kind of status-inconsistency effect. Studying the 1948 presidential election, Lazarsfeld, Berelson, and Gaudet (1948) introduced the concept of *cross-pressure* to refer to voters whose religion pushed them one way in voting but whose economic status pushed them in another direction; cross-pressure is another instance of status inconsistency. Lazarsfeld and his colleagues found that voters subjected to cross-pressures delayed their voting decision and generally showed less interest in the election than voters with minimal cross-pressures. Recall some of the reactions to imbalance or inconsistency that are available to the individual. The avoidance pattern seemed to characterize these 1948 voters, whereas those studied by Lenski seemed more moved to take an activist response to their own inconsistent position.

Lasswell and Lerner's (1965) analysis of the social characteristics of revolutionary elites confirms the point we are making. They found that both the Chinese Communists and the Kuomintang had a high status derived from high education and well-to-do fathers, but without a revolution in the society they could look forward to nothing better than unemployment in their own country: a condition that is status-inconsistent. Similarly, Lasswell and Lerner's study of the Nazis in Germany suggests the degree to which both the leaders of the movement and the followers were men *marginal* to their society; they were similar to others in the society on several rankings but were discrepant on others. A marginal man thus is conceptually similar to a status-inconsistent person.

If status inconsistency is analogous to other conditions of cognitive imbalance, providing a problem therefore both to the individual and to the collectivity, we would expect to find several other manifestations of displeasure about inconsistency in addition to desires for political upheaval or social revolution. Jackson (1962), for one, assumed that status inconsistency induces psychological stress that should be reflected in various psychological disturbances. Using national survey research data, he found that high symptom levels are associated with an inconsistency between the individual's ascribed status of race and his achieved status of occupation or education. In a somewhat novel related study Kasl and Cobb (1967) report a correlation between parental status inconsistency and the psychological and physical health of offspring. They suggest that status-inconsistent parents provide a general family instability and uncertainty, which plays a major role in producing negative health conditions in their children.

Status Inconsistency in the Small Group. Recall that in our discussion of the functional basis for the balance model (Chapter 8) I pointed out that a state of imbalance is both an *intra*personal and an *inter*personal problem. Several small-group studies of status inconsistency take as their major focus the interpersonal dilemma inconsistency provides. Picture a status-inconsistent person as the recipient

and sender of conflicting expectations for his behavior; a small group composed of such persons is likely to be beset with problems of trust and communication. Several studies support this expectation. In one of the earliest, Adams (1953) computed an index of status consistency on groups of Air Force flight crews. He related this index to measures of intergroup friendship, trust, and general satisfaction, and found that crews lowest in status consistency were generally lowest in friendship, trust, and satisfaction. Exline and Ziller (1959) conducted a study on ad hoc laboratory groups rather than the real groups of Adams' work; they found status-consistent groups to be more congenial and to show greater discussion agreement than status-inconsistent groups.

In a further series of laboratory studies Sampson (1969) and several colleagues sought to introduce real status inconsistency into the controlled setting of the social-psychological laboratory. A college setting provides opportunities to capitalize on group members' actual status differences; for example, there is a clear status ranking by year in school, with graduate students accorded higher status than seniors, who are in turn higher than freshmen. Likewise, although most people will not admit it, men occupy higher status, particularly in certain social contexts, than women. (Most women, by the way, recognize this kind of status differential, rightly complaining, for example, that it is difficult for a woman to get a job as a college professor at a top-flight university; they feel that as women they must be ten times better than the male competition.)

By introducing year in school into laboratory groups working on several experimental tasks that varied in the status of the job assignment (e.g., captain, sergeant, private), we created conditions of status inconsistency or consistency. Inconsistency would exist, for example, if three males differing in year in school were given role assignments so that the freshman was captain, the junior, sergeant, and the graduate student, private. Several such studies generally supported the notion that status inconsistency in such a group is an unpleasant state, producing tension and difficulty. One index of difficulty, for example, involves the group's ability to work effectively on its assigned task. In one study (Kardush, 1968) the group played a war game against a programmed enemy. Its moves were met by preplanned enemy attacks and countermoves. A successful group was one that was able to plan its own attacks better and thereby approach closer to its goal of capturing enemy headquarters. Data indicated that the status-consistent groups got significantly closer to the goal and planned a significantly greater number of moves in their limited time than did the status-inconsistent groups.

Other studies developing out of this same program of research lend additional support to this finding. A study by Brandon (1965) brought a male graduate student, an upper-division male, and a lower-division female student together to work as a group on a manufacturing task, producing "paper products" that if of good quality could be "sold" to the experimenter. Job roles were defined to vary in responsibility and difficulty. The role of *cutter* had the greatest responsibility and difficulty; he could facilitate or hinder group progress to a significant degree. Next in importance came the role of *draftsman*, who marked out lines for cutting and folding. At the bottom of this status hierarchy came the role of *folder*, whose only responsibility was to fold one piece of paper at a time into quarters. A status-inconsistent group would be one in which the graduate male was the folder, the undergraduate male, the cutter, and the lower-division female, the draftsman. In a consistent arrangement the graduate male had the job of greatest responsibility, cutter, the undergraduate male was the draftsman, and the female was the folder. Analyses of self-report data from this study highlighted the negative impact of status inconsistency on group harmony. In general the consistent groups felt less tension and hostility, felt the group's task was more important and felt the entire atmosphere was more pleasant.

JUSTICE AS A SECOND BASIS OF SOCIAL COMPARISON

In introducing this discussion of status inconsistency I indicated two factors that appear to explain the interpersonal problems inconsistency produces. In one, mastery or predictability, inconsistency in another person makes interacting with him a problem. In the discussion of the balance model a similar point was made; we have learned that a condition of balance—in which we agree with those we like and trust, and disagree with those we dislike and distrust —gives us a more stable, predictable hold on social reality than does cognitive imbalance (see Chapter 8). The second factor, which I termed justice, focuses our attention on yet another *functional* basis of the social-comparison processes: we compare ourselves with others not only to gain a hold on the nature of social reality but, in addition, to make judgments about the relative justice or equity that characterizes our situation. Others are comparison figures *both* for our assessments of what is true and correct and what is just, fair, and equitable.

Social exchange

It is helpful to consider P and O in terms of what has been called an *exchange theory* of social behavior. Here we apply an economic model of rewards and costs to our consideration of the interaction between P and O. Recall Thibaut and Kelley's discussion (pp. 97–99). In marketplace terms, P and O are persons with *investments* to be put into the relationship and *outcomes* to be attained from the relationship. Investments consist of such items as education, age, experience, training, skill, sex, social status, ethnic background, effort, seniority. Essentially, investments in the area of human behavior consist of any characteristic, either ascribed or achieved, that has market value in a given society or subpart of the society. One's sex, an ascribed personal characteristic, for example, can be an investment in a relationship when P values O because she is a *she* and not a *he*. Likewise, other ascribed characteristics, including age and race, have various values in human relationships. Outcomes include, on the positive side, such items as pay, intrinsic work satisfaction, affection, respect, status symbols; and, on the negative side, monotony, difficulty, strain, insult, rejection, and so on. Again, almost anything can be an outcome that persons in a relationship judge to be a value (either positive or negative).

When P and O come together in an interactive encounter, each brings with him certain investments and gets certain kinds of outcome. For example, P may be a long-time member of the group, whereas O is a new member. In exchange-theory terms, and for simplicity, say that P's investment involves this one quality, greater seniority over O. As an outcome, let us consider the one value of respect. The exchange or equity theory says that in a relationship P compares his ratio of investments to outcomes with O's ratio (and presumably O is doing the same vis-a-vis P), and on the basis of this comparison concludes that justice prevails or is absent. In our example, if for all of his seniority investment P receives only minimal respect from others compared to the respect the new member O receives, then P is likely to experience a feeling of inequity or the absence of justice. And it is assumed that inequity, comparable to imbalance, produces forces toward re-establishing equity in the relationship. Furthermore, not surprisingly, the various techniques whereby equity in a relationship may be achieved roughly parallels the listing of techniques (pp. 102–104) by which to achieve cognitive balance. (These are adapted from the discussion by Adams, 1965.)

1. One may *vary his investments*. In the seniority example this would be impossible. One cannot alter ascribed characteristics; they are an unalterable *given*. However, when the investment involves something such as the amount of work one does or the amount of energy or effort expended, one can alter the investment by working harder or less hard. For example, if P has been working hard and getting little pay as compared with O, who gets the same amount of pay for doing less, P may reduce his own amount of work output. It should also follow— and there is actually some evidence to support this conclusion (Adams, 1965)—that if P is working less hard than O but is getting more pay, he is likely to *increase* his work output to more closely approximate the equitable condition. The theory also suggests that if one

partner in a relationship is doing 75 percent of the giving, while getting back 25 percent satisfaction (assuming that we can really measure things this way), and the other is giving 20 percent for an 80 percent return, something has to change in this highly inequitable situation. The 75-percent giver might reduce his investment, or, in the best of all possible worlds, each might move toward a 50-percent giving level. Alas, however we are dealing with people, not with saints.

2. One may try to *vary the outcomes* in an effort to gain justice in the relationship by getting more for himself. This might involve trying to move upward in some status hierarchy, thereby gaining some social prestige as a return. How human a tendency this is, and how much others know it: "Give him a title and he'll be happy"; so they make him a second vice-president, giving the company a total of 500 such persons. He gets a tiny raise in pay, does even more work, but feels good because he has that new status symbol, the title on the door. Long live justice!

3. As with any perceptual process, one may *distort* either investments or outcomes and not see the inequity when comparing himself to others.

4. One may psychologically or physically *leave the field*. If the injustice is *that* bad, one may just pack up and go. That 75-percent giver, for example, may finally conclude that he's fed up with the whole affair and seek his pleasure elsewhere. Psychologically leaving the field, of course, would keep a person in the relationship but actively engaged in efforts not to think about the inequity. "Let's not talk about it."

5. One may begin a *search for hidden outcomes* that may have escaped an initial evaluation of the situation. P may suddenly realize, for example, that the San Francisco Bay Area is a glowingly beautiful place with all kinds of grand opportunities for living; it is worth a difference in salary to live there rather than in those parts of the country known as the Midwest, where his colleagues may be earning $5000 more. To move away from economically motivated examples, the 75-percent giver may look for all those good things that the other person really does give. "Why, the other night she stopped by and put on a frozen TV dinner for me. That's giving, isn't it?"

6. One may *try to influence the other person* to change his investments or outcomes. Union-management bargaining sessions usually revolve around such considerations; each seeks to influence the other to make some alteration in the investment-to-outcome ratio. Our 75-percent giver might eventually try to have it out with the other person, or at least try to discuss the situation with him, hoping thereby to alter the inequitable nature of the relationship.

7. One may *change the object of comparison* and cease viewing the situation relative to *that O. P* may reach a point of not comparing himself to a particular other person or group. For that matter, he may never begin to compare himself with certain others; for example, it is not typical for a normal person to compare his conceptions of reality with those of hospitalized schizophrenics. In matters of justice *P* may not compare himself to persons in another country or another culture, but rather restrict comparisons to those within his own culture; someone from another nation getting more money for exactly the same work may not evoke feelings of inequity. *P* is most likely to compare himself with those nearby and with those considered as part of his *reference groups*. Shortly we will look into this latter concept.

JUSTICE: EQUITY VERSUS EQUALITY

The exchange model of interaction gives the impression that *all* of our relationships with others in *all* contexts operate in marketplace terms; we come to look for investments and outcomes and their level of proportionality. On closer examination, however, justice is better seen as having two related but distinctly different meanings. The first is the one we have examined, justice as *equity* or proportionality of investments to outcomes. The second, however, suggests that in certain contexts the norm is not equity but rather *equality*. It is useful in understanding this distinction to place the equity-equality ideas into a broader context. I

shall differentiate the theme of the Protestant Ethic, out of which the equity notion emerged, from a political theme or ethic, out of which the equality idea has evolved.

Equity

Years ago Weber (1930) produced a monumental work in which he sought to demonstrate that the economic system of capitalism required for its fullest fruition the social ethic and set of ideas that was rooted in the Protestant religion. Of special interest to our present focus is an equation in that ethic between effortful work and rewarding outcomes. Work, in particular hard, effortful work, is taken to be a social "good," something of great positive value. By his works you will know the man; by his hard work and success the man will know himself to be among those chosen to live in the Kingdom of Heaven. Idleness is considered the workshop of the devil. This religious ethic preaches a marketplace ideology related to the exchange theory of interpersonal behavior. *P*'s hard work is his investment; his outcomes, especially monetary rewards and the benefits money brings, are the rewards of success. According to this exchange notion, without the investment of hard work no one should receive any rewarding outcomes. The norm in this ethic embodies a correlation between investment and outcome. This is the *equity norm*, telling us simply that one gets out of something only what he puts into it.

Equality

A very different ethic, which I suggest produces an *equality norm*, argues that the proper, harmonious state exists in a society when certain kinds of outcome are *not* related to one's personal investments. In this view the outcomes, especially of human respect and dignity, but perhaps monetary as well, accrue to all persons simply because they are persons, not as a function of effortful investments. Whereas the equity norm suggests that a man who does not work long and hard does not deserve respect or even human dignity as positive outcomes, an equality norm suggests that *all* persons ought to receive respect and be treated with dignity as rewarding outcomes, regardless of their investments. Taking this perspective one step further, we arrive at welfare-state notions for relationships in the larger society. Here it is argued that all persons, regardless of their investments into the system, ought to receive the rewarding outcomes of medical care, guaranteed annual income, proper housing, and so on.

In its most extreme form the equality norm argues that wealth ought to be distributed to all persons, so that everyone, regardless of the nature of his investment, has an equal share in the outcomes.

Two norms

Even if we do not consider the extreme form of the equality norm, it seems reasonable to maintain that justice as equity and justice as equality define two different systems of norms or expectations concerning the appropriate, harmonious state of human relationships. The economic exchange model of human interaction, although suitable for many kinds of encounter, ignores encounters that are governed by a different normative system. According to this more complex view of the social-comparison process, when we engage in an encounter with another we do not invariably evaluate our own situation by an equity norm, or feel cheated or disturbed if we note that our investment-to-outcome ratio is not proportional to the other's. Instead, many situations of human interaction, on the level of the dyad as well as on organizational and societal levels, are governed by a *comparison principle of equality*, leading us, in fact, to feel that a situation is disharmonious when equity prevails rather than equality.

In an experimental study relevant to this phenomenon Morgan and Sawyer (1967) created a bargaining situation involving subjects who were friends in one condition and first-time acquaintances in another. They included this friend-nonfriend distinction because they felt that most analyses of the social-comparison process in bargaining relationships assume that people are always out to gain maximal outcomes according to their own immediate investments, without regard to the other person. The equity notion would have us believe that when

two friends come together the one with the greater investment seeks the greater gain from the situation; Morgan and Sawyer argued, by contrast, that friends who wish to maintain a relationship seek to share more than they seek to fit investments to outcomes. In their experimental study subjects could choose an *equality strategy*—sharing monetary prizes equally with their partner regardless of initial investment—or an *equity strategy*, in which prizes were distributed according to investments. Their data, interestingly enough, strongly pointed to the choice of equality rather than equity among friends *and* nonfriends. In this study, at least, subjects with initially greater investments, and thereby greater likelihood of taking the lion's share of the prize, were willing to forego such a share in favor of equal distribution.

Other studies, somewhat on the order of the Morgan and Sawyer work, report similarly *altruistic* or *anticompetitive* behavior by subjects (see Gamson, 1964; Sampson, 1969, for a review and discussion of some of this work). We might imagine that certain persons always invoke an equity norm in their relationships with others, whereas other persons either exercise greater choice or emphasize the equality norm: one man may treat everyone as though he and they were in a competitive business relationship, carefully comparing his own investment-outcome ratio with theirs; another may deal in business relationships according to an equity norm, but use equality in his informal relationships with others; still another may build his entire life on a principle of equality, sharing with everyone else equally, regardless of who the other is or what kinds of investment have been made.

As a relevant aside, I must mention the degree to which some younger Americans in contemporary society have sought actively to rid themselves of the equity norm and put in its place the equality norm. Their notion is that each must share with everyone else; property is to be shared, not to be owned by one. Some have sought to live in communes in which one week or month one person works and shares his income with the others, and the next week another person does so. In some communes some individuals never go out and get a job for money but are still given an equal share of the rewards of others' work. This occurs without apparent resentment or guilt on anyone's part. In the mid-1960's a group known as the Diggers set up several free clothing stores as well as free food for anyone who wanted it. Outcomes were given without any consideration for anyone's investment; existence itself was sufficient investment to warrant receiving food and clothing.

During the summer of 1967 a free bus service was established between Berkeley and the Haight-Ashbury district in San Francisco. The bus made several round trips each day with absolutely no cost to anyone who wished to hop aboard. Often it would stop at a regular bus stop to offer those waiting there a ride into the city. Their reply was usually a startled, "How much will it cost?" They were puzzled at the straightforward reply: "Nothing. It's free." Those reared on the equity norm that governs most competitive business relationships could not understand this free service. They became suspicious and looked for the gimmick. Equality and altruism were something they simply could not comprehend: "You don't get something for nothing; where's the catch?"

The surprise that characterizes most of us when confronted by a stranger who invokes equality rather than equity is undoubtedly an interesting commentary on the state of contemporary society. Exchange theories of human behavior may become more understandable in this context; we are weaned on the competitive equity norm, applying it broadly, well beyond situations in which it may have been adaptive (i.e., in the competitive marketplace), in all of our relationships. That the modern American scene operates by an exchange principle, however, should not blind us to the alternative equality principle. As discussed in Chapter 15 on the sociology of knowledge, even our supposedly sacrosanct principles of human behavior are rooted in a particular sociohistorical context. Their universality thus is limited and should always be understood against the background provided by the era and persons who developed them.

REFERENCE GROUPS AND RELATIVE DEPRIVATION

Here are some apparently puzzling findings:

1. During and after World War II a study of the U.S. Army (Stouffer et al., 1949a; 1949b) indicated that the less the *actual* opportunity for promotion in a given branch of the service, the more favorable the *opinion* about promotion opportunity was. For example, comparing men in the Air Corps, where chances for promotion were high, with men in the Military Police, where chances for promotion were about the lowest of any branch of the Army, it was found that Airmen were far more critical of their chances for promotion than MPs. In that same study (a) married men more often questioned the legitimacy of their induction into the service than single men; (b) better educated military men were less optimistic about their chances for promotion than those less educated; (c) Negroes stationed in the South felt their life to be rather good, whereas nonmilitary Negroes in the South felt oppressed.

2. In a study on suicide and homicide Henry and Short (1954) found that (a) during periods of economic depression there is an increase in the rate of suicide among those of high status; (b) during economic prosperity there is an increase in homicides, especially among those of lower status; (c) during economic depression lynching of Negroes by lower-class whites increases.

As previously suggested, persons evaluate their own condition by comparing themselves with others. The point to be examined here is *which others*. It seems reasonable to assume that we all have a set of persons and groups to which we typically compare ourselves both for social reality (mastery) and justice. The concept of *reference groups* was developed by Hyman (1942) to encompass groups that serve as a social comparison, both those to which we belong as members and those in which we do not have formal membership. A reference group need not be one's own membership group; furthermore, it may be one with which we compare ourselves *positively* or *negatively*.

The Bennington study

In a study of the college experience and its impact on individuals' values Newcomb (1943; 1958) employed the concept of reference groups to explain what happened to coeds at Bennington College. Bennington was a hotbed of liberalism, both political and moral. Because of its expense and exclusiveness, it catered primarily to girls from wealthy, conservative families. Nevertheless, after a four-year hitch at Bennington the girls generally emerged filled with the liberal ideology of the college, although some did maintain their conservative ways. Through careful analysis of the girls' ideology as well as their group identifications, Newcomb was able to focus on the distinction between membership groups and reference groups and their impact on the girls' outlook. All girls were members of the Bennington community, but the community was not a reference group for all. Girls who retained their families as their major reference group—especially for political ideology—tended to retain conservative beliefs despite the liberalizing college experience. Some, in addition, adopted Bennington as a point of *negative* reference for their attitudes: "Probably the feeling that [my instructors] didn't accept me led me to reject their opinions"; "I wouldn't care to be intimate with those so-called 'liberal' student leaders"; "The things that I really care about are mostly outside of the college" (1958, p. 269).

For others, by contrast, the Bennington membership group was a positive reference group, and in some cases their families became points of negative reference: "I accepted liberal attitudes here because I had always secretly felt that my family was narrow and intolerant, and because such attitudes had prestige value"; "I came to college to get away from my family, who never had any respect for my mind. Becoming a radical meant thinking for myself and, figuratively, thumbing my nose at my family" (1958, pp. 272–3).

A valuable follow-up study 25 years later (Newcomb, Koenig, Flacks, & Warwick, 1967) indicated that most of the college-liberalized girls retained their liberalism over that 25-year period. What appears to have happened is that the girls married husbands with liberal views, which confirms the *P-O-X* balance model and, as importantly, indicates how once-changed persons maintain their new selves by means of social support (their liberal-thinking husbands).

Relative deprivation

For purposes of the reference-group notion the import of the Bennington study is its demonstration of the usefulness of the concept as an explanatory tool. But let us return to the seemingly puzzling findings cited at the beginning of this section. If one compares himself positively to certain reference groups and negatively to others, and if reference groups need not always be one's own membership group, perhaps we can understand Stouffer's American soldier data and Henry and Short's suicide and homicide findings.

Relative deprivation as used in this context refers to a comparison that leads one to feel that he is himself relatively deprived. A married soldier, comparing himself to his married civilian friends, felt that his induction into the army was a great sacrifice; relative to their escape of the fate he was suffering, he felt deprived. A Negro soldier comparing himself to Negro civilians in the South felt that he was relatively well off; his life in the army had much greater freedom and gave him a greater sense of dignity of self than he noted among the civilian Negroes. A more highly educated man *expected* to be promoted and saw himself more a failure in the eyes of his friends, his comparative reference group, than did a less educated man who was not promoted. A man in the Air Corps who did not get promoted, when actual promotions were frequent, would feel more keenly the frustration of his failure than an MP whose nonpromotion occurred against a background of generally low promotion rates.

A broadly instructive point to be extracted from this case suggests that as the expectations for upward mobility increase, one who doesn't make it is likely to feel worse off than one who is in a situation that holds little hope for promotion. In contemporary jargon this is called the *frustration of rising expectations*; it refers to the apparently greater sense of dissatisfaction among persons in developing nations of the world and among blacks and other minorities in the United States amidst a society in which others' chances for mobility toward success are greater than their own. With every new passage of civil rights legislation, blacks who see no change in their own status or life sense a greater amount of frustration and disaffiliation with the nation than they had experienced when they had less hope for upward movement. A concept such as relative deprivation may help answer the whites' plaintive query, "They're better off nowadays than they ever were, so why all those riots in the streets?" Those riots are a result of glimpsing hope and then not having it realized, or in Pettigrew's terms (1961), having the American dream deferred. One who has few hopes and dreams little is unlikely to feel frustration when nothing much happens. One who is led to dream, to hope, to expect more is likely to feel much the worse when he sees the familiar rats running through his over-crowded slum.

But upward is not the only direction in which one moves. According to the comparison process notion, one who has been riding high and falls will experience greater frustration than one who has never been up. In fact we would expect that the man on the bottom would experience a relative rise in his own status when he noted standing next to him in the breadlines the former Mr. Stockbroker of 1928. Henry and Short (1954) built importantly on the notion of relative deprivation to understand the data linking suicide and homicide as responses to the frustration of economic prosperity and depression. In times of depression the man who loses most relative to others is the man who has the most to lose. Because he has usually been in control of his life, he tends to blame himself for his failure. Thus one response to such loss on his part is the intrapunitive, anger-in response of suicide; during economic depression those of higher status are more prone to kill themselves. The image of the stockbroker jumping out of his office window in 1929 is not so far from correct. On the other end of the status scale, however, it is in times of economic prosperity that the man on the bottom feels most keenly the frustration of his lowly position. He is likely to have been a pawn and tends to blame others; his anger-out response to his

frustration becomes homicide. Lynching data (see Henry & Short's account) indicate that lower-status whites lynch more Negroes during economic depression than during prosperity. This provides further support to the relativity concepts with which we have been dealing. During depression, the barely discernible distinction between lower-status white and Negro breaks down. The white feels he has lost more relative to the Negro and may take out his frustration on those to whose status he is now too threateningly close.

The concept of reference group exists within the general context of social-comparison processes with which we have been dealing. Relative deprivation, one side of the picture, involves a sense of deprivation in comparison with those in one's reference groups. The other side is perhaps best called *relative gain* or *relative benefit*. We might expect that if frustration, annoyance, dissatisfaction, and envy are the feelings that go along with relative deprivation, something akin to guilt should be the likely counterpart for relative gain. It is often heard, for example, that the young, upper-middle-class white collegians who worked actively in the South during the civil rights protests of the early 1960's and who later worked in the ghettos of the North were giving expression to feelings of guilt over their relatively beneficent position; the argument is that they identified with the black ghetto as their reference group (for some unstated reason) and experienced guilt over their own position. In a sense this manner of discussing relative benefit emphasizes a negative reason for helping others rather than what is an equally plausible alternative, the positive passion of the altruist. It is very likely, in fact, that both sources of motivation occur in most upper-middle-class whites who seek to help the victims of their society.

The general balance model argues that imbalance is an unstable state, likely to produce forces toward change. Extending this notion into the discussion of relative deprivation or relative benefit, we maintain that in either case pressures toward change are present; a man who feels badly off relative to his reference groups or one who feels relatively well off are both in unstable situations. The frustration, envy, and anger of the former might lead him to try to change the situation; the guilt of the latter might likewise lead him to the same behavior.

CONCLUSION

Throughout Section III we have encountered a common theme: man's knowledge of his world and his interactions in that world are based on relative and comparative judgments. Input of all sorts is evaluated in terms of standards and within contexts. To understand how we know what we know at a given moment and how we operate on that knowledge, we must take into consideration where we are psychologically.

In this section we have concentrated primarily on locating that "psychological-at" within a relatively circumscribed context. Later, when we consider the sociology of knowledge, we shall expand our horizons and examine the involvement of sociocultural and historical relativity.

As is the case with other reference points, the broader social, cultural, and historical factors will play out their role in this unfolding exploration of the social psychology of man's knowledge processes.

Section IV

On selectivity

PROPOSITION IV

The perceptual-cognitive processes are selective

"In order to see anything at all, we must give
up the hope of seeing everything."

(Bruner, 1961, p. 197)

Chapter 10

General issues in selectivity

The issue of perceptual-cognitive selectivity may conveniently be examined in three ways. We select in the process of *registering* or attending to a given stimulus; in our *storage and retrieval* of the material; and in our *self-exposure* to particular stimulus material. In addition, the determinants of our selectivity range from internal, psychodynamic factors, including deep-lying conflicts, through aspects of personality, cognitive style, expectations, attitudes, and values, to factors more directly traceable to the external stimulus situation itself.

VERBAL REPORT OR PERCEPTUAL EFFECTS?

A problem we shall encounter as we explore selectivity, one that for the most part has not yet been resolved, concerns the nature of the data. Suppose you present a group of persons with a brief film of an accident. At the conclusion of the film you ask them to report what they just saw. You collect these reports and by careful analysis note how different persons saw different things. But is it that they saw different things or that everyone saw the same thing and reported it differently? Or did they differ in what they remembered? Does the selectivity occur, then, in the actual perception, or in the verbal reporting, or in the process of recall?

This is both an important question and one

that has been extremely difficult to answer satisfactorily. The matter is important because we hope to understand the conditions under which our perception is selective. To the extent that "what is seen" is confounded with "what is reported" or "what is recalled," we do not really know whether the conditions posited to account for selectivity are the conditions that affect the reports. For example, certain early studies (e.g., McGinnies, 1949) indicated that persons took a longer time to "see" "dirty" words than "clean" words. "Seeing" meant verbally reporting the specific word flashed on a screen; now, if the subject were female and the experimenter male, there might just be some hesitance by the subject to report the dirty words she actually saw. In this case has the experimenter been studying conditions that influence verbal reporting of perceptions rather than conditions that affect the perception itself?

Eye movements

In one technique that attempts to avoid verbal report in the study of attention and perceptual focusing the experimenter takes visual records of eye movements (Gardner & Long, 1962a, b; Luborsky, Blinder, & Schimek, 1965). In this way he knows where the subject's eyes *looked,* regardless of what he reports verbally. Of course there is no guarantee that he has actually *perceived* anything. If our interest is in the world P perceives, and if his eyes momentarily fall on a part of a picture but he perceives nothing, we are not especially interested in that eyeball location. We are interested in the perceptual world he has constructed, at least at some level of his awareness.

Stereoscopic viewing

In a second technique designed to get at actual perceptual selectivity a stereoscope is used to present different photographs simultaneously to each eye. A subject is asked to describe or report what he sees or in some instances to select from a multiple-choice set the photograph that is most like the "one" he has just seen. Although two different photographs are presented, subjects usually report one percept. Typically, this technique has been applied to individuals with known personality or social differences to uncover the relationship between the person's characteristics and his perception. For example, Pettigrew, Allport, and Barnett (1958) presented photographs to subpopulations of South Africans: Afrikaners (European descent), Indians, and Coloreds. The right eye received an image of a member of one of the ethnic groups while the left eye simultaneously received an image of a member of a different group. Which would these persons see as dominant? Colored and Indian photographs were seen most often by all groups of subjects. The Afrikaner subjects, however, tended to identify photographs as either European or Afrikaner, regardless of what was shown. Pettigrew and his colleagues interpreted this as indicating a concern for racial conflict that characterizes the Afrikaner group in South Africa.

A more recent study by Iverson and Schwab (1967) used this stereoscopic technique to uncover personality differences in prejudice. They reasoned that a person who was highly ethnocentric and dogmatic, as measured by standard psychological tests, would tend to dichotomize his perceptions and so view one of the disparate images as dominant. A low-ethnocentric-dogmatic person, by contrast, was thought to be better able to produce a compromised synthesis of the images reaching his eyes. To test this, Iverson and Schwab presented subjects with a series of stimulus photographs of drawings representing variations of several facial features such as shape, hair, eyes, eyebrows, ears, nose, mouth. A different photograph was presented to each eye. One stimulus set, for example, presented a white male with glasses to one eye and a light-skinned male with a mustache to the other. This was called the *neutral set*. A second set presented various sexual pairs such as a white male and a white female. A third set paired a light white with a dark black face. The subject was to select the photograph he had "seen" from a set of comparison photographs that included identical replicas of the original stimulus pairs and composites or fusions of the originals. For example, a composite would show a male face with glasses and a mustache, or a face with feminine hair style and lips but masculine jaws and eyebrows, or an in-between skin color and hair texture.

This method allowed the authors to determine whether subjects had fused the two disparate photographs into a composite or had seen one as dominant. Results indicated that the high-ethnocentric-dogmatic subjects reported significantly fewer fusions than the lows. The two subject groups had their greatest differences in perception in the area of race, the least differences in regard to sex. The data, therefore, offer substantial support to the theoretical expectation that links personality to perception.

Suffice it to say at this point that in much of the work that follows you should keep in mind the distinction between actual perception and verbal report. Most of the time we shall talk about what a person "sees," "hears," "feels," and so on, while the research methodology has mainly concentrated on what he reports about what his world is like.

Many concepts—one theme

Psychological writers from Freud to Piaget to those with more mundane credentials have been concerned with the phenomenon of perceptual *attention*. Theories of normalcy and psychopathology have evolved out of discussions of man's attentional equipment. Given the massive array of possible stimuli out there, to which does man turn his attention? Perhaps the earliest work in this area came out of the psychophysical laboratory in which perceptual and behavioral phenomena were being studied. It was noted that an individual's *set*, usually established by the experimenter in terms of the kinds of stimulus on which he should focus his attention, influenced his speed of reaction. Early work conducted in Germany at what has come to be called the Würzberg School focused particularly on the influence of various internal *determining tendencies* or *mental sets* on the things we see and to which we respond. It was argued that these sets guide our attention and provide organization for the otherwise confusing array of stimuli that exist out there in our world.

In 1904 Külpe presented subjects with groups of stimuli consisting of letters that varied in color, location, and the number and way in which they were clustered. Just before some presentations he told his subjects to note only one of the several possible dimensions; for example, attend to the colors you will be shown. On other presentations subjects were not given any specific set. Subjects were asked to report the characteristics of the stimuli as best they could. Results indicated that subjects were more accurate in reporting stimulus qualities to which they had been set to pay attention. It was suggested by Külpe, and later taken up by others, that set served to facilitate the *clarity* of the particular stimulus quality.

This idea implies a *perceptual tuning* or *perceptual enhancement* effect (Haber, 1966); what we are set to attend to stands out with greater clarity or greater vigor than nonset material, which becomes a background against which the attended-to figure is highlighted. Although the sets that Külpe and other early workers dealt with involved explicit instructions to subjects to "attend to *X*," it seems likely that one may give himself implicit sets to pay attention to certain attributes in an otherwise complex stimulus array. Thus the notion of set as producing a perceptual tuning effect was taken over by later workers to include any internal, implicit structures and mechanisms that heighten our sensitivity to particular kinds of attribute in our perceptual field.

In more contemporary usage aspects of the early notion of mental set are to be found in such concepts as *schema* and *attitude.* The concept of schema has gained widespread use through the work of Piaget (Flavell, 1963; Piaget, 1950, 1952). Basically a schema is an enduring framework or cognitive structure that organizes the manner by which we cognize our world. An attitude, as we have seen (p. 114), is a combined cognitive and affective orientation toward objects and events. In all cases, although the specific nature of the concept varies, sets, schemata, and attitudes take their place as an important class of internal determinants of our selective attention.

Other classes of internal determinants of perceptual attention usually referred to in the social-psychological literature include such things as expectancies, values, needs and motives, personality characteristics and styles. Essentially, each of us is composed of a variety of inferred internal states and structures that influence the manner by which we attend to and take in the vast array of potential stimuli in our world.

This variety of concepts with different shadings of meaning suggests the great historical diversity of interest in the determinants of perceptual-cognitive selectivity. The usual state of affairs in psychology is to find as many terms for roughly the same phenomena as there have been historical precedents and contemporary investigators. You should neither be cowed nor discouraged by this diversity of concepts; I will not engage in what would turn out to be a futile, fatiguing task of seeking the subtle distinctions among them. As we continue our discussion, however, the several flavors of meaning and usage will become apparent. Needless to say, this is not a neat way to run a business, but the business of psychology has never been noted for the neatness or parsimony of its concepts.

Chapter 11

Personality, needs, and selectivity

Let us begin where so much of this concern with selectivity all began, with the "new-look" approach to perception. This perspective had early precedents, achieved a high degree of vigor in the 1950's, and still exists in various contexts in today's social-psychological work. Its basic tenet is that our perception is influenced by internal physiological and psychological states that tune us in selectively to aspects of our environment. A hungry man, it is argued, should see food objects abounding in his environment; a fearful one should see otherwise neutral stimuli as hostile or in other ways distorted by his emotional state. The *content* of our perceived world is to be understood as a function of our personality and need states.

IN SOUTHERN CALIFORNIA

Although I was reared in southern California and spent most of my early years there, it was only when I went away to study that I became aware of a stereotype of the greater Los Angeles area. From a distance of both miles and maturity, Los Angeles, and especially its Orange County fringes, came to represent a politically conservative viewpoint. I developed tingling, boyish fears on crossing the Orange County line; I expected to see hordes of angry citizens shouting, "Get rid of the Commie rats!" Naturally

the scene was never so vivid as in my fertile imagination.

During 1965 I had the opportunity to spend a year in that area. Having been politically active for several years at Berkeley, which had stereotypes the polar opposite of southern California's, I began house hunting with a noticeable chip on my shoulder. I just knew that when "they" heard I was from Berkeley, they would cringe with horror and anger, color me Moscow red, and generally put me on the defensive. My shoulder chip was a predefensive defense.

I finally found a house I wanted to rent, and the deal was arranged through a realtor. When I met the owner later in the week we chatted amicably, mostly about the house. In the yard next door a man was watering his lawn. My new landlord looked at him, looked back at me, and said with a little laugh in his voice, "He's a Bircher." I smiled. He laughed. And that was it— but not really. A Bircher, I thought. How do you like that? My luck. The house I pick to live in for the year has as its neighbor a member of the ultraconservative John Birch Society. See, I told myself, my fears have been vindicated. Imagine, a real live Bircher for a neighbor. What would he think, I wondered, if he ever found out I was from Berkeley?

During much of the year I treated this neighbor rather coldly. I was not going to be friendly with the likes of him, I told myself. My house had a swimming pool; he and his wife had none. Would I invite them to use mine? Hell no! One night there was a public meeting of the Birch Society in a nearby community. I planned to attend and wondered whether my neighbor would be there. Sure enough, I looked out my window about 45 minutes before the meeting and there he was, getting into his car with his wife. Although I couldn't spot him in the crowd at the meeting, I knew he was there. After all, it all fit together in a perfectly consistent package.

Even I mellow eventually. About three months before I was to leave southern California my neighbor and I got into a friendly conversation. He happened at one point to mention that his wife was a schoolteacher and he was a butcher. I nodded. About five minutes later it hit me. Butcher . . . Bircher. What a fool I was! All along . . . it all had fit together so neatly, had been so consistent with my preconceived notion about the people I would find in southern California. I had distorted the sound of butcher to hear Bircher; who ever would have expected to hear butcher down there in Bircher country?

WISH-FULFILLING OR DIRECTLY FUNCTIONAL?

Two different arguments have been offered as the foundation of the new-look approach to perceptual-cognitive selectivity. The first derives primarily from a Freudian notion of wish-fulfill-ment: wishes that are not satisfied directly lead a person to distort his perceptions of the world to provide a *symbolic* fulfillment of the wish. This is rather like the "expectancy" argument; both suggest that we selectively distort in order to satisfy our needs or our hypotheses about how the world should be. A hungry man, therefore, wishing to find food in his environment, sees otherwise ambiguous material as the wish-fulfilling food. The second argument maintains that our perceptual apparatus is designed to facilitate a satisfactory adjustment to our world; a man in need would find it of inestimable value if objects that would satisfy his need state were in heightened focus compared with need-irrelevant objects. A hungry

man's perceptual vigilance to food objects thus has an *adaptive* feature.

It is not clear in any simple way whether the kinds of distortion that occur in the service of our wishes are functional in the terms of the second argument. A hungry person who, for the sake of wish-fulfillment, sees ambiguous blurs as food will in fact be deceiving himself. Research in this area of hunger and perception offers us several interesting leads. Typically, subjects are asked not to eat for a specified period of time and then are presented with a variety of stimuli for identification. The argument is that hungry subjects will report seeing more food objects than will a comparable nonhungry control group. Levine, Chein, and Murphy (1942) showed a group of subjects cards of ambiguous drawings, food objects, and general household articles. All cards were shown behind a ground glass screen, making identification of the objects difficult. Subjects in the experimental groups had been food-deprived for one, three, six, or nine hours; subjects in the control group were tested immediately after lunch. All were instructed to associate verbally to every picture. Results indicated a rise in food responses with one to three hours of deprivation, then a drop in food responses with six hours of deprivation and a further drop with nine hours.

The post hoc effort to explain these results called on a combination of the wish-fulfillment and functional arguments. Up to a certain point in need intensity there is a wish-fulfilling perceptual distortion, but beyond that point, when it is no longer functional to distort, reality processes take over.

Generally similar tendencies have been noted in several other studies that sought to link hunger to perceptual selectivity (e.g., Atkinson & McClelland, 1948; McClelland & Atkinson, 1948; Sanford, 1937). On the other hand—as we now know, there always is that other hand—one major study on relatively intense food deprivation in a long-term, controlled field setting rather than in a laboratory casts some grave doubts on the entire matter. Brozek, Guetzkow, and Baldwin (1951) studied a group of conscientious objectors who lived for 24 weeks on a diet that resulted in an average weight loss of 25 percent. These men were tested at several intervals. Of greatest interest was the finding that few food responses were given on most of the tests; and reports of food dreams were rare.

In an effort to reconcile the apparent inconsistency in these studies Saugstad (1966) and Spence and Ehrenberg (1964) suggested that the nature of the stimulus material must be considered when evaluating the effects of need states on perception. Saugstad's re-examination of several earlier studies suggests that perceptual distortion occurs primarily in response to material that is *relevant to the need* rather than to any ambiguous material. A hungry person is more likely to see food objects when the stimuli presented are food-relevant rather than totally ambiguous; an inkblot may not pull out the effects of his hunger as readily as a scene of a restaurant. Spence and Ehrenberg suggested that a hungry person should learn a paired-associates task better than a sated person when one of the stimuli in the pair involves a food object, and demonstrated how a need state combined with need-relevant stimuli produces the expected perceptual-cognitive effect. This is a refinement of the initial new-look propositions, at least in regard to hunger and perception: hunger leads one to see food objects in settings that are food-relevant. A hungry person does not fill his world indiscriminately with visions of food, but sees things in foodwise ways when food stimuli or associations are present. Man is *both* wish-fulfiller and reality tester.

Lest you get the feeling that social psychologists have spent most of their time examining food and perception, an interesting phenomenon but not all there is of what there is, let us turn our attention in other directions: one leads us toward the study of fantasy, imaginative material, and projective tests; the other more directly into the area of perceptual vigilance and perceptual defense.

THE PROJECTIVE HYPOTHESIS

The hypothesis that guides much projective testing maintains that the sense an individual makes out of otherwise ambiguous stimulus material is a reflection of the underlying structure of his personality and needs. This argument is much like the one we have just seen; the internal structure of needs, expectations, mental sets, personality traits, and so on, heightens awareness or attention to certain aspects of the environment and in addition leads us to reconstruct otherwise ambiguous situations in ways that are guided by these internal structures.

One version of this story has its beginnings in an Atkinson and McClelland (1948) study, again on food deprivation. As part of their daily routine groups of male trainees at a submarine base were tested after one, four, or 16 hours of food deprivation. The test was a series of modified Thematic Apperception Test (TAT) pictures: moderately ambiguous pictures of various settings and persons about which subjects are to make up a story telling what is happening, who the persons are, what they are doing, thinking, and feeling, what they want, what will happen, and what the outcome will be. McClelland and his associates developed a coding system to analyze the content of these imaginative productions. They sought to discover which of several needs were expressed in the story, the nature of the activity employed in the story to satisfy the need, whether the activity would achieve satisfaction or frustration, and so on. An example of a story and its scoring may help clarify this matter.

"The persons are a man from the black market and an honest citizen of a small southern town. The *citizen hasn't had any meat for a couple of weeks* and the *man from the black market thinks he can sell the meat for twice what it is worth.* The citizen doesn't want to buy the meat from the black market but *he is wanting the meat.* The citizen doesn't buy the meat and *reports it to the police*" (Atkinson, 1954, p. 67).

This story is scored for the presence of food imagery, for the presence of an obstacle in the environment to satisfying the need (he wants the meat but doesn't want to buy from the black market), and for an outcome that is doubtful in that we do not know whether he satisfies his hunger need.

By comparing the stories of men varying in degree of food deprivation McClelland and Atkinson noted how the need influenced the content of imaginative thought or fantasy life. Results indicated that with increasing deprivation of food from one to 16 hours the content of the stories to the TAT pictures increased in food-deprivation themes. In essence, the fantasy material reflected the state of the subjects' physiological need to such an extent that a psychologist trained in the analysis of TAT protocols could assess the subjects' actual state of physiological food deprivation with a reasonable degree of accuracy.

Assessing social needs

The Atkinson-McClelland crew, not being especially interested in food deprivation per se, felt that the same method of TAT story analysis could be employed to assess other need states. Such social needs as need for *achievement,* need for *affiliation*, and need for *power*, to cite only three of those they studied, should be measurable by TAT content analyses (see Atkinson, 1958, for a summary of much of this work). The problem became one of determining the conditions that would arouse each of these social needs and then measuring the effects through imaginative story material.

In one of the first efforts in this expanded direction McClelland and his associates (McClelland, Atkinson, Clark, & Lowell, 1953) studied the need for achievement, conceptualized in terms of a relatively enduring motivation to excel according to one's internal standards of performance excellence. A high need achiever is one who is driven to excel in these internal terms, whatever activities he engages in, ranging from schoolwork through competitive athletics, conceivably to his interpersonal relationships with others.

The McClelland et al. study of achievement introduced subjects to their TAT story-writing task after they had been put through one of several preliminaries; each preliminary aroused a need in much the manner in which food deprivation is said to arouse hunger. For example, in the *achievement-oriented* condition subjects were given several tasks to perform. Each task was introduced by an experimenter who was dressed formally and who treated them in a formal manner; subjects were told that their task performance indicated important abilities. In the *relaxed* condition, by contrast, the same tasks were given to subjects by a person who

had introduced himself as a graduate student doing some preliminary exploratory work. He treated them very casually, dressed casually, and in general played down the importance of the tasks. In a *success condition* subjects were led to believe that their performance on the tests had indicated good abilities compared to a normative group; in the *failure condition* they were led to believe that they had done relatively poorly.

After this experimental manipulation all subjects wrote stories in response to several TAT cards. In comparison with the stories written under relaxed conditions, those written under achievement conditions involved heroes who were more concerned with doing well or who were creating something innovative and inventive. In other words, the stories had achievement-oriented themes. A careful analysis of achievement-related themes in each of the several experimental conditions indicated that any of the ways of inducing a higher need for achievement produced stories with much greater achievement content than the relaxed or other control conditions.

Similar findings have turned up with respect to the need for affiliation—the need to be with others—and the need for power (e.g., Atkinson, Heyns, & Veroff, 1954; Shipley & Veroff, 1952). In all cases the social needs function in much the same way as hunger: the greater the aroused intensity of the need, the more the TAT fantasy material reflects the need state. One fascinating and instructive exception to this apparently consistent pattern occurred in Clark's (1952) study of sexual motivation. To arouse sexual motivation in a group of college men, Clark showed them a series of pictures of nude females; the nonaroused group saw pictures of landscapes. After viewing these pictures subjects were asked to write stories to the TAT cards. Unlike the other studies, Clark found that the sexually aroused group wrote stories containing significantly *less* direct sexual content than did the nonaroused group. In interpreting these results Clark suggested that the men felt guilty about their sexual arousal and inhibited it in a defensive manner in writing their stories. A further analysis of story content, this time looking for *symbolic* expressions of sexuality rather than direct expressions, revealed significantly more *latent* sexual content in the stories of the aroused group as compared with the control group.

It was felt that a similar experiment under conditions of a fraternity party at which beer was served would reduce the anxiety-and-guilt pattern and produce manifest sexual story content. Sure enough, this is what Clark found. The sexually aroused, beer-drinking group produced greater manifest sexual content in their stories than the nonaroused, beer-drinking control group. Personally, I'm never certain in reviewing this study whether it is more of a comment on the validity of the theory or on the generally immature quality of fraternity and college boys of the early 1950's.

So far the argument is that persons with particular internal need states will structure situations in terms of those needs when the needs are aroused and when the stimulus situation is relevant to the aroused needs. Someone who is hungry but sitting in a lecture carefully taking notes may not evidence in his behavior many manifestations of the need. However, as he moves out of the lecture to a situation in which the stimulus cues are more relevant to his hunger, the aroused need may begin to dominate the manner by which he perceives: what he attends to, what becomes dominant, and what fades into the background. Likewise, the more social or interpersonal needs of achievement, affiliation, and power will serve as guides to perceptual attention when the situational cues are relevant to the satisfaction of the needs. The moment a person high in the need for affiliation steps into the library to study, for example, he may scout around for a convivial and affiliative seating location rather than the achievement-oriented, isolated spot where real depth of study is possible.

Fear arousal and perception

What is life like for a person who is afraid? Does fear present a world that is peopled with danger and threat? Remember that time when a sudden surge of anxiety came over you just as you opened your eyes from a night's restless sleep? You may have had a vivid dream in which you were chased by assorted monsters

and your feet were too leaden to move, or perhaps that dream of falling and falling, suddenly to feel your body jerk you awake with a muscle spasm. Or it was the day of your final for *that* course. Yes, that clammy feeling is fear, and those sweaty palms denote anxiety. Your roommates greeted you on the day of that exam with a happy "Good morning," and you thought to yourself: "The bastards, bet they've studied and cooled every damn exam!" When you showed up in the examination room, did everyone else look rested and brilliant? And when Professor Mean arrived, did you note a smile of contempt curling around the corners of his lips? And what about time? Did fear make that time before the exams were handed out seem an infinity, and the exam period itself seem to shrink to a few moments?

Although this may sound like a commercial for some headache remedy, it is intended to expand our focus. The question to be answered through the use of fantasy material is whether a person afraid sees the world in a selective manner. The answer, as you well know if you've survived fearful episodes, is yes. Beyond our personal experiences with fear and anxiety, however, there are several interesting, more systematic studies. The classic one was performed by Murray (1933) at a child's birthday party in which the little girls present were asked to rate the maliciousness (quite a word for a little girl) of several photos both before and after playing the spooky game of "murder" in the dark. Murray found that maliciousness ratings increased after the game, as though the fear aroused in the girls led them to see their environment as filled with dangerous personages.

The children of psychologists, true to the popular stereotype, are never fully safe from investigation. Seymour and Norma Feshbach (1963) conducted a more refined replication of the Murray study in which they subjected their children's Halloween party guests to a similar experience. Their report makes both theoretical sense and enjoyable reading; and they found results roughly similar to those initially reported by Murray in his exploratory work.

The Feshbachs invited neighborhood children ranging in age from nine to 12 to a party. (The parents had been informed of the other purposes of the party.) The house was completely dark, with only the light from a jack-o'lantern casting eerie shadows. They formed a circle, initially about 11 feet in diameter. (Such investigator precision! It is not an easy chore to host a party for children and take psychological measurements at the same time.) They told horrendous ghost stories; the circle reduced itself, spontaneously, to about *three* feet. They also played the game of murder, after which the children told stories to a set of 16 pictures. As compared to a nonparty control group, the Feshbach's partygoing, fear-aroused children attributed greater maliciousness to the pictures. So far this finding directly supports the effect noted by Murray some 30 years earlier.

The Feshbachs, however, had hoped to demonstrate that the children, all young boys, would attribute maliciousness to adults but fear to other children. They argued that this follows from a view in which one's own emotional state is projected directly onto those who are similar (I am afraid, therefore other boys are afraid), while others (adult males) will receive a *supplementary* projection (maliciousness). To test this hypothesis they selected a somewhat different situation, again aroused fear, and noted that the boys did write fear-filled stories to pictures containing other boys, but malice-filled stories to pictures containing male adults. They did not write fear-filled or for that matter malice-filled stories to pictures containing girls. This led the Feshbachs to suggest that fear, and perhaps other emotional and need states as well, do not lead to an indiscriminate shading of the entire environment, but rather to a shading that is *object-specific*. Their argument follows a theme with which we are already somewhat familiar. The need, motivational state, or mood is one factor out of at least two that determine perceptual-cognitive selectivity. That all-important second factor is the nature of the stimulus or the cue context of the environment. Both the need and the context jointly influence the nature of the selectivity that occurs.

Before we take leave of the Feshbachs' Halloween extravaganza we should note one important side effect. Arousal of fear should be reflected both in the way fantasy material is perceived and in the manner by which one actually behaves in the environment. The Feshbachs report that after the spooky stories had been told and the game of murder had been played, the children gathered in the clean, white-walled dining room for refreshments. With unrestrained, hostile glee, the charming little boys hurled their dessert, chocolate ice cream balls, from hastily improvised slingshots, at those once-clean walls. Perhaps this was less a reaction to the spooky stories and game of murder than it was a direct attack on those psychologists who interrupted the otherwise social event to insist that the boys make up stories to those silly pictures.

One further study of more than passing interest (in Atkinson, 1958), relating fear arousal to fantasy storytelling, involved groups of soldiers taking part in maneuvers around an atomic bomb test center. Some wrote their stories 10 days before the blast; others the night before; others wrote stories in the field about one-half hour after the blast, and so on. Results from content analysis of the stories indicated a direct relation between need arousal and relevant thematic material. Those closest in time and location to the blast—presumably under greater need arousal—wrote stories with more fear-relevant content than those writing at a distance.

PERCEPTUAL VIGILANCE AND DEFENSE

Flowing almost directly out of earlier work on set and perception (p. 149), the concept of *perceptual vigilance* suggests that an individual's perception of certain events in his world is heightened as a function of his internal motivational state. The research paradigm for studying perceptual vigilance involves premeasuring a subject along some dimension of personality, motivation, value, or need, and then presenting stimuli by tachistoscope in varying degrees relevant to the measured state. The subject's task is to state what he sees, and the experimenter varies the speed of presentation so that he can readily determine the subject's threshold for a given class of stimuli. Perceptual vigilance is said to occur when a subject high in the need or internal state recognizes the need-relevant words at a lower threshold than subjects low in the need.

As we have seen, story content is a useful measurement device both for determining the state of a person's needs or the structure of his personality and for noting the manner by which he selectively structures—"sees"—his physical and social environment. Several different studies (Atkinson, 1958, has summarized some of them) have used TAT stories to assess individual differences in the strength of the need for achievement (*n*-achievement) and then compared high versus low achievers in terms of their recognition threshold for words that suggest success. A list of words that vary in degree of relatedness to achievement, success, and failure is presented tachistoscopically until the subject's threshold for accurate viewing is discovered. (A high threshold is indicated by a longer time to report seeing the word—say, 1/25 sec; a low threshold indicates "seeing" at a more rapid presentation speed—e.g., 1/100 sec.)

Results from several studies relating *n*-achievement to recognition threshold indicate that high *n*-achievers see achievement-related words at a lower threshold than those low in *n*-achievement (Moulton, Raphelson, Kristofferson, & Atkinson, 1958; McClelland & Liberman, 1949). This is an especially interesting finding because it suggests that a need state such as achievement can sensitize or make a person increasingly vigilant to need-relevant words and, by assumed extension, to other things and events in his environment.

In a related study Postman, Bruner, and McGinnies (1948) employed a paper-and-pencil test—the Allport-Vernon scales—to assess subjects' religious, esthetic, political, social, theoretical, and economic values. They noted that there was a lower threshold to value-relevant words; a person highest in the religious value, for example, had a lower recognition threshold for words relevant to religion than for those relevant, say, to political values.

The question to which Bruner and Goodman (1947) addressed themselves concerned the phenomenon of *perceptual accentuation*—the degree to which value enhances perception. They asked groups of 10-year-old children to estimate the sizes of various coins by adjusting a spot of light until they thought it was the size of a penny, nickel, dime, quarter, or half-dollar. In their first effort in this direction Bruner and Goodman found children tended to see the coins as larger than cardboard discs cut to the same size as the coins. Furthermore, it appeared that this tendency to overestimate coin size increased with the value of the coin, at least from the penny up to the quarter.

Bruner and Goodman (1947) repeated this study, this time selecting as subjects children from relatively wealthy and relatively poor homes. They found that the poor children tended to overestimate the coin sizes *more* than did the rich children, and concluded that value enhances perception. Coins have value, cardboard discs do not; thus one overestimates coins but not cardboard discs. If we assume that the poor children value the coins more than the wealthy ones do, then their tendency to overestimate the coin sizes provides further evidence for a perceptual-accentuation effect. It is also likely, however, that poor children have had fewer experiences with coins than rich children, which may lead to this misjudgment of size.

Efforts to replicate this Bruner-Goodman effect have varied from success to failure. One study (Ashley, Harper, & Runyon, 1951), for example, used hypnosis to create "rich" and "poor" kids and managed to find the same effect as Bruner and Goodman had reported. In another study (Lambert, Solomon, & Watson, 1949) poker chips were used instead of coins. The investigators permitted different chips to be exchanged for differing amounts of candy, thus creating different values. They found that size estimates of the chips varied as a function of their value. Carter and Schooler (1949) found that this accentuation effect worked when subjects made their estimates from memory but not when the coins were placed directly before them. This study, therefore, suggests a *nonperceptual, memory* effect, unlike several of the preceding efforts, which stressed perceptual accentuation.

Perceptual defense

Sharpened or vigilant perception is only part of the picture. Intuitively, we feel that some persons are psychologically blind to certain things in their environment. Furthermore, we vascillate in our common-sense psychology between the position that "it takes one to know one," which reflects the vigilant position, and the opposite, or defense, position: "He's so blind he can't even see the nose in front of his face." In the psychoanalytic framework this latter case may call on the mechanism of *denial*; an individual denies certain impulses in himself and thereby becomes insensitive to similar impulses in others. A person who denies his own aggressiveness may be the least sensitive observer of aggression in others.

Picture a situation in which you, as an observer, are asked to use a rating system to classify a sequence of interactions among four persons. The rating system, developed by Bales, asks you to determine who speaks to whom and in which of 12 categories their comments fall. See our later discussion of this system (p. 249 ff.). Several categories deal with expressions of positive emotion (I like you; That's a good idea) and several with expressions of negative emotion (I find you obnoxious; That's the dumbest thing I've ever heard). In theory, at least, if you deny such expressions of affect in yourself you are unlikely to be able to see them in others; you should not easily code interactions into these emotion-laden categories. This is defensive perception rather than vigilance.

Wrench and Endicott (1965) employed this interaction rating technique in a preliminary study of affect denial and conformity. They wished to use the concept of defensive perception as one of the correlates of conformity behavior; they argued that a person who denies affect in himself and is thereby unable to rate affect in others is alienated from his own emotions and likely to conform in a group-pressure situation. Their results showed low but promising correlations between their subjects' inability to code emotion-laden interactions in others and their tendency to yield in a social-pressure situation.

The Wrench and Endicott use of the Bales rating scales to assess an individual's estrangement from his own emotions—perceptual defensiveness—in a complex interactive situation

is novel and to my knowledge one of the few efforts to systematically study affect denial in a small group. More typically, perceptual defense has been studied by the use of tachistoscopic recognition thresholds. In 1949 one of the earliest and most controversial demonstrations of the defense effect was provided by McGinnies, who presented his subjects with a set of "dirty," or emotion-arousing, socially taboo words as well as the garden-variety, nontaboo types. McGinnies noted that his subjects took a longer time to report seeing the taboo words as compared with the neutral words; a defense effect.

Response Bias versus a Perceptual Effect. Rapidly on the heels of McGinnies' fascinating study came hordes of critics. With generally good justification, they focused on the methodological defects of his original study. The basic argument was that a *response-bias effect* rather than an actual perceptual effect could better account for the heightened thresholds to the taboo words. Two major kinds of response bias were suggested. First, it was argued that the frequency of occurrence in the English language of the neutral words that McGinnies used was far greater than the relatively low frequency of occurrence of the taboo words, so that subjects were more familiar with and more easily able to recognize the neutral words. Second, it was argued that subjects would be more hesitant to report verbally to the experimenter that they saw the taboo word, perhaps from embarrassment, perhaps from fear of error, even though they "saw" the neutral and taboo words with equal facility. A spate of response-bias studies (e.g., Solomon & Howes, 1950; Postman, Bronson, & Gropper, 1953) made it difficult to maintain a case for a perceptual-defense argument.

More recently, several efforts have been made to separate the effects of response bias from those more clearly attributable to perceptual defense. Although the conclusions are never without some degree of equivocation, the support for a real perceptual-defense effect does appear. The prime requisite for a study that could untangle these two effects is a condition in which both effects can be measured separately at the same time. One major method is to present the subjects with a list of the neutral and emotion-arousing words, having him select from that list the word he thinks is being flashed. In addition, most studies run a stimulus-absent condition; some subjects are presented the actual stimulus words while others, although expecting to see the words on the list, are presented only smudged slides or slides with typewritten marks rather than words. It is thus possible to compare recognition thresholds for neutral and emotion-arousing words between the groups. If subjects in the stimulus-present condition differentiate between neutral and emotion-arousing words to a greater degree than subjects in the stimulus-absent condition, we can infer a defense effect; however, if both groups report greater ease in seeing the neutral words than the emotion-arousing words, we are likely to infer a response bias.

Results of one study using this format (Goldstein, 1962) supported a response-bias effect. Goldstein's data indicate that the stimulus-present and the stimulus-absent groups have *equal* biases against the emotion-arousing words in the lists presented to them. On the other hand, several studies attempting even further refinements of Goldstein's approach report clear perceptual-defense effects that are greater than the response bias that they measure (e.g., Bootzin & Natsoulas, 1965).

Personality and Defense or Vigilance. Several studies of perceptual defense and vigilance have examined the relationship between perceptual effects and the personality of the perceiver. Unlike earlier work, recent efforts have attempted to relate the stimulus material to the personal conflicts of the perceiver (e.g., Bootzin & Natsoulas, 1965). An approach that relates explicitly to a personality theory is found in the work of Blum (1954; 1955). The personality theory is Freud's; more specifically, it is the Freudian model of psychosexual stages, according to which each person passes through several stages with varying degrees of success: oral, anal, genital. It is posited that individuals may have emotional conflicts at any of these stages.

Blum developed a test, the Blacky, that seeks to assess the nature of an individual's psychosexual conflict. The test consists of a series of TAT-like pictures showing a little dog, Blacky, in several encounters. Each encounter represents a potential psychosexual sore spot. For example, in one scene Blacky is witness to a knife falling on another dog's tail (castration anxiety); in another he is defecating between Mama's and Papa's house (anality); in yet another he is licking his sexual parts (masturbation). In Blum's studies, four pictures were used on each slide: oral sadism, masturbation guilt, oral eroticism, identification process (Blacky scolding a toy dog). The four pictures were arranged in different ways on each slide so that the position of any one picture could be at the top or bottom, on the right or on the left. The subject's task was to indicate the location of the picture that stood out most clearly.

Blum used an initial period of emotional arousal before presenting the subjects the pictures; he showed a couple of the Blacky cards, described the scene ("Blacky can't help licking his sexual parts even though he has been scolded for it"), and asked the subjects to spend a minute or so thinking about a similar experience in their own life. The slides were then shown at two speeds. In the original study Blum found that the subjects could locate the conflictful picture best at the faster exposure speed. This led him to argue that perceptual-defense mechanisms operate at higher levels of awareness; at the slower exposure time, presumably when the subjects had a higher awareness of the conflict picture, their defenses made identification more difficult than at the rapid time, when their awareness was lower.

In response to several criticisms leveled against Blum's original procedure, Mattson and Natsoulas (1962) provided an essential replication of Blum's study. After correcting some of the main methodological problems in the original study (e.g., Blum had not counterbalanced the order of presentation of the two exposure speeds), Mattson and Natsoulas found substantial support for the same effect: subjects were better able to locate the conflict picture at the faster exposure speed. This is an especially enticing experimental finding; it suggests that the perceptual-defense mechanism may operate on material that has been received at one level of awareness but does not function on material that "slips by." It is as though we first barely sense what we wish to avoid seeing and then avoid seeing it.

SUBCEPTION

You are in a movie theater watching a Hollywood production, when suddenly you feel a craving for popcorn. The word reverberates through your brain, becomes insistent. Popcorn. Buy popcorn. You dash for the lobby. A line of popcorn-starved patrons greets you, all demanding popcorn; the crowd grows. People tug, shove, push, pull, but in a few moments you look around sheepishly. Why are you out here acting like that? You don't even like popcorn, not even with hot, drippy butter! Along with the others you go back to your seat, and ever so slowly you begin to note a funny flash at the bottom of the screen. Soon you begin to make out some letters, and in a few moments you see the words, BUY POPCORN. So that's it! Subliminal advertising! In the next rush to the lobby you and the other patrons are hot in pursuit of the theater manager and his Madison Avenue crony. Of course such a thing could happen, but would it really be effective?

Despite the many valid criticisms of McGinnies' taboo-word study, one of his findings stimulated work in the area of subliminal perception, or, as it came to be called, *subception*. McGinnies (1949) found that his subjects responded physiologically, as assessed by their galvanic skin response (GSR), *before* their verbal report of the taboo word. This discrepancy between a physiological response of the autonomic nervous system, which is mainly outside the individual's conscious control, and the consciously controllable verbal report (as an index of conscious perception) was taken to indicate a phenomenon of perception without awareness.

Sensory threshold

The concept of subliminal perception is based on the idea of a sensory threshold, which is that point below which a person ceases to respond consciously to a stimulus about 50 percent of the time. You are presented with a light; on each trial the experimenter asks you to tell him whether you still see it. Every few trials you note that it is growing dimmer, but you can still see it. Finally your statement, "Yes, I see it," begins to change to, "No, I don't see it." The procedure is repeated several times. The value of brightness at which, 50 percent of the time, you report a change from "see" to "not see" is your threshold. Once this value is determined the experimenter can present brightness values well below the threshold and more or less guarantee that the stimulus is *subliminal,* or *below limen* (limen means threshold). When words are flashed on a screen, "buy popcorn" or words used in the McGinnies study, the threshold is the exposure speed on the T-scope (tachistoscope) at which the viewer changes his report about 50 percent of the time from "The word is . . ." to "All I see is a blur, I'll just have to guess."

Given that threshold is a statistical matter, and given that threshold values vary as a function of both individual and situational differences, it is usually no simple matter to state unequivocally that a given stimulus is subliminal. The location of the threshold for a particular person in a particular situation may be different from the threshold for another person in that same situation or for the same person in a different situation; and the same subject in the same situation may undergo a threshold change over time, toward either increased or decreased sensitivity. These are all matters to keep in mind in thinking about the concept of subception and in judging the plausibility of the "imagery" episode at the movies.

Back to subception

After McGinnies' opening move, the next significant study on subception was a classic by Lazarus and McCleary in 1951. And as with most classics, it was hotly disputed, with almost as many critics hovering about with methodological pickaxes as plagued McGinnies. Lazarus and McCleary conditioned their subjects to respond with a GSR to five-letter nonsense syllables by giving an electric shock whenever certain ones were presented. They then presented the conditioned set and a nonconditioned set to the same subjects, using a T-scope for exposure times ranging from a speed at which there was 100 percent accuracy of syllable identification to one at which accuracy was reduced to chance. In the final test situation a subject's GSR was recorded and his verbal report taken. The subception effect Lazarus and McCleary report showed that subjects responded with a GSR reaction to the shocked syllables before they could report a conscious recognition of the word. Thus they "saw" the traumatic event (shocked syllables) physiologically but not consciously. Several criticisms have been leveled at this study, among them: (1) the subjects were responding to fragments of the word but felt constrained about possibly making an incorrect guess immediately; and (2) all that has been demonstrated is that the GSR is a more sensitive measure of perception than is verbal report. Rather than pursuing the Lazarus and McCleary critics (e.g., Eriksen, 1956) further, let us look at some other data.

There are several types of systematic experiment. The first uses T-scope presentation of material at what are claimed to be subthreshold levels to influence subjects' perception of otherwise ambiguous stimuli. For example, in one interesting study (Klein, Spence, Holt, & Gourevitch, 1958) groups of subjects were presented a human figure rather ambiguous in sex; it could be either male or female. During the presentation, however, a T-scope flashed drawings of male or female genitals or the biological symbol for male or female. Klein et al. asked their subjects to draw the figures and to use an adjective checklist to describe them. Their data indicated that the subliminally presented sexual organs influenced both the drawings and the checklist descriptions. In a similar study Smith, Spence, and Klein (1959) used an expressionless face and the words HAPPY or ANGRY flashed subliminally to create subject descriptions of the face as either pleasant or unpleasant. A variety of other studies (e.g., Goldstein & Barthol, 1960; Zuckerman, 1960) indicated somewhat similar effects in which the T-scope subliminal presentation of a particular kind of stimulus influences subjects' perception of an ambiguous event, their verbal reports

of the event, and the stories they write to ambiguous fantasy material.

A second class of experiments, more directly related to our opening example of popcorn, attempts to affect choice behavior through subliminal stimulation. In one study of interest Champion and Turner (1959) showed a group of subjects a film; during the film a drawing of a spoonful of rice with the words WONDER RICE was flashed subliminally. A control group was shown only a meaningless array of lines. After the film they showed the slide of the spoon above threshold and asked the subjects to indicate if they had ever seen it or if they could identify the product with which it was associated. No significantly greater ability was found for the experimental group as compared with the control group, suggesting that subliminal advertising is by no means a surefire technique to capture the minds of the public.

A third kind of experimental examination of subception gets close to the heart of the matter of subliminal perception. Here the stimuli are *not* below threshold, but rather are presented in the background as non-attended-to, incidental stimuli; essentially they are stimuli that could be seen or heard if a person focused his attention on them. For example, in one study (Pine, 1960) subjects were asked to tell stories to pictures. In the next room, through a wall thin enough to convey the sounds of the neighbors, a passage was read. This incidental overheard stimulus passage was found to influence the content of the subjects' stories. In the classic verbal-conditioning work conducted by Greenspoon (1955), to which we have referred on p. 82, a similar effect of incidental stimuli was found: subjects could be influenced to increase their verbal output of a given class of words in response to approving nods and "uh-huh" grunts by the experimenter.

Work more directly in the area of attitude formation has employed incidental or background stimuli to influence the attitudes the subjects formed. Staats and Staats (1958) asked subjects to learn a list of nonsense syllables that were presented visually; the experimenter orally presented evaluative adjectives (e.g., good, bad) as certain of the nonsense syllables were exposed. The authors report a conditioning effect in which nonsense syllables that had been associated with "bad" evaluations were rated negatively in comparison with syllables that had been conditioned to "good." This effect occurred even when subjects who reported being aware of the purpose of the experiment were eliminated. It appears that the incidental evaluative stimuli, which were clearly above threshold, altered subjects' evaluations. Similar follow-up work, finding much the same effects, has been conducted by several other researchers (e.g., Blandford & Sampson, 1964). There also have been studies that examined individual differences in the use of essential background material. For example, assume that you have a problem to be solved and that certain incidental background stimuli contain elements that are helpful in solving the problem. If these incidental elements enter the focus of your attention, better problem solving will be the outcome. Work by Mendelsohn and Griswold (1966) suggests that persons rated high in creativity are better able to utilize incidentally presented information in problem solving.

The fourth type of study uses the classic psychophysical judgmental situation combined with subliminal *anchors* (standard reference points). Judgmental anchors are presented subliminally before the subjects evaluate the regular stimulus. An anchor above threshold influences the nature of the judgment (see p. 93 ff.); does the subliminal presentation of an anchor have this same effect? Several studies by Bevan (1964) suggest the answer is yes, within certain limits (see his pp. 93–97 for a summary and discussion). The work is provocative. According to Bevan, the research dealing with supposedly subliminal factors suggests that unconscious determinants restructure the *consciously apprehended* psychological field; that is, subliminal stimuli change our conscious frame of reference. His own work with subliminal anchor effects fits this model, as does much of the work on incidental stimuli and on verbal conditioning. It is not clear, however, that it applies as well to the "buy popcorn" variety of subception work.

Well, then, what can we conclude? Subception as a phenomenon does appear to have a reasonable degree of validity; clearly, however, it does not operate in as mysterious or manipulative a manner as we might have expected. It is unlikely that the popcorn panic will occur; it is likely, however, that many of our attitudes and judgments are shaped by factors beyond the range of our immediate attention in addition to those within our focused awareness. It is also possible, but not yet clearly demonstrated, that truly subliminal events—so far below the sensory threshold that no effort can bring them into awareness—influence our perceptions and actions. From a purely practical standpoint, man would live in disastrous chaos if he were to respond equally to subliminal stimulation and stimuli within the sensory range. I prefer to argue, along with Bevan, that subliminal events have their main effect by altering the structure of the supraliminal world.

What we call subliminal, then, is essentially just slightly beyond or outside the focus of our attention, rather than well below the sensory thresholds; and we have seen that material out of immediate focus, or material that gives partial cues, can and does enter to shape our conscious behavior. So if you are sitting one evening in a movie theater and feel a sudden craving for popcorn, you need not feel manipulated by wily advertisers as you go to the lobby to buy some. That flashing on the screen only served to remind you of your passion for popcorn, much as the fragrant odor of popcorn piped into the theater's ventilation system might have done. The barely seen flash or the delightful smell offered background cues that restructured the consciously available situation. You realized, perhaps rather suddenly, that you did want some popcorn. So give in. Get up. Go on out and make that purchase. It's good for the economy.

Chapter 12

Memory and recall

Our main concern up to this point has been the selectivity that occurs in the process of focusing on or attending to aspects of our physical and social world. In this chapter we shift our attention slightly to examine the processing of the data that "gets in." In the language of computers, we are interested in the selectivity that takes place in the *storage* and *retrieval* of material, whereas the previous focus has been on the selectivity of *registration* (perceiving and recording) or *encoding.*

The classic case is the accident witness. Several days after witnessing an accident you are called on to describe what happened. Let us say that several other persons also witnessed the accident; and just to keep the case simple, let us assume that you all registered the event in the same way. Two days later, however, each of you comes up with a different version of the event. Note the clause carefully inserted: "all registered the event in the same way." To attribute differences to the processing of memory and recall, we must assume equal initial learning (registration) or in some manner separate out any differential learning that may have occurred. Quite simply, if we wish to argue that an outcome is a function of *differential memory*, we must first show that each person "saw," "learned," or "registered" the same event. If selectivity has already occurred at the

point of registration—a very likely happening indeed—then it is just that much more difficult to tease out the effect attributable to recall.

In most live situations, of course, selectivity is undoubtedly a mixture of both differential registration and differential storage and retrieval. It is likely that any differences among individuals in the recall of a specific event arise from any or all of the following: differences in their understanding of the event; attention to different aspects or differential familiarity with the event; differences in motivation and mood at the time the event occurred as well as afterward; different sets or intentions concerning the use of the information from the event.

For example, *P* and *O* witness the same accident. *P* is new in town and doesn't want to get involved in any controversy with people he doesn't know; *O* has been around for a long time and has formed strong friendships and some intense antipathies. *P* prides himself on his excellence of memory and tries whenever possible to pick up all the details of any unusual event he sees. *O* is mainly concerned with the publicity he'll receive as a witness to the accident. At the time of the accident *P* had just been fired from his job; *O* had just spent hours in a delightful, ego-boosting encounter with some old cronies. *P* has excellent eyesight and hearing; *O* is getting slightly far-sighted and has trouble hearing anything less than a shout. It is possible to extend this list even further; it should be sufficient, however, to indicate how out there in the world any number of factors may, in an uncontrolled manner, affect P's and O's differential recall of an accident. Most of these factors are not attributable solely to differences in storage and retrieval but are inextricably mixed with differences in the initial impact of the event. I raise these matters mainly to point up the difficulty an investigator faces in trying to separate recall effects from other effects that may be operating.

RECALL AS A RECONSTRUCTIVE PROCESS

Memory and recall do not simply involve the verbatim replaying of some internal taped message passively stored in the brain; rather, when we dredge up an ancient memory (or for that matter the memory of that accident of only two days ago) we engage in a *reconstruction* of the past. In 1932 the English psychologist Bartlett published his work on remembering. He noted that the recall of a given event was different from the event itself. This suggested to him, as it had to others (e.g., Freud), that some kind of internal processing occurs to produce a reconstruction of the event. Bartlett turned to the conception of *schema* to explicate the major aspects of this processing. In Bartlett's usage a schema is like a setting, a general internal category or standard; it is the background against which the reconstructive remembering process is conducted. It mediates between the past and the present; the past is said to have no *direct* impact on our present behavior. Prior experiences, attitudes, emotions, and so on, produce schemata against which new experiences are compared and through which our recall is funnelled. When we remember a past event, we turn to our schema or active mass of prior reactions and reconstitute the past *as we imagine it must have occurred.*

We are already accustomed to thinking in terms of a schema in discussing the perception of events in the world. In an earlier discussion (p. 93 ff.) we noted that all incoming stimulus events are registered against the existing frames of reference or schemata. The process of remembering, as Bartlett presents it, functions in a similar manner. Thus we not only perceive but also we recall against a setting.

Freud's view

Freud (see 1954; 1964 editions) offered a view of the remembering process with which Bartlett's ideas had much in common. In the main Freud saw recall as a re-energizing of stored memory traces rather than as a passive process. Unlike Bartlett, however, Freud argued that rather complete, veridical (accurate) traces are laid down in memory; in recall they undergo a process that builds in many distortions. The end result is a reconstruction. Freud's essay on dreams (1954) and the concept of *primary process* provides a sense of the kinds of reconstruction that operate on the once-veridical memory traces. Primary process is an unconscious level of thinking at which everything that ever was still is; all is possible; time stands still so that past, present, and imagined future are equally vivid; not-*A* and *A* can exist in harmony, neither demanding release from its logical bondage with the other. This world of thought contrasts with the more logically consistent representations that exist in our conscious, everyday thinking. In dreams, in slips of the tongue, in jokes, in free associations, and often in the formation of neurotic symptoms, the analyst calls on the primary process for answers to what would otherwise be puzzling matters (see Freud, 1951).

One of Freud's masterful efforts was to make psychological sense out of dreams, filled as they are with content that at first blush seems to defy any reasoned understanding. Freud suggested how such mechanisms as *condensation, displacement,* and *symbolization* provide foundations for the distortions that appear within our dreams as we recall them. Condensation brings together into one idea material that existed initially as two separate thoughts; for example, in a dream two people may merge into one image. To operate, this mechanism requires the fluidity of boundaries that characterizes all thoughts in the primary process. Displacement involves changing the energy or wish invested in one idea or object to another. We are all familiar with displaced hostility, for example, when a man who is angered by his boss takes it out at home that evening on his wife; the target of the hostility has been displaced from boss to wife.

Similar displacements occur in the realm of thought. For example, a dominant idea may occupy a minor place in one's dreams. A person who loves his mother with a driving but unconscious sexual passion, for instance, may dream a scene in which the major elements are formal arrangements for a large dinner party. A minor element in this dream may be a brief, fleeting scene in which a young boy offers a bowl of chicken soup to his mother. Here the major theme has been displaced onto a relatively minor dream event. Symbolization is a primary-process mechanism by which one event or idea is represented by another. The example of phallic symbols is almost too well known to comment on; it was once said that the spire of the Washington Monument is a symbolically fitting tribute to one claimed to be "the father of our country."

In the recall of past events, especially those invested by an individual with more than casual meaning, the various distortions that characterize mechanisms of the primary process alter the memory traces and produce a reconstructed memory. A patient who recalls the events of an early seduction may be recalling an actual event, modified by the several mechanisms, or may even be recalling a *wish* for seduction rather than an actual event. In either case, the memory is a reconstructed past.

Piaget's view

Piaget also was concerned with the nature of recall as a constructive process (1950, 1952; Flavell, 1963). He argued that experiences are transformed through their assimilation into existing organized internal structures or schemata; recall is a function of the schemata to which our experience has been assimilated. Thus we neither "see" the event "as it is" nor recall it "as it was," but rather "see it" and "recall it" as it has become *assimilated* into an ongoing structure of mental organization. Reality is neither presented nor recalled, but rather is transformed in both acts.

SOCIAL-PSYCHOLOGICAL IMPLICATIONS OF THE RECONSTRUCTIVE PROCESS

In one manner or another the ideas of Bartlett, Freud, and Piaget have found their way into the social-psychological research laboratory. The common theme of reconstruction and transformation has had the greatest impact. It has been argued, for example, that a person both learns and recalls material that already fits his ongoing system of beliefs or expectancies (schema) better than he learns and recalls material that does not fit. It has also been argued that the transformational processes of recall produce a message at output that is systematically unlike the original input. Let us examine some of this work to get a better idea of the selectivity and reconstruction of recall in the arena of social psychology.

One of the classic studies was conducted by Levine and Murphy (1943). They selected two small groups of students at the City College of New York. One group was strongly pro-Communist, the other strongly anti-Communist. The experimenters selected two prose passages for both groups to read. One passage, as they describe it, was "excitedly" anti-Communist, while the other was "moderately" pro-. Each subject met individually with one of the experimenters. He first read one of the passages twice and then spent a 15-minute delay period in an informal chat with the experimenter about topics unrelated to the issue being studied. He was then given his first recall period and asked to reproduce the paragraph as accurately as he could. This procedure was followed for the second passage. The entire procedure of reading and delayed recall was conducted at weekly intervals for four weeks. This was referred to as the *learning period*. Finally, at weekly intervals for another five weeks each person's memory for the passages was retested without the rereading part of the procedure. This was referred to as the *forgetting period*. The results of their study indicated that the pro-Communists learned the pro- passage better than the anti-Communists did; in their turn, the antis learned the anti- passage better than the pros. For forgetting, the results again were striking, the pros forgot less of the pro- passage than the antis, who forgot less of the anti- passage. These results argue for a selective learning *and* a selective recall, with the basis for the selectivity being an individual's strongly held attitudes on a particular issue.

In this case the schema is the person's prior beliefs about Communism. Other material finds little existing structure into which it can be assimilated, and thus is forgotten more easily. Presumably, a person who strongly believes in a particular position on an attitudinal issue has a better-organized internal schema into which he can place corresponding material.

A rough analogy may be helpful. Imagine the mind as a filing drawer containing several folders that classify material; these folders are the schemata or inner organization. As we encounter new material we place it in already existing folders. Material that does not fit easily into any of the folders is more easily lost when we next search through the drawer; we cannot recall just where we filed it. In fact, as new material is transformed to be assimilated into one of the folders, we may change it sufficiently so that we are not certain any more of its initial form. On the other hand, material for which we already have a folder should be relatively easy to locate when we next rummage through the files.

In addition to the preceding *structural* argument, another basis for expecting selective effects on the recall of so-called controversial material focuses on *emotional mechanisms* of defense and distortion. The argument is that each of us seeks to protect his own views on matters of importance by defending against conflicting or threatening material. For example, individuals are said to forget material that threatens their existing attitudes, recalling only material that is supportive. When we venture into our later discussions this matter concerning the emotional bases of selective recall will crop up again.

Other researchers have uncovered the same kind of effect as that demonstrated by Levine and Murphy. Taft (1954), for example, reports that Negroes forgot more material unfavorable to Negroes and recalled more favorable material. Waly and Cook (1966) found support for

the Levine and Murphy effect in one of three experiments, but did not find this effect to be significant in the other two. A few studies offer nonconfirmatory results. Greenwald and Sakumura (1967), for example, failed to replicate the Levine and Murphy effect in three separate methodologically similar experiments. The issue they used was attitudes toward the war in Vietnam. They found no significant difference in learning or immediate recall among subjects purporting to be pro-U.S. involvement and those who were anti-U.S. involvement.

As with most studies that seek to replicate an effect and fail, it is possible to blame factors other than those directly involved in the phenomenon of selective learning or recall. In the Greenwald and Sakumura study several differences might have been operating. For example, Levine and Murphy used as subjects individuals with a known reputation for their political views—especially the pro-Communist group. We might gather, therefore, that they not only held their views strongly but in addition were more "public" subjects than "private" ones; that is, their performance might have involved their public image of themselves as supporters of a political position. By contrast, subjects in the Greenwald and Sakumura study were a random selection of college students. Although they professed a view, they might not have held it as strongly or with as great a public commitment as those in the Levine and Murphy study. Perhaps it is only with strongly held views, then, that true selectivity may be said to occur.

One further comparative point should be made before we move on. Levine and Murphy continued both their learning and their forgetting trials for several weeks, in contrast to the near-immediate recall of the Greenwald and Sakumara study. Perhaps it is only over a period of time that the internal processes become relevant. In fact, it is likely that the more complex the material and the longer we have to cogitate over it the more we assimilate it to a schema or operate on it. If someone gives us a brief passage—"Communists are pigs"—and asks us to repeat it immediately, it is probable that both pros and antis will yield equal recall scores. On the other hand, if the passage is longer and more complex, and if we work on it for a period of time, our reconstructive recall of a selective sort may be more evident. In the great world of reality out there, this complexity is undoubtedly more typical than the immediate recall of simple material that characterizes much laboratory research.

The Zeigarnik effect

As is the case with much that develops into systematic social psychology, a lunchtime observation (reported in Atkinson, 1964) inspired a theoretical basis for studies by Zeigarnik in 1924 to 1926 (later reported by Lewin, 1951). Lewin noticed that his waiter was able to recall every detail of his order until after he paid his check. After that point he could no longer remember the order. The theoretical notion that grew out of this observation was that the *intention to complete an activity* or a task sets up a tension within a person that is not relieved until the activity is completed, and further, that one reflection of the presence of this tension is found in recall. This idea led to a prediction that one would recall more incompleted than completed tasks. To study this, Zeigarnik, a student of Lewin's, gave her subjects a variety of tasks, interrupting some and allowing them to complete others. She then presented her subjects with a recall test and found that they recalled more of the uncompleted tasks. This has come to be referred to as the Zeigarnik effect.

The original work did not stop there; efforts were made to examine conditions under which the effect was reduced. It was argued, for example, that the effect would be lessened as the time interval between incompletion and recall increased; this was based on the assumption that the tension associated with the incompleted activity begins to dissipate over time. Experimental results indicated such a reduction after one day (Lewin, 1951). As another example, it was suggested that *fatigue* would serve to spread the tension around one's cognitive system, thus reducing the effect. Experimental data generally supported this expectation, with the effect being smaller for tired subjects than for those who were nonfatigued.

Another series of important early studies of the Zeigarnik effect focused on the issue of actual versus psychological completion (Lewin, 1951). If you have not completed a task but feel that you have gone far enough to have finished it, this psychological completion should operate as real completion. In one study the subjects were told that the experimenter was interested in finding out only if the subject could carry out the task and that he would interrupt as soon as he knew this. In this case subjects did not recall more incompleted tasks than completed tasks; their feeling of psychological completion erased the Zeigarnik effect.

More recently others have used the Zeigarnik effect in other contexts. One question of interest was whether another's completion of an activity would reduce one's own tension system. If you and I are working together and you complete some tasks that I was to complete, will my tension be reduced by your efforts? The answer seems to be affirmative, particularly when persons are in a cooperative venture (Lewis, 1944); here is the real meaning of psychological interdependence in a small group working together.

Horwitz (1954) added a further dimension by investigating the effects of group decisions about task goals on the reduction of an individual's tension. As part of an experiment in which a group worked cooperatively to complete jigsaw puzzles, he asked subjects to vote on whether they wanted to complete a particular puzzle. He rigged the experiment so that some groups were told that the group had voted to complete the puzzle and others were told the group had voted not to. His results generally supported the original Zeigarnik finding; the groups in which the yes-complete-it vote was followed by further task interruption recalled more tasks than the groups that voted yes and actually completed the tasks. Furthermore, the former groups recalled more tasks than the groups that voted *not* to complete and then stopped working. Essentially, therefore, the group decision to stop working sufficed to reduce the tension to complete the puzzles, as indexed by their relatively lower recall rate.

A more interesting finding involved Horwitz's analysis of situations in which an individual voted one way and his group another. Horwitz suggests that there are several avenues open to such an individual; two reactions in particular are of interest. First, he *accepts* the group's decision. Here, it is argued, if he voted "yes" but accepts the group's decision of "no," he should feel no tension to complete and thus should recall relatively few tasks. Second, he *rejects* the group's decision; his own decision "yes" results in tension to complete regardless of the group's vote of "no"; the rejector in this case should recall more tasks than the acceptor. This is in fact what the Horwitz results indicate. Again we note how the interdependence among persons working cooperatively in a group sets conditions for selective recall of the type studied originally by Zeigarnik. Selectivity, therefore, is not simply an isolated individual action, but usually occurs in social contexts in which joint efforts with others increase or relieve personal tension.

One especially important study of selective recall using the Zeigarnik approach was conducted by Atkinson (1954), who was interested in the relationship between task completion or incompletion and an individual's *motive system.* Persons high in the need for achievement presumably have a high task orientation under conditions that arouse their need. Atkinson varied the instructions to his subjects. Instructions to the *relaxed* group were designed to minimize the feeling that good performance on the tasks reflected something important about members' abilities. A second group, in an *achievement* orientation, was given instruction designed to emphasize the importance of the tasks. The *task-oriented* group was simply given instructions about how the tasks were to be performed, without emphasizing or de-emphasizing their importance as measures of the subjects' abilities. Results of major importance indicated little difference between the high- and the low-achievement subjects in their recall of *completed* tasks. However, for *incompleted* tasks, the high-achievement subjects in the achievement condition recalled a much greater percentage of the incompleted tasks than those low in need achievement. In great measure Atkinson's study suggests that whenever a Zeigarnik-type study is conducted under conditions of achievement arousal, the effect will hold more for high achievers than for low achievers. Working backward from this we might assume that subjects employed in the original Zeigarnik work were high in need achievement.

Repression

One of the features of the Zeigarnik situation that may have puzzled you is the possibility that subjects may be likely to actively forget (i.e., repress) incompleted tasks rather than persist in recalling them. It makes good sense, for instance, to suggest that we might feel a sense of failure about things we do not complete. If we repress failure-filled experiences, our recall should be the opposite of that uncovered by Zeigarnik. Although the situation is by no means clear, other researchers have been able to produce a repression effect in connection with the Zeigarnik-type situation. Rosenzweig (1943), for example, used puzzles with children and college students as subjects. One group was told that it was helping the experimenter standardize the puzzles while another group was told that the puzzles measured intelligence. Rosenzweig interrupted some of the tasks and let the subjects complete others. Those in the highly ego-involving intelligence-test condition recalled more completed than incompleted tasks, while the original Zeigarnik effect was replicated in the less involving condition. It is likely, as even Zeigarnik herself recognized, that if the psychological meaning of the task completion is changed, either through the instructions of the experimenter or the self-directed instructions of subjects with particular need and personality systems, the effect will undergo some modification.

Although I shall not devote much time or space to a discussion of what has now become part of the commonplace jargon of our society, clearly the several defense mechanisms that have been noted in psychoanalytic theory play a significant role in the selectivity of our perceptual-cognitive processes. A mechanism such as repression, for example, operates actively to relegate conflictful impulses and severely traumatic events to our unconscious. Although this body of repressed material continues to strive for expression, and may reveal itself in slips of the tongue, free associations, fantasy material, dreams, and such, when we engage in routine recall we are unlikely to have direct access to these repressed memories. Especially painful details in an event may not be recalled on retelling. In true repression, try as we may, we cannot dredge up painful recollections. Studies of repression in the laboratory usually are systematic but lack the forceful quality that truly repressed material possesses. On the other hand, studies of repression in the clinical setting of psychotherapy possess depth of meaning but are usually not very systematic. What this means essentially is that a failure to uncover a repression effect in the laboratory may be a failure of methodology rather than of theory. Obviously, the conviction held by those who have dealt with persons in the depth relationship of a therapy setting concerning the reality of a defense through repression will not be swayed by nonconfirmatory laboratory findings; nor, for that matter, should it be. I might add, however, that several more systematic studies have been suggestive in demonstrating the mechanisms of repression. Zeller (1950), for example, induced repression (i.e., nonrecall) of threat-associated material and later showed its recall when the threat was removed. This type of study meets some of the psychodynamics of repression in the Freudian model. High threat induces repression; removal of the threat allows the repressed thought to return again. In another study Flavell (1955) used a design similar to Zeller's, but introduced an individual "therapeutic" session to remove the threat that had been associated with the material to be recalled. Results generally confirmed the repression effect.

A reasonable conclusion, simply stated, is that recall is selectively processed in ways that have been discussed by psychoanalytic writers, particularly by means of the mechanism of repression. It is too simple and incorrect, however, to maintain that we selectively recall only the pleasurable and nontraumatic or that we repress all the unpleasant and traumatic events in our lives.

Chapter 13

Message transmission and reception

The usual situation involving recall of material, controversial or otherwise, finds most of us as one link in a communication network. Initially we are receivers of messages from other persons, from mass media, from our sense impressions, from our often vivid imaginations. In many circumstances we also act as transmitters, sending out messages to others. Given the selectivity of our perceptual-cognitive processes, it is likely that between receipt and transmission of a message certain kinds of change occur. Furthermore, the more emotionally charged the information is, the more personally involved we are with it, the more complex or ambiguous it is, the more likely there is to be selective distortion.

RUMORS

Rumors appear to undergo selective processing as they are transmitted from person to person. Several years ago Allport and Postman (1947) suggested that a rumor is likely to emerge and to be transmitted in situations that are highly *important* to the individuals involved and concern issues around which there is substantial *ambiguity*; it deals with the anxiety experienced about such important and ambiguous situations by offering an explanation. Allport and Postman

underplayed the *anxiety-enhancing* quality many rumors also possess. In fact, one of the insidious qualities of rumors is not that they relieve anxiety by offering helpful explanations, but rather that they may create conditions of even greater anxiety by planting seeds of doubt and fear, creating monsters where none formerly existed. Let's look briefly at a few rumors.

Almost immediately after the Japanese had bombed Pearl Harbor in 1941—an event both important and at that time relatively ambiguous —residents along the West Coast of the United States began to report stories of invasions, shellings, and air raids by the Japanese. These rumors often centered around Los Angeles. Many citizens swore that they saw Japanese planes fly over the city or that several submarines offshore had shelled the oil refineries along the coast. Some rumors reported an actual land invasion of troops. As these stories passed from mouth to mouth they were presented with greater certainty as to their truth. In some cases they made headlines in the public press; these stories were picked up by eastern news media, and relatives in the East began to phone families in the Los Angeles area and urge them to head inland where they would be momentarily safe from the invasion. Some families actually fled the Los Angeles area for the safety of Arizona and other noncoastal states.

A startling rumor in the late 1960's became an issue for excited public expression in 1967. The nation had witnessed several summers of violent upheaval in the black community. White middle-class war protesters had changed their tactics from polite marching in Saturday parades to more openly aggressive and militant attacks on officials and institutions associated with the Vietnam war. To many the nation seemed to be floundering as it rocked back and forth from one internal upheaval to the next, while resolutely conducting its unpopular war in Vietnam. The very survival of the national government became an issue of importance to all (some wanted it to survive, others wished to see it done in); ambiguity focused on the government's manner of dealing with these dissenting forces.

From this importance and ambiguity evolved a significant rumor: the government was rebuilding the camps it had used during World War II to house Americans of Japanese ancestry, and the reason for this rebuilding was to get ready to house black militants and campus draft and war protesters. The feeling among militant blacks and whites was that the government was just waiting for the right moment of public opinion to haul them away and thereby restore tranquillity to the internal scene.

Since there has not been any systematic study of this rumor, it is not clear what kinds of selective distortion it has undergone. From my own admittedly nonsystematic observations, it appears that certain details have crept in. For example, when I first heard the rumor the reference was only to the very general notion of relocation camps to house black and white militants. Some months later I heard specific references made to reports by residents in Tule Lake, a small community in northern California, of a great deal of building at the camp located nearby. In fact, on one radio phone-in program the announcer had been deluged with so many detailed calls concerning the rumor that he called Tule Lake to ask about the situation. Everyone he spoke to—including local officials and the person who actually leased the camp site from the government—expressed surprise at the rumor. Did this factual information stop the rumor's circulation? Not at all. First, not that many people heard the facts; they con-

tinued to operate under the assumption that the rumor was correct, especially as it applied to the Tule Lake camp. Second, true believers felt that even if the Tule Lake report was incorrect the government was still rebuilding camps in other, more secret locations.

I have the impression that the rumor comes to life each time there is another upheaval in the black community and every time a new youth protest occurs. Often it takes the form of friendly joking on the college campus; activist professors and students claim they will simply continue their courses in the camps. In the black community, especially among the militants, there is less joking but more serious preparation for their defense against what is felt to be the government's policy of black genocide. While professors and students arm themselves with reading material for their rumored imprisonment, black militants arm themselves with guns and ammunition; they will not go like sheep to slaughter.

Lest you imagine that a rumor such as this has absolutely no basis in reality, you should be aware of subchapter II of the Internal Security Act of 1950: the McCarran Act. This passage provides for the emergency detention of suspected security risks. Furthermore, on May 5, 1968, the House Un-American Activities Committee fueled the rumor by openly suggesting the use of detention camps for Negro militants as a means of controlling internal disorder. At times it becomes a mind-boggling exercise to differentiate pure rumor from fact.

The dynamics of rumor

To assess the selective transformations that occur during the course of a rumor's development and transmission we need a more systematic study than is to be found in the preceding accounts. Allport and Postman (1947) offer one of the classics in this area. They created an experimental situation in which they presented a subject with a slide of a complex social scene, had him describe the scene to another subject (who had not seen it), who described it to still another subject, who in turn described it to another, and so on through six or seven persons. Thus it was possible to evaluate the degree and nature of the changes that occurred as the story moved from one person to another.

As the story traveled, several processes occurred. One, *leveling*, involved dropping out details as the story moved down the chain. Somewhat like the dream mechanism of condensation, elements were combined and recombined into a more concise form. Another process, *sharpening*, involved the selective perception, recall, and reporting of certain details. Perhaps the most significant process was *assimilation*. Allport and Postman report several kinds of assimilation.

1. *Assimilation to principal theme.* As the story moved down the line of subjects, a leading theme emerged as the framework within which all other details were integrated, resulting in a more coherent story than originally existed. For example, one picture evoked a war theme in which successive storytellers introduced war-related elements to preserve the theme even though this distorted the facts in the original picture.

2. *Assimilation to closure.* The stories showed the Gestalt principle of closure or good figure. For example, in one picture a sign read "Loew's Pa . . ." Subjects completed this as "Loew's Palace." In another slide the background ad in a bus read, "Lucky Rakes." In the stories this was reported as "Lucky Strikes."

3. *Assimilation by condensation.* This process parallels Freud's concept of condensation and involves the fusing of several separate items into one. Instead of reporting several ads on a streetcar, subjects reported a "billboard" in the background. Instead of detailing the people present, subjects summarized the scene as "several people sitting and standing."

4. *Assimilation to expectation.* When arrangements and relationships that we expect do not occur in fact, our recollection often puts them back into their expected places. In one scene a drugstore was located in the middle of the block; in the stories it was moved toward its expected location, the corner. But perhaps the most startling assimilation of this type involved a streetcar scene. In the original picture two men, one black, one white, were standing in the streetcar; the white man held a razor in his hand. Allport and Postman report that in more

than half of their experiments the subjects moved the razor from the white man's hand to the black man's to fit the stereotyped expectation of a black carrying a razor.

5. *Assimilation to linguistic habit.* The tendency noted here is to fit events to linguistic cliches. For example, a professor might be reported as a "long-haired professor" or an Oriental gentleman as a "Japanese spy." Shorthand verbal cliches seemed to be employed instead of the full details of the presentation.

Although the Allport and Postman situation provides useful systematization of distortions likely in the transmission of messages from person to person, it does not embody the key ingredients of rumor transmission; there is little importance or ambiguity involved in their experimental situation, despite their statement that these are the basic reasons for rumors to emerge and to be transmitted. In addition, the nature of a rumor's spread in the laboratory is likely to be different from that encountered in live, field situations. In the field, for example, rumors are likely to spread along lines of friendship; you tell your friends the latest news. Furthermore, the pressure on accurate reporting that occurs in the laboratory is usually absent in live situations. How much more amazing it is, therefore, that Allport and Postman uncovered such extreme distortions.

A Field Experiment. Schachter and Burdick (1955) sought to provide a field study of rumor transmission, attempting to be both systematic and realistic in their work. They created an incident in a school that would be rumor-producing; that is, important and ambiguous. The principal entered a classroom and called out one of the students for the rest of the day. In some of the classrooms a rumor was implanted with two other students, ostensibly as part of an interview with their teacher concerning their progress in schoolwork: toward the end of that interview the teacher asked them if they knew anything about some papers that had been removed from the main office. The experimenters let the rumor spread "naturally" throughout the remainder of the day. Later a team of interviewers interviewed students from the classes in which the rumor had been planted.

All but one student interviewed had heard the rumor by the end of the day. Somewhat contrary to the Allport and Postman finding, Schachter and Burdick report only minimal distortions in the end-of-day stories. They did find, however, that although the planted rumor made it through the day relatively intact, many new, often bizarre rumors occurred in conjunction with it. Schachter admits that their rumor, unlike that in the Allport and Postman study, was relatively simple, and thus perhaps less likely to be subjected to the kinds of distortion originally reported.

Rumors in the crowd

It is clear to almost anyone concerned with collective or crowd behavior that rumors play a significant role. They incite, heighten intensity, direct. Because of the potent effects of rumors, especially during times of upheaval, rumor clinics have been established. During World War II they were much in evidence, and they have been in use again more recently during the periods of central-city racial upheavals. Chicago, for example, has set up a rumor clinic so that a person who hears a rumor can telephone the clinic and get the facts straightened out. In 1968 the police department and the local clergy in Norwalk, Connecticut, established a summer Rumor Clearing House and Control Center. Local residents were urged to telephone the center to get the truth about rumored reports that, if allowed to grow unattended, could lead to rioting.

Almost immediately after the tragic assassination of Martin Luther King, Jr., rumors cropped up across the nation concerning an uprising of the black community. Whites were fearful of blacks taking over their neighborhoods; blacks were fearful of white troops taking over their neighborhoods. Racial conflicts did occur, but there were many more rumors than actual encounters. The requisite conditions of importance and ambiguity were at a peak. Rumors grew faster than clinics could cope with them. A spiral of smoke in the distance became a mob moving toward one's own house. A car backfiring became a National Guard unit firing at citizens. Each ambiguous event was placed in the category of riot and spread like a brushfire. People

"heard stories" and locked themselves in their houses. Some "heard stories" and decided to flee the city. Some "heard stories" and rushed to their cache of arms to prepare themselves for a siege. The rumor clinics attempted to diminish these panic effects; a person could phone a clinic and check out the facts of the situation for his own neighborhood. The calm voice at the other end of the line often could help to stifle the fear and anxiety that nonfactual rumors created.

OTHER MESSAGES, OTHER SELECTIVITY

Rumors are only one class of message that may undergo selectivity in receipt, recall, and transmission. Given the conditions under which rumors arise and are transmitted, we would expect them to be especially prone to distortion. But what about other kinds of message? Let us refocus the question and look at the role of the person in the communication network. What is the nature of the perceptual-cognitive selectivity that occurs when an individual is prepared to be a receiver, as compared to the situation in which he is prepared to be a transmitter? Perhaps the easiest way to picture these two roles (receiver, transmitter) is to look at a typical classroom situation. The role of receiver is taken by the student; the professor is the transmitter. Our question, then, is whether different processing occurs as a function of these role distinctions.

Zajonc (1960b) provides one of the few systematic studies of what he calls *cognitive tuning*. He characterized a person who is *tuned* or *set* to receive a message as more loosely structured, having a more open system than a person set to transmit, who in turn is characterized as more organized and structured. To study this, Zajonc set subjects to be receivers or transmitters of a message concerning another person. He then assessed their cognitive system in terms of such dimensions as *differentiation* and *organization*. A highly differentiated cognitive system is one that makes or allows one to perceive many fine distinctions among elements; if you were to describe a friend and could only use two descriptive terms, whereas someone else could use 30 separate terms, we would consider you cognitively undifferentiated relative to the other person's high degree of differentiation.

Differentiation is only part of the picture. Two persons may be comparably differentiated but vary in the degree to which they organize distinctions into some more complex, integrated unity. One person may see each tree but not the forest; the other may see the trees *and* the forest. We would call the former highly differentiated but poorly organized or integrated; the latter is both highly differentiated and cognitively integrated. Zajonc found that subjects who were set to transmit had a more highly differentiated *and* more organized cognitive system as compared with those set only to receive.

Extending Zajonc's original study, A. R. Cohen (1961) found that "transmitters" who expected to communicate impressions to others maintained a highly differentiated view of the target person and therefore were less likely than "receivers" to integrate conflicting material contained in the impressions. If I may take the usually dangerous step of overgeneralizing, a professor's view of his material is more highly differentiated and organized than a student's view. But—and this is an important but—if the student were put in the professor's role and asked to transmit his knowledge (as occurs in seminars and small classes), his differentiation and organization of the material would be relatively greater than in his passive receiver role. As anyone who has taught knows, teaching (transmitting) is a very different way to learn from passively receiving information. When you prepare to transmit you have to think in ways that were not even imaginable when you were just a receiver. Students commonly have this experience when they hear something in a class that grabs their interest and then try to report it to roommates or friends. They quickly find that they had not grasped the material in the same differentiated and organized way they initially felt they had. They begin to stumble and hem and haw and finally give up or move on to another topic.

Zajonc's important study suggests that processing that could lead to selective recall occurs *more* as an individual prepares to transmit a message or a rumor than when he prepares to receive a message, for it is during the period of preparation to transmit that he begins to select out material to differentiate, to reshape, to reorganize. During this phase he may eliminate details that do not neatly fit into the organized theme he is developing, or begin to condense several ideas into a single thought. The openness and minimal structure that characterized him as receiver move toward closure as he becomes a transmitter.

SELECTIVE EXPOSURE

We are selective not only in what we see and recall but in addition in what we actively expose ourselves to. Attend a political rally and look around at the crowd. It is likely that the majority of the persons present will have opinions similar to those of the candidate they have come to hear—that is, if we discount that hearty band of loyal hecklers who come not to listen but to be heard; theirs is a different sort of exposure. Or inquire of yourself and friends about magazine reading habits. It is likely that *The New Republic* will be found in the homes of those of a liberal political persuasion, while more politically conservative individuals will be reading *National Review*.

It appears that we expose ourselves primarily to information that supports our present system of beliefs. This selectivity has been noted for some time among investigators concerned with the effectiveness of public communications in producing attitude change. During a political campaign, for example, the candidates wish to know where best to spend their money to reach the widest audience in order to win votes. Would a campaign that simply increased the amount of media coverage suffice to change voters' attitudes or, for that matter, even to have them "hear" the candidate's views? The answer seems to be an unequivocal "no."

Berelson, Lazarsfeld, and McPhee (1954) examined voter behavior in the 1948 election campaign of Truman against Dewey. Berelson and his colleagues noted a variety of psychological determinants of their subjects' political perception. For instance, they report that the stronger a voter's own position for a given candidate, the more likely he is to perceive his candidate's position on important issues as closer to his own than it actually may be. Furthermore, this strong partisan voter is likely to misperceive the opposition, denying or distorting any actual similarity between their stand and his on important issues.

In effect there are two political campaigns running simultaneously (Berelson et al., 1954). The first is the "objective" campaign of information and advertising carried on by the candidate and his aides. The second, equally important campaign is carried on in the voter's mind and involves selectivity of perception, recall, and exposure. There is no clear and simple correspondence between the two campaigns; some voters create a campaign in their minds that is more to their liking than the objective campaign is.

Hyman and Sheatsley (1958) provide corroborative evidence for these selectivity factors. They found evidence from a national survey that persons tend to expose themselves selectively to information that is congenial (i.e., supportive) to their earlier attitudes. They also suggest that in any information campaign some persons are more likely to expose themselves to information, while others form what they call a hard core of chronic know-nothings. This latter group seems to avoid, with a vengeance, exposure to any information, supportive or nonsupportive. Other studies, originating in a wide variety of information-spreading campaigns, provide added reams of evidence for a selective-exposure effect (see Freedman & Sears, 1965, for a review). We listen to what we want to hear; read what we want to read. Note that we are not dealing with selective perception or recall, but rather with the simple fact that people place themselves in contexts selectively to support rather than to undermine their already formed opinions and beliefs. The question, of course, is, "Why?"

Exposure: The consistency view

One of the major approaches to finding "reasons why" arises from the general body of material concerning cognitive consistency, in which, as we have seen (p. 100 ff.), it is main-

tained that we prefer balanced, consonant, or consistent cognitive systems. Recall that one of the functional bases for cognitive consistency lies in our efforts to entertain a coherent view of social reality. Assuming that our existing opinions and beliefs form one of the building blocks for any cognitive system, we can see why we might try to avoid the introduction of inconsistency into that system through exposure to counterattitudinal material. Nonsupportive information is not only cognitively inconsistent, but may threaten to undermine our very conceptions of social reality. In essence, then, this line of reasoning argues that selective exposure is a protective or defensive behavior, that we expose ourselves selectively to preserve our own status quo. Although this argument has a reasonable quality, individuals do vary in their demand for consistency; then, too, that very undermining a person may wish to avoid can provide one of the foundations for growth and for attitude change.

A straightforward derivation from the preceding line of argument is that the greater the inconsistency that would occur on exposure to a particular bit of information, the less likely a person will be to expose himself to it. This derivation can be studied systematically in the confines of the experimental laboratory; we need only give an individual a free choice between sets of information that will support his beliefs and sets that will undermine or challenge him, and note which he chooses. Freedman and Sears (1963) presented California voters with a choice among several pamphlets dealing with the 1962 gubernatorial election between Brown and Nixon. More than 58 percent selected a pamphlet that supported the election of the candidate they personally preferred. Here we have hard data that support the argument for selective exposure to avoid dissonant information; alas, however, a spate of other experimental studies do not demonstrate this same effect (e.g., Feather, 1963; Freedman & Sears, 1965, especially pp. 65–69). Some apparently ornery and undoubtedly very human subjects insisted on selecting pamphlets that argued for positions opposed to their own. Perhaps college students should not be used as experimental subjects. They may be the kind of population that prefers to read other arguments in order to be challenged to think; moreover, and perhaps because of this, they are noted for botching up the most elegant psychological experimentation.

An alternative explanation for the selective-exposure effect can be offered and tested systematically. It seems plausible to argue, especially with the conflicting results of earlier work, that persons who are most *confident* about their own position may actually seek non-supportive information. The least confident persons may prefer the unchallenging supportive material. In one test of this possibility Canon (1964) experimentally manipulated "confidence" by informing some subjects that their decisions about a particular issue were correct and had widespread support and telling others that they were wrong and unsupported. He found that his highly confident subjects preferred nonsupportive information, while those of low confidence favored supportive material. Before we cry out "hurrah, at last," I must mention that a later effort to replicate this study (Freedman, 1965) did not support Canon's conclusions.

A nonconsistency view

What, then, do we have? On one hand, persons do selectively expose themselves to material and are more likely to select supportive than nonsupportive information. On the other hand, it has not been demonstrated, in any simple way at least, that the cognitive consistency argument can explain this selectivity. As we consider selective exposure further, a host of other, less cognitive bases for the observed facts seem plausible. For example, the fact that more Democrats than Republicans attend a speech by a Democratic candidate may be attributable to economic and social factors in addition to any internal psychological mechanisms: it may be good business for an individual to be seen at a Democratic function; or, for that matter, he may simply be going along with his friends, for affiliative reasons rather than for political ideology or cognitive consistency. Nevertheless, for an information pusher working in politics, in advertising, in public service, in charity, or for whatever other purpose, the campaign on the psychological side is as important as the one waged objectively.

Man's delightful capacity to be selective in perception, recall, and exposure, which the information pusher finds an undesirable hurdle, undoubtedly provides individuals with one of the few shields by which they can maintain their integrity in a society and world that seem to be competing for the ownership of their opinion. At the extreme of "no selectivity" people would be completely at the mercy of the winds and currents of opinion. At the other extreme, "total selectivity," no one would grow or change but would only spiral more deeply into narrow private burrows. Somewhere between the poles, man may both grow and maintain his integrity.

SELECTIVITY: AN EXAMPLE

In July 1966 the entire issue of *The Journal of Social Issues* was devoted to a careful discussion and analysis of "Misperception and the Vietnam War." White, the author, utilized several principles of selectivity of perception, recall, and exposure to analyze positions on the war. His basic argument was that the insanity of war is initiated, maintained, and enhanced by psychological mechanisms of misperception, and that the direction of America's militaristic misperception has created several major types of distortion:

1. *The diabolical-enemy image.* The enemy is viewed in ways that are usually found in cases of paranoia. He is diabolical, fights dirty, is out to capture the entire world, and so on.

2. *The virile self-image.* The perception of America is of a country that is courageous, firm, and indomitable, and the perception of those who want us to get out is of traitors, weaklings, and cowards.

3. *The moral self-image.* America is seen as the defender of truth, goodness, and freedom, having committed itself to be guardian at the gates of worldwide freedom.

4. *Selective inattention.* This is a tendency to ignore or overlook negative aspects of U.S. policy or positive aspects of the policy of North Vietnam or the National Liberation Front.

5. *Absence of empathy.* Empathy is a capacity to put oneself into another's shoes and see through his eyes. An absence of empathy is a distortion that makes it impossible to gain an appreciation of a situation as the opposition might see it.

If it seems that White was arguing that Americans misperceived while the Vietnamese saw perfectly, note that he took great pains to indicate how this war involved *dual* misperceptions and distortions. Matching the U.S. diabolical-enemy image, virile self-image, and so on, was a Vietnamese counterpart; thus always the madness of war.

Of the several factors White discussed in this analysis of the selective clogging of the communication channel, he focused particularly on a factor he termed the *blindness of involvement*. White described this blindness or selective inattention as "a strong tendency on each side to ignore rather than refute everything on the other side that it is psychologically possible to ignore and to give too little attention to facts on the other side that are too obtrusive to be ignored completely" (p. 137). The tunnel vision that is produced as a nation becomes caught up in the blindness of involvement leads its citizens to stop thinking about what has become unthinkable—cessation of fighting and pursuit of compromise—and directs its thoughts instead toward revenge, recouping of losses, and, as Frank has argued, toward a primitive blood lust (reported by White, 1966, p. 138).

The concept of blindness of involvement or selective inattention that White used in his analysis of the Vietnam War has a long history in the psychological laboratory. Early researchers employed a similar concept, terming it *functional fixedness* (Duncker, 1935). Given a series of problems to solve, an individual soon happens on a format for solution. He becomes so wedded to this format that when later problems in the series are solvable by an easier method he overlooks the easier solution. Essentially, his flexibility as a problem solver becomes rigid; he no longer attends to better alternatives.

Selective inattention in the Vietnam War seems to operate analogously to selective inattention in other wars or, for that matter, in most conflict situations. To continue functioning in daily life, individuals put out of their minds the issues and problems that would be disruptive were they to ruminate over them. We can imagine citizens of towns in Nazi Germany who knew of the death camps, who could, if they would, see the smoke and smell the burning flesh, but who selectively inattended to these horrors so that their own lives could continue with what peace was possible. Likewise, during peak fighting periods in the Vietnam War taking place some 10,000 miles away, Americans went about their rounds of classes, work, cocktail parties, skiing, swimming, and so on, only occasionally interrupting their routine to become disruptively attentive to the war and its horrors. For some, though, it was difficult to lie peacefully on warm beaches, getting their bodies beautiful and tan, while people were dying in Vietnam and black ghettos were on fire at home.

Again we note the extremes; on one side are those who cannot selectively inattend, but live with their world inundating disruptively, each conflict plunging them to a new despair. At the other extreme are those who block out world and national conflicts, living blithely and blindly at peace in the midst of a storm. In the terminology of clinical psychology the former type tends to overempathize while the latter lacks any empathic ability at all. Imagine being operated on by a surgeon who overempathizes to such an extent that with each cut he makes he feels the pain so deeply that his surgical skills are disrupted. On the other hand, picture a nonempathic doctor who is completely unaware of his patients' pain. As White describes the selective inattention that characterizes the distortion involved in the Vietnam War he tends to use the low-empathy side of this dimension we have created. (Empathy is discussed again on p. 426 ff.)

Chapter 14

Personal styles of selectivity

So far we have been concerned with the contents of our world as we select them according to certain internal determinants. Independent of these contents, however, is the *individual structure* or *style* of selectivity. What manner or style of attending to the world do individuals use? Are certain persons characteristically selective or narrow in their focus while others are more generally broad?

ATTENTION DEPLOYMENT

An analogy regarding attention deployment may be helpful to point out the route on which we are heading. This analogy derives from the writings of Hernández-Peón (1964) and Wachtel (1967). Picture each of us as a beam of light playing about the world as we wander through it; the beam represents our attention to aspects of that world. The central, bright part of the beam is the precise area of the environment on which we are focusing our attention. Other things occupy a fuzzy area along the edges and are barely discernible; still others lie outside in the dark, invisible to us without a shift in focus. Individuals may be characterized in terms of the *width* of their attention beam and in terms of its *scanning* or movement around the field. A person we might say has a wide beam brings a relatively large area into focus; one with a narrow beam attends only to relatively small areas at a time. A high scanner is one who deploys his attention around the field, focusing on many different areas; a limited scanner deploys attention around only a few areas of his psychological field.

An individual may be characterized by a tendency to scan a great deal of material; he may seek a broad sampling of information before he ventures to take action. The same person may, however, attend to specific details of this sampling, rather than to the relationships between the parts of the field. Thus, although he checks out his world extensively, he comes up with separate bits and pieces rather than with a more organized, coherently integrated picture. In clinical terms such a person is said to have an *obsessive* personality. Recall our example on pp. 172–173. He never sees the forest; all he notes are the separate trees, their limbs, their leaves, their height, their form. He loses the relationships, so that his world view is characterized by its high degree of *differentiation*—many aspects are seen—but low degree of *integration* of the elements.

DECENTERING

A concept of Piaget's (Feffer, 1967; Piaget, 1950) that has much in common with the preceding discussion is *decentering* or shifting one's focus. Piaget's perspective is developmental. Early ways of focusing (centering) on the environment are highly concrete and dependent on immediate sensory stimuli; a young child focuses first on this item, then on that, then on another. He cannot center on more than one stimulus at a time. With development, however, these immediate and discrete stimulus-bound impressions become subordinated to more abstract thought, which allows a person to entertain simultaneously several separate *centrations* or points of focus. This is called *simultaneous decentering*; it is characteristic of developmentally mature thinking.

Conservation

The Piagetian studies of *conservation* will help us to clarify this concept. Piaget presents his subjects (usually children of various ages) with two containers of exactly the same size and shape. He has them fill both containers with equal quantities of water or beads and then presents a container of a noticeably different size and shape. The subject pours the water or beads from one of the initial containers into the new one. Piaget then asks the subject to tell him which container now has "more." Note, of course, that the quantity in both containers is the same; the new container has been filled by emptying the original one. But if the new container's size and shape is such that it appears to be more filled (if, say, it is taller and thinner so that the water or beads seem to be at a higher level), subjects at a certain age will report that the new container has "more." Beyond that age, however, subjects *conserve quantity*; that is, they are able to think in more abstract ways to note that the quantity remains the same even though the shapes are different.

Piaget suggests, in essence, that a young child lacks constancy because he is bound up with more concrete aspects of the situation and is unable to consider its several parts simultaneously. Thus he focuses on the increased height of the water in the new container and is unable to note other parts of the situation, such as the fact that it is the same water. A conceptually more mature child, who conserves

quantity, does so because his abstract thinking —simultaneous decentering—allows him to overcome the immediate sense-bound impressions and thus to consider the several aspects of the situation simultaneously and in relation to one another.

In another Piagetian research situation a child is presented with a number of wooden beads, most red, a few blue. He is asked to indicate whether there are more *wooden* beads or more *red* beads. Young children report more red beads, often saying, "See, there are only two blue beads and a bunch of red ones." Their difficulty with this task is said to stem from their inability to decenter; they center on one aspect of the total, such as "more red than blue." Older children, however, are able to report that there are more wooden beads, some of which are red and some of which are blue. They can simultaneously consider various aspects of the situation.

In terms of our discussion of attention deployment, the work of Piaget and his associates suggests a case of differentiation without integration. Aspects of the field are differentiated (scanning is high), but interrelationships are not noted (narrow focusing).

Decentering: An interpersonal application

Any effective encounter with another person requires simultaneous awareness of a wide and complex number of interrelated elements. For example, Mead (1934) indicated that an individual must keep in mind both his own role and that of the person with whom he is interacting. Recall that in Mead's discussion of "the game" (pp. 25–26) he argued that each team member is able to take the role of every other player, to anticipate what is likely to occur, and thereby able to modify his own behavior. This requires him to integrate several perspectives into a larger, more abstract whole. The implication is similar to the implications of the Piagetian conservation studies. A young child or, for that matter, a concretely thinking adult who is less capable of solving the conservation problem would be less capable of solving the interpersonal problem; that is, his narrow focus on *one* aspect of the situation would work against his noting the essential interdependence of his and the other's actions and adjusting his behavior accordingly.

Feffer (1967) and Feffer and Suchotliff (1966) have attempted to apply notions derived from Piaget and others to interpersonal contexts and to provide a systematic, empirical test of decentering in the interpersonal arena. They developed a test of a person's ability to adopt several integrated social perspectives. They placed persons with this ability in a cooperative interactive encounter and scored their performance for quality.

Decentering was measured by a projective role-taking test (RTT). Subjects were presented a TAT-like picture in which several persons were present; they were to spend about four minutes writing a dramatic and imaginative story about that picture, indicating what was happening, what the persons in the picture were thinking and feeling, and what the outcome of the story would be. After completing this initial story they were asked to rewrite the story, this time taking the point of view of each of the persons in the picture. Scoring assessed the degree to which subjects were able to refocus the original story as they wrote it again from each character's perspective *and* to maintain continuity between the various versions. For example, if the original story were about a father who had a difficult time at work, and if the refocused story, written from the father's perspective, described him as "hungry," this was taken as indicating an inconsistency in the subject's ability to refocus with continuity. If the refocused story described the father as "anxious" or "unhappy," the subject was scored as having refocused appropriately. The assumption was that persons who could refocus successfully in this hypothetical test situation were capable of simultaneous decentering in live interaction with another person, and should be able to work well in a cooperating team.

Feffer and Suchotliff arranged subjects in either high-scoring or low-scoring pairs and had them play a game called Password, in which a sender has to communicate a word to his partner by means of single-word cues; for example, I might communicate to you the word "relax"

by the one-word clue "rest." Feffer considered this task suitable for assessing decentering because good team scores required a sender to be able to adopt his partner's perspective as well as his own in order to select the best clue words. The theoretical prediction was that high-RTT pairs should score better in the Password game than low-RTT pairs. Two indices of success were developed: the time required to solve each of 36 words and the number of clues required to solve each word. RTT scores were correlated with these two indices of team performance, and significant correlations indicated that the pairs who showed the greatest decentering abilities were most capable of effective teamwork.

It appears that both the conceptual notion of decentering as extended to the interpersonal arena and the measurement technique of the projective RTT offer a potentially useful link between a more purely individualistic cognitive-style variable and social behavior.

CONCRETE AND ABSTRACT FUNCTIONING

The concrete, stimulus-bound style by which Piaget characterizes primitive thinking, and the high-differentiation, low-integration style we considered in terms of attention deployment link several areas of psychological inquiry. In work with the brain-damaged, for example, Goldstein (1963; 1944) distinguishes concrete and abstract attitudes: a more concrete person is highly dependent on a stimulus as immediately given in its specific and unique context, while a more abstract person is capable of subordinating the specific and immediate to the more general.

The concrete extreme

Several separate studies conducted by Harvey and his associates (e.g., Harvey, Hunt, & Schroder, 1961; Adams, Harvey, & Heslin, 1966; Harvey, 1966; Harvey & Ware, 1967; White & Harvey, 1965) have yielded the following descriptive characteristics of a *concretely* functioning person.

1. On a dimension ranging from simple to

complex cognitive structure, he scores on the simpler, less highly differentiated side. In addition, those few differentiations he does make are poorly integrated; they exist as more or less isolated, discrete elements.

2. He evidences a tendency to make both extreme and highly polarized evaluations of objects, events, and persons in his world. He tends to see in terms of good versus bad or right versus wrong, an all-or-none view that does not take shades of gray into consideration.

3. He shows a tendency to be intolerant of novel and ambiguous situations, forming rather quick judgments in such situations.

4. Related to this tendency to structure a novel situation quickly and thereby shut out alternative possibilities, the concrete-styled person tends to form and generalize impressions of others from relatively incomplete bits of information about them.

5. He tends toward rigidity in thinking. Once he has himself set he has difficulty in changing as the circumstances change; this leads him to a greater degree of stereotyping in judgment and makes it difficult for him to modify his behavior in response to new information.

6. He is characterized as having a generally poor capacity to act "as if," a capacity so essential to being able to take the role of the other and thereby to gain a sense of perspective about himself and to be empathic.

The abstract extreme

The other side of this picture is a person characterized by a tendency toward overabstraction. Optimal functioning in both the physical and social environments requires a combination of differentiation and integration; but the overly abstract person tends to gloss over differentiations in pursuit of larger categories into which everything fits. For him, there are no trees, only forests. The world of the abnormal provides the richest examples of thought disorders at such extremes: a certain patient, asked to classify several different things, placed Jesus, cigar boxes, and sex into the same category *because they were all encircled:* Jesus by a halo, cigars by the tax band, and woman by the sexual glance of man (Feffer, 1967, p. 19). In extremes this tendency to be overinclusive can

lead to interpersonal conflicts when an individual treats all members of a perceived category the same way. For example, a person may treat the members of his family in the same manner he treats his employees, including them all in the category of "status lower than mine"; he may discount differences in social situations by being as loud and aggressive at a formal dinner as he is while drinking beer and watching television around his house with a few cronies.

FIELD DEPENDENCE AND INDEPENDENCE

A somewhat different conception of attention deployment concerns an individual's ability to focus his attention on *relevant* parts of the stimulus field while shutting out, ignoring, or keeping in the background those aspects of the total field that are irrelevant and interfere with the task at hand. Witkin and his associates (1954; 1962) introduced the concepts of field dependence and field independence to describe two modes of perceptual functioning that seemed to be consistent characteristics of individuals and to have broad relationships with other areas of psychological concern.

Generally, to distinguish the two types of perceptual style, an individual is put in a situation that requires him to respond selectively to one part of the field while he ignores interfering cues from other parts. The rod-and-frame test (RFT) is one such situation. The subject is seated in a darkened room and is asked to adjust a luminous rod to a position he sees as upright within a luminous frame. The situation is varied: for one series of adjustment the subject's chair and body are tilted in directions opposite to the frame; for other series either his body and the frame are tilted in the same direction or his body is erect and the frame tilted. Both dependents and independents solve the problem by selectivity weighing the different cues they experience. Field-dependent subjects deal with the task (and other, related tasks) by giving special weight in their judgments to the location of the external field cues provided by the positioning of the frame within the room. Field-independents, by contrast, attend primarily to cues that emanate from their own bodily sensations.

Extensive research conducted with field-dependent and -independent subjects indicated several interesting psychological correlates of these cognitive styles. A field-dependent person is characterized by a generally global, undifferentiated organization of his psychological field. His style of perceiving is dominated by his over-all response to the entire field, whereas a field-independent person tends to perceive his psychological field in ways that indicate both greater differentiation and integration of the competing elements. In drawing the human figure the field-dependent person is likely to draw a less highly articulated figure, that is, one with fewer parts interrelated and formed into a definite structure, than those drawn by a field-independent person.

It is usually maintained that one develops from the global to the more highly differentiated and integrated. Recently Witkin, Goodenough, and Karp (1967) reported data from a developmental study including both longitudinal and cross-sectional analyses. Their cross-sectional data derived from subjects ranging in age from eight to slightly over 21 years. Their longitudinal study obtained data from one group over the 14-year period from age 10 to age 24 and another group over the five-year period from eight to 13 years of age. The general development was toward increasing field independence, without a single reversal. A further analysis of the data provided the interesting finding that at about age 17 there was a leveling off of the over-all developmental trend. The general finding of a sex difference was upheld in this study: males tend to be more field independent than females. Finally, and importantly, analysis of performance for the longitudinal samples, in which scores were correlated over time, indicates a high degree of stability in perceptual style. For example, for the males, scores at age 10 correlated highly (.66) with scores at age 24. This means that those who are relatively field dependent as children, while developing generally greater field independence with age, are still relatively field dependent as compared with their peers at age 24.

One question that is not answered in these data, but for which there are suggestive data elsewhere, concerns what may be called de-differentiation. Do we begin to return again to a less highly differentiated state as we get older? Studies of older groups report high field-dependent scores; this suggests a return to more primitive perceptual functioning with older age. Perhaps even more fascinating to contemplate is a study reported by Witkin et al. (1967, p. 299) in which he found that older subjects who were still actively engaged in working scored as more field independent than those who had retired.

SIMPLICITY-COMPLEXITY

Each person's cognitive system can be characterized by its degree of complexity. A system with many elements, which allows an individual to make many differentiations among and between objects, persons, and events, is said to be complex; but this is only part of the picture. It is argued (Crockett, 1965; Zajonc, 1960) that the concept of cognitive complexity should be reserved for a system that is *both* highly differentiated *and* integrated.

In their study on the authoritarian personality, which we shall consider shortly, Adorno, Frenkel-Brunswik, Levinson, and Sanford (1950) defined a character who lives in a world of two values. For him, there are good people or bad people; women are either good or bad; politically, you are either with him or against him. This *dichotomous thinking* is characteristic of cognitive simplicity. As Rokeach (1956; 1960) pointed out in his discussion of dogmatism, such thinking occurs in political extremists of the left or the right; although the content or specific ideological referents may differ, both structure their world view in a highly similar manner, dogmatically and simplistically. This factor has been of special importance in the study of person perception and impression formation.

Impression formation

We are concerned here with the nature of both the selectivity of attention and the selectivity of processing that occur as one who is cognitively simple (or complex) forms an impression of another person. To the extent to which each of us is capable of being "read" in a wide variety of ways, a cognitively simple person will do us a disservice in his impression formation; the few concepts he has to structure persons are likely to give him a somewhat distorted, erroneous impression of us, at least compared to the impressions of a more cognitively complex person. Furthermore, each of us gives off potentially conflicting or inconsistent images; a cognitively complex person, with greater capacity for integrating differentiated elements into larger, more coherent wholes, should find it easier to deal with such contradictions than a cognitively simple person.

Ambivalence. Sometimes we hate, with nearly equal intensity, a person we love dearly. This is *ambivalence*, a feeling of both approach and avoidance, positive and negative. Resolving an ambivalent attitude requires integration of the two opposing orientations; we would expect a cognitively complex person to be better able to do so. Let's look at some relevant research.

Ambivalence is usually studied in the laboratory as *resolution of conflicting impressions*. In one such study (Nidorf, reported in Crockett, 1965, pp. 69–70) subjects were given a set of traits that presumably described a single O— PESSIMISTIC, INTELLIGENT, COMPETITIVE, SENSITIVE, KIND, SELF-CENTERED—and were asked to write their impressions of O. These were evaluated to determine whether the subjects had integrated traits that had opposite connotations into some broader framework, perhaps by calling on a concept such as social role, or had simply retained them unintegrated. An unintegrated impression was one in which subjects either restated the opposing traits without trying to deal with them, or formed impressions by including only traits that had the same value and direction (positive or negative). A correlation was computed between the subjects' cognitive complexity scores (measured separately) and the degree of integration of impressions. A significant although admittedly low correlation of .36 supported the prediction that persons who were more cognitively complex would be better able to produce integrated impressions.

Ambivalence is, in essence, a state of cogni-

tive imbalance (see p. 100 ff.). *P* like both *O* and *X*, but has to live with the fact that *O* does not like *X*. What is the relationship between cognitive complexity and tendencies toward balance? The theoretical prediction is that the cognitively complex individual, as compared with his simple counterpart, should be better able to handle situations that are cognitively imbalanced. One study of this matter was conducted by Scott (1963), who asked subjects to sort nations into several clusters. When he examined their groupings he found that those who were more cognitively complex were able to group into the same cluster nations that had oppositely valued characteristics; in essence, they were better able to tolerate cognitive imbalance. In another relevant study Campbell (reported in Crockett, 1965, p. 66) found that subjects who were cognitively simple were more likely than those who were cognitively complex to see relations between their friends as balanced; that is, if friend *O* liked *X*, they would assume friend *M* would also like *X*. In other words, there is some evidence to indicate that cognitively complex persons do not fit the paradigm of cognitive balance in precisely the way the theory would demand; if anything, the tendency toward cognitive balance and consistency is lived out more by cognitively simple persons.

AUTHORITARIANISM AND DOGMATISM

After the world-shocking events that marked the rise and fall of Nazism in Germany before and during World War II, including a form of obedience to authority of such extremes that massive crimes against humanity were committed in the name of the *fatherland*, concern for a Nazi-like personality type became the focus of social-psychological inquiry. Was it possible that a particular clinical syndrome, the *authoritarian personality*, existed? If so, what qualities did this personality possess? And did this authoritarian personality exist in the United States as well?

A group of researchers (Adorno, Frenkel-Brunswik, Levinson, & Sanford, 1950) at the University of California applied clinical case history and social-psychological attitude-measurement techniques to discovering the authoritarian personality. They felt that an individual's political, economic, and social views formed a broad and integrated ideological pattern that reflected underlying trends in his personality. The anti-Semitism that characterized the Nazi regime, they argued, was not an isolated belief, but rather was part of a fascistic *ideological system*. It was theoretically possible to assess anti-Semitism without ever directly inquiring about specific anti-Semitic sentiments; such research would focus on the person's total ideological pattern.

To this end, therefore, they developed several scales that measured different components of a basically antidemocratic ideology. One scale assessed attitudes of *ethnocentrism (E)*, a tendency to see things and evaluate them in terms of in-groups, which are good, versus out-groups, which are rejected. Another scale dealt with *political-economic conservatism*. A more direct measure of anti-Semitism was an *A-S* scale, in which items focused on attitudes towards Jews and things Jewish. An *F* (fascism) scale was also developed to measure attitudes toward self, family, sex, people in general, and so on. Intercorrelations between these scales and clinical case histories produced an interesting, provocative picture of the authoritarian personality, a personality type predisposed to accept an antidemocratic ideology such as fascism.

The authoritarian has been described as having the "bicyclist's personality": "Above they bow, below they kick" (Adorno, 1951). This conveys their tendency to be concerned with the power aspects of relationships, readily acquiescing to those in superior positions while domineering, often ruthlessly, those who have less power.

The authoritarian personality tends toward rigidity in thinking. He stereotypes. His sexual views are puritanical; conventional sexual values are nearly sacred to him and deviation from sexual norms is to be severely punished. The authoritarian is preoccupied with virility, with being rough, tough, and aggressive; men should be rugged and masculine, much in the image often conveyed in television commercials. While

men are out doing battle in the jungle-like world, women are to be petite and soft and feminine, dutifully and delicately fulfilling their obligations as housewives. His views of life, the world, and human nature tend to be pessimistic. Every man is for himself in a dog-eat-dog world. Others are not to be trusted. People are evil, dirty, and dangerous. He thrives on order and is intolerant of ambiguity; everything has a place and everything must remain in its place, neat and well ordered.

In terms of psychological dynamics, the authoritarian is characterized by his opposition to introspection; he dislikes looking inward and examining his motives and feelings. He tends to use such defense mechanisms as denial, repression, and projection: he denies his own impulses, especially those concerned with hostility and sexuality; he represses feelings to such an extent that he has little contact with his own inner world of emotions; through projection he casts out onto others the unwanted and denied impulses he possesses. The world out there is a hostile projection outward of his own burning hostility.

Follow-up efforts of several sorts have focused on the factor of intolerance for ambiguity. One type of investigation used one or more of the scales of the Adorno et al. study (e.g., the *E* scale, the *F* scale) and noted the behavior of high versus low scorers. One such effort was a study by Block and Block (1952). They placed high and low authoritarians (as measured by the *E* scale) in two kinds of situation. First they gave subjects meaningless tasks to perform, and the authority (the experimenter) instructed them to continue every time they paused. As expected, high authoritarians continued this meaningless activity for a longer period than lows. In the second situation the Blocks evaluated the rapidity with which highs and lows structured an ambiguous autokinetic situation (see p. 125). As expected, the highs, less tolerant of ambiguity, sought structure earlier than the lows.

A second kind of follow-up study is exemplified in the efforts of Budner (1962) to develop a separate scale to measure intolerance for ambiguity. Budner defines an ambiguous situation as (1) so new that there are no familiar cues with which to structure it; (2) so complex that there are many cues to be evaluated; (3) one that yields contradictory cues. A person who is highly intolerant of ambiguity is threatened by such situations. Budner developed a 16-item scale on which a subject was to indicate his degree of agreement or disagreement with each item; for example, "An expert who doesn't come up with a definite answer probably doesn't know too much"; "What we are used to is always preferable to what is unfamiliar." He reports that scores on the scale correlate positively with self-descriptions as "conventional," "cautious," and "ordinary." He also reports a significant positive correlation between high intolerance for ambiguity and a highly religious belief system, and that those who are intolerant of ambiguity generally approve of strong censorship, especially on issues of morality.

Enter the critics

The Adorno et al. book *The Authoritarian Personality* was carefully scrutinized and analyzed in another book (Christie & Jahoda, 1954), smaller but equally compelling and rather critical of the parent work. Objections ranged from bias in the Adorno et al. sampling procedures to the possible confounding effects of *agreement-response set*. This latter concept was simplicity itself, and set in motion a wave of similar critiques of a variety of personality and attitudinal test scales (e.g., Bass, 1955, Couch & Keniston, 1960). Someone who marked "extreme agreement" with every item on the Adorno et al. measures would be scored as a high authoritarian, but Christie and Jahoda claimed that an unknown factor, *tendency to agree,* might be the characteristic that was really being measured. This eventually resulted in the development of revised scales to measure authoritarianism (Christie, Havel, & Seidenberg, 1958). In these scales questions were worded in such a way that one would have to indicate strong agreement with half of the items and strong disagreement with the other half in order to be scored as highly authoritarian.

Other objections centered on spurious correlations among the several subscales making up the test. For example, Christie and his as-

sociates pointed out that the *F* scale and the scale to measure political-economic conservatism contained items of highly similar content, so that correlations need not indicate anything more than a similarity of test items. Objections were also raised concerning the method of using clinical case-history and projective-test data; coders of the case-history data were biased through familiarity with the subjects' test responses, so that any correspondence between the two could be attributed to a halo effect rather than to any real content correspondence.

Right and Left Wings. The major focus of these criticisms and much subsequent work was on the methodological faults of the original study. On the more conceptual side, however, major criticism was concerned with what seemed to be an anti-right-wing bias of the study. Shils (in Christie & Jahoda, 1954), for one, argued that there may be an authoritarianism of the political left in addition to the authoritarianism of the right emphasized by the Berkeley workers. The essence of this argument is that the structural pattern that underlies the authoritarian syndrome may be applicable across ideological content areas. That is, although the ideological content of the right and the left may differ, extensively in many cases, the manner of thinking and approaching the world may be very similar.

Rokeach (1956; 1960) directed his own efforts to this point. He employed the concept of *dogmatism* to describe a general intolerance or general closed-mindedness that was independent of any specific issue, and developed scales to measure this general stylistic tendency. In one (1960) he presented 20 items that measured Right Opinionation and 20 that measured Left Opinionation; persons who were nondogmatic would reject *all* the items. Later validation studies showed that samples tending toward the political left or right scored more highly on the corresponding opinionation items; for example, a sample of British Communists scored an average of 108 on the Left-Opinionation items, but only 47 on the Right. By contrast, a group of British student conservatives scored 83 on the Right and about 56 on the Left.

Rokeach correlated *F*-scale scores (as a measure of authoritarianism) with the Right- and

Left-Opinionation scores. As expected, he found a Right-winged bias of the *F* scale. He reports, for example, a correlation of .54 between *F* and Right Opinionation, but only .02 between *F* and Left Opinionation. This confirms in data form what others have noted, the bias of the *F* scale toward the political right.

Working-Class Authoritarianism? Another conceptual direction that evolved from the original work on authoritarianism was concerned with a somewhat disconcerting relationship between *F*-scale scores and socioeconomic background factors such as education and social sophistication. Authoritarianism as originally conceived and measured had not only a right-wing bias, but also a social-class bias. According to critics of the Adorno et al. studies, high *F* scores among the working class were not so much a matter of disturbed psychological dynamics that characterized the antidemocratic personality as they were a reflection of stunted opportunities for learning that realistically confront the poorer members of a society. Kelman (Kelman & Barclay, 1963), in particular, thought it useful to differentiate two typically confounded aspects of authoritarianism. One is the authoritarian syndrome in its clinical-pathological sense; the other is better seen as an index of a person's socioeconomic background, to which Kelman refers as the individual's *breadth of perspective.*

If we assume, along with Kelman, that the *F* scale more aptly measures a person's breadth of perspective than it does a pathological condition, then a high scorer would be described as one who moves in relatively narrow and confined social circles. We would expect him to be intolerant of differences, having had little experience with them. His minimal contacts with others make it difficult for him to recognize and appreciate a wide range of values and variety of different ways and styles of living.

Kelman (1963) next argued that authoritarianism, so conceived, is a function of an individual's *psychological capacity* and his *social opportunities.* An authoritarian individual may have a limited capacity or he may have the psychological capacity for a broad perspective but have lived too long in an environment with stunted opportunities for growth and development. Those who live in a constricted and homogeneous environment, who have minimal contact with diverse values, beliefs, and types of people, may develop intolerance and rigidity in dealing with others. According to Kelman, such authoritarian attitudes could be minimized by new opportunities; but if authoritarianism is seen strictly as a psychological incapacity, its reduction requires a more directly therapeutic encounter.

Kelman and Barclay (1963) sought to provide a test for this expanded conception of authoritarianism. As a measure of psychological capacity, they asked their subjects to complete a test of intolerance for ambiguity; highly intolerant subjects were assumed to have a low capacity. They assumed that certain social-background factors would produce a broad or a narrow range of opportunity. For example, they assumed that females woud have less opportunity for breadth of experience than males; that Negroes would have less opportunity than whites; lower class less than middle; the less educated less than the more highly educated; those from rural backgrounds less than those from urban backgrounds. They scored their sample on each of these background characteristics and divided the resulting distribution into a high-opportunity and a low-opportunity group.

Kelman and Barclay argued that persons who have both a high psychological capacity and a high opportunity should have the widest breadth of perspective, and, with the *F* scale as an index of authoritarianism, the *lowest F* score; those who suffer both from low capacity and low opportunity should evidence the greatest amount of authoritarianism. To test this, they computed the mean *F*-scale score for subjects who were high in both capacity and opportunity, low in both, or high in one and low in the other. Table 14.1 shows these data. Their expectations were borne out, but because the numerical

Table 14.1 Mean authoritarianism of persons varying in psychological capacity and social opportunity

	High Capacity	Low Capacity
High opportunity	3.97	4.55
Low opportunity	4.43	4.95

difference was not great this effort really must be taken more as provocative and instructive about the usefulness of this conception of authoritarianism than as a precise proof of its validity.

Applications

Before leaving authoritarianism and dogmatism as personal styles, we may gain a better perspective on the operation of these cognitive personality factors by briefly examining two interesting applications.

The Peace Corps. The qualities ascribed to the high authoritarian, especially rigidity, ethnocentrism, and conventionality, appear to be the sort that would be detrimental to effective overseas work in the Peace Corps. Smith (1965) examined Peace Corps teachers who trained in Berkeley in 1961 and later were sent to Ghana to teach in secondary schools. He addressed himself to two related issues: the construct validity of the test measures of authoritarianism, as related to scores on other assessments, and the predictive validity of the concept, as related to ratings of job effectiveness. As we shall see, his data indicate construct validity of the test measures; but, at least in the situation studied, there is no confirmation for predictive validity.

To assess the relationship between test-measured authoritarianism and other ways of evaluating the authoritarian personality syndrome, Smith examined descriptions that psychiatrists made of high and low authoritarians. Early in the training each corpsman was seen by psychiatrists in two 50-minute sessions. At the conclusion of each interview the psychiatrists made various ratings and wrote a narrative summary of the interview. These narrative summaries became Smith's source of psychiatric data. Block (1961) had developed what is known as the *California Q-deck*, which consists of 100 items, each printed on a separate card and each containing a description of a person. Judges sort these cards into piles ranging from items that are most descriptive of a given person to those that are least descriptive. Smith asked his judges to read the narrative summary for a given corpsman and then conduct a descriptive Q-sort. When this was completed it was clear that the description significantly differentiated the high from the low authoritarians.

A sampling of some of these descriptions will indicate the value of this technique. High authoritarians as compared to lows were described as (1) uncomfortable with uncertainty and complexities; (2) tend toward overcontrol of needs and impulses and delay gratification unnecessarily; (3) moralistic; (4) tend to project their own feeling and motivations onto others. By contrast, low authoritarians were described as: (1) tend to be rebellious and nonconforming; (2) verbally fluent, express ideas well; (3) have a wide range of interests; (4) have insights into own motives and behavior.

Even a cursory glance through this small sampling of data will indicate an amazing correspondence between these descriptions and the original conception of the authoritarian personality. Recall, these are ratings made from narrative reports of psychiatric interviews that were in no way focused on authoritarianism. The data thus offer strong support for the validity of the construct of the authoritarian personality.

When it comes to predictive validity, however, the story is different. Evaluations of the corpsmen's success as teachers in Ghana did not in general differentiate between high and low authoritarians. That is, Smith's expectation that low authoritarians would show a better performance in the Peace Corps was not upheld by the ratings. As Smith himself noted, we must consider both the personality and the social context in which a person plays out his drama. It is possible that the rather predictable and controlled setting teachers faced in Ghana (perhaps unlike many Peace Corps settings) was not the kind of situation that would be a problem to a high-authoritarian individual. On the other hand, if a setting demanded flexibility, and a high authoritarian were left on his own to define his job, perhaps we would find greater predictive validity for authoritarianism.

In addition, we must keep in mind that it is likely that those who scored as high authoritarians in this very selected and screened sample were higher relative to their colleagues, but perhaps not very high in relation to the general population. Needless to say, both of these factors undoubtedly operated to cut out whatever predictive usefulness the measure may have had. We as social psychologists must always take into consideration the person *and* the situation in making behavioral predictions.

Cognitive Change and Prejudice Reduction. A fascinating nine-year follow-up study by Kutner and Gordon (1964) really goes beyond the measurement of authoritarianism and dogmatism. Nevertheless, it is concerned with cognitive factors contained in both authoritarianism and dogmatism, and seeks to relate outgroup prejudice to these cognitive styles. Methodologically, I hasten to note, there are several problems with the study. However, it offers us one of the few glimpses into the possible relationship between changes in cognitive style and prejudice.

In 1950 Kutner studied a group of 60 seven-year-old children who were rated as either high or low in prejudice toward several minority groups. At that time he found that children who were rated as highly prejudiced were characterized by a cognitive style reminiscent of authoritarianism and dogmatism; they tended to be rigid in their thinking, to overgeneralize, to dichotomize, to be more concrete than abstract, and to be intolerant of ambiguity.

Early in 1959 Kutner and Gordon had the opportunity to restudy about half of the 60 children. They used measures of cognitive-style variables that were roughly similar to those used in the first study, plus new ratings of prejudice. Were those who had been prejudiced at age seven also prejudiced at age 16? They compared high- and low-prejudiced subjects at the two age levels, reporting *no* pattern of consistency: 18 children retained the same high or low prejudice over the nine-year period, 15 changed.

Their second question was by far more interesting and complex; their concern was to relate *changes* in cognitive functioning to *changes* in prejudiced attitudes. They hoped, of course, that subjects who became cognitively healthier (less rigid, less dogmatic, less intolerant of ambiguity, etc.) over the nine-year period would also have become less prejudiced, and expected also that those who became cognitively sicker over the nine years would show greater prejudice. To test this they computed rank orders on the cognitive tests (high score was in the healthy direction) for children who were low in prejudice at both seven and 16; those who were high at age seven but low at 16; those who were low at seven but high at 16 and those who high at both seven and 16.

The data in Table 14.2 indicate general sup-

Table 14.2 Mean rank on cognitive tests

	At Age 7	At Age 16
Low prejudice at 7—Low at 16	1.7	1.3
High prejudice at 7—Low at 16	3.1	2.3
Low prejudice at 7—High at 16	1.7	2.3
High prejudice at 7—High at 16	3.5	4.0

port for the theoretical expectations. The first group, consistently low in prejudice at both seven and 16, retained its high (healthy cognitive style) ranking on the cognitive tests. The group whose prejudice decreased over the nine-year period showed a corresponding change in ranking on the cognitive tests: cognitive abilities improved. On the other hand, the group that showed an increase in prejudice decreased in its ranking on the cognitive tests: cognitively these children had become relatively more rigid and intolerant. Finally, the group that remained highly prejudiced over the nine-year period retained its relatively poor ranking on the cognitive tests. With so small a sample size and so rough-hewn a measure as relative group rankings, these data should be taken only as suggestive of support for a model that links *changes* in attitudes of prejudice to *changes* in the kinds of cognitive factors embodied in the authoritarian and dogmatic personalities.

Conclusion

Undoubtedly part of this search for "the authoritarian" was based on the assumption that it took a certain personality to yield the horrors of Nazi Germany. This pursuit of an evil personality type tends to play down social conditions that can bring out the beast in all men.

Likewise, it obscures the pressures toward compliance that make men yield out of fear, and the pressures of social reality that lead men to yield because everyone else, including those in political power, in the churches, and in the universities, has defined a new base of legitimacy. In other words, it may be erroneous to assume "it can never happen here" just because we do not have *that* type of character structure. The development of facism within a nation depends on more than the presence of "the authoritarian."

PERSONAL STYLES:
REGRESSION IN THE SERVICE OF THE EGO

As we have seen, several approaches to personal styles of selectivity refer to different stages of development, each with a different type of transaction with the environment (e.g., Piaget; Harvey et al.). In general these approaches consider a developmentally earlier, more primitive mode of relating and a later, more mature process. In Freud's original formulation he also offered a developmental distinction in thinking. He differentiated between a mode he termed *primary process* (see p. 163). and one he called *secondary process*. Basically, primary-process thought is more primitive, secondary process more developmentally advanced. Dreams and fantasy material are characteristically framed in primary-process terms, whereas our waking life, with its efforts to deal with the reality around us, characterizes the secondary process.

Regression in the service of the ego is a movement backward from the secondary to the primary mode in an effort to solve problems in the ego's world of reality. A creative act, for example, is seen to involve a regression of this sort: a person moves backward into the fanciful realm of the primary process and emerges with a combination of elements unavailable to his more rigid, reality-centered secondary process. His regression has provided a solution, a creation, a new emergent in the service of his ego in its efforts to deal with reality.

In terms of perceptual-cognitive style, the ability to utilize primary-process material in this way would presumably characterize an individual who has what Schachtel (1959) called an *openness to experience*. Such a person would face his world and deal with its objects in ways not conventionally bound by rules and expectations. He would reshuffle objects and experiences so that they could be viewed from a variety of angles. We would expect him to be tolerant rather than intolerant of ambiguity; he should not be driven to create a logically consistent or simplified picture of the persons and events he encounters daily.

Systematic research has been difficult to undertake for many such psychoanalytic notions. For example, how might we measure regression in the service of the ego? One effort to do so, which I find of both interest and potential value, involves the use of a word-association technique. Word association—rapid response to the presentation of a stimulus word—has been used for some time as a technique to uncover unconscious material (e.g., Jung, 1918; Rapaport, 1945). In its usual use the time taken to give an association and the nature of the association are thought to offer clues to an individual's underlying areas of conflict and personality difficulty.

Another use involves a determination of an individual's ability to *shift sets* in the word-association task; here it is assumed that such an ability can indicate regression in the service of the ego. Essentially the procedure is as follows. First an individual's associations are obtained under normal or *uninstructed* conditions. Next he is given a brief description of a conventional person and is asked to respond *as if he were that character*; this is termed the *regulated set*. Finally, he is given a description of a rather unconventional, novel sort of person and asked to respond as he would; this is the *unregulated set*. A *shift score* indicates his ability to switch from a conventional to an original response.

Wild (1965) used this technique with three samples of subjects: art students, teachers, and schizophrenics. She reports that the art students showed the greatest ability to shift from conventional to original responses, the teachers next, and the schizophrenics the least. In a separate and important analysis Wild had expert judges rate the art students on their creativity;

she then correlated the ratings with subjects' shift scores. In general, compared with those rated low on creativity, the more creative art students were better able to shift from conventional to nonconventional associations.

Wild reports anecdotally that the art students gave the impression of being intrigued by their own responses and what they revealed about their inner life. By contrast the schizophrenics, and to some extent the teachers, tended to be cautious and fearful about what they were revealing about their inner world in their responses. Wild's technique seems validly to differentiate between those who are more and less creative, and, because regression in the service of the ego—openness to the inner world of experiences and fantasy material—is thought to be a quality creative persons possess, her study furthers our understanding of the concept.

Another effort to develop a valid measure of openness to experience was undertaken by Fitzgerald (1966). Fitzgerald developed an *experience inquiry*, a paper-and-pencil test with several subscales that communicate the sense of the concept. For example:

1. *Tolerance for regressive experiences:* "I like to indulge in emotions and sensations with the feeling of just letting go."

2. *Tolerance for logical inconsistencies:* "There are things and events that cannot ultimately be explained logically."

3. *Constructive use of regression:* "I have had experiences that inspired me to write a poem or a story, or make up a humorous tale or paint a picture."

4. *Altered states:* "At times I have focused on something so hard that I went into a kind of benumbed state of consciousness, or at other times into a state of extraordinary calm and serenity."

5. *Peak experiences:* "I have been so strongly in love with someone that I somehow felt that my own self was fading and I was at one with the beloved person."

Scores on this test were correlated with scores on a variety of other instruments. Of particular interest to our discussion is their correlation with the technique developed by Wild. Fitzgerald had his subjects give word associations under uninstructed, regulated, and unregulated sets, just as Wild had done. He reports that subjects who scored highest on this test of openness to experience gave significantly more original associations under all conditions as compared with the low scorers. In addition, the highs showed a greater ability to shift from conventional to original associations under the two instructional sets. This work adds further to the developing interest in the concept of regression in the service of the ego; another perceptual-cognitive style that enters importantly into the manner by which each of us selectively transforms and deals with our physical and social environments.

Section V

The sociohistorical roots of cognition

Proposition V
The perceptual-cognitive processes are sociohistorical as well as individual events—the sociology of knowledge

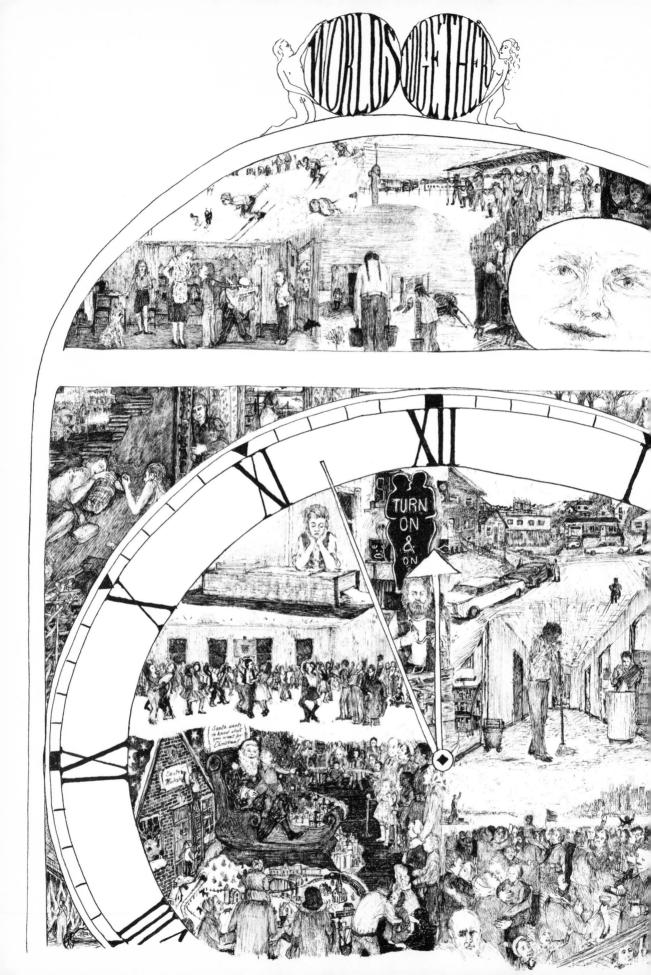

Chapter 15

The sociology of knowledge

An Arab proverb states that men resemble the times more than they do their fathers (Ryder, 1965, p. 853). We call it a generation gap. It is nothing new, but it can and does vary in scope and intensity. The concept of an age-graded generational gap between historical groups in a society is only one instance of the topic of concern to us in this chapter. Our more general concern is with the field called the sociology of knowledge, the essence of which is the link between knowledge and society. The assumption is that our knowledge, including our values and even our personal styles, can best be understood in their relationship to certain definable aspects of society. These social aspects to which our knowledge is referred can include the entire society, subunits in the society such as social class, or, more extensively, historical epochs. In each case the argument is that what we think, what we know, what we accept to be true and valid, what morality we accept, are all to be understood in their relationship to one or more of these substrata of the sociohistorical system.

We might say that the sociologist of knowledge does to knowledge what the psychoanalyst does to dreams. The analyst assumes that the manifest or directly observable content of dreams is to be understood only by uncovering its systematic relationship to the substrata of wishes and impulses that comprise its latent content. Likewise, the sociologist of knowledge assumes that the observable expressions of knowledge, belief, or ideology are to be understood only when their relationship to sociohistorical substrata (the latent content) is uncovered. That is the task he sets for himself.

MARXIAN INFLUENCE

Any review of the historical developments of the field known today as the sociology of knowledge inevitably pauses to pay respects to Karl Marx. Marxian theory argues for an *economic determinism:* the course of history and the lives of men are influenced extensively by the nature of the economic production system within a society. An individual's relationship to the mode of production in his society provides the real foundation for his system of ideas and beliefs. An owner, Marx argued, by virtue of the fact that he *is* an owner and has a vested interest in a particular system of economic production, thinks in a particular manner; a worker, by virtue of the fact that he *is* a worker, thinks in a different manner.

To put the Marxian sociology of knowledge another way, it may be argued that a person's economic position determines the *specific* manner of his thinking about social reality; this may lead to a more general belief. In time the person believes that his specific condition of existence and consciousness *should* be the general condition of existence and consciousness for all; and, in fact, that his own beliefs and knowledges *are* the same beliefs and knowledges that all other persons have, regardless of their particular economic class position.

Millhands and preachers

Although there are many who argue against Marx's view of history, in particular pointing to its failure to deal adequately with the contemporary class situation in the United States, his sociology of knowledge offers us some interesting possibilities. One fascinating study within the Marxian perspective appeared several years ago in a work by Pope (1958) entitled *Millhands and Preachers*. Pope studied a small southern milltown of the 1920's and 1930's. This town, like so many similar small towns, was almost entirely owned and operated by the mill owners, who controlled property, housing, stores, and other such facilities. In addition, and importantly to Pope's analysis, they supported the local churches. The rich churches with their large buildings and fine trappings catered to the town's upper class of mill owners and managers; the poorer churches catered to mill workers.

A gift of money from the mill could make or break a church; an interesting economic *symbiosis* developed between the mills and the preachers. In a symbiotic relationship each member gives and gets, and each needs for his own survival what the other gives. In this town the churches gave a doctrine of morality that kept the mill hands thinking and acting in ways essential to their being effective workers in the mills. The preachers urged the workers to adopt a morality that stressed the godly virtues of hard and responsible work and decried the evils of late nights, excessive drinking, tardiness, and so on. In other words, anything that might make a millhand a less viable worker was deemed immoral by the churches. The churches, in turn, got from the mill owners sufficient capital to maintain and enhance themselves in the community. In that community, at that time at least, there was competition among several churches for the largest congregations and the best physical facilities. The capital gained from the mill owners' donations entered usefully into this competition.

During one period efforts were made by the national union movement to unionize the workers in this town. What worse fate could befall the mill owners, or so they imagined, than to have their workers unionized? They knew all too well that a strong union could break their hold over the community, could force them to increase pay and improve working conditions, and could thereby threaten their profits in an already competitive national market. In fact, these particular mill owners had a competitive advantage in the national marketplace primarily because of their control over the workers' lives, pay, and working conditions. Any change would reduce and possibly even eliminate this advantage; unionization was something they wished to fight off. It takes little to guess how the battle was fought. The preachers spent many Sunday sermons arguing against unionization. Union organizers were outsiders; they were Communists; they embodied all the evils the church was fighting against. The preachers clearly were not about to bite the hand that was feeding them.

This example offers some insights into an economic view of community relationships and a glimpse into the manner by which knowledge, especially concerning right and wrong and the proper way to live one's life, are understood in their relation to substrata in a community. It is also a key example of the manner by which a ruling or dominant group can determine the ideology that shapes the consciousness of others. It was this matter that so concerned Marx; he noted that dominant classes feel that the specific conditions requisite for their own economic well-being are the general conditions necessary for the survival of everyone. In the milltown the dominant ideology of the mill owners, fed out through the churches, created a general state of belief and value that helped the dominant group maintain its own specific advantages.

Source credibility

It is not a very great leap from Pope's analysis of the milltown to the long-standing political concern with the issue of objectivity versus conflict of interests. In the government of the United States, as in most similar bodies, it is assumed that one cannot render impartial judgments while at the same time maintaining an interest—primarily of an economic sort—in the areas being judged.

As interested citizens we are not likely to look on dispassionately when a lawmaker's responsibility is to protect the general public's interest on a matter in which he has a clearly marked private interest. We doubt his impartiality; soon we may come to doubt his credibility as a legislator. It would be like hearing a television newscast on the health benefits of smoking and later learning that the program was sponsored by several large cigarette companies. Some early experimental work under the able leadership of Hovland has systematically demonstrated the effect of *source credibility* on interpretation of message content (see p. 312 ff.).

In one such endeavor Hovland and Mandell (1952) compared two types of communication that were identical in all respects. In one condition of their experiment, however, subjects were led to believe that the communicator had something to gain if they accepted his arguments and point of view; in another condition they were led to believe that the communicator was an impartial university professor. Results indicated that the communicator with an axe to grind was rated as less fair and honest than the apparently impartial professor. Furthermore, the professorial message, although precisely the same as that given by the biased communicator, was rated as a better-quality presentation.

In another endeavor Hovland and Weiss (1951) presented identical messages to groups of subjects and systematically varied the source purported to have advocated the message. For example, on the issue "Is the steel industry to blame for the current shortage of steel?" the high-credibility source was the *Bulletin of the National Resources Planning Board* and the low-credibility source was a "widely syndicated antilabor, anti-New Deal, "rightist' newspaper columnist." As expected, subjects considered the low-credibility sources as less fair and impartial than the more highly credible ones.

Essentially, our understanding of the truth value of a bit of knowledge is facilitated when we come to see the relationship that exists between the proponent of the knowledge and his socioeconomic position. McGuire's review (1969, especially pp. 182–187) of much of the experimental work on the topic suggests, interestingly enough, that although a communicator with a vested interest may be rated as less fair than one who is impartial, at least insofar as laboratory research is concerned, this "partial" source may still be effective in changing attitudes. (See p. 312 ff. of this text for a discussion of some of McGuire's ideas on this matter.)

MANNHEIM

Of the figures who have contributed to the sociology of knowledge none is more sweeping in his point of view than Mannheim. In *Ideology and Utopia* (1936) he set forth his sociology of knowledge. Unlike his predecessors and even some contemporary workers in this area, Mannheim called into question nearly all knowledge and ideology; he did not restrict his focus, as Marx did, to the relationship between knowledge and the economic substrata of society.

Mannheim's principal argument was that there are forms or modes of thinking and belief that can never be fully understood without taking their social origins into consideration. These forms he referred to as *ideological thought*. He rejected a purely logical or rational approach to thinking. Rather, he saw that knowledge is inevitably rooted in the particular kind of collective activity in which we participate; like language, thinking is a social act. What we believe to be true, correct, and valid comes from our efforts as members of a society to deal with common life situations. And it follows, said Mannheim, that men whose collective activity occurs in different social contexts will arrive at different ideologies. This line of reasoning led him to conclude that thinking is inevitably different in different social and historical contexts. For example, when man's collective activity was embedded in an agrarian society, his beliefs about his life and the world were different from those he presently possesses in modern, industrialized society.

Mannheim did not claim that *all* knowledge derives from collective activity and so can only be understood in its relationship to these social origins; 2 + 2 = 4 is not rooted in socio-historical origins. But he argued that it would be erroneous to believe that true knowledge is *only* knowledge that is devoid of any human element. The natural sciences may deal with forms of knowledge that only minimally reflect sociohistorical origins; but for the social sciences and day-by-day, man-on-the-street knowledge, we lose more than we gain by obscuring social and historical foundations.

This last point is interesting; again it calls our attention to a distinction between the kinds of knowledge in the natural sciences and those in the social sciences. It is made even more interesting by Kuhn (1962), who argued that it is also fruitful to discover the social and historical foundations of the accepted knowledge in the natural sciences. For Kuhn, each science develops a particular paradigm of its knowledge, a world view, during each phase in its development. The paradigm defines a certain range of knowledge as scientifically legitimate and indicates what lies outside this range. Kuhn argued (see p. 16) that the development of a science does not proceed in so smooth and simple a manner as most textbooks would have us believe; a new paradigm comes about by a near-revolutionary upheaval in a discipline, the result of which is an entirely *new* way of viewing the world of interest to that scientific discipline.

In fact, and perhaps not surprisingly, Mannheim and Kuhn have presented very similar arguments about the evolution of knowledge. Mannheim argued that the sociohistorical origins of any idea are always relevant to our understanding of its validity unless these origins have no effect on either the form or the content of the idea. If this statement were so, any two historical periods would be distinguishable only because the earlier period lacked specific, more complete details of knowledge uncovered in the later period. But, as Mannheim suggested, "Every epoch has its fundamentally new approach and its characteristic point of view, and consequently sees the 'same' object from a new perspective." He went on to indicate that just as we date art forms according to their style, so we may date knowledge styles according to their historical origins.

In a sense Mannheim's analysis urges us to make *ad hominem* arguments, which we are usually urged to avoid in normal discourse. An ad hominem argument is one that questions the validity of a point by making reference to the personality, social position, or vested interest of the man making it. According to Mannheim this type of questioning and uncovering is what we, as sociologists of knowledge, *should* be doing. Lest you now feel totally justified in raising ad hominem arguments against your opponents, however, Mannheim warns that we must apply a similar analysis to our own arguments. It is not only our opponent's beliefs that are to be understood in their relation to his person, his group, and his historical period; our own beliefs are similarly rooted.

What does a sociologist of knowledge do? Essentially, he endeavors to discover the correspondence between beliefs and social structure and between beliefs and historical epoch. For each bit of knowledge, belief, ideology, or justification he encounters he asks himself how that bit arose from a particular sociohistorical context. He does not regard it as a source of error that such beliefs are rooted in a sociohistorical context; he considers it a fact of human social and psychological functioning that each person, group, and period should have its own particular perspective or ideology, and that each possesses only a *relational* quality, a partial view. His function, in addition, is to attempt to gain a sufficiently detached perspective that he can minimize the binding demands of his own background and epoch. The point, simply, is that no individual can hope to understand the relational quality of the knowledge of others without having insight into the relational quality of his own thinking.

The detached perspective

Mannheim suggested several ways to attain a detached perspective. First, a person gains some detachment from his own perspective by *vertical or horizontal mobility*. Movement upward in a status system in a society offers an opportunity, at least for an individual who pays attention, to gain detachment by contrasting the ideologies of his former position with those of the position into which he has moved. This is a phenomenon that may befall a college student, for example, who moves from a working-class family background into a social class of professionals and academicians. The relational quality of his initial beliefs may become apparent to him as he visits his home during vacations and sees the often glaring contrasts between where he is now and where he was.

Horizontal mobility, particularly across cultural boundaries, offers another way in which a detached perspective may evolve. It is a commonplace experience among persons who visit other cultures to note substantial differences between themselves and members of a new culture. It is rumored that American tourists abroad (frequently called the ugly Americans) note these differences but, rather than gaining perspective on the relational quality of their own ideas, continue to see theirs as "one true way" and other ways as primitive or funny.

Some examples are cited by Segall, Campbell, and Herskovits (1966) that emphasize this often unfortunate ethnocentrism. During World War II U.S. military personnel viewed Algerian laborers with whom they had contact as filthy because they seemed to care little about bathing. The Algerians, however, were shocked that American soldiers used the same hand for eating that they used in urinating. For the Algerians this was a taboo, and indicated severely poor manners and filthy habits. Americans were revolted to see Hindu peasants blow the mucus from their noses onto the street. On their part, however, the Hindu peasants regarded it as a disgusting and unclean habit for Americans to blow their noses into small pieces of cloth that they wrapped up and stuffed into their pockets. In these two examples it seems clear that although cross-cultural contact can produce sufficient detachment to gain a new view of the way in which a person's beliefs are related to his own culture, such contact in no way guarantees that anything other than ethnocentric support will actually evolve.

A second manner by which Mannheim saw that detachment may come about involves relatively *rapid social change*—for example, with the impact of a new technology (see Chapter 24) that changes the basis for collective existence. The automobile brought about the possibility for new forms and kinds of social relationships and collective activities in the American way of life. These new forms, in turn, brought about a shift in beliefs and values. The family became mobile. People came into contact with a greater number and variety of other people and their different ways of life. An entire system of economics developed around the automobile. People could move out of cities and into suburbs. Television is another technological event that produced a change in the structure of relationships, and with this change the possibility for a detachment of perspective again emerged.

Note at this point that these technological innovations have occurred within the lifetime of many individuals. It is theoretically possible for these individuals to gain sufficient detachment to understand the relationship between their pre-innovation views and their post-innovation views. Such detachment, presumably, is more difficult to attain if an individual has been brought up entirely within the period of the automobile or television, nuclear power, rapid air transportation, or any other significant technological innovation.

It is not directly to our present point to discuss the many-faceted nature of the impact of technology on society. The point rather is that a change in the traditional structures of a society can bring about the kind of detached perspective requisite to the analysis made by a sociologist of knowledge. The argument is that beliefs are related to social structure; if social structure changes, resulting thereby in a change in beliefs, a person who undergoes such change is capable of gaining a sense of detachment and of seeing his beliefs in their sociohistorical context.

A third manner by which detachment may be obtained, according to Mannheim, is the *clash between disparate perspectives* within the same society. There is perhaps no better way to state the case than to let Mannheim's own words speak for him:

"What seems to be so unbearable in life itself, namely to continue to live with the unconscious uncovered, is the historical prerequisite of scientific critical self-awareness. In personal life, too, self-control and self-correction develop only when in our originally blind vital forward drive we come upon an obstacle which throws us back upon ourselves. In the course of this collision with other possible forms of existence, the peculiarity of our own mode of life becomes apparent to us. . . . Even in our personal life we become masters of ourselves only when the unconscious motivations which formerly existed behind our backs suddenly come into our field of vision and thereby become accessible to conscious control. Man attains objectivity and acquires a self with reference to his conception of his world not by giving up his will to action and holding his evaluations in abeyance but in confronting and examining himself. In such moments, the inner connection between our role, our motivations, and our type and manner of experiencing the world suddenly dawns upon us." (1936, p. 47).

We might say that this quotation indicates Mannheim's basic trust and good feeling about human behavior. He argued that we recognize the blinders of our own perspective (i.e., we gain detachment) when we collide against another perspective. As in the ethnocentrism of some Americans in other countries, it is possible that the outcome of such a collision is not enlightment but rather retrenchment; instead of gaining a sense of the relational quality of his own position, a person may emerge from the collision with blinders pulled on even more tightly than before. Nevertheless, we must agree with the general focus of Mannheim's argument, that one's own views *potentially* are called into question when they collide with those of others who look at the same world from another perspective. The discussion of social reality and conformity pressures (p. 126 ff.) offers several examples of some reactions to this clash of disparate viewpoints.

THE SOCIOLOGY OF KNOWLEDGE LOOKS AT ITSELF

Nothing is sacred in Mannheim's point of view other than the virtue in examining all that is sacred. One of the tenets of the sociology of knowledge is that most knowledge has a relational quality, and this holds for the field itself. In essence, what sociohistorical events have made it possible over time for the field of sociology of knowledge to develop? What is there about contemporary society that makes it plausible to argue that ideology is relational?

Mannheim attempted to trace several changes in the sociohistorical climate or *Zeitgeist* that forced on people the realization that the same world can be represented differently by different observers. Historically, there are several ways by which order has been attributed to the world. A person may experience in an ordered manner what already exists. This view was characteristic of the medieval Christian conception of an objective organization and patterning to the world—God's meaning and order. One checked the validity of his own beliefs by an appeal to the all-knowing divine. With the breakdown in the predominance of the Church as the body that defined and gave meaning, and with movement toward the age of enlightenment, the basis for world order and organization began to move inward to the perceiver. Validity became a function of the constructive activity of the mind of a perceiving and knowing subject; one gained access to valid knowledge by acts of pure logical and rational contemplation, a la Descartes and Kant.

The movement from the objective unity provided by God to a more subjective conception of knowledge permitted the first crucial step in the evolution of the sociology of knowledge. Once it is agreed that knowledge is a subjective act of the individual, it is not so great a leap to imagine that as the individual changes over time, location, or historical period, so do conceptions of knowledge. Hegel and later Marx entered here. Hegel introduced historical depth, while Marx, as we have seen, brought us to a consideration of class consciousness or class knowledge rooted in a given economic grouping.

As Mannheim noted, the full-blown conception of *his* brand of the sociology of knowledge could not appear until several further steps had been taken. Of these further steps, perhaps the most significant, according to Mannheim, is the realization that one's own perspective reflects his social position as much as his opponent's does.

As long as a society remains relatively stable, especially if the stability is based on the authority of a single group, there is little cause to question the social basis of knowledge. Essentially, investing one segment of the society with legitimate authority is analogous to accepting as true only what God or the Church validates as true. As long as a society is autocratically structured, therefore, the field of sociology of knowledge is unlikely to develop fully, if at all. To develop, the field requires democratization of the society; that is, a breakup in traditional lines of authority and legitimacy and a growing equality among the members of the society.

This democratization calls into question the ideology of the once-autocratic regime by contrasting it with the ideology of lower strata. In other words, democratization of a society makes others' perspectives *equally legitimate*, and with such legitimization comes a clash of disparate points of view that forces an awareness of the relational nature of each perspective. Thus Mannheim saw it as no accident at all that the sociology of knowledge as a field has blossomed in present generations.

The God-is-dead theme that has come into vogue recently reflects a state of thinking that encourages a sociology of knowledge to grow. If God is dead, Church dogma no longer can validate or legitimize a particular ideological system. By extension, when God symbolizes all authority, and when therefore the meaning of the statement is that "all authority is dead," no authoritative conception of truth or reality can occupy a position of absolute legitimacy, and the arena is free for competing views. Each claim to ideological legitimacy then clearly reflects the social position and historical period of its holders.

With democratization pushing decision making back to the individual, and with travel and communications media allowing greater contact with divergent ways of life, the once-solid stability of society has begun to crumble. People have become skeptical not only of others' knowledge, but also of their own. As Merton has stated it,

"In a society where reciprocal distrust finds such folk-expression as 'what's in it for him?'; where buncombe and bunk have become idiom for nearly a century and debunk for a generation; where advertising and propaganda have generated active resistance to the acceptance of statements at face value; where pseudo-*Gemeinschaft* behavior [see p. 373 ff.] as a device for improving one's economic and political position is documented in a best seller on how to win friends who may be influenced; where social relationships are increasingly instrumentalized so that the individual comes to view others as seeking primarily to control, manipulate, and exploit him; where growing cynicism involves a progressive detachment from significant group relationships and a considerable degree of self-estrangement; where uncertainty about one's own motives is voided in the indecisive phrase, 'I may be rationalizing but . . .'; where defenses against traumatic disillusionment may consist in remaining permanently disillusioned by reducing expectations about the integrity of others through discounting their motives and abilities in advance; in such a society, systematic ideological analysis and a derived sociology of knowledge take on a socially grounded pertinence and cogency" (1957, p. 459).

THE END OF IDEOLOGY?

Up to this point we have seen that ideological inquiry developed almost directly as a function of the breakup of legitimate authority within a society. When no group maintains a greater claim to the legitimacy of its ideas than any other, persons come to question the sociohistorical basis of all ideas; thus a *Zeitgeist* is established within which the field of sociology of knowledge can evolve.

As with the God-is-dead theme, the world has been rocked by the end-of-ideology theme (see especially Bell, 1960), especially in the United States. "God is dead" made it possible for a sociology of knowledge to develop by bringing down traditional forms of authority and legitimacy; "the end of ideology" argues for a shift in society away from ideology and toward a new form of authoritative legitimacy. Basically, as conditions have shifted to produce what Lane (1966) has called the "knowledge-able society," the "domain of ideology was thereby shrunken by the dominance of knowledge." To the extent to which a society is founded on scientific advances in such a way that what were formerly political decisions made on the basis of interest-group ideology are now made on the basis of cold facts, that society has become one in which science has become the new source of truth, replacing both God and the subjectivism of the "thinking" mind. The argument is that factual knowledge has increasingly replaced biased or error-ridden ideology.

Although this argument has much merit, critics note that scientism is an ideological position in its own right (e.g., Mills, 1961; Zinn, 1968; Chomsky, 1967, 1969). Each of these critics in his own way maintains that governmental planning by scientific experts is ideological: facts and statistical charts by themselves do not speak; they require an interpreter; and his interpretations are based on values that consider and rank competing priorities. Chomsky is the most severe, applying to the scientist-technician the same kind of argument that Marx applied to the owner class: each of these technicians or knowledge makers assumes that his conditions of survival are the conditions necessary for the general good of all mankind (e.g., what's good for social science is good for mankind). This is hardly a nonideological position.

More of this matter will be discussed in Chapter 23. Let us simply note here that in psychology, sociology, anthropology, political science, economics, and so on, we still find the "distortions" of ideological thought running rampant through the pages of so-called science. For example, as we saw on pp. 139–141, notions of equity theory seem rooted more in ideology than in passionless science. For that matter, it is not really clear whether the human sciences can ever detach themselves from an ideological bias. Computers, statistics, and empirical facts —the keynotes of modern society—produce a knowledgeable society but not necessarily one in which ideology is a dead issue. There remains much work for the sociologist of knowledge.

Chapter 16

Sociology of knowledge: some applications

A sociologist of knowledge working in the Mannheimian framework generally conducts an extensive historical analysis. He attempts to trace the origins of particular ideas to certain sociohistorical themes and structures. For example, he might take the orientations Parsons and Shils (1951) termed *collectivistic* or *individualistic*, and relate the prevalence and legitimacy of one or the other of these to certain features of sociohistorical structure.

INDIVIDUALISM AND COLLECTIVISM

The orientations refer to the focus of an individual's loyalties, and the two comprise broad themes within historical periods and socioeconomic structures. A collectivistic orientation legitimizes the cooperative efforts of each for all; team effort is emphasized and individual prominence is played down. A more individualistic orientation emphasizes and legitimizes each person's work for his own gain and prominence.

A cultural example

Benedict's (1934) study of the basic orientations of American Indian tribes pointed out this kind of difference, for example, between the collectivistic Zuñi and the much more individualistic Kwakiutl. Benedict borrowed from

Nietzsche the terms *Apollonian*, referring to a person who spends his life in pursuit of the middle road and commits himself to his people and to tradition, and *Dionysian*, referring to one who pursues personal experiences and excesses. She called the Kwakiutl Dionysian, the pueblo-dwelling Zuñi, Apollonian. As she described the Zuñi, "... those influences that are powerful against tradition are uncongenial and minimized in their institutions, and the greatest of these is individualism" (p. 73). On the other hand, great emphasis on strong individualism, as manifest in the importance of private ownership of personal possessions, is evidenced among the Kwakiutl. In Benedict's descriptions of the Kwakiutl there are repeated references to the importance of such ownership. The Kwakiutl *potlatch* feasts were ceremonies in which property was destroyed as a means of gaining victory over one's rival by shaming him into destroying an equal amount of his possessions. The Dionysian pursuit of individual supremacy, "this will to superiority ... was expressed in every detail of their potlatch exchanges" (pp. 180–181).

Benedict also cited the Dionysian practice of seeking supernatural power in visions, often brought on by severe deprivation or personal tortures, the excesses of which were personally pleasurable to members of Dionysian tribes, who sought the sensory experience for its own sake as well as to outdo others in their tribe. The Apollonian Zuñi also sought visions, but did not relish the personal torture or sensory excesses that might have been used to achieve them: "If ecstasy is not sought by fasting, by torture, or by drugs or alcohol, or under the guise of the vision, neither is it induced in the dance" (p. 84). Zuñi dances were not the frenzied routines or individual boastings in dance so characteristic of other groups.

Example upon example highlight this differential philosophy and way of life. In each cultural practice the Zuñi manifest their Apollonian posture while the Kwakiutl and many other North American Indian groups demonstrate the personal, experiential aspects of the Dionysian. Although they own private property, the Zuñi work their fields together cooperatively and store their food in a common shed. Religious ritual is likewise a collective activity. The Zuñi ideal "is a person of dignity and affability who has never called forth comment from his neighbors" (p. 90). By contrast, the Kwakiutl ideal "was drawn up in terms of these contests [potlatch ceremonies] and all the motivations proper to them were reckoned as virtue" (p. 185). In death as in life the Zuñi practices were the moderate Apollonian ideal devoid of the passionate extremes that characterized the Dionysian's life and his response to death.

Note that these broad cultural themes of private ownership and individual prominence on one hand, communal ownership and minimal prominence for any individual on the other, establish patterns of legitimacy for individual thought and action. A Zuñi who sought personal prominence and gain, for example, was censured; he was as much in violation of the cultural view of what proper behavior should be as a Kwakiutl who decided to give up private ownership and opt out of his tribal potlatch rituals.

In more contemporary societies these basic orientations of collectivism versus individualism can be seen to operate in the distinctions often made between the United States and other Western nations and nations of the Communist bloc, particularly Russia and China. In Russia,

or so we read and hear, a man may be sent to prison for engaging in personal moneymaking activities. He is not supposed to be an entrepreneur. In the United States a person who acts to share his wealth is usually not punished, but is treated with vast amounts of suspicion. In the so-called hippie scene of the late 1960's some young hippies, called Diggers, would offer free food and drink to office workers in San Francisco during their lunch hour; they were met with almost universal suspicion. It was as though the workers said to themselves, "I wonder what he really wants from me." This suspicion suggests how much we are imbued with a noncollectivistic view; anyone who behaves collectivistically is interpreted in individualistic terms. What does he *personally* want from me? A hippie who has the audacity to hand a flower to a "straight" citizen is similarly met with suspicion. Sharing is not one of the prime concepts of an individualistically oriented society.

To the sociologist of knowledge the issue is not which—if either—of these two orientations is correct, but, rather, why it is that persons in one kind of social system believe one to be legitimate and valid in comparison to the other. He attempts to uncover the relationship between these cultural orientations and sociohistorical factors in the society.

The sheer complexity of uncovering such linkages, however, makes a direct test of such cultural themes difficult to undertake; one would have to be a sociologist, political scientist, historian, economist, *and* psychologist. It is possible, however, for someone with less lofty aspirations or training and skill to examine a key component systematically. The question boils down to the possibility of systematically creating different ideologies by manipulating certain features of the social structure. Such an *experimental* test, if it could be done, would be a much more forceful demonstration of the framework of the sociology of knowledge than the usual *correlational* analysis in which one hopes at best to demonstrate a correlation between belief and social structure.

In correlational analyses it is usually difficult to determine the direction of causality. Did the social structure create the ideology or did the ideology create a particular form of social structure? Did some third factor as yet unaccounted for create both ideology and social structure? It is likely that a social structure *both* is made possible by a particular system of beliefs and *in turn* creates or reinforces that system. For example, in Weber's (1930) discussion of the relationship between the Protestant Ethic and the rise of capitalism he argued that the particular ideology of the Protestant Ethic was a requisite condition to the development of the socioeconomic structure of capitalism, which in turn reinforced the ethic. In an experimental approach the investigator hopes to demonstrate that by creating a social structure he can thereby create a particular ideological system.

A Laboratory Approach. An effort in this direction was undertaken by Breer and Locke (1965). Much in the manner of Mannheim, who argued that our thinking evolves out of our collective activity in society rather than out of pure contemplative reasoning, Breer and Locke maintained that individuals who underwent a particular kind of experience working on a task with others would develop attitudes that had features in common with the demands of those tasks. For instance, suppose you and several others are given a series of tasks to perform, and you are allowed to work on each of these tasks once as a group and once alone. Furthermore, suppose you find that group work produces greater success on the tasks than individual work. If all other things are equal, might you not then feel favorable to cooperative group work? Essentially, this is a method employed by Breer and Locke. I shall report only one of their series of seven studies; in basic design the studies all gave subjects differential success experiences with tasks worked on individually or jointly. Attitudinal measures were obtained both before and after the tasks.

In 1962 at Cornell University Breer and Locke used 93 freshman students, 33 in a pretest and 60 in the experiment proper. Subjects were brought into the laboratory in groups of seven or eight. All were asked to complete a "before" questionnaire, and then were told that they would be given some tasks to work on for the afternoon and would be paid $5 for their efforts. They were informed that they would have a chance to try the tasks together as a group and

once again alone. Half the subjects were given tasks that pretesting had indicated could be completed more efficiently by a group of persons in close cooperation than by individuals working alone; the other half were given tasks that could be performed better by individuals working alone.

At the conclusion of their task experience, all subjects completed the "after" questionnaire containing several subtests designed to measure aspects of collectivism versus individualism. Thirteen items measured attitudes toward small work groups; 11 items measured attitudes toward groups in general; 16 items were concerned with the individual's way of life; 10 were concerned with the family; and 10 with fraternities. A sample of these items follows.

Small Work Groups:
   1. Ordinarily I would rather work with others in a small group than work alone.
   2. Members of small work groups should be encouraged to do their work as independently as possible rather than cooperating as members of a tightly knit group.

Groups in General:
   1. In general, the most efficient way to organize a group is to allow each individual to work on his own rather than in close cooperation with other members.
   2. In any group an individual's first responsibilities should be to himself, and only secondarily to his fellow group members.

Family:
   1. Children should be trained to put their obligations to the family above their own personal interests.
   2. Family tasks should be arranged so individual members can do as many things as possible on their own with a minimum of joint cooperation.

Fraternity:
   1. Given the choice, I would rather be an independent than join a fraternity.
   2. Fraternity members should cooperate as much as possible in joint activities involving the fraternity as a whole instead of pursuing their individual interests independently of one another.

Way of Life:
   1. I prefer a way of life which calls for cooperation among men rather than independent achievement.
   2. Societies should encourage their members to be more concerned with independent achievement and less concerned with group cooperation.

Data analyses examined the direction of change in the before-after questionnaire responses for subjects who experienced successful group work in contrast to those who experienced successful individual work. Breer and Locke report statistically significant differences in the predicted direction for all five attitude areas. Subjects who underwent the successful collectivistic task experience showed a change in their attitudes toward greater collectivism when compared with the change toward greater individualism on the part of subjects who experienced the successful individualistic task experience. As we might expect, the greatest differences were obtained for items that were most closely associated with the actual task experience, small work groups, and groups in general.

As the authors carefully note, the changes in attitudes they produced involve a generally *nonpersuasive* change technique. In a typical laboratory study of attitude change an experimenter may make obvious efforts to induce a subject to change his attitude by offering rewards, threatening punishments, using prestigeful figures, arguing persuasively, and so on. In this study, however, the change produced seems to be very much in line with our common, everyday kinds of learning experience; the success-failure feedback we receive can shape our behavior and eventually lead us to generate more abstract principles or ideologies. When we find greater success working individually than with others, we are likely both to continue to prefer individual work and to generate an abstract principle, possibly even a set of justifications, opting for individualism over collectivism.

What Breer and Locke offer us is a systematically controlled approach to studying certain derivations from the sociology of knowledge. Their data indicate how an individual working within a particular kind of social structure that provides differential experiences of success or failure may generate a system of beliefs or attitudes supportive of that system. A society of many such individuals may develop a particular ideology in which each person's individual experience is merged with others; each reinforces the others to develop a firm ideological

system that legitimizes and declares as valid individualism or collectivism. To be sure, it is a huge leap from the Breer and Locke laboratory out into that inordinately complex real world; nevertheless, their study allows us to leap less gingerly than before.

ENTREPRENEURS AND BUREAUCRATS

As most of us know, the family as a social group does not exist in isolation but, like other small groups, is intimately related to the society of which it is a part. One of the systems of the surrounding society that has an important effect on the organization of the family is the economic system. Several years ago a psychologist (Miller) and a sociologist (Swanson) examined the implications of this relationship between a society's economic system and the organization of the family (Miller & Swanson, 1958). Their theory falls within the purview of the sociology of knowledge in that it relates certain ideological outcomes to structural aspects of the society as mediated by the family.

Family integration setting

The focus of the Miller-Swanson theory is on the kinds of child-rearing practice and husband-wife relationship that occur as a function of the economic relation between the family and the larger society. They argue that there are two major types of what they call *family settings:* one reflects an *entrepreneurial* economic situation, the other, a *bureaucratic* situation.

The entrepreneur competes individually in the open marketplace; his success determines the family's status within the society. The bureaucrat succeeds in an organization either through seniority of position and management-labor negotiations (blue-collar) or by presenting a good front and by demonstrating, at least partially through his family relationships, a smooth and happy interpersonal pattern (white collar). An interesting laboratory experiment conducted by Berkowitz and Friedman (1967) offers us a view of some ideological consequences of this distinction between entrepreneurs and bureaucrats. Recall our earlier discussion of equity theory, or the concept of distributive justice, in which we suggested that equity notions are founded on the Protestant Ethic's ideology of receiving in proportion to what one has given (pp. 139 ff.). Berkowitz and Friedman reasoned that an ideology of this sort should operate differentially as a function of an individual's entrepreneurial or bureaucratic family background. They suggested that entrepreneurs, being more involved with a money economy and its emphasis on proportional giving and getting, should operate more in accordance with an equity notion as compared with bureaucrats. This latter group, they argue, "... growing up in a society prescribing that people should help those who are dependent upon them should therefore be more willing than middle-class entrepreneurs to assist other persons in need of aid regardless of the benefits he can derive or has obtained from the situation" (p. 219).

Berkowitz created an experimental situation in which high-school-student subjects received varying degrees of help from a partner and later had the opportunity to reciprocate or not. They were informed that the subject who was most effective in supervising his partner's work would receive a $10 gift certificate. In the *high-help* condition they were told that the partner had worked very well and thus had helped them a great deal; in the *low-help* condition, the experimenter indicated how little the partner had done in response to supervision. The second part of the experiment provided subjects the opportunity to reciprocate through their own work efforts, with someone else supervising. Half of the subjects were led to believe that their supervisor was the same person who had just been their partner.

The key analysis of the study concerned the degree to which subjects reciprocated in the second part of the experiment as a function of their entrepreneurial or bureaucratic background (determined by father's occupation and organization size). The prediction was that those from entrepreneurial backgrounds should reciprocate more in the high-help condition than when the partner provided little help, and that the bureaucratic youngsters, by contrast, would not be so greatly influenced by the level

of help they received. Results generally confirmed these expectations.

Achievement and entrepreneurship

For the most part, other efforts to relate family integration setting to ideological or behavioral outcomes have turned to personality variables rather than to the broad social and political ideologies of special interest to Mannheimian sociologists of knowledge. McClelland's (1961) work on the need for achievement is suggestive. Although personality variables and ideological values are not the same order of concept, it is reasonable to adopt the working assumption that ideology and values influence the factors that psychologists have studied as personality. In fact in certain areas—the need for achievement is one—there is reason to believe that the psychological need is itself a reflection of a broader cultural or subcultural (social-class) value or ideology. In particular, some sociologists (e.g., Kahl, 1965; Scanzoni, 1967) have argued that achievement values and achievement goals are subcultural phenomena and vary by social status.

In *The Achieving Society* McClelland presents interesting data relating need for achievement to the economic development of a society. He selected children's readers dating from 1925 from several nations, scored these readers for the existence of achievement imagery and themes, and gave each nation a need-achievement score based on this analysis. Even this methodology, note, reflects more of an ideological or value framework than the usual kind of individual technique employed to assess the need for achievement as a personality variable. As an index of the nation's level of economic development McClelland selected electrical output, assuming that more technologically advanced countries would require greater energy output. He was thus able to correlate the existence of achievement themes in children's readers of the past with actual economic development in the present. His results indicated a positive correlation; nations with children's readers emphasizing achievement in 1925 were nations that 25 years later in 1950 manifested a high level of economic development. He argues that children reared at that time developed a high need for achievement, which in turn predisposed them to take the kinds of risk in capital investment required for surges in economic development. When these risk-takers grew up they became the entrepreneurs of the society, accounting for its advanced economics.

McClelland claims to be able to show how peaks and troughs of economic development can be correlated with peaks and troughs in achievement imagery; a peak in achievement imagery in children's readers in a society is associated with a peak in economic development *years later* in that society; an achievement trough in readers in turn is followed by a *later* economic trough.

McClelland (1958) presents some additional data that indicate a relationship between high need achievement and so-called entrepreneurial behavior (risk-taking) on laboratory tasks. High achievers prefer to take moderate risks when the outcome is of the 50–50 sort. By contrast, low achievers (Atkinson calls them high-fear-of-failure types: 1964, Chapter 9; Atkinson & Litwin, 1960) prefer to take extreme risks when the outcome probabilities are either near certainty (e.g., 90 percent chance of success) or near impossibility (e.g., 10 percent chance of success).

McClelland (1965) has also uncovered a relationship between need achievement and a preference for entrepreneurial occupational position. In a longitudinal study he examined the occupational choices of Wesleyan University students who had been measured for need achievement in 1947. About 14 years later, when they varied in age from 31 to 46, all had presumably settled into a more or less stable occupational choice. Their occupations were classified as entrepreneurial or nonentrepreneurial; for example, a job was classified as entrepreneurial if there was individual responsibility for *initiating* decisions rather than just making decisions when presented with problems; there was individual responsibility for decisions and their effects without supervision or committee review; there was more objective feedback concerning the success or failure of decisions; and the job entailed some risk or

challenge because errors were potentially observable. Data from this study indicated that 83 percent of those classified as entrepreneurs had been measured high in need achievement 14 years earlier, whereas 79 percent of the non-entrepreneurs in business had been low in need achievement. This is a striking finding, and an effort to cross-validate it (McClelland, 1965) generally confirmed the results.

I would do a real disservice to the field not to mention, if only briefly, the cost side of the ledger outlined by McClelland's theory. Rudin (1965) correlated the McClelland themes of achievement *not* with the value-positive outcome of economic advancement, but rather with the value-negative outcomes of societal sickness. He measured societal sickness by societal death rates from "psychological" causes: murder, suicide, ulcers, hypertension, and alcoholism. Although he found no significant correlation between 1925 achievement imagery and deaths in 1950 caused by alcoholism, murder, or suicide, Rudin's results show a positive correlation between achievement imagery in 1925 and deaths in 1950 from ulcers and high blood pressure (e.g., hypertension). An achieving society, it seems, pays the price for its achievement.

Conceptual note: Circular causality

It is of value to pause at this point and examine two questions the preceding material suggests. Do ideology or personality-level variables influence social structure and the economic system? Do the social structure and the economic system influence ideology and personality-level variables? The initial question, based on a *personal-causal model*, is answered affirmatively both by McClelland and by Weber in his seminal work, *The Protestant Ethic and the Spirit of Capitalism*. Their argument essentially is that a person's system of values (e.g., the Protestant Ethic) or his personality (e.g., *n*-achievement) determines the structure of the society's economic system. It is to be noted that McClelland's work adds to Weber's thesis by making the family the mediating link. Presumably the Protestant Ethic creates a family context in which children are reared to possess the appropriate entrepreneurial qualities, including especially a high need for achievement.

The second question, based on a *social-causal model*, is also answered affirmatively by such persons as Marx, Mannheim, and others involved with the sociology of knowledge, and by the Miller-Swanson thesis. Here ideology and personality-level variables are derived from a socioeconomic fact. But is there a real contradiction between these two viewpoints? I think not. In Figure 16.1 the models are represented. The ingredients in (c) are represented in terms of a circle rather than in a linear, cause-effect chain; this circular representation is intentional. In a model of this sort the point at which you break into the circle and call one thing a cause and the other an effect is somewhat arbitrary.

This model is perhaps most simply seen as it applies in a dyadic encounter. A couple with a marital problem comes for counseling. You, the counselor, place them together in a situation where you can observe their interaction. As you watch them over a period of time you note

that the wife keeps nagging her husband, finding constant reason to criticize his every deed; even his *inaction* seems to wear on her, so she nags him more intensely. The husband's response to this nagging is a tendency to withdraw further into a passive or submissive pose. After a while you break in and talk with them. The wife says she keeps nagging because "he just sits there so damn passively; he never gets up and does anything." The husband maintains that his withdrawal is only a defense against her incessant nagging. You see the situation as one big vicious circle: husband withdraws because wife nags; wife nags because husband withdraws. Just what causes what? Clearly, in an arrangement of this sort, to pull out one factor as the cause and the other as the effect is not only arbitrary, but, worse, entirely misses the point: each causes each.

In Figure 16.1 I intend the circular representation (c) to convey the idea that each component adopted as causal in (a) and (b) enters into the societal melting pot as *both* cause *and*

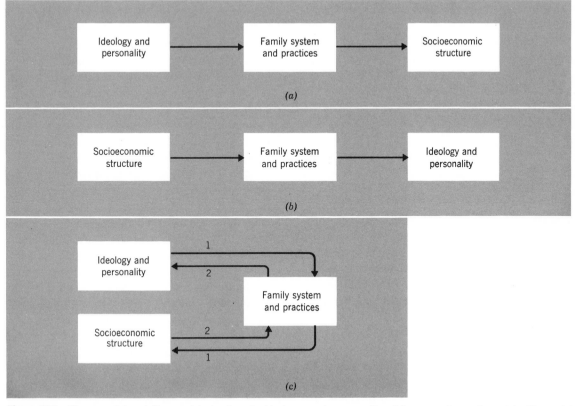

Figure 16.1 Three models relating social structure to ideology and personality: (a) personal-causal model; (b) social-causal model (c) circular-causal model

effect. Each element feeds back into the other in much the same manner as in our family example. Thus ideology and personality affect the family system and its socialization practices and in turn affect the structure of the society, *and in addition* are affected by the society's socioeconomic structure; and so on around. The congruence between these several models occurs at the family link. In all views the family mediates between the socioeconomic structure and personality-ideological outcomes.

Keep the diagram in mind, but recall that the links between knowledge or ideology on one hand and social-structural factors on the other are of special interest to the sociologist of knowledge. He would be most concerned, for example, with how a change in the socioeconomic structure from entrepreneurial to bureaucratic induces a change in ideology and perhaps personality. If a society becomes increasingly bureaucraticized in order to deal more efficiently with the complexities of advanced technology, this should produce a particular kind of social character well suited to think in terms required by this bureaucratic living. If an entrepreneurial system demands and produces the social characteristics of high-*n*-achievers and adventuresome risk-takers, a bureaucratic system may very well demand and produce a social character more concerned with security than with taking risky chances.

Need achievement of course, is only one of the variables of personality and ideology that may be seen as outcomes of a particular entrepreneurial or bureaucratic social system. As the Berkowitz work suggests, another outcome may very well be a less equity-oriented personal philosophy. The kind of other-directedness of which Riesman (1950) spoke is yet another important outcome factor. If, as Miller and Swanson indicate, success in a bureaucracy demands a concern with good front and smooth interpersonal relationships, in contrast with the more inner-directed qualities demanded of the entrepreneur, then to the extent to which a social system moves toward increasing bureaucratization, we would expect an increase in over-all other-directedness. These points are raised at this time primarily to indicate the direction a sociology of knowledge would have us pursue.

REACTIONS TO DEVIATION

The sociologist of knowledge tells us that we live in different worlds as a function of our locations within the various structures and substructures of a society. These worlds define the normal, the usual, and the proper, and often the deviant, the improper, the excessive. One area of growing interest to social-scientific investigators concerns the relationship between an individual's location in a social structure and his attitudes and reactions toward deviance or the unusual.

An early effort of apparently enduring relevance was a study by Stouffer (1955) during the McCarthy era of the 1950's. This era, as many will recall, was named for that U. S. Senator who spent much time, before he was eventually denounced, undertaking Communist witch hunts the likes of which this nation had not seen since Salem. During that period a study entitled *Communism, Conformity, and Civil Liberties* was a natural.

Stouffer examined the relation between various social-structural variables and attitudes toward dissent and political deviance. For example, he made inquiries concerning feelings about allowing a Communist speaker in a community, a Socialist speaker, an atheist, and so on, and feelings about having the local library stock books written by known Communists. Stouffer's interest was not simply in what people felt about each of these matters, but more specifically how their attitudes related to such structural factors as their leadership position in the community, their age, and their education. His results indicated several striking differences in attitude toward political "deviants" between community leaders and the general population: whereas 51 percent of the leadership would permit a Communist to speak, the corresponding figure was only 27 percent for the general population; whereas 84 percent of the leaders felt a Socialist should be permitted to speak, only 58 percent of the general population agreed.

Stouffer computed a composite *index of civil libertarian tolerance* by combining his several items. He found that persons who were most tolerant of political deviance were *younger* (47 percent of those in their twenties compared to

18 percent highly tolerant in their sixties), *better educated* (66 percent of college graduates versus 16 percent with grade-school education), and came from *urban* as compared with *rural* settings.

Attitudes toward political deviance are only one of a class of attitudes that can be examined in relationship to position in the social structure. For another example, how are attitudes toward *mental disorder* influenced by structural factors? It should be clearly understood that views about mental health and illness, even in a society like the United States where such views are built on mass media and often enlightened information, can and do vary as a function of the viewer's position in the social structure. A man who is highly educated, perhaps even a community leader, may hold attitudes about who is "sick" and what should be done to the "sick person" that are unlike those of a less-educated, working-class person.

One view of this matter, which seems to conflict with Stouffer's findings on tolerance, claims that the *lower* socioeconomic classes are more tolerant of deviant behavior. This view is propounded by Hollingshead and Redlich in their classic study, *Social Class and Mental Illness* (1958). This apparent discrepancy may result from a difference between responses (i.e., attitudes) to political deviation as compared with mental deviation. On the other hand, it is also possible that the lower classes are really intolerant about mental deviation but define mental illness differently than do members of higher socioeconomic classes. If the latter is true, the lower classes may be very intolerant, but only of behaviors that *their* norms define as deviant.

A more systematic manner of studying differences in conceptions and treatment of mental disorder involves the presentation of cases to persons of different social backgrounds. Star (1955) developed a listing of six psychiatric cases.

1. *Paranoia.* I'm thinking of a man—let's call him Frank Jones—who is very suspicious; he doesn't trust anybody, and he's sure that everybody is against him. Sometimes he thinks that people he sees on the street are talking about him or following him around. A couple of times, now, he has beaten up men who didn't even know him. The other night he began to curse his wife terribly; then he hit her and threatened to kill her because, he said, she was working against him, too, just like everyone else.

2. *Simple schizophrenia.* Now here's a young woman in her twenties, let's call her Betty Smith . . . she has never had a job, and she doesn't seem to want to go out and look for one. She is a very quiet girl, she doesn't talk much to anyone—even her own family—and she acts like she is afraid of people, especially young men her own age. She won't go out with anyone, and whenever someone comes to visit her family, she stays in her own room until they leave. She just stays by herself and daydreams all the time, and shows no interest in anything or anybody.

3. *Anxiety neurosis.* Here's another kind of man; we can call him George Brown. He has a good job and is doing pretty well at it. Most of the time he gets along all right with people, but he is always very touchy and he always loses his temper quickly if things aren't going his way, or if people find fault with him. He worries a lot about little things, and he seems to be moody and unhappy all the time. Everything is going along all right for him, but he can't sleep nights, brooding about the past, and worrying about things that *might* go wrong.

4. *Alcoholism.* How about Bill Williams? He never seems to be able to hold a job very long, because he drinks so much. Whenever he has money in his pocket, he goes on a spree; he stays out till all hours drinking, and never seems to care what happens to his wife and children. Sometimes he feels very bad about the way he treats his family; he begs his wife to forgive him and promises to stop drinking but he always goes off again.

5. *Compulsive-phobic behavior.* Here's a different sort of girl; let's call her Mary White. She seems happy and cheerful; she's pretty, has a good job, and is engaged to marry a nice young man. She has loads of friends; everybody likes her, and she's always busy and active. However, she just can't leave the house without going back to see whether she left the gas stove lit or not. And she always goes back again just to make sure she locked the door. And one other thing about her: she's afraid to ride up and down in elevators; she just won't go any place where she'd have to ride in an elevator to get there.

6. *Juvenile character disorder.* Now, I'd like to describe a twelve-year-old boy, Bobby Grey. He's bright enough and in good health, and he comes from a comfortable home. But his father and mother have found out that he's been telling lies for a long time now. He's been stealing things from stores, and taking money from his mother's purse, and he has been playing truant, staying away from school whenever he can. His parents are very upset about the way he acts, but he pays no attention to them.

What happens if these six cases are presented to a variety of samples of persons, and each is asked to indicate whether he feels the person described has some kind of mental illness, how severe each illness is, and finally, his view of just what kind of action should be taken in each case? Star's data indicated that, in 1950 at least, only the paranoid case was seen as mentally ill by a majority of a national sample. In the 1960's Dohrenwend and Chin-Shong (1967) used these same six cases and reported several differences between their data and those initially uncovered by Star. See Table 16.1. One of the first things the data reveal

Table 16.1 Percentage reporting case as mental illness

Case	1950 Data, U.S. Sample	1960's, Cross-Section	1960's, Leaders
Paranoia	75%	90%	100%
Simple schizophrenia	34	67	72
Alcoholism	29	41	63
Anxiety neurosis	18	31	49
Juvenile character disorder	16	41	51
Compulsive phobia	7	24	40

is a change in sophistication about mental illness over the 10-year period. Recalling that the cases are descriptive of psychiatrists' conceptions of illness, the data indicate a general movement toward greater congruence between the public's view and the psychiatric view. Perhaps the mass media and mental-health education programs have an effect after all.

A second finding of relevance to our immediate concern, however, is the difference between the cross-section's and the community leaders' views. Leaders included state senators and assemblymen, judges, police officers, school principals, businessmen, clergymen, and heads of community-service organizations. Almost three-fourths of these leaders were college graduates; many had done graduate work as

well. The data reveal a closer correspondence between the psychiatric view of illness and the leaders' view than between the psychiatric view and that of the general cross-section.

It appears that an important factor in accounting for the definition of a given behavior pattern as mental illness is educational level. A separate analysis to check out this point was undertaken by Dohrenwend and Chin-Shong (1967), who found that the higher the educational level, the closer the correspondence with the psychiatric definition of illness. For example, whereas 60 percent of those with 16 or more years of schooling saw something wrong with *all six* cases, only approximately 29 percent of those with 11 or less years of education did so. Analyses of ethnic-group views added to the picture, leading the authors to conclude, "...much of the behavior viewed by members of the mental health professions as serious departures from norms is not seen this way by large segments of the community—especially the lower-class members of the most disadvantaged ethnic groups" (p. 427).

So far it appears that what is defined as mental illness does vary as a function of position in the structure of society. The next question concerns the treatment of persons seen to be mentally ill. Are those of lower educational and general social-class background more or less tolerant in their view of how those they define as ill should be handled? In the one case (the paranoid) on which there seems to be general agreement in all classes and educational levels about the presence of mental illness it is possible to see how community standing and educational level contribute to views concerning the handling of the illness.

If the recommendation of mental hospitalization represents a lesser tolerance of the deviance than, for example, recommendation for outpatient treatment, we note that the cross-section and those of lower education are less tolerant of the paranoid than are the community leaders. Whereas about 61 percent of the cross-section favored hospitalization of the paranoid, only 47 percent of the community leaders agreed to this form of treatment. Likewise, whereas only 47 percent of those with 16 or more years of schooling favored hospitalization, the figures are 85 percent for those with seven years or fewer and 61 percent for those with eight to 11 years. It is a paradox, at least regarding treatment of the paranoid case, that the psychiatric recommendation is also for hospitalization!

As one further measure of toleration of mental deviation, Dohrenwend and Chin-Shong presented their subjects with a social-distance scale. Table 16.2 shows the scale items and the responses of the leaders and the cross-section. If we take social distance as a measure of toleration, it seems apparent from these data that community leaders adopted less distance (i.e., were more tolerant) from former mental patients than the cross-section sample. Even within the cross-section, however, years of schooling made a difference. As with the other findings, the greater the number of years of schooling, the less the social distance. In fact, whereas college graduates among the cross-section, like the community leaders, would accept a former mental patient in a marriage or child-care situation, those of lower educational levels were unwilling even to allow the former patient any closer than minimal entry into their community.

From these data we can conclude that higher-status groups tend to be more tolerant about mental deviation than lower-status groups, especially when we consider the kinds of deviance that *both* high- and low-status groups define as serious. However, those of lower status tend to have a narrower range of definition of serious mental illness, and so may *appear* to be more tolerant.

Education and Tolerance. Thus there appears to be a consistency between Stouffer's findings concerning toleration of political deviation and findings concerning toleration of mental deviance. Recall that a key ingredient in both is educational level; it seems that education is one of the essential social-structural factors influencing the kind of ideological outcome of concern to us here: reactions to deviance. The greater the number of years of formal education, in general, the greater the tolerance of deviation.

Stouffer argued that education had a *freeing* effect in that it placed an individual in contact

Table 16.2 Percentage willing to accept an ex-mental-hospital patient on seven social distance items: leaders and cross-section samples

Social-Distance Item	Response	Leaders ($N=87$)	Cross-Section ($N=150$)
It would be wise to discourage former patients of a mental hospital from entering your neighborhood.	Disagree	94.3%	82.0%
It would be unwise to encourage the close friendship of someone who had been in a mental hospital.	Disagree	89.7	72.0
You would be willing to sponsor a former patient of a mental hospital for membership in your favorite club or society.	Agree	86.2	67.3
If you were a personnel manager, you would be willing to hire a former patient of a mental hospital.	Agree	85.1	62.0
If you were responsible for renting apartments in your building, you would hesitate to rent living quarters to someone who had been in a mental hospital.	Disagree	86.2	54.0
You should strongly discourage your children from marrying someone who was formerly in a mental hospital.	Disagree	39.1	37.3
It would be unwise to trust a former mental hospital patient with your children.	Disagree	55.2	26.7

with a variety of people who had a variety of points of view. In Mannheimian logic, as we have seen, it is out of this potential clash of disparate viewpoints that one can gain a sense of perspective, and this relational perspective yields a greater toleration of differences.

Trent and Craise (1967) report a study in

which a national sample of high-school students were tested for general intellectual disposition as well as for their degree of openness and flexibility (i.e., nonauthoritarian thinking). When measured in 1959 the seniors scored approximately the same on all of these standardized psychological scales. Four years later, when some had completed college and others had gone directly to work, the group differences were extensive. In almost every case those who had gone on to college became more intellectually disposed, more open and flexible. In other words, they became more nonauthoritarian and more generally tolerant. What is of even greater interest is the discovery that those who went into employment actually became *less* tolerant over the same four-year period!

Before we get too excited about these results, recall our earlier discussions of the Schachter and the Sampson and Brandon experiments (pp. 126–129). When their worlds of social reality were threatened by a deviant attitude (Schachter) or a deviant characterization (Sampson & Brandon), college students responded with rejection. Without comparable experimental data from other subject populations we cannot gain insights into this finding. Perhaps other populations would have been more severe in their rejection of the deviant. Or perhaps most persons react negatively when their own little world, up close and personal rather than out there and abstractly distant, is brought into confrontation with differences. It is one matter to answer a survey questionnaire with socially liberal attitudes; it is another matter to act on such attitudes. (See p. 326 ff. for a discussion of the discrepancy between attitudes and behavior.)

Chapter 17

Top down versus bottom up: perspectives from the master-slave relationship

By now it must be apparent that the perspective of a sociology of knowledge has an extremely wide application. There is one further area into which we should poke our inquisitive noses before concluding and then moving on. Realize, however, that this is not the end of the story, or of this approach, but just another chapter, often neglected.

The view of the world from the top and the view from beneath are not the same. This statement is valid whether we are talking about organizations, social institutions, or the entire society. In particular, I would argue that these views vary when the top-to-bottom relationship is one of master to slave. The master-slave terminology denotes a situation in which one person or group occupies a position of near-total authority over a group of other persons. This relationship is noted most clearly in historical examples in the United States and some other nations; the analogy to the contemporary scene, however, has received increasing application, especially by militants in minority racial groups (see, e.g., Cleaver, 1968).

The history of what has been called America's "peculiar institution" (Stampp, 1964) of slavery marks one of the bleak points in the history of mankind. In the United States especially, the peculiarity of slavery is found in its obvious contradiction with the avowed ethic, as declared by the founders of the Republic. In his classic work on race relations in the United States Myrdal (1944) noted and carefully documented what he called *An American Dilemma*, the discrepancy between the values of the nation and its treatment of its minority citizens. If *all* men are "created equal and endowed by their creator with certain inalienable rights," how could anyone account for slavery in pre-Civil-War America? Today, how can anyone account for the lowly social position of the minorities?

Thomas Jefferson is a significant case in point. Jefferson was a slave holder, yet he was one of the framers of the basic values of the American creed. Consciously or not, Jefferson's pained solution to his dilemma was to provide an ideology that justified unequal treatment. Although he seemed to abhor slavery and wish all men to be free, some of his writings indicate lingering doubts concerning the fitness of the black man for the rigors of freedom. For Jefferson, nature had created a distinction between blacks and whites:

"Negroes seemed to 'require less sleep,' for 'after hard labour through the day,' they were 'induced by the slightest amusements to sit up till midnight, or later' though aware that they must rise at 'first dawn.' They were 'at least as brave' as whites, and 'more adventuresome.' 'But . . . this may perhaps proceed from a want of forethought, which prevents their seeing a danger till it be present.' . . . Negroes were 'more ardent,' their griefs 'transient.' 'In general . . . their existence appears to participate more of sensation than reflection. To this must be ascribed their disposition to sleep when abstracted from their diversions, and unemployed in labour. An animal whose body is at rest, and who does not reflect, must be disposed to sleep of course' " (quoted in Jordan, 1968, p. 436).

Jefferson's ideology, very influential both in his day and in the periods that followed, also stressed a basic intellectual difference between blacks and whites.

" 'Comparing them by their faculties of memory, reason, and imagination, it appears to me, that in memory they are equal to the whites; in reason much inferior, as I think one could scarcely be found capable of tracing and comprehending the investigations of Euclid; and that in imagination they are dull, tasteless, and anomalous. It would be unfair to follow them to Africa for this investigation. We will consider them here, on the same stage with the whites, and where the facts are not apocryphal on which a judgment is to be formed. It will be right to make great allowances for the differences of condition, of education, of conversation, of the sphere in which they move. Many millions of them have been brought to, and born in America. Most of them indeed have been confined to tillage, to their homes and their own society; yet many have been so situated, they might have availed themselves of the conversation of their masters; many have been brought up to the handicraft arts, and from that circumstance have always been associated with the whites. Some have been liberally educated, and all have lived in countries where the arts and sciences are cultivated to a considerable degree, and have had before their eyes samples of the best works from abroad. . . . But never yet could I find that a black had uttered a thought above the level of plain narration; never see even an elementary trait of painting or sculpture' " (Jordan, 1968, pp. 436–437).

Although Jefferson's account has hints of a societal or environmentalist position, attributing the mental capacity of the black to his condition of living under slavery, he was not able to take this position very far. Rather he argued for a more basic (i.e., innate) difference in mental ability between the races. As Jordan indicates, ". . . he went to great lengths to prove that the Negroes' lack of talent did not stem from their condition" (p. 438).

Jefferson was not alone among the "heroes" of U.S. history to maintain an ideological separation of blacks and whites. Shocking as it may be, Abraham Lincoln in an 1858 debate with Douglas boldly declared,

" '. . . I will say . . . that there is a physical difference between the white and black races which I believe will ever forbid the two races living together on terms of social and political equality. . . . I as much as any other man am in favor of having the superior position assigned to the white race' " (quoted in van den Berghe, 1967, p. 79).

Oh, where have all our idols gone!

If the ideology maintains that there is an intrinsic difference between whites and blacks, is the American dilemma not thereby made easier to tolerate? That is, this view of the master-slave relationship from the top down, from the perspective of the masters, eases the burden of those who carry on the institution of slavery in the midst of a nation that declares all men to be free.

Not all men were satisfied to accept a Jeffersonian-type justification. Some were directly at odds with him, maintaining that any apparent intellectual dullness the Negro displayed was a function of the miserable state of his existence rather than of any innate differences between the races. (See Jordan, 1968, for a further discussion.) Still others sought to bolster the environmentalist position through tortured logic, erroneous facts, and rather disastrous conclusions. Rush, for example, likened the Negro's skin color to a disease akin to leprosy:

" '. . . all the claims of superiority of the whites over the blacks, on account of their color, are founded alike in ignorance and inhumanity. If the color of the Negroes can be the effect of a disease, instead of inviting us to tyrannize over them, it should entitle them to a double portion of our humanity, for disease all over the world has always been the signal for immediate and universal compassion' " (in Jordan, 1968, p. 519).

Another aspect of the dilemma facing the master is the matter of a slave rebellion. If one assumes that all men desire freedom and thereby are prone to rebel against oppression, it follows that slaves must have this desire and the corresponding potential for rebellion. Paradoxically, however, it is possible for masters to develop and maintain an ideology in which the slaves are seen as happy and contented; it follows from this view that the Negro, rather than desiring freedom, must have an instinctive tendency to obedience; it follows but one pained step further that any rebellion or dissatisfaction that occurs must be the work of "outside agitators."

The contented-Negro ideology was held by most whites in pre-Civil-War America. Negro slaves were regarded as children who needed the paternal guidance of a kindly master to keep them in line and out of trouble:

"Negroes were regarded as immature, irresponsible, unintelligent, physically strong, happy-go-lucky, musically gifted, grown-up children. They were treated at best like a 'stern but just' father would deal with backward children, at worst like special and expensive species of livestock whose labor was to be exploited for the greatest economic gain" (van den Berghe, p. 83).

And just as children were expected to treat their elders with respect, so too the slaves were expected to be submissive and respectful. They were addressed by first names, or called "boy," or sometimes "uncle" or "aunt." In turn they were to keep a happy, childlike countenance turned up in obedience to the paternal and caring masters.

So deeply entrenched is this ideology that my own college history textbook (used in the mid-1950's) contains the following revealing passage:

"The lot of the slave on the southern plantation was ordinarily quite tolerable. . . . By and large, the conditions of his life represented a distinct advance over the lot that would have befallen him had he remained in Africa.

"Indeed, the slaves got much positive enjoyment out of life. Extremely gregarious, they delighted in the community life of the plantation, and on special occasions were permitted to indulge in picnics, barbecues, and various other types of celebration. They loved to sing and dance, and contributed ideas

along both lines that the whites, at least of a later generation, were not too proud to appropriate. They were generally blessed with a keen sense of humor; they rarely fretted, when treated well, because of their state of bondage; and they were often deeply devoted to their master and his family" (Hicks, 1943, p. 291).

Given this master's-eye view of slaves, any sign of discontent or, heaven forbid, any move toward rebellion, could only be understood in terms of an outside-agitator theory. Adults with the malleable minds of young children, instinctively obedient and easily led astray, could presumably fall easy victim to those whose interest would best be served by a slave rebellion.

That same college history textbook, reporting on the impact of the Nat Turner slave uprising of 1831, says, ". . . the incident served to unsettle the good relations between many southern masters and their slaves for years to come" (pp. 292–293). What is revealing about this analysis of slave rebellion is that it takes the ideological perspective from the top down—that is, the master's perspective—and fails to understand the natural and reasonable response of an oppressed group. In the ideology of the master, "our blacks never had it so good; their rebellion just serves to unsettle a pleasant situation." Pleasant for whom? For the masters, of course! From the perspective of the man on the bottom, unsettling the oppressive relationship is just what he seeks.

Note that somewhat the same top-down reasoning occurred during the turbulent 1960's, with regard both to black urban revolts and student demonstrations; the contemporary rationale for Negro unrest and campus turmoil cited the "outside agitators" of Communism. Moreover, during the slave period in the Old South, outside agitators were said to have come from the North to make trouble; during the civil rights demonstrations of the early 1960's in the New South, similar pronouncements could be heard. Once again some felt that the only reason for "our colored" to get so riled up must be those Northerners down here to make trouble. Not everyone in contemporary society maintains this perspective. Although some hang on to the obedient-child view of the ignorant, happy-go-lucky black man who is stirred up only by intrusive outsiders, others take a more environmentalist stance and view blacks as oppressed victims of a racist society; they interpret black rebellion as an understandable response of oppressed persons who need little "outside" motivation to rebel.

We also find these competing perspectives on the campus scene. The collegians of today are viewed by some in much the same way the masters viewed their slaves: impressionable young children needing the careful guidance of a strong but compassionate father. Thus when collegians revolt it is understood in terms of outside troublemakers, say, Communist professors who have led the young innocents astray. In the alternative perspective the collegian is considered mature, sensitive, and critical, neither extremely impressionable nor plastically malleable. In fact, he is undoubtedly more critical in his thinking and thereby more resistant to propaganda than the average citizen. When *that* young citizen revolts, on and off his campus, we must look for the conditions of society and of his institution that create the conditions for dissatisfaction and change-oriented rebellion (see Chapter 23).

ON COLONIALISM

So far I have been discussing a kind of master-slave relationship in which the former group adopts an ideology that legitimizes and supports the exploitative nature of the relationship. I could as well have taken examples from the U.S. period of westward expansion, with the consequent master-slave relationship involving the American Indian. Here, as in Negro slavery in the South, the defining group of masters established an ideology that supported its program of grabbing and settling. As Carmichael and Hamilton (1967), two contemporary representatives of the black liberation struggle, note, "In the wars between the white settlers and the 'Indians,' a battle won by the Cavalry was described as a 'victory.' The 'Indians' ' triumphs, however, were 'massacres' " (p. 36).

With the mass media and all too many history books adopting the perspective of the white settlers, the Indians came to be seen as un-Christian savages, hell-bent on the senseless destruction of innocent whites, whom they massacred at whim, collecting scalps as prizes of their pagan battles. Few, however, pause to structure history from the perspective of the Indian, whose land was being invaded ruthlessly by white settlers. When the master writes the history the Indian looks like a savage who needs to be tamed by beneficent, compassionate whites; but in the Indians' own texts any success in fighting off those invaders of his homeland could only be recognized for the victory that it was.

Recall for a moment the British view of the American Revolution as a riotous uprising of some dangerously foolish colonists; compare this with the American view, which sees the same actions as "our fight for freedom." Enough said.

The relationship between master and slave has been explored even more broadly in a fascinating and personal account by Memmi, *The Colonizer and the Colonized* (1967). The colonial relationship has many of the same qualities as the master-slave relationship. The European colonist enters a colony and adopts a status within it that places him in a power-superior position to the natives. Memmi's analysis is concerned with North Africa around the time of the Algerian revolt that led to the departure of the French from North Africa. He notes the near universality with which colonizers maintain the view that the colonized is characterized by his laziness:

"It [the trait of laziness] seems to receive unanimous approval of colonizers from Liberia to Laos, via the Maghreb. It is easy to see to what extent this description is useful. It occupies an important place in the dialectics exalting the colonizer and humbling the colonized. Furthermore, it is economically fruitful.

"Nothing could better justify the colonizer's privileged position than his industry, and nothing could better justify the colonized's destitution than his indolence. The mythical portrait of the colonized therefore includes an unbelievable laziness, and that of the colonizer, a virtuous taste for action. At the same time the colonizer suggests that employing the colonized is not very profitable, thereby authorizing his unreasonable wages" (p. 79).

Memmi goes on to note that this trait of laziness is imputed not only to the colonized laborer, but also to those among the colonized who are professionals: professors, doctors, engineers, and so on; the colonizer tends to see laziness in the colonized as an innate endowment. How similar this perspective is to that held by some masters during the slave period in the United States, and even more similar to the views some whites hold today about "those shiftless blacks."

Assuming that the colonized is lazy, perhaps even weak and childlike, the colonizer then sees himself as serving a positive function when he takes over the role of protector. A person so lazy, so weak, so irresponsible could never make it in a position of management; the colonizer must take care to save for himself all managerial functions. Furthermore, once the colonizer maintains that the colonized is a backward person tending toward thievery and violence, he has justified the use of a strong, even repressive police force. As Memmi put it, "After all, he must defend himself against the dangerous foolish acts of the irresponsible, and at the same time—what meritorious concern!—protect him against himself!" (p. 82).

If the colonizer views the colonized as lacking drive and initiative, and as caring little for comfort or convenience—he lives in squalor and still retains a happy look, so naturally he must not care about how he lives—why should the colonizer be concerned with trying to improve the lot of the colonized? "If he doesn't care, why should I?" Furthermore, the colonizer notes how ungrateful the colonized is whenever the colonizer, out of the goodness in his heart, tries to be charitable. His acts of decency go unrewarded, basically because the colonized are not grateful.

Although the ideology by which the colonizer justifies his presence in a colony and his treatment of the colonized contains inconsistencies, Memmi notes that this bothers him little. For example, the colonizer sees the colonized

". . . as frugal, sober, without many desires and, at the same time, he consumes disgusting quantities of meat, fat, alcohol, anything; as a coward who is afraid of suffering and as a brute who is not checked by any inhibitions of civilization, etc." (p. 83). This apparent illogic, according to Memmi, has a deeper logic: the colonizer defines the colonized in terms that serve his own needs.

Memmi argues further that one of the essential building blocks of the ideology of the colonizer is a *negation*; he refuses to allow into his thinking anything that would give a properly positive picture of the colonized. One of Memmi's examples is instructive. Arab hospitality initially receives accolades from visiting European tourists. However, when a tourist settles into the community and begins to take the role of colonizer, he sees the Arab's once-pleasing hospitality as "a result of the colonized's irresponsibility and extravagance, since he has no notion of foresight or economy" (p. 84).

FROM THE BOTTOM UP

In a relationship there are always at least two parties involved. As Memmi so succinctly puts it, "colonization creates the colonized just as we have seen that it creates the colonizer." If the man on top of the heap, whether we call him master, colonizer, or oppressor, sets the definitions for the entire system, the man on the bottom—the colonized, the oppressed, the powerless, the victim—creates his own unique world of response.

It is helpful to consider two separate and general kinds of reaction. On one hand, continued oppression may effect psychological changes in the victims that make a person psychologically similar to the terms the dominant group uses to define him. That is, growing up as a victim of oppression produces a person with a lesser amount of creativity, curiosity, initiative, achievement, and so on, who may rightly be said to be childlike in many of his reactions; he may be lazy, need prodding to be productive, lack imagination and a vision of the future. Some evidence for these consequences can be found in discussions of social deprivation and its effects on intellectual and motivational development (e.g., Deutsch, Katz, & Jensen, 1968; Dreger & Miller, 1968; Pettigrew, 1964).

On the other hand, continued oppression can create psychological *resistance*, which takes a form hardly distinguishable from actual psychological change; the oppressed person resists the oppressor by putting on a *face* of stupidity, laziness, and childlike dependency. Table 17.1

Table 17.1   Responses to oppression

Psychological change
1. Change toward *being* the expected image; long-term role playing produces actual psychological change.
2. Wishing to be like the dominant group; emulation of the master group, usually with concomitant hatred and denigration of one's own group.
3. Direct psychological effects of living in a low-opportunity environment; effects especially on intellectual development, achievement aspirations, physical health, and well-being.

Psychological resistance
1. Open resistance or revolt.
2. Passive resistance; especially the use of the put-on both as passive resistance against the dominant group and as a technique to maintain one's own sense of dignity.

presents a rough outline of these two general classes of reaction to oppression along with several specific examples of response.

In the discussion that follows I shall concentrate primarily on the world view from the perspective of those on the bottom, especially in terms of their tactics of psychological resistance. In Part Two of this book I'll have more to say both about psychological change and mass movements of more directly open resistance.

In concentration camps

Bettelheim (1958) spent 1938 to 1939 as a victim of oppression in the German camps of Dachau and Buchenwald. In describing conditions at the camp and the responses of the prisoners Bettelheim concentrates primarily on the first kind of reaction of the victims, actual psychological change as a result of continued

role-playing and identification with the aggressor. Prisoners were expected to act out the role of dependent children while in the camp: they were expected by guards and fellow prisoners alike to become dependent on the guards; they were to use the "thou" form when addressing one another—a form used only between children. Like children, the prisoners lived in the present, forgetting both their pasts and any hopes for the future. They were given nonsensical tasks such as carrying rocks from one place to another, only to return them to the original place, with no explanations for these activities. Guards even controlled the timing of visits to the latrines. All sense of dignity as human adults was taken away. Bettelheim reports that actual regression to infantile behavior could be observed over time as the prisoners were subjected to this treatment.

After a substantial period of time in the camps, the prisoners made what Bettelheim saw as a final adjustment; they *identified with their aggressors*, adopting as their own personality and system of values those of their Gestapo guards.

"From copying the verbal aggressions of the Gestapo to copying their form of bodily aggressions was one more step, but it took several years to make it. Old prisoners, when in charge of others, often behaved worse than the Gestapo because they considered this the best way to behave toward prisoners in the camp. . . . Old prisoners tended to identify with the Gestapo not only in respect to aggressive behavior. They tried to arrogate to themselves old pieces of Gestapo uniforms. If that was not possible, they tried to sew and mend their uniforms so that they would resemble those of the guards. . . old prisoners boasted that, during the twice daily counting of the prisoners, they had stood well at attention . . . [they] prided themselves on being as tough as the Gestapo. . . . This identification with their torturers went so far as copying their leisure-time activities. One of the games played by the guards was to find out who could stand to be hit longest without uttering a complaint. This game was copied by old prisoners" (1958, p. 309).

In parallel fashion, as Memmi notes, one of the responses typical of the colonized "is to change his condition by changing his skin." He adopts the colonizer as his model and seeks to become just like his master. And just as the colonizer rejects him and those of his ilk, so the colonized rejects himself and his brothers. Self-hate and self-denigration become patterns that mark the life of the colonized.

"A blonde woman, be she dull or anything else, appears superior to any brunette. A product manufactured by the colonizer is accepted with confidence. His habits, clothing, food, architecture are closely copied, even if inappropriate. A mixed marriage is the extreme expression of this audacious leap" (Memmi, 1967, p. 121).

How similar the descriptions of the response of the colonized and the POWs in Nazi camps are to the response noticed by observers of the American Negro. Identification with whites takes the form of seeking to become white. For some who are light-skinned, *passing* is possible. For others of darker skin, however, there is overabundant use of hair straighteners and skin bleaches. The horrible consequence of self-hatred and the sense of self-inferiority develops. White definitions and white standards are applied across the board. One is said to succeed only to the extent to which he becomes like whites and middle class. To succeed, therefore, one must deny his history, his culture, his racial heritage. On the strictly ideological level, the psychological transformation is complete when the oppressed black man adopts the ideological perspectives of those on top and sees himself fully through their eyes: He *is* inferior; he *is* unworthy; he *is* intellectually a dullard, he *is* noncreative except in a few things such as music and athletics. Shall we yell in anger at this contemporary Uncle Tom, shuffling along with a smile firmly planted on his face? No. With compassion we recognize in him the scars of the victim, so very difficult to heal in one who has lived in such a way for so long.

In Genet's *The Maids* (1954) there is a situation in which two servants, Claire and Solange, appropriately servile in their mistress' presence, enact her life when she is absent. In one scene, when Claire plays her mistress, the full force of the contempt the servant has of himself is revealed:

"I said the insults! Let them come, let them unfurl, let them drown me, for, as you well know, I loathe servants. A vile and odious breed, I loathe them. They're not the human race. Servants ooze. They're foul effluvium drifting through our rooms and hallways, seeping into us, entering our mouths, corrupting us. I vomit you!" (1954, p. 86).

In another passage Claire and Solange enact a plot to kill Madame; Solange unveils the truth secreted behind the false mask of her servitude:

"... Yes. I dare speak of these things. I do, Madame. There's nothing I won't dare. And who could silence me, who? Who would be so bold as to say to me: 'My dear child!' I've been a servant. Well and good. I've made the gestures a servant must make. I've smiled at Madame. I've bent down to make the bed, bent down to scrub the tiles, bent down to peel vegetables, to listen at doors, to glue my eye to keyholes! But now I stand upright. And firm. I'm the strangler . . ." (p. 92).

When we think about it, the reaction to oppression that takes the form of psychologically passive resistance, the putting on of an Uncle Tom manner for "Whitey," or The Colonizer, or Madame, or perhaps even for The Professor, is often what we have come today to call the put-on. When conditions of life are so oppressive that direct, open resistance can only lead to punishment, including death—as during the slave period in this nation—resistance of another sort can be observed. To the master slaves were by nature stupid, indolent, dependent, childlike, and lazy; he had trouble getting a good day's work out of them. For the slave, however, being stupid and lazy meant getting away with much less hard work; he would be given fewer responsibilities and have fewer demands made on him. We might even go so far as to maintain that the put-on is one of the few dignifying tactics that an oppressed person retains; he keeps some sense of his own integrity as a human being by playing out a role that he knows is a put-on but that the master takes to be real.

Realize that we are talking about a situation in which an individual has few avenues by which he may relate to his oppressor and yet retain a sense of himself as real, as a man like other men. To his master and perhaps later to himself, he is invisible:

"I am an invisible man. No, I am not a spook like

those who haunted Edgar Allan Poe; nor am I one of your Hollywood-movie ectoplasms. I am a man of substance, of flesh and bone, fiber and liquids—and I might even be said to possess a mind. I am invisible, understand, simply because people refuse to see me. Like the bodiless heads you see sometimes in circus sideshows, it is as though I have been surrounded by mirrors of hard, distorting glass. When they approach me they see only my surroundings, themselves, or figments of their imagination—indeed, anything except me. . . . That invisibility to which I refer occurs because of a peculiar disposition of the eyes of those with whom I come in contact. A matter of the construction of their *inner* eyes, those eyes with which they look through their physical eyes upon reality. I am not complaining nor am I protesting either. It is sometimes advantageous to be unseen, although it is most often rather wearing on the nerves. Then too, you're constantly being bumped against by those of poor vision. Or again, you doubt if you really exist. You wonder whether you aren't simply a phantom in other people's minds. Say, a figure in a nightmare which the sleeper tries with all his strength to destroy. It's when you feel like this that, out of resentment, you begin to bump people back. And, let me confess, you feel that way most of the time. You ache with the need to convince yourself that you do exist in the real world, that you're part of all the sound and anguish, and you strike out with your fists, you curse and you swear to make them recognize you. And, alas, it's seldom successful" (Ellison, 1952, p. 7–8).

The put-on

An article in *The New Yorker* (Brackman, 1967) provides a valuable discussion of the technique of the put-on as it is used increasingly in modern America. In the article the technique is discussed in a variety of exchanges that extend well beyond the master-slave relationship of our immediate focus; nevertheless the author perceptively discusses the use of the put-on in Negro-white interchanges, noting that one advantage this kind of portrayal allows is feigned innocence when caught. Unlike the openly resistant behavior that would lead to punishment or ostracism, a put-on enactment of the expected stereotype permits its user to be hostile and resistant without running a risk.

"If the victim chooses to notice the put-on, the perpetrator can always feign absolute innocence. A put-on may even be veiled in expressions of injured purity:

A: What are you trying to do—make fun of me nigger?

B: Oh *no*, suh. No *suh*, Boss." (Brackman, 1967, p. 57).

Brackman discusses two options that are available to a put-on user engaged in a conversation with a member of the out-group: he may offer a caricature of the out-grouper, who in this interchange is *his* victim; or he may offer a caricature of the victim's view of himself (the minority-group put-on artist):

"Black vs. White: A benevolent progressive tries to express his questioning support of civil rights. The militant Negro responds;

"(1) 'You're two hundred percent right. I mean, with freedom goes responsibility. You can't just grab everything right off. Some demonstrations can only hurt our cause, you know what I mean? Like Dr. King says, our people've got to meet body force with Soul Force. He sets a good example. Like Joe Louis. He was a helluva fighter, huh? But he knew his place. Now, a man like Adam Clayton Powell, he's overstepping his bounds. He takes advantage. Ralph Bunche. That was a good nigger. 'Cept he couldn't sing and dance. What do you think?'

"(2) 'Don't make your superego gig with me, ofay baby. Your grandaddy rape my grandmammy, and now you tell me doan sleep with your daughter? Well, beat up side my black head and whup my humble black back, but don't offer me none of the *supreme delectafactotory* blessings of equalorama, 'cause when this bitch blows you gonna feel black man's machete in the soft flesh of your body, dig?' " (pp. 57–58).

Self-presentations

Although he hasn't involved himself directly in the study of the put-on per se, Goffman's perspective, especially as reflected in his work on self-presentations (1959) and what he has called the "management of spoiled identities" (1963b), is relevant to our discussion. Goffman adopts the perspective of a *dramaturgic* analysis, conceptualizing human encounters in terms of the metaphor of the theater. An encounter is viewed as a performance; P enacts a routine in which he creates a character and manages the impression he conveys to his audience, O. P may use props, including other people, employ a particular style of dress, adopt certain personal mannerisms, speak in a particular manner, and so on. He may stage his performance in a location containing scenic properties requisite to his creating and maintaining the character. All of these are designed to create for O a certain impression that P wishes to maintain.

Certain classes of Ps possess attributes that set them apart from the population of "normals." These *stigmatized* persons, to use Goffman's term (1963), may possess such characteristics as abnormalities of the body, "blemishes of individual character" such as mental disorders or so-called character disorders such as addiction, alcoholism, homosexuality.

"Finally there are the tribal stigma of race, nation, and religion. . . . The attitudes we normals have toward a person with a stigma, and the actions we take in regard to him, are well known, since these responses are what benevolent social action is designed to soften and ameliorate. By definition, of course, we believe the person with a stigma is not quite human. On this assumption we exercise varieties of discrimination, through which we effectively, if often unthinkingly, reduce his life chances. We construct a stigma-theory, an ideology to explain his inferiority and account for the danger he represents . . ." (Goffman, 1963b, pp. 4–5).

On his part, a stigmatized individual is expected to stage his performances (his self-presentations) in a manner designed to fit his audience's stigma theory. As Goffman suggests, he is

". . . warned against 'minstrelization,' whereby the stigmatized person ingratiatingly acts out before normals the full dance of bad qualities imputed to his kind, thereby consolidating a life situation into a clownish role:
"I also learned that the cripple must be careful not to act differently from what people expect him to do. Above all they expect the cripple to be crippled; to be disabled and helpless; to be inferior to themselves, and they will become suspicious and insecure if the cripple falls short of these expectations. It is rather strange, but the cripple has to play the part of the cripple, just as many women have to be what the men expect them to be, just women; and the Negroes often have to act like clowns in front of the 'superior' white race, so that the white man shall not be frightened by his black brother. I once knew a dwarf who was a very pathetic example of this, indeed. She was very small, about four feet tall, and she was extremely well educated. In front of people, however,

she was very careful not to be anything other than 'the dwarf' and she played the part of the fool with the same mocking laughter and the same quick, funny movements that have been characteristics of fools ever since the royal courts of the Middle Ages. Only when she was among friends, she could throw away her cap and bells and dare to be the woman she really was: intelligent, sad, and very lonely." (1963b, p. 110; in Carling, 1962, pp. 54–55).

To be sure, it is difficult to imagine that one could still gain a measure of human dignity by putting on performances for the master or the defining population of normals that fall neatly between the extremes of "minstrelization" and "normification"; yet for those stigmatized there may be few other avenues of resistance of which they are aware. From the perspective of the man on the bottom, living out his life in the midst of a society that defines him *to him* as well as to all others, and all in *their* terms, the character he presents may be indeed just that, a character that is always "on" before the master, and he may laugh contemptuously behind the master's back when he is with his brothers.

It depends on where you stand

A group of American Indians in the Midwest were offered a deal by the U. S. Government (Wellman, 1968): "We'll give you several cows and a few bulls to get a herd started; all we want in return is the first calf born." Sounds like a great deal as The Man from Washington explains it. But these are hungry people: they desperately need and want meat to eat now. So when The Man leaves they up and kill all the animals and have themselves a feast. The Man returns sometime later and wants to see the herd. They tell him, with deep innocence etched on their craggy faces, that they killed the animals and ate them. The Man is hurt, puzzled, a little angry. But then, "what can you expect from these dumb savages? Poor devils, they don't know any better." So off he goes and they have one hell of a good laugh. From his perspective, they are dumb; from their perspective, he's the dumb one; they've gotten precisely what they wanted.

A group of black youths in a California community are to be paid $5 per day to learn how to get a job (Wellman, 1968). The gig is to learn how to pass as a middle-class white during an employment interview so that if there should be any openings for a garage mechanic or a janitor a black kid can get this work. There aren't any jobs available—possibly a few for unskilled laborers—but these kids are to be taught how to act during an interview. For them it's a gas: $5 a day for this kind of play; why not? So they put on the white staff. Whites tell them that playing games like dominoes is useful for learning simple arithmetic, so they ask to play dominoes most of the day. The whites protest that they have other things to do. "But teach," they proclaim self-righteously, "we're just learning our math." The whites think them stupid: "They can't seem to understand why they are here." They, however, read the situation all too well. Antagonistic? Yes. Resistant? Indeed. But stupid? No.

A white employer comes in to help out. He is going to conduct a role-played job interview, just to test them. One of them asks him for real for a job. He's flustered. "Why, we're only here to give you practice in being interviewed; there are no jobs, at least not yet." So they put him on too. They act up during the role-played interview. The employer gets indignant. "They just don't want to work; they're just lazy good-for-nothings." But are they? From their point of view, he's there playing some white man's game with them; he's asking them to adopt his rules and his definitions and play completely on his terms. All they have left to do is resist by putting him on, by making the game-like quality of the situation blatant. And as anyone who has tried this knows, when you call a game a game master gets himself uptight and angry and pulls out his theory of the blacks and. . . .

CONCLUSION

Where you are in the hierarchy of status and power thus produces different perspectives on the world. We live, it seems, in several worlds simultaneously. What the perspective of the sociology of knowledge offers us, in essence and by way of summary, is a social and historical dimension to our consideration of the processes of perception and cognition. It forces us to consider the individual not only as a member of a society but also as a member of a historical epoch. This individual knows his world not only uniquely through his own eyes and particular background, not only socially or culturally through the eyes of the groups and subgroups to which he belongs, but also, and importantly, through the eyes of the historical period in which he was reared and in which he lives. We know what we know because of *who* we are, because of *where* we are, and finally, because of *when* we are.

Part Two

CHANGE AND DEVELOPMENT

A man who spends his entire life in a world that is only blue is completely unaware that the color blue exists. Yet if his world has variations in hue he may recognize the sea as blue and the sky as turquoise. In contrast we gain awareness of the context within which we live. So it is with the study of change.

If we were to live out our lives in Shangri-La, and in that setting we were to write a textbook in social psychology—why anyone in Shangri-La would want that task is puzzling indeed—it is likely that, without a strongly vivid imagination or vigorous contact with mass media, ours would be a text of quiescence and stability. On the other hand, living in a society and a world that seem to turn pages as though they had just graduated at the top of their speed-reading class, we cannot help noting the vital importance of the topic of change. Wherever you look you come in direct contact with a life in process, a flow, sometimes small, more often broad and sweeping. Fads and fashions change: skirts short, hair long; hair short, skirts long. Nations change, as do the relative positions of persons in those nations. Attitudes change, values change, people change, institutions (presumably) change. Technology advances and spins off a new image of man.

Caught up in all of this is man, paradoxically reflecting a passion for stability and predictability and at the same time welcoming the nuances of difference, the variety that slashes boredom and peppers one's life. For the young, it is exciting never to know what tomorrow will bring; for the old, it is frightening to see things once known and familiar rushing off just ahead of their grasping hands.

From the perspective of the sociology of knowledge (Section V), change must be a vital topic of concern in all of the social sciences. We no longer live in a stable time; ours is a time in flux, and our theories and concepts about man and about society must inevitably reflect these facts of our social existence.

I think our purposes will best be served if we differentiate among three types of change: life-history or developmental change; spontaneous, un-planned change; and planned change. In addition, it will be helpful to differ-entiate the *contexts* within which change occurs. We shall examine such

223

contexts as the individual, the group, the organization, and finally, the community and society.

DEVELOPMENTAL CHANGE

Life history or developmental changes are those that occur as one grows from youth to maturity; or, as Shakespeare noted, as one passes through his seven ages: from the "mewling and puking" infant to the "last scene of all, that ends this strange eventful history ... second childishness and mere oblivion, sans teeth, sans eyes, sans taste, sans everything" (*As You Like It*, III, 2).

The young child arrives on earth one day neither a totally blank tablet on which experience writes nor a miniature preprogrammed adult, awaiting only the proper moment of maturation to bring to flower seeds already planted. His growth, rather, involves an interaction between structuring tendencies within and the variety of experiences he encounters.

It is possible to differentiate a maturational view of development, a learning view, and an interactionist or cognitive-developmental view. According to the maturational argument development occurs as the innate patterns and structures of an organism meet their proper moment of environmental stimulation. Critical periods in development trigger the release of these structures at just that key moment in time. If there is early environmental stimulus deprivation the organism ages without encountering external stimuli requisite to the maturation of certain perceptual and cognitive functions.

In the learning view the organism develops through accretion of new internal structures and patterns as he learns external structures that are presented to him. In this view the structure exists in the external world to be learned and thereby taken in to form an internal structure. As Kohlberg, a critic, puts it (1969), in this view the child is like a miniature adult, missing only the information skills and associational complexity the adult possesses.

Thus the maturational argument says structures of the mind evolve from within, and the learning view sees them originating from outside. By contrast, the cognitive-developmental view is of a vital interaction between internal tendencies to structure and transform experiences and the actual structure of those experiences. Recall our discussion of cognitive theory in Chapter 1. Early, primitive structures transform experience—inputs from the external world—in ways that create a newly experiencing and thinking organism. The individual *both* transforms the external world in accord with these internal cognitive structures (a process termed *assimilation* by Piaget) and transforms the structures on the basis of this encounter with the external world (Piaget's term is *accommodation*). We have come around full circle: man is involved in a *dual transformation* in which he both assimilates experience and accommodates to it; he both transforms external reality and is transformed by that reality.

In a similar manner groups and organizations, communities and societies, develop out of the interaction between their structures and the external realities they encounter. Such larger analytic units, then, may also be said to undergo dual transformations. In the first, primitive or early forms of social structure and social organization (the collective counterpart to individual cognitive structure) transform external reality. In the second, external reality operates on the structures, which seek to accommodate to it.

When the unit is the individual we typically view external reality as the structures, belief systems, and organizations of the society in which he is reared. When the unit is a society itself, however, external reality typically is said to include such diverse things as the economy, technology, population size or density, ideas.

For example, we can assume that a society must both assimilate and accommodate to a technological innovation. The introduction of the wheel is one such technological innovation. We would be interested in the manner by which the wheel was integrated or assimilated into the existing social structure and organization, and we would want to examine the effects of the wheel on social structure and social organization—accommodation. The wheel changed relationships among persons. As McLuhan noted (1965), distance took on a different meaning. Persons could live less clustered together;

thus patterns of interaction changed. Later innovations in transportation had similar striking consequences on social structure and organization. The invention of the high-speed elevator, coupled with advances in construction material, made it possible to develop the skyscraper, which in turn facilitated population growth of relatively high density in central cities. The invention of the internal combustion engine and the automobile made it possible for persons to live increasingly distant from their places of employment; in turn, social relations were changed. The jet engine likewise has had a startling impact on social organization.

McLuhan, of course, is especially concerned with the effects of the electric media of computers and television in changing man's conception of himself and nature and in affecting the very forms of social organization that develop within a society. But more of these later.

The point, then, for both individual development and for the development of organized collectivities, is twofold: first, existing structures and organizations affect the manner by which external reality is assimilated by the individual or by the collectivity. Neither simply responds passively and totally to what is out there; rather, each transforms external reality in terms of its existing structures and levels of development. Second, external reality, although shaped by extant structures, has an effect on those structures as they are modified to accommodate to these intrusions of reality. The life experiences of a growing individual leave their mark upon him; likewise, the encounters between social organizations and the realities of technology, population, ideology, and so on, effect a change in those organizations. Developmental changes are carved out of these interactions between internal structure and external reality.

SPONTANEOUS CHANGE

The second type of change is spontaneous or unplanned, in particular the kinds of change that arise from natural events, often outside the system. For example, an accident can effect a sudden, even drastic change in an individual. If the context is a community or even a society, an earthquake or flood or some other natural and unplanned occurrence can produce significant changes. In such cases the change is *precipitated* by an unplanned occurrence, but the changes that occur may follow a planned program; after a disaster relief programs do not occur randomly but follow a plan, often conceived by a government relief commission.

PLANNED CHANGE

Planned change has been of primary concern to social psychologists on one hand and to clinical practitioners on the other, and to all kinds of action-oriented persons, including some in government. Planned changes occur as part of an intentional effort to intervene in the ongoing state of a system (individual, group, etc.) in order to produce a new state. Although developmental changes *may* flow from an intentional act—as in developments of technology—a key difference between developmental and planned change involves the use, in the latter, of self-consciously applied change techniques and specific knowledges. The changes themselves may occur with or without the consent of the person, the group, or other system. For the individual, planned changes occur in such areas as attitude change and propaganda in social psychology and therapy in clinical psychology. Although the fit is not so elegant as I might wish, I include under this same canopy the entire topic of social movements, whether directed at a radical reformation of an organization (e.g., a university), a community, or a society, or, for that matter, even at a radical change in an individual, as in some religious or youth movements. Likewise, I place the mass media under this topic of planned change, although media effects have certain nonplanned, unintentional qualities about them.

A category system for the three types of change or the several systems or contexts in which it occurs is a helpful guide to the territory rather than carved firmly and forever in stone. This manner of categorization is helpful in outlining the territory covered in the rest of this book. To be specific, we shall concentrate on the complex and highly differentiated topics of planned change; look somewhat at life-history or developmental change; and, frankly, not at all at unplanned or spontaneous change.

Section VI

Planned change

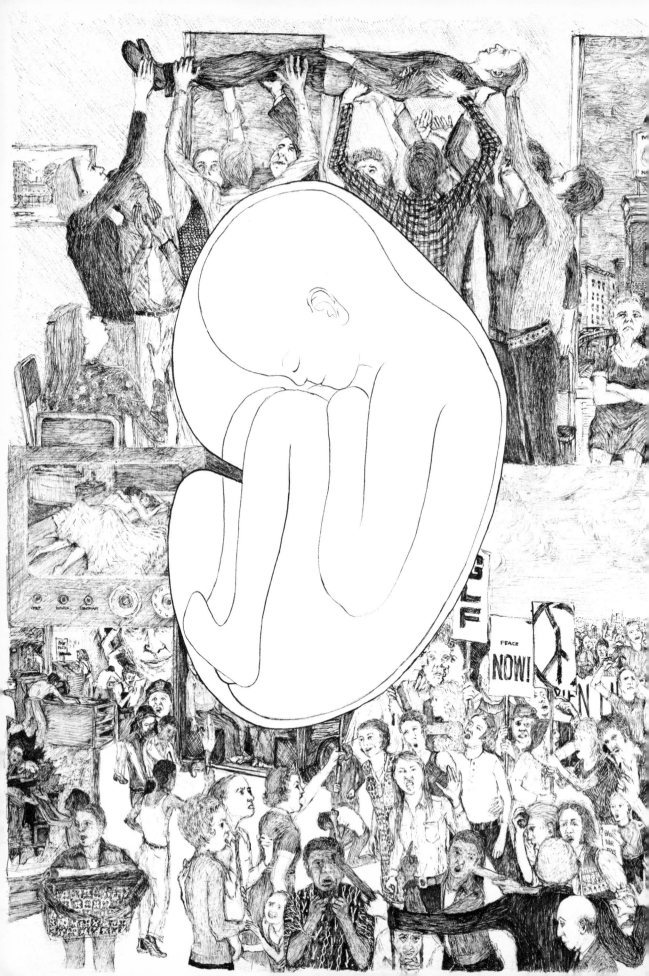

Chapter 18

Some issues in planned change

Whether you are an advertising man, complete with ulcer, contemplating your newest sales pitch in a Madison Avenue office complete with fancy carpeting, or a psychiatrist in a Beverly Hills wood-paneled office listening to someone place his soul in your hands, you are interested in planned change. It is likely that in the former case your interests and the interests of the one to be changed are not so congruent as in the latter case. In one case the object is on the receiving end of a pitch thrown by one who wishes to effect a change in him, whether or not he wants to cooperate. In the other case a client has entered your agency in a presumably fully aware and cooperative venture in change.

Planned changes, of either the cooperative or the less cooperative sort are of interest to both practitioner and theoretician. A *practitioner* is concerned with the application of knowledge to produce an effect in the real world; he is concerned with curing the ill, molding public opinion, engaging an organization in a program of human relations training to increase its overall effectiveness, in selling a product, and in any number of other ways dealing with a specific practical problem. For a *theoretician* planned change is an endeavor that has a special relevance to a theory he is testing, usually in the dark recesses of his laboratory.

The distinction between applied and theoretical interest in change is almost as rough-and-ready as some of the other distinctions we have made. The theoretician, examining the process of change in order to test some aspect of a theory such as attitude change, may uncover material of directly practical value to the practitioner; in turn, although his concern is whatever will work to effect a change, a practitioner is likely to uncover rich material of use to those who develop the theories. Too often, of course, those who spend their lives in the sterile white gown of the social-psychological laboratory frown on those who muddy their hands in the trials of everyday man, and the muddy practitioners look with horror on pure theoreticians who live in isolation from the full complexity of real dilemmas. Lewin often said that there is nothing as practical as a good theory. In this simple Confucianism he captured the sense of the relationship between the practical and the theoretical.

The distinction, however clouded it may be in any specific instance, is nevertheless useful; it marks out two broad areas in social psychology with different traditions and approaches to the study of planned change. The theoretical tradition offers an extensive literature of careful research. An example is the very successful program of laboratory research in social psychology undertaken by Hovland (e.g., Hovland, Lumsdaine, & Sheffield, 1949; Hovland, Janis, & Kelley, 1953; Hovland, 1954; Hovland, Mandell, Campbell, Brock, Luchins, Cohen, McGuire, Janis, Feierabend, & Anderson, 1957). His laboratory became the setting for exacting and systematic investigation of variables in producing attitude change in response to controlled kinds of communications. Hovland and his co-workers produced volumes of significant social-psychological research that succeeded in testing a theory. Mostly, however, it was oversimplified and often too detached from reality to have much generality beyond the context of the laboratory with its motivated, captive audience.

Practitioners, not in a position to subject isolated variables to systematic exploration, had some immediate social problem to deal with. The niceness of a theory, the neatness of a variable, or the precision of the measurement was of less concern to them than getting the job done, the problem solved, or the product sold. They produced some of their own conceptions of the practice of planned change. To be somewhat crude, but to offer a hint of the direction in which we are heading, picture Hitler and his very skillful propaganda minister Goebbels, who created some of the most impressive displays of propaganda with which the modern world is familiar. They undoubtedly had some conceptions to guide them, but we could hardly maintain that they were staging their performances, especially the Nuremberg Party rallies (see Burden, 1967 for a discussion), to test a theory of planned change. Yet apparently they were enormously successful.

FIELD APPROACH

For our applied model of planned change we turn to the writings of Lippitt, Watson, and Westley (1958). Although their approach emphasizes practical applications, keep in mind that Lippitt was importantly influenced by Lewin, whose dictum linking the theoretical to the applied we have already mentioned.

Lippitt and his associates offer us a model of planned change under conditions in which the target or client is a knowing cooperator. As with any change model, two parties, or two systems, are involved; one is called the *change agent*, the other, the *client system*. The change agent may be another person, say a psychotherapist or a community worker; or it may be an entire organization devoted to producing social change (e.g., the Peace Corps, the C.I.A.). The client system may be a single individual or may encompass such larger systems as small groups, organizations, or entire communities. In any case the concept of the client as a system means that there are parts and interdependent relationships that comprise the whole. As a client *system*, for example, an individual presumably has such psychological "parts" as motivations, needs, inhibitions, emotions, skills, styles of thinking. Lippitt examines aspects of the client system and aspects of the change agent itself that are relevant to planned change.

The client system

Two factors are pertinent to the client system: the client's *motivation* for change; and the client's *resistance* to change.

Motivation for Change. What factors influence the client to seek change? Lippitt and his colleagues suggest several issues to be examined. First, the client system may be disturbed in its present situation and want relief. A person, for example, may feel wrapped up in anxiety and seek relief through a therapist; or a community may be suffering from a crime wave and seek aid. Second, the client may detect a discrepancy between his present state and what he imagines or hopes might be. For instance, he may notice that he's not getting all that he deserves, or that his community preaches equality but practices discrimination, depriving him of what he is rightfully owed. He may seek change in the form of legal or court action, or perhaps in some grass-roots community organization. Third, the client system may be under outside pressure to change. For example, technological advances may put pressure on an organization to update its procedures; or an individual may enter a new community and be under pressure to conform to its (to him peculiar or novel) demands. Finally, a significant factor providing the initial impetus to change is an innate drive toward growth. Lippitt recognizes what Maslow (1954) and Rogers (1951) have suggested, that persons have an internal and natural drive toward health, sometimes called self-actualization; this drive state induces forces toward growth and change.

Resistance Forces. Several factors act either to prevent or to inhibit change. Some of these resistance forces originate in the *interdependence* of the several parts of the client system; others result from what Lippitt calls *interference* rather than resistance per se.

An interdependent system is one in which a balance is achieved among several differentiated subparts, all of which function together as a whole. Each part of the system serves a different need or purpose; a change in one part therefore may knock the whole system out of whack by disrupting the balance. Resistance to such change is likely. For example, an individual's psyche can be conceptualized in Freudian terms as consisting of an id, an ego, and a superego; the three subparts exist in a rugged harmony or compromise. Therapy might induce a change in the forces of the id, which might put additional strains on the controls of the superego or the ego and thus threaten to upset the system's balance. This threat could be sufficient to set up resistance by the individual against the therapeutic encounter. A similar analysis can be made for a group, an organization, or a community. For example, if a community is organized so that the financial success of one segment is vitally dependent on the exploitation of another, any effort to change the condition of the exploited section may be met with substantial resistance because the stability of the entire community is threatened. Rising hopes and aspirations set the exploited group to questioning the inevitability of the present predicament; balance and harmony undoubtedly will be upset.

As this example suggests, a condition of stability or harmony among the subparts of a system is not always seen as the desired state. A community or a society that functions by a system of exploitation is somewhat like an individual who keeps himself together by repressing too much that is significant within him. Notice in both examples how the same forces that can produce resistance to change may also serve to initiate change.

An interdependence not unlike the preceding, but with a slightly different emphasis, is seen in the almost neurotic relationships that evolve among parts of a system. A family, for example, may be so structured that its maintenance depends on a continuation of the sickness of one of its members; the thread that ties a husband and wife together may be their sick child. Each parent places a burden on the child, enacting his or her own peculiar life drama: "If it weren't for our child, I'd have left you ten years ago." "*Our* child! You mean *your* child!" The thought of bringing the child for treatment will be met with considerable resistance by the parents, who need the sick child rather than a healthy one.

This same pattern occurs in small groups. One member may adopt the role of "poor suffering child" and be reinforced by the group for maintaining this role. Efforts to break him out of this pattern are met with great resistance both on his part and on the group's part; only so long as he maintains that role can the group relate to him and to one another.

Not all resistance forces have their origins in the interdependencies in a system. One source of resistance occurs in the initial phases of an encounter between a change agent and a client system. It arises from the abundant reservoir of fear and ignorance clients may have concerning change; they may be afraid that "I can't do it"; "I don't have the strength"; "I don't have the skills."

Resistance may arise from the dogged adherence of a system to its present satisfaction; the system hauls these satisfactions out whenever the subject of change is broached. It may also arise from the kind of relationship that grows between the change agent and the client. In psychotherapy, in fact, the interpretation of these resistances forms a significant basis for the therapeutic process itself. Resistance can emerge anywhere en route, when obstacles originally unnoted suddenly become apparent:

"I didn't realize I'd have to do *that* in order to change...." Finally, the approaching end of a relationship between the change agent and the client may set up resistance forces that operate against either further change or the maintenance of the change that has been accomplished: "I don't see how I can do it without you...."

The category of *interference* forces, in contrast to *resistance* forces, refers more directly to the notion of competing priorities. For example, a client system may have a listing of desired goals, but have such limited resources that it cannot get everything it wants. Establishing priorities based on time, energy, skill, and other such resources, while inducing change in one direction, serves as a source of resistance to moving in other directions.

The change agent

The client system is only half of the picture of planned change. Lippitt, Watson, and Westley (1958) suggest that several change-agent variables are also of particular importance: the agent's assumptions about the client's problems; his conception of his role, his personal motivations for inducing change.

Assumptions about the Problem. As I have suggested throughout the book, the orientation or kinds of assumption that a person makes about himself, other people, or his world, influences his actions. Lippitt similarly suggests that the assumptions the change agent makes about his client's problems will influence the nature of the cure he offers. Lippitt differentiates between assumptions that pertain to the client's internal problems and those that focus more directly on his external relationships.

If the agent assumes that the client's problems are internal, the cure must involve some change of this internal condition. One assumption he may make is that there is a poor distribution of power within the client system. On the individual level, as Lippitt notes, this may mean that the agent (e.g., a psychotherapist) assumes his client lacks sufficient ego strength to deal with demanding id impulses; therefore his goal as a change agent is to help the client deal more effectively with these impulses, that is, to

help him redistribute the power so that the ego has more of it. On the organization level, the agent assumes that the organization's problem is a faulty distribution of power; for example, too much power at the top, too little at the bottom. University crises of late have involved this kind of analysis. Students and faculty lack power to decide important matters; administrators and trustees have all the power. The cure: redistribute the power within the organization (good luck!).

In commenting on the application of this perspective to the community Lippitt cites the efforts of Saul Alinsky as a community organizer. Most of his work has been directed toward helping communities organize themselves to gain more grass-roots power with the "downtown establishment."

A second assumption the change agent may make is that the client's problem is primarily one of channeling and mobilizing energy. He may decide, for example, that an individual has been wasting too much of his time and energy in internal conflict; he sees his goal, then, as helping the client reorganize this wasted energy.

Finally, the change agent may assume that the primary source of the client's difficulty lies in a breakdown in communication, ranging from an inability to communicate to distorted communication. His efforts here are to increase the client's capabilities as a communicator or to sharpen the accuracy of his self-perception as a communicator. Much of the work in human relations or sensitivity training is based on this kind of assumption.

Client systems often suffer from a problem in dealing with their surrounding world. Here the change agent may assume that the client is suffering from social blindness, lack of information, or insufficient skills. Social blindness is a difficulty in seeing the environment with a reasonable degree of accuracy. The client system may be so wrapped up in defensive postures that he cannot see the world as it really exists. An agent who interprets this as the client's problem would seek to place him in a situation in which feedback provides ample opportunity to validate reality, say, a human relations training program.

On the other hand, the change agent may assume that the client's troubles stem primarily from a lack of good information on which to base decisions. His efforts then are aimed at providing the client with, or helping him learn how to acquire, the kind of information that will permit him to act in ways that produce a change. A college professor may guide his students toward the kinds of reading and critical thinking that give information on which they can decide to act in ways they would not have thought of; and, with action, a change in both attitudes and values can soon evolve. Students who take philosophy courses often discover readings that suddenly crystallize their thinking and send them off and running in a new direction with a new shading to their lives. This even happens in some courses in psychology; even in social psychology.

Finally, the agent may simply assume that the client system lacks sufficient skills to handle situations in its environment. He sees the cure in helping the client gain requisite skills. As Lippitt, Watson, and Westley note, many change agents believe that instead of any particular skills, they should help the client achieve the general skill of *flexibility*; they believe that a system that is sufficiently open and flexible can effectively solve any external problems that it will encounter.

Assumptions about His Role. Not only does the agent have conceptions about the client system and its problems, but also, and as importantly, he has some conception about himself and his own role in this endeavor. Lippitt suggests five role-conceptions an agent may adopt. The agent may see himself as an outsider with a unique perspective on the client's problems. He enters to mediate conflicts or offer a slightly different view, one that is usually unavailable to a client caught up in the midst of some pressing issue. Or he may enter the picture as someone with expertise, in particular over matters of organization and procedure. Third, he may join the client system in an effort to provide strength from within, for example, as a community organizer who becomes a member of the community and works from the inside. He may function to create a special

setting in which change can come about more readily, or to introduce learning experiences into the client system's life. Finally, he may adopt a supportive role by encouraging the client system to try out a new way, by supporting him when the going gets rough, by assisting him in his efforts to keep his eye on the goal, and so on.

The Agent's Motivations. Although the point is extremely important, especially when we consider the social significance of planned change, we shall make only brief mention here of the change agent's own motivations. As Lippitt, Watson, and Westley put the matter,

"Presumably the change agent is motivated by a desire to help other people. But why does he want to help them? Is he genuinely interested in their welfare? Or—and this is sometimes the case—does he enjoy giving help solely because it inspires feelings of power, assurance, or self-righteousness in him? Usually, of course, motivation is complex and involves both altruism and self-interest. This is not bad in itself. The danger comes at the point where the change agent is so busy creating a situation which will satisfy his own needs that he is unable to respond to the needs of the client system. When this happens, his 'help' may actually be a hindrance..." (1958, p. 93).

Anyone who involves himself in planned change at some point or another—and one hopes this is before, not during or after—has to come to a careful self-examination. His own motives need as much (or more) self-conscious laying on the table as those of his client.

Responsibility to whom?

In their focus on collaborative efforts at planned change Lippitt and his associates did not deal very much with another important matter, the broader social responsibility of the agent who seeks to change another's behavior, attitudes, values, or whatever. Presumably the change agent intends to help work out a program that he feels is most beneficial to all concerned. *All concerned* is usually a relatively small cluster of persons or groups out of a larger potential array; what is his responsibility to the larger body?

One aspect of this matter can perhaps best be highlighted by an example suggested by Frankel (1967). Suppose you were a psychiatrist to whom Hitler came for relief from his feelings of guilt. As a change agent in a collaborative endeavor with Hitler, you might well seek to give him some kind of supportive therapy, enabling him to deal with the guilt experienced over his activities as a mass murderer. On the other hand, you might view your social responsibility more broadly and believe your role is not to help him overcome his guilt, but rather to force him to experience it sufficiently to change his behavior and make him less an insane dictator and more a benign German citizen. In doing so you would be seeking to change your client in a direction you (and maybe many others) felt was beneficial, disregarding his own request. If you should follow his request, however, you would be helping him learn to live with his guilt as a mass murderer.

For those who love to find flaws in examples, let me assure you there are many in this one. However, it is useful for making a point. To whom does the change agent bear allegiance and responsibility? Is he to help his client and disregard the social consequences of this help? Or is he to consider a larger social responsibility and forget the client? Or is there some hoped-for compromise? Most persons would argue that in Hitler's case the agent's responsibility is to the society; he should not attempt to make *that* man feel happier with his guilt—assuming that he ever experienced any guilt. But what about this next case?

A young man comes for treatment. He is rather rebellious; he gets along well with a few close friends; he has difficulty staying in school; he finds too much fault with "the system"; he is in trouble with the draft, having decided to refuse military service; he uses some drugs. His parents think of him as a real problem. The school authorities feel that he keeps making trouble for them; he helps organize student uprisings. The government thinks he should be compelled to serve his hitch in the military. You talk to the young man and find that he is anxious and disturbed by events around him. As a change agent, should you try to make him fit in better with society? Or should you try to make him feel happier with his rebellious and clashing ways? What about your responsibility

to society itself? If you make him a happy rebel, are you not helping to undermine the social order? In fact, are you helping him to keep on drugs (clearly illegal) and to keep refusing military service (again, illegal)? Whose side are you on?

Does this sound far-fetched? Take a draft-refusal case that came up in California in 1968–1969. A mother refused to permit her son, who had just turned 18, to register for the draft. Her first son had registered, was inducted, refused induction, and went to jail. The mother argued that, as the agent responsible for training her children to be moral and to follow their consciences, she could not permit them to engage in actions that ran counter to their consciences and would put them into legal jeopardy. She maintained that her training led her children into the dilemma of confronting the law. If anything, she said, *she* should be put in jail. If you were a psychiatrist assigned to that case; would you applaud that mother, arguing that she and her kids were all in great shape and that the society needed change? Or would you want to try to convince them to adapt to society's demands?

We need not consider only draft cases or young political rebels against society. What would you do about a homosexual who comes in for treatment? Would you help him become a better, more comfortable homosexual or try to help him change to a heterosexual pattern?

The dilemma extends from the individual client through small groups and organizations into the community, and even more broadly into the society; any society exists in a world that provides an even larger context to consider when pressing for change within that society. Perhaps, then, change agents should simply withdraw from the field, deciding that things are too complex to be decided by any eternal truths or professional ethics. But then what about the social responsibility of each man to every other? Change will in fact come about, one way or another, for better or worse. Should the change agent shirk these difficult problems and allow change to happen randomly, when in fact he might participate as a responsible citizen?

It seems that the poor change agent stands

to lose on all counts, for as soon as he begins to think—something, I passionately argue for—he confronts these various dilemmas head on. And there are no neat, nor hard-and-fast, nor elegantly simple rules for him to follow. Each case will present a different perspective on the matter of responsibility. In some he will refuse the agent's role entirely or will inform the client frankly that his aims may differ from theirs: "Adolph, I think you are guilty. If I'm to take your case, you'll have to stop this killing before we can deal with your guilt." In other cases he will self-consciously refuse to adopt society's perspective; he will pursue goals he and his client feel are best, producing happy rebels, or adjusted homosexuals, or whatever, despite societal demands to the contrary. In each case these are value choices; he does not cop out; he does not act dispassionately, without concern for the consequences of his activities. He tries to be fully aware of his *role* and his *responsibilities* and, as importantly, his *values.*

Lest this sound as though the change agent makes his choices on a purely individual, idiosyncratic basis, I hasten to point out that a consideration of one's own role and responsibilities extends well beyond the notion that "If I like it, it must be good; let each man do his own thing." In Chapter 25 I discuss moral development, concentrating especially on Kohlberg's scheme. Although I shall postpone a detailed discussion of that scheme until later, let me suggest here that I subscribe to a view based on the notion of universal principles of morality that guide the decisions a change agent has to make. Decisions based on such principles take into consideration much more than the agent's personal passions, the client's demands, or even any specific society's imperatives. Rather, these decisions are based on an evaluation of more general views of justice and equality that cut across time and place. Keep this matter in mind when I come later to discuss moral development. The issues I discuss in Chapter 25 and those I've just referred to here in examining the responsibility of the change agent should be carefully read and reread together, as part of a whole rather than as separate, unrelated matters.

LAB APPROACH: COMMUNICATIONS MODEL

We see many of the same factors or variables in the research laboratory as in the field approach; but at the same time we notice a greater distance between planned change and the dilemmas of social responsibility. Not all laboratory research on planned change has called on the communications model we shall examine. For example, some systematic psychotherapy research has employed live therapy situations that have not been systematically altered to fit a communications paradigm. Experiments in group dynamics (which we shall examine shortly) typically do not employ this model in any systematic fashion. However, a considerable amount of the attitude-change literature in social psychology proper, as McGuire (1969) has demonstrated, can be helpfully organized in terms of this model. I shall call freely on McGuire's talents to indicate just what is meant.

In a manner roughly analogous to the Lippitt scheme of planned change, the communications model considers factors associated with the change agent and with the client system. In the former category the model offers a *source*, a *message*, and a *channel*; in the latter category are the *receiver* and the *destination*. In attempting to understand what these terms mean and what this model is all about, it is best to think of a situation in which O is communicating with P. We call O the source; what he has to say, the message; the media employed, the channel; P is the receiver; and the kind of change in P that is sought is the destination.

The source has been examined in terms of its *trustworthiness* or *credibility*, its *expertise*, its *power*, its *intent to influence*, its *attractiveness to P*, and its *similarity to P*; the communications model attempts to control four of the factors, systematically vary the fifth, and examine its effect. The message factors include the *content* of what is said, its *structure* (e.g., its order of presentation), the *kind of appeal* that is used (e.g., soft sell versus hard sell, fear-arousing or neutral), whether a *conclusion* is drawn, and so forth. The channel or medium may include any of the senses, or a combination. The receiver, or the client system, P, has been studied in terms of its *personality*, its *ability*, its *degree and kind of participation* in the process of change. The destination is concerned with the aspect of *P* we seek to change. Is it *P*'s verbal behavior? His action? Do we wish to produce short-term change? Long-term?

We shall have more to say about the communications model of planned change when we come specifically to examine the contribution of the social-psychological investigation of attitude change (Chapter 21). It is important at this point, however, to note that although both the field and the lab models discuss a client system and a change agent, they focus on different aspects of each. With their origins in different contexts and with different professional audiences (the models' own client systems), each model has a different emphasis.

For the laboratory model, for example, the change agent or source is relevant primarily as he fulfills his role in a mechanistic equation. Is he credible? Is he powerful? Is he expert? How does he structure his messages? What channels does he employ? The concern is with the relationship between source factors as independent variables and change as a dependent variable. For the field model, on the other hand, the change agent is relevant primarily in terms of the diagnostic orientation he takes, the role he adopts, and the motivation he possesses. What is important here is to provide potential change agents with a listing of alternative conceptions of themselves and of their clients.

Another way of stating the different emphases is to suggest that the lab model takes an *external* view of what the field model focuses on *internally*. It is as though the lab model is a handbook for an outside observer who is watching an incident of attempted change occurring; the field model is a handbook for the change agent (or the client system) who has been hired to engage in the process of planned change.

A paradox explained

Hovland, a leader in the laboratory study of planned change, puzzled for a time over the

seeming paradox that lab studies invariably produced much greater change than field studies were able to demonstrate. He noted, for example, that field studies that examine the effect of information campaigns in producing change in voting behavior result in only about 5 percent actual change, whereas the lab figure is always significantly greater (Hovland, 1959). He suggested seven key ways in which lab studies differ from field studies.

1. The lab study involves a captive audience with forced exposure to the material designed to produce attitude change, whereas the field study involves persons who can voluntarily expose themselves to or ignore the communications.

2. Laboratory studies typically use simple messages in a one-shot appearance; field studies typically involve large campaigns, with repeated efforts to hit the potential audience.

3. In lab studies there is usually a very brief time at which the measure of change is taken. In the field, by contrast, there is usually a longer time interval between exposure and the measure of its effect.

4. In the lab the typical communicator is an experimenter, or a teacher, or someone known to the subjects. In the field the communicator may be remote from the subject or known outside the usual context a schoolroom study introduces.

5. The laboratory is a special context within which to conduct work; recall our earlier discussion of experimenter effects (see p. 79 ff.). The field, as the natural habitat of the audience, lacks experimenter effects and adds a dimension of social reality testing. The subject in the lab is isolated from contact with persons to whom he usually turns when he has questions to be answered; the man in the field has friends and associates with whom to discuss the issues raised by the communications of the information campaign.

6. Whereas the lab population is usually from a restricted range in terms of education, social class, and so on, the typical field study takes a random sample of the entire population.

7. Finally, lab studies usually deal with issues that are not very ego-involving to the subjects, in comparison with the more personally relevant issues selected for information campaigns studied by field researchers.

To Hovland's listing I would add that the laboratory usually studies issues that, although they may on occasion be involving to the subjects, have little relevance to public policy and action. Thus what the individual says or does usually matters little. On the other hand, change-oriented efforts that field researchers typically study involve matters that entail a definite social consequence. Changing or not changing in the field context is more consequential than changing or not changing in the lab context.

Although Hovland's major effort was an examination of the differences in lab and field methodologies, with the conclusion that they are complementary rather than contradictory, the factors he has brought to our attention are useful in still another way. These seven or so factors that differentiate the methodologies and influence the effectiveness of a particular change-oriented technique are of the same sort that give rise to the models of planned change we have examined. A man who deals with a captive college-student audience is likely to arrive at an approach to the study of change and to its conceptualization that is different from what a man directing a politician's campaign is likely to develop. The man in the laboratory is also likely to arrive at a conception of change and of his role in the endeavor different from that of a social worker, a community organizer, or a psychiatrist.

CONCLUSION

Well, we have now come around full circle and are ready at last to launch our examination of planned change. In the chapters that follow we shall examine various approaches and aspects of planned change, looking at the theories, the research, and some of the broader social implications of these efforts. If you tend to get bored easily, remember that social scientists are being called on increasingly to help government and private businesses introduce change in a carefully programmed and planned way. If you will not be a change agent yourself someday, at least remember that you, I, and everyone else are and will continue to be part of somebody's client system. If this sounds as though I'm warning you about 1984, and Big Brother is planning to change you, maybe I am. Needless to say, the study of planned change is much more than a simple exercise in ivory-tower game playing. Social implications arise from these theories and studies. There are few areas in the social sciences in general or social psychology in particular in which there are greater social consequences than in the study of how to produce change or how to prevent it.

Chapter 19

The participation approach

Somewhere someone has said that one's work as a scientist must be objective and value-free. This has been taken by some to mean that rigorous work in science must necessarily be devoid of passion and values. Clearly, for anyone who has ever engaged in the complex enterprise of scientific investigation, passion is, or should be, right at your finger tips. There is the excitement of playing the game properly, of trying something out and sometimes making it, sometimes not, but learning even when you don't quite make it. This is hardly an absence of passion. And anyone who can spend much of his life in scientific investigation and be without passion in this endeavor must be a dull boy indeed.

Few could deny that a person's values or interests or backgrounds influence the kinds of problem he selects for study, and may even influence the methodology he chooses to study those problems. Likewise, in today's world it is difficult to be completely valueless about the outcome of one's work, especially if that work has an important consequence in the real world of people, their lives, and their problems. There are fewer and fewer aspects of research that do not soon enter the public's arena; values, whether denied or recognized, therefore are at play much of the time. Social psychology in particular, and especially the social psychology

of planned change, rushes headlong into the world of passions, controversy, and values.

A LEWINIAN VIEW

Lewin said it well in 1947:

"The social scientists, perhaps more than the natural scientists, have to learn to be unafraid and at the same time fair-minded. To my mind, fair-mindedness is the essence of scientific objectivity. The scientist has to learn to look facts straight in the face, even if they do not agree with his prejudices. He must learn this without giving up his belief in values, that is, without regressing to the pre-war cynicism of the campus. He has to learn to understand how scientific and moral aspects are frequently interlocked in problems, and how the scientific aspects may still be approached. He has to see realistically the problems of power, which are interwoven with many of the questions he is to study, without his becoming a servant to vested interests. His realism should be akin to courage in the sense of Plato, who defines courage as wisdom in the face of danger" (1947b, p. 153).

And, as importantly, Lewin and the students and colleagues he inspired *did* it well in the late 1930's and up to the present. Lewin was born in 1890 and studied psychology under the influence of the Gestalt tradition in Berlin. In 1932 he left Germany for the United States.

Perhaps it was his background in prewar Germany, with fascism's challenge to free men; perhaps it was his deep commitment to research and to social action; regardless of why, Lewin carried with him a passion for democracy. His work at Iowa with Lippitt and White (Lippitt & White, 1958), and his later efforts as part of the social scientists' contribution to the U.S. war effort in the 1940's, all reflect this keen concern (see Lewin, 1958).

Democracy versus autocracy

Lewin, Lippitt, and White studied the effects of leadership style on group behavior. Their classic study (1939; see 1958) varied the style of the adult leader in several children's groups and examined the consequences of these different styles on the groups' behavior. Leadership style and the atmosphere it creates provide a group variable, in contrast to the individual variables that had typically formed the basis for group dynamics up to that time. The study was thus significant in the over-all history of the social psychology of small groups, for it was one of the earliest efforts to study systematically the effects of such group-level variables. As importantly, this study began a chain of studies in what has come to be known as the group-dynamics approach to planned change.

Lewin, Lippitt, and White experimentally created three leadership styles: *democratic, authoritarian,* and *laissez-faire.* The democratic leader was to engage a group in discussion and involve it in group decisions over matters of concern to the group. He was to help keep the group's over-all goals in mind and clarify the relationship between its specific activities and these goals. In spirit he was to be a regular group member; but he was instructed not to do much of the actual work of the group. The authoritarian leader was to establish the general policies of the group and to make specific decisions. He was to keep the group in the dark, to a certain degree, concerning its long-range goals and how its present activity fitted into this larger picture. He was instructed to remain fairly aloof from any participation in group work. The laissez-faire leader was to play a passive role, responding primarily when asked, never taking any initiative to facilitate group activity or

clarify goals (unless asked). He was to be more friendly than aloof, yet not participate much in group work.

It should be apparent that Lewin was examining factors in this small laboratory study that had extensive social significance. Surely it was no coincidence that the authoritarian pattern of leadership marked the country he had left in 1932, whereas the democratic style characterized the country to which he now felt allegiance.

The groups studied were several clubs of 11-year-old boys. They were put through a program in which the adult leader was changed every seven weeks; some began with a democratic leader and shifted to an autocratic one, and others reversed this procedure. Measures were obtained through observational records and interviews with the participants, their parents, and their classroom teachers.

In addition to its normal routine each club was to experience three rigged events. In the first the leader arrived late for a meeting. The second required that he be called away during one of the sessions. Finally, a stranger—either a "janitor" or an "electrician"—came into the room while the leader was gone and began to criticize the work the groups were doing.

Lippitt and White (1958) report several findings of particular importance. They noted two distinct responses to the authoritarian leadership style. Most of the groups under an authoritarian leader reacted passively and dependently, showing low levels of either tension or frustration, but one club was more actively aggressive, demonstrating both frustration and aggression toward the adult leader. We shall return to this shortly.

In the authoritarian group there were greater feelings of general dissatisfaction than in the democratic groups, more efforts to gain the adult's attention, less personal, friendly, or intimate conversation between members, greater intragroup irritability and hostility. This last finding also differentiated the democratic from the laissez-faire style; the laissez-faire groups were more like the authoritarian than the democratic in generating expressions of irritability toward fellow group members.

The groups responded differently to the three

rigged events as a function of the style of leadership employed. The democratic groups were able to work well on their own, being minimally disrupted either when the leader arrived late or was called out during a meeting, but the authoritarian groups did not take any initiative to start without their leader's presence. The laissez-faire groups were reported to be active but not productive without the leader present. The arrival of the critical outsider in the authoritarian-led groups was met with greater hostility toward the intruder and higher inter-member tension and scapegoating than in the democratic or laissez-faire groups. When transferred from the autocratic to the democratic structure, groups acted as though they were letting off steam; this suggests that the authoritarian leader served both to create frustration and to act as a lid on the resultant bubbling caldron.

Undoubtedly we should not rush from these results into an entire theory of democracy versus totalitarianism; on the other hand, these 1939 data offer us some interesting food for social-action thought. The authoritarian leader took control and directed the group. Its reaction was either to withdraw into apathy or to react with rebellion and aggressiveness. When The Man wasn't around, little work was accomplished, and often all hell broke loose. When faced with an outsider who annoyed them, the authoritarian-led groups tended to deflect their anger from the object of their annoyance (the leader) toward the out-grouper.

By striking contrast, the democratically led groups were freer to make their own decisions about how their clubs would be run; the leaders were helpful resource persons. The groups were sufficiently independent to be able to initiate their own work when a leader was late or was called out. They were self-directed and self-governing. When an intruder annoyed them, they tended to react directly toward him and not bother scapegoating. They were in both a more productive and a more personally satisfying setting.

Picture a classroom in what may be a typical school. One day Mrs. Scrunch is ill and a substitute teacher is sent in. Kids begin to pick fights with one another; they hassle the sub-

stitute, who soon finds that most of her time is spent keeping order and praying that poor old Mrs. Scrunch will get healthy quickly. Perhaps Mrs. Scrunch has managed to create in her class the kind of authoritarian atmosphere Lewin and his associates noted; perhaps her students are reacting with frustration and tension; some are generally apathic, giving up the fight, and others maintain a watchful waiting, looking for their moment to erupt with rebellion.

With rebellion there usually comes stricter authoritarian leadership; with that comes a greater move into apathy or harsher rebellion, beginning the vicious circle. Is there any wonder that by the time students from Mrs. Scrunch's classrooms get to a university they are not self-directed, eager learners, but are either grade-seeking, knowledge-avoiding apathetics or passionate rebels, shouting often just to know they are still alive?

Fortunately for Lewin's democratic value bias, this early study offered the results it did. Imagine how distressing it would have been to have found the authoritarian style producing happier groups than the democratic. But it didn't, so we can go on to a more direct consideration of planned change using the group-dynamics techniques revealed in that early study (but see p. 257 ff. for a more complex analysis).

GROUP PROCESSES AND CHANGE

World War II arrived, and social scientists who were not carrying guns found themselves swept up in the nation's cause. Lewin and others were engaged in several programs designed to examine techniques of planned change. He was faced with the problem of changing actual behavior in such a way that, once changed, it would stay put; no easy feat. In his now-classic study (1958), the behavior to be changed was eating habits; the goal was to produce a change in eating behavior so that those delectable chunks of meat necessary to serve the fighting men would be replaced on the home tables by more esoteric cuts like beef hearts, sweet-breads, and kidneys. How do you convince a housewife to serve *those* foods rather than steaks and chops?

First, you conceptualize the problem. You note that the housewife is a *gatekeeper*, occupying a critical link in the chain of events that brings food from the market to the table. To induce change you must head for such key figures, whose behavior must be changed in order to effect a new level of activity in the system as a whole. It might be easier to get a three-year-old to cry loudly for kidneys; but until mamma is ready to buy kidneys there will be no kidneys served in that house.

Once you have found the key to the system's structure, your next problem is to figure out why she does what she is already doing. Lewin recognized that most eating behavior involved social habits that served as strong obstacles to change; a social habit does not exist in isolation, but rather in a social context that supports and maintains it. That the housewife serves the particular food she does is not an accident; it is a behavior that is maintained and reinforced in a social context. This understanding led Lewin to state,

"Perhaps one might expect single individuals to be more pliable than groups of like-minded individuals. However, experience in leadership training, in changing food habits, work production, criminality, alcoholism, prejudices, all seem to indicate that it is usually easier to change individuals formed into a group than to change any one of them separately. As long as the group values are unchanged the individual will resist changes more strongly the farther he is to depart from group standards. If the group standard itself is changed, the resistance which is due to the relation between individual and group standard is eliminated" (1947a, p. 34).

The essential point is pleasantly simple and thus all too easily overlooked: our habits, attitudes, and so forth, all exist in a social context. That context, usually a group or groups to which we belong, supports our continuation of the habit or our maintenance of the attitude. Deviating from the group's level of habit or opinion is usually cause for the application of sanctions. Any process of individual change must overcome the group standards that support a particular level of behavior. If we can work to change the standards of a group, we can thereby effect a change in the behavior of individual members of that group.

In an updating of Lewin's views Cartwright (1951) indicated three ways in which a group enters the process of change. He argued that a group could be a *medium*, a *target*, or an *agent* of change.

As a medium of change the group has the ability to exercise power over its members either to conform to or resist efforts toward change. Presumably, the more strongly an individual is attracted to membership in the group and the more cohesive the group itself is, the stronger those influence forces are. Several studies support this argument. Recall the Schachter study in which cohesiveness was experimentally varied (p. 128). The more highly cohesive groups placed greater pressures on their members to conform to their standards. Studies by Festinger and others (e.g., Back, 1951; Festinger, Schachter, & Back, 1950) have likewise demonstrated that the more cohesive the group or the more strongly the member wishes to remain a member, the greater power the group has either to produce conformity with the change agent's efforts or to resist his efforts. More on this later.

The notion of the group as a target of change is one I have previously mentioned. Here the standards of the group are the target of the change agent's efforts. He assumes that if he can change the group's standards, and if the group has power over its members, then he will have successfully altered individual behavior.

Finally, the group as an agent of change exists whenever a group as a whole becomes the change agent working to alter some other group. For example, a neighborhood group might form to achieve change in city government policies involving recreation facilities in that neighborhood.

For Lewin the group standards were to be changed in order to change individual members whose behavior was anchored by those standards. His method had to be both effective and, as importantly, ideologically democratic. Lewin was vitally concerned that change agents be self-conscious and moral. His work with children's groups had suggested that a democratic style of leadership was effective in gaining the intelligent participation of all members in the decisions affecting their club. In addition, decisions that were made by the group appeared to be independent of the adult leader. By contrast, the adult leader in the authoritarian groups was essential in keeping them going. For one who wanted to induce permanent change that was arrived at by an agreement among equals rather than forced from above and that did not require continued surveillance by an authority, the democratic group-decision method seemed preferable.

Unfreezing and refreezing

In his food-habits research Lewin (1958) saw the change process as involving three stages: *unfreezing, movement, refreezing*. Unfreezing, as the term suggests, conceptualizes the behavior to be changed as frozen in a social context. Lewin noted that unfreezing might require breaking "open the shell of complacency" or deliberately bringing about an "emotional stir-up." Movement involves actual change in the group's behavior from its former position to a new level. Finally, refreezing firms up the standards again so that the change will be permanent.

In the 1940's Lewin and his co-workers undertook a series of investigations in which they tested this conceptualization of change by contrasting group decision with lecture technique as devices for inducing planned change. In one food-habit study (reported in Lewin, 1958), for example, Red Cross volunteers in groups ranging from 13 to 17 members were targets of efforts to get them to serve beef hearts, sweetbreads, and kidneys. Some of the groups were given lectures "... which linked the problem of nutrition with the war effort, emphasized the vitamin and mineral value of the three meats, giving detailed explanations with the aid of charts. Both the health and economic aspects were stressed" (1958, p. 202). In addition, these lectured groups were given recipes for preparing the foods in a most tasty manner.

The groups in the group-decision condition met with a democratically oriented leader who engaged the Red Cross volunteers in discussion, covering most of the same topics dealt with in the lectures the other groups had heard. Toward the end of the discussions a show of hands indicated how many of the women were willing to try the new foods.

Follow-up interviews showed that whereas 3 percent of the lecture groups served at least one of the new meats, 32 percent involved with group decision served them. Thus, although the lecture was interesting, well conducted, and meaty, it was relatively ineffective in producing any behavior change.

As part of that same research program, Lewin reports several further studies, all of which indicate the relative effectiveness of the group decision over the lecture method for producing behavior change. Klisurich (in Lewin, 1958), for one, attempted to get housewives to increase home consumption of milk. Follow-up at intervals of two weeks and four weeks after either the lecture or the group decision indicated that the group method was more effective after both time periods than the lecture approach. In yet another study (in Lewin, 1958) group-discussion methods were more effective than lecture approaches in getting mothers to use orange juice and cod liver oil for young children.

Decision or discussion?

Progress does occur in social psychology. In 1955 Pelz (in Bennett, 1955) brought the complexity of Lewin's group-versus-lecture methods under careful scrutiny. She was concerned, as others had been, with the precise distinction between these apparently contrasting methods. To tease out the differences she isolated four factors in the group-decision approach: (1) *group discussion to convey information*; in Lewin's group methods the discussion was a means of getting the same information to the group that the lecturer presented to assembled individuals. (2) *Decision making*; in the group approach the housewives typically were asked to make a decision to do something, for example, to try out the new meats. (3) *Commitment*, or the degree to which the decision was made publicly for all to see. (4) *Degree of consensus*, the extent of agreement in the group about trying out the new behavior.

Pelz's change goal was to get introductory psychology students to become more willing to volunteer for psychology experiments. She experimentally varied both the *type of influence* attempted (discussion or lecture) and the *level of commitment required* (no decision made; decision made anonymously; partial anonymity about the decision—subjects briefly raised their hands; public commitment—subjects raised their hands and publicly gave their names as being willing to volunteer for psychological research if asked).

An analysis of her data led Pelz to conclude that of the four factors initially thought to be crucial only two were in fact critical elements of the group method as compared with the lecture approach. These were the actual *process* of making a decision and the *degree of perceived consensus* concerning that decision. Neither group discussion alone nor public commitment appeared to be essential in producing behavior change. As Pelz herself suggests, "In the light of the findings here reported, therefore, 'group decision' might profitably be redefined as 'decision about individual goals in a setting of shared norms regarding such goals'" (Bennett, 1955, p. 219).

If we generalize her suggestive results more broadly, these two factors shed further light not only on group decision as a technique of change, but, as importantly, on the possible dynamics of behavior and opinion change. It appears that the anchoring of opinion and action in a social context in which norms of enforcement are present and sanctions are applied for deviation serves as a strong resistance force against individual change. The techniques of group dynamics call on this reality and seek to induce change by working on the very group that supports the behavior in question.

In a real sense, then, the application of democratic or participatory methods engages the members of a group in an active re-examination of their present position. It places the individual and the group in a position of coming to a decision about themselves; the decision is made from within rather than dictated from without. From Lewin's value bias as a change agent this point is critical. The democratic leader as a change agent is a guide, a resource person, a procedural expert who assists persons in discovering whether some change is needed, the implications or consequences of that change, and how best to accomplish the change if it is decided on. Notice that although the lecture method *could* allow for both individual decision and perceived consensus—the two factors

Pelz finds significant—it cannot as conveniently allow for group participation in the discussion and in reaching a decision as the group method.

Individual autonomy and group pressure

The theme that runs through these several studies concerns the role of an individual in directly affecting decisions that have some consequence for him and for his life. Lewin, Lippitt, and White created a situation in which the democratic leader urged group members to play an active role in determining their groups' policies. The food-habit studies varied the degree of active involvement in the process of change. One of the strongest effects in Pelz's study was in the comparison of subjects who were asked to make some decision concerning their future behavior (I will or will not volunteer for future studies) with those who were dismissed after the influence was attempted but before any decision was required. The personal activity of making the decision was more effective in producing behavioral change than was the degree of publicity concerning the decision. It seems plausible to suggest that democratic or participatory techniques allow individuals greater leeway in making a personal decision to change than does the authoritarian leadership style of a typical lecture. As a passive member of a lectured audience or of an autocratically led group, one need not make a decision.

I suggest that Lewin's program of planned change argues for both an *individual autonomy effect* and a *group-pressure* or *consensus effect*. The individual autonomy effect derives from active participation that allows an individual to be an actor who affects his environment. He is an active, causal agent, an origin rather than a pawn. For Lewin individual autonomy in the process of change is ethically appropriate. Furthermore, it helps overcome resistance to change. If I participate in the decisions affecting the future course of my actions, I should be less resistant to undertaking those actions; after all, it is my own decision. The change that eventually comes about as a function of individual autonomy and participation also tends to be less dependent on the change agent than change that is induced with minimal individual involvement. We shall return to this matter later;

at this point, however, it is important to keep in mind Lewin's contrasting findings. Recall that those who worked with a democratic leader worked independently and on their own when he was no longer present; those with an authoritarian leader were so dependent that they ceased effective work when he was absent or late. Finally, when an individual is involved in decision making he has a greater sense of personal responsibility for the decision or the new actions. It makes good common sense. Contrast the apathetic response of those under the autocratic leader with the stronger sense of camaraderie and group responsibility that the democratic-participatory leader created.

Not only is it common sense, but this conclusion also seems to jibe with various impressions of the state of our nation and its large-scale organizations. We often hear complaints (or praise) of a silent majority, a do-nothing, apathetic citizenry. Too often we hear stories of persons standing by and watching some horrible fate befall one of their fellows, proclaiming calmly after a knifing in the street, "I just didn't want to get involved." Active involvement in the affairs of the nation, its organizations, or an individual's own groups seems to be at a low ebb. Let George do it; don't bother me. Likewise, the attitude of social responsibility, of being my brother's keeper, seems to be lost in the shuffle as each person looks out for himself and his own, leaving others to get by as best they can.

Let us speculate that these quiet, seemingly uncaring ones are victims of a relationship to society in which they feel themselves effectively cut off from significant participation in the process of change. Decisions are made somewhere out there. Even writing letters to a congressman or placing complaint slips in an organization's suggestion box may seem to make little dent on those who bring about change. If this is the way a person views his relationship to his government, his organization, his university—seeing himself as powerless—it comes as no surprise that his response is apathy, silence, and minimal responsibility. Lewin and his associates, as potential change agents, would involve individuals sufficiently in the process of change so that they feel they are active agents responsible for whatever comes about, not passive, irresponsible victims of someone else's decision.

Group pressure or consensus, the second factor, is based on the fact that opinions and behaviors are all rooted in social contexts. To the extent to which an individual is strongly attached to membership in a group, as that group's norms change, as it comes to redefine social reality, it brings pressures to bear on him to view things in a different way, or to take actions that formerly were difficult, or unlikely, or taboo. The effects of group pressure need not be seen as an all-or-none matter or as a newer, more insidious form of dictatorship. As a member of the group an individual participates in redefining its boundaries and its perspectives, and thus is actively involved in the process of change.

Autonomy or Manipulation? The same themes that characterized Lewin's prewar and wartime efforts characterized his and his associates' programs of change in the postwar era. But did the studies really use group decisions? Let us look at another classic study, conducted by Coch and French (1948), to examine another ideological underpinning of the participation approach to planned change.

American industry undergoes many changes in production as technology advances. With each change the workers are required to unlearn the old and relearn the new way of working. Usually management, apprised of the change, informs the working force, and that's that, other than the usual round of grumbling complaints and employee turnover. When management is psychologically sophisticated, however, it takes a somewhat different look at this matter.

For a psychological sophisticate the issue is *planned change*, or how to introduce a change procedure in such a way as to minimize expected resistance. Coch and French sought to use the Lewinian participation approach in a pajama factory in Virginia. The Harwood factory used an individual incentive system, paying employees according to piece rates determined by time study. Whenever an employee was changed from one type of work to another he was paid a *transfer bonus*, computed so that the transfer would not produce a loss in pay during the period of relearning. However, the employees' attitudes toward any job change were negative; some preferred to quit rather than change.

Coch and French selected subgroups from the factory to undergo separate change treatments in which the employees' amount of involvement with the decision to change varied. They used three procedures: (1) *No participation*. In this group the employees were informed in the usual manner about their job change. The production department set a new piece rate, a meeting was called in which the group was informed about the need for a new rate in order to keep up with competition, questions were answered, and the meeting was dismissed. (2) *Participation through representation*. In this group management met with the workers and, to quote Coch and French, presented the need for change "as dramatically as possible." Management then presented a change plan for the workers to discuss: workers were to select several of their number to undergo new training; importantly, the new piece rates would be set on the basis of this representative group's experiences. After the training period another meeting was held with all the workers; the new rates were presented and the representatives were assigned to train the other workers. (3) *Total participation*. These groups were smaller in size and more intimate in member association. A dramatic presentation of the need for change was offered. However, all members of the group participated in designing the new job, rather than just selecting a representative few.

Coch and French studied these groups' production rates over 30 days after the transfer to the new job. Their results are striking. All groups showed an initial drop in productivity when the transfer was first instituted, but the two participation groups returned to their former level and even beyond, whereas the no-participation group retained a low level.

In one further experimental variation Coch and French selected members of the no-participation groups who were still working at Harwood (17 percent had quit!) and used a total-participation technique before transferring them to still another job. Whereas this group

of persons had transferred so poorly under no participation, under total participation they transferred with ease and recovered their former levels of efficiency or even went beyond. Furthermore, there were fewer expressions of aggression after the participation technique as compared with the higher level of hostility expressed when the transfer was made without employee participation.

The evidence seems to be piling up, then, that the participation approach to planned change is more effective in terms of both productivity and morale than methods that call on less individual responsibility and initiative. An important question, however, is a distinction between *real* participation in decision making and *psychological* (perhaps illusory) participation. That is, are we discussing situations in which the members actually *can* effect a change in their environment? Or do they only *believe* that they are effecting a change? Could the total-participation group, for example, decide that it did not wish to change jobs and that management should find itself some other patsy? Or was it really that management had decided what was the best policy and that the workers were to *feel* that they were participating in this decision?

In the Coch and French study it is likely that both real and illusory participation occurred. The participation was illusory in that it seems unlikely that the workers could have decided to refuse any change in job. It was real, however, in that they did determine for themselves the new piece rate they would be earning after transfer. The distinction nevertheless is important. Often someone at the top makes a decision and introduces illusory group participation as a technique to convince the workers, or the students, or whoever, that they are playing a part in determining their own fate. This kind of participation, even though it may work—that is, make the change more effective—is unlike Lewin's bias and the implications of Lippitt's collaborative approach to planned change.

I think that if I may recapture the spirit at least of the participation approach, especially as Lewin envisioned it, the change agent, who may be more expert or more experienced than his clients, does not try to put something over on them for his own benefit, but rather tries to work with them in a collaborative adventure of change. In this endeavor participation becomes essential, especially as it allows those who will be affected by any change to see and evaluate the need for it, to understand its consequences for them and their lives, to assess the relationship between this change and other change, and thereby to evaluate the connection between the change and the values and priorities they feel are important. Experts in time study, in medicine, in economics, in education, and so on, serve as resource persons responsible for conducting the research or developing the skills that help an informed public participate more intelligently in evaluating the need for change and their role in its production. At the same time, and as a direct consequence of the collaboration between the experts and the public, resistance to change is diminished, any change that finally occurs is better stabilized, and, as importantly, those who have changed are autonomous and independent rather than continually dependent on the change agent.

Although Lewin worked primarily on the scale of the small group, I daresay he felt these techniques to be applicable more broadly, including organizations and communities. The mechanics of participation in a large and complex society, although extraordinarily more difficult to achieve than in a small group, nevertheless are not beyond feasibility. Public-opinion polls, for example, can more rapidly link elected representatives with their constituents today than ever in the past, and thereby permit greater public participation in setting priorities concerning public policy. Decentralization or overlapping social organizations offer yet another way of bringing more persons into the arena of decision making.

An Organizational Example. An effort to apply the participation approach in an organization was undertaken by Morse and Reimer (1956). Although Coch and French's work was in an organization, they concentrated on small groups within that organization; Morse and Reimer actually sought to restructure the organization to allow greater or lesser amounts of worker participation in decision making. Essentially,

they restructured the divisions of an organization so that two divisions increased rank-and-file participation and authority in decision making and two other divisions increased upper-level decision making; these were the *Autonomy* program and the *Hierarchically controlled* program, respectively. They followed the organization for one and a half years, including a pre-measurement of employee satisfaction and productivity, a training period to produce the two experimental conditions, and one year of functioning under the new organizational structure, before the final measures were obtained.

Morse and Reimer expected to find that both satisfaction and productivity measures were higher in the Autonomy program than in the Hierarchy program. True to their expectation, they found greater satisfaction with the self and the organization in the Autonomy program; satisfaction actually decreased under the conditions of Hierarchy. *Both* programs resulted in greater productivity; if anything, the Hierarchy condition showed a greater increment in productivity than did the Autonomy condition. In essence, however, introducing significant decision-making participation to lower levels of the organization increased *both* satisfaction and productivity. A manager's and an employee's dream come true.

Although not concerned with productivity, Miller (1967) offers further confirmation of the relationship between personal autonomy in an organization and level of general satisfaction. Miller studied professional scientists and engineers in two divisions of a large aerospace company. He correlated measures of alienation from their work (e.g., I really do not feel a sense of pride as a result of my work) with the type of organizational control structure encountered, differentiating between a directive structure—unilateral decision making and low interaction rates—and a participatory structure—joint decision making and high interaction. His data showed a positive correlation between structure and alienation; the most alienated scientists worked in the most directive structures.

We would not expect, however, that every flat organizational structure (one in which decision making is shared) would produce an equally salutary effect. Workers (including scientific professionals) might enjoy their increased autonomy, but management personnel who have lost some of their organization power and privilege might feel less joyful about the entire matter. Recall the problem of interdependence that Lippitt, Watson, and Westley suggested (p. 231). Giving joy to one part of an interdependent relationship while simultaneously giving sorrow to another can produce an unstable situation that will not endure for long.

OTHER VIEWS OF PARTICIPATION

There are several lines of research that offer further perspectives on this matter of participation in decision making and planned change. One approach comes out of the lab studies of communication networks; another derives from some of Bales' work on interaction patterns within small groups; a third derives from the tradition of industrial psychology.

Communication networks

If you can imagine the most asceptic and artificial method of examining communication in a problem-solving group, you will have in mind the communication-network studies. Bavelas (1950) and Leavitt (1958) created a variety of communication networks in small groups. To accomplish this feat, you need a group of people, a table, preferably circular, and partitions separating the individuals from one another. Oh, yes, you also need a variety of colored or numbered slots into which subjects can put written notes, set up so that the experimenter can close or open them as conditions warrant. Figure 19.1 shows several networks you can

create with this equipment and personnel. These patterns differ in terms of who gets to communicate with whom and the varying degrees of distance between members. In (a), for example, each person gets to communicate with two others directly, without relaying his message through someone else. In (b) the end people have to send messages through all the others to reach each other; each position must go through others to get messages across. In (c) one person can directly reach all the others.

In addition to the *distances* between members, Bavelas has suggested that the patterns differ in terms of the *centrality* of positions in the network. The position of highest centrality in a network is the one closest to all other positions. In the circle pattern (a) all positions occupy the same degree of centrality; everyone is comparably close to everyone else. In the chain (b), in the wheel (c), and in the Y (d), however, position C is the most central in that it communicates most directly with all the other positions. It has been suggested that centrality in position should correlate highly with perceived leadership in a problem-solving endeavor. If the groups have a problem to solve, and the solution requires a pooling of pieces of data that each member holds individually, the person who occupies the most central position should emerge as everyone's leader. Data from several studies indicate this is generally the case. For example, in the circle there is no expected correspondence between network position and leadership ratings; data substantiate this. But in the wheel pattern there should be a high correspondence between position C and recognition as group leader. Again, data

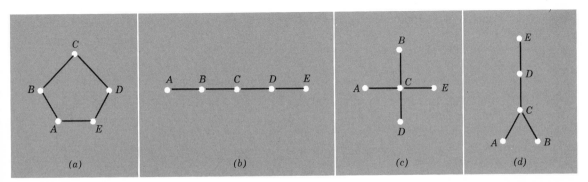

Figure 19.1 Communications networks. Leavitt called (a) the circle; (b) the chain; (c) the wheel; (d) the Y

substantiate this expectation: in the wheel, position C receives 23 leadership nominations, whereas *no* other position is so rated; in the Y, position C receives 17 leadership nominations, whereas each other position has none or at most only one (see Bavelas, 1950).

It should by now be apparent that the most central positions have the greatest participation permitted within the structure, and the peripheral positions have the least. In terms of autonomy in decision making, centrality implies independence, peripherality implies dependence. As Leavitt informally describes his results,

"We may grossly characterize the kinds of differences that occur in this way: the circle, one extreme, is active, leaderless, unorganized, erratic, and yet is enjoyed by its members. The wheel, at the other extreme, is less active, has a distinct leader, is well and stably organized, and yet is unsatisfying to most of its members" (1958, p. 558).

This distinction between task efficiency and personal satisfaction is discussed more fully in the next section.

In terms of member morale as a function of position in the network, those in most peripheral positions were much less satisfied with their jobs than those who occupied positions of greatest centrality. People do seem to like to be where the action is, to be involved in making decisions about the work they and the group are doing, to be kept informed about what's going on.

Additional research has indicated that the circle, being more democratic in its form and thereby allowing freer member-to-member interaction and discussion, actually works more effectively than the autocratic patterns when a problem is changed and its solution requires a new way of thinking—that is, breaking the former set. Interestingly enough, in a study with the same kind of task Leavitt employed, but permitting the groups a two-minute period between trials to re-organize, the circle pattern sought a more hierarchical structure (Guetzkow & Dill, 1957). Still other research has indicated what happens when a person accustomed to one structure is changed to another. Cohen, Bennis, and Wolkon (1962) report that promoting a person from a peripheral position in one network to a more central position in another

(i.e., to a position of more equal participation) produces positive effects on measures of satisfaction. Demoting a person from a position of greater centrality to one of less centrality has the reverse effect: all indices of satisfaction drop significantly.

Interaction process analysis

Bales' empirical data and its theoretical underpinnings offer us still further insight into the participation approach to planned change (Bales, 1950a, b; 1955a, b; 1958; Borgatta, Bales, & Couch, 1954). On the theoretical side, Bales offers us a functional view of small-group dynamics. He views the small group in much the same way he views the total society: both are social systems with problems of adaptation to an external world and an internal world. The external world or outer situation involves the kind of task to be completed or goal to be achieved. One group may have been formed to outline plans for a community recreation project; another may have been organized to plan a class party; another, to prepare a protest demonstration; still another to paint a house. These all define the external situation to which the group must adapt. The internal world involves relationships among members. This internal world has variously been referred to as the groups' *maintenance* system, its *internal* system, or its *socioemotional* system.

In Bales' theoretical model (1955a) there is a basic opposition between successful efforts to adapt to the external or task system and successful adaptation to the internal system. He envisions chains of events that give rise to problems: a group that attempts to deal successfully with its task problems acts in ways that create internal problems, and a group that directs its major efforts to solving its internal problems produces a problem in successful task adaptation.

Task Adaptation. The theoretical argument maintains that successful dealing with a task (adaptation) demands a division of labor in a group. This means a differentiation of roles and jobs. One member might take on secretarial duties, another might handle publicity, another sign making, and so on. Bales argues that as this differentiation is carried on for some time it becomes more hierarchical and formal. In a long-lived group or social system over time a preliminary, even informal division of labor tends toward increased formalization. Furthermore, a hierarchy of importance or prestige begins to emerge: certain jobs have more power and responsibility; others are cleaner; others require manual work; certain jobs give a person greater access to rewards; others may cast a person into the background. If you have ever worked with a group planning a demonstration or affair (of almost any sort), you know that some persons get all the publicity and seem always to be in the limelight, and others, who may in fact do most of the envelope stuffing and dirty legwork, are shoved into the background; their rewards, although present, are often less than those of the person in the public's eye.

Bales suggests that as this differentiation begins to occur, all in an effort to deal better with the group's external problems, forces that are antagonistic to group solidarity are created; with formalized role differentiation and with a hierarchy, especially one in which authority, prestige, and rewards are increasingly vested at the top, antagonisms arise within the group.

Internal Adaptation. In Bales' theory a similar outcome occurs to a group that seeks to solve its internal problems. In this chain of events a group tries to keep itself harmonious, happy, and conflict-free, equal in power, status, and rewards. Such a group prides itself on its inner harmony and full equality; but at the same time it cannot do what may be necessary to deal adequately with its external or task problem. As Bales states it,

"As solidarity increases between those in authority and those subjected to control, strains are created toward a more diffuse, less differentiated, and less formal exercise of authority, which in turn may interfere with the adaptation and integration of the whole group by making it difficult or impossible for the persons in authority to require or demand that which is necessary but unpleasant, difficult, or dangerous" (1955a, p. 130).

Essentially, he argues that to get a job done often requires someone to take charge and dole out unpleasant, lower-status jobs to others. This, in turn, may create dissension in the group.

On the other hand, a group that seeks to keep everyone happy and equal may indeed succeed, but soon no one is willing to take on responsibility for doling out the dirty work that may have to be done. To keep itself happy the group may sacrifice the task; to get the task done efficiently, it may sacrifice people.

Interaction Coding. In his empirical work Bales examined actual patterns of interaction in small groups dealing with a problem. He had observers record member-to-member interactions over time, noting who interacted with whom and what the nature of their interaction was. He employed a 12-category coding system (Bales, 1950a; 1950b):

1. Shows solidarity
2. Shows tension release
3. Agrees
4. Gives suggestion
5. Gives opinion
6. Gives orientation
7. Asks for orientation
8. Asks for opinion
9. Asks for suggestion
10. Disagrees
11. Shows tension
12. Shows antagonism

Six of these categories (1, 2, 3, 10, 11, 12) apply to the internal system and involve the nature of relationships among members; the remaining six apply to the external system and deal more directly with matters involving the group's task. A further differentiation indicates three that apply to *positive* internal factors (1, 2, 3) and three that apply to *negative* internal factors (10, 11, 12).

This system makes it possible, at the end of a group's session, to order or rank the members in terms of their participation or interaction activity. In addition, it is possible to ask members questions about who they liked most and who offered the best ideas in the group, and then to relate these rankings to interaction rankings. This is precisely what Bales did (1958).

He found that those who are high in their total interaction are rated by fellow members as contributing good ideas for the group's task problem. On the other hand, the contribution of the most active member (through his helpful ideas) does not lead to his being very highly liked. Integrating the finding with the theory, there seems to be an opposition between contribution to the external or task problem and solution of the group's internal problems. In fact, a man who contributes most to the task seems to be relatively lower in his ranking on liking.

Leader and Member Types. These provocative findings led Bales to posit the notion of *complementarity of leaders* (1958). He defined five theoretical kinds of group member and leader in terms of the functions they serve for the group: (1) The *great man* leader, an empirical rarity in Bales work, is a person who is highly active in his participation, but ranks highly *both* in task ideas contributed and in likability, his contribution to group solidarity. He is a great man in that he somehow manages to overcome the opposition between the external and internal problems. In a moment we will examine how this apparent magic is accomplished. (2) The *task specialist* is high on over-all activity, ranks high on ideas contributed, but seems less able to fulfill the functions of group maintenance; he ranks lower on likability. (3) The *social specialist* ranks high on likability but lower both on ideas and over-all participation. He seems to work toward keeping harmony, in contrast to the task specialist. (4) The *overactive deviant,* a type Bales suggests is common, participates a great deal but contributes little by way of ideas or likability. That is, he talks a lot but says little that is helpful to the group in solving either its external task problems or its internal, socioemotional ones. (5) The *underactive deviant* ranks low on total participation, ideas contributed, and likability. He's there in the group, but that's about it.

Complementarity of leadership occurs in groups—by far the majority—in which there does not exist a great man leader. Here the task specialist and the social specialist must work hand in hand to deal with both kinds of group adaptive problems; the task-specialist concentrates on task matters, and the social specialist deals with the disharmony that too much task concentration can produce.

Few Great Men. Why is it that few great men leaders emerge? Bales suggested that the task specialist tends to talk a great deal and to offer many ideas, but may allow little interaction.

He tends to be a one-way street, possibly even somewhat authoritarian, giving out a lot of helpful material but keeping himself inaccessible and aloof. This creates disharmony. Bales' research technique (1958) allows us to examine individual differences in what may be called the *feedback ratio*, the ratio of communications sent out to communications received. A person with a high ratio is one who is very active in his participation and in turn allows much interaction to be directed to him. A member with a low feedback ratio sends out a great deal, but takes in very little in return.

Examining his data in light of this feedback ratio, Bales comes up with the very important finding that task specialists with a high feedback ratio are better liked than those with a low feedback ratio. Those with a low ratio tend to be disliked more the more they talk.

This finding is important because it indicates one manner by which the basic opposition Bales posited between task and maintenance functions may be overcome. It is even more interesting and important when we realize that the participation and group-decision techniques we have considered point out a similar factor, although it is not referred to as feedback ratio. Inducing change by means of a democratic leadership style creates a context of equality of involvement, unlike the one-way flow of the authoritarian style or lecture format. A high feedback ratio, as Bales notes, allows "objections, qualifications, questions, and countersuggestions to occur" (1958, p. 444). It allows all to contribute to a group's functioning. From Bales' perspective this kind of member involvement allows a leader to deal with both external and internal problems of adaptation; it is an exercise of authority that does not bring about internal disharmony, so that both morale and task efficiency are met. From the Lewinian perspective, as we have seen, member involvement overcomes resistance to change, produces a sense of responsibility and involvement, induces change that is independent of the change agent, and is ethically appropriate. In other words, participation increases group efficiency (or produces effective change) while maintaining high satisfaction. Both Bales' and Lewin's perspectives indicate the positive virtues of democratic, participatory leadership, whether within a group or by a change agent.

Industrial psychology

Roughly paralleling Bales' differentiation between the task system and the socioemotional system we have in the history of industrial psychology two contrasting theories of organization. One, the classic theory, is relatively non-psychological and emphasizes the kinds of structural arrangement in an organization that will make it a smoothly efficient machine (e.g., Dennison, 1931; Sheldon, 1923; Taylor, 1911; Urwick, 1944). The concern is with task factors and work efficiency. Structures such as chain of command, unity of command, and specialization of function are considered essential. Modern organization theory, by contrast, tends to de-emphasize the machine qualities of the organization and to concentrate on psychological factors within and among individuals. The concern is with training in human relations, motivating workers, keeping morale high, and so on (e.g., Argyris, 1957, 1964; Likert, 1961; McGregor, 1960, 1966).

The machine-like approach of classic organizational theory envisions the worker as a cog in the machine needing careful supervision and control, responding primarily to monetary incentives. He is relatively unthinking, uncaring, lazy, not terribly responsible; nor is he particularly creative. The modern approach sees him as a person with needs for security, personal growth, and self-actualization. His involvement with the organization is not as a cog but as a thinking man with complex motivations. As Bennis (1959) summarized the distinction, the earlier view talks about "organizations without people"; the later tends to discuss "people without organizations."

It is not clear just when the person focus became more central than the machine view, but no doubt the classic studies undertaken by Roethlisberger and Dickson in 1939 at the Western Electric Company in Hawthorne, Illinois, contributed something positive in this regard. This early study highlighted the importance of human factors in employee productivity and morale. Plodding dutifully ahead in their classic manner, the investigators sought to relate certain

physical features of the work environment to employee productivity. Perhaps, they argued, if illumination were increased, productivity would increase; perhaps if rest pauses were lengthened, productivity would rise. Other physical or environmental factors were similarly posited to be related to productivity. To study this they isolated a group of workers and introduced the physical variables thought to increase productivity. They compared the test group's rates with those of other groups in the plant as well as with its own rates over time and under different experimental conditions. Puzzling findings emerged. For example, it seemed that productivity went up with *decreases* in illumination. If anything, it seemed that isolating the group produced an informal social structure that effectively influenced members' behavior toward either increased or decreased productivity; the productivity effects were caused by informal group pressures rather than solely by systematic modifications in the physical environment. Alas, it seemed that human factors were more important than physical factors.

The Successful Supervisor. During the last 20 or 30 years substantial effort has gone into the examination of human factors in industrial motivation. In a review of motivation in organizations, Katz and Kahn (1951) have suggested several qualities successful supervisors possess (*successful* here refers to high productivity records). First, a successful supervisor plays a more differentiated role than a less successful supervisor. Rather than doing the same kind of work as the men he is supervising, he spends more time in planning work and performing specialized tasks. Second, more successful supervisors do not supervise as closely as less successful ones; they do not check up on their men as often; they limit their workers' freedom less. In essence, they give the men greater personal freedom and autonomy, delegate more authority, and still perform supervisory functions. They begin to sound like Lewin's democratic leaders or Bales' great man. Third, successful supervisors show greater employee orientation, as distinguished from production or institution orientation, than less successful supervisors. They spend more time on employee motivation, especially involving themselves in supportive personal relationships, in being more understanding and less punitive. Employee orientation sounds much like a characteristic of Bales' social specialist and includes some of the qualities of Lewin's democratic leader.

Organizational Structure and Employee Behavior. A more recent effort to document the importance of organizational structure and employee behavior is reported by Porter and Lawler (1964). They indicate how several factors of organizational structure that have direct relevance for worker autonomy and participation in decision making are related to positive job attitudes and behavior. Of special relevance is their analysis of *tall* versus *flat* organizational structures. A tall structure has a number of levels of responsibility in a hierarchical arrangement; a flat structure is less complex and more decentralized with respect to control over decision making. Worthy (1950) had maintained that flat structures were better in that they

". . . tend to create a potential for improved attitudes, more effective supervision, and greater individual responsibility and initiative among employees. Moreover, arrangements of this type encourage the development of individual self-expression and creativity which are so necessary to the personal satisfaction of employees and which are an essential ingredient of the democratic way of life" (p. 179).

Porter and Lawler noted that there really had been no systematic tests of Worthy's argument for almost 12 years after it was published. One of the first (Meltzer & Salter, 1962) showed no particular relationship between organizational shape and worker satisfaction or productivity, but in two studies reported by Porter and Lawler (1964) organizational *size* interacted with shape, and shape and type of need satisfaction were correlated. Although no over-all effect emerged, in small companies (fewer than 5000 employees) there was greater managerial satisfaction in flat rather than in tall structures; in larger companies tall structures produced self-reports of greater satisfaction.

As Porter and Lawler argue, organization size seems to be a reasonable conditioning variable to the relationship between shape and satisfaction. In a smaller organization, where communication and coordination are easy,

the flat shape allows for greater individual autonomy and responsibility, but when size gets unwieldy, so that coordination is a problem and communication is difficult, some tallness may be essential. In these larger structures there may be a need for what Likert has referred to as *overlapping* structures; here an important degree of individual autonomy is preserved and at the same time a structural arrangement is created in which coordination is possible. Each level is linked by an overlapping directorate to lower levels; decision making thus does not simply flow from the top down, but rather through a series of overlapping centers of decision-making control.

The second interaction effect in Porter and Lawler's study involved the relationship between organizational shape and the kinds of need that were best satisfied. They differentiated *security needs* (e.g., feeling secure in my management position); *social needs* (e.g., opportunity to give help to others or to develop close friendships); *esteem needs* (authority of position, opportunity for independent thought and action, or opportunity for participation); *self-actualization needs* (opportunity for personal growth or feeling of self-fulfillment or feeling of worthwhile accomplishment). Their results indicated that a tall structure was especially satisfying to security and social needs; a flat structure was superior in producing satisfaction of self-actualization needs; the remaining needs were comparably satisfied in both types of structure. Although there are some puzzling aspects to these findings—really nothing that an inventive mind with a bent toward the post hoc couldn't easily handle—in general they suggest that the picture gets increasingly complicated when it comes to applying participation procedures to larger industrial organizations. The size of the organization, the kinds of need satisfied, and (a factor not systematically explored) the level of the person in the organization (manager, as in this study, worker, or what?), and undoubtedly even more variables, must be taken into account.

Despite these important qualifications, it appears that investigators most directly involved with industrial psychology have turned to the same kinds of factor as those in the participation approach to planned change. Note that their efforts are indeed oriented toward producing planned change; specifically, they are interested in how best to create happier, more creative, and more productive workers in large-scale organizations. It seems realistic, albeit unfortunate, to assume that some kind of complex organization will form a basic part of our lives for some time to come in this highly technological world in which we live. The question then is how to change these structures to bring out the best in people. The participation approach to planned change, as reflected in human relations programs in industrial psychology, is not simply idle game-playing by academicians, but has strikingly important social applications.

Recall that a university is often a large-scale organization. Recall further that students and others spend a significant part of their lives in such institutions. Then note that many large universities seem to be hard-line adherents to tradition, resisting the very kinds of change with which most business organizations have long since involved themselves. Finally, note that many efforts today are being made—usually at the noisy insistence of students—to change the structure of universities, to bring them into greater congruence with the ideas embodied in this participation approach. Paradoxically, the academicians who study organizations, consult with them for outrageous fees, and urge them to change, return to their own universities and seem to put on the black boots and uniform of the autocrat. Who changes the change agents?

HUMAN RELATIONS OR HUMAN RESOURCES?

In the discussion of the participation approach I differentiated between psychological or illusory participation and real participation in the decision-making or change process (pp. 245–246). Miles (1965) made a similar point in differentiating between what he called the *human relations* and the *human resources* perspectives of business managers. Recognizing the impact that modern organization theory has had in focusing businessmen's attention on human factors in organizational behavior, Miles suggested that a human relations approach captured the imagination of business managers. In effect, this approach tries to give workers a sense of being useful and important. As Miles states it,

"Participation . . . is a lubricant which oils away resistance to formal authority. . . . The manager 'buys' cooperation by letting his subordinates in on departmental information and allowing them to discuss and state their opinions on various departmental problems. . . . Implicit in this model is the idea that it might actually be easier and more efficient if the manager could merely make departmental decisions without bothering to involve his subordinates. . . . In many instances, this model suggests, the manager might do better to 'waste time' in discussing the problem with his subordinates, and perhaps even to accept suggestions that he believes may be less efficient, in order to get the decision carried out" (pp. 149 & 151).

Clearly, as Miles suggests and as we have previously noted, this approach seeks to give a sense of participation in order to gain better worker cooperation, but basically does not consider other aspects of participation; the other possibilities form the basis of the human resources model.

As the term suggests, a human resources view of participation is based on the assumption that talents, ideas, and skills exist throughout an entire population of workers; the function of the manager, the group leader, or the change agent—whatever the specific case may be— is to create an atmosphere in which this reservoir is tapped.

". . . the manager's job cannot be viewed merely as one of giving direction and obtaining cooperation. Instead, his primary task becomes that of creating an environment in which the total resources of his department can be utilized" (Miles, p. 151).

Miles' own research, not unexpectedly, indicates that managers view their relationship with their superiors in terms of the human resources model but relate to subordinates in terms of the human relations model. That is, managers feel that their superiors should allow them to participate in organizational decision making because they have good, creative ideas. They don't want to participate in an illusory way merely to *feel* important; they want their ideas to be heard and perhaps to be acted on. However, when they confront their own employees, too often they tend to see them in human relations terms: how could *they* have any good ideas? How could *they* take the initiative to direct themselves? Let's just let them feel good through these human relations gimmicks.

How often throughout this text have we encountered this same general point? An individual wants others to treat him in ways that he does not feel can be applied to them. He wants his superiors to assume he is capable, creative, self-directive, but cannot grant these same qualities to his subordinates. And in the international arena we have noted how we define as beneficent actions of our own nation that we define as evil in another: if we do it, it is to defend freedom; if they do it, it is to convert the world's people to Godless Communism. In the master-slave context, if our side wins, it's a glorious victory, if their side wins, it's a massacre. Perhaps we need a resurrection of the Golden Rule, which defines relationships between persons, or groups, or nations in a reciprocal context: do unto others what you would have them do unto you. If you would be treated according to a human resources model, why not apply this same model to those with whom you interact? If you feel that taking another's life is shocking regardless of who does it, you can make no easy distinction between a glorious victory and a hideous massacre. You cannot celebrate one and mourn the other.

Human resources:
Leadership style and minority opinion

The human resources model offers us another perspective on the participation approach. There are several important facets to this notion: (1) More people involved in a process open up a broader range of ideas and bring up combinations that might otherwise have been ignored. (2) More people actively involved offer the possibility for a system of checks and balances, a screening of ideas. If the first point suggests that real participation opens floodgates to new information, this point indicates a kind of combined ego-superego function that provides some checks on the potential flood. (3) Real participation in a group may increase the level of individual motivation. (4) Real par-

ticipation opens up the possibility for a creative clash of disparate perspectives, out of which may emerge a more innovative program than would be possible without full use of human resources.

Several lines of research will clarify and amplify various aspects of the human resources perspective on participation. Maier and Solem (1952) presented discussion groups with the following problem: "A man bought a horse for $60 and sold it for $70. Then he bought it back for $80 and again sold it for $90. How much money did he make in the horse business?" About half of the discussion groups had a leader whose only function was to be an observer, listening to the discussion but not contributing any views of his own. The other half had discussion leaders who were to encourage everyone to participate; they too were to refrain from expressing their own views, but were to be more democratic in their style. All group members recorded their estimates of the correct answer both before discussion and after. Both types of group began with about the same number of correct answers; both increased correct answers after the discussion, but the democratic-leader groups increased significantly more than the observer groups.

Maier and Solem were particularly interested in testing the proposition that the positive benefit of a democratic leader is that he allows minority opinion, which may be correct but unpopular and therefore inhibited, to be expressed. That is, by encouraging everyone to participate he makes maximal use of the group's resources and thereby increases the quality of its problem-solving ability. They conducted a careful analysis of their data by dividing the groups not only by leadership type but also in terms of minority with correct answer before discussion versus majority with correct answer before discussion. In this manner it was possible to see if the leader was helpful in permitting the correct minority view to sway the group. The general trend of their data suggest this was the case. When the majority holds the correct answer at the beginning, the presence of a democratic leader does little; however, when the minority has the correct answer, a democratic discussion leader helps by guaranteeing them a hearing and by reducing the normal social pressure exerted against minority or deviant views.

Oh, yes—the answer to the horse-trading problem. A frequent answer is $10, but that's incorrect. The answer is $20.

A conclusion similar to that proposed by Maier and Solem was put forth by Torrance (1954). During his investigations of bomber crews given survival problems to solve he found that crews with a rigid structure prevented those lower in the command hierarchy from using their full talents in dealing with the problem, whereas more flexible crews facilitated communication between members and called on a wider range of crew resources and member skills. In yet another study Maier and Hoffman (1961) found that foremen in a simulated work situation who thought of their workers as idea men had groups that produced more innovative solutions to the issue they faced than foremen who defined their subordinates as problem people. In essence, then, the way the leader views his men influences the over-all quality of their performance. In each of these cases the leader who viewed his group as a resource or acted (usually democratically) to increase the likelihood that various opinions, skills, and ideas would come forth contributed to a better group performance.

Human resources:
The release of deviant perspectives

It is interesting to note the relevance of an apparently different research tradition to this matter of human resources. Recall that Maier and Solem suggested that a person holding a minority opinion in a group might be hesitant to express it—even though he could be correct—unless someone like the leader created the proper atmosphere. Some classic laboratory studies of conformity behavior come up with much the same point. These conformity studies have involved the conditions under which a minority member (minority in opinion or perception) feels capable of expressing his unique point of view. In some cases the person is free to defy social norms rather than majority group opinion.

Asch examined this first effect in one of the several variations of his classic study (1952, pp. 450–501). One naive subject faced groups of up to 15 stooges who gave the incorrect judgment on several key trials of a perceptual task. Picture yourself seated in a room with five others. As far as you can tell they are, like you, subjects serving in some kind of psychological experiment. The experimenter tells you all that on each trial you will be shown a standard-length line and three comparison lines; your task is to indicate which of the comparison lines is closest in size to the standard. A simple task, you think. The first critical trial is the one on which the stooges give a clearly incorrect answer: they say a line that is clearly the wrong size matches the standard. Suppose the standard line is about 8 inches, comparison line 1 is 6 inches, comparison 2 is 8 inches, and comparison 3 is 6½ inches. You are confident in your choice of comparison 2 as the correct one. On each trial each subject announces his answer out loud; subject 1 announces line 1; subject 2 announces 1; subject 3, 1; subject 4, 1; subject 5, 1; and now it's your turn. More than one-third of the subjects in this experimental treatment gave erroneous judgments; control subjects not subjected to this false majority judgment achieved more than 90 percent accuracy, but the experimentals' accuracy dropped to about 67 percent. To examine even more extreme deviations from objective reality Asch used comparison lines that were more radically different from the standard. For example, if the standard were 10 inches, the comparison lines would be 3, 10, and 2 inches. Again the controls achieved almost perfect accuracy in this easier perceptual judgment, but the experimentals' accuracy was only about 72 percent. In fact, whether the judgment was difficult or relatively easy as in this latter case, the difference in accuracy between the controls and the experimentals remained about the same.

In a variation of this study that is of particular interest to us, Asch had one of the stooges become a "deviant partner." Instead of the naive subject facing a unanimous majority in opposition to his perception, he had a partner who saw as he did. Under these conditions Asch found that subjects were courageous enough to stand up in opposition to the majority and utter the correct answer. It appears that the validation of his own conception of social reality helped a minority subject with the correct answer feel free enough to state his opinion.

Milgram's (1963 study of obedience, discussed on pp. 76–77, offers further instructive confirmation of this effect. Recall that Milgram's basic experimental situation involves a subject presumably administering electric shocks to a poor learner (the stooge) to help improve his learning. Although no actual shocks are administered, the subject is led to believe that he is administering progressively more severe intensities. Even when the learner cries out in pain, at the urging of the experimenter the subject continues giving shocks. The variation of this design that is relevant to our present discussion is one in which there are three teachers and one learner (Milgram, 1965). Two of the teachers, like the learner, are stooges; they play a defiant role at several specified points in the experiment. The subject and the two teacher-stooges begin shocking the learner for each mistake; shocks are increased in intensity for each error. Finally, at around the 150-volt level, when the learner-stooge makes his first vigorous protest about what is presumably happening to him, one teacher-stooge informs the experimenter that he is quitting. He goes to sit in the back of the room, refusing to participate further. The experimenter urges the subject and the other teacher-stooge to go on. When the shock level reaches about 210 volts the second teacher-stooge quits, in defiance of the experimenter's request to continue.

What is the effect on the live subject of having help such as the defiant stooges? Milgram's results indicate that these conditions produce a figure of 90 percent defiance, in contrast to 35 percent defiance when the subjects faced their ordeal alone. Milgram concludes that group pressure can be liberating to the individual.

In addition to the apparently liberating effects a partner in deviation can provide against pressure from a group or from a psychological experimenter, researchers have uncovered liberating effects from more general social norms. For example, you are walking down the street, window shopping perhaps, when you come to a stoplight at the corner. You stop,

prepared to wait for it to change. (Here we must assume that you are not in New York City, where there seems to be a norm against waiting for lights; pedestrians and autos vie in a match against death.) While you are waiting, someone begins to cross against the light. Do you just stand there? After all, there are no cars coming. After all, he's just crossed in violation, so why don't you? Investigations of this situation (in Blake, 1958) have indicated how another's rule violation acts as a releaser, making it easier for you to go ahead and break the rules. More refined examination indicated, furthermore, that a well-dressed rule violator liberated more souls than one who was poorly attired.

In still another situation (in Blake, 1958) subjects were given soda crackers treated with a thirst-inducing drug and told to wait a few moments in the hall. Sure enough, out in the hall there was a drinking fountain, and sure enough, over the fountain was a sign indicating that it was not to be used. Along came that stooge and took a drink, and sure enough, the thirsty subject followed right along. Another liberating effect. It should be noted that naive subjects who were *extremely* thirsty drank anyway, managing to disregard both the stooge (who sometimes did not violate the rule) and the sign.

In a perceptive and fascinating psychoanalytic account of the dynamics of leadership Redl (1955) suggested several kinds of group leader or *central person* who serve this releasing or liberating function. One is called a *seducer*. Although this individual may not be much respected or liked, he commits the first act and thereby releases others' inhibitions. As Redl views the situation, there is a buildup in the intensity of some forbidden drive such as sex or aggression. The drive is kept in control until the seducer commits the initiatory act. An example Redl offers is a boys' classroom in which there had been some buildup of anger toward the instructor. He arrived and the students rose to stand at attention. Suddenly one student began shouting aggressively; shortly thereafter the rest joined in, with an intensity that seemed puzzling. It appears that the initiator's action had released the forbidden impulses.

Another type of central person relevant to this analysis is the *bad influence:* "These children do affect the others, not overtly—quite in contrast to the 'seducer type'—but by their presence in the same room, something happens to these youngsters which makes them unruly, full of 'dirty' ideas, or just difficult to manage." (Redl, 1955, p. 84). Redl's example is a class of 11-year-olds in which a word reminds those in the know of a sexual situation. Those who have this association look knowingly at one boy in particular. They begin to grin and he grins in return. The next day that boy is absent; the same kind of situation occurs, but this time there is no exchange of knowing glances, no division of the classroom into those who "know" and those who remain in the dark. Unlike the seducer, who actually carries out the initiatory act and thereby releases others' inhibited impulses, the bad influence need not *do* anything. He *represents* the forbidden; he is someone who seems less confused and conflicted than the others. He is infectious; he offers the group a quality around which it can form. His very presence serves as the releaser of the forbidden impulses the others are experiencing.

As these general lines of investigation suggest, there are conditions that give an individual permission to express his views, even when he is in the minority, or to defy authority, or to violate broader social norms. In terms of the human resources model we have been examining, this research highlights both the social reality factors at play in inhibiting and later releasing minority perspectives and the potential benefits that accrue both to the individual and to the group from such release. Of course a leader or change agent who confidently knows himself to be correct is not likely to wish or to endure the release of such minority perspectives. After all, he is less interested in maximizing human resources than he is concerned with getting his own point of view across and accepted.

Human resources and leadership style: Complicating factors

Saying that the issue we are examining is complex is one matter; demonstrating it is another. A program of research undertaken over the last 20 years by Fiedler demonstrates the complex collection of factors that must be considered before we can state boldly that participatory or democratic leadership is the best (most of this work is summarized and discussed in Fiedler, 1964). In his initial efforts Fiedler sought to relate a leader variable to group productivity. The variable he selected was the leader's attitudes toward his workers. Leaders were asked to rate qualities such as pleasantness, friendliness, and enthusiasm, both in those they most preferred to work with and those they least preferred to work with. The discrepancy in ratings between most- and least-preferred was called the *ASo* score, meaning *assumed similarity of opposites.* If the leader made only a minimal differentiation between them the discrepancy score would be low and we would say that his ASo score was high; he made a high assumption of similarity between opposites. However, if he strongly differentiated between the most liked and the least liked, the discrepancy score would be high and his ASo score would be low.

Fiedler viewed the ASo score as a measure of the leader's psychological distance from his workers. Those who differentiated a great deal (low ASo) were assumed to be more distant than those who saw the most-liked and the least-liked as very similar. In an updated reconceptualization, Fiedler (1964) viewed the low-ASo leaders as being more task- than person-oriented, whereas high-ASo leaders were thought to be more member-oriented. He also determined that the rating of the least-preferred co-worker (LPC) was most indicative of the leader's style: a leader who rated LPC highly tended to use a permissive or considerate style; one who gave LPC low ratings was more controlling, managing, or directive. This distinction is somewhat like Bales': on one side is the leader with distance and task orientation (low LPC or ASo); on the other is the leader who is oriented toward equality and interpersonal relationships (high LPC or ASo).

Fiedler sought in a lengthy series of studies to relate the leader's ASo score to evaluations of group effectiveness (see Fiedler, 1964). Although he initially expected that interpersonally oriented leaders would be more effective, ratings of high-school basketball teams and a later study of survey teams indicated just the reverse: ASo was *negatively* correlated with measures of team performance. Better basketball teams (they won more games) and survey teams receiving high ratings were led by *low-ASo*-type leaders who were psychologically distant, more task-oriented and directive.

As though matters were not complicated enough already, Fiedler insisted on a continual refinement of both his theory and the data. On the theoretical side, he argued that the leader's ASo score is only one ingredient in the mix that produces an effective group. Moreover, for some kinds of group and some kinds of task a more directive leader is better, whereas for other groups and other tasks less directiveness is more effective. Specifically, he maintained that three situational factors would interact with the leader's ASo and LPC scores to produce high or low effectiveness for the group: (1) the liking relationship between the group members and the leader; (2) the power the leader's position carries with it; (3) the degree to which the task is highly structured. When the liking relationship is good, the task unstructured, and the position of power strong, the leader is in a favorable situation to be influential. When the liking relationship is poor, the task unstructured, the leader's power position weak, the situation is deemed unfavorable.

A convenient way of examining Fiedler's theory and supporting data is found in Figure 19.2, which indicates the nature of the relationship Fiedler found between leadership style (as indicated by the leader perception scores, including the ASo and the LPC) and group effectiveness under varying situational conditions (as outlined in the octants). The bow-shaped curve indicates what Fiedler discovered in reanalyzing his data: that directive leaders (low ASo or LPC) are most effective in situations that are at either extreme of favorableness, whereas permissive leaders (high ASo or LPC) are most effective in group conditions in the middle range, moderately favorable (octant IV) or moderately unfavorable (octants V and VI). In Fiedler's words,

"In very favorable conditions, where the leader has power, informal backing, and a relatively well-structured task, the group is ready to be directed on

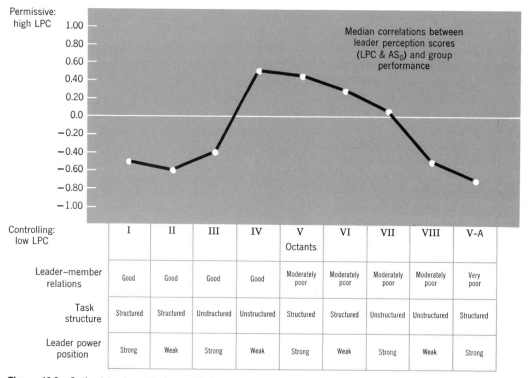

Figure 19.2 Optimal leader attitudes and behavior required by various group situations (adapted from Fiedler, 1964, p. 175)

how to go about its task. Under a very unfavorable condition, however, the group will fall apart unless the leader's active intervention and control can keep the members on the job. In moderately unfavorable conditions, the accepted leader faces an ambiguous task, or his relations with group members are tenuous. Under these circumstances, a relationship-oriented, nondirective, permissive attitude may reduce member anxiety or intra-group conflict, and this enables the group to operate more effectively (i.e., the members would not feel threatened by the leader, and considerate, diplomatic leader behavior under these conditions may induce group members to cooperate)" (1964, p. 165).

In a recent study to test these ideas further Shaw and Blum (1966) created a situation in which directive leadership style could be contrasted with nondirective in a situational context that sought to vary favorableness:

". . . the results of this experiment show clearly that directive leadership is more effective than nondirective when the task is highly structured; that is, when there is only one solution and one way (or only a few ways) of obtaining this solution. . . . However, on tasks that require varied information and approaches, nondirective leadership is clearly more effective. On such tasks the requirements for leadership are great. Contributions from all members must be encouraged, and this requires motivating, advising, rewarding, giving support—in short, nondirective leadership" (p. 241).

The resource of conflict

Another aspect of the human resources approach to participative change is related to the preceding sections yet sufficiently unique to warrant separate consideration. This is the use of *constructive conflict* as a group resource. Although we commonly view conflict within a group or between groups as something negative and to be avoided, several sociologists have called our attention to the positive functions conflict can serve. Coser (1956) and Simmel (1957) talk of conflicts that help growth and development or serve as a positive force of cohesion:

"An absolutely . . . harmonious group . . . not only is empirically unreal, it could show no real life process. The society of saints which Dante sees in the Rose of Paradise may be like such a group, but it is without any change and development; whereas the holy assembly of Church Fathers in Raphael's *Disputa* shows if not actual conflict, at least a considerable differentiation of moods and directions of thought, whence flow all the vitality and the really organic structure of that group" (Simmel, 1957, p. 195).

The relationship between conflict and participation is straightforward in theory if somewhat troublesome in practice. A structure of communication that maximizes individual involvement and participation should allow for conflict of ideas to emerge in a group; an autocratic structure should tend to inhibit diversity or to view conflicting ideas as negative rather than as potentially positive. An overly simplified but not unreal example is an autocratic schoolteacher who resists intrusions of student ideas that might clash with her own or churn up the smooth sea on which she is trying to sail this classroom of hers. She maintains peace and order at the expense of potential growth that a conflict of ideas could offer in her classroom.

The point of balance between conflict that produces growth and conflict that forces retreat or disruption and incapacitation is most delicate indeed. Often we turn to history with the intelligence of hindsight in order to point out where, when, and how the balance has been tipped in either direction. I say either direction because either too much or too little conflict in a social system can lead to destruction of the system on one hand or to stagnation on the other.

Universities have seriously pondered this balance point in the early 1970's. It seems that what one day is considered too much conflict the next day appears as a pleasantly hospitable environment. In 1964 the Berkeley campus erupted with the Free Speech Movement. A sit-in of 800 persons in the administration building brought citizen complaints. Faculty were annoyed. Administrators pulled out what few remaining hairs remained: too disruptive; too much conflict; threatened the entire system of higher education; clearly a disaster. Time passed, and by 1970 those same citizens, faculty, and administrators looked back with fondness on the good old days of 1964, when students were idealistic and peaceful; they looked back from windows boarded up, across a campus swarming with police and clouded with teargas. I wonder what 1970 will look like from the perspective of the late 1970's.

A comparable line of development occurred in the movement for civil rights. When it began, with the Montgomery bus boycott and subsequent sit-ins and protest marches, many persons were incensed. They saw these nonviolent actions as clearly going too far, as too much conflict, as threatening the core of society. But later, when boycotts, sit-ins, and marches were replaced by shouts of Black Power, when ghettos began to organize to fight back with force against the police and many whites, a call came for a return to those halcyon days when the movement was peaceful and idealistic.

Although the balance point is difficult to specify, and undoubtedly even more difficult to study systematically, a glimpse of it may be attained by looking at a classic study in group dynamics conducted by French (1941). French brought two differently structured types of group into his laboratory for study. One type, which he termed *unorganized*, was made up of unacquainted college students. The *organized* groups, by contrast, included members of intramural sports teams, many of whom had known one another for some period of time. French presented both types with a puzzle that could not be solved or with a fear-arousing experience. Observational and questionnaire data revealed that the organized groups expressed more aggression and hostility when faced with the frustrating situation; in addition, they tended to experience greater minor disruptions. On the other hand, they did not tend to split into subgroups as the unorganized groups did. Although French did not have any measures of group productivity, the descriptions he presents strongly suggest that the organized groups kept together, used fuller member participation, took pride in their group; in other words, they acted more like an effective group than did the more splintered and divided unorganized groups.

In seeking to understand these findings French turned to an idea that most of us intuitively sense, that the stronger the forces that initially hold a group together, the more frustra-

tion, hostility, and conflict it can tolerate without splitting apart. With little positive to tie them together, and the negative qualities of frustration driving them apart, the unorganized groups tended to split into factions and subgroups. The organized groups, although clearly annoyed by their failure, kept together and continued trying to deal as a group with the troublesome situation.

How true this all seems for an intimate relationship between two persons—as in marriage—and for relationships that exist in the larger society. Marriage partners who have little in common to hold them together can little afford even the minor conflicts that a more strongly united pair can withstand; one little fight and it's, "I'm going home to mother." "Good, I'm going to become a bachelor again!" On the national scene, a society with little cohesiveness will find most kinds of conflict troublesome and potentially disruptive. Such a society would have to resort to force to keep a semblance of togetherness in the face of conflict; totalitarian states spin out their lives in this manner. Democracies, presumably, call on each man's good will and respect for all to keep themselves together when conflicts burst forth. When that good will is lacking, when man faces man as though in a jungle rather than in a cooperative community of shared trust and love in which justice for all is a valued principle, then force comes into use.

An interesting approach to the study of "naturally" occurring conflicts in real groups demonstrates some of the complexities of the issue. Guetzkow and Gyr (1954) studied a series of conference groups, dividing them, on the basis of observer ratings, into high- and low-conflict and in terms of the type of conflict—interpersonal or task-oriented—expressed. Their aim was to come to some understanding of the processes by which groups in conflict achieved decision-making agreement. Some findings of particular importance indicate that many expressions of self-oriented needs hindered the achievement of consensus. On the other hand, whether the conflict were interpersonal or substantive (task-related), a pleasant atmosphere within the group facilitated the achievement of final agreement. Likewise, even when conflict was present, if members examined one issue at a time in an orderly fashion, they were likely to be able to come to some final decision. Substantive conflicts could be effectively reduced and consensus achieved by a helpful chairman directing the group to factual matters, but interpersonal conflict was best handled by withdrawing from the problem or from one another.

To this point achievement of consensus has been assumed as the reasonable end state to which a decision-making group should be striving. Of course, groups that are set up merely to generate ideas need not be concerned with final consensus, but most groups have somewhere they are trying to go; they need a degree of consensus in order to move. Conflict does not necessarily prevent consensus, but it is clear that much higher consensus is reached in low-conflict groups than in high-conflict groups. Conflict can be usefully overcome; much depends on the atmosphere created in the group, minimization of self-oriented or personal need expression, approach to facts, and withdrawal from personal conflict. This last point may strike many persons as annoying, for it suggests retreat. As we shall see in Chapter 20, sensitivity training seems to make its living from confrontation rather than withdrawal. However, sensitivity-training or encounter groups rarely have a decision-making agenda to get through; they can afford the luxury of in-fighting. Conference groups may have to put personal battles aside to make any progress at all.

Conflict in Ideas. The notion of actively inducing conflicts in a group to broaden its resource base is interesting to contemplate. Theoretically, the view is that bringing potentially disparate perspectives together in a setting in which they can be freely expressed can increase the resources for problem solving and thus come up with a better, more innovative solution. Note that disparate perspectives must both be brought together and allowed to gain expression. The latter point, as we have noted, argues for a group structure or leader style that is democratic and participative.

Hoffman, Harburg, and Maier (1962) sought experimentally to develop conditions that would produce conflict and creative group problem solving. They reasoned that one of the problems a potentially creative group faces is overcoming the dominance of its leadership. If divergent ideas are present in a group but a strong leader keeps them unexpressed, the group will not be able to use them effectively. How do we reduce the leader's importance? One technique we've already seen is to instruct leaders in democratic techniques. Another is to strengthen the commitment of subordinate group members to their own opinion; the more strongly committed a person is to a particular point of view, the more likely he is to express it, even if the leader tries to dominate. Hoffman and his colleagues created a role-playing work situation in which instructions were used to increase or decrease a member's commitment to a particular opinion, and used role-playing instructions to vary the dominance of leaders. The prediction was that greater conflict would exist in groups in which the role players were strongly committed to divergent points of view, and that when a leader's role was less dominant, and he thereby permitted the conflict to gain expression, high-quality problem solutions would be offered.

The task situation was a meeting in which a foreman was to discuss a change in work procedure with several of his workers. Hoffman, Harburg, and Maier differentiated three kinds of solution to this work-change problem: (1) the foreman wins by convincing the groups to change; (2) the workers resist his efforts and wish to retain the old method; (3) in an *integrative* solution both individual demands and company requirements are met in a unique manner. The last, most creative solution is rare in most studies using this kind of problem.

Results from this study indicate that integrative (creative) solutions were produced in about 48 percent of those groups in which workers were strongly committed to a particular point of view concerning the job change, whereas only 18 percent produced the integrative solution in presumably low-conflict (low-commitment) groups. An analysis that combined type of foreman and commitment of worker indicated that the highest percentage (54 percent) of integrative solutions were offered in groups in which there were strongly committed workers and a less dominant foreman. When workers were only minimally committed to a position the foreman dominated the group even when he was minimally dominant (66 percent of the solutions were in line with the foreman's request whether he was more or less dominant).

Conflict in Personality and Cognitive Style. In the realm of the human few things are simple. In the Hoffman, Harburg, and Maier study conflict occurred in divergent perspectives between role-playing workers and role-playing foreman. Conflict can also exist among the members of a group. Furthermore, as Guetzkow and Gyr (1954) note, it can exist in terms of personality or cognitive development as well as in specific ideas or opinions.

If we examine the group dynamics literature on the problem of homogeneity versus heterogeneity of personality and its effects on creative group problem solving, a somewhat mixed picture emerges. Haythorn (1958), for example, composed groups that were homogeneous or heterogeneous in the degree of authoritarianism (as measured by the *F* scale) between the appointed leader and his followers. In a homogeneous group the leader and his followers were comparably high or low in authoritarianism; in heterogeneous groups the leader was high and the members low, or vice versa. Haythorn reports that leaders in the homogeneous groups were more aggressive and autocratic than their counterparts in the heterogeneous groups. Followers in the homogeneous groups were described as seeking group approval and withdrawing more than followers in the heterogeneous groups. Finally, Haythorn reports more conflict in the heterogeneous groups.

Although he presents no measure of group problem solving, Haythorn's results for the homogeneous or low-conflict groups agree with other work that suggests such qualities might produce less innovative solutions. For instance, the more autocratic leader behavior and the greater member withdrawal in the homogeneous groups would undoubtedly reduce effective use of the groups' human resources, but the clashes between member and leader personality in the heterogeneous groups could be sufficient to incapacitate the group as an effective problem-solving force. The work of Schutz (1960), of which I will say more in Chapter 20, also suggests that homogeneity of interpersonal orientation allows for compatibility and consequently for performance efficiency.

An effort that I find hopeful, in that it combines a plausible theory with some interesting data, is a study conducted by Stager (1967). Stager's approach is based in part on the theory of conceptual development initially proposed by Harvey, Hunt, and Schroder (see Chapter 14) and an information-processing version of that theory proposed by Schroder, Driver, and Streufert (1967). The idea is that each of us has moved through life to a particular level of conceptual development, and the level affects the manner by which we structure and process information from our environment. Persons at a high conceptual level tend to make many alternative differentiations of their environment; those at a lower conceptual level differentiate minimally and in terms of a few fixed categories.

Stager argues that a group composed primarily of persons who are high in conceptual development should make few demands that the group structure itself into carefully defined roles and form a hierarchical arrangement; should generate diversity and conflict; should synthesize and evaluate the alternatives that are generated; and should conduct a search for novel information. That is, persons who are conceptually high in development see the world in many alternative ways, tolerate the uncertainty of an absence of rigid structure, generate conflict because of the variety of alternatives they create, but at the same time synthesize these divergent views. In toto, they should be better able to produce innovative solutions than persons low in conceptual level.

To test these notions Stager obtained measures of individuals' level of conceptual development and varied the number of high conceptualizers in four-man groups: *100-percent* groups had all four members at a high level; *75-percent* groups had three high; *50-percent* groups had two, and *25-percent* groups had only one. Note that a homogeneous group is theoretically expected to be the most conflicted, to produce the greatest diversity of ideas. Clearly, therefore, we cannot simply speak about the effects of homogeneity versus heterogeneity, but must of necessity specify both the characteristics being considered and the situational context involved. Stager presented the groups with a complex decision-making problem involving a tactical military situation. He recorded individual and group behavior and assessed the group structure that emerged. Uncertainty of group structure exists when members play a variety of decision-making roles throughout the duration of the study; high uncertainty suggests lack of structure and low uncertainty indicates a more highly structured arrangement.

True to the theoretical expectation, as the number of high conceptualizers increased from 25 to 100 percent, uncertainty also increased. That is, the more high conceptualizers in a group, the more open and flexible its structure was. Groups with many low conceptualizers tended to structure themselves into definite roles rather quickly and thereby reduce uncertainty. An analysis of conflicts that were generated offers further support for the theoretical predictions. The 100-percent or all-high-conceptualizer groups produced more conflict than any of the other conditions. In terms of ability to form a new synthesis from the divergent material that was generated, the 100-percent groups again ranked significantly higher than the other conditions. Other expectations were similarly borne out by the data.

Stager's concern with relating level of conceptual development as a variable of group composition to the groups' subsequent information processing and decision making is relevant to our concern with the human resources approach to participation. Most importantly, his data indicate that the kind of group in which conflicting perspectives are both generated and effectively utilized in decision making is a group in which hierarchical structuring in terms of specific roles is low and member participation is equal. Furthermore, both equality of participation and conflict generation and utilization seem to occur, in this situation at least, as a function of the members' level of conceptual development. Although in practice we cannot yet easily control compositional factors, these data indicate a condition in which conflict in a group of a particular composition seems to offer a potentially creative use of the group's human resources, and, of course, a condition in which too much conflict might be more detrimental than helpful. It seems plausible from these data that conflict in a group composed primarily of low conceptualizers would be disruptive because the group would be relatively incapable of using divergent ideas in a helpful manner.

Brainstorming. This approach to human resources was built on a conflict-free, non-evaluative, ad-agency idea. (See especially Osborn, 1957. Other relevant references are Gordon, 1961; Mason, 1960, 1962.) It caught on like the Hula-Hoop and soon was part of the repertoire of many industrial consultants. The basic technique is pure simplicity. Give a group a problem to solve—for example, what would be the benefits if people were born with an extra thumb on each hand? Then rule that absolutely no one may be critical of any idea. The object is just to pour out ideas in quantity; time enough later for evaluation and quality. The rules of this game essentially are directed at letting go verbally and seeing what happens.

On the surface brainstorming is a participative approach that calls on human resources. However, what it lacks is another vital human resource, man's critical ability. This ability is honed by the clash of disparate perspectives; it is likely to decay in the fully id-like setting that brainstorming fosters. Brainstorming was finally put to the test of systematic research. By comparing individuals using brainstorming rules with brainstorming groups, Taylor, Berry, and Block (1958) found that individuals produced a greater number of ideas, and ideas that were more original and unique, than did the groups. In fact it appeared that rather than being as open and freewheeling as hoped, groups thinking together adopted an idea set that restricted the range of members' ideas. Like so many fads desperately grabbed by eager-to-make-a-buck businesses, it seemed that group brainstorming was somewhat worse for generating ideas than individual brainstorming. Even individual brainstorming does not seem very likely to create an Einstein or a Mozart; it is by no means clear that simply generating ideas can substitute for thinking, discipline, or hard work, whether we are talking about individual or group problem solving.

Alone-together

A human resource not to be overlooked is motivational in character. As mentioned earlier (pp. 18–19), Allport and others had noted that persons working together seemed to do quantitatively more than persons working alone on the same kinds of problem. A sophisticated version of the motivational consequences of working together has been presented by Zajonc (1966), who examined a wide variety of studies involving animals or men working together and concluded that such work does indeed induce a higher level of performance output. But—an important but—this motivational effect seems to heighten output for well-learned behaviors, but to impair new learning.

Although I have tastefully avoided mentioning most animal studies in this text, I cannot help mentioning a fascinating and relevant study that Zajonc reports. In 1937 Chen (see Zajonc, 1966, pp. 16–18) observed ants building nests; he observed them alone and in groups of two or three. His measures involved both the speed with which they began excavation for their nest and the weight of dirt excavated. Table 19.1 indicates the striking outcome of this study.

Table 19.1 Nest-building behavior of ants alone and in groups (from Zajonc, 1966, p. 7)

	Alone	Groups of 2	Groups of 3
Latency	192 min.	28 min.	33 min.
Weight	232 grams	756 grams	728 grams

Clearly, ants together started to work sooner and excavated more dirt than ants working alone, an effect, by the way, that is matched in most studies of people together.

On the other hand, as Zajonc demonstrated in his review, the presence of others during a learning phase seems to interfere. As he notes, one practical implication for students is not to study in groups while learning, but to take tests in groups once the material is learned. For purposes of the human resources view, what this material suggests is that an approach that places people together where they can interact openly and freely potentially ups the level of individual motivation.

Risk-taking

Unkind observers of mob or mass behavior (e.g., Le Bon, 1896) long ago suggested that even a cooly rational, reasonably conservative individual could become a hypercharged, irresponsible, risky madman when in the company of his fellows. Of course it is a long way from a mob storming the Bastille, or an induction center, to a small group sitting comfortably in a scientist's laboratory, but certain aspects of this apparent change in the individual have been noted in lab work as well.

Festinger, Pepitone, and Newcomb (1952) studied the concept of *deindividuation*, the loss of individual identity within a group so that an individual does not feel that he is singled out and identified to others. They argued that deindividuation contributes to a loss of individual restraint; no longer feeling himself to be readily identifiable, that is, feeling somewhat anonymous, an individual is released from former inhibitions and may do things that alone or with more individuation he would not do. Festinger's group created a laboratory procedure designed to induce this state of deindividuation and generally found data supportive of the expectation.

A somewhat related program of research was undertaken by Kogan, Wallach, and several others (e.g., Wallach, Kogan, & Bem, 1962, 1964; Kogan & Wallach, 1967a, 1967b). They presented subjects individually, and later in a group, with a variety of hypothetical risk-taking situations. In each situation a central person had to choose between two courses of action that varied in degree of risk and in the reward if the character were successful. Twelve situations such as the following were presented.

1. An electrical engineer may stick with his present job at a modest but adequate salary, or may take a new job offering considerably more money but no long-term security.
2. The captain of a college football team, in the final seconds of a game with the college's traditional rival, may choose a play that is almost certain to produce a tie score, or a more risky play that would lead to sure victory if successful, sure defeat if not.

In each case the subject was to indicate the "lowest probability of success he would accept before recommending that the potentially more rewarding alternative be chosen" (Wallach, Kogan, & Bem, 1962, p. 77). That is, he was to check the probability statement that he would favor; for example, the chances are 1 in 10 that the risky play will succeed, 3 in 10, 5 in 10, 7 in 10, 9 in 10. He could also refuse to try the risky alternative, no matter how high its probability of success.

After subjects completed this questionnaire individually they were brought together in groups to discuss each situation for about five minutes and reach an agreed-on group decision. In many repeated tests with this general experimental format it was found that individuals shifted toward a riskier position after group discussion and decision. In other words, comparing individuals who had merely gone through the stories twice with those who had gone through a group procedure, it was found that the group-processed individuals became more risky in their choices. This was called the *risky-shift* phenomenon.

But why did this happen? Several explanations were put forth. Originally Kogan and Wallach and their colleagues argued for two plausible interpretations: first, that high risk-takers in the group exerted more influence than others; second, that something akin to a de-individuation effect was operating. They referred to this as *diffusion of responsibility*. Basically the argument was that to fail as an outcome of a group decision would not be an individual's failure, but rather would be the more general responsibility of the abstraction, *group*; when responsibility was spread around, the group could afford to be riskier.

This latter interpretation is especially interesting; it seems to run counter to the Lewinian view of the effects of participation in decision making. Recall that one of Lewin's points is that individual participation in decisions can increase a sense of involvement and responsibility. Yet Kogan and Wallach interpret the risky-shift effect as a diffusion of responsibility in group decisions. These seem to be conflicting viewpoints, but it is possible that the kinds of group decision with which Lewin and his colleagues dealt—having a direct personal con-

sequence—and decisions of the hypothetical and personally inconsequential sort with which Kogan and Wallach dealt operate differently. Both perspectives, of course, may be true, the particular circumstances determining when and if responsibility is diffused or etched more deeply than ever into the individual.

If we accept the responsibility-diffusion interpretation, the picture becomes frightening. If group decisions are no one's responsibility, so that groups can take greater risks than individuals, and if an increasing number of our societal and organizational decisions are being made by groups, then may we not entertain some anxiety over the consequences of decisions by *that* group in the State Department or *that* group in the Pentagon? Arendt (1969) aptly captures a sense of this condition in her description of the bureaucratic rule by Nobody (see p. 375 for a discussion of Arendt's perspective).

Although the risky-shift phenomenon has been observed consistently, especially when the same or highly similar kinds of hypothetical situation have been employed, the interpretations originally offered have been modified. It is important to note that in modification newer, often simpler interpretations have been added, rather than discarding the older ones.

Following Rettig and Turoff (1967), it is helpful to distinguish between information and value interpretations and those based on factors of group structure. Brown (1965) suggested that it was not diffusion of responsibility that produced the risky shift so much as it was information exchange in a group discussion that resulted in an awareness of the high value of risk in this culture. Brown's notion is that we value being risky. In a group discussion people realize that although they personally wish to take risks, from what they hear they have not really been risky enough, so they become more so.

Research by Levinger and Schneider (1969) and by Wallach and Wing (1968) supports this argument. They demonstrate that subjects seem to place a high value on being risky. Levinger and Schneider, for example, find that subjects most admire persons who make choices that are riskier than their own, and see their peers as being more conservative than they are. It seems reasonable, then, that group discussion would make each person aware of how risky his peers in fact are, and that he had better become more risky himself to keep up with the values.

Another testing of the information and value interpretation was undertaken by Lamm (1967), who had subjects simply witness a group discussion concerning hypothetical risk situations. They, too, manifested the risky shift. Lamm argues that witnesses to a group discussion are not likely to experience the diffusion of responsibility that members are presumed to experience. It is more likely, he maintains, that witnessing the information exchange allows them to realize that they should become riskier in line with what they personally value.

An interesting variation on this same theme involves a study by Rabow, Fowler, Bradford, Hofeller, and Shibuya (1966), who argued that groups were neither more nor less risky than individuals. Rather, group-developed norms or more general social norms influenced the direction of a group's choices. According to this argument groups could manifest either a *risky* shift or a *conservative* shift. If norms support a conservative rather than a risky choice, the effect of group interaction should be to change individuals toward the conservative position. This argument is consistent with the information exchange and value notion.

To test their hypothesis, Rabow and friends used several of the same hypothetical situations that Kogan and Wallach had employed originally. In addition, however, they introduced the following two situations, which they felt would pull normatively for the more conservative choice, or at least not so strongly for the risky choice.

"A successful businessman with strong feelings of civic responsibility must decide whether or not to run for Congress on the ticket of a minority party whose campaign funds are limited. He must also consider his children, who have felt deprived of his companionship."
"A very small community has sponsored the medical education of a young doctor in order to replace the older and only doctor of that community. The young doctor must decide whether or not to follow up

a research idea which may produce an important medical advance, a decision that will prevent him from returning to the small community."

The argument is that these situations are filled with conflict between taking the risk and being more conservative, in contrast to the original work in which risky choices were more clearly the valued ones. Rabow's results indicate a risky-shift effect for the stories originally used by Kogan and Wallach, but a decided conservative shift for their own stories. This finding, combined with the entire information and value argument, places the risky-shift phenomenon right back in the camp of group dynamics; at least it begins to seem that the same factors of social influence and social reality influence whether an individual will become more risky or more conservative after participating in a group discussion or after gaining access to the information and points of view such a discussion generates. Although none of this research really disproves the structural argument—deindividuation and responsibility diffusion—the material casts some serious doubts on the full merit of this kind of interpretation.

Responsibility-Diffusion or What? The diffusion-of-responsibility interpretation just examined does not really encompass the meaning of group discussion that Lewin intended. Lewin sought participatory approaches to group decision making to overcome rather than feed the impersonal and autocratic decision making of centralized, bureaucratic society. He sought a rule by Everybody where a rule of few had existed. What a bitter pill to swallow if participatory democracy diffuses responsibility so that nobody feels himself a part of a decision; this I find truly puzzling and difficult to accept as true. I do wonder, however, (and have no ready answers) under just what conditions the original Kogan-Wallach interpretation would pertain, for in common experience both personal involvement and a sense of responsibility and bureaucratic diffusion of responsibility have emerged out of participation in group discussion.

I wonder sometimes if we are really talking about what Kohlberg discussed in terms of individual moral development. In Chapter 25 we shall examine some of his ideas more fully, but now I think it relevant to plant a seed. There is a stage in an individual's moral development at which he responds to a moral dilemma by choosing what his institutional role dictates. He says, for example, "I must kill because I am a soldier." The social order exists for him as a prime end, a guide to carry him over moral hurdles. He feels himself personally less responsible for his actions, for he is enacting his obligation to society. But there is another stage in moral development at which the social order is subordinate to more general principles; when dilemmas arise, decisions are made on the basis of these principles rather than in terms of duty to a social order that is presumed to serve them. The individual says, "I cannot serve in the military; I cannot take another's life; I must go with my conscience even though it places me in conflict with my society and its demands." The individual at this stage sees himself as a personally responsible agent, one who causes, one who has effects.

I cannot help feeling that a person of principled morality could not function by a diffusion-of-responsibility notion, but that a person of more conventional or institutional morality would be more likely to fit the initial Kogan-Wallach interpretation. It seems to me that the diffusion-of-responsibility interpretation of the risky-shift phenomenon, presently of some dubious empirical merit, needs to be questioned more broadly. To maintain that subjects become more risky in a group because they pass responsibility off their own shoulders is to make a shocking commentary on human morality. Can this be true for all men? For some men? For whom? When? Even the simplest of psychological inquiries carries serious moral implications.

BY WAY OF SUMMARY AND PREVIEW

There is more to come, but much already covered, so let us pause a moment and see where we have been and where we are going. Figure 19.3 is a shorthand summary indicating that the participation approach to planned change is a technique that has the potential to produce positive outcomes both in terms of

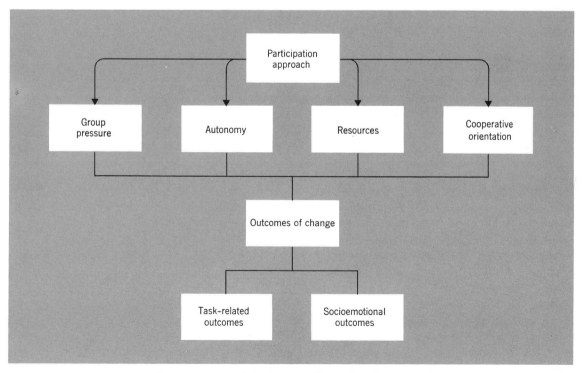

Figure 19.3 Potential outcomes of the participation approach

task-related matters (e.g., productivity, creativity, efficiency) and in terms of socioemotional factors (e.g., morale, satisfaction, personal growth, self-actualization). This approach operates through the several kinds of mediation that we have examined. *Group pressure*, the group dynamics view of participatory change, is based on the notion that our ideas, opinions, and actions are embedded in social contexts. Change of a context of support therefore can produce a change in an individual who dwells in that context, especially when he is strongly attracted to membership or is sufficiently removed from other, conflicting sources of support so that the context becomes a major determinant of his conceptions of social reality. *Autonomy* is based on the idea that individual participation in the processes of planned change reduces resistance to change, increases the extent to which change is independent of the change agent, and provides an ethically appropriate means of introducing change in a democratic society. The *human resources* perspective argues that the participation approach to planned change increases the likelihood that the full range of resources available to the individual and the group will be employed; these include such resources as a broad base of ideas or alternative perspectives, a system of checks and balances whereby ideas are evaluated, increments in motivation, and use of minority and deviant views. *Cooperative orientation* is another mediator to which we now turn our attention.

COOPERATIVE ORIENTATION

We know from the first part of this book that when a person is involved in decisions about planned change or in almost any kind of decision-making activity, the manner in which the situation is defined, the world perceived, or persons viewed importantly affects what is likely to happen.

One of the bases of resistance to change involves prior commitments to a policy or course of action, or vested interests in certain kinds of activity. A group that feels itself caught up in some turmoil, realizing that a change *must*

come, may yet be resistant because commitments or conflicts of interest limit alternatives. Members may accept the change as long as it doesn't remove or reduce the benefits that each personally has been receiving. One member may feel that a change in a particular direction is good because he gets to keep what he already has; unfortunately another member may lose by a change in that direction.

Let's take the homely example of the university in crisis, especially that delicate relationship between the faculty and the students. To protect the guilty, let us talk about a mythical university involved in a mythical crisis. Correspondences between this description and reality are purely probable. Students feel that their interests lie in getting good teachers who can devote substantial time to teaching them. Some faculty members feel that, although teaching is indeed important, research, especially publication-oriented research, is vital to their own careers. Some even feel that teaching time, especially teaching undergraduates, is stolen from their more personally important research activities. We wander by that campus one day and notice picketing, shouting, rallies, sit-ins, crisis faculty meetings, captured (or liberated) campus buildings, hordes of police, and so on. Ah ha, we mumble, change is needed; brilliant deduction. But look more closely. The students see a sharp conflict between their demands for better teaching and more time devoted to them and the faculty's demands for more time for research and less for teaching. Faculty likewise see a conflict, but from the opposite perspective; teaching and research are at variance—the more of one, the less of the other—and their career interests are in research. Students shout, "I came to old Big U in order to take a class with Professor Noble Laureate, but he's too busy making bombs to teach us lowly undergraduates." Professor Laureate shouts back, "I was enticed to Big U by the offer of my own building, full lab facilities, all the secretaries and grad students I needed, and freedom from the drag of undergraduate teaching."

We perceive a conflict of interest that makes change difficult. But we are wise men. We know that an order from the college president telling faculty to think more about their teaching will have little effect, although it may bring the students out of his office and back where he feels they belong on a lovely, warm Saturday afternoon in fall. On the other hand, a participatory approach, bringing Professor Laureate and student Morris Militant face to face, shocking as it may be to both, may result in a redefinition of the situation and some resolution to the conflict. In other words, a technique that enables the warring factions to sit down and talk things over, to examine the nature of their conflict, to participate jointly in any resolution that occurs, even perhaps to use a third party as mediator or helpful perspective giver, is potentially useful. For one thing, this participatory approach might actually place the conflict in a cooperative rather than a competitive context. And, as I shall argue, this context becomes all-important in determining the outcomes that are possible.

Cooperation versus competition

Deutsch, cut straight from the cloth of Lewin, is our guide on this trip. In 1949 Deutsch (see 1953) published his classic study of cooperation and competition. In the early 1960's Deutsch and Krauss (1960, 1962) published the outcome of a series of experimental studies of bargaining and conflict. In 1969 Deutsch combined these several works and themes into an analysis of conflict reduction in a context of cooperation.

The early work on cooperation and competition (Deutsch, 1953) indicated several important advantages that accrued to cooperative group behavior. Whenever two or more persons are *promotively interdependent*, so that if O gets to his goal P does too, the conxtext is *cooperative*. When they are linked in terms of *contrient interdependence*, so that if O makes it P does not, the context is said to be *competitive*. Clearly, these define two extremes of a relationship. At one extreme, if I get there, so do you; we both gain when either of us moves forward, and we both lose when either of us is set back. At the other extreme only one of us can win; and if I'm the one, tough for you buddy. Deutsch created a competitive classroom context by rating individual behavior on selected discussion or puzzle problems; the person who contributed most to the discussion or to the puzzle's

solution would be ranked 1, the next would be ranked 2, and so on. At the end a summed ranking would determine who was the best in the classroom. This individual would be excused from a term paper and would get an automatic high grade for that paper. In this situation it is apparent that if O is ranked 1, no one else can be; the relationship between class members is competitive. In our student-faculty example a competitive context exists if each side believes that if the other side wins, its own side loses; that is, if faculty do more research, students' concern over teaching quality is a lost cause, so research is bad, or, from the faculty perspective, if teaching load is increased, research suffers, so teaching is bad.

To create a cooperative context in another classroom Deutsch informed the members that the entire group's performance was to be compared to the performance of other groups. The group that performed best each week would be ranked 1, the next, 2, and so on. At the end of the term all members of the best problem-solving or discussion group would be excused from writing one term paper and all would receive a high grade. It is clear that in this situation if O contributes a great deal, P benefits. Their relationship is one of cooperation.

Key findings indicated that the cooperative context produced groups that showed

"(a) more coordination of efforts; (b) more diversity in amount of contributions per member; (c) more subdivision of activity; (d) more achievement pressure; (e) more communication to one another; (f) more attentiveness to fellow members; (g) more mutual comprehension of communication; (h) more common appraisals of communication; (i) greater orientation and orderliness; (j) greater productivity per unit time; (k) better quality of product and discussions; (l) more friendliness during discussions; (m) more favorable evaluation of the group and its products; (n) more behavior directed toward helping the group improve its functioning; (o) greater feeling of being liked by fellow members; and (p) greater feeling of obligation and desire to win the respect of others" (Deutsch, 1962, pp. 284–285).

Of special importance are the findings that involve open communication, the development of trust, friendliness, and confidence, and the sharing and evaluation of ideas in a relatively nonthreatening context. Rather than vying competitively in a jungle of I-win, you-lose, persons in the cooperative context could work together toward common, shared ends, as though one bright and sunny day both faculty and students saw that they shared more than either at first had imagined. Working cooperatively, they might find a resolution to this conflict and bring about constructive planned change in which each side gains satisfactions. Of course, for the sake of simplicity, I have left out the other parties (e.g., the ill-informed but angry public; vote-seeking politicians) that tend to complicate the picture. In many real situations it would be a much happier state of affairs if those others stayed out.

Games: Zero- and Nonzero-Sum. The kind of interdependence that Deutsch considered can be represented in game theory terms as well. We can speak of a *zero-sum* game, like baseball, in which one side's winning means the other side's losing. Or we may speak of a *nonzero-sum* game, in which both parties can profit jointly if they manage to work well together. Nonzero-sum games are of particular interest to social psychologists because they allow for psychological processes to intervene either to facilitate or to hinder the game player's achievement of the maximally satisfying solution. Furthermore, they characterize a great many human bargaining and decision situations, although parties may not see themselves as standing to gain by cooperative bargaining even when such mutual gain is possible. Thus they may face off in a zero-sum battle when a nonzero-sum venture would benefit all. A change agent's role in this case is to help the participants psychologically view their possibilities for nonzero-sum cooperation rather than the inevitable, usually escalating destruction that the competitive context produces.

One typical nonzero-sum game has been called the Prisoner's Dilemma (e.g., Minas, Scodel, Marlowe, & Rawson, 1960; Sampson & Kardush, 1965; Scodel, Minas, Ratoosh, & Lipetz, 1959; Terhune, 1968; Rapoport & Chammah, 1965). Two persons, O and P, are suspected of commiting a crime. Individually each is informed that he can confess or not. If both confess, their sentences will be relatively light;

if both refuse to confess, they'll be booked on minor charges. However, if one confesses but the other does not, the confessor, having turned state's evidence, will get off with a minimal sentence, but the other will get the book thrown at him. They cannot communicate with one another and bargain openly. Each must decide, on his own, how much he can afford to trust the other. The dilemma of these prisoners then, is how to maximize their joint outcomes, in this case, without having any chance to communicate openly with the other person.

The Prisoner's Dilemma does not only face prisoners. Picture a nonzero-sum game situation in which O and P are seated on opposite sides of a partition so that O cannot see what P does, and vice versa. Each has a red card and a black card, and they are to hold up one of the cards on each trial. They know that if both hold up the red one, each will get 3 points, but if both hold up the black one, each will get only 1 point. However, if one holds up red and the other black, the one who chooses black will get a payoff of 6 points, while the other suffers with 0 points. These possibilities are shown in Figure 9.4.

Suppose you are O. What do you do? If you hold up red, can you trust your unknown friend, P, to hold up red so that you both will win 3 points? Or do you suspect that he's a competitive sonofabitch like you, so that if you hold up red he's just as likely to hold up black so he'll get 6 points while you get nothing. (Remember that O and P are not communicating with one another; this dialogue is going on in one mind.) On the other hand, if you hold up black, the best that can happen is that you'll get 6 and he'll get 0, and by you that's fine; if he too holds up black, you'll both get 1, which is not too bad, but it's not too good either. The joint solution that most pairs settle on is the 1-1

	P	
	Choose Red	Choose Black
Choose Red	O wins 3 P wins 3	O wins 0 P wins 6
Choose Black	O wins 6 P wins 0	O wins 1 P wins 1

O appears at the left of the rows.

Figure 19.4 Payoff possibilities for a nonzero-sum game

payoff; apparently the kind of cooperative trust required for both to maximize their joint gains by making the 3-3 choice is not likely in the restricted confines of the game situation, at least unless the trials continue for a substantially long time.

I hasten to add that not everyone is equally untrusting. Deutsch (1960) found a negative relationship between authoritarianism and trusting behavior in the game situation. Wrightsman (1966) reports that trusting subjects in his game experiment "had more generally positive attitudes towards human nature . . . saw people as more trustworthy . . . more altruistic . . . and more independent than did distrusting subjects. . ." (p. 330).

Acme and Bolt. From the perspective of Deutsch's approach to cooperation and competition, the nonzero-sum game, although more cooperative than the competitive zero-sum game, retains aspects of both cooperation (if we both choose red, we both maximize our outcomes) and competition (if I choose red and you chose black, I get 6 and you get 0). This situation as described does not allow for bargaining communication to help the pair move toward the maximally satisfying solution.

Deutsch and Krauss (1960; 1962) constructed a fairly elaborate game board. Subjects were to imagine that they were in charge of a trucking company, Acme or Bolt. Each company had a route over which it could move its trucks from their point of origin to their destination. Figure

19.5 roughly indicates this situation. The plot thickens. Note that each company had two routes available, one considerably longer than the other. The most direct route was a one-lane road on which both trucks could not pass at the same time. Each company controlled a gate to this road. Deutsch and Krauss saw the presence of this gate as a *threat potential.*

The object of the game was very simple: get your trucks efficiently from their origin to their destination. Payment was made for each successful trip with operating costs deducted; these costs were computed in terms of time. A player could earn 60 cents for each trip; costs were figured at the rate of one cent per second. If it took 30 seconds to complete a trip, the profits for that trip would be 30 cents. Clearly, players could cooperatively help or competitively hinder one another's attainment of a maximally satisfying resolution.

Deutsch and Krauss studied several variations in the basic design. They systematically varied the threat potential, having conditions of *bilateral threat* (both controlled the gates), *unilateral threat* (only one gate was controlled), and *no threat* (neither gate could be closed). In another variation they ran a *bilateral communication* condition (both sides could talk) and a *unilateral communication* condition (only one side could talk). In still a third variation they introduced *compulsory communication* on every trial.

Results indicated that the greatest difficulty in

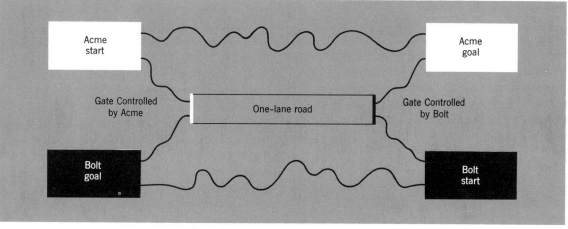

Figure 19.5 Routes for Acme-Bolt game

coordinated activity and consequently greatest monetary loss occurred in the bilateral threat condition; unilateral threat was second worst. In fact, only in the no-threat condition did players make a profit. It appears, then, that the potential to use threat against another to accomplish one's ends produces a mutually destructive, competitive relationship rather than a potentially constructive, cooperative one. It is as if one player says, "You think your threats are going to intimidate me! Hell, I'll show you!" And both plunge into mortal combat, forgetting that a better solution would be possible.

Somewhat contradictory findings and a different interpretation are reported by Shomer, Davis, and Kelley (1966). They partially replicated the Deutsch and Krauss situation, but made it possible to separate a threat from the act of blocking the other person's movement. Shomer and his associates note that when it was possible to make a threatening gesture, as opposed to actually engaging in combat, persons used warnings to force negotiations. Under these conditions the joint payoff was not necessarily as low as the original study suggested.

The Deutsch and Krauss communication variable was also interesting. There was no essential difference in task performance between the bilateral and the unilateral communication conditions, for the most part, apparently, because the players tended *not* to communicate even when the possibility existed. For this reason Deutsch and Krauss introduced the *compulsory communication* condition. Forced communication was effective, but only under conditions of unilateral threat. If anything, forcing persons to communicate under conditions of bilateral threat resulted only in verbal repetition of threats made in action. Thus when people communicate and have the potential to threaten one another in a competitive context the communication may facilitate threat-oriented messages, and this only intensifies the conflict, helping little to attain cooperative efforts.

Inducing trust

On examination, it seemed to Deutsch that the kind of orientation that existed was a significant determinant of the manner by which conflicts between Acme and Bolt or between any

groups could be resolved. An orientation that fostered trust, showed potential for shared interests, minimized threats—in other words, a cooperative rather than a competitive orientation—should facilitate the achievement of mutually satisfying solutions to conflict dilemmas. Deutsch continued with his experimentation on these themes, introducing a cooperative or competitive orientation into a two-person nonzero-sum game situation. His results (1962) indicated that joint gains, satisfying to each, occur when persons are given a cooperative orientation, whereas mutual loss results from a competitive orientation. Communication is helpful primarily when it focuses on the better outcomes likely through cooperation; under these conditions it increases the mutual trust between the players. Not one to be shy in generalizing to broader social implications of his work, Deutsch states,

"We live in a time when international cooperation is required to avert nuclear catastrophe. Yet cooperation founders because of the inability of one side to trust the other and the inability to resolve bargaining deadlocks. . . . We must each develop a genuine stake in the other's security and welfare, in the other's doing well rather than poorly, and we must promote cooperative endeavors which will foster the development of an interest in the other's successes rather than failures" (1962, p. 316).

In that passage are the guiding directives for change agents. Unlike the experimenter, the change agent cannot *give instructions* to be cooperative and to look for mutual points of gain and joint benefit; he cannot *insist* that each must take a concern in the other's winning rather than pleasure in his losing; he cannot *demand* that communications be directed only toward outlining a cooperative venture rather than toward saber-rattling threats and tactics of intimidation. Yet he can be aware that the participative approach is more likely than autocratic or nonparticipative ones to produce mutual friendliness and trust, to allow for legitimate influence sharing rather than illegitimate or inappropriate influence giving, to aid the weaker partner to gain the confidence that is basic to true cooperation, and indeed to create an atmosphere in which awareness of the benefits of exchange and a commitment to maximizing everyone's gain far outweigh insensitivity or the passion to be a winner at another's expense.

A fascinating field study conducted by Sherif and Sherif (1953) on groups at a summer camp further demonstrated the validity of these co-operative notions. After systematically creating tension between two groups in the camp, the Sherifs facilitated harmony by forcing the groups to cooperate. Instead of telling the campers that cooperation was the best way, the Sherifs created a camp emergency that compelled the one-time opponents to work together to solve the new, joint problem. Out of distrust and tension this need to cooperate produced a harmonious camp.

Some implications

As Deutsch (1969) has so aptly noted, a competitive context favors the escalation of conflict rather than its reduction. It sets people against one another as warriors out for blood, blind to anything but their zero-sum goals. Competition feeds on faulty and decimated communication; it induces suspicion and distrust; it magnifies small disagreements into major wars; it calls out aggression and hostility; it legitimizes differential judgment and differential sanctions. This last point is one we have seen crop up in several other places. If my side does *X*, then *X* is good; if your side does *X*, then *X* is bad. If *X* is legitimate when my side does it and illegitimate when yours does, and if legitimate actions should be rewarded and illegitimate ones punished, then it follows that your side needs a good whomping. This passion to destroy the other side for the same deeds we commit becomes magnified in a competitive context in which "win or lose" is carved on every wall. In a context of cooperation, however, we may gain clarity on the psychological principle that links act to origin and makes my acts seem good and yours bad. It is difficult to think in these narrow terms in a context in which we are more friends than enemies, more trusting than suspicious, more open than threatening and defensive.

Conflicts between persons, between groups, or between nations are not simply going to fade away. This should not be taken as a totally pessimistic assessment of the future of man or of society. Deutsch's argument is compelling. When viewed from the perspective of cooperative problem solving, conflicts become a challenge, a vital force for growth and change. The contrasting perspective, however, involving competitive conflicts that escalate cancerously, threatens to destroy rather than affirm life.

If we follow Deutsch's views and those outlined in this lengthy chapter, the *minimal* task that lies ahead is to facilitate conflict resolution and social change through cooperative and participative means. A real challenge exists both for the social scientist and the concerned citizen. How can we overcome the narrowness of individual or national self-interest and move toward an awareness of the things we share rather than the things that separate us? How can we move from a zero-sum to a nonzero-sum definition of our situation? Would that I could outline a program of social action designed to effect such change. At this point I view the material in this chapter (and those to follow) as providing a broad framework within which any such program must operate.

Chapter 20

The T-group movement and planned change

Describing a T-group is not easy. It is a collection of people. It is a task-free group; or, better stated, its major task is to examine itself rather than to accomplish something external to itself. Its leader usually sits quietly, more nondirective than directive; he is less a leader than a screen onto which members may project whatever they wish or imagine. It is a very ambiguous situation; few roles, rules, or directions exist, at least in its early life. It is a challenging situation; its major resources consist solely of the people present, somewhat like being trapped on a desert island and having little else to do than to deal with one another. It is a potentially frightening experience; it demands that individuals begin to examine themselves and their manner of relating to others, and few things pass by politely; almost everything is open to challenge, to examination, to scrutiny.

To the member of a group it is vividly experiential, best described in the language of phenomenology. Yet it is still understandable to others in the less personal conceptual language of the observer or researcher. To a researcher it is a setting in which human relations can be studied, a microcosm of life wrapped up in a tiny package. To a change agent it is a setting that holds out much hope for introducing change through the use of group processes. To an instructor of a course in group dynamics it is a

laboratory for the various concepts and theories his students are studying; they need no longer discuss the development of norms and the application of group pressure merely as abstractions, but rather, can personally witness the norms emerging and experience the application of sanctions against those who violate these norms.

For a variety of intertwined reasons the use of T-groups, once relatively small in scale and located at a few places in this country (e.g., the National Training Laboratory in Bethel, Maine), has mushroomed amazingly, finding its way into the lives of an increasing number of persons and organizations. For some the T-group has become a way of life, in fact a substitute for living. For others it has become a panacea, an answer to all their own ills, the ills of their organizations, the world's problems; for still others it seems a conspiracy hatched in Communist China and designed to brainwash. Others also oppose the T-group movement, but more benignly.

Me? Well, I've called this a T-group *movement* because I am impressed with the wide-scale growth of these groups, called T-groups, encounter groups, sensory-awareness groups, game groups, or whatever. I am impressed with the almost religious fervor with which people pin their hopes on the groups or with equal fervor are hostile to them; and I am impressed with the mystique that has grown up around the groups, leaders, styles, and so on, and with the outcomes that are sought through a group experience.

T-groups shed light on a wide variety of topics of interest to the social psychologist, although not uniquely to him. First, they provide an opportunity to look at one kind of contemporary social movement. More will be said about social movements in Chapter 23, but we cannot easily look at T-groups today without widening the over-all perspective to include its "movement" qualities. Second, they offer a deeper look at human interaction. Finally, they provide still further insights into the dynamics of planned change through the use of group techniques.

INPUTS TO THE T-GROUP MOVEMENT

There exist a variety of inputs or factors that have given the T-group movement the unique shape it presently has: Lewin; ego psychology, especially through Sullivan, Rogers, and Maslow; dramatists and symbolic interactionists, including Moreno and Mead; existentialism; societal transformations.

Lewin

In its origins in the 1940's the T-group movement showed the Lewinian touch. We have examined Lewin's contribution in our discussion of the participation approach (Chapter 19); in essence, he was vitally concerned with making social psychology and group dynamics into action-oriented disciplines. He and his associates saw the use of group techniques as a vehicle for successfully inducing social change by democratic, participatory methods. A group in which the members spent most of their time analyzing group process was useful in the Lewinian framework, for it both facilitated change in the individuals and taught the individuals about the operation of groups. Assuming that many community action programs require individuals to work in and with groups, Lewin and his colleagues felt that group techniques, including the T-group, would be useful in sensitizing them to the various roles and functions required.

The idea was not so much to use the T-group to treat an individual's personal problems as it was to help him gain insights that were necessary for him to be a more effective group member and leader. These insights for example, would lead him to see the advantages of a democratic leadership style, of full group participation in decision making, and of open channels of communication; the problems of defensiveness and threat and of achieving consensus; the emergence of functional roles; the manner by which norms are created and enforced, and so on. These are mainly insights into group behavior rather than personal insights that one may gain from intensive group psychotherapy. The line between these two is rough and rarely drawn easily. For example, a man might find that his resistance to authority in a group is based on some earlier experiences. As he works through his difficulties in the group, he may simultaneously gain insights that facilitate working through his personal underlying problem.

One Lewinian emphasis is his concern with contemporary rather than historical explanations of phenomena. In the T-group this led to a focus on the *here and now* rather than the *then and there*; rather than retreating into the past to explain a member's present action, it is better to concentrate on how he is behaving in the group right now. Much of the early life of these groups is spent in developing members' facility in working in the present rather than the past, and this is no easy matter. You may say the reason you cannot get along with the leader is because you have always had a problem with authority. Fine. But right here and right now you are not getting along well with this present leader. Why are you relating to him in this way, *here and now*? Is he really like your father? You know he isn't your father. What are you going to do about this immediate representation of your past problem? The T-group's focus on the here and now is an attempt to work with the social field as it exists. This is disconcerting to the members, especially if they are accustomed to being let off the hook once they introduce a past problem.

In the main the Lewinian-type approach embodies an entire conception of education, an activist, participatory view. Rather than educating change agents by lecturing to them and having them spend hours buried in books studying concepts about groups in some abstract manner, this approach offers them an active encounter, a participatory educational experience. Thus participation comes to have two meanings: member involvement in the processes of group decision making; and member involvement in learning by doing and experiencing.

In this general approach T-grouping is directed primarily toward the gatekeepers of change in a community. It seeks to train members of a community who occupy positions that are critical in community decisions; these include teachers and educational leaders, religious leaders, Chamber of Commerce types, local businessmen, service club members, and so on. In other words, the idea is to bring these gatekeepers and potential change agents into a T-group educational experience, where they can learn about groups and about themselves directly and actively.

The format of planned change thus is much like that employed in changing food habits (p. 240 ff.): first find the gatekeeper. In the food-habit work the housewife was the key; if she could be changed, the larger unit to which she provided entry would be affected. Similarly, rather than bringing in each member in a community, it is possible to have key members undergo the educational experience of the T-group. When they return to their communities, it is argued, they will relate differently; hence the community itself will benefit from this educational encounter of some of its key personnel. In a similar manner, business and industry send key managerial personnel to training laboratories to learn by means of T-group participation. And what all persons presumably learn is a way of relating to others, a way of working more effectively with groups and in groups, a way of becoming a democratic change agent back home.

Ego psychology

Under the heading of ego psychology I lump together Sullivan, Maslow, and Rogers, all of whom have contributed importantly to the contemporary versions of T-groups. First, note

a change in terminology that reflects a change in emphasis. The "T" in T-group stands for "training," and this is essentially what the Lewinian crew were attempting; they used these groups as an educational tool to help train key personnel. Rogers preferred to call his groups *basic encounter groups*. Although training and education might indeed be an outcome, the emphasis was on the encounter, the meeting of persons in a setting that helped them to explore their relationships with one another.

Sullivan (1947; 1953; 1954) emphasized the interpersonal quality of personal problems; we are not so much personally caught up in some intrapsychic battle (a la Freud) as we have gone astray in our relationships with others. We have moved toward distortion and a faulty perspective on reality. The cure to such interpersonal problems should best be found in the context of a group. Furthermore, if problems center on perceptual distortions, resolution requires the testing of reality by gaining free and open communication in which feedback from others helps the individual see himself and these others in sharper focus. Therefore one of the key functions of T-group experience is to provide *consensual validation* for each member's conception of himself and of reality. Open and nondefensive communication becomes of primary importance within the T-group, for it is only communication of this sort that permits the group to achieve a stage of consensual validation.

Maslow (1954) emphasized self-actualization as a force that exists in each of us for self-enhancement and development. Somewhat like White in his discussion of competence motivation (see pp. 19–20), Maslow stresses positive forces in the individual, not simply tension-reducing, negative forces. Men are basically active and good, not passive or filled with surging passions in need of constant surveillance and control. They have within them the possibility for self-help. All men may be teachers; all may be competent to help others in a shared context. This perspective on man feeds nicely into the developing ideology of the T-group. Here is a setting in which no one person leads, but all share leadership jointly. People working together can help one another achieve their creative potential. They can be self-directing and self-guiding; they need not face off against a strong leader.

Rogers, like Maslow, emphasized man's positive potential. He saw the encounter group as a setting wherein forces for positive growth could be stimulated. As an individual psychologist Rogers (1942; 1951) is usually connected with the *nondirective* school of psychotherapy, according to which the individual himself can evolve in a healthful direction; he is an active agent for positive growth. The therapist is to be nondirective to permit these inner forces their own development. He is to reflect back feeling and to create a permissive atmosphere in which the individual feels no need to become distortive and inauthentic to himself. The T-group, or encounter group, offers such a setting.

The emphasis in ego psychology on man's ego capacities, his abilities to adapt, to cope, to be competent, to explore, to grow, to self-actualize, or whatever terms we choose, must be considered along with the more specific contributions of Sullivan, Maslow, and Rogers if we are to understand the rapid growth and the subtle shift in orientation in the T-group movement. The *Zeitgeist* in the professional field was ripe, the conceptions of man were ready; all that was needed was the proper setting. This came in the form of the group, especially the T-group, which seemed to embody all the qualities of mankind about which these men and these theories had been speaking. It emphasized the interpersonal rather than the intrapsychic; self-direction rather than leader direction; the positive features of self-actualization and personal growth rather than the more negative qualities of impulse control and tension avoidance; it argued that man was an active agent rather than a passive victim; it emphasized open and honest communication with feedback rather than the distortive or defensive communication that cut man off from the inner core of positive self that he possessed.

The Lewinian utilization of groups, although experiential and direct, nevertheless emphasized *cognitive* sensitivity. Knowledge of concepts and theories about groups were every bit as important as any deeper-lying motivational changes that might occur. As times changed,

and as Maslow and Rogers and others of this school got into the business, the emphasis came around increasingly to the emotional encounter often substituted for any cognitive or intellectual learning. Maslow spoke of the *peak experience* an individual might have; Rogers emphasized the *reflection of feeling over content*. In groups the emphasis soon came to center on *having an experience* (with a capital E), having an encounter and feeling deeply, rather than on a more total cognitive-emotional experience within the group. This is not to say that Rogers or Maslow or others denied the importance of intellectual processes, but rather that their own focus combined with the spirit of the times, with its emphasis on the nonintellectual, to redirect the T-group program away from the cognitive and straight into the heart of the emotional encounter.

In this renaissance of the group movement *authenticity*, to be gained through open, honest, nondistortive communication, came to mean "letting go." The idea seemed to be that a "good" group member was noisy, brash, bold, outspoken. He was authentic who made the most outrageous comments; after all, he was genuinely expressing himself. As T-groups spread around the country, some became more like games in which persons literally let go at one another. Health would presumably emerge if persons let it all come out, got it off their chests, and struck out verbally—in some groups, even physically—saying just what they felt, just when they felt it. A new set of norms was instantly created, at least among the growing cadre of experienced groupers. These persons would arrive along with the initiates to their first group meeting. Rather than the giggles of anxiety, the fear of the unknown, and the slow emergence of this group's own unique norms and patterns of communication, the old-timers would instantly turn on the letting-go game. The norm for them from day one was to be authentic in the peculiar sense I've indicated, so they would begin to say just what they felt—usually a vivid combination of 85 percent hostility and 15 percent intimacy—and manage to frighten the hell out of the newcomers.

This is an especially revealing conception of authenticity, which in all fairness, cannot be attributed to the thinking of either Maslow or Rogers, but seems to derive both from the membership and a handful of some group leaders. The conception links honesty and authenticity with total release of feeling, typically hostility, as though the authentic person is one who wears feelings on his shoulder in the shape of a spear. There seems to be an inability to recognize that restraint is also an authentic aspect of an individual. I shall examine this matter briefly under the section on societal transformations, but let me indicate here that as feeling and impulse release took center stage in some conceptions of the T-group, it all began to look more like a modern-day, upper-middle-class religious ritual than an educational experience in the sense that the Lewinians originally intended. But more of this later.

The dramatists and symbolic interactionists: Moreno and Mead

Actors once were trained to put on roles by matching a list of almost stylized qualities of voice and body alignment to a list of characters or emotions they were to convey to the audience. If you were to play an old man, you were taught how an old man walked and talked; if you were to act surprised, you were taught what the mouth and eyes looked like under surprise. Stanislavski, the director of the Moscow Theater, introduced striking changes into the theory of acting (see Cole, 1955; Moore, 1965, for a discussion of the Stanislavski method). He trained persons to create an authentic representation on stage by *becoming* what they were to depict. Rather than imposing qualities of an old man on a young actor, the actor began by making careful observations of old men, their movements, their speech, their mannerisms. He would then think himself *to be* old, to get into the role. Much of his training time was spent in learning methods for doing so, rather than specific techniques of specific roles. The acting genius is the man "who sees life and is able to recreate it on the stage" (Moore, 1965, p. 79).

This approach comes into social psychology and the T-group movement through Moreno (1934; 1944; 1946; 1947; 1959), who introduced *psychodrama*. Moreno's idea, much like Stanis-

lavski's, was to use dramatic techniques of role-playing to aid individuals to become sensitive, gain perspective, and eventually become spontaneous and free in expression. The relation between the method school of acting and Moreno's psychodrama is best captured in the following passage.

"The Stanislavski method aims to develop in the student those abilities and qualities which give him the opportunity to free his creative individuality—an individuality imprisoned by prejudices and stereotyped patterns. The liberation and disclosing of the individuality. This must become the principal aim of a theatrical school. A theatrical school must clear the way for the creative potentialities of the student—but he must move and proceed along this road by himself: He cannot be taught" (Cole, 1955, p. 116).

If we were to substitute "psychodrama" or even "T-group" for "the Stanislavski method" or "theatrical school" in the quotation, the meaning would shift very little.

Moreno established a *theater of the spontaneous*; persons would come on stage to create, with props and a cast of assistants, a dramatic encounter in their own lives. One might play a scene of himself as a child in an encounter with his father or mother or some sibling. He might first take his own role, later shifting into the other's role. He might confront a father—usually one of Moreno's assistants—who acted just as his did or who acted in an entirely different manner. In each case conditions were established so that the person could recreate a life experience. Just as with the Stanislavski method, Moreno's clients were not to put things on or simply act, but rather were to undergo an actual experience.

Role-playing of this sort in the context of a psychodrama was intended to reveal things to an individual that would otherwise be unavailable—feelings he held toward himself or toward significant figures in his life that would emerge during the course of the enactment; he could gain sensitivity to himself. By taking the other's role, by seeing himself through another's eyes, perhaps he could better understand the interactive nature of his problem. In addition, as he developed the capacity to become various people and to open himself up, he would become freer in his forms of expression and more generally spontaneous in his behavior.

Recall Mead's (1934) conceptions of the self-concept and the manner by which it develops (see pp. 25–26). He argued that the self develops by taking the role of another and viewing the self as object. This capacity to role-play that Mead saw as essential to the development of the self Moreno saw as basic to the development of a freer, more spontaneous self.

Moreno's emphasis on spontaneity and openness and his use of the technique of role playing fit neatly into the work of T-groups. One of the problems Lewinian-type T-groupers face is generalization of the change that is produced. To achieve change they have created a cultural island. How can they make behaviors in this island relevant to situations they encounter back home? One way of dealing with this problem is for the groups to introduce role-playing at various points so members can try out back-home problems with the presumed insights gained from group experience. Role-playing becomes an important adjunct to the group experience itself.

Existentialism

Several themes that have been expressed in existential philosophy and some of its applications to psychology—themes that involve the concepts of commitment, action, responsibility, and choice—are given life in the context of the T-group. The group is literally nothing but a collection of people and a nonleading leader. They have no place to go; they have nothing to do; they have no purpose for being beyond whatever purpose they provide. Their situation is artificial, awkward, in essence absurd. It has no past but exists in the immediate present. Without each person's commitment of his time, his interest, his concern for others in the group, his concern for the group itself, nothing happens. Unless the individuals decide to take the initiative and responsibility to act, to discuss, to lead, to make things happen, nothing happens: the group becomes a mere shadow. In fact, it is not uncommon for groups to live their brief lives waiting for Godot, as in Beckett's play. But he never comes, and on the last day of a group's life the members turn and depart in sadness, still puzzling about why they have failed.

Sartre argues (1953; 1956) that man's existence is no more than the choices he makes; there is nothing of value, nothing means anything, everything is absurd except insofar as each of us makes choices and accepts the responsibility for what he has chosen. There is no truth and no reality outside of our choices and actions. Look at the typical T-group. There is, in fact, little meaning or value, little to pin one's hopes on, other than what each person in the group actively chooses to do and to make of the group and the situation. The entire meaning of the group is caught up with the actions and choices of its members. The T-group turns out to be the essence of an existential encounter; in many ways it is a combination of *Waiting for Godot* and *No Exit.*

One further existential quality of the T-group is the manner by which we come to know another person. In many existential views, for example that of Jaspers (1947, 1948; Tymieniecka, 1962), one cannot know another person conceptually (i.e., through the application of external categories of description or analysis). Rather, *P* comes to know *O* only through a process of participation with *O*, as in an act of communication or through an intuitive, empathic apprehension of *O*'s experience. In this view *P* cannot know *O* by placing him in a psychological category (*O* has an Oedipal complex), in a sociological category (*O*'s from a working-class background), or, for that matter, in an astrological category (*O*'s a Sagittarian). *P* can know (i.e., understand) *O only* by sharing experiences with him. In the *T*-group this process has the potential of being realized as *P* and *O* face off as persons, not conceptual categories, and together seek to give meaning to an otherwise absurd encounter.

Societal transformations

I shall keep this section relatively brief; books can be and have been written on the complex topics I touch on lightly. (See Chapters 23 and 24 for a more detailed discussion.) Why has the T-group movement cropped up and spread so rapidly at this time? Why has it taken on the particular form that it presently has? I argue that certain changes in the society have contributed significantly to the rise of T-groups and to their form.

Technology and bureaucracy, with their emphasis on the rational, the planned, the logical, and the cognitive, often ignore the more emotional and nonrational side of man's total existence. This other side is bound to crop up somewhere, as in art, movies, dance, clothing styles, protest, and in the T-group movement. I think that much of the emphasis in contemporary T-groups on the nonrational and on experiencing and feeling comes from a group of persons —mostly white, mostly middle- and upper-middle-class—who lack these experiences in their workaday worlds. They seek relationships in groups that offer what is otherwise missing but felt to be needed. In addition, I think that a more affluent society, emerging in the 1960's from a silent and security-conscious postwar era of restraints and inhibitions, is oriented toward greater freedom and individuality. As with any emergence from restraint, a sudden push to the opposite extreme occurs. All barriers are cut away; impulse release is legitimized in the context of the T-group. The good life is the uninhibited life. The message comes through loud and clear; the group is to provide a location in which release of aggressive and sexual impulses is viewed positively; unlike the world of technology and organization, it is to permit freedom from the restraints of social politeness, manners, and decorum.

In my view, just as the church was intended to satisfy man's spiritual questing and fulfill needs that were not being met by other social institutions, T-groups and similar phenomena today are filling unmet needs of a small but growing segment of the population.

The housewife who finds little intimacy in her relationship with her husband, the salesman who finds little that is fulfilling in his work, the student who remains puzzled by the empty promises of his university, all come flocking to the T-group seeking a sense of belonging and a momentary closeness to other human beings. Some come to experience a sense of potency

and power, for at least they can hope to be effective in their group even if they cannot alter the course of history or change the direction of their nation. In a real sense, then, the T-group movement is like a new religion for these persons and is helpfully understood in that context.

Although this is a somewhat negative view of the reasons for the rapid rise in T-groups, a positive reason emerges from roughly the same nexus of societal transformations. Increasingly in this technological age we have all become specialists, narrowly focused in our expertise. To the extent to which problems require broad-based knowledge for solution, *teams* of specialized experts with complementary patterns of knowledge are required; team and group work are essential. It is not unusual therefore to find interpersonal relationships emerging as critical issues in today's society. Industries, business, government, educational institutions, community groups and so on are all seeking ways to train their employees to be more effective in working in teams and small groups. The training programs the T-group offers thus have a growing appeal that has much less to do with meeting new personal needs than it has to do with meeting new societal and organizational needs.

By way of summary

It is helpful to summarize these several themes by placing them in a simple input-outcome flow chart (Figure 20.1). As I have presented them, the several sources of input are factors that gave the T-group its initial form, plus factors that have modified it to yield its contemporary forms and varieties. The outcomes range from those that emphasize training of leaders and community or organizational change agents, through those that focus on personal growth and the resolution of interpersonal problems in an interpersonal setting, to those that emphasize the purely experiential, the sensory, or the communal escape from alienation and isolation. As noted, the Lewinians originally viewed the T-group as serving training functions, and the Sullivanians, Rogerians, and others of their ilk viewed the T-group (or encounter

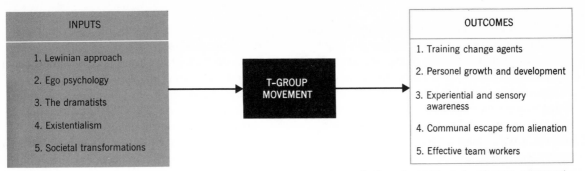

Figure 20.1 Origins and contributors (inputs) to and impact and contributions (outputs) of the T-group movement

group) as a setting for personal growth, self-actualization, and development. A combination of factors has produced varieties of T-group that have come to have quasi-religious functions, meeting needs that are apparently abandoned in the flurry of today's modern society.

I have tried to make two points in this discussion. I wanted to provide a general view of the T-group as a vehicle for planned change and to suggest its usefulness as a locale for studying topics of interest to the social psychologist (communication and social influence; development and enforcement of social norms, etc.). Second, I wanted to show the variety of T-group-type programs that exist by indicating some of the changes that have occurred as the initial conception of the T-group met other theories and philosophies in a society that seemed ripe for an emergent social movement.

THE T-GROUP AS A MICROCOSM OF HUMAN RELATIONSHIPS

As I suggested in the opening paragraphs of this chapter, the T-group is not simply a vehicle for introducing planned change, but, as importantly, may be seen as a miniature model for basic human relationships. Just as one may learn much about human relationships from a therapy session, even when the session is oriented toward healthful change in the patient, one may also learn much about social relationships from the careful analysis of T-groups. I have always been impressed, in fact, by the extreme usefulness of the T-group as a laboratory for gaining knowledge and understanding; often more impressed, I might add, than I have been by its success as a laboratory for change.

A considerable body of theory and research has evolved out of this perspective on the T-group or some comparable type of group. We shall spend some time examining several of the major contributions.

Freud speaks

Although the great Sigmund did not deal in T-groups, and, for that matter, his offerings in group psychology (e.g., Freud, 1922) were not greeted with hearty acceptance by the establishment of the field, he nevertheless outlined the territory in a way that influenced many theories that followed. In his analysis of group formation Freud turned to the bonds that developed between members and a leader or some central figure and to bonds among the members themselves. It was Freud's thesis that the bond that united members in a group was founded on a shared identification with the same person, object, or concept. Using the church as a prototypical example of group formation, Freud suggested that the members are united through their love of Christ: "There is no doubt that the tie which unites each individual with Christ is also the cause of the tie which unites them with one another" (1922, p. 43). Freud maintained that groups also may be formed on the basis of shared hatred of a person, an object, an idea, or whatever; the essential component is the existence of a central theme around which members align themselves, either in love or in hate, much as the P-O-X model suggests (p. 100 ff.).

Notice how Freud's conception of group formation builds on a two-stage developmental model. The first stage is each individual's attachment through identification with a central person or a leading idea. Until this identification with the *leader* occurs there cannot be any group. Once it has occurred the individual is bound in with others who share the same object of identification. To paraphrase Freud's own terms, the developmental argument implied is that before the genital character can develop, one must have passed through oral stages of dependency and anal stages of counterdependency. In language other than Freud's we might say that the first stage in group formation is the relationship of each member with *authority*; the second stage is the relationship of each member with every other in terms of *intimacy*. Until a resolution of authority issues occurs there can be no intimacy.

Bennis and Shepard

Bennis and Shepard (1956) spent more than five years observing T-groups in a course they were teaching; on these observations they based a theory of group development. Their description of the developmental stages is one of the best accounts I have read on T-group development; it manages to capture much of what in my own experience seems to happen when you bring a group of persons together, present them with a task-free situation and a nondirective leader, and urge them to focus on themselves and on their own processes.

Much as Freud did, Bennis and Shepard argue that two areas of uncertainty exist in human relationships: relationship to authority and relationship with peers in terms of intimacy. A person may deal with authority by submitting (dependence), by rebelling (counterdependence), or by acting independently. Submission and rebellion are said to reflect problems with authority in that they are essentially blind reactions; independence, on the other hand, indicates a relationship based on more reasoned consideration. When a person in charge says "follow me," the submissive one does so, the rebel runs in the opposite direction, and the independent looks over the situation and may or may not follow, depending on where the leader is leading and why, and what he himself wants to do.

Difficulties likewise arise in the area of in-

timacy. Bennis and Shepard suggest that we find conflicted *overpersonals* and *counterpersonals*, both of whom are basically antipersonal or opposed to true intimacy. Both say, "I am no damn good; if others knew the real me, they'd reject me, so . . . ." The overpersonals try to be all-loving and all-accepting, making it difficult for anyone to dare to reject so loving a creature. The counterpersonals take the other tack, rejecting everyone before anyone can reject them.

The dynamics of group development, according to Bennis and Shepard, involve conflicts within the group that derive from members' different orientations to authority and intimacy. Following Freud's outline of group formation, they maintain that the initial phases of group development deal with the issues of power and authority. For example, in their initial effort to deal with an unleading leader, part of the group (the dependents) move toward him, awaiting leadership bids that rarely come. His lack of leadership leaves them feeling helpless and disturbed. The counterdependents feel angry with a leader who won't lead—what can they rebel against?—but who, they suspect, is really trying to manipulate them to accede to his wishes.

By refusing to take a dominant leadership role, a T-group leader thus provides a ready target or screen on which each member may project his own particular manner of relating to authority. Presumably in a context of this sort members can gain insights into their own manner of relating to persons in authority. One of the functions of the T-group, in fact, is to make members sensitive to the way in which their own difficulties with authority emerge in the context of a group.

Bennis and Shepard argue that until these troubles with a nondirective leader are satisfactorily resolved the members cannot focus their attention on themselves and their relationships with one another. They note that their observations were based on groups that ran for 17 weeks, and that it was not uncommon for these groups to be in the authority phase throughout this entire period.

If the group progresses, however, the second

phase of development now centers on members who have difficulties in dealing with relationships of intimacy. The overpersonals demand unconditional love; the counterpersonals worry about getting too close and too involved. With luck, perseverance, helpful awareness of one's own difficulties, and a handful of relatively unconflicted members, the group may move on to achieve the nirvana of this conception of T-groups, *consensual validation:*

". . . what ensues is a serious attempt by each group member to verbalize his private conceptual scheme for understanding human behavior—his own and that of others. Bringing these assumptions into explicit communication is the main work. . . . Some of the values that appear to underlie the group's work during this subphase are as follows: 1. Members can accept one another's differences without associating 'good' and 'bad' with the differences. 2. Conflict exists but is over substantive issues rather than emotional issues. 3. Consensus is reached as a result of rational discussion rather than through a compulsive attempt at unanimity. 4. Members are aware of their own involvement, and of other aspects of group process, without being overwhelmed or alarmed. 5. Through the evaluation process, members take on greater personal meaning to each other. This facilitates communication and creates a deeper understanding of how the other person thinks, feels, behaves; it creates a series of personal expectations, as distinguished from the previous, more stereotyped, role expectations" (Bennis & Shepard, 1956, pp. 432–433).

It is enlightening to read over that list of five values presented as the potential outcome of a successful T-group experience; it includes those qualities thought to be beneficial in all human relationships; presumably, therefore, it has application well beyond the T-group. Formal task groups in business presumably would benefit if people related in terms outlined in the list; likewise, relationships in smaller, less formal groups, including dyads, or even in larger groups might benefit. The list is somewhat like a Golden Rule or a Ten Commandments of interpersonal relationships.

In summary, then, the T-group approach builds in a sense on the concept of implicit personality theory with which this book began. It assumes that each of us has an implicit theory; that this theory has as central foci ways of relating to authority and of dealing with intimacy; that, in great measure, our views of authority and of intimacy derive from the familial context; that a hidden agenda of personal involvements and emotional hangups tends to be recreated in our contemporary relationships and interferes with progress on a *task* agenda; and finally, that the T-group is a setting within which the distortions and projections of our personal hidden agendas are highlighted in bold relief, and consequently may be dealt with so as to minimize their potentially destructive effect.

Interpersonal orientations

One point that clearly emerged from the Bennis and Shepard approach to group development was that individuals have *characteristic* ways of relating themselves to authority and to intimacy. Several other investigators have made substantial contributions to this study of interpersonal orientations, using the T-group as a setting both for discovering the orientations and for testing their validity.

Bion and Thelen. In 1948 Bion published his first "experience" with a therapy-type group. In 1951 his concluding article in the series, entitled "Experiences in Groups," found its way into print. Like any good scientist in any discipline, Bion kept his eyes and ears open, and at the top of his mind kept asking the nagging question, "What the hell is going on?" He had a vast amount of experiential data to organize and explain in some fashion. The theory he developed in those articles between 1948 and 1951 expressed his efforts to explain the complexity of human interaction that presented itself to him.

Bion viewed the group as a miniature society caught up in internal conflicts over the basic assumptions by which it should operate. The assumption of *work* focused on efforts to deal with problems to be solved; this was the group's cognitive state, its conscious task orientation, if you will. The assumption of *emotionality*, by contrast, was more primitive and unconscious, and was concerned both with helping to maintain the group and with avoiding certain realities. In any one moment of its life the group was thought to be dealing with both assumptions. Therefore Bion saw his therapy groups as doing essentially what Bales had seen his task groups doing: dealing with task and socio-emotional issues (see p. 248 ff.).

Bion's major contribution was to posit separate psychological states or *cultures* by which a group functioned. He assumed that the behavior of an individual in a group, although a reflection of his own psychological needs, was always activated by, and thus to a certain extent an expression of, the psychological state or culture of the group as a whole. He proposed four major needs a group culture could have that could be reflected through individual behavior: fight, flight, dependency, and pairing. *Fight* is any expression of aggression toward the problem at hand, the leader, the group, outsiders, one's self. *Flight* is behavior such as running away, leaving the field, daydreaming, rambling discussion, overintellectualized abstract discussion, joking, avoidance. *Dependency* is any behavior that seeks aid from outside, from the leader, the minutes of earlier meetings, tradition, experts, and so on. Finally, *pairing* is any approach to intimacy, especially remarks made privately to another group member, efforts to reach out to another, expressions of warmth or approval, and so on.

In Bion's scheme the group as a whole is said to be in flight when, for example, one or several members are engaged in out-of-field conversation or are joking. He maintains that a group that permits several members to engage in flight does so because the behavior satisfies the culture or psychological need state of the group as well as their own personal needs. In like manner, Bion argues, individual behavior in any of the other modes reflects the psychological needs of the group as a whole.

Notice some of the similarities and points of contrast between Bion's view of group behavior and the view of Bennis and Shepard. Both reflect the seminal conceptions of Freud. Dependency in both views is a way of relating to authority; Bennis and Shepard call it intimacy, Bion calls it pairing. Unlike Bion, Bennis and Shepard discuss points along dimensions of dependency or pairing. Whereas Bion argues

that individual behavior always *reflects* the groups' needs, Bennis and Shepard see individual needs as *creating* group process.

Thelen (1954; 1959) built on Bion's main concepts to achieve dimensionalization of dependency and pairing; he conceptualized dependency and counterdependency as two points along one dimension and pairing and counterpairing as two points along another: the dependent seeks aid but the counterdependent shouts, "I can do it myself"; pairing is meant to seek intimacy, counterpairing is meant to avoid involvement. Second, Thelen argued that these psychological needs or group cultures (now six in number: dependency, counterdependency, pairing, counterpairing, fight, flight) were individual orientations or *predispositions*; an individual could be predisposed toward dependency, fighting, or pairing, or toward their opposites. Finally, he developed two techniques for determining these orientations, a sentence-completion test and a Q-sort. In the former an individual was asked to complete sentences such as, "When George attacked the group, Bob. . ."; "When the leader offered to help him, Pete. . . ." The Q-sort consisted of 60 items (10 for each orientation) that an individual was to sort into piles ranging from "most like me" to "least like me." In both cases it was possible to determine an individual's score on the six orientations and from this score make predictions about his behavior in a group, or, knowing the composition of the entire group, to make predictions about its behavior.

In one study (reported by Stock, 1964), for example, observers rated the behavior of groups that had been composed intentionally of persons of differing orientation. Just as we would expect, a group containing many members oriented toward flight was rated as uninvolved both with the task and with one another. In another study (Stock, 1964) groups with and without pairing-oriented members were observed; as expected, the groups differed most in expressions of pairing (closeness and intimacy).

A study that I undertook with a colleague, Ned Levine, is also helpful (Sampson & Levine, 1963). As part of a course in small groups, students were divided into T-groups to meet for an entire semester. In one such class there were four T-groups. In the early part of the semester all students were given a variety of tests, including the self-descriptive Q-sort developed by Thelen to measure the six orientations he derived from Bion. At the end of the semester all were asked to complete a role or *behavioral description* questionnaire, 23 descriptions of behaviors that might have occurred during the course of their semester-long T-group. They were to use a five-point rating scale, ranging from "most describes" to "least describes," and fill out this questionnaire for every member of the group including themselves. If there were 10 persons in their group, each had to make 230 separate ratings: 10 persons × 23 descriptions.

We scored these forms by computing the group's average rating of a given member on each of the 23 traits. We termed this the *average-other* rating. Now all that remained was to relate the Bion orientations from the Q-sort to these average-other ratings. To do this we divided the students at the median or midpoint on each of the six dimensions. We then found "pure" cases on each dimension. A pure case on the dependency dimension, for example, is a person who scores high in dependence *and* low in counterdependence. Table 20.1 presents results of this analysis.

Several things emerge from an examination of these data. First, it is apparent that the Bion-Thelen orientations inventory measures qualities in people that are expressed and noticed in group behavior. In fact it is heartening to note the generally close correspondence between an individual's test score, obtained early in the term, and his group's average rating of his behavior at the end of the term. Second, the table gives some further flavor to the meaning of the several kinds of interpersonal orientation that Bion and Thelen offer. It seems clear, for example, that fight-oriented persons are active energizers, keeping things moving, whereas those who prefer flight as a mode of dealing with difficulties do in fact fade away from their group. The counterdependents likewise seem to be sparkplugs that keep the group moving right along, even though they tend to dominate.

Table 20.1 The relationship between interpersonal needs and individual T-group behavior

I. Persons who were high counterdependent and low dependent, as compared with persons who were high dependent and low counterdependent, were described as follows.
  1. Energized discussion; motivated members to participate.
  2. Tended to orient group to various problems.
  3. Tended to initiate discussion.
  4. Tended to keep the discussion harmonious.
  5. Tended to dominate the discussion.
  6. Gave out many opinions.
  7. Tried to control others.
  8. Were not followers; did not go along passively.
  9. Tended to express negative feelings about the leader.

II. Persons who were high pairing and low counterpairing, as compared with persons who were high counterpairing and low pairing, were described as follows.
  1. Wanted to be close and personal.
  2. Not detached in manner; inclined to form special friendships.
  3. Especially warm and friendly toward one or two members.
  4. Tended to seek recognition.
  5. Not uncomfortable when feelings were expressed.
  6. Tried to be close and personal.
  7. Primarily interaction oriented.
  8. Wanted to be included in discussions.

III. Persons who were high fight and low flight, as compared with persons who were high flight and low fight, were described as follows.
  1. Energized discussion; motivated members to participate.
  2. Did not want to be controlled.
  3. Tended to orient the group to various problems.
  4. Tended to seek recognition.
  5. Took aggressive role in discussions.
  6. Tended to start arguments.
  7. Tended to dominate the discussion.
  8. Disinclined to follow the suggestions of another group member.
  9. Gave out many opinions.
  10. Tried to control others.
  11. Tended to express negative feelings about the leader.
  12. Tended to use the group to further his own personal needs; self-oriented.

Recall that Bennis and Shepard say that movement of the group derives from some of the internal battles that develop over these "types." We can almost see the counterdependents lined up on one side, pushing, arguing, trying to take charge, attacking the nondirective leader, and, on the other side, the dependents quietly waiting for their inactive leader to rise phoenix-like from the flames. There are so many hidden agendas that we sense the group could continue to generate activity almost endlessly; yet members soon begin to decry the fact that they have no task to accomplish, no stated or formal agenda; they are bored. Among people who have different orientations to one another and to authority, it seems unlikely that there is nothing to do; boredom undoubtedly is more a measure of flight from the hidden agenda than it is true boredom.

Schutz. FIRO is the name of the book Schutz published in 1960; it stands for *Fundamental Interpersonal Relationships Orientation.* In this book Schutz developed what he termed a three-dimensional theory of interpersonal behavior. He argued that each of us orients himself in characteristic ways to other persons; and if we knew what those interpersonal orientations were we would understand much about both individual behavior and the interaction among persons as members of a group.

Schutz posited the existence of three interpersonal needs (needs that require good relationships with others for their satisfaction); these he termed inclusion, control, and affection. *Inclusion* is an issue of in versus out; the need is to interact and associate with people, to belong, to affiliate. *Control* is an issue of top versus bottom; the need is to achieve, to influence, to have power, to be independent. *Affection* is an issue of close versus far; the need is to love, to be close and intimate with another. An individual may be high or low in any of these needs.

In addition to defining three interpersonal needs, Schutz does what none of the other theorists has done; he defines two *modalities* for each need. One modality is the behavior that *P expresses* toward others; the second is the behavior that *P wants others to express* toward him. This results in six separable need-modality combinations or interpersonal orientations (see Table 20.2). An individual theoretically might be high in C^e but low or middling in C^w.

Table 20.2 Need-modality combinations

	Expressed	Wanted
Inclusion	I^e	I^w
Control	C^e	C^w
Affection	A^e	A^w

This person would express a great desire to control and dominate and want others *not* to act in controlling ways toward him.

To assess these six orientations Schutz developed a simple, straightforward paper-and-pencil test. The flavor of the test and the meaning of the concepts can be seen in the first six items:

I^e "I try to be with people."
I^w "I like people to include me in their activities."
C^e "I try to be the dominant person when I am with people."
C^w "I let other people decide what to do."
A^e "I try to be friendly to people."
A^w "I like people to act friendly toward me."

Most empirical research using the FIRO scales has been concerned with the effects of group composition and compatibility. The variety of orientations that Schutz posited permitted him to compute several kinds of compatibility score for two persons at a time. *Interchange compatibility* is based on the notion of need similarity. To compute this score you take O's and P's expressed and wanted scores and sum across the three interpersonal needs. This yields a score that indicates the over-all similarity between O and P in the three needs. *Reciprocal compatibility* is essentially a need-complementarity measure. If P expresses in his behavior what O wants others to express toward him, O and P are said to have a high *reciprocal compatibility*; if P's expressed behavior (as measured on the test) does not reciprocate O's wants, their reciprocal compatibility is low.

Schutz (1960) reported data indicating that groups composed to be compatible are both more cohesive and more productive. For example, in a study of fraternity roommates Schutz found, as expected, that persons chosen as roommates were generally rated as highly compatible with the chooser. In the same study he found that the more of the three needs on which there was compatibility, the more likely the person was to be chosen.

In another study Schutz (1960) replicated earlier results. He composed groups that were compatible and groups that were incompatible, whether the compatibility was in terms of high scores or low scores. Thus it seemed to be the compatibility (in this case interchange compatibility) rather than the particular need system that facilitated group productivity.

In still another effort Schutz (1961) sought to determine whether members could identify their own group's composition. He composed T-groups to be homogeneous in interchange compatibility. Toward the conclusion of the training experience he presented them with descriptions of groups and asked them to select the one that was most like their own. Results indicated that in general members were able to determine the composition of their own group.

One interesting application of the FIRO theory and methodology was attempted by Pollack (1967), using the T-groups run as part of a group dynamics class at Berkeley. Pollack argued that a change toward balance between what an individual expressed toward others and what he wanted from them was a positive or healthful change. A person, for example, who wants affection from others (high A^w) but who expresses little toward them (low A^e) is more likely than a balanced person to be frustrated or annoyed, or to behave in a self-defeating manner.

Pollack next argued that a heterogeneous T-group would produce more positive change than one that was homogeneous; he based this on Harrison's view of change as requiring both confrontation and support (Harrison, 1965; Harrison & Lubin, 1965). Confrontation is necessary to unfreeze an individual, to shake him from his complacency, to indicate other ways of looking at people. Too much confrontation, without an atmosphere that is generally supportive, would be likely to put him in a hardened and defensive posture; with a supportive atmosphere, however, he may be emboldened to step out of his old shoes and experience new ways of relating with others. To test this Pollack formed several groups that were homogeneous in the FIRO dimension of control and several

that were heterogeneous. He obtained change scores by computing the discrepancies for each person's expressed and wanted scores on each of the FIRO orientations both before and after the T-group experience. The hypothesis generally received confirmation; the heterogeneous FIRO groups produced greater positive change —greater change toward balance between the wanted and the expressed modes for each orientation.

In addition to his concern with compatibility and group-composition effects, Schutz applied his three-need scheme to group development. He argued that the focal issues in T-groups move from inclusion to control and finally to affection. Initially a group is wrapped up with the matter of inclusion and group formation, setting up boundaries, determining who is in, who is out, who has made a real commitment to the group and who seems to have done little yet to earn membership. Although the issue of inclusion is usually settled beforehand in formal groups with a structure supplied externally (e.g., a work group in business), this becomes a key matter in most informally structured groups such as the T-group. In fact, when we think of inclusion as involving commitment to the group, especially in terms of willingness to take on the jobs and responsibilities expected of members, it is not unusual to see most groups, both formal and informal, pass through an inclusion phase. Loosely structured, small, informal groups, ranging from dyadic relationships to groups of 15 or so persons, usually have to come to grips with the inclusion matter early in their lives. I have seen many T-groups haggle endlessly over inclusion issues, using such symptoms as showing up late to a meeting, not talking, or missing a meeting as signs of low commitment and thus as *out*; members who show up eagerly on time, never miss a meeting, and talk often are assumed to have made the proper commitment and thus are *in*. To be in is not simply an idle matter. To be in means to come under the normative rule of the group; to be out, especially when membership roles await, very importantly conveys rejection *of* the group, so that the uncommitted are threatening to the group.

Control concerns power and decision making. Schutz indicated that once a group has passed through its issues of inclusion it is ready to focus on power matters, including leadership; and only when it has moved beyond control is it prepared to deal with affection (intimacy in the Bennis and Shepard scheme; pairing in Bion-Thelen). Notice how Schutz's developmental outline parallels that of Bennis and Shepard, positing authority issues as prerequisite to intimacy issues, and how his approach, like theirs, derives from the Freudian theory of psychosexual development: oral stage—inclusion; anal—control; genital—affection. It appears that a rose by any other name will still carry the scent of Sigmund Freud.

Unlike Bennis and Shepard, and for that matter unlike most theories of development, Schutz suggested a sequence that occurs when a group is ready to come to a close: a reversal of the order of development. As the relationships in the group are about to terminate, the first bonds that must be severed are the ties of affectional intimacy that presumably have evolved. These may be broken (*decathected*) in several ways. A person may antagonize others so that they will come to reject him; this I have seen occur often and vividly. Leaving is indeed difficult, especially if positive bonds have been strong. One way to leave, although not with much grace or dignity, is to become so hostile and antagonistic that others finally say "good riddance." Then the individual may say smugly to himself, "I'm not casting adrift from them; they have rejected me."

Other members decathect affectional bonds by coming late or not showing up, or, when they come, by reducing their participation to a minimum. Still others leave by devaluing the group, shouting in their protest-too-loudly voices, "Who cares! Who really gives a damn about this group and you people!" Some manage to leave by never having entered in the first place. That is, for some persons investment and commitment are so threatening and so potentially filled with danger and pain that they never make the initial investment of themselves in the group or in other people. Leave-taking for them is relatively easy.

The next relationships to go are those involving power and leadership, and finally inclusion disintegrates. But often the group does not depart without one final effort to continue, even when the term (in the case of classroom T-groups) has been completed. "We'll all meet at 8:30 right here just as we always have, right after Christmas vacation." "Yes!" they all shout in agreement. Christmas comes and goes, and 8:30 arrives that day and no one shows up. But the carefully made plans to keep things going have helped stave off the great difficulties that are encountered when one must leave a group or depart from a relationship.

Summary

I think that even this relatively brief run-through indicates that in essence Schutz and the others are not talking simply about T-groups. Rather, their theories apply to all forms of human relationships. It so happens that the T-group provides in capsule the entire spectrum of human dilemmas that emerge in any relationship, whether a one-to-one dyadic encounter or more formally structured, work-based relationships. There is a beginning, there is a course of life, and there is a closing. Certain issues arise at each of these points in every relationship. In the T-group we may study human relationships as they form and finally as they terminate.

TWO DIMENSIONS OF RELATIONSHIPS

By now the similarities in conception that run from Freud through Bennis and Shepard to Bion-Thelen and finally to Schutz should be apparent. At minimum each defines a two-dimensional space within which one can map out interpersonal relationships. One dimension is defined in terms of authority or control; the other is a sphere of affection or intimacy. At their root, these two dimensions are little different from the two major dimensions of task and socioemotional functions that guided much of Bales' work.

Perhaps even less surprising is the rough parallel between these two kinds of relationship in a group and the role configuration assumed to exist in the traditional family structure. The husband carries the instrumental or task functions, with the emphasis on power and authority; the wife carries the expressive or socio-emotional functions, with the emphasis on affection and intimacy. It is of more than passing interest to note that when Bales' methodology of interaction analysis was modified and applied to the T-group setting, a role patterning was uncovered that embodied these two dimensions plus several interesting residuals.

A program ominously called the General Inquirer was developed (Stone, Dunphy, Smith, & Ogilvie, 1966) in order to permit computer analysis of subjective material including diaries, letters, stories, and so on: a special dictionary of concepts is formed; the data to be analyzed are coded, and everything is run through the computer. The computer *tags* or labels clusters of concepts (for example, *actions* or *roles*) that are mentioned in the subjective report material, yielding frequency counts for each concept.

It is possible thus to content analyze complex material and abstract the dominant themes that occur in a group or in a particular kind of relationship. Dunphy (1966) applied this program to the analysis of diaries T-group members had written after meetings. His analysis revealed several clusters of typical roles or patterns of behavior that emerged at various phases in a group's life. A *father-figure* role emerged; the emphasis was on emotional distance, task orientation, and judging others. A *mother-figure* emerged; this role was more emotional and supportive, like the traditional mother. Two *dominant siblings* emerged. One, called the seducer, continually tried to direct the discussion to topics of sex and intimacy; this member was physically attractive and seemed seductive in his or her manner of relating to others in the group. The other, called the aggressor, seized every opportunity to create disharmony and strife. The final role pattern to emerge, which Dunphy called the *weak sibling,* was the scapegoat, who became the object of the attacks of the aggressor and of almost everyone else in the group. We see in this brief view of the General Inquirer the same two dimensions of human relationships, authority

and intimacy. Even the aggressor and the seducer join this picture; only the scapegoat stands aside as the victim of others' relationships to authority.

In other efforts to classify interpersonal relationships several authors have latched onto similar dimensions. Leary (1957) for one, examined interview protocols and actual therapy sessions and from these derived a two-factor system for classifying behavior. He termed one factor *dominance-submission* and the other *affiliation-hostility.*

On a somewhat different tack, Jackson (1959) sought to understand the meaning of group membership. He reasoned that a person may be a *formal* member of a group if his name is on its roster, yet he may not be a *psychological* member; that is, he may not consider himself as part of the group, or, for that matter, others in the group may not consider him to be committed to their program and values. To deal with the apparent complexity in the meaning of group membership, Jackson presented two dimensions that could be used to characterize a wide variety of relationships between an individual and a group. One dimension he termed *attraction;* an individual could be *positively* attracted to the group, *negatively* attracted, or be located at some *indifference point.* The second dimension was *acceptance;* Jackson defined this dimension in terms of the degree to which role expectations existed within the group regarding that individual. He suggested that acceptance involved the extent to which a person came into the power field of the group— the degree to which he was subject to its sanctions and influences. Thus this second dimension is defined in terms of authority or influence. As with attraction, acceptance was dimensionalized into *positive, negative*, and *neutral* acceptance. Positive acceptance is readily understood as the existence of a place for *P* in the group. In neutral acceptance, an indifference point, there neither is nor is not a role for *P.* Negative acceptance is not simply the absence of a role, but is the rejection of *P* from membership; the group actively refuses to open itself to him.

Jackson suggests that the two dimensions

are independent, at least in theory. He presents a graph (Figure 20.2) that plots a variety of relationships that may exist between the individual and a group. From reading the figure it is apparent that a psychological member of a group must have both high positive attraction to the group *and* acceptance into its power field. A person who is highly attracted to a group but is not an accepted member is said to have a *preference group* relationship. He likes the group he is not yet in. A *rebel* is defined as an accepted group member who does not like the group. *Caste* relationships exist when acceptance into the group is negative—rules exist against admitting the individual. Jackson suggests that one type of caste relationship involves positive attraction (the individual admires the group to which he is barred entry); another involves indifference. The former exists, for example, among Negroes who wish to be accepted into white society, its clubs, its restricted neighborhoods, its schools, and so on; the latter exists among those who care little about white groups and accept a separate-but-equal philosophy. Other relationships are relatively easy to trace in the figure.

One laboratory effort to test certain aspects of this theory was attempted by Jackson and Saltzstein (1958), who experimentally created varying conditions of attraction to a group and varying degrees of member acceptance. Four such conditions were created: *members*, who were both highly attracted and accepted; *marginals*, who although accepted had lower attraction; *preferences*, who were not accepted although they were attracted; and *nonmembers*, who were low both in attraction and in acceptance. All groups were presented with a modified Asch-type situation (see p. 255 for a discussion). They were shown maze-like figures and asked to indicate the shortest route from start to finish on notes that they wrote to one another. On several trials the experimenters changed the notes to give subjects false information about the group's opinion. It was hypothesized that the degree of conformity to the group would vary as a function of the relationship between the individual and the group. For example, it was felt that persons who were psychologically members of a group should be under more pressure to conform to group perceptions than persons who were nonmembers.

It was further reasoned, following Festinger's ideas (1950); that there were two separable sources of pressure to conform. One, *group locomotion*, involved getting people sufficiently in line so that the group could make successful progress toward its goals. The other, *social reality* (a factor we have discussed on p. 122 ff.) arises from individual processes of social comparison. If a group were rated in terms of the accuracy of its performance on a task (the *normative* condition) there should be more conformity pressure than if individuals were scored separately (the *modal* condition).

Results from this study were revealing on two counts. First, as predicted, there was greater pressure on psychological members and greater conformity under the normative as compared with the modal conditions. Second, however, persons who were not accepted as group members unexpectedly also showed a high degree of conformity to group opinion. To explain this outcome Jackson and Saltzstein suggested that rejection from membership might have created a need for social reassurance that led a rejected individual to overcome the disturbing experience by conforming closely to the group's judgments; he sought to ameliorate his disturbed feelings by showing what a good group member he really would have been. This

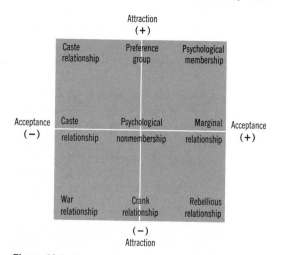

Attraction
(+)

Caste relationship	Preference group	Psychological membership

Acceptance (−)

Caste relationship	Psychological nonmembership	Marginal relationship

Acceptance (+)

War relationship	Crank relationship	Rebellious relationship

(−)
Attraction

Figure 20.2 A space for conceptualizing relationships between the individual and a group (adapted from Jackson, 1959)

result is interesting because it suggests that Jackson and Saltzstein created a caste relationship rather than a nonmember relationship; and in a caste relationship we may actually find conformity to the dominant group's opinions even when the caste member is not allowed entry. He may become whiter than white—or in this case he conforms every bit as firmly as a good group member should.

So once again we see two useful dimensions, sharing much with those we have already examined, providing a system for classifying social relationships. Although it is tempting indeed to suggest that intimacy and authority are two dimensions that characterize all human encounters, as much of the preceding research and theory have suggested, it seems premature to oversimplify to that extent.

BUT DOES IT WORK? THE RESEARCH EVIDENCE

The question posed in the title of this section is more easily asked than answered, and its simplicity of statement conceals some monumental research problems. When we ask if "it works" we assume that we really know to what "it" refers and what "works" means. Presumably "it" is a training program that involves T-groups and may include reading, lectures, papers, analyses of case histories, and other more traditionally academic forms of study. But even if "it" is only a T-group, we might want a narrow approach to answering the question or a diffuse one. The narrow approach would attempt to tease out parts of the total T-group experience that could be held primarily accountable for any change that occurs. We might, for example, claim that it was the leader's style that was primarily responsible; or the group's composition (as in Pollack's work); or the level of conceptual development of the individual members; or a variety of specific independent variables hypothesized to be responsible in some manner for the change. We would undoubtedly wish to set up an experimental paradigm in which each variable was systematically varied and its effects noted. We might compare a T-group with a nondirective leader with one that has a directive leader; we might

construct groups of varying composition and examine the consequences of these compositions on change. In a broader approach we would not concern ourselves with relating specific internal factors of the T-group to our change measures; instead we would compare the T-group as a whole with other, non-T-group experiences. This assumes, of course, that we know what a so-called standardized T-group is.

Clearly, both approaches are complementary and essential to any systematic endeavor. The initial question that we typically ask, however, focuses on the broader approach: Does going through a T-group produce more change in people than not going through this experience? Presumably if we note change, we will be motivated to look at the factors in the group that play a major role in producing this change. This might lead us to examine the personalities of individuals who are most and least receptive to the experience; the group-composition variables that are related to change; the style of leadership that most facilitates change. Lest you think that the complexity ends there, let me note that external factors are also likely to be important. Thus the context within which a T-group is introduced is relevant to consider in evaluating its effectiveness as a change-inducing technique. T-groups may work better in some cultures or subcultures than in others; they may work better in some kinds of organization than in others.

Assuming that we now know what "it" is— quite an assumption as you can see—the question remains of what "works" means. What is it that we take to be a change? It may be helpful to think of several *domains* within which change may occur. On the individual level, a person's attitudes may change, his personality, his defenses, his behavior, his interpersonal orientations, his values, and so forth. The change may be temporary or enduring. It may occur during the course of the group, or immediately on its conclusion, or it may not show up until sometime later. The change may be positive and constructive or negative and destructive. Even this is no simple matter. A change that is positive and healthful for an individual might in fact set him in opposition to the goals of some larger unit of which he is a member (recall the discussion on p. 231). For example, an organization may send some of its personnel to a T-group program. After the experience they may come back to the organization with more open expression of resistance to organizational practices than they had evidenced before. This may be deemed a personally positive change, but the organization does not particularly enjoy it.

Changes may also occur on the group level. Although any one individual may not evidence change, what actually is affected by the experience is how these individuals now work together. They may become more cohesive; lines of communication may be more open and function better; they may become more creative in their problem solving. Or the group may split apart, being unable to work effectively because it is so caught up in interpretive struggles and motivational analyses that it no longer gets any external jobs completed.

It should be apparent by now that once we have in mind the meaning of "it works," we still have to consider how to measure any of the variables or factors. Obviously, if we want to predict behavioral change, our measurement will be somewhat different than if our predictions are for attitudinal change. Likewise, our measurement problem is different if we examine immediate change as opposed to long-term change; and if we focus on individual-level change we face a different problem than we would encounter if we focused on group-level change.

In the typical research paradigm we obtain premeasures, introduce the change procedure, and obtain postmeasures. At times, if it is safe to assume that before the change experience people were pretty much alike (say they were randomly assigned to the T-group or to a comparison group), we may just obtain postmeasures. Before we can make any measures, however, we must first know the kinds of variable we want to examine and the nature of the change on which we intend to focus. Suppose, for example, we simply compare T-groups with non-T-groups. We may randomly assign persons to both groups. In a non-T-group there

may be no special group experience. That is, the T-group may be compared with one that simply goes through life or work in a "natural" way without any special change procedure, or with a lecture course in group dynamics, or with a task-oriented group.

Suppose the change to be examined is behavioral; we want to see if persons who go through a T-group actually return to work as better supervisors or managers than they were before the T-group or as compared with non-groupers. We set up criteria for evaluating good supervisors; these may include supervisor ratings or even employee ratings once the person is back on the job. Naturally, if ratings are used and if those doing the rating know that a person rated has undergone some special training, this may affect their ratings; they may hope to see more change than there actually is; or their hope may lead them to expect so much improvement that they miss subtleties. This can be overcome by having raters rate individuals about whom they know very little.

Up to this point, then, we have some persons randomly assigned to T-groups and some assigned to non-T-groups; and we plan to have their superiors and their employees rate their behavior. Have we taken ratings before the change as well? Probably not; we just compare the two groups afterward, assuming that because they were randomly assigned their previous ratings as a group would be highly similar. Do we plan to get behavioral ratings immediately on their return to work? Do we plan to get them at six-week intervals for a year? What do we plan to do to measure the duration of the change? Let me assure you that the research problem involved in evaluating any change procedure, including the T-group, is a complex matter indeed. I have presented this relatively brief peek at some of the complexities involved in order to provide a context within which to evaluate the research more intelligently.

Anecdotes

Perhaps the most extensive source of data concerning the effectiveness of T-groups derives from word-of-mouth advertising. Mrs. Klutch has been through six groups and swears by them. Mr. Tilk has had his first group experience and feels he is a new man. Mrs. Wirthmore already knows that this is a worthless experience. Sally Finch had a nervous breakdown that required intensive psychotherapy after her T-group. Marge and Ted Munch got a divorce shortly after each went through a T-group. Most of this anecdotal evidence indicates that the groups do have some effect, often positive, at times negative or personally disastrous. Some persons are disappointed; they come looking for a miracle and leave feeling much the same. Others find their miracle.

I do not want to ignore these anecdotes; if they were collected and organized they could form an important source of data. Usually, however, they remain just informally stated views. Depending on the number and variety of anecdote merchants a person has contact with, then, he comes to see the effectivenes of T-groups in different ways. If everyone you know—all two of them—has had a bad experience, you may conclude that T-groups are no good. Or if all two of them have had great experiences and now feel changed for the better, you may conclude that T-groups are great.

Systematic work

Systematic T-group research, sparse but growing rapidly and tied into the multitude of methodological problems just mentioned, offers us some material to aid our evaluations of T-groups as a technique of planned change. Several studies suggest attitudinal and perceptual changes as an outcome of T-groups. In one effort Burke and Bennis (1961) obtained pre- and postmeasures on persons in a laboratory T-group. They report significant changes in the degree to which these persons report satisfaction with themselves; the movement is toward greater congruence with their ideal self-image. In addition, they report positive changes in the degree to which their views of others are valid.

Harrison (1962) asked members of an organization in which some employees had gone through a T-group to describe persons in the organization. Comparing descriptions of those

who had been through the T-group with those who had not, Harrison reports significant effects of the T-group experience, especially the degree to which members' perceptions of one another were affected. In general the T-group experience increased the use of interpersonal and emotional categories in descriptions. Haiman (1963) reports a shift toward increased open-mindedness as a function of a college course in sensitivity training. In still another effort Bass (1962) had T-groupers and a sample of others complete sentences concerning a movie they had just seen. The focus of the questions was primarily on the motivations of the characters. Results indicate that T-groupers became more sensitive than nongroupers, as determined by comparing their scores with expert opinion.

Interestingly enough, fairly well-conducted, systematic efforts to study the effects of T-groups on behavioral change generally tend to find positive results. Bunker (1965) gave a questionnaire to raters at the conclusion of a T-group; they were to use it to evaluate each participant of the T-group and of control groups. Raters' evaluations of change were compared with members' perceptions of change. In general Bunker found good agreement between these two independent assessments, and found more reports of change in the T-groups than in the control groups. Even more importantly, evaluations of these individuals back on the job indicated positive effectiveness of T-groups in producing better job ratings.

Underwood (1965) asked raters to report any changes they noted in several sets of employees in an organization. They were not told which of these had been through a T-group program and which were part of the comparison group. The raters found much more change in the behavior of those who had been through the T-group than in the control group. In addition, by rating the changes in terms of their contribution to positive or negative on-the-job effectiveness, Underwood found 15 changes rated positively and seven negatively (contributing to a decrease in effectiveness). Probing more deeply, he uncovered what is not really surprising to anyone who has worked with T-groups: many of the negative changes involved emotional expressiveness. One effect commonly noted in anecdotes is that going through a T-group loosens an individual up so that he can vent his feelings more openly. Back on the job such venting might be rated as a negative change, at least by those doing the ratings in Underwood's study. Clearly, however, the T-group had impact.

A comparison of T-group training with a lecture course covering group dynamics material revealed more ratings of change in the behavior of those in the T-group (in Buchanan, 1964). Observers rated these as primarily positive changes, although T-groupers were also rated higher in negative or undesirable changes. Once again, in a job situation the kind of opening up that a T-group provides may be rated as undesirable.

Argyris (1962; 1965a, b, c) has done a considerable amount of work attempting to evaluate both perceptual and behavior changes as a function of T-groups. He reports data that are positive on both counts. T-groupers alter their perceptions both as they report them and as their subordinates rate them; in this case the subordinates rate the increasing consideration of their supervisors as positive. Likewise, using behavioral ratings, Argyris reports long-term effects of T-group training, especially regarding interpersonal categories such as openness, concern, and consideration for others.

An especially valuable contribution to the examination of the effectiveness of T-group training involved a well-controlled study by Rubin (1967). Rubin reasoned that persons high in self-acceptance would show less ethnic-group prejudice than persons low in self-acceptance; and that one of the consequences of a T-group experience is higher self-acceptance. It would follow that after being involved in a T-group individuals should show a reduction in prejudice. To study this, Rubin premeasured individuals' ethnic prejudice and general level of self-acceptance; after the T-group experience he obtained postmeasures on the same variables. A similar before-after measure was obtained on a control group that did not go through T-group training. Rubin's results, confirming both his expectation and the efficacy of T-group training,

showed substantial change both in self-acceptance (it became higher) and prejudice (it became lower) for those who were in the T-group, but relatively no change for those in the control group.

In a lengthy review, in which much of the research literature is reported, House (1967) concludes:

"One of the most striking results . . . is the lack of contradiction among the findings. All . . . revealed what appear to be important positive effects of T-group training. Two of the studies report negative effects as well. These findings take on special significance when one considers the rigor with which the studies were conducted" (p. 18).

On the other hand, in another review article Dunnette and Campbell (1968) found less to praise and more to criticize about research data that demonstrated the efficacy of sensitivity training. Dunnette and Campbell concluded that T-group training

". . . has not been shown to bring about any marked change . . . on objective measures of attitudes, values, outlooks, interpersonal perceptions, self-awareness, or interpersonal sensitivity. In spite of these . . . negative results . . . individuals who have been trained . . . are more likely to be seen as changing their job behavior . . . in the direction of more openness, better self- and interpersonal understanding, and improved communications and leadership skills. Unfortunately, these behavior reports suffer from many possible sources of bias and must, therefore, be taken with a grain of salt. . . . Primarily . . . our review has brought out weaknesses and gaps in the research related to the effects of laboratory education" (pp. 23–24).

It appears to me that although some contradictory findings are reported, and although the methodological problems are still monumental, evidence that points to certain kinds of effectiveness of T-groups as change agents remains impressive. Combining the research data with anecdotal reports leads me to conclude that the T-group can be a powerful tool for changing perceptions, attitudes, and behavior. Whether business, industry, or our educational institutions can tolerate the kinds of change that occur is another matter. It seems reasonable that consideration for others and a concern for their well-being, their ideas, and their contributions are all positive changes. How we evaluate the openness and emotional expressiveness that is also observed as an outcome of T-group training depends, I suppose, on our position and over-all time perspective. Undoubtedly it is uncomfortable to lead a group of individuals who feel an obligation to vent their feelings about you and about the task and about everyone else. I am certain there are times the leader would like to yell "shut up," and rues the day he ever heard of T-groups and sensitivity training. On the other hand, perhaps it is a short time perspective that yields this discomfort and these negative ratings; it may be that, with a longer time perspective, what seems distressing today, tomorrow becomes most highly valued. It is difficult to know about that today, of course. But the deluge of T-groups is here, a social phenomenon, an interpersonal revolution that may someday rank alongside other technological and ideological revolutions as significant driving forces of history and as shapers of our way of life.

Chapter 21

Social influence, conformity, and resistance

I suppose that if we did a simple number count, we would find social psychology abundantly filled with laboratory studies and accompanying theories, all dealing with the topics of social influence, conformity, and attitude or behavior change. There is no area in the field that has occupied more time, interest, and federal funding. The range of researchers extends from those with a basic curiosity about the foundations of behavior and attitude change to those whose interest is more directly practical. Theories formulated to account for social-influence effects run the gamut from strictly behavioral to intensely psychoanalytic. Most of the research itself is rigorous and experimental, usually performed on college sophomores, but the conclusions tempt one to generalize to the moon and beyond.

THE COMPLEXITIES OF CONFORMITY

Conformity implies a change in P (P can be a person, a group, or some larger social unit) from one state to a new state as a function of some act of O. The change may be toward a congruence in thought, perception, or action between P and O; for example, in the Asch situation (p. 255) P changes his judgments to see (or report seeing) as O does. The change may be congruent with the intentions or desires of O, as

when P follows an order O gives him, or succumbs to a suggestion from O, or yields to O's persuasive message. Changes may be behavioral or may involve a shift in attitudes or perceptual judgments.

Lest we forget the full picture, of course, P may not change, or may change to *increase* the incongruence between himself and O. For example, if O is a norm that indicates what one *ought* to do or think or see, P may stand pat, or change toward congruence with O, or change away from O, or he may not noticeably change, in the usual sense of that term, but rather may find the intensity of his conviction reinforced or undermined. In Asch's study, for example, it was noted that although some subjects did not change their judgments to coincide with the false majority, they reported being less confident in their own abilities. A child may know what he thinks, but, on encountering differing parental opinion, may come to question his own point of view. The opposite is also true; knowing how O thinks is sufficient cause for P to feel more convinced of the rightness of his own opinions. A member of the John Birch Society, hearing the views of the SDS, may feel a reconfirmation of his own views. It seems reasonable to suggest that changes toward O be called *conformity*; that standing pat be referred to as *passive resistance*; and that moving away be called *active resistance* to an influence attempt.

Not that I want to complicate the picture needlessly, but I hasten to add that a change in P toward O, or active or passive resistance to O, may not be attributable to O. In that case we would be wrong in calling the change conformity or resistance in response to social influence. Of course the matter becomes imponderably complicated if we allow the possibility for P to misperceive O and conform to or resist something that was never really offered by O. For example, suppose P reports seeing a card with seven dots on it. O reports seeing 10 dots, but P thinks that O has said six—please don't ask how this perception is possible; we can be sure that in the realm of the human almost everything that can happen will happen. So P does not change his judgment, and we think of him (erroneously) as passively resisting O's influence. We may think this example absurd, but when we realize that many influence attempts are concerned with complex issues and that people retain the right to be selectively distortive in their perceptions, it seems less absurd.

Some would have us count conformity only when P *intends* to change toward O; others concentrate primarily on the behavior change (see Hollander & Willis, 1967; or Nord, 1969, for a discussion). Most of the research is not especially helpful in this regard, at least in any systematic manner; it manages to mix behavioral change with and without phenomenological intent. Perhaps it is less important at this point to become hung up on definitions than simply to indicate, as I have, the several complications.

Marching to a different drummer

A point of view in popular vogue is that what passes for rebellion or resistance is really conformity. The argument, especially as it applies to the fads and fashions of youth, runs: Young persons dress strangely and wear their hair long because they think they are nonconforming to society. But aren't they *really* conforming more than most? Whether youth is conforming more or less than the older generation is perhaps an idle point to worry about for very long.

That resistance to one group may be conformity to the norms of another is not *really* a surprising piece of information; the sociologist Merton (1957) reminded us that resistance in one context may be seen as conformity to another. We do not all march to the same drummer. In his book on social movements Toch (1965) cites a relevant passage from Chayefsky's play *The Tenth Man:*

"A deaf man passed by a house in which a wedding party was going on. He looked in the window and saw all the people dancing and cavorting, leaping about and laughing. However, since the man was deaf and could not hear the music of the fiddlers, he said to himself: 'Ah, this must be a madhouse.' Young man, because you are deaf, must it follow that we are lunatics?" (p. 186).

Both conformity and resistance are best seen as relative concepts, most usefully applied when we keep in mind the social context (or historical era) that provides the reference point for each.

Reducing complexity in the laboratory

The study of social influence in the laboratory usually eliminates many complicating factors. There the basic paradigm is for O to seek to gain conformity from P. O's characteristics may be varied systematically, including his relationship to P and the manner by which his influence is attempted, or P's personality may be varied. In these ways it is possible to decrease the impact of complicating factors outside. For example, if you neatly restrict the possible responses that P can make, and if you insistently barrage him with the social influence attempt, you can be fairly certain that any change in his behavior is attributable to what you've done. No guarantees, of course; but probabilities that please the reasonable man.

McGuire (1969) pictures a chain that links the independent variables introduced in the experimental lab (e.g., the persuasive communications) with the dependent variables (e.g., P's change in attitude) as involving a series of five mediators—*attention, comprehension, yielding, retention,* and *action*—through which P must pass before O's efforts to influence him can be said to be effective. First, his attention must be caught; if his attention wanders, no message from O gets in. Second, he must comprehend the message; it is difficult indeed to influence with a message in Chinese a man who speaks only English. Third, P must (or must not) demonstrate the impact of the influence attempt in immediate yielding (or resisting) behavior. Retention and some action beyond the verbal involve longer-term impact of the independent variables.

The first three mediating stages can be studied in the laboratory, where we can provide some guarantee that P will glue his attention on the message from O, that it can be presented in a manner that should maximize his comprehension, and so on. Of course, we cannot guarantee that O will yield, or that he will remember for long what was done to him, or that he will take behavioral action; but we can provide a much more controlled setting than we are ever likely to encounter in life.

PUBLIC VERSUS PRIVATE CHANGE

It is useful to differentiate between a change in P that retains its dependence on O (a *public* change, depending on O's surveillance) and one that eventually becomes independent of O (a *private* change that, although initiated by O, becomes part of P). In this distinction we have an important instance in which the *same* behavior can have different underlying psychological properties. To an observer both Peter and Larry have just conformed; each has changed his view toward congruence with their teacher's. On closer examination it turns out that Peter has changed both his publicly stated view and his private belief as well; Larry, however, has complied publicly, but has not accepted the teacher's influence on the private level. If we treat these two instances of conformity in precisely the same way we shall miss an important difference in psychological meaning; Peter's conformity is likely to endure when the teacher is no longer present, but we can expect Larry to revert to his old ways once the teacher is removed from the scene. It is also apparent that the conditions that have led to Peter's conformity are different from the conditions that inspire Larry's. We shall deal with this matter shortly.

Several combinations of public versus private conformity are possible: public conformity with private acceptance; public conformity without private acceptance; public resistance with private resistance; public resistance with private acceptance. The first and third demonstrate consistency; the second and fourth indicate discrepancy. The second is easy to understand. Like Larry, this person may be under threat of punishment for resistance, so he conforms publicly in view of threatening Os while retaining his freedom on the private level. A liberal during the Communist-witch-hunting era of Senator Joseph McCarthy may have yielded publicly to McCarthy's anti-Communism, fearing consequences to his career for open defiance, but privately he may have retained his liberal or even leftist attitude.

Imagine living in a society in which all your actions were continually under surveillance. Trusting no one to conform privately, "big brother" would insist that for each man there must be a policeman with the power of the State to punish transgressions. You would be living under conditions of public conformity with—perhaps—private nonconformity. In a truly totalitarian regime private nonconformity could be in thought only, for deeds can be publicly noted and thus are liable to punishment.

The fourth situation may strike you as unlikely, for why would a person publicly resist O's influence while privately accepting it? One reason might be that he wishes to appear rebellious or independent. Or, in a debate or discussion, he may intentionally adopt a public stance that is contrary to what everyone else maintains, primarily to stimulate discussion and to force others to tighten their thinking. Privately, of course this devil's advocate may hold beliefs that are congruent with O's.

It should be apparent, both to the theoretician and to the practitioner of planned change, that this distinction between public and private modes of response is basic, if not *the* most basic issue in the matter of social influence. Most parents hope their youngsters can become sufficiently independent of their constant attention to act reasonably on their own. Most brainwashers hope to induce a change that is permanent, one that will remain with the person when they, his keepers, are no longer around to harass and threaten. Most advertisers hope to convince their audience to make purchases and to accept products when they are not immediately inundated with commercials. A democratic government trusts its citizens to have internalized the ground rules for social living sufficiently that they can exercise social control from within rather than have it imposed externally. Every therapist or psychoanalyst hopes to be able to assist his client in changing internally so that he will no longer require the therapist's presence. And every change agent hopes that he can assist his clients, whether they are persons, organizations, or communities, to produce change that no longer depends on him. In every case the issue is how to produce an enduring private change so that P no longer requires the continued surveillance of O.

Kelman's model

Kelman (1958; 1961) presents one of the best discussions of this matter of public versus private change. He differentiated three processes by which social influence could be accepted by P: *compliance, identification*, and *internalization*.

Compliance. Compliance occurs when P is influenced by O in order to obtain rewards for his conformity or to avoid punishment for nonconformity. He does not privately accept O's influence because of its intrinsic merit, but rather because acceptance is *instrumental* to attaining or avoiding something he likes or dislikes. Clearly, if conformity is instrumental to gaining rewards or avoiding punishments, P will conform only to the extent to which O has some knowledge about his conformity or resistance; compliance is dependent on O. Keep in mind that rewards range from tangible rewards, such as money, food, or candy, to psychological rewards of acceptance by O, liking by O, praise by O, and so forth. Punishments range from "the whip" to social rejection or isolation.

Identification. Identification is acceptance of O's influence in order to maintain an important relationship with O. Kelman calls this a *self-defining relationship*; if P identifies with O, essentially he adopts O as the model for defining himself. In this case we would expect P to conform under conditions in which the relationship is most salient. For example, Festinger (1947) found that individuals changed their votes for election of a group leader when they learned of the religious affiliations of the candidates. Changes were generally toward their own religion. Charters and Newcomb (1958) conducted a laboratory study in 1952 with much the same findings. They presented groups of students with statements they were to rate, either as members of a psychology class or as members of reference groups (religious groups). When the religious reference groups were experimentally made salient, subjects rated the statements in a way congruent with the ideology of those groups.

Changes that are mediated by identification, unlike those of compliance, involve both a public and a private shift. The change is not dependent on continued surveillance by O; it does require, however, that the relationship between P and O be active and remain important for P if he is to express the new position under different circumstances. Thus, although O's presence is not required, P must *reproduce* the relationship in a new context in order to maintain his changed perspective. To this extent, therefore, the change remains dependent on O, although clearly less so than with compliant change. The change that occurs, as Kelman sees it, is never fully integrated with the totality of P's values, but remains encapsulated and to the side. This will become clearer when we examine internalization.

Internalization. Internalization occurs when P accepts O's influence because the *content* of the influence is congruent with P's value system. Unlike compliance, P does not conform to gain something external to himself; unlike identification, he does not conform to maintain a relationship with O. Rather, he conforms because of the intrinsic merit of the influence attempt. The change becomes part of P, fully independent of O.

Kelman warns us, however, not to assume that internalization is always grounded in rationality. As he states it,

". . . I would also characterize as internalization the adoption of beliefs because of their congruence with a value system that is basically *irrational*. Thus, an authoritarian individual may adopt certain racist attitudes because they fit into his paranoid, irrational view of the world" (1961, pp. 65–66).

Reward and Punishment. Festinger (1953), whose contributions to social psychology cover a broad range, adopted a position in this issue that deviates slightly from Kelman's. Kelman talks of compliance as a response either to reward or punishment. Festinger stresses punishment as the major factor in determining public compliance without private acceptance. It appears, however, that Festinger and Kelman would agree that changes under reward, especially psychological reward, that begin as compliance may over time shift toward identification; with such a shift there is less dependence on O and greater correspondence between private and public behavior. Thus rewarding P for complying with O's influence attempts may in time lead to a more permanent change than is possible with continued threats of punishment.

Zipf (1960) provides some support for this contention. Her subjects were threatened with monetary fines for noncompliance with a "supervisor's" orders or were promised rewards for compliance. Over several work periods she was able to compare the impact of punishment and reward in maintaining a new level of behavior. Toward the end of her study she had the "supervisor" inform the subjects that for the next work period they would be neither rewarded nor fined. Results indicated that those who had previously been threatened reduced their conformity, whereas those who had been rewarded maintained their previous level, suggesting that rewards had produced changes that became independent of their initial instrumentality.

Some Relevant Research. Although Kelman suggested that the three processes rarely occur in isolation, and in fact that all are present in some degree in almost every social-influence situation, he nevertheless attempted (1961) to test part of his model experimentally. He varied one antecedent variable, O's source of power, and examined its consequences for P's behavior. Negro college students heard a recording of an interview on a school desegregation case before the Supreme Court. Four

different versions were presented; the content was always the same, but the introduction of the communicator (O) was systematically varied. Kelman created communicators who had (1) high power to reward or punish, (2) high attractiveness, (3) high credibility, (4) low power, attractiveness, and credibility.

In one condition students filled out questionnaires under conditions in which O was relevant to P and had surveillance over him; in another, relevance but no surveillance; in a third, neither relevance nor surveillance. The theoretical predictions were: (1) Social influence from an O with power to reward or punish should be expressed only under O's surveillance. This is compliance. (2) Social influence from an O who is attractive should be expressed when P's relationship with O is salient. This is identification. (3) Influence from an O who is credible should be expressed when the content is relevant, regardless of surveillance or salience of the relationship. The process is internalization. Data were consistent with these predictions, lending encouraging support to Kelman's model.

Unfortunately, not all data from all sources lend comparable support to Kelman's conceptualization. For example, although we would suppose from the theory that highly credible sources would produce enduring attitude change based on the content of the message, McGuire (1969) reports several studies in which attitude change occurs somewhat independently of content learning. In one such experiment Watts and McGuire (1964) presented subjects with sets of persuasive messages over a six-week period. They measured the extent to which subjects' initial opinions were influenced by the messages and also obtained a variety of recall indices: several weeks afterward they asked the subjects to recall, if they could, the general topic that had been discussed in each message; they also presented subjects with the general topics and asked if they could recall whether a pro or con stand had been advocated; and they told subjects the nature of the topic and the position advocated and inquired about the source of the message; finally, they tested to see if subjects could recall the specific arguments in each message.

Watts and McGuire related opinion change to

these several indices of recall. They found, in general, that opinion change diminished over time at a different rate than recall; subjects forgot specifics of the messages faster than they moved toward their original opinion. This suggests a degree of independence between message content and its effectiveness in producing opinion change; a message still had impact even if most of it had been forgotten.

One fascinating finding of this study, substantiated by others (e.g., Miller & Campbell, 1959), was that those who show *immediate* recall of the message's topic show high opinion change, whereas as time passes those who show the *least* recall show the most opinion change. Imagine you are a student whose professor is trying to induce opinion change (those who think professors do not do this should return to college) in your attitudes toward psychological experimentation. One week later those in your class who remember his lecture are most influenced, while those who have forgotten much of it are least influenced. By the end of the term, however those who remember the lecture the least are the most influenced. Does this mean that those who receive A's on the final examination have been the least influenced by the professor's lectures, but that those who flunk the final have been influenced to a greater degree?

The interpretation is that if you can't recall its content immediately after hearing a message, you have probably not attended or comprehended it sufficiently to be influenced. However, as time goes by, a *sleeper effect* occurs (Hovland, Lumsdaine, & Sheffield, 1949). That is, you forget the context within which you heard the message (you may have resisted it, say, because you considered it just a propaganda session) and only remember enough to experience its impact. Essentially the effect is a delayed impact of persuasive messages. To understand this, Hovland (Hovland, et al., 1949; Kelman & Hovland, 1953) turned to the notion of *discounting cues*. He maintained that over time we forget cues that initially led us to discount the message or the source; with such forgetting the message can have a fuller impact on us. For example, say you did not exactly revere that professor (he had too many ties to big business,

big labor, and big government to be considered an impartial expert). Once you have forgotten he was the source of the message you may recall only enough to be influenced—at least as long as the original context is not too vividly restored.

For the other measures of recall Watts and McGuire report a positive relation between recall of the arguments and opinion change; those who recall more arguments change their opinions more, *provided* that they are informed of both the topic of the message and the side taken by the message. When the source of a message is positive (esteemed and credible), those who recall him also show greater opinion change. When he is negative, however, there is no relation between recall and opinion change.

The implication of these findings for Kelman's theory is not too difficult to see. Kelman maintains that internalization occurs when one attends primarily to the content of the influence attempt (the persuasive message), ignoring the source's power to reward or punish and his relationship to P. These data, however, suggest the matter is more complex; especially revealing is the independence between recall of content and opinion change. Presumably, if the content is so important in producing opinion change via internalization, P should have some recollection of that content; at least he should recall the general topic. In the sleeper effect those who are most influenced in the long run do not even recall having heard any persuasive message. However, once they are reminded of the message ("Don't you remember hearing a message on topic X?"), their recall of specifics is generally related to opinion change; this does substantiate Kelman's notion of internalization. Even here the picture is complicated; recall of the source is positively related to opinion change, indicating that content factors are not operative entirely by themselves.

Before we leave this instructive experiment, let us consider again the puzzling finding of a short-term *positive* relation between topical recall and opinion change and a long-term *negative* relation. In a sense this finding may provide more support than refutation of Kelman's concept of internalization. The long-term opinion changer does not even recall hearing a message, yet his opinion is changed. Isn't this, in fact, the very essence of internalization? The individual undergoes a change in his opinions that is independent of the originating circumstances; that he cannot recall any persuasive messages may be taken as supporting this degree of independence. In fact, those short-termers who change most when they recall the message may be evidencing compliance or identification, in contrast to the internalization that characterizes long-term changers.

Independent processes or a blended mixture?

One of the implications of Kelman's theory is that a change agent who wishes to produce relatively permanent change that is not dependent on him should focus on antecedent factors that produce internalization. He should present himself as a credible (expert and trustworthy) source of information. However, by focusing on separate mediating processes, Kelman has drawn our attention away from a blended mixture of the three. Just as a positive or rewarding source may eventually produce internalized change (or change based on identification) rather than compliance, there is also a body of literature that suggests that compliance can eventuate in internalized change. We shall examine some material on dissonance, the effects of role playing, the consequences of role changes, including social mobility, and the effects of brainwashing and hospitalization. In each case a changed situation, often founded on compliance, creates conditions that can lead to a permanent internalized change.

Dissonance Again. The dissonance-theory formulation that we examined on p. 108 ff. reverses the usual attitude-change paradigm, including Kelman's proposals. The typical paradigm builds on the notion that because attitudes affect behavior, changing those attitudes can produce a change in behavior. That this notion is itself an oversimplification, more often incorrect than correct, will concern us later (pp. 326 ff.). Festinger (1957) and the dissonance model, however, boldly argue that if we can first produce a change in behavior, we can produce a change in attitude. The logic by now should be familiar. If I *do X*, it is dissonant to maintain attitudes that are inconsistent with my action, so I

change my attitudes. Recall the studies (p. 112 ff.) on forced compliance with insufficient justification; *P* was induced to eat grasshoppers or lie to a waiting subject, and doing so produced a change in *P*'s attitudes.

According to this dissonance theory, compliance, under certain conditions, will produce a change in attitude that over time presumably becomes independent of the influencing agent and so looks more like internalization than compliance. The *degree* of reward or punishment is a relevant factor in such matters. The more a person feels pressured into taking a specific action, presumably, the less dissonance he will experience, so the pressure will be less to change his attitudes toward congruence with his actions. This means that a change agent must manipulate the situation to create an atmosphere in which *P* more or less *voluntarily* behaves in a particular manner. Holding a gun to *P*'s head to make him conform is a case of raw compliance that is unlikely to produce internalization when gun-toting *O* has left the scene. Flooding *P*'s coffers with money, in theory at least, also should not lead to internalization. However, rewards seem to function differently than punishments; for example, one may come to like a benefactor and change out of identification with him.

Nevertheless, the problem for the change agent is to produce voluntary behavioral compliance. Changes in laws that result in changed patterns of relationship between people may, in time, produce a shift from compliance to internalization; a person who holds negative attitudes about eating at the same restaurant with blacks may find himself eating frequently at such restaurants after laws are passed concerning integration of public facilities. As he continues eating at integrated restaurants he may come to change his attitudes, saying, in essence, "Well, since I eat here all the time, it would be inconsistent to keep my negative beliefs."

A recent study of the attitudes of physicians toward Medicare legislation offers further insights. Colombotos (1969) contrasts two approaches that relate legal change to attitude change. The first, akin to the dissonance formulation, argues that a change in law produces a change in behavior and that a change in behavior in turn produces a change in attitudes. The second argues that a change in law by itself is sufficient to produce a change in attitudes; it educates the public and legitimizes a new set of values, and attitude change occurs as people come to internalize the newly legitimized views. To study this distinction as it applied to physicians, Colombotos interviewed 1205 New York State physicians in private practice. He interviewed them in 1964 and early 1965 *before* the Medicare legislation was passed; in 1966 *after* the legislation was passed but before it went into effect; and in 1967, after physicians had had about six months experience *behaving* under its main provisions. In 1964 38 percent of the physicians favored Medicare; in 1966 70 percent favored it; in 1967 81 percent favored it. These results show clearly that the passage of the law had a significant effect on physician's attitudes even before they had any behavioral experience, and implementation of the law further boosted favorable attitudes.

Although this research does not permit us to conclude unequivocally that law alone or behavior alone is sufficient to create attitude change, I think that it nicely demonstrates how a combination of legal change and new behaviors under the legal change can produce striking attitude changes. As we shall see (pp. 326ff.), however, the picture is neither so simple nor so rosy as these examples suggest. The reasons for a given individual's attitudes especially of prejudice) may be more deep-seated and may encompass an entire psychological syndrome not easily changed by placing him in a forced compliance situation.

The dissonance-theory formulation concerning a shift from compliance to internalization emphasizes the voluntary commitment of an individual to behave in a particular manner. Let us look at an example from many turbulent campuses. Students who are committed to demonstrate their support for a change in their university's curriculum picket in a boisterous, disruptive manner. This demonstration naturally draws a large crowd of noncommitted onlookers who have come to watch today's antics. The demonstration grows in size and intensity. In a moment of outrage, campus administrators

call for the police; the police arrive and begin to clear out the demonstrators, shall we say, a bit vigorously. Some demonstrators do not take kindly to being pushed away, and small-scale scuffles occur. The situation erupts; police and demonstrators clash openly. Clubs are raised to beat at heads; rocks and cans fly at the police. One bystander is caught in the middle, being chased and struck by the police. He shouts out his innocence, but deaf ears and blind eyes see only enemy in time of battle. He is outraged; he hits out at the police, and eventually runs. When we talk to him later we discover that he only came to watch the demonstration; at first he hadn't supported it, and in fact had been a staunch law-and-order, bring-the-police-quickly type. But now he's changed his attitudes; not only does he support the demonstrators, but also has developed real hate for the police.

Now, don't get me wrong. I am not saying that dissonance totally accounts for this person's change of attitude; things are not that simple. However, it is possible to see aspects of dissonance at work in that situation. This individual found himself behaving voluntarily in a particular way in a situation that suddenly changed its character. He saw himself strike back at the police; he felt anger and outrage at the scene he was witnessing. Indeed it would be dissonant for him to retain antidemonstrator and propolice beliefs under those circumstances. The wise "demonstrator" understands this effect all too well; he knows that onlookers become ready converts if the situation surrounding them changes, so that they make behavioral commitments they would never have dreamed of. Once that first commitment is made, attitudes are likely to change, paving the way for further, more dramatic behavioral commitments.

Role-Playing. A relative of the forced-compliance notion of dissonance theory derives from conceptions of role-playing. The idea is simple. If a person takes on a role that varies from his usual ones, he may change his attitudes after this experience. For that matter, if the role-playing is intense, extends through time, and is nearly total in its impact, the personality of the individual may undergo a basic change.

Suppose you are asked to play a person who

sincerely advocates a position that you yourself do not believe. Is it possible that you will convince yourself? Do salesmen come to believe in products that they thought absurd initially? Do debaters come to believe in the positions they advocate? According to some work by Janis and King (1954), the answer is yes. They had experimental subjects improvise and role-play attitudes that were more extreme than their own, and found that improvisational role-playing resulted in more opinion change than occurred by passively reading a set of arguments. On the other hand, several studies (e.g., Jansen & Stolurow, 1962; McGuire, 1961) indicate either no difference or a difference in favor of the passive rather than the actively involved group.

Scott (1957) asked students to debate by taking a side that differed from their own. He rigged the situation so that some debaters were declared winners by the rest of the class, and others were declared losers. The winners showed more attitude change in the direction of the role-played position; interestingly, the losers seemed to become slightly stronger in their original convictions.

The dissonance interpretation for these role-playing effects is clear and parallels the interpretation of the forced-compliance paradigm: one changes his beliefs toward greater congruence with his behavior. This, of course, may be a momentary shift in attitudes, rather than anything long-term, but the general principles apply. Another interpretation of these effects is that through role-playing a person gains new perspectives and new insights. The use of role-playing as a training technique is based on this thesis. By trying on another's shoes, P gets the feel of the world from a different angle; this can be an enlightening experience. P may see things he never before thought of; he may even shake himself up as he creates arguments that were originally foreign to him.

Role Changes. The new-perspectives argument is expanded by adding the concept of role expectations. Picture a situation in which P's role in an organization changes. The new role entails an array of new responsibilities, a different public, new perspectives on the entire situation, and a new set of expectations concerning his behavior. Take a familiar example. A student completes his doctoral dissertation and is graduated in June. That September he finds himself a member of the faculty at Big U, standing before a class of 300. He attends faculty meetings with those *names* he had just finished reading about in his doctoral work. He has responsibilities that are different from those that faced him as a student. Our faculty man sees things he may never have known fully before (e.g., the political infighting and petty squabbles that he'd assumed could not touch the life of a scholar); he has insights that can shatter his youthful and idealistic naïveté.

He finds himself playing before students as an assumed expert in his field, before his colleagues as a still-wet-behind-the-ears new Ph.D., before the community as a college professor, before his neighbors as an egghead intellectual, and so on. He finds that people have different expectations about his behavior now that his role is changed. They may expect him to wear a proper suit and tie, to abandon the levis and boots that marked him as a graduate student. They may expect him to speak with confidence and firmness, citing chapter and verse, and always in eloquent and perfect English. They may expect him to behave with dignity, decorum, and restraint; after all, he is a member of the faculty.

It is difficult indeed not to imagine that a role change of this sort would have an effect in altering an individual's attitudes as well as other aspects of his life style. Lieberman (1956) took advantage of a real-life situation to offer us some systematic evaluation of the effects of such role change on attitude change. He assessed the attitudes of a group of workers before some were promoted to shop foremen and others became union stewards as a natural part of a factory's operation. He did not know in advance which workers would move to which roles. Some time later Lieberman remeasured the attitudes of 23 men who had become foremen and 34 who had become union stewards. In addition he obtained attitude measures on comparable persons who had not changed roles over this period.

His data significantly indicate that changes in role altered individuals' attitudes; men who had had similar attitudes before the role change showed divergent attitudes after it. Specifically, those who became foremen, with responsibilities to management, took on attitudes congruent with that role; those who became union stewards, with responsibilities to the workers and working conditions, changed toward congruence with that kind of role; that is, they became more generally critical of management, whereas the foremen became more generally supportive.

Even more striking is Lieberman's analysis of a small subgroup of foremen who several years later were switched back to their former positions as workers. He reports that their attitudes reverted to their original positions, apparently as a function of the role change. As workers they had been moderately critical of management; as foremen they became supportive; when demoted they again became moderately critical.

Social Mobility and Attitudes. Lieberman's study indicated how mobility within an organization affects an individual's attitudes. In the larger scale of society there has been an enduring interest in the relationship between mobility and attitude change, in particular between mobility and attitudes of racial prejudice. In 1950 Bettelheim and Janowitz reported that persons who were socially mobile, especially downward, were more prejudiced than persons of more stable social position. In a 1964 revisitation of their earlier results they reached much the same conclusion: occupational mobility downward, affecting a person's entire economic position, is related to ethnic intolerance.

There are several interpretations of this apparent relationship. First, after Durkheim (1951), we could propose a *mobility* thesis: any change in social class position, any move from one group to another, introduces frustrations of adapting to a new way of life without the kinds of control that formerly served as normative guides. These frustrations may lead an individual to vent hostility toward out-groups, especially those that still give him a sense of superiority and thus partial control. Second, mobility places an individual in a marginal position between his class of origin and his class of destination. Marginality makes for tension, uneasiness, and anxiety, which may be reflected in out-group

hostility. Third, we may posit a direct social-class thesis, much like Lieberman's argument, that maintains that a person conforms to the norms, including the attitudinal norms, of those groups in which he holds membership or with which he identifies; that is, change is mediated by identification, as in Kelman's model. For example, there is evidence that competition between lower-class whites and Negroes for scarce jobs has produced a general anti-Negro attitude among lower-class whites (e.g., Henry & Short, 1954; Hodge & Treiman, 1966). If we know the class position of a person, we are able to make a reasonable prediction about his prejudicial attitudes.

Efforts to find substantiation for this effect have not been uniformly successful, although several confirmatory studies are worth brief mention. If we take as our measure of social mobility the discrepancy between an individual's own occupational level and that of his father, we find, for example, that about 63 percent of downwardly mobile persons, as compared with about 56 percent of stable manual workers or 60 percent of stable nonmanual workers express anti-Negro attitudes (Greenblum & Pearlin, 1953). The differences between these groups are not great, although they are in a direction consistent with the Bettelheim and Janowitz finding. Silberstein & Seeman (1959) also find mobility, especially downward, to be related to anti-Negro attitudes.

A national survey conducted in 1963, reported by Hodge and Treiman (1966), attempted to separate the mobility effect per se from the effect of class position. The first finding is a positive correlation between both a subject's own class and his father's class (as measured by occupational ranking) and pro-Negro attitudes: the higher the class, or the higher the father's class, the more pro-Negro attitudes are expressed. There is some slight indication of a relationship between pro-Negro attitudes and mobility, with the mobiles—both down and up in this case—being less pro-Negro than the stables. Hodge and Treiman predicted an attitude score on the basis of a knowledge simply of *P*'s class of origin (father's social class) and his class of destination (his own present social class), and compared this expected score with those actually obtained. Results indicate that mobility per se does not play a major role, but it does play some role, in predicting anti-Negro attitudes.

Although the picture remains mixed, certain consistencies across studies suggest moderate support for a relationship between downward mobility and prejudicial attitudes toward Negroes. These differences, small as they may be, reflect an important relationship between a change in social class and a change in attitudes. Whether the relationship is mediated by a frustration-aggression hypothesis (the pure mobility thesis) or by a normative social-class interpretation (based on identification), or parts of both, has not been settled, but the relationship is there and its implications are especially significant in a rapidly changing society. If mobility itself leads to instability of the sort that produces prejudice, a society undergoing rapid social change should experience great upsurges of high prejudice. If, however, it is not mobility but rather social-class norms that relate to prejudicial attitudes, then there can exist a rapidly changing society in which norms are not insistently prejudicial of out-groups.

Both social mobility and organizational role changes seem to involve a mixture of compliance and identification, with the latter weighing more heavily than the former. The possibility exists that changes initially mediated by identification may shift over time to an internalized change. Lieberman's evidence, however, that those who shift back again to their former roles also change to their former attitudes, argues against internalization. The case is by no means either simple or clear. Recall that role changes (including mobility in a class system) offer an individual new perspectives and new knowledges. New attitudes that develop from these new perspectives have the quality ascribed to internalization rather than to either compliance or identification. I think that these several examples plus those to follow more than adequately point up the blending of these separable processes that occurs in any live situation.

Brainwashing. If one has near total control over the physical life of another person or group of persons, as occurs in mental institutions, prisons, and prisoner-of-war camps, it is possible to combine compliance-inducing techniques with role-playing techniques to produce long-term, internalized behavioral and attitudinal change. Brainwashing was studied especially during the Korean War (Schein, 1958).

The intent of brainwashing or thought reform is to create a new being out of the old. In this case the new being would be friendly to a particular political ideology, Chinese and Korean Communism. With control over an entire society such thought reform can work in the institutions of socialization, especially the family and the systems of formal education, to produce a new being by shaping the young into the character type sought for the society. With an already developed person, on the other hand, the problem is to break down the old patterns (unfreezing), move the person to a new position, and solidify this new stance.

Assuming near-total control over rewards and punishments, as in a POW camp, it is possible to demand compliance to force behavior change. A prisoner can be drained of his physical strength and well-being by a diet carefully controlled at a minimal level, by being kept awake or standing for endless hours, by interrogation, and by painful punishment. He can be cut off from his buddies to face these tortures alone; he can be placed with prisoners who extol reform of his beliefs. He can be humiliated; he can experience a loss of his sense of personal worth and dignity as a human being; he can be forced to confess, to recite his sins, to prostrate himself, to undergo a never-ceasing self-critical examination. In so structured and controlled an environment everyone can relate to him as a helpless, dependent child or an incompetent. Soon he may come to think of himself in these terms, and cry out for the aid and succorance his captors are willing to provide if he will only confess once again, if he will only change his beliefs.

Schein reports that in Chinese and Korean POW and re-education camps techniques of this sort did produce collaborative behavior—signing confessions of war crimes, making broadcasts, and so on—but often did not produce underlying changes in an individual's beliefs, primarily because there were too many ways open for him to rationalize his behavior.

As in the forced-compliance paradigm of dissonance theory, he did not feel sufficient personal responsibility for his collaboration to modify his inner beliefs. Thus when most of the prisoners returned home they did not retain for long the belief systems that had been tailor-made for them in the camps. Schein suggests that the Chinese and Koreans, although seemingly effective, were basically inefficient in their techniques of indoctrination. They did not control the situation sufficiently to unfreeze most POWs to the point of complete thought reform.

A follow-up examination of Western prisoners in Chinese prison camps who were subjected to brainwashing, including businessmen and professionals, is also interesting. Schein reports that several prisoners, when released and returned home, could never fully understand why their extreme attitude changes had occurred. Others retained evidence of conflicting loyalties, and sought to find a midpoint between the Communist position and their older beliefs. Still others, however, were reported to have undergone extensive personality changes and to have adopted an enduring new set of attitudes and supporting values; in some cases, then, the brainwashing techniques were effective in producing permanent, internalized behavioral change.

We would expect that the usual domestic prison situation creates more compliant change, based particularly on threats of punishment, than it produces either identification or internalization. On release prisoners are further restrained through a probation system that tries to ensure conformity to societal norms; again the change is based more on compliance than on internalization.

Mental hospitals have been criticized for providing a setting that deters good mental health and independence (see Etzioni, 1960; Goffman, 1961; Henry, 1954; Stanton & Schwartz, 1954). The argument is that the role of mental patient and the punishment he receives in the institution force conformity and good behavior that is both superficial and potentially harmful. Depriving an individual of his rights as a human being, humiliating him, removing his sense of personal worth and dignity, denying him privacy, treating him as a unit in a large and impersonal bureaucratic institution, are all parts of an initiation into the role of mental-hospital patient that can have negative consequences; it is questionable whether under such conditions a person can improve his state of mental well-being. He may feign health in order to get out of a situation that is far worse than the illness for which he was committed in the first place. Threats of punishment, at times in the form of electric shock therapy, force compliant conformity while undoubtedly creating a storehouse of resistance that makes health-producing therapy much more difficult.

It can similarly be argued that military basic training is carefully designed to unfreeze individuals and make new men, soldiers, out of rag-tag civilians. Compliance techniques, based primarily on threats of punishment, are used in conjunction with role changes that seem to share much with the POW approaches to brainwashing. Unlike the POW approach, however, in which efforts are directed at breaking apart all organization, military training is an effort to build up a strong group organization.

Summary. It appears that compliance-based approaches over time can create changes that are internalized and no longer dependent on the surveillance of the change agent. If we think of role-taking in an organization, or social mobility in society, as having some of the properties Kelman assigned to the process of identification, we see how identification too may in time produce internalized change. Recall, however, that in Lieberman's analysis those who changed roles back from foremen to workers reverted to their initial attitudes; this suggests a maintenance of attitudes more in terms of identification than internalization. In a total institution, a miniature society such as a prison camp that exercises nearly absolute control over all aspects of life, compliance approaches and role-taking combine, often effectively, to produce a new personality complete with new attitudes, new values, and new behaviors.

The impression at this point may be that man is a fragile flower with little ability to withstand the windstorms that happen his way. Leaving aside the important matter of individual differences, if anything the impression actually should be of a character who is no easy pushover, especially when we think of permanent change. Every man may have a purchase price for conformity based on compliance—although history offers us examples of men who refused to yield their principles for money or death—but even in a POW camp designed for change, more long-term resistance than facile change is the outcome.

SOME BROADER APPLICATIONS: THE MATTER OF SOCIAL CONTROL

To this point our examination of the influence relationship between *P* and *O* primarily has included cases in which each is a person. It will be profitable to our broader understanding of the influence processes to go beyond the individual case to examine several investigations of the issue of social control in a society.

Riesman

Most students have some vague familiarity with a scheme proposed by Riesman (1950; 1952). He attempted to describe the character types or basic personalities that develop in various societies and that serve to maintain the order and stability of those societies; these characterological types were derived from the bases of social control to which they responded. Riesman differentiated three kinds of social control: *tradition-orientation, inner-orientation, external-* or *other-orientation*. Social control based on tradition is achieved by reference to values and directives that have existed in the history of that society. Inner-orientation, somewhat like internalization in Kelman's scheme, achieves social control through standards, guidelines, or values that exist in each individual. Other-orientation or other-direction achieves social control by conformity to standards that exist in other persons and groups. Each of these creates a different character type in a society. A tradition-directed character is oriented toward history and the ways in which things have always been done; an inner-directed character is oriented toward his own internal values; an other-directed character is oriented toward ways by which others act.

A significant point that Riesman makes is that an entire society at a given point in its develop-

ment may have its mechanisms of social control centered on one or another of these three; he maintains that the United States today is other-directed. We have little tradition to speak of, in comparison to the long history of European nations. We have few shared internal standards, things we believe in with sufficient depth and commitment to guide our actions. We are left then to flounder on the sea of changing whims and social fantasy. As other-directed souls, we keep our antennae carefully tuned in to public opinion to know what we should believe this week. The mass media, especially television, are helpful in bringing into each home a listing of the new fads, fashions, beliefs, and life styles. There can be little argument that many persons today fit Riesman's description of the other-directed man. Wolfe's (1965) account of American life is as revealing and insightful in this regard as his title is amusing: *The Kandy-Kolored Tangerine-Flake Streamline Baby.*

A test to measure Riesman's character types was developed by Kassarjian (1962), who provided some successful validation for the test by correlating scores with activities thought to reflect inner- or other-directedness, including such things as hobbies, sport preferences, and social activities. Data analyses indicated that neither sex, age, year in school, race, religion, nor father's occupation was correlated with a person's inner- or other-directedness. Undergraduates in college, as compared with the general population, however, tended to be slightly more other-directed. Using the same scale, Centers (1962) reports an age trend, with younger persons being more other-directed than older persons. These last two findings were taken by Centers to be consistent with Riesman's argument that the United States is becoming increasingly other-directed. Yet with so much revolt in the late 1960's, initially based on inner values rather than on conformity to fleeting group norms, it is difficult to imagine the hordes of other-directed persons that Riesman described back in the 1950's when the Silent Generation grew up with barely a whisper to mark their tenure at Big U. However, collegiate revolt cannot be equated simply with inner-directedness. The first protestors may have been guided by inner values, but those who followed their lead may have been responding in an other-directed way to the evolving norms of their peers.

Another technique employed to assess the hypothesized rise in other-directedness and the corresponding decline in inner-directedness is reflected in the work of several authors who conducted content analyses of various "popular" written material.

DeCharms and Moeller (1962) scored children's readers for achievement imagery—which they assumed to be an index of inner-direction—and affiliation imagery—taken as an index of other-direction—from 1800 to 1950. They report a rise in achievement imagery from 1800 to 1900 and a drop from 1900 to the present, and a tentative increase in affiliation imagery. Although several other studies using a similar methodology (e.g., Henley, 1967; Strauss & Houghton, 1960) have confirmed the decline in achievement imagery, replication of the affiliation results is much more equivocal. In an analysis of other-directed appeals in advertising Dornbusch and Hickman (1959) report a rise. On the other hand, in her analysis of stories appearing in the *Saturday Evening Post*, Henley (1967) found a decrease in achievement imagery but no significant trend over time for affiliation.

Content analysis offers a useful way to get at the kind of imagery that is expressed in popular cultural material. However, the assumption that links inner-direction with achievement and other-direction with affiliation may itself be questioned. For example, does the decline in achievement imagery mark a decrease in over-all inner-directedness or a decline in only one kind of inner-directed value? These studies do not help us in this regard, although their results to date are interesting and provocative and their methodology important to keep in mind as further work is conducted.

Riesman's scheme is similar to Kelman's and to most other approaches, in that it emphasizes a difference between internal and external bases of behavioral control; recall that Kelman's concept of compliance pictures a more or less external source of social influence and control. In both of these schemes is embedded a value bias: it is better to be guided by that voice from within than to yield to momentary social currents. Riesman clearly does not take kindly to the other-directed person. Kelman is less evaluative in his discussion, but we sense that for him *good* lies in internalization. In thinking about the application of his ideas to an entire society there can be little doubt that a free society, presumably something we all value, must be based heavily on internalization techniques rather than on external sanctions that produce compliance.

Weber

The sociologist Weber (1946; 1947) also offered an analysis of the types of authority in a society. A basic problem for any society or collectivity is the coordination of the activities of many different kinds of person; this in turn involves both the use and the maintenance of authority. Weber differentiated the following three types of legitimate authority (*legitimate* means that P accepts O's rights to exercise authority over him).

Rational-legal authority is based on a belief that those in positions of authority have a legal right to issue commands in their efforts to provide a rational approach to accomplishing certain ends or goals. This kind of authority is exercised, for example, in an organization in which members agree that the social order is legal and that the normative controls exercised in it, given the particular arrangement of role relationships (e.g., P is the worker and O is his boss), are to be followed.

Traditional authority is based on the belief that traditions of a society have a sanctity that demands they be followed. Traditional leaders are granted the rights of a chieftain or a king to rule in accordance with the authority their status has traditionally permitted.

Charismatic authority rests on the devotion of persons to the exceptional and infectious qualities of a particular individual. A charismatic leader rules by virtue of a mystical and emotional quality that his followers attribute to him.

It is interesting to note that the two sociologists, Riesman and Weber, introduce a basis for authority that has its roots in societal tradition, whereas Kelman, the one psychologist we have examined, includes this basis less clearly. Of course we might say that tradition establishes the role relations that produce the kind of identification of which Kelman speaks. It is likewise interesting to note Weber's introduction of charisma as a basis for authority and social control. Although others talk about attraction or identification, the notion of charisma carries with it a flavor beyond attraction that we can intuitively grasp. Gandhi's influence could not be based on so sterile and lab-coated a concept as attraction; but charisma is an entirely different matter!

Whiting

Whiting (1959), who brings together the perspectives of psychology and anthropology, sought to examine three bases of social control in a variety of less complex societies. He argued that sorcery, sin, and the superego provided three mechanisms by which a society controlled its members. *Sorcery* is based on a belief that any member of a society may have mystical powers of witchcraft that can be used to destroy or injure another. There exists a strong fear that others may retaliate for any misdeeds; this fear of retaliation serves to deter actions that violate societal norms. Whiting (1959) cites the Paiutes, who have no chief or council of elders to decide matters of social control for their tribe. However, there is a very strong belief in sorcery among the Paiutes, and this belief helps maintain order within the society. Kluckhohn (1944) presents similar material from his work with the Navajo, suggesting how the belief in witchcraft not only serves to maintain order within the society but also channels disruptive aggression to outside groups. Witches always live just over the next hill; if trouble comes it is possible to get even by casting a spell outside the necessarily closely knit living group.

Sin focuses on the belief that any transgressions against the gods or ghosts of departed spirits are recorded and will be punished in the afterlife. This kind of fear serves in many societies to maintain conformity. After all, if you are afraid of offending the gods, who are all-knowing and all-present, and perhaps even can read your evil thoughts, you will watch over your own behavior with great care. Of course

we need not wander that far from complex technological societies to see some aspects of this same belief. Children are warned that if they are not good Santa Claus will bring them nothing for Christmas. Others are told by parents, who seem no longer to believe this for themselves, that God is watching everything and will punish them. One day a little child, for once escaping Mommy's eternal surveillance (Daddy is at work, naturally) looks carefully all around him. He doesn't see any God. He suspects those stories anyway. So he does just what Mommy said God doesn't like any kid to do. And he gets away with it. But, no, he trips and falls. Just then Mommy comes out, sees what he's done, and sees his skinned knee and tearful face. "See, God punishes," she says. You'd better believe that kid now knows what happens to sinners.

The *superego* as a source of social control in Whiting's scheme involves a sense of guilt that a person has violated standards of his own conscience or moral values. The argument is that a given society bases its control mechanisms on guilt induction; persons become wracked with feelings of guilt over something they have done or experience a twinge of guilt over the thought of doing something and thereby experience sufficient motivation not to do it.

It is common to differentiate "fear," "guilt," and "shame" as three separable mechanisms. Fear is readily understandable in terms of concern about getting caught and punished, but the distinction between shame and guilt may be more difficult to grasp intuitively. The essence of shame is a violation of a cultural norm in the presence of others, either a real or imagined audience. One is shamed if he is ridiculed (or rejected) by those who see his transgression. Benedict (1946) has described Japan as a shame culture. By contrast, guilt is experienced as a response to an internalized standard; it does not require any other presence; an ever-watchful conscience (superego) will do just perfectly.

There is a rough parallel (with emphasis on rough) between Kelman's trilogy and these three mechanisms of social control that have general currency in anthropological circles. Fear seems to parallel compliance; it is externally based and focuses on punishment. Shame and identification have a degree of similarity in that violations committed in the context of an important relationship with the identification model would produce a sense of personal shame: "If my revered leader could see me now, he would reject me forever." Guilt and internalization likewise are roughly parallel in that both involve a reference to internal standards. However, whereas internalization as Kelman uses it seems to emphasize cognitive factors, guilt places a much heavier stress on strong affect.

I suppose that one of the first ideas to emerge from this brief overview is that the several approaches examined all emphasize *three* factors or *three* mechanisms. Second, each offers a dimension that ranges from external control (compliance, other-directedness, fear, and sorcery) on one side to internal control (internalization, inner-directedness, guilt, and the supergo) on the other. Several mixed cases stress a relationship that ranges from external to internal; these include identification, shame, sin, and charisma. In these cases control is achieved by reference to the maintenance of a relationship between *P* and *O*.

Those who are keeping careful records will wonder what has happened to tradition-directedness, traditional authority, and rational-legal authority. It seems to me that these add a dimension that is not captured by any of the others. In a chart such as Table 21.1 most of these conceptions fit without stretching their meaning. However, unless we maintain that tradition establishes role relations of identification, the table would not as easily include tradition and

rational-legal authority, both of which seem to be factors contributing to social control. (The table recognizes this facet of tradition-direction but leaves it open to question.)

Don't misunderstand this table. The parallels between the several different conceptualizations are not fully precise. Items in the same columns have roughly the same outlook, although, as I pointed out earlier, the flavor is often very different; for example, the cognitive emphasis of internalization and of rational-legal authority is different in tone from the strong affective sense that guilt and the superego convey. It is nevertheless interesting to notice some general similarities in the thinking that has taken place in several disciplines and in several historical periods.

ACQUISITION AND CHANGE

In the pages that follow the discussion of social influence is built on a simple foundation: if you have a conception of the process of acquisition you have a formulation of change. If we can come to an understanding of how attitudes are formed or what functions they serve, we will have gained access to an understanding of change or resistance to change.

Attitude change: Behaviorists versus functionalists

This discussion could be subtitled *Yale versus Michigan*, if we allow that Michigan's functionalism combined with several other varieties, and that Yale's behaviorism and communications theory has spread beyond its ivy covered walls. By the way, *versus* does not mean hot and heavy competition but rather differing perspectives on a large area of inquiry. The group from Yale preferred to think in learning theory terms; the functionalists worked best in terms of individual personality. Standing on different platforms, the two groups tended to see different things about the processes by which attitudes were formed and changed.

Toward the end of World War II, under Hovland's guidance, a group at Yale undertook an extensive series of investigations of persuasive communications, undoubtedly inspired by wartime concerns with public opinion and propaganda. Their methods came from the ex-

Table 21.1 Various mechanisms of social control

	External	Relationship	Internal
Kelman	Compliance	Identification	Internalization
Riesman	Other-directedness	(Tradition creates role-relationships)	Inner-directedness
Weber		Charismatic authority	(Rational-legal authority)
Whiting	Sorcery	Sin	Superego
Cultural anthropology	Fear	Shame	Guilt

perimental laboratory; their theory drew heavily on behavioristic accounts of how man and animals learned. With this methodological and theoretical foundation, it is no wonder that they examined change from an outside perspective.

That same war stimulated psychological investigation of attitudes that were most resistant to change, especially pervasive attitudes of prejudice. The concept of an authoritarian personality emerged from these endeavors, as did several other approaches to attitude formation and change. The theories that developed around these investigations drew on psychoanalytic and similar conceptions of personality functioning; methods were influenced by those commonly encountered in the clinic. It is no wonder, then, that this work examined change from the inside structure of the person.

The Behaviorists' Model. Hovland's group focused much of its initial effort on relating qualities of the communicator, the message, and the audience to attitude change in response to persuasive communications. The research paradigm was simple experimental elegance. Independent variables were defined, one at a time. Communicator factors: Was he of high prestige or low? Was he expert or not? Was he objective, or did he stand to gain by persuading others to adopt his position? Message factors: Was it based on fear arousal or was it more neutral in tone? Were both sides of the argument presented or only one? Did the message draw conclusions or leave that up to the audience? Audience factors: What were the intellectual or self-esteem characteristics of those who were most easily persuaded by the message? Once these independent variables were defined, the experimenter took premeasures of audience attitudes on a given issue, introduced treatment (the independent variable), and obtained paper-and-pencil postmeasures of attitude change, the dependent variable. What did they discover?

1. *The communicator.* Although their view of communicator factors was relatively undifferentiated as compared with work done today, the Hovland group nevertheless supplied evidence to support the principle that high-prestige communicators were more influential than low-prestige communicators, (Hovland, 1954, 1959;

Hovland, Lumsdaine, & Sheffield, 1949; Hovland & Weiss, 1951; Hovland & Mandell, 1952; Hovland, Janis, & Kelley, 1953; Hovland, Harvey, & Sherif, 1957; Hovland, Mandell, et al., 1957; Hovland & Pritzker, 1957; Hovland & Janis, 1959), regardless of whether the content of the communication fell within the communicator's area of high prestige. A well-known source who was generally admired could pontificate on matters well beyond his known expertise. For those who wonder if things have changed much, may I simply call your attention to California politics of the late 1960's, when becoming a celebrity through the mass media seemed to be a prerequisite to becoming an influential political candidate.

McGuire has pointed out (1969) that although an unbiased, objective communicator may be rated as *fairer* than one who stands to gain something from persuading P to adopt his position (see p. 195), a wide variety of studies suggests a more complex picture relating fairness to O's ability to change P's attitudes. McGuire reports that there is very little evidence to indicate that P is turned off by a biased O, and that there is some evidence that knowing O's biases *increases* P's conformity to his messages. He suggests that a soft-sell approach may never really communicate O's persuasive message to P; such an approach would actually produce less rather than more opinion change. McGuire's conclusion: "... resistance derives more from the subject's inability to learn what the source wants him to believe than from his unwillingness to yield to the source's pressure" (1969, p. 186). He adds, "In communication, it appears, it is not sufficient to lead the horse to the water; one must also push his head underneath to get him to drink" (p. 209).

The image of man that is derived from these statements would drive a good man to drink (or whatever), were it not for the realization— both ours and McGuire's—that the conclusion is based primarily on laboratory work with passive or ingratiating subjects. I suppose it is true that with a subject dragged into the lab to "volunteer" for science, presented with some trivial communications with little real impact on his life or behavior, from a communicator who is on tape or in a mockup of a news story, you had better shout long and loud into one ear to guarantee that the message is heard and well understood. The subject is just dying to comply if you'll only let him know more clearly what you want.

As Hovland himself noted (see pp. 236–237) the captive and apparently accommodating audience in the laboratory produces change effects that the researcher in the field has never even seen, although surely he has dreamed about them. On the other hand, before putting that bottle (or whatever) away, do you really think it that unreasonable to imagine some of these same forces at work out there in TV land? Are there not many people who would be more than willing to accommodate the persuasive communicator—especially one of high prestige seen nightly on the tube—if they could just figure out what he wanted from them? Not everyone, to be sure; but many, perhaps. When we realize how public relations firms have taken over political campaigns, can we retain our doubts much longer?

2. *The message.* The Hovland group's focus on message factors generated several interesting studies and effects. One classic effect (Hovland et al., 1949) related the one- or-two sided nature of a message to its persuasive impact. A one-sided communication gives only one side of the issue; a two-sided one gives the persuasive side and also challenges some of the arguments of the opposing side. One-sided and two-sided messages seemed equally impactful, but certain specific effects were uncovered. First, for those who initially agreed with the message, a one-sided message ignoring the opposing point of view was better. Why raise doubts in the minds of those who are already convinced? Remember, the interest here is in producing attitude change in response to persuasive communications, not in providing a challenging education. For those initially opposed, however, the two-sided approach was more effective. Second, giving one side was more effective with a less intelligent audience; presenting two sides worked better with a more intelligent audience.

In what is perhaps one of the most quoted classics from the Yale school, Janis and Feshbach (1953) conducted an experiment in which they apparently demonstrated that communications that aroused high fear produced minimal opinion change. They were concerned with changing attitudes about dental health care; they presented groups of subjects with communications that varied in degree of fear arousal. Some groups received a fierce display of the consequences of poor dental care; others received less arousing messages. Findings indicated that high arousal led to less change than low arousal. The plausible interpretation turned to the learning theory concept of interference; it was argued that when drive level is too high it actually disrupts behavior. With high fear arousal, presumably, hearing the message or learning its content was disrupted, and no change resulted.

In what by now is one of his favorite professional roles, McGuire (1969) debunked with a great flourish the myth that has grown up around this classic study. In essence, Janis and Feshbach reported a negative relationship between fear and change. However, McGuire summarized a variety of studies indicating a *positive* relationship as a preliminary to his own tentative compromise solution. Positive relationships were uncovered in studies involving high-fear-arousal messages about seat belts and auto accidents and smoking and cancer (e.g., Leventhal & Niles, 1964; Leventhal, Singer, & Jones, 1965; Leventhal & Watts, 1966). In general, the more fear-arousing the message, the more change reported.

McGuire's compromise model is based on a two-factor conception in which fear *cues in* avoidance and also serves to *motivate* learning. His argument is that high fear arousal may inhibit the *reception* of the message—attention and comprehension—but at the same time may motivate an individual to learn its contents; at some intermediate level of arousal, both cue and motivating functions are at the optimal point at which the message should have its greatest persuasive impact. Too little fear arousal will not motivate; too much may lead the cue-avoidance function to override the learning. For example, you are presented an extremely dramatic, frightening message relating smoking to cancer and heart disease. Although motivational arousal may be very high, if that message is too scary the cue functions may be reduced. You may be too frightened to receive (hear and understand) the message. The outcome could well be minimally effective. On the other hand, with a message that is overwhelmingly dull, although cue functions are served (you hear it), motivational arousal may be so slight that you do not bother to learn or to act on the message. Again, minimal effectiveness is the outcome. At some moderate level, in which you are both motivationally aroused and still able to see, hear, and understand clearly, the message is maximally effective.

By positing two separable functions McGuire hoped to bridge the gap between studies, such as Janis and Feshbach's, that have demonstrated a negative relationship and those that have demonstrated a positive relationship between the fear-arousing properties of the message and its persuasive impact.

3. *The audience.* The factor of the audience that most intrigued the Yale group was self-esteem (Hovland & Janis, 1959). Research (e.g., Janis, 1954; Kelman, 1950) indicated that the higher a person's self-esteem—that is, the more confidence he had in himself and in his abilities—the less likely he was to be influenced by persuasive messages. As is usually the case, what began clearly as a negative relationship—high esteem, low influenceability—was turned by other researchers into a positive relationship—high esteem, high influenceability (McGuire, 1969, reviews several of these).

Before you throw in the last remaining towel, give up completely on social psychology, or rip another page out of this book, let us pause a moment, scratch our collective heads, and think. There are several things that can be done when we run into conflicting experimental data. The typical response—I must admit this is often *my* typical response—is to say, "What the hell; that's just the nature of the messy beast!" Another response, equally adaptive but requiring more disciplined work, is to look carefully at the specifics of the controversy to see if a new plotting of relevant variables is possible. This is what McGuire did when confronted with the conflicting results relating fear arousal and attitude change. The idea, essentially, is to seek some *superordinate principle* or theory that

will make sense out of seemingly conflicting results. With the self-esteem literature we might find, for example, that at certain intermediate levels self-esteem is positively related to attitude change, whereas at other levels of esteem an individual may be more resistant. If we think of an individual who is defensively high in self-esteem, cocky and arrogant in his manner, we can imagine a situation that permits him to drop these defenses a bit and give in to a persuasive communication. The relationship here would be positive; that is, high self-esteem correlates with high attitude change. Similarly, it is possible to imagine a context in which a person who is characteristically low in self-esteem feels sufficiently comfortable to resist influence attempts. Of course it is also possible to imagine a situation that washes out all self-esteem variance completely, being too straightforward and simple to allow for any meaningful individual variation. Conflicting experimental data should provide fuel for thought, not just fuel for abandoning a field.

The Functional Approach. The Yale group stood outside the individual, plugging him into a communications system and studying his attitudinal print-out; the functionalists gnawed their way into the individual's guts and saw his attitudes as propping up the foundations of his personality.

Work on the authoritarian personality (see p. 182ff.) more than amply demonstrated how attitudes of prejudice toward out-groups formed a coherent cluster—the authoritarian or antidemocratic syndrome—and, as importantly, were intimately tied in with the underlying dynamics of personality, in particular, defense mechanisms. A prejudiced authoritarian held attitudes that did not exist on the surface but rather in deeper layers of his personality; they encompassed so much of him that the implications for attitude change were clear. One- or two-sided messages from a high- or low-prestige communicator, high fear appeals, or, for that matter, almost any of the more rational techniques studied by the Yale group, would not be likely to dent the armor protecting his less rationally based attitudes. The rational-man model that much of the original Yale approach built does not seem adequate to handle such attitudes.

Perhaps only some depth technique, including psychotherapy, could ever reach and affect this person.

In psychology there also exists a less rationalistic model of man. Man is seen as driven by impulses, as lacking the ability to make decisions by considering all facets of a matter. The functionalist approach sought to bridge the gap between these apparently disparate concepts by viewing attitudinal dispositions in terms of the functions they serve. This functional approach argues that man is sometimes rational, sometimes irrational. His attitudes, then, sometimes serve functions involved with knowing the world in which he lives and sometimes serve more defensive functions. In the former case—the one generally of interest to the Yale group—attitude change can proceed by rational argument. In the latter case, however, resistance is more typical; change requires a different approach.

In 1956 Smith, Bruner, and White—combining both social-psychological and clinical talents—published a classic work entitled *Opinions and Personality*. It was based on an intensive clinical study of a small sample of individuals that sought to uncover the relationship between the opinions they expressed and their personalities. Smith and his colleagues classified the relationships they found in three broad categories, each expressing a different function of an attitude or opinion.

1. *Object-appraisal function.* Attitudes serve cognitive functions by providing ready structures into which incoming information can be organized. A man who has a set of attitudes about objects in his world has, in effect, a series of categories for processing information; he knows how to respond, how to think, how to feel. He need not continually go through an entirely new reappraisal process, but rather can slip new information into the old molds. The implication for change is straightforward: the function is fairly rational; new information, then, should be helpful in altering an individual's perceptions. A prejudiced man defined in these terms is one who dislikes blacks primarily because of misinformation he possesses. He believes that all blacks are lazy, superstitious, and dangerous.

New information or new experiences, if properly presented, should facilitate his change in attitude because the attitude serves object-appraisal functions rather than anything more deeply distortive.

2. *Social-adjustment function.* Attitudes not only function to provide meaning to our world, but in addition serve to link us to others who share those attitudes or remove us from those with whom we have sharp attitudinal disagreements. One example of this function is Pettigrew's discussion of the *latent liberal* (1961). Unlike individuals for whom discriminatory attitudes are deeply rooted in their personality, the latent liberal's attitudes are rooted in the norms of his reference groups. He is a *latent* liberal in that events that effect a liberalizing change in the norms of those groups will effect a change in his discriminatory attitudes. For instance, the Supreme Court's 1954 school-integration decision changed the normative climate for groups of law-abiding citizens. This change allowed a reduction in individuals' discriminatory attitudes toward blacks.

3. *Externalization and ego-defensive functions.* An individual has certain unresolved inner conflicts that are externalized and come thereby to color his view of other persons and issues. The kinds of attitude measured in the *Authoritarian Personality* (Adorno et al., 1950) were of this sort. In effect, an individual's anti-Negro or anti-Jewish attitudes, based on an externalization of his own inner conflict, serve as a psychological crutch to keep his balance roughly intact. Such crutches are not likely to be changed by rational appeals. How absurd it must be to this kind of individual to listen to those who would appeal to his sense of humanity. Humanity? Insofar as his personal stability rests on his hate of Negroes and Jews and other out-groups, such appeals must naturally fall on deaf·ears.

In a similar vein Katz (1960) proposed a four-fold system to classify attitudinal functions. There is substantial overlap with the system proposed by Smith, Bruner, and White.

1. *Instrumental or adjustive utilitarian function.* Each of us develops favorable attitudes toward those things in our world that provide satisfaction to our needs and unfavorable attitudes toward things that frustrate or punish us. This is a basic utilitarian or self-interest view of attitude formation and change. It is to a worker's self-interest, for example, to support the political party that satisfies his economic or security needs. The implication for change is clear: change the degree to which an individual sees that his values will be satisfied if he adopts specific attitudes. The approach employed by Carlson (pp. 115–116) in altering the perceived instrumentality of an object in attaining satisfactions for *P* is based on this function.

2. *Value-expressive function.* Some of our attitudes provide an affirmation of our identity or our values. For example, an individual likes to think of himself as a radical in political matters. He adopts attitudes that express this self-image or that express the values of radicalism he espouses.

3. *Knowledge function.* Akin to Smith, Bruner, and White's object-appraisal function, attitudes give coherence and meaning to our world. They provide standards against which we make judgments, frames of reference within which we interpret and understand the meaning of specific persons, events, and issues.

4. *Ego-defensive functions.* The point is much the same as the Smith et al. conception of externalization. Each of us utilizes certain defensive mechanisms and strategies to manage our internal affairs and to minimize what we take to be disastrous or threatening encounters with our external world. These ego-defense mechanisms are adaptive—they keep us afloat—and at the same time nonadaptive because they narrow our focus and provide us with a world that is more rigid and more distortive than need be. Attitudes that serve ego-defensive functions help bolster the ego while protecting it against real and imagined threats.

The most unique contribution of the functional approach lies in its delineation of the ego-defensive functions. There are several important implications of the ego-defensive framework. First, the object of the attitude *symbolizes* the individual's inner conflict; there may be only a minimal connectedness between the object's

real attributes and the choice of it as a symbol for the individual's distorted hatred (or love). Second, related intimately to the preceding, attempts to change such ego-defensive attitudes typically run headlong into a wall of resistance and denial, often so thick that one thinks of compliance techniques rather than anything more benign.

To provide a systematic test to the ego-defensive concept, we must examine attitudes on issues that potentially serve such functions. Although, given man's vivid psychological makeup, the range of possibilities is great, racial attitudes have a long history of serving ego-defensive functions. Next we must introduce a technique of change that has psychotherapeutic qualities about it, a technique that offers the individual some insights into his psychodynamics rather than one that merely provides new factual information. Katz, Sarnoff, and McClintock (1956) provide us with one of several such efforts. They selected a group of college students as subjects for three sessions and measured attitudes toward Negroes during the first session. One week later subjects were assigned either to an *informational* or an *interpretive* session. In the informational session they received factual information designed to influence a change in their attitudes. In the interpretive session they were provided with a discussion linking anti-Negro attitudes to mechanisms of ego defense. At the conclusion of this second session all subjects completed another attitude questionnaire. Finally, in the third session, six weeks later, they again completed an attitude questionnaire about Negroes.

Results were interesting and provocative. First, those who were subjected to an interpretation designed to undermine their ego-defensive attitudes changed more toward favorable attitudes over the six weeks, compared with either a control group or the informational group. In immediate impact (after the second session), however, there seemed to be no difference between the interpretive and the informational appeals.

A second finding of note related the individual's degree of ego defensiveness to his change in attitude: the higher his ego defensiveness, the less amenable he was to attitude change, and this held even in the interpretive condition. This was not unexpected; the insight gained through the interpretations offered in the second session were not of sufficient depth to reach those who were most highly ego-defensive. For those of moderate or low defensiveness, however, interpretation worked more effectively than information.

Other work by this same Michigan-based group (e.g., Stotland, Katz, & Patchen, 1959) further substantiates the usefulness of the interpretive, insight technique for inducing attitude change when the attitudes under consideration serve ego-defensive functions.

I do not know of any good statistical breakdowns that would help us determine the percentage of the U.S. population whose prejudiced attitudes primarily serve ego-defensive functions. Clearly, however, the insight techniques that are proposed as the most useful approach to altering such attitudes take great time and demand almost individual attention. It seems unlikely that large groups of persons could be offered the kinds of enlightening insight that such an approach demands. Furthermore, the more defensive the person, the less likely we are to reach him with *any* change-inducing program; or, having reached him, we may still find it difficult to help him overcome these basic prejudices. If the percentage of ego defenders is large, and informational campaigns ineffective, we are left with a predicament. Perhaps the best solution is to work on the generation in the making rather than trying to invest our aid in present generations. And it is here that the laws of the land, the systems of education, and the mass media can play their proper social role in helping to remove from tomorrow's generation the need for the psychological crutch of prejudiced attitudes.

Campbell's learning approach

Campbell (1961) views attitudes or opinions as a type of behavioral disposition acquired according to the basic principles of learning. He outlines six ways in which all kinds of disposition are acquired, including attitudinal dispositions.

1. We may learn through blind trial and error,

stumbling about until our behavior produces success.

2. We may learn by observing a situation carefully. The example Campbell offers is a child given the problem of figuring out which of several containers holds the piece of candy he wants. In trial-and-error acquisition he stumbles about until he hits on the correct container. With perceptual learning by observation he looks through the open container tops to see which one has the candy.

3. We may learn by observing the trial-and-error efforts of others. The child may watch another child's random efforts and note which container has the candy.

4. We may learn by observing the responses of another person who already knows his way about. In (3) the child learns by watching a newcomer explore his environment; in (4) he learns by watching an experienced person and imitating his actions.

5. We may learn through verbal instructions about the characteristics of objects in the environment. O may tell P to look into the green box.

6. Finally, we may learn by being given verbal instructions about the kinds of response we should make. O tells P to move several steps forward, then turn right.

Essentially, Campbell informs us that we may learn behavioral dispositions either through a personal mode (1 and 2), acquired on our own, or a social mode (3, 4, 5, 6), acquired by reference to others. In acquisition of behavioral dispositions verbal instructions usually are the significant social mode. Unlike a chimp who has solved a problem but cannot inform the chimp in the waiting room, a human problem solver can verbally tell his waiting friend just what to do to figure the whole thing out.

To understand P's responses to social influence, according to Campbell, we need a *weighted composite* of the contribution of each of the two modes. That is, P's conformity or resistance is an outcome of the contribution of the personal mode relative to the contribution of the social mode: the greater the weight of the personal mode, the less likely P is to conform or yield to social influence; the greater the weight of the social mode, the more likely he is to yield. This formulation allows Campbell to summarize neatly a considerable amount of the literature on conformity. It is instructive to present several generalizations taken from Campbell's discussion (1961) of the conformity literature that fit this model.

1. The more frequently the personally acquired disposition has been activated or practiced in the past, the more resistant *P* will be to social influence. As Sherif noted (see p. 125), subjects who had made their judgments alone first in the autokinetic situation were more resistant to moving toward a group norm later.

2. The more difficult the subject matter, the less well learned or the more unfamiliar the task, the more *P* will rely on social modes and thus the greater his conformity will be. An early study by Coffin (1941) indicated that persons were more likely to follow up hints in solving difficult rather than easy math problems.

3. The greater *P*'s knowledge in a particular subject, the less he will conform to social pressures.

4. Public commitment to an individual position before receiving social information will weight the personal mode and thus reduce conformity.

5. The more competent *P* is, the stronger his personal modes of learning will be and thus the less he will conform. Although the relationship is not always as clear-cut as stated, there is some empirical evidence (reported by Campbell, 1961) to support the contention that persons of greater over-all intelligence and competence are more resistant to influence than those of lesser ability.

6. The clearer and less ambiguous the situation, the stronger personal modes of acquisition will be and thus the less the conformity. Ambiguous situations generally pull for the greatest yielding to social influence.

7. The more *P* has been rewarded in the past for nonconforming or for innovative behavior, the more likely he is to be resistant to social influence. Conversely, the less he has been rewarded for innovative or nonconformist activities, the more likely he will be to yield.

This listing of generalizations could easily be extended for many more pages, but I think

these examples convey the flavor of Campbell's approach. There are several implications of this approach for the matter of social influence and change, including both conformity and resistance. In developmental terms, the scheme suggests ways in which dependence on the social mode and thus conformity can be increased. Take a child carefully in hand and reduce the learnings that derive from his own explorations. Punish him for every act of disobedience and reward him splendidly for every act in which he yields. Reduce his self-confidence to a low level so that he comes to depend more on what others say and do than on anything he can pick up on his own. Assuming this is the kind of extreme we want, send him to a school that does not teach him how to think critically or creatively.

On the other hand, if you want to increase the likelihood that a youngster will develop the personal mode, without dismissing the collected wisdom of the ages that the social mode may offer, give him reasonably wide freedom of movement. Don't let him jump out of third-story windows just to learn a lesson for himself; on the other hand, don't do everything for him or punish him when he tries something alone and it doesn't come out admirably enough to show off at the Ladies' Tea that afternoon. Urge him to explore, to invent, to create, to innovate. Help increase his confidence in himself by tailoring his chores to his level of competence. Don't expect a youngster of three to function like an adult; but don't expect him to be as dependent and helpless as an infant. There are activities within and slightly beyond his range of abilities that can challenge and stimulate but not thwart him so that fear of failure becomes his dominant point of view. If possible, get him to a school that reinforces personal exploration, autonomy, and the development of personal creativity. Good luck with that one.

With an adult the general formulation remains the same. To induce conformity, work to undermine the personal mode while simultaneously heightening the importance of the social mode; reverse the process if resistance is the desired outcome. In doing all of this, of course, remember not to be as offhand and casual as this section sounds. We are talking about people and their lives. The brainwasher (we reserve that term for changes we don't like; if we like the change we call it psychotherapy or education) may care little about ethics or morality. He is interested in undermining a man's personal modes of learning, his self-confidence, his normal supports, and driving him against a wall until he finally grabs for the social modes his captors provide. In therapy and in education, presumably guided by more humane ethics than is brainwashing or even advertising, any change is one that invites the participation of all parties.

Walker and Heyns: Anatomy for conformity

"If one wishes to produce Conformity for good or evil, the formula is clear. Manage to arouse a need or needs that are important to the individual or the group. Offer a goal which is appropriate to the need or needs. Make sure that Conformity is instrumental to the achievement of the goal and that the goal is as large and as certain as possible. Apply the goal or reward at every opportunity. Try to prevent the object of your efforts from obtaining an uncontrolled education. Choose a setting that is ambiguous. Do everything possible to see that the individual has little or no confidence in his own position. Do everything possible to make the norm which you set appear highly valued and attractive. Set it at a level not too far initially from the starting point of the individual or group and move it gradually toward the behavior you wish to produce. Be absolutely certain you know what you want and that you are willing to pay an enormous price in human quality, for whether the individual or the group is aware of it or not, the result will be CONFORMITY" (Walker & Heyns, 1967, p. 98).

The need–instrumental-act–goal formulation expressed in the Walker and Heyns scheme shares much with Campbell's conceptualization. Both derive from a learning theory model. Walker and Heyns argue that conformity is a behavior that can be manipulated like any other: create a need and make conformity an act that is instrumental to satisfying that need. For example, an individual high in the need for achievement can be made to conform when he is placed in a situation in which doing well— which satisfies his need for achievement— means yielding to O's influence attempts.

Walker and Heyns' approach, along with Hovland's and Campbell's, has a mechanistic

quality. All convey the impression that if you, the Grand Manipulator, simply do A, B, and C, you'll get poor P to move this way and that. The functionalist approach, by contrast, especially in its concern with ego defenses, conveys the impression of a somewhat more actively involved character, even if the involvement is of a distortive and defensive variety. In great part these impressions are conveyed by the *concept language* that is employed. When we talk about communicators, messages, audiences, acquired dispositions, and need-act-goal sequences, we create an impression of a mechanical, push-pull model of human behavior. On the other hand, when our language introduces concepts of coping, denial, ego defenses, adaptation, and so forth, our organism-man takes on a more delightfully active, enigmatic, we might say *human* posture.

Although the distance between behaviorists and functionalists is much less today than earlier in this century—especially since behaviorists have introduced some of their own internal concepts—it is nevertheless clear that their concept languages tune them in to different worlds. Another way of relating the sense of this difference is to suggest that the former live in a world of Dick and Jane primers: "See Dick run." "Jane has a red wagon." "Throw the ball, Dick." "Run Spot run." The latter live in a world cast by some New Wave French film maker in a production directed by Bergman from a script by Pirandello.

The consistency approach to change

For this discussion I can be brief. In the last several years consistency theory has taken off with a vengeance in numerous journals and several texts and has drawn our attention at many conventions and symposia. The only reason I can be so brief, given the vast amount of material from this approach, is that we have already covered most of the essentials in earlier sections of this book (see p. 100ff.).

Recall that the essence of the consistency approach is man's presumed preference for psychologically consistent relationships between elements of his attitude system. Inconsistency motivates action to change toward consistency. To create change, then, is to create conditions that produce inconsistency; this may be done by several means we have already examined, for example, by inducing P to engage in actions that are at variance with his attitudes or values; by introducing new information to P of the sort that will conflict with his present attitudes; or simply by pointing out to P the existence of inconsistencies. In all cases the principle remains the same: introduce conflict into P's world by bringing about a condition that is inconsistent with his status quo.

THE EXCHANGE MODEL
OF INFLUENCE AND CONFORMITY

Is it not fitting that a society of the marketplace, with economic theory and practices living intimately in every household, should eventually compose an economic version of social psychology? We have already seen hints of this approach in the writings of Thibaut and Kelley (pp. 97–99); another hint occurs in the Walker and Heyns conception of conformity as a behavior that is instrumental to obtaining rewards. The hint, of course, is that one acts to *exchange* conformity behavior for need satisfaction. A notion of social exchange is at the core of the economic theory of social behavior.

In simplified terms, the marketplace is a location in which exchanges occur; for example, P gives money to O in exchange for some goods he wants to purchase. If we think of social behavior in similar terms, we can talk about P voluntarily giving "something" to O in exchange for "something" that O gives to him. But what are these "somethings" that are exchanged? In an effort to build a model of social influence and conformity based on economic theory Nord (1969) offers us some provocative answers. He argues that in the social arena *conformity* is the commodity and *social approval* is the money paid for this commodity. One exchanges his conformity behavior to obtain the rewards of social approval or to avoid the costs of rejection and disapproval. Unlike money, social approval cannot actually be transferred in a physical sense. Unlike money, which seems to hold its value regardless of the source (although I suppose a man of high principles would frown

on money received from illegal sources, say from selling drugs to grade-school kids), the value of social approval can vary as a function of the source that provides it.

In economic exchange terms both conformity behavior and social approval can not only be *exchanged* but also can be *invested* as though they were credits for future exchange. In his work on ingratiation (see pp. 42–43) Jones (1964; Jones, Gergen, Gumpert, & Thibaut, 1965) suggested how P may conform to O as one of several ingratiation tactics. P ingratiates O, creates a good impression of himself by yielding to O's demands. This tactic may place P in a better exchange position vis-a-vis O when P wants to draw some positive benefits from his account later. For example, a student ingratiates his naive-innocent-idealistic instructor by conforming to his every wish: assignments are eagerly turned in on time or even a little early; in class, when the instructor asks for questions, P always asks one that shows off his instructor to good advantage; P always comes up after class and plays the game of fascinated scholar. Later P may wish to draw from this account and get a favor from his instructor, who, remembering all these past delights, grants it.

Hollander (1958; 1960) introduced the interesting concept of *idiosyncrasy credits*. He argued that one could build up deviation points against future nonconformity by conforming early in a relationship. He suggested that conformity to group norms earns an individual status and prestige credits in the group. Like a savings account, such credits build up investments that the individual can "spend" later on greater freedom to deviate, to innovate, to do things that other members are forbidden to do. Hollander examined this notion in an experiment on problem-solving groups. He found that early conformity to agreed-on procedures of operation gave an individual more freedom to be innovative later in the group's life, whereas early disagreement over procedures reduced the leeway for later effective innovation. Other work (e.g., Hollander, 1961) indicates, however, that such idiosyncrasy credits apply more strongly to certain norms than to others. An early conformer could not get away with murder (figuratively speaking); rather, he was allowed to deviate later on certain norms, especially those most salient to his initial conformity.

Intuitively, this approach seems valid. A person who conforms early and rises within a group, a community, or a society, a man who plays the game of life by the approved book of rules, does seem to build up some account against which he may later draw. He is less likely to be caught for later indiscretions; he is less likely to go to jail when caught, or less likely to remain there long. His deviations, in fact, are more likely to be dismissed or labeled as eccentricities rather than as severe violations of social norms.

However, an alternative to the idiosyncrasy approach also seems valid. We build up certain expectations about the behavior of other people. We come to expect our leaders and high-status persons who have played by the rules for so long to continue to do so; likewise, we expect those who have deviated early to keep playing the same kind of role. Do we not then reward persons for fulfilling our expectations? If so, it seems that we would *disapprove* of a deviating high-status person, while a deviating low-status person fits our expectancies and thus is not to be further rejected.

I raise this question because it seems reasonable that *both* sides of the picture are correct. We do reward persons for early conformity by giving them more freedom of movement than we provide for those who kick up their heels too early in the game. However, we also reward people for conformity to the role expectations we have built up for them and punish them for their deviations. Undoubtedly there is some optimal point at which these two tendencies (and probably others we have not considered) yield maximal payoff to an individual in terms of freedom of movement. We would expect, however, that at some point the credit runs out, countermanded by his failure to live up to role expectations based on his early conformity.

Social approval itself has investment properties. Jones noted how P may give O his social approval as a tactic designed to set up a better exchange with him. P builds up O's ego in such a way as to make himself seem very attractive;

later he can draw on this account. It has been noted, however (e.g., by Blau, 1964), that P must beware of giving so much social approval that it is no longer worth anything. A man who loves everyone and compliments all with equal vigor soon finds few who are willing to receive his approval as either an investment for future payoff or as rewarding right now. I have been involved fairly often in evaluating applications for graduate study in psychology. In these applications we find letters of recommendation from colleagues around the country. Certain individuals have earned reputations with the selection committee as always writing overwhelmingly favorable letters filled with vividly positive adjectives. A positive letter from such persons earns the candidate no points in our evaluation; they send out too much approval, without discrimination, to be believed.

In his discussion of social influence and conformity Nord (1969) goes on in marketplace terms by analyzing the issue of *supply* and *demand*. P supplies conformity to O, the consumer who demands a certain level of conformity. Remember that both P and O can be persons, groups, or larger social units. As a group O may demand conformity from its members either to accomplish its goals or as a sign of loyalty. As a supplier P may give O his conformity if the conditions are right, or withhold his conformity if the deal is not to his liking. Nord hypothesizes that P will *reduce* his supply of conformity to O if the cost of conforming is high, if the rewards of conforming are low, if the costs of nonconformity are reduced, or if the rewards for nonconforming are high. On the demand side, Nord argues that if conformity is like a commodity, the demand should be *high*— O increases his pressure on P to shape up— when the present level of conformity is low and conformity is scarce. To this we add that the demand should be higher as more uniformity is needed to achieve group goals.

Once we begin to think of influence and conformity in exchange terms, several interesting implications develop. Let us make two assumptions. First, nonconformity is often painful and costly; at minimum, when discovered, it can place an individual in an interpersonally uncomfortable situation. Conformity may be less costly and often more rewarding; its reward value is that it both serves to validate our conceptions of social reality and gains us social approval and acceptance by others. Second, however, in the U. S. culture at least, conformity also carries with it a cost component, especially with regard to an individual's sense of personal worth and self-respect. Independence is valued positively as rewarding to the individual. These assumptions indicate that both conformity and nonconformity have reward and cost components. If we assume that P is an economic man out to maximize his reward-cost outcomes, the implication is that he will not conform unless its rewarding qualities can be established as greater than its cost to his sense of self-respect. Nord outlines several factors that contribute to shifting the reward-cost values of conformity, or nonconformity, or both.

1. The type of influence attempted and the type of task or issue involved can play a significant role in determining the reward-cost values. For example, on an issue that is ambiguous or one about which P is uncertain of his own knowledge or abilities, the costs of yielding are less, and thus the likelihood of conformity is greater. Note that Campbell reaches much the same conclusion but from a different model.

Both the type of influence used and its style of usage should be relevant as well. Deutsch and Gerard (1955) differentiated two types of influence. *Informational influence* occurs when P takes the information that O offers about the nature of reality. For example, we hear that a group of experts have determined that the earth is not flat but tends to be rounded. This information may sway our own view about the nature of that reality. *Normative influence* occurs when P seeks to go along with O in order to meet O's expectations. One finding of special interest in Deutsch and Gerard's study showed that individuals under normative pressure to stick to their own judgment conform less to the demands of others. The point is that when group norms define your own judgments as important, it is more costly to yield to others than when the norms demand conformity or offer no definition of your judgments.

As for the style of the influence attempt, given the reward-cost assumptions we have made, it seems likely that efforts to play on or make salient the cost side of yielding will decrease P's conformity. If O comes on very strong and demanding, making it plain that if P yields he will give up all his own control to O, the cost of doing so should be greater than if O's style is less gross. Although this seems reasonable, I can recall all too vividly that this effect was not borne out in my doctoral dissertation (Sampson, 1960). In that case O sought vigorously to demonstrate that he could control P's behavior regardless of what P wanted to do; he did so primarily to produce strong resistance. Unfortunately, this attempt to control did not produce the resistance I had expected. Recall that suggestion situations, including the sort used by hypnotists, build on P's willingness to yield to O; perhaps we will have to modify the clear-cut cost side of the conformity ledger. There are times, there are situations, and there are persons to whom some of us may delight in yielding, apparently without feeling that we have deprecated ourselves.

2. Characteristics of the source (O) will play an important role in affecting the reward-cost outcomes. As the preceding example indicated, there are some Os for whom yielding is not the costly matter we might expect it to be, and there are other Os whose every wish we want to thwart. As we have seen, however, in both Hovland's and Campbell's views, the more positive, prestigeful, expert, or competent the source, the more likely it is to be rewarding and the less likely it is to be costly for us to yield. In addition, of course, if we are thinking of conformity in terms of an ingratiation tactic, to conform to a man of high prestige may be quite a good investment to make. Undoubtedly it is a better investment in terms of potential later payoffs than to yield to someone of lesser status. If we think of conformity more in terms of validating social reality, the payoff of accurate validation is undoubtedly higher the more expert and knowledgeable the source.

3. Clearly, the payments for conformity or nonconformity will effectively juggle the reward-cost matrix. Payments may be in the form of reward for conformity or punishment for nonconformity or vice versa. Rewarding one or punishing the other will change the values in our matrix to make one more desirable. This, of course, leaves aside the issue of permanence of the change (p. 298ff.).

Nord incorporated a result into this discussion that we have considered earlier. Recall in the Asch situation and other contexts (see pp. 255–256) that the presence of a single deviate helped P overcome the pressure from the group and increase his resistance. In exchange terms, the costs of nonconformity are reduced by the presence of another person who acts defiantly. In addition, depending on the reaction P receives, it may even prove rewarding to follow the deviant model. If the group rewards a lone nonconformist, it inspires others to try it out as well. It is often for this reason that groups and organizations choose to punish some kinds of nonconformity. In campus uprisings, for instance, college administrators feel they are in a bind if they reward disruptive behavior by giving in to student demands. Their reasoning is simple: if we reward these acts of rule-breaking and defiance, will we not inspire others to join in? On the other hand, if there is no compromise, surely a rigidly held administrative policy will also inspire others to protest. Alas, the lot of the administrator is not easy. But then, whose lot is?

4. Another factor in reward-cost outcomes is the degree of pressure that is brought to bear. The more pressure to conform, the more costly it is to continue to nonconform and thus the greater the chances that conformity will result. Recall the Schachter study of opinion deviation and rejection and the Sampson and Brandon replication and extension (p. 126ff.). The costs of standing out there alone are indeed often severe; it takes a person of great principle to face off alone against such odds.

A body of laboratory research relating opinion discrepancy to pressure for conformity is relevant in this context. The argument is that, within broad limits, the greater the discrepancy between P's position and that advocated by O, the greater will be the pressure on P to change and thus the more he will change. Hovland and Pritzker (1957) experimentally created three levels of distance—slight, moderate, and extreme—between P's position and the position a communicator advocated, and they used a variety of issues. They compared the amount of opinion change in P for each of the three levels, finding a progression: more change with greater discrepancies. Others (e.g., Fisher & Lubin, 1958; Goldberg, 1954) report generally similar findings, suggesting that there is a greater cost for P to remain more distant from an advocated position than there is for him to remain at a minimal distance.

In live situations things may not operate that simply. If we assume that the issues involved are vitally important to P, then greater distance between himself and O may come to mean that O is to be discredited, rather than P's experiencing the cost of his being so discrepant. Recall from consistency theory that being distant from a disliked O in fact is cause to rejoice rather than to feel pressure to conform (see p. 125ff.). Nevertheless, in general, the greater the pressure on P to conform, whether the source of this pressure be O's communications, P's distance from O, P liking O, or P seeing O as a credible source, the greater will be the cost of nonconformity to P.

5. Another entire class of factors that influence the reward-cost values of conformity or nonconformity pertains to individual differences in personality. Certain personality traits increase the likelihood that P will find conformity rewarding; for example, the need for social approval as measured by Crowne and Marlow (1964) shows a relationship with conformity. On the other hand, needs such as the need for independence or autonomy should place a negative cost on conformity. Some provocative work by Schachter (1959) related position in family, need affiliation, and conformity to social influence.

He suggested that firstborns, when anxious, prefer to affiliate with others; this can lead them to find it rewarding to follow others' views. Firstborns do conform more than later-borns. Whether the relevant personality variable is affiliation—as Schachter suggests—or something else, for example, achievement—which some of my own data (1965) and those of a study done with Hancock (Sampson & Hancock, 1967) suggest—remains to be seen. The picture is complex. In general, however, it is reasonable to argue that such personality factors color the environment, making some situations rewarding and others costly. In exchange terms, some kinds of person under specifiable conditions will be willing to exchange conformity behavior for need satisfaction, whereas others will maintain their nonconformity.

It is likewise correct to maintain that a person's consciously held self-image will color the environment in much the same manner. For example, an individual who prides himself on being independent will find obvious yielding to another's influence too costly a behavior. An individual who feels himself to be as lowly and ignorant as a human being can get will find yielding much more rewarding; for him, independence may be unthinkable.

Social standards

One of the issues raised by an exchange model of influence and conformity, discussed in regard to the Thibaut and Kelley model of social interaction (pp. 97–99) and to which we have alluded briefly here, involves the determination of the value to P of O's social approval and to O of P's conformity. We are not dealing with a scale that has absolute values as money does. Ten dollars in money is twice as valuable as five dollars. But what are the comparable value units in social exchange? Recall that Thibaut and Kelley defined two concepts that both P and O employ in evaluating the outcome (rewards minus costs) of their encounter. One standard, the comparison level (CL), was employed in gauging how good the good (reward) was and how bad the bad (cost) was. Comparison level for alternatives (CL_{alt}) was the standard used to compare the outcomes of the present relationship with available alternatives.

Baron (1966) found it useful to define an individual's *social reinforcement standard* (SRS), which he hypothesized as an internal standard built up on the basis of past reinforcements (rewards and punishments); the SRS was assumed to provide structure to an individual's ongoing relationships. Simply, a person who has received many positive reinforcements in the past—you're a good kid, a talented kid, a brilliant kid; here, have an A; here, have some money; here, have a job; here, I'm dying to date

you—will have built up a standard that places heavy demands on all who would win his conformity through reinforcement now. Compare him with an individual whose past history has led him to expect the worst or at least very little out of life; a tiny amount of approval from O may be sufficient to win his conformity.

It seems reasonable to maintain that just as P has his internal SRS by which he comes to evaluate the value of O's handout of social approval, so too does O have a standard by which he gauges the fairness of this exchange. O is not going to hand out gobs of approval for low amounts of conformity just because P's own SRS is so high. Some breakdowns between P and O undoubtedly have their source in different bargaining prices based on different SRS levels. Whereas money provides generally agreed-on standards with an absolute zero point, social exchanges lack any zero point, and, as importantly, may not even build on a common framework of standards. It is roughly analogous to P working in dollars and O working in cowrie shells.

Personality and SRS. The notion of an SRS allows us to introduce personality dispositions into the exchange model in yet another way. Low self-esteem, for example, may be conceptualized as establishing a low SRS. The individual comes to expect little and exchanges his conformity to O for a lesser cost than someone whose self-esteem, and consequently his SRS, is high.

A personality variable of interest recently is the *internal* versus *external locus of control* of reinforcement (see p. 36ff.) for another discussion of this trait). Some persons, called *externals*, characteristically view themselves as lacking control over their environment. Things happen to them; rewards are just given to them, as are punishments; and there is little they feel they can do about controlling these reinforcements. *Internals* generally see themselves as in control of things in their environment; specifically, they feel themselves capable of creating conditions that yield positive reinforcements or avoid negative reinforcements.

If you were an external you would be living in a world of fate where little you did mattered much, so why do much? If you were an internal, your world would be amenable to change; effort rather than apathetic withdrawal would reflect this sense of personal responsibility and personal causality. Through reinforcement schedules and variations in experimental situations, even animals can be internals or externals. There is a fascinating study in which ulcers were experimentally induced in rhesus monkeys (Brady 1958). Those monkeys (internal) who could avoid a painful shock by pressing a lever developed the ulcers; their noncontrolling partners (external), who could only receive the shock but do nothing about it, did not get ulcers. Perhaps that explains the relationship between ulcers and other stress-related symptoms and executive responsibility in people as well as in monkeys.

Research on locus of control has offered some fascinating findings. Strodtbeck (1958), for example, found a social-class difference in this dimension: middle and upper classes felt more in control than lower classes. Another study with important social implications was conducted in a southern Negro college (Gore & Rotter, 1963). Gore and Rotter report that internals indicated interest in taking civil-rights-oriented social action; externals expressed little interest in such actions. If we think of participation in social change as requiring at minimum a sense of personal efficacy—I am in control of my fate; I must act—these data suggest that internals are more willing than externals to take change-inducing actions.

Some studies have related locus of control to conformity and related behaviors (e.g., Crowne & Liverant, 1963). Externals tended to conform more than internals. In terms of SRS we can state something about both the *level* of the standard that differentiates internals from externals and the degree of pertinence of the standard to these two types. The external feels he has minimal control over reinforcements in his environment; it is likely, therefore, that he has few expectations about gaining reinforcements and that the SRS therefore is not of great pertinence for him. The internal, however, should be more actively involved in seeking out positive reinforcements; both his SRS level and its pertinence should be much higher.

In a sense the internal is like an entrepreneur who can wheel and deal in his world. He doesn't confront O as some hapless soul with little to offer; rather he hopes to be able to engage in a successful exchange with O. This implication is interesting; it suggests that the internal might well wish to exchange conformity for social approval, thus appropriately complicating any simple prediction from locus of control to conformity. Just as in the marketplace, you have to know more about the deal before you make your prediction.

If the internal is an entrepreneur, the external is a petty bureaucrat who feels his fate is out of his own hands. He does not wander about looking for deals; he does not make effortful advances to gain rewarding reinforcements. Que será, será: what will be, will be. At least he doesn't get any ulcers, that is, if we may generalize from monkeys to bureaucrats.

The norm of reciprocity

Although the language and the meaning of the marketplace approach to influence and conformity may incite some to fury (and excite the imagination of others), the notion of social behavior as an exchange has wide applicability and a sense of subjective worth when examined in slightly different terms. Gouldner (1960) defined a norm of reciprocity that governs all human relationships. This norm, he maintained, ". . . makes two interrelated, minimal demands: (1) people should help those who have helped them; and (2) people should not injure those who have helped them" (p. 171). His argument is that this norm is at the root of all cultures' moral principles and value systems. It establishes a set of reciprocal demands and obligations that provides stability to a social system. That a norm exists does not mean that it will always be followed without violation. The implication, however, is that when violation occurs strains are created that may eventually lead to a disruption of the entire social system.

Clearly, the norm of reciprocity builds on an exchange model. It obligates P to exchange help with O to reciprocate for help received from O. The demanding quality of this norm is not simply based on man's good will to his fellow man; but, as Gouldner notes, ". . . if you want to be helped by others you must help them; hence it is not only proper but also expedient to conform with the specific status rights of others and with the general norm" (p. 173).

The other aspect of the norm of reciprocity requires that punishments *not* be exchanged as reciprocation for rewards. If *P* helps *O*, *P* can expect to receive help rather than injury or punishment in return. Imagine the chaos that would result in any society if this were not so. Every time you did something positive for another, you would have no way of knowing whether something positive or negative would be returned. Soon you would cease to offer positive help, preferring perhaps to withdraw into self-centered isolation. A society of such persons would indeed be in a state of potential war of all against all; hardly a condition conducive to social integration.

In his analysis of the norm's operation between persons of different power Gouldner suggests that reciprocity tempers any tendency for those in high power to engage in exploitative behavior. Exploitation would occur if *O* expected help (or gain) from *P* without any exchange on his part to *P*. The norm, however, demands that *O* exchange with *P*. Again, this does *not* mean that the norm will be followed and that exploitation will never occur. Rather, it argues that when the norm is violated—when *O* gets *X* from *P* without any reciprocation—the system will begin to experience strain. Eventually it will collapse or be wrapped up in an internal revolution. Adherence to the norm thus offers stability to a social system.

ATTITUDES AND BEHAVIOR

At long last the budding young social scientist feels he is equipped with his doctor's kit, ready to plunge into the world and change it. If we do this, this, and that, attitudes will change. But so what if *attitudes* are changed? The question is twofold: (1) What is the relationship between *P*'s attitudes and *P*'s behavior? (2) What is the relationship between a *change* in *P*'s attitudes and a corresponding change in his behavior?

The relation between attitudes and behavior

I fear we have come to that moment when we must get off our honeymoon express and see the world of attitudes in the harsh glare of empirical reality. But let us begin by being naïve and hopeful; let us blandly assume that there is a simple correspondence between attitudes and behavior. The classic work in this genre was that by La Piere (1934), who traveled around the country with a Chinese couple, stopping at a variety of restaurants and hotels. Later La Piere sent a questionnaire to the manager of each place, asking whether they would serve Chinese. Approximately 92 percent said that they would not, although all but one *had* served the Chinese couple. Several other studies show similar inconsistencies between stated attitudes and actual behavior. Minard (1952) compared southern white coal miners' attitudes toward Negroes in the mines and more socially outside. Inside there is considerable integration; outside separatism is the rule. About 60 percent of the white miners reported attitudes inconsistent with their behavior. Minard's conclusion emphasizes the importance of situational norms in influencing behavior. Still another example (Saenger & Gilbert, 1950) demonstrates a discrepancy between shoppers' expressed attitudes (refusal to have a Negro salesperson wait on them) and subsequent behavior in a department store, when they did, in fact, allow a Negro to wait on them.

Although the evidence of inconsistency between reported attitudes and more overt behavior is impressive, there is an interesting study by DeFleur and Westie (1958) that offers a bit more hope. They measured the attitudes of a large group of college students toward Negroes. From this larger sample they selected two extreme groups, one indicating strong anti-Negro attitudes, the other indicating pro-Negro or unprejudiced attitudes. They next created a believable behavioral situation; each person was asked to sign a paper permitting use of a photograph of him sitting with a Negro. A variety of purported purposes for the photograph ranged from restricted use in further experimental work all the way to its use in a national campaign. Data indicated that those who were more prejudiced were less willing than the less prejudiced subjects to have the photograph taken or used. Here, at least, is a small indication of consistency between attitudes and behavior; the majority of the data, however, is not terribly heartening to the naïve researcher who expects a simple correspondence.

The Methodological Side. Up to this point I have accused our researcher of naïveté. What would a more sophisticated investigator have to say? I think he would have comments to make both on the methodological and on the theoretical level. Methodologically speaking, the problems that militate against any simple attitude-behavior correspondence may occur in several places (see Ehrlich, 1969, for a similar analysis).

1. When it comes to measuring attitudes, especially on hot or controversial issues such as prejudice, investigators may pick up factors other than an individual's "true" attitude, such as subtle experimenter effects. For example, a Negro interviewer will be less likely to uncover anti-Negro attitudes than a white interviewer (see Pettigrew, 1964); "Jewish-looking" interviewers are less likely to get admissions of anti-Semitism from their subjects (Robinson & Rhode, 1946).

2. We may not really know how to get at attitudes that have an important ego-defensive or unconscious component through the use of paper-and-pencil tests. Our measurements may only cut at the surface, leaving much of the iceberg well out of sight. Predictions from such measured attitudes to behavior would be likely to lead us, like the Titanic, crashing against the hidden portion.

3. In many cases we measure general or abstract attitudes and then try to predict to very specific behavioral incidents. For instance, we seek individuals' attitudes toward Negroes by using scales that pick up general anti-Negro sentiments; then we pick out some minor behavioral situation that may or may not have any relationship to the general attitudes measured. So we find that P doesn't like Negroes, yet he gets his shoes shined by a Negro every week. Methodologically, we social psychologists have invested much in measuring attitudes but little in measuring behavior-in-situations.

4. If we assume that the behavior of an individual in a particular situation is a function of many different factors, including the specific attitudes we have measured, it follows that we

are being naïve to assume any simple correspondence; at minimum we should measure more attitudes or more components than the one we pick out. *P*'s attitudes may indeed influence his behavior toward Negroes. But other things also influence his behavior. These remain unmeasured; thus our predictions are incomplete.

Much this same point was raised by Rokeach (1966), who argued that there are always two attitudes involved: the individual's attitude toward the object; and his attitude toward the situation. As Rokeach puts it:

". . . we have scales that measure attitudes toward the Negro, the Jew, liberalism-conservatism, and religion. But we do not have scales that measure attitudes toward such situations as managing or being a guest in a Southern hotel, being a passenger or driver of a bus, buying or selling real estate. As a result, the study of attitudes-toward-situations has become more or less divorced from the study of attitudes-toward-objects" (p. 531).

His point is that before we can hope to predict from attitudes to behavior we have to measure *P*'s attitudes *both* toward the object (e.g., Chinese) and the situation (e.g., being a hotel manager). Although an individual may think negatively of Chinese, he may think positively of being a manager who serves all comers.

The Theoretical Side. Rokeach's last point provides some overlap between the methodological and the theoretical arguments. On the theoretical side, however, there are again several arguments that caution a naïve investigator against expecting any simple attitude-behavior correspondence. For example, there is good theoretical reason to believe that *P*'s attitudes toward *X* do not exist in isolation, but rather form part of a larger system of relationships in which *X* is but one element; it is overly simple to predict from an attitude toward *X* to behavior without considering the variety of other attitudes that become activated once *X* is aroused. This is the essence of consistency theory, which argues that our attitudes form an interdependent system so that a change in one element implies changes in other elements. For predicting behavior the implication is much the same: a given situation may activate *X* and all of its associates; behavior is complexly determined. There is also a theoretical basis for maintaining that *not all aspects* of P's attitudes are relevant to his behavior. That is, if we assume that his attitude toward X is complex, then not all of its components may be related to his behavior toward X.

It is both a methodological and an important theoretical point to note that what a person says and what he does are two different orders of behavior. What he says occurs in one context with one set of behavioral determinants; what he does occurs in another context with its own set of determinants. He may say or do things in one context that are little related to his words or actions in another context, and he need not feel much dissonance if the contexts provide different, internally consistent justifications for his statements or his actions. He may say, "I hate Negroes and would never even want to sit near one," in the context of a KKK meeting, and later sit next to a black couple at a movie. He may justify these seemingly disparate events to himself in ways that make each internally consistent and thus consonant to him. The demand for simple consistency is undoubtedly more the rule of the psychologist than that of the nimble-psyched individual.

It does not demand a far stretch of our imagination to picture the kind of situation that sociologist Yinger (1965) proposes in his discussion of prejudiced attitudes and their relation to P's behavior. Along one dimension we have four separate social contexts: a liberal university community; a northern city; a southern city; the rural south. We picture these as representing variations in permissiveness or constraints about expressing nonprejudicial attitudes toward blacks. Along a second dimension we can place four kinds of individual; the all-weather liberal; the fair-weather liberal; the fair-weather illiberal; the all-weather illiberal. In general we would expect both the all-weather types to express their attitudes in all contexts, although we should not picture them strutting about with their attitudes on their shoulders. By contrast, the fair-weather varieties have a breaking point at which context interacts with attitude to determine what they are willing to express in their behavior. Thus the fair-weather liberal may be proudly pro-black in the university commu-

nity and the northern city, but find it too hot for him to act on his beliefs in the southern town or rural area; much the same kind of analysis could be made for the fair-weather illiberal. I might add that before you pounce on these people, considering them evil and without backbone, you should pause one moment to examine your own attitudes and behavior. If you are a student at a large radical-to-liberal urban university, is it not relatively easy to express and act on your pro-black attitudes? How might you fare at a smaller southern community college?

An Experimental Case. An interesting and valuable experimental effort to study this complex interaction between attitudes and social context was undertaken by Warner and DeFleur (1969). They hypothesized that there were two contextual factors that were important determinants of whether a person would express his pro- or anti-black attitudes. The first of these factors they called *social constraint.* The concept is much like one we've already discussed as *surveillance* or *observability* (see p. 298ff.): social constraints are high if our behavioral expressions are open to scrutiny by members of our own positive reference groups; if they will not know what we have done, low social constraint operates. If P is a member of a fraternity that preaches strong anti-black attitudes, he is under high social constraint to express this attitude whenever members of his fraternity are around to see him or learn about what he's done; however, if they'll never know, constraints are much lower.

Warner and DeFleur called the second situational factor *social distance.* Behaviors may serve either to reduce or maintain P's social distance from another group, for example, blacks. Some actions place P and a black in a context in which the social distance between them is minimal; for example, P takes a black home to dinner or out dancing. Other actions retain whatever social distance presently exists.

Warner and DeFleur argue that these two factors interact with P's attitudes to determine his behavior. Thus knowing P's attitudes alone is a poor predictor of his behavior until we also know the kinds of social constraint operating on him and the implication of the action for reducing or maintaining social distance. In their study P was asked to sign and mail in a pledge in response to a letter sent out by the experimenter, who represented a fake campus organization. The pledge was to involve P in one of a variety of actions with a Negro, ranging from having a date to making a contribution to an educational charity. It was assumed that signing this pledge and mailing it back was a behavioral commitment and not simply another verbal attitude. The form indicated either that subjects would engage in the action outlined *or* that they disapproved of it entirely. Subjects had been premeasured on their attitudes to Negroes.

The authors report that the general collegiate context in which their study was carried out provided an environment "hostile toward integration" (p. 156). Social constraint was experimentally manipulated by indicating to subjects either that their action would be entirely private and anonymous (low constraint) or would occur in public and would be disclosed to the rest of the campus (high constraint). Some of the actions were of the sort that would reduce the social distance between P and Negroes; some would maintain presently approved (in that college) social distance.

The specific question to which this study addressed itself, then, was how P's attitudes toward Negroes related to his pledge-signing behavior in contexts that varied constraints and distance. Several detailed findings are worth mentioning.

1. Regardless of his pro- or anti-attitudes, the presence of social constraints reduced P's willingness to sign the pledge. When behavior was open to public scrutiny, then, most persons' behavior was inhibited. Almost independent of the attitude focus of this study, there is an implication of this finding for bargaining and negotiation sessions between groups. Negotiating in the fishbowl of public scrutiny can inhibit each party's ability to negotiate a compromise; each must play for his viewing audience of reference groups. Most negotiators know this and prefer to deal behind the scenes.

2. Under low social constraint—the privacy of nonobservability—persons were more willing to act in accord with their attitudes; the low-

prejudiced were more willing to sign a pledge and the high-prejudiced were less willing. Behavior was consistent with attitudes.

3. High constraint was more inhibiting to less prejudiced subjects than to the highly prejudiced. Recall that the actions to be taken deviated from college norms. Thus when these actions were to be public the group most likely to engage in them by virtue of their pro-attitudes felt most constrained by publicity. Those who were disposed by their attitudes *not* to engage in these activities did not mind publicity, for others would note their refusal to do things that were generally disapproved.

4. Under conditions of low constraint, interestingly enough, the more prejudiced as well as the less prejudiced subjects felt freer to engage in pro-Negro actions. Recall Pettigrew's notion (p. 315) of the *latent* liberal (fair-weather illiberal) who is constrained by social norms to engage in discriminatory behavior. Change that context (or minimize the publicity of his action) and his latent liberalism pops out. In much the same way, the context that assured anonymity permitted some illiberals to manifest more liberal behaviors. For them, then, there was an inconsistency between attitudes and behavior under conditions of low social constraint.

5. Warner and DeFleur report that reducing the social distance had an inhibiting effect on all subjects, regardless of initial attitudes. It appears that maintaining the social distance produced greater behavioral compliance (pledge signing) among less prejudiced subjects; this condition, then, produced consistency between P's attitudes and his behavior. For those who were more prejudiced, however, attitude-behavior consistency occurred at both levels of social distance; that is, they refused participation in any activities regardless of whether these implied reduction or maintenance of social distance.

6. Perhaps the most refined and complex analysis—one, however, that reduced the sample size considerably—sought to examine the interactions of all three factors: verbal attitude, social constraint, and social distance. This three-way analysis indicated the following. (a) Unprejudiced subjects under high constraint were willing to engage in behaviors that maintained social distance. Under these specific conditions, therefore, there was a correspondence between their attitudes and their behavior. (Note that behaviors that maintained distance were approved in that college context. Our fair-weather liberals were willing to engage in distance-maintaining, approved behaviors when others would see what they had done.) (b) The prejudiced subjects were most eager to show their refusal to engage in distance-reducing behaviors under conditions of high constraint. That is, they were willing for everyone to note that they were not going to engage in distance-reducing activities. Under these conditions, therefore, there was a consistency between their attitudes and their behavior.

I have spent some time going over this study because I think it demonstrates both the exciting possibilities of systematic and meaningful research on this important topic and the complexities of relating attitudes to action. It should be clear by now that only the most foolhardy would rush into the world equipped solely with a measure of someone's verbal attitudes.

Attitude change and behavior change

The second main question we raised concerned the relationship between attitude *change* and behavioral *change*. The assumption is that if *O* can induce a change in *P*'s attitudes, he can effect a subsequent change in *P*'s behavior. For most of the reasons already given there is no simple basis for this expectation. If attitudes are themselves complexly related to behavior, we should expect a change in attitudes to be comparably complex in relation to behavior change.

Festinger (1964) addressed himself to this question, coming up with a shocking conclusion. In the first place, he reports very few (three, in fact) systematic investigations that relate attitude change to behavior change. In the second place, these few studies do not offer any very heartening evidence. One study, for example, was undertaken by Maccoby, Romney, Adams, and Maccoby (in Festinger, 1964). They interviewed a sample of mothers with one child between three and 12 months old; the focus was the age to begin toilet training. They then had the mothers in the experimental group read

material intended to persuade them to start training at 24 months. The mothers were re-interviewed several times afterward, both to gauge the impact of the communication on their attitudes and to find out when they did, in fact, begin toilet training. As expected, the mothers in the experimental group went through a striking attitude change on the change measure obtained immediately; even after some time had passed they still showed signs of the impact of the persuasive message. However—and this is the key point—when their actual behavior is compared with that of the control groups,

"There is, if anything, a reverse relationship between attitude change and behavior. The mothers in the experimental group actually started toilet training 1.2 months later on the average than they had initially advocated. But the mothers in the control group, who had never been subjected to any experimental persuasive communication to change their opinion, started toilet training 2.0 months later than their initial opinion would have indicated" (in Festinger, 1964, p. 409).

What we have, then, is evidence for attitude change without subsequent behavior change. The reversal itself is puzzling: the group without persuasive communications to get them to train later actually trained later than the experimental group. But, leaving aside the slight reversal that is reported, Festinger offers an interesting explanation for the apparent failure to find a relationship. He suggests that any attitude change is inherently unstable until it is reinforced by a behavioral change that sustains it; a change in belief that is not supported by an appropriate environmental change congruent with it will tend to revert back again. If you brainwash someone in a POW camp and then return him to a less controlled environment, he may slip back into his old "capitalistic-imperialistic" ways. Recall Newcomb's finding about Bennington College graduates after 25 years (p. 142): their attitude change was supported by an environmental change; the girls married men with comparably liberal political views. In the Maccoby et al. study Festinger's argument is that the mothers' attitude change did not receive behavioral support requisite to maintaining it.

Although this general point strikes me as valid

and valuable, I have little confidence that this is what occurred. I find it easier to assume that the attitude change was more of a friendly, helpful gesture to the interviewer (experimenter effect, as discussed on p. 75ff.), giving him what he wanted, rather than any real effect; this might be true even of the maintenance of the attitude change on remeasurement. Very likely, of course, both experimenter effects and some actual influence effects were inextricably confounded, making any simple interpretation impossible. Nevertheless, regardless of whether the behavioral-support interpretation applies in this case, it is a reasonable analysis of a factor that is basic to the maintenance of an attitude change and of its translation into a behavioral change.

I would add that normative change without subsequent attitude and value change to support and maintain it is likewise unstable. There are two systems to be changed: the personal and the normative or social. To live out in practice the attitudes that one holds may require that one undergo a personal restructuring in a social context that *itself* has undergone a normative restructuring. Picture a child in therapy. In the therapy session he changes his attitudes, but goes home to an environment that supports his earlier, sicker attitudes and ways of relating to people. Thus we find no correspondence between attitude change (in therapy) and behavior change (back home) because of the instability of changed attitudes without behavioral support. To effect a real change the social context (his family) must also be restructured.

I am certain that some of you still have that nagging question at the back of your heads: "So, if there is no correspondence either between attitudes and behavior or between attitude change and behavior change, why study attitudes and why try to change them?" Lest you forget so soon, there is every good reason *not* to expect any simple correspondence between attitudes and behavior, but there is every good reason to expect that attitudes are an important component of our behavior. Recall the interaction effects in the Warner and DeFleur study; they clearly showed the important but not determining role that attitudes play in influencing

behavior. Recall also our discussion of cognitive theory (see p. 11ff.). The point was made that the manner by which one construes a situation importantly influences how he will behave in that situation. Attitudes enter into the construing process. Their change, therefore is no idle matter, but can have very significant consequences both for how we see situations and how we behave in them. Simple it isn't.

THE AMERICAN DILEMMA REVISITED

In 1944 Myrdal introduced America and the rest of the world to a basic dilemma of the society and its people. On one hand, the American creed preached democratic and Christian ideals; on the other, reality indicated a pattern of racial inequality and discrimination. How could one profess to be a rational human being and at the same time live with this dilemma, this discrepancy between attitudes, values, and behavior? It was Myrdal's thesis that we in America dealt with our dilemma by finding *supportive justifications* and *culture myths* that helped to rationalize away the apparent inconsistency. Thus, although our ideal speaks of equal educational opportunity for all, we turned our backs on integrated schools, arguing that blacks were intellectually inferior and could never benefit from the same kind of educational experience; that furthermore they'd just hold the whites back.

This inconsistency between attitudes and behavior is no mere theoretical puzzle for the social psychologist to entertain himself with. We are dealing with the essence of an entire society that does not practice what it preaches. The consequence of this discrepancy is not simply that someone's predictions are incorrect, but rather that the viability of the society is open to serious question. For the victims it is always a curiosity as to why social scientists must try to demonstrate in research what to them is a living truth. For the safe citizenry it is often annoying that the social scientist should attempt to *demyth* a system that has been so good to them. But the social scientist must explore the obvious as well as the hidden; he must cast up the truth for all to see, although it gives fuel for revolution to some and wakes others from complacent slumber.

In 1965 Westie published a study designed to test several facets of Myrdal's thesis. In particular he sought to discover how persons dealt with inconsistencies between their general values and their specific application in behavior. Westie's study built on verbal measures to get at behavioral manifestations of attitudes. His sample included 103 heads of household who were interviewed in Indianapolis in 1957. The date is important, especially in the area of civil rights. After 1957 the decade of protest began; the impact of this decade on the character of the American dilemma undoubtedly is significant. Westie's data, nevertheless, are revealing.

He presented his subjects with a series of statements reflective of the general values of the American creed, for example: everyone should have equal opportunities; public facilities should be equally available to everyone; I believe in the principle of brotherhood among men. In addition, he presented a series of specific manifestations of these values, for example: I would be willing to have a Negro as my supervisor; I would be willing to stay in a hotel with Negroes; I would be willing to invite Negroes to a dinner party. Both the responses to these statements and the subjects' general, spontaneous comments were recorded and later analyzed.

Whereas most persons (an average of 81 percent) agreed with the general values, only an average of 56 percent agreed with the specific reflections. Westie took this as evidence supporting Myrdal's thesis; although people subscribe overwhelmingly to the general values of democracy, they are not willing to support specific reflections. Look at a few examples:

General: Everyone should have equal opportunities. 98 percent agree
Specific: I would be willing to have a Negro as my supervisor. 60 percent agree
General: Public facilities should be equally available to everyone. 83 percent agree
Specific: I would be willing to stay in a hotel with Negroes. 61 percent agree

General: I believe in the principle of brotherhood among men. 94 percent agree
Specific: I would be willing to invite Negroes to a dinner party. 29 percent agree

One especially important finding indicated that when a specific item represented a *fait accompli*, for example, the existence of Negro jurors or congressional representatives or the reality of school integration, there was a greater correspondence between the general values and endorsement of the specific behavior. Think about this for a moment. What it says is that when society has already allowed Negroes into certain occupations or social relationships, in other words, when specific aspects of the dilemma have been resolved, persons are more willing to accept it. According to the dissonance view (p. 108ff.), a behavioral *fait accompli*, including a change in the law, could induce attitude change toward congruence with the behavior; the Supreme Court's school-integration decision was a *fait accompli* (in many districts, at least) that allowed people to agree in their attitudes with integration. The same position derives also from a sociological view that people conform to the norms of a situation; change those norms, as with legal sanctions, and behavior will be changed (e.g., see Lohman & Reitzes' 1952 discussion of race relations; it is also part of Pettigrew's thesis—see p. 315).

Another question to which Westie addressed himself concerned his subjects' awareness of any inconsistencies and the manner by which they dealt with these. He reports that approximately 42 percent of the inconsistencies were freely admitted; 42 percent, however, were denied as being inconsistent; 16 percent were not recognized as being inconsistent. Furthermore, when subjects gave explanations for their views, a majority sought to explain their inconsistencies by adjusting the specific behavior to minimize its conflict with the general value (e.g., yes, everyone should have equal opportunity, but Negroes aren't trained enough yet to be good supervisors); but at least 25 percent of the explanations were efforts to explain and justify the *consistencies*. Persons were very concerned that the interviewer understand why they were consistent in the specific reflections of their general values. What real dilemma must exist when people have to justify practicing what they preach! Does this not reveal something about the norms of a society? Imagine someone at a university who believes deeply in his religion and in going to church but who always feels obliged to explain his churchgoing. We would suspect that the norms of that university community make churchgoing sufficiently unusual that it needs justification; the believer who acts consistently is forced to explain his consistent behaviors. What an American dilemma this is, then, when equal treatment of Negroes, consistent with the credal American values, needs to be explained and justified.

SOCIAL INFLUENCE: A TWO-WAY STREET

One often gets the impression in social psychology of a static scene, frozen in space and time; the full, exciting, dynamic flow of interaction, the give and take, are often clouded over by frame-stopping concepts and approaches. Although hints have already appeared in our discussions, you may still think social influence is a one-way street flowing from the origin, O, to the destination, P. Nothing could be further from the truth. As we have seen, the exchange model brings the dual nature of the influence process into sharper focus; likewise, the functional model offers us a view of P as an active, even resistant being.

Social influence and power are inevitably relational concepts, dealing with an aspect of O's relationship with P. Lewin (1951) recognized this quality when he defined O's power over P in terms of two sets of forces: those that O induces and those that P offers in resistance; the outcome of these forces gives us P's conformity to O or his resistance to O. O may build his efforts to induce forces that influence P on one or more of several of what French and Raven (1959) called the *bases of social power*. He may offer to *reward* P; he may threaten to *punish* P. He may base his efforts on the *legitimacy* of his position, which gives him agreed-on rights to influence P and also establishes limits to his influence. He may base his inductions on *referent power*, the relationship of liking or identification with P. He may base his efforts on his *expertise*, seeking to get P's conformity by affecting the knowledges P has.

In a scheme outlined by Gamson (1968) and derived in part from some of the ideas of Parsons, O may seek either to exercise control over the *situation* or to affect P's *orientations*. In controlling the situation O may add *disadvantages* (e.g., threats of punishment) that constrain P's activity; or he may add *advantages* (e.g., rewards) that induce P to comply. In affecting P's orientations O may attempt to persuade him by focusing on the *content* of his arguments, his *expertise*, or their *relationship*. As can be readily seen, Gamson's scheme includes almost all of the same bases of power as French and Raven's.

We should recognize that P may likewise utilize similar bases to establish counterforces to resist O. Gamson suggests that the relationship between P and O—he calls P the *potential partisan* and O the *authority*—as regards social influence and control is one of opposites:

"Authorities are the recipients or targets of influence and the agents or initiators of social control. Potential partisans have the opposite roles—as agents or initiators of influence and targets or recipients of social control. Thus the influence and social control relationships are the inverse of each other" (1968, pp. 36–37).

Read that passage again. According to Gamson's analysis, from P's perspective O is attempting to get him to do something. P would like to have something to say about O's exercise of this control, so he tries to influence O. From O's perspective, he is giving out control-oriented messages while receiving messages from P that seek to influence what O does. If we think of O as a member of a university's administration and P as a group of students, this relationship will become even clearer. The administrator is trying to keep a demonstration under control so that he will not have to call off-campus police and thus escalate the crisis.

He may try to achieve this control by persuasion, by calling on his expertise as a college professor who understands the students' grievances, or by appealing to their relationship to him and to *their* university (referent power). He may try to persuade them that demonstrations are not the way to get what they want. He may call on their compliance because he is the college president and they are supposed to follow his requests (legitimate power). He may toss in the towel on persuasion and decide to work on the situation. He may introduce constraints by threatening to call the police unless the building is emptied, undamaged, in two hours. Or he may offer inducements, promising to hold a personal meeting with the aggrieved students and to withhold all punishment if they'll leave the building. His problem is to control their behavior; he is the initiator of social control.

The students want to get a new program set up in their college; they want to have more say over curricular matters. Right now they are occupying the administration building in an effort to influence the administrator. Perhaps they could have tried to persuade him, just as he might have tried to persuade them. However, he might not have accepted either their expertise or their legitimacy. Because it is a large university, they may not have sufficient relationship with him to build on referent power. Presumably they could have tried to influence him by promising him a tranquil year ahead. Or they could attempt to influence him by taking a building and threatening to remain, perhaps even threatening to take other buildings, or damage the one in which the computer is located. I hasten to mention now what I hope is self-evident, that O's initiating controlling forces does not mean that he will effectively control P's behavior; nor does the fact that P attempts to influence O mean that his efforts will be effective.

Looking at P's resistance in terms of efforts to influence O's decisions lends a meaningful social dimension to the concept of resistance. We can see that P's resistance is not inevitably a simple passion for rebellion, but rather can have an important rational basis in his efforts to be effective. Realize that in many situations in

which O exercises his power he is not acting entirely on his own, but rather sits at the center of a circle of forces seeking his attention and seeking to have something to say about how his power is used.

The college administrator, for example, has many audiences—faculty, trustees, the public, and others—who seek to affect his decisions and the ways in which he controls those under his jurisdiction. These form his circle of influence. That the students wish to be taken seriously into consideration, then, seems reasonable; they, too, want to have some influence. However, unlike those who presently form part of this administrator's circle of influence, the students have to start from scratch. They must gain power before they can hope to join that circle. In exchange terms, they may be willing to give him some control if he'll give them some influence. From his perspective, the administrator is hesitant to add yet another member to that circle. He may prefer to exercise control without receiving influence in return; or he may be willing to grant some influence, provided he can use techniques of control that fit his office. He may find persuasion or inducements preferable to constraints, especially in the context of a university.

To the extent to which the students remain outside the system in which he can use these techniques, the administrator may be forced to deal in constraints. However, he may find it possible to bring them into his system by allowing them some influence, for example, by permitting student participation in some aspects of university decision making. Through this process of *cooptation*—a term Selznick (1948) introduced to describe the absorption of new elements into the leadership of a system—he gains an advantage of being able to exercise control by using persuasion and inducements. After all, they are now in *his* system; and he knows very well how to play that game. Thus there are benefits to be gained by giving the potentially disruptive students entry to his circle of influence.

It may look as though through cooptation the students have sold out, but they too experience certain advantages from the inside that they lack out on the cold streets or up at the barricades. As Gamson notes, cooptation gives the partisans access to resources and potential influence; it gives them a certain legitimacy that may in turn swell their ranks.

". . . Cooptation does not operate simply as a control device—it is also likely to involve yielding ground. For this reason, there are likely to be parallel fears on the part of authorities. They may worry that the act of cooptation represents the 'nose of the camel' and be fearful of their ability to keep the rest of the camel out of the tent" (1966, pp. 136–137).

As even this brief discussion indicates, the dynamics of social influence are clearly more involved than any one-way street could hope to handle.

INDUCING RESISTANCE

From the perspective of the social psychology of planned change, the conception of social influence as a process involving reciprocal efforts to control and to influence opens a fascinating door (or a Pandora's box) to an issue, as yet not very fully explored, of inducing resistance rather than conformity. Recall that resistance in the sense developed here is not blind opposition, but focuses on P's efforts to influence O.

Perhaps I am being a bit cynical, but it seems that too much of traditional social psychology has emphasized conformity to social influence and, as significantly, conformity to persons in positions of authority. A passage from Deutsch's address in 1968 on receipt of the Kurt Lewin Memorial Award captures this sentiment.

"Suppose . . . that as social scientists we were consultants to the poor and weak rather than to the rich and strong. . . . Let me note that this would be an unusual and new position for most of us. If we have given any advice at all, it has been to those in high power. The unwitting consequence of this one-sided consultant role has been that we have too often assumed that the social pathology has been in the ghetto rather than in those who have built the walls to surround it, that the 'disadvantaged' are the ones who need to be changed rather than the people and the institutions who have kept the disadvantaged in a submerged position. . . . It is more important that the educational institutions, the economic and political

systems be changed so that they will permit those groups who are now largely excluded from important positions of decision-making to share power than to try to inculcate new attitudes and skills in those who are excluded. After all, would we not expect that the educational achievements of black children would be higher than they are now if school boards had more black members and schools had more black principals. . . . Again, would we not expect more civil obedience in the black community if Charles Evers rather than James Eastland were chairman of the Senate Judiciary Committee and if the House had barred corrupt white congressmen as well as Adam Clayton Powell? Let us not lose sight of what and who has to be changed; let us recognize where the social pathology really is!" (pp. 32–33).

Inoculations for resistance

Thinking in terms of a quasi-medical model, McGuire wondered if you could *inoculate* a person against persuasion by giving him an attenuated dose of the counterarguments, just enough to stimulate his defensive systems (e.g., McGuire & Papageorgis, 1961; McGuire, 1961, 1962; Papageorgis & McGuire, 1961). The medical notion is that you provide the individual with a sufficient amount of the disease for him to develop the proper antibodies to fight off the real thing. Suppose P believes X; but you know he will shortly undergo a massive propaganda campaign designed to change his belief in X. You present him small doses of that campaign, just enough to arouse his defenses against changing X but not enough to effectively persuade him to change; you have thus inoculated him and made him resistant to change.

McGuire undertook a series of experimental studies to test this idea. In its basic format the attitudes he sought to inoculate against change were "cultural truisms"; for example, everyone should visit his doctor once a year; everyone should brush his teeth after each meal if it's possible. It is assumed that such beliefs live an insulated life; they rarely, if ever, come in for attack. It is assumed therefore, that the individual is not likely to have developed defenses against changing them; he is out of practice, so to speak. To help inoculate him, therefore, break the insulation; present him with tiny doses of arguments that challenge the truisms, and see if he is resistant to changing them when presented later with the big campaign.

In one such study McGuire and Papageorgis (1961) demonstrated that arguments that *refute* the beliefs (why you shouldn't brush your teeth after meals) work better than arguments that support them. If the function of the inoculation is to stimulate P's defenses, they should be more stimulated by challenging counterarguments in small doses than by further supportive material. Anderson and McGuire (1965) demonstrated that threatening P about the validity of his beliefs stimulated greater resistance to change than offering him reassurance that his beliefs were correct. Again this fits the inoculation model. Threats stimulate defenses that can be activated later; reassurance does not help build defenses, as pleasantly unchallenging as such support may be at the moment. In a further examination of this matter McGuire (1962) expanded the time interval, noting that refutational methods that threatened rather than supported P's beliefs conferred resistance to change immediately after receiving the "shot" as well as two days or even one week later.

The entire concept on which McGuire's approach is based is interesting. Recall that his efforts have been directed primarily toward beliefs that are cultural truisms, beliefs he assumes typically are insulated and thus not well defended. This same effect may not hold for beliefs that are more adequately defended or that are challenged almost daily; we would expect the latter to be well defended and relatively resistant to change.

From the models we have previously examined, several other notions emerge if we wish to help P develop resistance to social influence. We noted that the greater an individual's self-esteem and self-confidence, the more resistant he is likely to be. A community that feels itself weakened and incompetent is not likely to be able to resist intrusions on it from the outside, nor is such a community likely to view itself as capable of exercising counterinfluence over O. Recall the idea of internal versus external control of reinforcement (p. 324ff.); a community of individuals who lack self-esteem and are externally oriented is not likely to see

that it can have an influential role in policy decisions. Aiding that community and its inhabitants to gain a sense of confidence and a sense of internality becomes an essential part of helping it resist social influence.

Although the preceding point is simple, it is often overlooked, especially by academic consultants who fail to recognize that not everyone is as internally directed as they may be. One problem in helping others develop resistance is that the downtrodden too often have given up all efforts to be effective in modifying their environment. They have experienced the victim's position so long that they cannot think of themselves as capable of mounting a countermovement. Even the simple notion that authority can be questioned or challenged is something that has escaped them as a possibility. One of the first steps in creating resistance, therefore, is to help them gain a realization of the real possibilities that exist for them to flex their muscles. They can be helped to go down to City Hall, to complain to the police department, to bring their arguments before governmental officials. Even a small success at muscle flexing can have wondrous effects in stimulating a group to think that it may in fact be able to exercise some control over the environment.

The several contemporary "power" movements have this quality, whether their focus be Black Power, student power, Chicano Power, or whatever. Such movements help give people a sense of personal worth and self-esteem; these are essential to any power relationship. P must approach O not as a poor humble victim but as a man who counts, who has the potential to influence O. Black Power inestimably aids in providing a sense of dignity in a historical scene that has deprived blacks of that sense. In addition these "power" movements offer people a chance to take an active rather than a passive role. Through the exercise of their organized power, they come to occupy a negotiating stance vis-a-vis O; they become a part of his circle of influence, another factor that he must consider in his decision making.

The essence of this argument is that resistance originates in a position of power. Persons who can be the most resistant to influence are those in positions of power; they can enter into a social exchange with O and bargain in terms of reciprocity. When they exchange with O they can get a better deal if they are influential in ways that are important to O. To reverse the Walker and Heyns formulation, from *P's* perspective we note that when P has the power to satisfy *O's* needs, P has a better chance of resisting *O's* efforts to control him. For those in the *down* position, often the only needs of O over which they have any control are his needs for peace and order. Thus their power lies in their ability to disrupt. They can exchange this with O, giving him assurances of minimal disruption in exchange for certain benefits.

If power allows for resistance, the other side is also true: resistance confers power. That is, P's resistance provides a basis for power over O. Short of using brute physical force, O must work to get P's compliance. To the extent to which P can refuse to comply, he has power to influence O; his resistance forms a basis for pressuring O into an exchange position. If I refuse to comply with you, and if you need my compliance and hesitate to get it by brute force, then I have gained an ability to influence you. If you want my compliance, you had better come sit down and talk. I think we can make a deal. Of course in a cultural climate in which O does not hesitate to use brute force to gain compliance, P's resistance through noncompliance is vastly limited. Yet I believe that in the long run, at least in our contemporary situation, O needs P's cooperation and must eventually come to yield some of his power to P.

We in the United States have recently come to realize the important limitations to the actual power of the powerful in dealings with the less powerful. The application of brute coercion to gain compliance usually brings about so many other negative consequences that the powerful resist the temptation to bomb the hell out of "them" and be done with it. This limitation (especially of coercive power), helps the less powerful to gain a better bargaining position; in a sense, their lack of power works to their advantage, just as possession of great power can work to the disadvantage of the powerful. In spite of the horrors committed in Vietnam or in the streets of the United States during the long, hot summers, the full coercive power available has seldom been used. A powerful nation or a powerful person, then, may receive counter-influence from the weaker party that is out of proportion to the power differential.

For the person in authority, O, there is a lesson to be learned. Since he wants P's compliance, and since, as we shall assume, he does not want continual disruption, he will be helped to his goals by providing other means than disruptive ones for P to influence him. By taking P into his circle of influence he brings him off the streets and allows him to exercise his influence in more constructive ways. To paraphrase something that John F. Kennedy said, a nation that does not allow for peaceful change will find itself beset by violent change. In other words, until P is permitted access to O, until lines of communication are opened and participation assured, the streets rather than the council chambers are likely to be the loci of change.

Chapter 22

Mass media

On one hand,

"It was an unnecessary war. It was the newspapers' war. Above all, it was Hearst's war. It is safe to say that had not Hearst, with his magnificently tawdry flair for publicity and agitation, enlisted the women of America in a crusade they misunderstood, made a national heroine of the jail-breaking Miss Cisneros, made a national abomination of Depuy de Lome, made the *Maine* a mistaken symbol of Spanish treachery, caused thousands of citizens to write their Congressmen, and dragged the powerful *World* along with him into journalistic ill-fame, the public would have kept its sanity, McKinley would have shown more spunk, at least four more Senators would have taken counsel with reason, and there would have been no war" (Swanberg, 1963, p. 172).

On the other hand,

"A tremendous amount of applied research has been carried out to test the effectiveness of the mass media. . . . The outcome has been quite embarrassing for proponents of the mass media, since there is little evidence of attitude change, much less change in gross behavior. . . . Indeed, some of the results make it appear that mass media campaigns may even have the reverse of the intended persuasive impact . . ." (McGuire, 1969, p. 227).

Once again we encounter what on the surface appears to be a paradox. We have historical accounts, often combined with our personal intuitions of contemporary events, that indicate a strong relationship between the use of mass media (television, radio, newspapers, books, movies, or for that matter, even cultural pageants with wide coverage; in essence, a communications network linking people together by sight and sound) and a change in attitudes and behavior; and we have evidence that casts serious suspicion on such apparently overwhelming effects. The truth lies somewhere between the two extremes. By this point in this text we cannot easily imagine that man is as passive, malleable, and uncritical as he would have to be for the media to mold his opinion with instant success. Nor can we imagine that he is so isolated and devoid of constraining and supporting social ties that he will alter his attitudes and behavior without appropriate social support to maintain any such change. In other words, it is difficult to plug in a simplistic stimulus-response model, calling the mass media the stimulus and man's attitudes and behavior change the response. We expect selectivity to intervene at several points in the process: exposure to the media, reception of the message, recall, and so on. Likewise, we expect personal relationships to exist as important mediators of media effects, sometimes modifying an effect, sometimes supporting it, sometimes refuting or destroying it.

Yet, coming back to our intuitive common

sense, we cannot help noting the potential array of variable effects that are attributed to the media. We *know* that certain books have had striking effects on public opinion and eventually on policy changes. Nader's account (1965) of auto safety hazards had an effect both on public opinion and eventually on congressional legislation. Carson's accounts (1962) of man's pesticidal pollution of nature also affected both opinion and legislation. Harrington's book on poverty in America (1962) shocked the nation and apparently laid the groundwork for legislative action.

Intuitively we all suspect that television affects public attitude and governmental policy. Investigations have sought to relate violence in people to violence on television (or in movies or comic books). A CBS-TV exposé of hunger in America (in May 1968) shook national complacency and drew both criticism and praise from implicated Federal departments. Advertising, as it appears on television, in newspapers, and on the radio gets fantastic financial support, presumably because someone somewhere feels the money is wisely invested; public buying habits are assumed to be shaped by such advertising.

DIRECT MEDIA EFFECTS

Klapper (1960), a long-time student of the mass media, outlined five different effects the mass media could have: (1) create opinions; (2) reinforce opinions; (3) produce minor change; (4) produce conversion; (5) no effect. To understand these effects we must imagine a situation in which the media convey a message whose intent is to persuade the public (*P*) to change either attitudes or behavior, or both.

Creative effects

If we can assume that the public has no opinion on a particular issue, or a minimally differentiated opinion, the media presumably can create something where nothing initially existed, perhaps simply by calling public attention to some matter that was unknown before. For example, the books of Nader, Carson, and Harrington, plus television and newspaper exposés, call public attention to social ills and at the same time offer a direction for opinion to take.

In the political realm, media, especially television, can create instant fame for potential candidates. Persons can rise from relative obscurity in the public's eye to sudden and vast popularity. An instructive example involves S. I. Hayakawa of San Francisco State College, who took over as acting president of the college in November 1968, during a period of high turmoil. By taking a popular hard-line position against faculty and student protests, Hayakawa earned himself many interviews and spot news coverage on television shows locally, statewide, and even nationally. Few people knew of him before November; less than six months later, according to a California survey, he ranked second only to the governor in popularity as a political figure and in terms of familiarity to the public. More persons knew about Hayakawa, in fact, than knew about Edmund G. Brown, a former governor of the state. A striking media effect!

The creative effect of the media can also occur through the socialization of children or, for that matter, of adults. Both children and adults view role models, a style of life, and a manner of conflict resolution that television writers decide represents reality. Several investigators have examined these effects of television on children. Gerson (1964), for example, asked adolescents whether they ever got any ideas about dating from television and other forms of mass media. Of special interest was the finding that those who were least well integrated into either a home or a school context relied most heavily on media advice and models.

Although systematic evidence is not available, television is often seen as a source of radicalization in the black ghetto. Television presents images of the "Good American Life" with which one can compare his own sorry lot. Out of such comparisons a social movement can arise. It has been suggested that the transistor radio has had a similar radicalizing or politicizing effect, especially on native populations in underdeveloped countries (e.g., Brazil); it brings news into backwater native communities deep in the jungles. Opinions and needs are created; a population, now informed, begins to ask questions; and the seeds of political discontent and perhaps of a social movement are sown.

As any good advertiser (or a bad one, in fact) will tell you, another creative effect of the media—for which systematic evidence is scant—is its creation of new needs, thought to be essential to the operation of the U. S. economy. The housewife sees a new product advertised, or a new packaging of an old product, and suddenly it becomes a must for her. The child, a recipient of much advertising, sees a commercial for a new kind of toy; that becomes his first demand when Christmas or his birthday rolls around. A house without one of those thingamawatchits is no house at all. Whether advertising works or not, millions of dollars are plugged into it in hopes that potential buyers will demand the product.

There is evidence both for and against the effectiveness of such advertising. Sponsors of television programs believe that if a new advertising campaign correlates with a rise in their sales, *ipso facto*, the advertising has caused the sales increase. Any good social scientist will tell you that simple correlation does not necessarily mean a direct causal connection. However, if you are selling thingamawatchits you don't much care whether the advertising works directly or indirectly; you just want sales figures to rise. If going to a magician who casts a spell always correlates with a sales increment, no doubt you will go to that magician.

Media and Violence. Television has been blamed especially for creating and reinforcing violence. British studies (in Larsen, 1964) suggested a real impact of television on a nation, including its level of violence. Differences in impact among groups were also reported. Delinquents seemed to use television as a source of excitement as compared with nondelinquents, who turned to it more for its entertainment value. If television forms a person's major contact with social reality, as it seems to with delinquent youth and others who have stunted social contacts, its impact could be both considerable and horrendous.

Systematic laboratory investigations undertaken by Berkowitz and some of his associates (e.g., Berkowitz, 1962, 1964, 1968; Berkowitz & Geen, 1966, 1967; Berkowitz & LePage, 1967)

indicated that the mere presence of violence-associated stimuli such as guns, which were irrelevant to the task at hand, induced experimental subjects to administer more severe electric shocks to what they assumed to be another subject. Objects not associated with violence did not produce this effect. If violent stimuli can incite to violence, is it not likely that violence on television and in other media can have similar effects?

This argument and this evidence appear to run counter to the argument and evidence that maintain that fantasy material—such as encountered on television—vicariously *absorb* violent impulses. In this view television episodes would *reduce* violence by allowing a person to discharge it through fantasy identification with characters in the stories. The evidence for this position is by no means unequivocal. Maccoby's (1956) efforts in this area produced some contradictory findings in separate investigations. Emery (1959a, b) showed a western movie to children, giving them a projective test one week before and immediately after the film. He reports a slight increase in fantasy aggressiveness after viewing this film. If anything, Emery argues, the final test situation seemed to allow greater permissiveness for expressing aggression. The experimenter appeared to accept more playful aggression afterward than before. Assuming that the kids picked up these adult cues, they would be expected to feel freer to express hostility in their fantasy projective stories, not necessarily because they *were* more aggressive, but rather because the situation seemed to permit it.

Other work examining the cathartic effects of fantasy material has produced some limits on the general proposition. For example, a movie or television program must be *relevant to the aroused need* in order to reduce it effectively through catharsis. Thus if a person is angry and witnesses a bland program, it will not release any of his anger; however, if the program is filled with hostility, discharge of his own anger is more likely. Others (e.g., Pytkowicz, Wagner, & Sarason, 1967) have suggested that fantasy be treated as an ability that persons have in varying degrees. The notion is that some persons spontaneously produce fantasy material as an adaptive mechanism for coping with internal and external stress. These persons presumably should be better able than nonfantasizers to use fantasy exercises to reduce their aroused needs. Some empirical evidence substantiates this possibility. In bold generalization, these data suggest (but by no means prove) that persons who use fantasy as an adaptive technique are better able to reduce vicariously any tensions they are experiencing. Low-fantasizers do not show the opposite effect; that is, they are not incited by such material, they are just less able to release pent-up feelings through it.

By now, of course, we should know enough not to ask which position is correct and which is incorrect; rather, we should ask about the conditions under which television violence incites and those under which it reduces violence. In this case, as the discussion has shown, conditions include both situational factors and qualities of the individual.

Situationally, constraints set up prohibitions against the expression of violence, and disinhibitions work to permit it. One derivative hypothesis of some import then, suggests that an atmosphere or general social context of violence serves to disinhibit violence. More specifically, when adults use violence generally to settle their affairs, children and other adults should pick up cues that violence is permitted. I wonder if a nation that is frequently at war or one that invests much in the machinery of warfare thereby instills violence in its citizenry as a legitimate means of social expression. Do war and weaponry create a context that disinhibits violence? This is an interesting question, especially now. Television was under attack for contributing to the violent mood in the United States during the 1960's; is it not also likely that a state of war and a large defense budget contributed an atmosphere that played an even more important role than television? Yet it was television that came under national scrutiny.

As for the more systematic, experimental evidence, Berkowitz suggests that film violence that is *justified* ("he got what he deserved") does not vicariously reduce subjects' aggressiveness, but actually can increase it. As Berkowitz notes, this finding provides a paradox;

the consequences may well be to *increase* the hostility level on the part of the audience.

"Seeing the fantasy villain 'get what he deserved' may make the angered individual more inclined to hurt the villain in *his* life, the person who had angered *him*. In essence, our findings point to possible dangers in movie and television adherence to the Mosaic injunction of an 'eye for an eye.' An aggressive villain should perhaps be punished, but apparently not aggressively" (Berkowitz & Rawlings, 1963, p. 411).

Another of Berkowitz' efforts was equally revealing. Berkowitz and Geen (1966; 1967) introduced accomplice-subjects called "Bob" and "Kirk" to other subjects in a task situation. In the first part of the experiment each accomplice worked to arouse anger in some subjects and to minimize it in others; they applied shocks to the subjects in evaluation of their performance. All subjects then were shown film clips, ostensibly introduced to study the effects of diversion on problem-solving ability. Half the subjects saw a fight scene from the movie *The Champion*, starring Kirk Douglas (and the experimenter was careful to point out the similarity of the star's name and the accomplice's); the others saw an exciting racing film in which the main character lost badly. Subjects then returned to the tasks; it was now the subjects' turn to apply shocks to the accomplices. To make a long story short, the angered subjects gave the greatest number of shocks to the accomplice Kirk. As Berkowitz and Geen suggest, the name Kirk apparently served to mediate feelings of aggression toward the accomplice. Of further interest was the apparent lack of a significant difference in aggressive behavior (number of shocks administered) between the Bob-fight movie and the Bob-racing movie; the fight movie in itself did not produce significantly greater aggression, although in another study Berkowitz reports a more substantial effect from this film.

The presence of provocative stimuli alone is not sufficient in most cases to trigger overt behavior, although their presence may be important. Social restraints keep much of our behavior in check; we are not always in a situation that allows us to be violent. Similarly, for those who contact reality by means other than or in addition to television, other sources of information are present to moderate behavior. However, individuals who rely on television—or any single medium with a dominant message of violence—to a high degree as a source of their beliefs and as a guide to their actions may respond much as Berkowitz' subjects did. Whether this is a situation in which the media create a new condition in *P*, reinforce a state that already exists, or trigger a reaction, is not clear, although all three are likely.

The *boomerang* is yet another possible creative media effect. Of course television producers do not intend to create an attitude of violence (as the term boomerang might imply); but even if television does prove to have that effect in some persons, others may see sufficient violence on television and in the media in general to be turned off by all forms of violence. For example, news reports showing the horrors of war may serve less to excite the citizenry to violence than to create an attitude in which violence and warfare are abhored.

Media Models. Another relevant line of investigation that offers further leads into the potential creative impact of the media—especially television and movies—is a series of experiments by Bandura, Walters, and several associates (Bandura & Walters, 1963). Their work is based on a social-learning theory that argues, in part, that we acquire new modes of responding or modify our old ways through observation and eventual imitation of others. Thus if *P* sees that *O*'s actions are rewarded, *P* is said to have learned vicariously to act in ways similar to *O*'s under presumably comparable circumstances. Bandura and Walters' work covers a variety of areas; here we shall consider the work involving the expression of aggressive behavior.

In their research paradigm the subject—usually a child—sees a television presentation of a model engaging in a variety of aggressive acts for which he is rewarded or punished. The subject later finds himself in a situation in which he can imitate the model. For instance, Bandura, Ross, and Ross (1963) studied nursery-school children ranging in age from 38 to 63 months. While "waiting for the experiment to begin," the children saw one of three brief television episodes: aggressive model rewarded; aggressive model punished; nonaggressive model as control condition. In the aggressive model rewarded condition Rocky, the aggressor, had an encounter with Johnny in which Rocky's aggression won the day for him. In the punished condition Rocky's aggressive behavior did not quite make it and Johnny left with the desirable toys they had been fighting over. In the control condition the two characters played vigorously but nonaggressively with the toys. Some time after viewing the television program the children were taken to another room where they could play with a variety of toys, some designed to elicit aggressive responses (dart guns, baton, Bobo punching-bag doll, etc.) and some to elicit nonaggressive responses (blackboard, doll house, building blocks, etc.).

The children's behavior was observed, with careful records indicating responses that were a direct match for those of the model and those that were nonimitatively aggressive. In the film Rocky spent some time kicking the poor Bobo doll around the room, so kicking it was a direct matching response; punching or slapping it was a nonimitative aggressive response. Results indicated that the children tended to imitate the rewarded model more than the punished model, both in direct matching of their behavior to his and in nonimitative aggressive behavior.

Reflect on these results for a moment. Children tend to copy the aggressive behavior of a television model who is rewarded for his aggression. This finding is made even more interesting when coupled with the results of an investigation by Larsen, Gray, and Fortis (1963), who concluded that the dominant theme of most television programs examined was the *achievement of an approved goal by illegitimate means.* If we assume that among these illegitimate means was the use of force and violence, then a dominant theme of television programs is to reward violence by showing how its use can lead to the attainment of socially approved goals.

Reinforcing effects

Although there is substantial debate concerning the degree to which the media have creative consequences, in general there is less disagreement about their reinforcing effects.

Reinforcement is the bolstering or intensifying effect that the media have on the opinions and beliefs that a person already possesses or on practices in which he presently engages. Like the creative consequences of the media, reinforcing effects may be unintended byproducts. For example, television news covers a protest demonstration. Mr. and Mrs. Viewer watch intently, noting the number of long-haired, bearded, weirdly dressed participants. Mr. Viewer announces to his wife, "See, I told you it was only those dirty beats and hippies." In this receiver selectivity a pro-police viewer sees dirty demonstrators provoking the police, whereas the pro-demonstrator or anti-police viewer pays most attention to incidents in which the police club the demonstrators; each goes away from the set reinforced in his beliefs, even though the media may have sought to present a more impartial coverage of the event.

Whether the media are impartial, of course, is a complex matter. Selectivity occurs in the eyes of the news reporter or cameraman as well as in the eyes of the viewer. Media may intentionally play up the unusual element in the demonstration to reinforce the stereotypic picture of the contemporary protestor, or they may wish to be impartial but find more interest and local color in the unusual types than in the straight housewives with children. I have seen many demonstrations in person and watched them later on television. In talking with the television crews more often than not I find them sympathetic to the causes of the demonstrators. However, they feel their job is to capture the exciting, "newsworthy" events and people. Thus, when I watch the demonstration later at home, I notice that more violent confrontations have occurred than I noted in person. I recall that the only time the cameras were running was when an "incident" occurred. Five such incidents—during a five-hour demonstration—are strung out, end on end, in the news, making the day seem terribly violent to the viewer who has only television coverage as his source of information. This selective view may either create new attitudes or reinforce old ones.

Another media reinforcement involves the support and maintenance of existing ideology. If popular presentations of social situations are represented consistently in the same manner—as, for example, in family situation comedies—a certain system of values may be reinforced in the viewers. If father is always represented as incompetent while mother has the family's brains—or if father is the noble, staunch head of the household and mother is a featherbrained little housewife—this may both create and reinforce particular family patterns. Likewise, the manner of presenting sex roles, male-female relationships, cultural heroes, cultural villains, and so forth, can sustain and reinforce the status quo rather than challenge the existing ideology. Until a few years ago the movies and television never showed even a married couple in bed together. To some extent their representation of married couples in single beds reinforced, and to some extent it reflected, a puritanical sexual morality. For the most part television still does; but it gradually has become difficult to find a movie that doesn't have everyone in bed together.

Racial roles, even in these days of more "enlightened" media, tend more to reinforce traditional stereotypes than to introduce new forms. Although you will undoubtedly not find the shuffling Negro houseboy role depicted much anymore, you are still likely to find a basic dishonesty in the way in which racial roles are handled. For example, an upper-middle-class white family situation is created and Negroes play the parts. Or racial incidents may be handled so gingerly and unrealistically that no challenge to the dominant societal values ever appears.

Support of the political status quo is yet another possibility. If books, magazines, television, and movies present a dominant political and economic theme (e.g., hard work makes anyone a success; big business protects free enterprise; big government threatens democracy) it is likely that these representations reinforce the status quo rather than introduce elements of change. In fact, the less daring the media, the less likely new elements are to be introduced that challenge old ways and old philosophies.

Television dramatizations have almost always portrayed small-time individual crime or organized Mafia-like crime, but have ignored the crimes of government and of business. Business, for example, may earn large profits while polluting the water and air; state governments may maintain segregated schools in violation of Federal laws. These crimes may receive some small news coverage, but are rarely considered in the popular crime series. A viewer thus might come to think of a criminal either as a gangland mobster or as some poor devil who has lost control for a moment. Occasionally, of course, we get the romantic view of the daring young criminal-hero, always robbing from the rich, sometimes giving to the poor. These representations reinforce a particular concept of America's criminal element and a particular theory of crime.

Media Differences. Media differ among themselves both in their audiences and in the kind of representation they typically allow. Television news coverage, for example, attempts to depict incidents visually, leaving commentary and analysis to a bare minimum. The person who gets his information primarily from television, therefore, is likely to get only a surface perspective. This is especially important when we realize that studies of voting behavior have shown that television has now become the main source of political information for the U. S. voter (Campbell, 1968). Even newspapers have limited space to devote to intensive analysis of situations and events. Often they seek to sell copies by playing up the sensational, so a crime may be gruesomely detailed while a political or social issue may receive only surface attention. Magazines and books, on the other hand, usually can afford greater depth of coverage, and since they do not come into one's living room uninvited, as television and radio do, they can afford to be more flexible, more open, more controversial, and freer to cater to a more limited range of audience.

I have so far left out of this discussion of media differences McLuhan's (1964) provocative, though puzzling, analysis of *hot* versus *cool* media. McLuhan defines hot media as those with an overabundance of information, which thereby require little participation; cool media, on the other hand do not have much information and therefore call on a considerable amount of individual participation. He considers radio, movies, photographs, and lectures hot; television, seminars, the telephone, and cartoons cool. For McLuhan the rapid growth of television indicates a movement in the society toward coolness, which for him "retribalizes" modern man and makes the world a global village. Thus the postindustrial modern era in McLuhan's theory is understood as a function of a change in the media of communications. In addition to difficulty in determining criteria for classifying media as hot or cool, I find it a troublesome oversimplification to attribute to the media, especially television, the entire motive force behind social change. McLuhan's ideas, nevertheless, offer a provocative manner of viewing media effects and in particular differences between several of the mass media.

Not only do media differ among themselves, but in addition different media attract different audiences. Studies of the political impact of media have indicated that magazine readers, as compared with television viewers, radio listeners, or newspaper readers, are better educated, rely on more diversified media (use other media in addition to magazines), show greater familiarity with political issues, are more willing to take sides and express opinions on political matters, and are more likely to be concerned with U. S. involvement in international affairs (see Key, 1961). Even within each medium an individual has further choice. He can examine the *Reader's Digest* or turn to the *New Republic*; he can read the *New York Times* or some flashier, sensation-oriented newspaper. And within each of these he may further select material to which he wishes to attend. He may read only the sports page; or turn to the business section; or he may find the editorial page more to his liking.

In any case it is possible for an individual to choose media and parts of media that suit his tastes and reinforce rather than challenge his views. Whenever he encounters that horror of dissonant information, he can flip to his favorite rag or tune in his favorite commentator and have his original views bolstered. Moreover, as we noted on p. 173ff., selectivity does not occur simply to avoid dissonance, but rather encompasses a life style, importantly influenced by educational and social background. A stock-broker is more likely to read the *New Yorker* than is a mechanic, who may prefer the *Reader's Digest* or *Life*. This is not necessarily because they are trying to avoid an encounter with dissonant information; rather, these are differences in taste having roots in educational and social factors.

Even if a person selects a particular medium, he may feel somewhat dubious about its actual validity as an objective source of information. One study (reported by Rivers, 1965) indicated that 50 percent of a sample trusted television as a source, whereas newspapers were rated as trustworthy by only 23 percent; 42 percent ranked newspapers first as media *not* to be trusted in political matters. Thus, even when a person watches television and reads newspapers, he may selectively reinforce his views by rejecting contradictory information that he feels to be untrustworthy. In any case, individual selectivity makes it difficult for the media to be more effective.

Prevention of Defection. The media can be said to have a bolstering or reinforcing effect in any number of ways. A political campaigner may feel that he cannot reach the audience he needs to change, but uses the media to guarantee that there will be no defections among those already interested in him. Likewise, a commercial sponsor may have less hope that persons will switch from *A* to *B* than hope that those who already use *B* will not be swayed to use *A*. Prevention of defection, then, is another potentially important reinforcing effect.

This function is especially important in planned change. Assume that a change agent has been successful in producing a change in a group's attitude or practice. As you are by now well aware, the maintenance of this change is as important as is its induction; the media can help support it. Say a sensitivity-group procedure is employed to get smokers to stop smoking. The group meets, analyzes why each person smokes, and makes a group decision to try to stop for a period of one week. The next evening Mr. Puffer is sitting and watching the telly, fidgeting nervously in his chair, dying to grab a soothing cigarette. He feels torn between

this surging need on one hand and the commitment he has made to the group on the other. Then he sees a series of commercials by the American Cancer Society. They combine fear-arousing appeals with a variety of other approaches, all designed to get people to stop smoking. Although the commercials as such may not induce change, in Mr. Puffer's case they may provide just enough support to help him get through one more nonsmoking day.

It is important to keep in mind that although we have offered instances primarily of positive reinforcement, the media can also negatively reinforce; they can *undermine* a change that has occurred, for example, by tempting one with the delights and pleasures of smoking. They can provoke defections as well as prevent them. If another politician mounts a particularly exciting, attention-grabbing, and seductive campaign, he may in fact induce defections from the first. This we would consider a *conversion*; it involves a change from *A* to *B*. The media can introduce doubts in the mind of a voter who has already decided for whom to vote but is not firm in his choice. They can likewise undermine *P*'s confidence in his beliefs, negatively reinforcing them before inducing conversion.

During the 1960 presidential election between Kennedy and Nixon, popular opinion had it that the debates cost Nixon the election by attracting Republican voters to Kennedy. A study of that election by Campbell, Converse, Miller, and Stokes (see Rivers, 1965, pp. 14–15), however, indicates that the debates were relatively ineffectual in changing *committed* Democrats or *committed* Republicans; each felt his own candidate did quite well. Kennedy did lure the still-sizable proportion of independent voters almost two to one. Among the decided voters Nixon was leading; Kennedy's last-minute surge among the undecided carried the election for him. If media effects are related to change in this case, we note their general ineffectiveness among true believers and their relative effectiveness among the undecided. If reinforcement effects were examined systematically, however, they might have shown how the debates helped firm up both Kennedy's and Nixon's support and kept defections from occurring.

Minor changes and conversion effects

Klapper (1960) differentiates minor change as an effect of the media and actual conversion from *A* to *B*. A minor change occurs if someone's position on a given issue is "neutralized" by the impact of the media; a conversion occurs if the media actually manage to get someone to vote Republican rather than Democrat or to switch from Camels to Brand *X*. An anecdotal account of what sounds like a conversion effect appeared in *Newsweek* (May 1969). Ridicule directed at Youngstown, Ohio, on a popular comedy show (*Laugh In*) reportedly changed the public's vote on a school tax increase. The media made this city a national joke for its refusal to vote a tax increase and the subsequent closing of its schools. Youngstown citizens did not relish being the butt of such a joke, so they went out and voted a tax increase by a margin of some 7000 votes. *Newsweek* indicated that persons who were antitax at this time (they had been in the majority before the media took them to humorous task) kept quiet lest they be run out of town.

In general, conversion effects such as the preceding are rare. Unfortunately, however, systematic studies that examine the effects of media exposure over time have not been undertaken. Simple before-after studies may not turn up conversions as an immediate consequence of exposure, but it is conceivable that follow-ups over time would indicate sleeper effects. Constant repetition over a long time also might eventually break down an individual's resistance to maintaining a given position, ripening him for a conversion (see Zajonc, 1968). Repetition in a setting that controls all other sources of information input, that derives from sources that are both highly prestigeful and credible, surely will weaken even the heartiest of souls. The massive spectacles of Nazi Party rallies catered primarily to those who were already true believers, so their effects were mainly reinforcing (Burden, 1967). Yet an antagonistic spectator, seeing the near-hypnotic quality of the pageantry, sensing the symbolic strength that the movement conveyed through its massive architectural structures, and noting the hordes of dedicated followers shouting their loyalty to their *Führer*, might have moved slightly toward conversion to this apparent tide of the future.

Narcotization effects

A media effect discussed by Lazarsfeld and Merton (1948) but not included in Klapper's array of effects is *narcotization*; the media so inundate our senses that rather than becoming aroused to action we become hypnotized, confused, and eventually apathetic. As the flood of information rises, we may come to believe that being knowledgeable is sufficient, that action taken in support of that knowledge is irrelevant. So we sit home reading the newspaper and watching television, absorbing great quantities of information, but never acting. An alternative to narcotization has been called *privatization* (Larsen, 1964). Here an individual is so overwhelmed by the media that he turns inward to areas of his personal life and ignores the massive and unceasing displays of advertising, news, entertainment, and so on. He may turn to private thoughts or sit hypnotically entranced.

If narcotization and privatization are effects of the media on an individual, we would not expect minor change, conversion, or, for that matter, reinforcement to take place. We might look at these effects as unintended creations of the mass media, more functional perhaps to an individual who is struggling to keep his world in order and under some control than to the media entrepreneurs and their clients. How distressing it would be for a political campaigner to find that his extensive use of the media has brought about a well-informed but narcotized public who forget to vote for him on election day.

INDIRECT EFFECTS

Much of our discussion so far has focused on media effects that reach the recipient, in particular the general public, directly from the source. Indirect effects are those that eventually reach the public after passing through one or more other avenues or channels.

Opinion makers

One such indirect effect involves what Lazarsfeld, Berelson, and Gaudet (1948) have called the *two-step* flow of communication. In step one the media directly influence certain key persons in a community; these are opinion leaders or *influentials*. Step two involves *personal influence* by which these influentials personally effect a change in the opinion and behavior of others in their community; the public is reached by the media indirectly through the opinion leaders. Lazarsfeld et al. studied the 1940 presidential election in Erie County, Ohio, noting that most persons who changed their votes claimed that this change had been influenced by personal contacts with friends and associates. Recall that a change in our reference groups can effect a change in us. Although the media may not hit us directly, they may hit those in a group to whom we turn for our information and opinion validation, and thereby indirectly reach us.

Key (1961) summarizes some relevant data on personal influence and the two-step communications flow. It is possible to classify persons as *convincers* (they try to convince others of their opinions) or *advisers* (others ask for their advice), and to compare both groups with all others in terms of exposure to media as a source especially of political information. Only 9 percent of these groups sought information from friends; 29 percent of other persons did so. Whereas 63 percent of the convincers and advisers obtained information from the media, only 41 percent of the others did so. Thus there is some evidence for a group of influentials who get their main information from the media and pass it on to others more ready to use personal sources for information. Other studies have suggested that the flow of communication runs downward in a status hierarchy. Persons low in occupation and education tend to call on those somewhat higher for their information; those in higher positions use the media.

As Key noted, if we assume a two-step flow to be important, especially in political matters, it becomes increasingly relevant to uncover the characteristics of the influentials. Data from national surveys in 1950 suggest that persons of high political activity are scattered through all economic levels; however, in comparing the very actives with the very inactives, the upper strata appear to be more politically active. Furthermore, although all educational levels are represented by persons who talk to others about political matters, within each level those who are more exposed to the media do more talking in an effort to convince others. The evidence, then, does not indicate a single set of political influentials, but rather points to potential opinion leaders in each economic and educational stratum. There is an indication that those who try to be influential are in more contact with the media.

The media elite

Another way of looking at the influentials is to focus on differentials within the leadership itself. A two-step model is undoubtedly an oversimplification. Picture a model in which certain media and certain persons are more highly regarded as primary sources; these would be *true influentials*. They in turn influence a second or third line of influentials who represent *other media*. The flow moves from these secondary or tertiary sources to community leaders and thence via personal influence to the public. In essence, then, there exists a hierarchy of influentials and opinion makers in the media itself. Rivers (1965) reports several ratings by media personnel that shed some helpful light on this more refined picture. Correspondents were asked to rate newspapers other than their own that they relied on most often in their own work. In surveys both in the 1930's and in the 1960's the *New York Times*, the *Washington Post*, and the *Washington Star* were the highest ranked, with the *Times* far and away the most influential newspaper source for other correspondents. Newspapers were also rated on fairness and reliability. Again the *Times* topped the list; interestingly enough, whereas about 70 percent reported using the *Washington Post* in their work (in the 1960's), only 15 percent reported it as fair and reliable.

A similar ranking of magazines indicated that *Time* was consistently rated at the top of the *use* list in both surveys. The top three in the 1960's study included *Time, U. S. News and World Report*, and *Newsweek*. Comparatively, however, there was more consensus by media men about newspapers than about magazines; the reason emerges when we note that reliability and fairness ratings of the magazines were very low. As Rivers points out, many correspondents interviewed commented that although they might read the magazines, they considered few to be trustworthy sources of information. Twenty-four percent did not list any magazine as fair or reliable; 17 percent wrote that none was fair or reliable. Seventy-five correspondents listed *Newsweek* as the fairest, whereas *Time*, although regularly read by about 34 percent of the mediamen, received only nine votes for fairness.

Within the newspaper and magazine world there are individuals who form an elite. In particular, Walter Lippmann and James Reston were ranked highly in Rivers' analysis of the nation's political opinion makers. On the television front, Rivers found David Brinkley one of the elite influentials; Walter Cronkite and Eric Sevareid were likewise generally held in high esteem. *Time* and columnist Drew Pearson were both highly influential and outcasts among professionals.

Diffusion

Anthropologists and sociologists have been interested in the phenomenon of *diffusion*, whereby one society picks up the innovations of another, or innovators within one society spread the innovation throughout the entire society. Diffusion of invention, technology, and symbolic and ritualistic material has been of special interest. In most cases diffusion from one culture to another occurs as travelers bring back to their homeland ideas or inventions picked up elsewhere. Early exploration of the Americas, for example, facilitated the introduction of tobacco and smoking throughout the European continent. Diffusion of innovation by culture contact of this sort is thought to be a major contributor to social change in a society; and new technology may be introduced more rapidly by this means than by evolutionary development within the society. The introduction of the trappings of Western civilization to the far outposts of primitive civilization have often radically altered those societies, at times beneficially, at times disastrously. World War II contacts between American GI's and certain natives of

Micronesia left behind in residue *cargo cults* (See Burridge, 1960; Worsley, 1957). Natives waited longingly for their planeload of Western technology to arrive and save them. But the planes never came.

A somewhat amusing example of culture contact and diffusion is reported by the anthropologist Hoebel (1966). As was their custom, American missionaries sought to bring their brand of enlightenment to otherwise "poor but humble savages." In western New Guinea they sought to discourage the native practice of cannibalism by introducing the more civilized practice of eating canned goods. The natives soon came to learn that a tin with the picture of a bean on the outside meant beans on the inside, that a pear outside meant pears inside. One fine day shortly after one of the missionaries' wives had given birth, the natives saw a jar of Gerber's baby food being served; and on the jar there was pictured a healthy young baby. Need we guess the natives' assumptions about the missionaries' favorite foods?

In general, the concepts employed by sociologists and anthropologists interested in the study of diffusion have much in common with those we have just reviewed in our discussion of the two-step flow of communication. Katz, Levin, and Hamilton (1963) offer a useful definition of the process of diffusion that highlights some of these concepts and important dimensions:

"Viewed sociologically, the process of diffusion may be characterized as the (1) *acceptance*, (2) *over time*, (3) of some specific *item*—an idea or practice, (4) by individuals, groups, or other *adopting units,* linked (5) to specific *channels* of communication, (6) to a *social structure*, (7) to a given system of values, or *culture*" (p. 240).

We can apply this concept of the diffusion process to a relatively contemporary example: the fashions, music, and life style of the hip community of the middle and late 1960's.

1. *Acceptance.* This is commonly taken as the dependent variable in diffusion studies: *who* adopts the practice or the idea, and *when*. The innovators in this case began in the mid 1960's in San Francisco and to some extent in New York City (although we could argue that the "true" beginning was in England). The media got hold of the concept of "hippie" in early 1967, spreading it around so that by September of that year general-circulation magazines such as the *Saturday Evening Post* ran feature stories and cover articles on "The Hippie Cult." Meanwhile, the folk music and rock tradition that had begun to swell during the late 1950's grew and changed in the 1960's, with the rise of Bob Dylan, the Beatles, and the San Francisco sound marking highpoints in the "new music" that became associated with this growing cult of the young. In addition to magazine stories about the hippie cult in 1967, the airwaves carried the music; soon television and movies showed personalities who sported the clothing, styles, and language of "the movement." Not long thereafter, Americans in general began to acquire the accoutrements of hippiedom. The broader acceptance of long hair, sideburns, beads, medallions, and bright colors for men occurred quickly after the media publicized the innovators' message. The early acceptors were mostly the young; but style in dress and dance caught on even among those over thirty.

2. *Over time.* Transmission of innovation takes some time. Anthropological studies of culture contact and innovation often take years, often generations, as do sociological studies of the spread of technological innovation. The mass media, however, condense the time factor to a bare minimum for some kinds of innovation, especially nontechnical symbolic and cultural matters. The diffusion of certain of the items of hippiedom, especially clothing, music, and personal appearance, spread out rapidly from the innovators, via the media, to the acceptors. If we assume that the hippie innovators surfaced in 1966, then the media carried the ideas to the population of acceptors after about one year. It is interesting to note that even though beards and very long hair on males had not achieved widespread acceptance even by 1970, sideburns, moustaches, and hair longer than crewcut had become distinctly fashionable.

3. *Specific item.* In most cases of technical diffusion the specific item is relatively easy to identify; clothing and personal appearance are a particularly noticeable and relevant item in this case. Music is another relevant cluster of items. Life style and attitudinal variables, which form important items in the cluster that was picked up by the media and spread around the nation, are usually much more difficult to pinpoint and to define. The middle-class use of drugs, especially marijuana, also forms an important part of this cluster. We could expect that, as with diffusion in general, the diffusion of hippiedom's items depended on such factors as ease of communicability and the risk involved in their adoption. Items that were directly observable—such as dress and personal appearance—could be more readily diffused than any of the vaguer attitudinal and life-style items. And items of apparel are less risky to adopt than are certain practices like smoking marijuana.

4. *Units of adoption.* The unit of adoption may vary widely. A single individual may respond to the call of hippiedom, or an entire society may find itself caught up in the acceptance of certain major items that have diffused from the centers of innovation. In the example we are examining I think it is safe to say that much of society has experienced the infusion of many items of this innovative movement.

5. *Channels of communication.* As suggested in the discussion of the two-step flow of communication, influentials or innovators are tuned in to mass media while others are tuned in to group values and personal influence. Much the same fits the example we are discussing. Some persons were turned on by television; others awaited their friends' gentle or vigorous push before deciding to go along and try out the new fashions and perhaps even the new life style.

6. *Social structure.* As Katz, Levin, and Hamilton point out, the structure of a group, a community, or a society offers boundaries or limits within which diffusion spreads. Some practices do not spread across lines of social class or education; others easily pass through these boundaries. Other practices are limited by age-grading within a society; children may find rapture in a Hula-Hoop, for example, but adults may not be comparably influenced. Professional and occupational boundaries likewise provide limits to diffusion. These structural limits apply both to receiving an innovative practice or idea and to accepting it.

In the diffusion of hippiedom we have a case of the young spreading a practice to young and to old, in reverse of the direction we commonly—though erroneously—expect for the transmission of new practices. Age does, however, establish some boundaries. We also find class limits to the diffusion; if anything, the hippie style marks the middle and upper-middle classes rather than those lower on the socio-economic ladder. Even within the adoptor classes, occupational boundaries provide further restrictions. Stockbrokers, insurance salesmen, bank managers, and the military seem to be among the last holdouts. Yet even they have been seen in public with inching sideburns and an occasional moustache, and, shocking as it may seem, a fringe of brightly daring color.

7. Values. As Katz and his colleagues note, there is an issue of the degree of fit or compatibility between the items of the innovation and the group's, the society's, or even the individual's values. *Selective borrowing* is a concept from anthropological investigations; one culture does not adopt everything from another, but rather picks and chooses in terms of the compatibility of the new practices with the ongoing system. Similarly, we would expect an individual to accept a new practice that fits his values more readily than he would be willing to adopt something entirely new and alien to him.

Many styles and customs of hippiedom are compatible to a substantial number of young persons but at the same time alien to the older generation. For example, older persons, who worked hard in hard times to get to their present positions, could not easily understand a value that dismissed routine work and called for each to do his own thing. They felt obliged to do their duty, their work, and to deny themselves their inner passions in order to get ahead. On the other hand, for a group of reasonably affluent young persons, the idea of hard work as an essential in life was itself foreign. Many grew up in conditions that did not demand that they work to get ahead; nor would many of them easily be able to find work even if they wished to do so. They were the generation of tomorrow, when more leisure time would be available and when hard work as a criterion of a man's worth would be meaningless; thus they were more predisposed than their elders to adopt the new outlook being diffused.

In many other ways the diffusion of hippiedom ran counter to or was congruent with societal, communal, and organizational values. Long hair, which many persons associated with femininity, was not easily diffused to those who maintained that older system of beliefs. Those who were younger and not yet fully integrated into a system that equated hair length with sexual identity found the adoption of long hair relatively easier; at least it did not run counter to their personal values, even though they undoubtedly encountered much opposition from their elders. We might also note that for the generation that grew up on the music of Lawrence Welk, that grooved to Kostelanetz and to Mantovani and his 1000 violins, and that found salvation in Scotch or bourbon, Dylan, the Beatles, the San Francisco sound and the use of drugs rather than alcohol were incompatibilities nearly impossible to overcome. In essence, the more a person is wedded to one value system, the more difficult it is to change in response to the diffusion of innovation.

Indirect media effects: The third party

I would now like to introduce a different perspective on indirect media effects. In this case P is affected directly by the decision-making power of O; O's decisions, however, are influenced by what he assumes to be a direct and potent relationship between the media and P. Picture a not-uncommon situation in which the relationship between the decision leaders (O) of a community or a society and the public (P) they presumably serve is mediated by a third party, the media. O reaches P through the media, while P reaches O through public-opinion polls, letter-writing campaigns, and eventually the vote on election day. A congressman, for example, may be very sensitive to the thinking of his constituents; he learns about their views primarily from opinion surveys and from letters they write to him. The media bring the congressman's activities back to the public. His image is represented, his opinions are aired or written about.

The media in this situation serve a *controlling* function. The congressman is concerned about the impact on his constituents of the media representations of his stands and policies; he may feel compelled to modify his behavior to conform to his assumptions about his constituency. We can say that he assumes the media to have a greater impact on his public than they actually may have; thus its controlling influence over him is based on a type of *pluralistic ignorance*. The term describes a situation in which no one believes, but everyone believes that everyone else believes. In an early study reported by Schanck (1932), for example, the residents of a small town all believed that the church norms that dictated against smoking, card playing, and drinking were shared by everyone in their town. However, in fact, most persons in the town did not adhere to these beliefs in their own homes. Breed and Ktsanes (1961) examined this notion of pluralistic ignorance in the context of southern segregation. Within certain limits they found that persons generally felt others in their community to be very conservative on the integration issue, although the real attitudes uncovered were not so conservative.

The congressman's pluralistic ignorance involves his assumption that the media affect the public to such a degree that it is ready to pounce on every wrong move. The media presence serves, therefore, to provide boundaries or limits to his activities in the political arena.

Much this same media role exists in national and international politics. The opening quotations in this chapter recall the role Hearst's massive publicity campaign played in locking President McKinley into a war with Spain. Political decision makers are constrained in their actions by media that publicize items that may force a premature hardening of positions. Thus the media generally are barred from secret negotiations to avoid public feedback. Later, however, they are courted, for once an issue is settled and a press statement is framed in language designed to appeal to the public, they become an essential vehicle for politicians to gain access to the public. In Vietnam peace negotiations the fear was that the public would not take kindly to any aspects of the negotiating that made either side seem to have lost face. Negotiators therefore sought to keep such information from the public until it could be put forth as a *fait accompli* in some palatable form.

Even though the founding fathers of the United States were personally hesitant about disclosing the processes that took place during the Constitutional Convention of 1787, most of them felt a free and open press was essential to the democratic society they were bringing into being. The media, then, offer some degree of assurance that the public's views will enter the circle of influence of each community or societal decision maker. This public opinion may force a decision that is more punitive than might otherwise have emerged—as with repressive legislation directed against campus protests— or it may force a leader to withdraw from a course of action that he would otherwise pursue. Public opinion about the Vietnam War compelled one president to step down and not run again and set limits on his successor's ability to escalate the war or seek a military victory. In each case the media kept the public informed.

During the antiballistic missile discussions of 1969, Senate committees that were opposed to a large monetary investment in an ABM system held public hearings: they broadcast live on television. The coverage in other media was extensive. Regardless of whether there was any real impact of these public hearings on opinion, decision makers thought they were important enough that those supporting the ABM had to stage their own hearings. Once again, even though actual public interest and opinion formation may have been minor, each side eagerly sought to use the media to reach the public and thereby to convince their colleagues in Congress and the President that the public did or did not want an ABM system. If what we know from other studies applies in the ABM case as well, we would expect those already opposed to watch one set of hearings, and those already in favor to watch the other set. In other words, we would not expect major conversions in public opinion; reinforcement of opinion and perhaps some creation of new opinion is likely. Yet it is not so much the *reality* of the media's impact that moves the decision makers as it is their *assumption* of a significant impact. In an important sense, therefore, the assumed effects of the media in shaping public opinion can override the reality of their effects; in this way they enter as a third party, with consequences for behavior and attitudes well beyond those encompassed by the usual study of direct or indirect, two-step media effects.

MEDIA IN POLITICS

Clearly implied in the previous discussion is another tack that the investigator of the media can take: examine the use of the media by those who wish to create change in a society. Whether they base their actions on illusion, reality, or parts of each, most political decision makers (and many members of the public as well) grant a considerable degree of power to the media. The press and television in particular have come to occupy a vital position in U. S. politics matching in that realm their already significant role in advertising and general entertainment. Rivers' account (1965) of the Washington press corps and of the relationship between Congress and the press provides more than ample testimony to the power of the media:

"Naturally, the Washington press corps also has the trappings of power. Privileged as no other citizens are, the correspondents are listed in the *Congressional Directory*; they receive advance copies of speeches and announcements and read documents forbidden to high officials; quarters are set aside for them in all major government buildings, including the White House; special sections are reserved for their use in the House and Senate galleries and elsewhere in the Capitol. In all, fantastic quantities of government time and money are devoted to their needs, desires, and whims. There are White House correspondents who talk with President Johnson more often than do his own party leaders in the House and Senate; there are Capitol correspondents who see more of the Congressional leaders than do other Congressmen" (p. 19).

The picture that emerges, then, is of the media standing between various persons and agencies of decision-making power, a linkage that provides avenues of communication and interpretation. Lest we so easily forget, the media are not simply a conveyor belt, moving information from one locale to another; rather, they select, interpret, emphasize, omit, commit, and in any number of ways *create* as well as *convey* information.

Media control: News and image management

With the media occupying so central and so significant a position in public affairs, it is no wonder that individuals or groups who can control the media, or at minimum control their own representation in the media, become very powerful indeed. But it turns out here, as in so many other aspects of life, that more power goes to those who already possess power.

It is far easier for a man who is already in power to obtain media coverage and to *stage* his performances than it is for a man or group on the bottom. At the bottom of the social hierarchy, one gets media interest by being outrageous or at least somewhat destructive. At the top one gets media coverage through more benign means: public speeches and press conferences rather than riots in the street.

Let us not imagine that access to the media is equated with control over the media. Media control as I use the term in this discussion refers either to *news management* (e.g., controlling the news items that reach the press and/or their timing) or *impression management* (e.g., controlling the representation of one's public image). Presidents and their staffs have recently developed as specialists in the field of news management. Nor are they slouches when it comes to managing the impression they convey in media coverage.

News Management. Rivers (1965) suggests that modern news management came into its own under the able hands of Franklin Roosevelt. He cites Lincoln, however, as no mean manager when he waited more than two months for the proper moment to announce his Emancipation Proclamation. Timing becomes one manner by which a public official can control news, "orchestrating relations with the Washington correspondents, both courting and commanding them" (Rivers, 1965, p. 132). FDR began an important tradition that subsequent presidents have followed: the Washington press conference. He likewise made extensive use of the radio, especially in his reassuring "fireside chats," when each American could feel himself to be an intimate of the President. FDR managed the news by dominating the news, by controlling the glimpses that the public gained of him, by courting reporters through his press conferences.

Truman continued the press conferences; his vigorous, uncourtly, but direct manner showed a spirit that little men everywhere found appealing. Eisenhower sought to control the media by staging nonspontaneous press conferences and by concealing himself behind a professional staff of news aides and television directors. Kennedy returned to Washington a tradition of live and spontaneous conferences, and at the same time earned himself a place in the history of presidential news managers. Eisenhower had wanted press conferences taped so that they could be edited; Kennedy stood live before the press corps and the American public. Much of his popular image was carried by his wit and charm at these public gatherings. The Johnson years saw off-the-cuff conferences replace regularly scheduled formal ones, and with Nixon live but carefully staged coverage became the rule. In each case the president controlled the news. He is news, wherever he goes, whatever he does, whatever he says. If he chooses to speak live in the State Department auditorium or suddenly in a moment of sunshine in the White House rose garden, he has in his hands the media men and through them the public.

News management in the form of deliberate deception or occasional lying also marks the history of the American presidency. From Eisenhower's U-2 spy-plane incident to Kennedy's Bay of Pigs, presidents, sensing that media control gives power to shape public opinion, have sometimes sought to work in opposition to a free press. Kennedy, for example, urged the *New York Times* not to print a story that would reveal the Cuban Bay of Pigs invasion. No president or no government official, however has been shy in his efforts to assist the media in covering his own administration. After all, he thinks, who is better suited than he to interpret his policies and his actions?

A somewhat amusing example of news management and censorship involves the Greek government's effort to ban the West German weekly *Der Spiegel* in September 1968 (as reported in *Newsweek*, June 16, 1969). The government bought up all the newsstand copies. *Der Spiegel*, however, quickly replaced the copies, forcing the government to buy additional copies. The circulation of *Der Spiegel* rose threefold during that time, proving that some forms of censorship can be profitable after all.

Impression Management. Impression management in today's era of the instant candidate (just add television and a winning smile) has become every bit as important as the direct management of news content. Whether it swayed any votes is not known for a fact, but there were few reporters and subsequently few citizens who did not comment on the heavy shadow beard that Nixon sported during his televised debates with Kennedy in 1960. His television advisors and makeup men, entrusted with his image, failed to cover it up adequately with makeup. When they put on too much face powder the shadow was covered, but the man looked pale and sickly by comparison with the freshly tanned (chemically perhaps), healthful image of the young Kennedy.

Public relations firms now handle candidates on the campaign trail, and experts from television and the movies are responsible for maintaining images of elected officers (see McGinniss, 1969, for a revealing account of the management of a presidential candidate). Of special interest is that public relations firms not only handle the *personal image* that their man presents in the media and thence to the public, but also handle the *content themes* he will play up or play down. The business of psyching out the audience, a business learned by those in advertising, has moved into the political arena.

Lighting, makeup, staging, verbal presentations, style of dress, gestures, voice, you name it; all have become a fairly integral part of contemporary politics. No wonder, then, that those who made headline careers in Hollywood tend to think of themselves as politicians. In advertising a winning product is one that customers readily identify; so too in politics. If Crest toothpaste with Fluoristan can become a household word, why can't television and advertising make a candidate's name another household word? And it's easier to begin with someone whose name is already well known.

Too often we think of the political public today in the same terms those investigating media effects thought of it years ago. At that time the public was thought to be a passive recipient of media campaigns; today there is a comparably facile tendency to imagine that a public relations firm can make us buy almost anyone as president, governor, congressman, senator, or mayor. If there is anything we do know about the effects of media, it is that they are not simple, or direct, or the entire story. A candidate on television, for example, always risks coming off badly. No amount of paint or makeup or coaching can make a sow's ear look like a silk purse. On the other hand, the public often seems to want sow's ears; and these are readily forthcoming from the pens and wardrobe closets of PR firms.

In essence I am suggesting that the public is not easily fooled, by the media-borne image, into buying a candidate. Impression management can enhance positive features and play down negative ones; it can present the candidate in a good light as a family man, as one who likes children, as one who wanders among the people. It can help make a fool appear less foolish and an abtruse intellectual appear less wise and more earthy. But whether people buy candidates as they are said to buy products, on the basis of such packaging frills, as popular impression strongly suggests, or whether they buy on the basis of more substantive issues, remains a question not yet answered by systematic investigation. Although impression management is a vital part of politics today, it is my impression that the public chooses the best-packaged candidate whose substantive views represent a fulfillment of their needs.

THE BUSINESS OF THE MEDIA

It is so simple and self-evident that we sometimes forget that the media are business ventures in addition to whatever public service they may perform. As such, they not only enter as agents that affect public opinion but also as agents that are affected by public opinion. No business long endures that does not capture sufficient public interest to pay its way eco-

nomically. For most of the media the public's economic impact is through advertisers who buy space or time. Although a magazine or a newspaper may have many subscribers, it will soon fold unless it can capture advertisers willing to buy space to reach those subscribers. Costs are high; subscribers alone rarely suffice to cover such expenses. On television and radio sponsors are the vital ingredient that keep the business enterprise going. And sponsors are in business as well; they want the media to sell their products. They want to sponsor programs that provide a proper showcase for their products, programs whose image enhances theirs. As an FCC member once commented, "Many broadcasters are fighting *not* for *free* speech, but for *profitable* speech" (*San Francisco Chronicle*, July 5, 1965).

Television costs are enormous, profits potentially great. In 1965 the total advertising billing on the three major television networks was more than $1.6 billion; in 1964 CBS reported a net income of approximately $50 million (Aurthur, 1965). In the early days of television, it cost about $60,000 to produce a dramatic show; today those costs have risen to $100,000 or more per show. A television columnist (O'Flaherty, *San Francisco Chronicle*, May 7, 1969) reported that one episode of "Bonanza" cost $188,000 to make, *plus* $172,000 per hour for air time. Another show, "Bewitched" cost $85,000 to make and another $80,000 to get on the air. These are mid-1969 figures. Some estimates place the cost of a one-minute commercial in prime time (i.e., greatest audience coverage) at about $40,000. During 1965 and 1966 NBC reported earning over $27 million for the Huntley-Brinkley newscast alone. Sponsors, of course, footed the bill and allowed such earnings.

There is no wonder, then, that sponsors initially were vitally concerned about program content. Aurthur (1965), a novelist and playwright, reports his effort to do Kafka's *Metamorphosis* as a television show. The producer he approached with this idea was concerned with this type of show's advertising appeal; he wondered whether Aurthur could have the character change into a dog rather than a cockroach. The show aired in New York at 9 P.M. and on the West Coast at 6 P.M.; he felt that it might be offensive to viewers eating their dinner to deal with the transformation of a man into a cockroach.

The economic issues involving the media become especially critical when we attempt to uncover the relationship, if any, between economics and media control. I suppose the most blatant form of control that we can imagine is one that demands that editorial pages and news stories conform to a single party line. In the case of television there are governmental controls that attempt to guarantee fairness of news reporting; a station can lose its license to broadcast if it does not engage in some reasonable degree of political balance. News commentaries, however, although requiring equal time for opposing viewpoints, can offer direct expressions of the station's or the network's point of view. Blatant controls over the content of reporting are less likely than the application of more subtle controls. These can be efforts to slant news stories or to conceal important material while emphasizing other aspects of a situation. Television control can extend beyond news coverage and into the realm of entertainment and specials.

News distortion or slanting, whether from the wire services, television newscasts, or newspaper and magazine accounts, is something nearly all of us take for granted, even though detailed proof is not easy to obtain. Rivers (1965) reports a study done in the 1930's that indicated that 60 percent of the correspondents interviewed were aware of pressure on them to slant their stories; 55 percent indicated that they had actually had stories cut or modified for "policy" reasons. Even Lippmann indicated that some of his own early stories were entirely deleted after they were written.

In Rivers' view the heavy-handed editorial tyrants of yesteryear are no more. Even so, he reports, whereas the editorial position of most newspapers is Republican, most of the reportorial staff are independents or liberals. If you followed the editorial pages, then, in the seven presidential elections up to 1960 you would find a ratio of Republican to Democrat support of 3½ to 1. In news reporting, however, there are fewer reports of news slanting today than in the 1930's. In fact, Rivers reports in 1965 that

only 7 percent of reporters indicated that they had ever had a story modified or killed for reasons of editorial policy.

None of this should be taken to mean, however, that news slanting does not occur. Rather, the link between slanting and the economics of ownership seems less today than it was in the 1930's and before. Reporters remain human beings with the same kinds of selectivity biases we all possess. Some, in addition, may wish to garner the favor of their bosses, adding just another flavorful touch to their stories. In the main, slanting takes a form that Rivers outlines in the following contrast of a news story carried by AP and the same event covered by Baskin of the Washington Bureau of *Dallas Morning News*: AP reported, "Students picketing for peace marched four abreast. . ."; Baskin reported, "Left-wing student peace marchers— with a definite beatnik tinge—marched. . . ."

IN CONCLUSION

This chapter began with an example in which a nation was pushed to war by a provoking press. Throughout the chapter we have examined the range of effects as well as the limitations of the media in effecting change. Given what we have seen, should we burn the presses and switch off the television sets lest we be seduced by the media as Trilby was by Svengali or the U. S. by Hearst? I think not. It takes more than the media to light a fire under a nation's people. As one of several sources conspiring together, the media play out their intriguing role in affecting man and in changing his life and society. If anything, today, while most of the public pays homage to the vast wasteland, a few are moved to action by the rapid-fire images of poverty, war, hate, and injustice. The unintended effects of the media, joining as brothers persons separated by miles and custom, making your wars mine and my anguish yours, may yet inspire a people to mass action.

But have the media created the action? Or, rather, have they made it possible for time and space to become condensed so that we act in the knowledge that it is our *own* town that is now infected by an illness that needs immediate attention? In other words, may it be simply that the mass media have brought to our attention the ills that once were concealed or removed from our awareness? In 1898 Hearst used the press to help create a war with Spain by whipping up the sentiments of the public and thereby constraining avenues of peaceful diplomacy. In the 1930's Goebbels helped Hitler stage the Nuremberg rallies that laid the foundation for the Nazi takeover of Germany. Today the media may be laying the groundwork for the growth and maintenance of a self-conscious radical social movement. A volcano may exist in the midst of that wasteland.

Chapter 23

Social movements

Let me put my cards face up on the table before this game gets under way. In this chapter I plan to discuss some general points about collective behavior and some specific points about social movements as one form of collective activity. I plan to examine in detail the application of these points to two interrelated contemporary social movements: the radical student and Negro protest movements. I have personal experiences and definite points of view on both of these. I do not trust anyone who purports to discuss these controversial topics but disclaims bias or personal interest; indeed, it is difficult to live today without some opinions on students and blacks who protest.

Biases are usually a mixture of conscious knowns and a hodgepodge of more or less unconscious motives, dreams, and blinding defenses. The latter I cannot hope to talk about short of placing myself on the analyst's couch; the former I can hope to reveal, although incompletely: with the few reservations that any man of reasonable intelligence and good will must have, I rank myself among those who find hope in the visions of these two social movements. At times I was among those professors who actively joined and supported the protests around Berkeley; at other times I felt myself to be more a reporter observing the scene. In what is by now not an atypical collegiate ex-

perience, I have been tear-gassed, clubbed, punched, nearly arrested, threatened by phone and by letter, and in any number of other ways been involved as a participant-observer.

I write this chapter, then, not entirely from the outside as some presumably dispassionate observer might. Of course, I cannot really write entirely from the inside either, for after all, I am over 30; of a different generation, and thus not fully a part of the student movement; also, being white, I am not really a direct participant in the blacks' struggle. The advantages to a student of social movements that derive from being a spiritually (and at times physically) involved participant in my opinion far outweigh the disadvantages. One exchanges some spots of blindness, hopefully, for some otherwise unobtainable knowledge and sensitivity.

COLLECTIVE BEHAVIOR AND SOCIAL MOVEMENTS

It is no wonder that the study of collective behavior grew rapidly during the late 1960's. You needed only to turn on your radio, look at the evening news on television, examine the morning headlines, or perhaps even examine your own bruised body to bear witness to the fact that collective activity in the United States and around the world had risen to a peak. Summers

357

of strife in the central city were followed by school years of disruption on the campus and often in the surrounding community.

The traditional study of collective behavior, including panics, crowds, riots, and fads, followed a fairly descriptive, case-history methodology, which, however, did not meet the more rigorous demands for experimental science. Moreover, the *Zeitgeist* over the last several decades emphasized the more cognitive aspects of man's behavior and focused our attention away from collective behavior; such behavior was considered irrational and noncognitive.

Two developments helped to modify the purely cognitive emphasis and to offer a hospitable background for the study of collective behavior. First, noncognitive aspects of behavior began to show their gaudy heads in the legitimate circles of social-psychological inquiry. Increasingly, people were seen as more than dissonance-reducing logicians. Second, new theoretical accounts of collective behavior began to emerge; these versions offered a perspective that made greater sense out of the many forms of collective activity than did the earlier, less accepted theories.

Theories of collective behavior

Turner and Killian. Turner and Killian (1957) differentiate three theories of collective behavior: *contagion, convergence*, and *emergent-norm*. The contagion theory argues that collective behavior derives from the more or less automatic transmission and uncritical reception of moods and emotions from person to person. Le Bon's account (1896) of the crowd built on this idea; in a crowd an individual was thought to be relatively unthinking and irrational, to pick up the mood at hand and run raving through the streets. Convergence theory, somewhat akin to Freud's notions of group formation (1922), envisions a collection of persons who share similar qualities and have their attention captured by a common event or another person. A collective enterprise (e.g., a crowd or a lynch mob) develops as these persons focus on a common object of love or hate.

Turner and Killian's own emergent-norm theory places collective behavior in a less irrational framework. They argue that collective behavior, like all human behavior, occurs in a social context with its own norms and its own form of emergent social structure. Unlike contagion or convergence theory, emergent-norm theory allows for wide individual variation in the degree of activity, expression, and commitment in any collective phenomenon. For instance, some persons in a crowd are spectators, others are actors; some are highly committed to the activity, others merely curious or minimally committed; some have lost themselves in the flood, others have managed to retain full critical capacities. The notion is that pressures to conform to the norms that have emerged operate in collective behavior in much the same way such pressures operate in all forms of social and group behavior. It takes a courageous man, indeed, to resist the norms of a crowd in which he is caught up. According to emergent-norm theory, following the crowd need not be based on a loss of individual uniqueness or critical sense, but rather on conformity to group pressures of which the individual is critically aware and knowledgeable.

You can readily see that this view of collective behavior emphasizes its more rational aspects and at the same time places collective activity in much the same theoretical bag as other, known forms of social or group behavior. As such, it becomes less mysterious and more an integral part of social psychology.

Smelser's Value-Added Theory. Smelser's sociological account of collective behavior (1963) likewise places collective behavior more readily in the mainstream of social-psychological inquiry. Briefly at this point (we shall examine this view again later), Smelser offers a value-added theory of collective behavior, with six determinants. A value-added situation is somewhat like a production line; each step must be accomplished before the next one is possible. Each of Smelser's six determinants represents such a step or stage. All six together become sufficient cause for a collective episode to occur.

1. *Structural conduciveness.* Social conditions must permit a collective episode to occur. For example, before a riot or a campus demonstration occurs, there must be a population of individuals gathered in one spot. Their gathering by itself, however, is not sufficient to cause a collective outbreak.

2. *Structural strain.* Strain exists whenever there is a conflict between persons, between norms or values that groups maintain, or between persons and scarce resources.

3. *Growth and spread of beliefs.* Beliefs or ideology focus on the strain and justify action against an outgroup that is held to be responsible for the present predicament. The belief often spreads by rumor, which indicates both the source of the strain and the kinds of action necessary to overcome it.

4. *Precipitating factors.* A single incident, for example the arrest of a black by a group of white police, the shooting of a black, or the assumed rape by blacks of a white girl, can precipitate an outbreak of collective behavior, given the preceding conditions.

5. *Mobilization for action.* The existence of a crowd, strain, belief, and precipitation are not enough unless there is some leadership or direction that mobilizes the restless and milling collectivity into action.

6. *Social control.* Unlike the previous determinants, social control refers to the reaction of the establishment to the imminent outbreak. Rapid and strong control may nip a collective episode before it begins; delay in exercising control or weak control may permit the determinants to bubble into a full-blown crowd, panic, mob, or social movement.

It should be apparent even from this preliminary overview that Smelser's theory is sufficiently organized and systematic by comparison to earlier accounts (e.g., Le Bon's) to permit more rigorous investigation. Contributions like Smelser's and Turner and Killian's, therefore, facilitated the return of the study of collective behavior to a respectable place in several social-scientific disciplines.

The social movement: One form of collective behavior

The term collective behavior is offered in particular by Smelser and by Turner and Killian; others, for example Brown (1954), have referred to much the same activity by the term mass phenomena, and still others (e.g., Lang & Lang, 1961) have talked about collective dynamics.

In all cases the referent is the generally spontaneous actions of a collectivity that arise at particular points in time and for some time are in a state of flux, as differentiated from collective actions that are more routine or institutionalized, including stable groups, organizations, and institutions to which we all belong.

Although we could get caught up in the endless task of naming and classifying forms of collective behavior, carefully distinguishing crowds, publics, panics, fads, and social movements per se, I prefer to avoid that somewhat tedious and often fruitless activity, and concentrate entirely on the form of collective behavior that most authors agree to call a social movement. Toch (1965) defines a social movement as "an effort by a large number of people to solve collectively a problem that they feel they have in common" (p. 5). He emphasizes that social movements are directed toward either producing or resisting change, and, unlike crowds or panics, are relatively long in duration and have a purpose or change-oriented program to accomplish. In much the same way, Killian (1964) sees a social movement as the collective effort to bring about a cultural or social change and as having certain definite features, four of which he briefly outlines (p. 430): (1) a system of shared values, a program, or purpose for the existence of the movement; (2) a sense of belonging or "we-ness"; (3) a normative framework of rules concerning how members are to relate to one another and to those outside the movement; (4) structure, including a division of labor into "members" and "leaders."

What is apparent from these two conceptions of social movements is that we are dealing with a form of collective activity that is directed toward *producing change* in a society or *resisting* change; has a career *over time* and thus is relatively enduring, although not so stable or long-lasting initially as the institutionalized forms of society; has a *purpose, program*, or *goal* and an *ideology* that defines itself and its values; has a definable *structure of norms and functional roles*, although the structure usually lacks the stability of institutionalized social structures. Social movements, then, are not the mad, screaming, irrational mobs that Le Bon described or that most persons imagine. A movement may, however, evolve out of such less stable forms of collective behavior and, in turn, may use other such forms during its own life.

ANATOMY OF A SOCIAL MOVEMENT

If we examine the several efforts to deal either with social movements specifically or collective behavior in general, we notice certain key similarities. I think it helpful if we group these key factors into three clusters: *origins, structure* or *organization*, and *career* or *life history* of a social movement.

Origins

Although a casual observer might feel that a social movement has arisen spontaneously and without apparent cause, to an experienced analyst the origins of any social movement must be seen against the background context a society provides. Smelser (1963) calls our attention to structural conduciveness and structural strain as two relevant background determinants. Toch (1965) emphasizes the existence of a problem on one hand and a state of susceptibility on the other, so that people come to feel that their action can alleviate the problem. Turner and Killian (1957) similarly trace the genesis of a social movement to the existence of unsatisfied needs that produce shared frustrations among a group of people and lead to a vision of a better state that is possible and to organization to attain that vision.

The imperfections of a stable social order and the variable processes of socialization whereby we enter society create numbers of persons who experience frustrations and unsatisfied needs. During periods of rapid social change this problem-bound cadre increases. When individuals realize that they share their problems with others, a state of political consciousness has evolved. A change-oriented social movement can develop from this consciousness. Structural conduciveness, in Smelser's theory, can facilitate or hinder the development of this common consciousness. In a society where all its parts are in touch, for example, through the mass media, distant souls join easily into one potential body. Likewise,

a large congregation of persons, as in a ghetto or a university, brings individuals into direct personal contact who may soon come to see themselves as sharing a common source of frustration.

Beyond the shared consciousness, however, lies an organization and a vision, a hope that joint action can alleviate the problem and produce satisfaction. A body of frustrated persons, each of whom notes that he and others stand on common ground, will not evolve into a movement until they also share a common vision and a sense of *efficacy*; a sense that change is possible and that their organized actions can bring about a new and better world. Frustration can lead to apathy and withdrawal as well as to activism; the vision and the sense of efficacy make one man fight while another, without these assets, gives up and retires.

In his account of his efforts to organize migratory farm workers in California during the 1960's, Cesar Chavez points out several of these essential elements in his own movement (see Matthiessen, 1969). He began his serious organizing efforts with workers in the Delano, California, area, not because they were the worst off economically, but because they were the least transient of the grape workers in the state and as such could be organized more easily. Chavez notes that the fact that they were the best paid of the farm workers (averaging $2400 per year) itself was a helpful organizing device. Had they been less well off—and understand that $2400 a year does *not* make a man with a wife and family very well off at all—they would have been too desperately poor to be inclined to act: "unlike people who have glimpsed a spark of hope, the destitute are often too defeated to revolt" (Matthiessen, 1969, p. 46).

Structure

Although a social movement may be less neatly organized than a typical social institution, and although it may lack any great degree of differentiation of structure, there are still several structural features of a social movement that we can examine. In particular, it is helpful to consider the structure in terms of leaders and members and in terms of norms and ideology.

Leaders. Those who have sought to understand social movements of the past have differentiated several types of leadership. A leader is a man who is able to take a crowd of like-minded individuals and build their mass dissatisfactions and frustrations into a movement with a program, values, goals, and activities. Killian (1964) specifies three main types: *charismatic, administrative*, and *intellectual.*

A charismatic leader captures the vision of the movement in his very being. He is worshipped almost as a god, embodying the essence of each man's hopes and dreams. Hitler, Gandhi, and Martin Luther King held their followers together by their strong charismatic quality. Persons outside a movement tend to define it entirely in terms of this charismatic leader. He comes to represent for everyone, both inside and out, the meaning of the entire movement. He builds his strength, and the strength of his movement, on his character and, as importantly, on the grand or dramatic gesture, the bold move. Showmanship in the best sense of the term is his forte; he uses his intuitive talents to clarify the muddied, to simplify the complex, to resolve the nagging questions that many still have. In his presence there can be no doubt. His pure feeling, pure intuition, pure subjectivity, rings true each time. King's bus boycott and later his Selma march were precisely the gestures that captured the moment and won the hearts of his followers. His strength, his courage, his gestures became theirs. They were at one with him in his life and even in his martyr's death.

An administrator is a leader whom Killian describes as a pragmatist. He is concerned less with show and drama than with the details necessary for any large movement to progress. He may be less in tune with the movement, in fact, than most members; yet he oversees the essentials of money, organization, and even diplomacy. He is ready to compromise, to bargain, and to deal; he attempts to carve out a balance point between the dogmatic idealism of the movement on the one hand and the threatening gibes of the outside society on the other.

An intellectual leader provides the justifications, the rewrite of history, the theory of the movement. He manages the symbols and gives logical coherence to the movement's vision. He sees the place of the movement in history and justifies actions that are taken in terms that communicate both to outsiders and, importantly, to the members.

Clearly, no social movement functions on the basis of any one of these leader types alone. All three types operate in different ways to give the movement direction and meaning. Outsiders may see only the charismatic leader blasting across their television screens nightly; he, in turn, uses the theories created and elaborated by the intellectual and pays the bills with the pragmatic administrator's bookkeeping.

Members. Hoffer's *True Believer* (1951), much in the tradition of early theories of collective behavior, describes a relatively undifferentiated type of movement follower. In this view all followers are fanatics, deeply and blindly committed to a movement's goals and tactics. Yet when we look more closely, the membership of any social movement is as highly differentiated and structured as is the leadership. Not every member is either a blind fanatic or as deeply committed as might be imagined. Some are hard-core and activist; others remain on the fringe, giving tacit support to the movement by their presence. A relatively small handful may perform all the duties, while many more drift into some actions and out of others. For some members, as Killian (1964) has noted, the movement is the dream of tomorrow; their involvement is only sufficient to guarantee that they'll ride into that future. Others root the hard core on, but participate minimally in any other way. Still others may be termed opportunists; in the language of the day, the movement gives them a great ego trip. The movement for them is a moment of excitement, providing a chance to be the someone, if only for a brief time, that they could otherwise never be.

Norms and Ideology. Another aspect of a social movement's structure concerns its norms, its internal culture, its manner of relating to other social movements and to the outside society, its system of values, and, finally, its schema of justification or ideology. Smelser (1963) differentiates between *norm-oriented* and *value-oriented* social movements. The first attempts to change the way things are done in a society without requiring a radical change in the society's basic values; the second attempts to change the basic values of the entire society. We might say the first is a *reform* movement, the second a *revolutionary* movement. In reform the aim is to extend the values of the society to a segment as yet deprived. For example, it has been suggested (e.g., Katz, 1967) that the Poverty Movement and the Civil Rights Movement are both norm- or reform-oriented, whereas the more radical forms of student protest are value-oriented or revolutionary. Such a neat classification is tempting, although we might question the degree to which the Civil Rights Movement can achieve its goals within the present value system of American society. Some (e.g., Cleaver, 1968) maintain that it will take a revolutionary change before Negroes can attain equality and justice. But more on that later.

The ideology or belief and justification system of a social movement may be carefully outlined in a formal philosophy and definite program (e.g., the origins of the Nazi Movement) or may consist of a loosely linked, ill-defined, almost intuitive sense of frustration and malaise (e.g., student protest). In the former case a challenge of "what do you really want?" can readily be met; in the latter the challenge often goes unanswered.

Career and life history

Social movements have a birth, a life, and either a death or an assimilation into the societal mainstream. Two facts often overlooked, but of prime importance to anyone who would attempt to understand the career of a social movement, are that any movement may be one of several social movements in a society and the fate of one may hinge on its relationships to others; and that the kind of relationship between the movement and conventional society importantly affects the life history of the movement itself. A politically left protest movement, for example, relates not only to conventional society but also to other social movements, including those that may be politically far to the right; the careers of the left and of the right in some sense form a symbiotic bond, each feeding the growth of the other. Regardless of its relationship to other social movements, the life history of any one movement is vastly affected by its manner of relating to conventional society. The

world the movement faces is, as Blumer (1951) noted, almost always opposed or resistant, at best, indifferent. The movement may grow and flourish or be suppressed and forced underground, almost entirely as a function of the manner by which it is received by the larger society.

The Killian Formulation. Killian (1964) considers three ways in which the conventional society may relate to the movement. First, it may consider the movement a worthy opponent. If this is the case the movement gains legitimate entry into the public forums of the society and engages in socially sanctioned forms of growth and development. A movement that gains this degree of acceptance, of course, may lose some of its missionary zeal as a change agent because those elements within it who are too defiant must either be constrained to fit the established forms of debate or else be repudiated.

Chavez relates a relevant episode involving his efforts to organize farm workers (in Matthiessen, 1969). During its early life, when his organization was engaged in traditional civil rights activities, many outside groups came around to help. These included clergymen, members of SNCC, CORE, SDS, and an array of hip student types. Chavez noted that many of these helpers needed more help than they could themselves provide. Some became financial burdens to his poor organization; others became sources of embarrassment because of their manner of dress and behavior. Chavez finally had to act decisively to get rid of "those kids." It was not an easy decision; they were friends. Yet, in terms of the larger aims of the organization, their behavior could not be tolerated.

Society, of course, may seek to subdue the more threatening elements of a movement by granting legitimacy to some of its more benign demands. This seduction by the society may successfully divide and eventually conquer those in the movement. In this case, some of the movement's original goals will have been achieved, while others, still outstanding, form the basis for the evolution of another movement.

A second form of relationship between a movement and society involves a movement that the society considers "safe" and nonthreatening, but at the same time, rather odd or peculiar. Certain religious cults would fall into this category, as would, say, flying-saucer societies. In this case the movement is isolated, perhaps through ridicule or apathy, and becomes even farther out and more peculiar, living out its life increasingly by the wayside, making hardly any impact on the society.

Third, a social movement may be defined as a danger to the stability of the society, and thereby evoke strong opposition and concerted efforts both to discredit and destroy it. Conventional society, still in charge of the major justifications and media, defines the movement as revolutionary, with designs on the violent overthrow of the established government. Pressures are created to do away with it. This treatment, in turn, pressures the movement to gain power and control through *any* means it can. It becomes increasingly dependent for its survival on its ability to move underground, to emerge on occasion to wreak havoc on the society that threatens its existence. Terror, violence, and conspiracy may take over; rhetoric of the movement may claim that the end—which all in the movement agree is good—justifies any means necessary to obtain it.

This turn to tactics of terror includes the use of violence as a pure act of destruction and its more limited use to gain positions of counter-power and eventually control. Violence and terror, however, are not of the movement only; the stable society resorts to violence and particularly to the use of terror to snuff out resistance and maintain its own control in the face of the threatening movement. The leaders of the movement in a hostile society, rather than being taken into the council chambers for discussion, are constantly wary of their very survival; they become conspirators leading a band of hearty freedom-fighters (their terms) against the fascistic society (their terms) that seeks their removal.

Notice that this direction of a social movement occurs in a society that seeks forcibly to oppose its growth; conventional society's reaction to the presence of the social movement casts it in a more violent mold. There is little wonder, then, that many black militants claim they will be only as violent as the police and the establishment demand. What they mean is that they would prefer to attain their movement's goals through nonviolent means; but if repression is the society's response, the society has called the tune and it must pay the piper when, for its own survival, the movement turns to violence.

When this third alternative is reached in a society's relationship with a movement, polarization has become nearly complete—you literally are either for us or against us—and myth-making on all sides becomes a major undertaking. The movement develops its own myths and martyrs about as rapidly as does the large society. Each side sees its myths as true and its opponents' myths as clear lies. A battle for purity and idealism usually rages. As Killian suggests, efforts are made by the movement's adherents to cloak themselves in a mantle of idealism and altruism; but the movement is not alone in seeking such cloaks of credal values and basic human decency. Society wraps itself even more tightly into God, flag, motherhood, or whatever else is held in high value. It is into this arena, by the way, that college professors wander, waving on high their banners reading, "A pox on both your houses"; they retain "total objectivity" while Rome burns.

Katz's View. Another effort to relate a social movement to the mainstream of society is Katz's (1967) comparison of the Civil Rights Movement and the anti-Vietnam War movement during the sixties. Katz maintains that in terms of members, individual motivation, tactics, and values, these two movements are much the same. They differ, he maintains, in the manner by which each relates to the values of the outside society. Katz suggests that the Civil Rights Movement has values that are congruent with key forces in mainstream U. S. society, especially in regard to American ideals of equality, American industrial and military manpower needs, and the United States' relationship to a world containing a nonwhite majority. This congruence gives the movement an important degree of legitimacy on which even the intellectual justification makers of the main society focus and thereby validate.

By contrast, according to Katz, the antiwar movement flies in the face of some major forces in the U. S. industrial and military system. Katz sees these forces as oriented toward an extension of U. S. national interests and power around the world. The antiwar movement argues against such an expansion; thus it receives less legitimacy and less support from the society. As we shall note later, much of the same analysis can be applied to the student protest movement, whose legitimacy is questioned even by the most sympathetic of observers. What is important in Katz's analysis, at least for our present consideration, is his argument that two movements that appear to be much the same undergo different careers as a function of their relationship to the mainstream society.

Toch's Analysis. Toch (1965) calls our attention to the death that awaits a movement as it pursues the three P's of *prosperity, power*, and *popularity* and finds itself just another institutionalized form in a society. He sees these three P's as a mixed blessing. With them, on one hand, a movement can be a major change agent with significant impact on a society; on the other hand, these are the very qualities that may lead to disaffection of members who had seen something different in the movement's earlier vision.

The temptations conventional society holds out are seductive indeed; it takes a strong man to turn them down. Many a movement leader has found himself called to Washington or to some statehouse where he is wined, dined, treated to the intimate secrets of those in established power, and finally offered a cushy position on some establishment board, committee, or whatever. Chavez, penniless, was offered a job at $21,000 per year as a Peace Corps director in South America. He turned this down to continue organizing farm workers, to the delight of some and the economic chagrin of others.

As Toch noted, the process of becoming a member (conversion) and later disaffecting from a movement is a further feature of the life history of a social movement. Just as a movement does not arise mysteriously as some freakish, irrational occurrence, but rather evolves in an understandable manner from the normal social order, persons, too, convert to movement membership as part of an explicable process over time, even though the experience may be one of suddenly, mystically, "seeing the light."

The convert undergoes a variety of disillusioning encounters with reality that lay the groundwork for later conversion. These may be contradictions between what he is taught and what he sees; in the American dilemma (p. 331ff.), between ideals and reality. The precipitating event, the final disillusionment, may suddenly provide clarification. Conversion, then, is a point of *transition*, a sudden takeoff from a well-prepared field.

In much the same process, disaffection builds up over time and over a series of disappointments and disillusionments. Toch outlines four ways in which it may develop. First, a person may have joined a movement with some reservations, making his own special unmeetable demands on it. When his unique personal needs are not met he becomes disillusioned and finally drops out. Second, his disaffection may represent reservations he had on joining but that remained concealed even from himself. An event may rapidly bring these latent reservations to the fore; suddenly he realizes this is not for him and out he goes. Third, a crisis situation in the movement may precipitate a personal crisis situation in P. Finally, P may undergo some cognitive reorganization in which he attempts to find alternative solutions to his problems, abandoning the movement as something not worth his while.

Note well that the picture of a social movement that even this brief outline provides is very different from what too readily comes to mind when we hear "right-wing movement," "student protest movement," or "Negro protest movement." We usually react to these terms in a highly undifferentiated manner, eliminating the complexity that is an intimate part of any social movement.

Outcomes. A movement that begins out of frustrated need, that spends its life seeking redress of its grievances, may eventually be examined in terms of its outcomes or consequences for change. Its death may lay the seeds for yet another movement; or, perhaps, like the characteristic fate of third parties in U. S. politics, its programs may be incorporated into the platforms of one of the major parties and thus be preserved. It is possible, of course, that a social movement's vision may come true.

The revolution may succeed and the movement one day emerge in control of the society; and even in this action are the seeds of still other social movements; on it goes, man's eternal struggle to change the social order—even the new one—to meet his questing needs. As Killian has said, "The study of social movements reminds us of the irrepressible conviction of sentient men that they can collectively, if not individually, change their culture by their own endeavors" (1964, p. 454).

PROTEST MOVEMENTS OF THE 1960'S

Civil rights

In 1942 in Chicago the Congress on Racial Equality (CORE) employed a nonviolent sit-in to protest segregation in public facilities. Between 1940 and 1944, 17 similar, small-scale, nonviolent protests were recorded. Between 1956 and 1957 King led the Montgomery, Alabama, bus boycott, developing the Civil Rights Movement. In 1960 the CORE sit-in technique was employed in the South, again to protest segregation in public facilities and accommodations. The nonviolent protest movement, led primarily by King, grew rapidly in the South during the early 1960's. Sit-ins, swim-ins, eat-ins, walk-ins, and protest marches became a regular occurrence. Shortly the compass point would swing northerly; the focus would shift from public facilities to housing and employment.

In 1857 the U. S. Supreme Court ruled in the Dred Scott case that a Negro born to slavery could not enjoy the privileges of citizenship; he had none of the constitutional rights that a freeman possessed. In 1883 it ruled that Negroes were not guaranteed equal rights in public accommodations. In 1896 it approved the doctrine of "separate but equal," which legitimized segregation in education, housing, and public facilities. On May 17, 1954, however, the Court voided its 1896 decision, declaring in essence that separate was *not* equal. The legal groundwork was laid for the integration of the black community into the mainstream of American life.

In 1948 the military was integrated. In 1961 the Interstate Commerce Commission ruled that all rail and bus terminals involved in interstate travel must be racially integrated. In 1962 a Kennedy executive order declared that no federal loans would be given to builders who excluded Negroes from employment. In 1964, after much haggling and many protest marches, including a massive march on Washington, D. C., President Johnson signed the Civil Rights Act. Its several key provisions provided for equal voting rights for blacks and whites, prohibited segregation in all public facilities that involved interstate travel, prohibited discrimination in all programs that received federal aid, and so on.

Other than two outbreaks in Harlem (1935 and 1943), Negro-white encounters in the United States historically have been initiated primarily by whites and directed at the black community. Whites rioted particularly whenever blacks sought entry to white neighborhoods; during these riots the white community used bricks, guns, and Molotov cocktails against the blacks. In the mid-1960's the pattern changed. In 1964 Harlem erupted in a summer's storm of riot. In 1965 Watts, a black ghetto outside of Los Angeles, treated the nation to an upheaval of intensity and proportions unimaginable to most Americans. The summers of 1966 and 1967 saw dozens of cities, notably Detroit and Newark, torn by ghetto upheaval. Some called it riot; others, civil insurrection; others, the beginning of the new American Revolution. Whatever it was called, there was extensive property damage and, more importantly, much damage to the body and spirit of a nation. In 1968 the President's Commission on Civil Disorders issued its report arguing, all too convincingly, that the nation was rapidly becoming polarized into two societies, separate but unequal, one black, the other white.

In November 1963 President John Kennedy was shot to death in Dallas. In April 1968 Martin Luther King was murdered on the balcony of his motel in Memphis. In June 1968 Senator Robert Kennedy, just victorious in the California presidential primary, was shot to death in a Los Angeles hotel. Nonviolence was dying, its leaders killed, its followers enraged. Black Power and black militancy were replacing King's SCLC; Black separatism challenged the notion of integration. The Student Nonviolent Coordinating Committee (SNCC), haven of white students and others who had traveled South to join civil rights protests during the early 1960's, changed its leadership and its nonviolent stance. Stokely Carmichael and Rap Brown challenged the moderate rhetoric of the past with the potent rhetoric of black revolution.

Campus protest

In 1964 on the Berkeley campus of the University of California the silent generation of the 1950's gave way to the turbulent, protesting, and demanding generation of the 1960's: the Free Speech Movement was born. The training received by white students in civil rights sit-ins found its way to the campus, and campus life would never again be the same. In 1968 some students at Columbia University in New York City, using the vigorous protest techniques that marked the new mood among militant black Americans and their student brothers of France, seized campus buildings, threw out faculty and administrators, copied confidential papers, and created a new form of white college student protest. Nonviolence seemed to be dying; the friendly sit-in of yesterday had been replaced by the militants' naked power plays.

In the fall of 1968 the Democratic Convention at Chicago included, live and in glorious color, the nation's youth on parade, doing battle with police and National Guard forces. In May 1969 the nation was shocked to see black militants emerge with loaded rifles from a seized building at Cornell University. Later, in 1969 and in 1970, both on the campus and in the nearby community, the turn toward militancy saw ROTC buildings attacked and burned, other buildings threatened or bombed, and at least in one case a branch of the Bank of America burned to the ground.

If 1964 at Berkeley was the beginning of contemporary protest on campus, and if 1968 at Columbia saw the introduction of heavy militancy to the campus, the Chicago Democratic Convention of fall 1968, the Berkeley Peoples' Park scene of spring 1969, and the Jackson and Kent State deaths of 1970 manifested a new direction in society's response to campus protest. This is not to say that before this time protestors had been met with open arms, but rather to indicate a new intensity, direction, and breadth

of societal outrage. From the indiscriminate use of tear gas sprayed from a National Guard helicopter at Berkeley to the killings of two students by the police at Jackson State and four by the National Guard at Kent State in 1970, the established society was loud, clear, and in its own way extremely violent in speaking out against campus protest.

By mid-1969 state and federal legislators were seeking to control the "rioters" and "mobs" by passing or threatening to pass restrictive legislation and, in several notable cases, applying new legislation drafted to prohibit movement across state lines to incite to riot (e.g., the 1969–1970 Chicago 8 Conspiracy trial). By June 1970, 32 states had passed laws designed to prevent further disorders, including measures to eliminate financial aid to students and to dismiss faculty members involved in protests. While legislators fumed, police and military forces took over, making a police state just that much more a reality in parts of the United States. And much of this met with the approval of many citizens who were concerned about what seemed like anarchy around them.

A sense of the scope of protest during the mid- and late 1960's can be gleaned from the figures reported by the President's Commission on the Causes and Prevention of Violence; see Table 23.1. More than a match for campus turmoil in the United States, students around the

Table 23.1 Protest in the United States: June 1963–May 1968 (adapted from the *New York Times Almanac* 1969, p. 236)

Type of Event	Number Events	Number Participants	Number Casualties	Reported Arrests
Civil rights demonstration	369	1,117,600	389	15,379
Antiwar	104	680,000	400	3,258
Student protests on campus issues	91	102,035	122	1,914
Anti-school integration	24	34,720	0	164
Segregationist clashes and counter-demonstrations	54	31,200	163	643
Negro riots and disturbances	239	200,000	8,133	49,607
Terrorism against Negroes and rights workers	213	2,000	112	97

world rocked their campuses, their communities, and their governments. In France, in Japan, in South America, in Australia, and elsewhere, a generation of young were rising up in protest. By examining the origins, structures, and careers of these protest movements we shall not only learn about social movements in general, but also gain access to the often-concealed under-belly of the society.

ORIGINS OF THE PROTEST MOVEMENTS

A social system creates both the conditions of its stability and the sources of strain that cause the development of change-oriented social movements. Lasswell (1965), for example, defines, under the familiar heading of life, liberty, and the pursuit of happiness, eight values essential for the maintenance of human dignity: well-being (life); shared power, shared enlight-enment, shared rectitude (liberty); wealth, re-spect, skill, affection (happiness). When the social institutions of a society present these values to one segment of the population while systematically denying them to another, the conditions are ripe for the stirrings of revolt.

Likewise, and intimately related to the preced-ing, the stable institutions of a society can create personal and social strain by frustrating what I shall call basic human needs. The tendency in contemporary social science has been to assume that man is highly malleable, capable of being socialized in numerous ways by the variety of cultures and social structures in which he is reared. In this view man has few, if any, basic needs other than those of his biological inheritance; whatever needs he has are usually seen as direct derivatives of a given society's socialization practices.

The sociologist Etzioni (1968), whose view is similar in structure but not in content to that of some psychoanalytic writers (e.g., Freud's instinct concepts), and similar in both structure *and* content to some existential authors, argues, in contrast, that there are certain basic human needs that different societies' socialization practices and institutional arrangements satisfy or frustrate to varying degrees; societies can be rated (theoretically at least) on the extent to which their institutions and practices are costly to the satisfaction of these basic needs. Some societies, presumably, pay heavily for frustrating individual basic need satisfaction; they must expend considerable time, energy, and money to control those who express their frustration in illness, crime, apathy, reform, and revolution. In particular Etzioni argues that in-dustrial societies of today create conditions that frustrate the basic needs for affection and recognition. I will use this same argument shortly to examine the origins of the student protest movement. At this point, however, note that the popular view of man's near-infinite malleability places the burden of illness and trouble on the man who does not bend to meet society's demands, whereas a notion of basic human needs allows for an entire society to be ill (in the sense of frustrating many person's basic needs) and calls attention to the po-tentially healthy qualities of human rebellion. A man who does not bend with the institutions of his society may be the mainstream's deviant but history's true hero.

Black America

The protest movement of black America is deeply rooted in a social system that for cen-turies has systematically denied to one segment of the population the rewards and values of equality and justice that other citizens are guar-anteed. Economic insecurity has been cited as a cause for many social movements, both in the United States and around the world. Zeitlin (1966), for example, found that workers in pre-Castro Cuba who had been the least eco-nomically secure were the ones most likely to support the revolution. In the United States the historically based economic insecurity of the black population provides a fertile field for the kinds of strain that can give birth to a social movement. Let's examine some of the relevant statistics.

Employment. Employment and unemployment figures are particularly striking. Between 1958 and 1963 in northern industrial cities one out of every three Negroes experienced unemploy-ment for varying periods of time. Just before the 1964 Harlem disturbance, Clark reports (in Hill, 1965), almost 50 percent of all black workers in New York City were in dead-end jobs—jobs that would shortly be eliminated; thus those who are employed are often in jobs that have no future. A 1960–1961 study in Chicago (reported in Hill, 1965) indicated that the unemployment rate of white males between 25 and 44 years of age was 2.2 percent; the Negro ghetto rate was over 15 percent. National studies consistently indicate that the unemployment rate of Negro youths is twice that of whites. The Labor Department reported in 1969 that Negroes, 10 percent of the total population, make up 20.6 percent of the national unemployment figures. A study of textile workers in South Carolina (see Hill, 1965) indicated that while the total working population increased from 48,000 in 1918 to 122,000 in 1960, the percentage of Negroes in the textile industry *fell* from 9 percent in 1918 to 4.7 percent in 1960.

From 1960 to 1968 there was a general decline in unemployment rates for both whites and nonwhites. However, the nonwhite rate remained double that of the whites even in its decline; Table 23.2 gives a good sense of this.

Table 23.2 Unemployment rates by color (adapted from *New York Times Almanac*, 1969, p. 652)

	White	Nonwhite
1960	4.9	10.2
1961	6.0	12.4
1962	4.9	10.9
1963	5.0	10.8
1964	4.6	9.6
1965	4.1	8.1
1966	3.3	7.3
1967	3.4	7.4
1968	3.2	6.7

Wages and Income. Wage statistics are equally revealing. In 1951 the median wage of black workers was 57 percent that of whites. In 1966 the ratio of Negro-to-white median income was .58. It ranged from about .74 in the North Central states to a low of .51 in the South (*New York Times Almanac*, 1969, p. 300). Wage figures in 1963 indicate that nonwhites consistently earn less than whites of a comparable educational level (*U. S. Books of Facts,* 1965). In 1963, high-school graduates, if white, earned an average of $6997; if nonwhite, only $4530. White college graduates earned $9857 on the average; nonwhite college graduates earned $7295. Wage differentials over time are strikingly illustrated in the following figures: in 1950 the difference in median income between whites and nonwhites was $1576; in 1960 this difference grew to $2602; in 1963 to $3083; and in 1966 to $3259. These figures are even more striking on a per capita basis by family; in 1966 the black family (averaging 4.38 persons) had a per capita income of $1000, compared to the white family (averaging 3.62 persons) figure of $2100 (*New York Times Almanac*, 1969).

Reporting on a government study of the income distribution in the United States, the columnist T.R.B. (*The New Republic*, May 11, 1968) noted how the rich get richer and the poor, poorer. The bottom fifth of American families gets only 5 percent of the national income pie; the top fifth gets 45 percent; much the same distribution existed in 1947 and 1962. In another analysis T.R.B. noted that the top 5 percent of the nation gets 20 percent of its wealth, while the bottom 20 percent gets only 5 percent.

Of course you need not be black or nonwhite to be poor in America. But it helps. In 1959 22 percent of all families were classified as poor by Social Security Administration standards. White poverty was at 18 percent; the nonwhite figure was 55 percent. By 1967 over-all poverty dropped to between 11 and 13 percent. Nonwhites still were overrepresented: 31 to 35 percent, compared to 8 to 10 percent for white families (*New York Times Almanac*, 1969).

If you were a migratory farm worker you were near the bottom of the poverty heap, earning an average of only $1016 a year. An analysis by Schmid and Nobbe (1965) is revealing. They found that over two decades (1940–1960) the Chinese and Japanese ranked highest in income among nonwhites, while both Negroes and Indians remained *consistently* at the bottom.

It has been estimated that advances in technology and the increased use of automation will displace nearly two million unskilled and semiskilled workers each year (see Lekachman, 1966). The displacement will primarily affect the black community. In economics there is a curve called the Phillips curve, relating unemployment figures to inflation rates. It indicates that a nation's level of unemployment is inversely related to inflationary price spirals. Some economists have suggested that a 4 percent unemployment figure is the closest a society can get to full employment without adversely affecting wage-price stability. Beyond this point, a tradeoff—of unemployment for reduction in inflation—must occur. More refined analyses, however, suggest that this becomes primarily a black tradeoff. For example, an effort to reduce by half an inflation rate of 3.50 would result in an over 8 percent rise in black unemployment, a much higher figure than for whites. Much of this sharper rise in black unemployment occurs as unskilled and semiskilled workers are cast out of work (from *San Francisco Chronicle,* December 17, 1968).

Education. Education has become the port of entry into the mainstream of American society, even though, as some of the figures above indicate, education alone is no guarantee of "making it." Statistics on years of schooling completed indicate, once again, a striking differential between whites and nonwhites. Table 23.3 presents the median number of school years completed by sex, color, and year. Nonwhites consistently complete fewer years of schooling than whites. Although median education for both whites and nonwhites increased from 1960 to 1964 and from 1964 to 1968, nonwhites nevertheless remain below whites. If we restrict our examination to persons 25 to 34 years old, the gap is still present but is less than Table 23.3 indicates. In this age group the median is 12.5 years for whites and 12.1 for blacks. On the other hand, whereas 15 percent of whites between 25 and 34 completed college, only 6 percent of the blacks had done so. As we head into the seventies it is likely

that pressures introduced in the sixties will take effect and lessen this educational gap.

Schmid and Nobbe (1965) found that between 1940 and 1960 Chinese and Japanese maintained relatively high educational status, along with whites, whereas both Indians and Negroes continued to hold the lowest positions. In a study of predominantly white universities Egerton (1969) reported that less than 2 percent of the students and about 1 percent of the faculty members were Negroes. Although about 10 percent of the U. S. population is black, not one of the institutions he examined had that high a percentage of black students. In the western part of the United States Negroes made up about 5 percent of the total population, but the 26 state universities and land-grant colleges enrolled only about 1.34 percent Negroes. On the other hand, in the school year 1968–1969 Ivy League colleges showed an average increase of 89 percent in black enrollment. Changes can and do take place.

Life at the Bottom. If you are poor, and black in addition, you look on a bleak present and bleaker future. If life at the top is one mad round of cocktail parties, galas, ulcers, and heart attacks at 55, life at the bottom, if you make it past childhood, is hunger, illness, poor housing, welfare, and a pervading hopelessness. The cycle, once engaged, persists, dragging one generation down on the heels of the one before. A Blue Cross survey conducted by pollster Harris (1968) compared the health conditions of the poor and the affluent. He found that the poor have three times as many serious illnesses as the population as a whole. Nervous tension concerning economic and health issues is reported by 49 percent, as compared with 33 percent of the affluent sample. In response to an inquiry about getting up in the morning, 40 percent of the poor indicate that they are too tired to rise each morning; only 25 percent of the total sample report comparable fatigue.

American Indians live in poverty and are the one group even more underprivileged than most black Americans. Conquered, placed on reservations, then neglected, they show the shocking disarrangement of economic, social, and psychological security that presently exists in the world's most affluent nation. Progress has been

Table 23.3 Median years of schooling by sex and color for persons 25 years old or older (adapted from *N.Y. Times Almanac,* 1969, and *U.S. Books of Facts,* 1965)

| | White | | Nonwhite | |
	Male	Female	Male	Female
1960	10.7	11.2	7.9	8.5
1964	11.9	12.0	8.7	9.1
1968	12.1	12.1	9.0[a]	9.6[a]

[a]Figures are for Negroes only

made, especially in health, although their state is still beyond belief. Although infant mortality has been reduced in the last years, of the 1700 Indian infants born in a given year, 500 will die in their first year, of illnesses that medical science could prevent (Rusk, 1966).

The incidence of influenza and pneumonia is twice as high among Indians as in the general population. Death from tuberculosis is five to seven times greater than the national average (*New York Times Almanac*, 1969). More than 50 percent of the American Indian population presently have to haul their drinking water a mile or more, usually from unsanitary sources. Only a small number have indoor plumbing. Indian death rate from accidents is three times the national average; 50 percent of these deaths result from overcrowded living conditions and fires caused by gasoline or kerosene lighting and heating. Unfortunately, I could cite page after page of such statistics.

Although living conditions in the big-city ghetto do not compare in objective horror to those of the American Indian, or in many cases to that of the migrant farm worker, the ghetto black's existence is filled with psychologically comparable misery. Between 1950 and 1960 the number of below-standard housing units for whites diminished by 53 percent; for nonwhites, the decrease in substandard housing was only 20 percent.

In 1960 roughly 14 percent of all housing units were rated by the census as deteriorating and roughly 5 percent as dilapidated; but the figures for nonwhite housing were 30 percent and 18 percent respectively, *double* in the case of deteriorating housing and over *triple* in the case of dilapidated housing (*U. S. Book of Facts*, 1965). Those same census figures indicate that roughly 22 percent of nonwhite housing units are occupied by six or more persons, compared with 10 percent for the total housing units in the nation. On a persons-per-room basis, the census figures indicate that approximately 28 percent of nonwhite housing has more than one person per room as compared with 10 percent for all occupied units.

A nonstatistical portrait of poverty is provided in the following description:

"Mr. Perez is 47 years old. For the last two months he has been feeding and clothing himself, his wife and their four young children on $1 a day. . . . Mr. Perez lives with his 42-year-old wife and four children ranging in age from 7 to 11 in five small rooms. . . . The living room, about 10 feet square, contains the only furniture Mr. Perez has bought—blue couch and two orange chairs. . . . They are covered with clear plastic to protect the upholstery. . . . The three bedrooms are barely big enough to contain their double beds. A metal filing cabinet in one room serves as a chest of drawers. The room shared by the boys . . . has no window. They receive compensation, however, by having the only bed with sheets on it. . . . The girls . . . have three changes of clothing between them. . . . The kitchen—containing a sink, gas stove, refrigerator, and a bare cupboard—is the largest room. The bathroom, off the kitchen, is the size of a large closet and has a bathtub and a toilet. Mr. Perez thinks the apartment has certain advantages. There is always heat and hot water. The rats come only at night. . . . For breakfast yesterday the family had bread and milk. For supper there was rice and beans. . . . For entertainment there is an old television set . . . and a radio. There is no money for newspapers or books. . . . Movies are out of the question. Once a year the family goes to Coney Island . . ." (*New York Times*, January 10, 1964, p. 17).

The 1960 census demonstrated that 27.4 percent of the population of the nation's 10 largest cities is black. The figure for Washington, D. C., was 52 percent. Central city growth has been primarily Negro growth while suburban growth has been primarily white; 55 out of every 100 Negroes lived in a metropolitan area in 1967, compared with 27 out of every 100 whites. By contrast, 37 out of 100 whites lived in the surrounding suburbs (*New York Times Almanac*, 1969); less than 6 percent of the suburban population outside of these 10 cities was black. In fact, the white suburban growth rate between 1930 and 1960 outdistanced the black by 30 to 1. If we couple these figures with another set, a picture of a lost dream begins to emerge. In 1900 the proportion of Negroes in the South was 90 percent; by 1960, this proportion had dropped to 52 percent. Negroes had migrated northward, especially around World War II, seeking a better life in urban America. The American dream, our myth of success by which any man could be president, any man could start on a shoestring and rise to the heights of wealth, power, prestige, and the good life, however, was denied to them. The central city not only became their home, it became their prison. How very ripe, then, were the conditions of strain that are basic to any form of collective behavior, including urban riot and the evolution of a social movement.

Structural Strain and Conduciveness. Two further points need to be made before we move from the roots of Negro protest to those of the New Left. First, we should note that although strain and problems exist among blacks, Indians, Mexicans, Puerto Ricans, poor whites, and others, a vigorous social movement did not develop equally in each group. A social movement, recall, does not spring up solely on the basis of need or strain; other factors must be present. Strain may be reflected in withdrawal, say suicide and alcoholism (as it is among the Indians), rather than in a change-oriented social movement.

It is likely that the relative deprivation experienced by blacks in the central city, coupled with the hope that new legislation provides, ripens them more for a protest movement than the conditions of utter despair and resignation that mark most Indians. Furthermore, as split and torn as it has been, the black community has retained a semblance of strong leadership, especially among its religious leaders. These men were able to help channel the strain in the direction of a social movement. Only recently, with the rise of persons such as Chavez among the farm workers in California and Tijerina in the Southwest, have other groups begun to organize themselves into more effective social protest movements. The leadership helps organize individuals into a collectivity and, as importantly, helps give concrete meaning to the vision of a better tomorrow. A man who feels totally resigned to his miserable life comes slowly to see the possibilities for improvement. Perhaps it is primarily among the young that a movement first gets its impetus; older members of the community are either too fully resigned or are too fearful of losing what little they have. In this regard it should be noted that, as compared with the white population, blacks are

younger on the average: median age for blacks in 1967 was 21.2 as compared with the white median of 29.0 years (*New York Times Almanac,* 1969).

Second, conditions that Smelser has called structural conduciveness importantly affect the development of the Negro protest movement. In the United States Negroes not only are vastly underprivileged but also are the largest identifiable minority group in this "down" position. The congregation of large numbers in the central city permits communication among like-minded persons. The constitutional guarantee of freedom to assemble, it turns out, even in this mass-mediated society, is a condition essential to the formation and organization of a social movement. One of the first regulations to be put in effect during a period of emergency is to forbid persons to congregate in groups larger than two or three, and the use of sound-amplification equipment is usually denied. In this way it becomes difficult for persons to organize, communicate their dissatisfactions, and plan some retaliatory action. In a ghetto, however, large masses of persons come together where they are visible and where they can be reached and organized.

Another set of structural factors conducive to the formation of a social movement is the development in the ghetto of indigenous social structures. Soul music radio stations carry the message to the people; black newspapers range from moderate to radical. Churches, meeting halls, civic groups, neighborhood clubs, and so forth, develop in a ghetto community. These help create a complex that ties persons together within the community while setting them apart from the mainstream of the society. The larger community contains its power structure and communication networks; the ghetto has developed its own patterns, ready to function when the moment is ripe.

In a society that controls its mass media— mainland China, for example, or Russia to a considerable degree—movement-fomenting images and stories can be deleted. American freedom of the press and media, however, can help foster a climate for protest or even revolution. Each night the ghetto dweller sees the nature of his deprivation. White images on television harp on the style of white suburban living that is not a part of his life, although it may become a part of the dream that motivates his protest. To a resident of Watts who sees someone like Martin Luther King on television, leading a march in the South, making an inspirational speech in Washington, or challenging the President and Congress in a news conference, the hope for a better life is further kindled. The media in a free society thus help sow seeds of rebellion within that very society. For all this society's faults, it is this kind of perversity of democracy and freedom that gives one some hope for the future.

Conditions conducive both to the formation of the Negro protest movement and to specific manifestations of collective behavior, especially urban riots or revolts, are rooted as well in the history of approaches to conflict resolution. Locales differ in this regard. Police-ghetto contacts, for example, are a key sore spot in the relationship between the black ghetto and the surrounding white community. For the average white suburbanite the police are protectors of his private property and friends of the community. For the average Negro in the ghetto the police symbolize in concrete form the distant and unreachable agencies of control and frustration. They are the prison guards, keeping the lid on a bubbling caldron.

We would expect that communities that make special efforts to deal with conflicts through discussion, participation, and negotiation rather than through repressive police tactics or continued harassment would be less likely to experience outbursts of collective behavior such as riots or to provide a fertile ground for the formation of a strong social protest movement. When conflicts are resolved primarily by repressive means, we would expect conditions to be especially conducive to collective behavior, including both riots and protest movements.

Lieberson and Silverman (1965) provide some confirmatory evidence regarding race riots. In a comparison of 38 pairs of riot cities and roughly comparable nonriot cities on a variety of indices, 24 nonriot cities had more Negro policemen than their riotous matched partner. Lieberson and Silverman argue that the exist-ence of Negro policemen importantly reflects a city government's attitudes toward race relations. The more Negro policemen, presumably, the better the attitudes, and the less the conditions are conducive to collective action. In 14 of 22 pairs, the cities in which the population per city councilman was large were more likely to have riots than in cities where the ratio was lower. In other words, the closer the people are to the city government (low population per city councilman), the more likely the government is to be responsive to the needs of the people, and thus the less conducive the governmental structure is to the development of collective episodes. As Lieberson and Silverman conclude, "Populations are predisposed or prone to riot; they are not simply neutral aggregates transformed into a violent mob by the agitation or charisma of individuals" (p. 897).

A summary of the variety of causes for ghetto upheavals was provided in the 1968 report of the U. S. Commission on Civil Disorders, which outlined three levels of community grievance, including at the level of highest intensity the following three items: (1) police practices; (2) unemployment and underemployment; (3) inadequate housing. At the second most intense level were (4) inadequate education; (5) poor recreational facilities; and (6) ineffective political structures and mechanisms for handling grievances. Finally, on the third level were (7) disrespectful white attitudes; (8) discriminatory application of justice; (9) inadequate Federal programs; (10) inadequate local services; (11) discriminatory credit practices; and (12) inadequate welfare systems.

These 12 grievances provide a cookbook for urban revolt and for a movement of social protest. When such problems are present in significant degree for a significant number of a society's citizens, we need not look to a theory of outside agitators.

Young America

The black protest has its origins in centuries of slavery and a contemporary ghettoized existence. Statistics and tragic portraits sharply outline the disparity between the haves and the have-nots, pointing to the key factors that fuel the movement's fire. Young white Americans, primarily on college and university campuses, although sharing those origins indirectly through empathy and a keen social conscience, trace the origins of their own movement to the frustrations of basic human needs that have been shunted aside by structures and institutions that now disturb more than they satisfy. Although we can generally understand a movement arising from injustices that produce hunger, poverty, and physical want, I think that to grasp the essence of the campus protest movement of the sixties we must recognize man's psychological needs as well; their frustration, although difficult to document in statistical tables, is a root source for the protest movement of many young Americans.

There are two major issues to be examined. First, in what manner, if at all, do contemporary social structures and institutions frustrate basic human needs and thereby create the strains that give rise to a social movement? Second, what conditions of contemporary society, and in particular of the modern educational institution, are conducive to the growth and perpetuation of a social movement?

From Community to Society. In offering a preliminary answer to the first question we turn to a combination of social theory and criticism and to several basic themes of the movement itself. Many authors have commented on a shift in the forms and quality of human relationships as society moved from its simple communal form to the more complex, industrialized type. Tönnies (1940), for one, described the shift as one from *Gemeinschaft* (a close, reciprocal community relationship) to *Gesellschaft* (an impersonal, mechanistic social relationship). Although differing in certain specifics, the distinctions drawn by Durkheim (1933) between societies integrated in terms of *mechanical solidarity* and those based on *organic solidarity*, and by Maine (1861) between *status relationships* and *contract relationships* are similar to Tönnies' notion.

In general, each discusses a shift of relationships from those based on an identity of the individual in a relatively small, homogeneous community to relationships in larger, more highly differentiated urban contexts where persons become roles and relate to others in a more impersonal, segmented manner. Redfield's

distinction (1947) between *folk* and *urban* societies and Cooley's discussion (1909) of *primary groups* in contrast to other kinds of group relationships likewise captures the flavor of this difference. A folk society is small, isolated, homogeneous, with a strong sense of group solidarity. We think readily of primitive villages that exist today, or even of American rural life of decades ago—small-town America, where everyone knew everyone else; where there was a sense of *our* town, *our* school; where traditional ties of family and kin provided an integration imagined but rarely experienced in the canyons of our large urban centers. In these centers we are strangers far from home, from kin, from intimate involvement in the life of others. Cooley's primary group was an entire web of close personal relationships bound tightly together by a strong identification of each with all, a "we-feeling" in his terms. Secondary groups, by contrast, are impersonal, more distant, and removed from the intimacy and sense of belonging that primary groups provide.

In his own analysis of the advent of *modernism* the sociologist Nisbet (1966) outlined five key qualities of life that have undergone change as society moved from traditionalism (*Gemeinschaft*, mechanical solidarity, status) to modernism (*Gesellschaft*, organic solidarity, contract):

"*Community* includes but goes beyond local community to encompass religion, work, family, and culture; it refers to social bonds characterized by emotional cohesion, depth, continuity, and fullness. *Authority* is the structure or the inner order of an association, whether this be political, religious, or cultural, and is given legitimacy by its roots in social function, tradition, or allegiance. *Status* is the individual's position in the hierarchy of prestige and influence that characterizes every community or association. The *sacred* includes the mores, the nonrational, the religious and ritualistic ways of behavior that are valued beyond whatever utility they may possess. *Alienation* is a historical perspective within which man is seen as estranged, anomic, and rootless when cut off from the ties of community and moral purpose" (p. 6).

The basic argument is that modernism has moved us toward opposite poles of these relationships. Opposed to community is society, in which relationships are impersonal, distant, and segmented. Whereas authority derived its legitimacy from the personal association among individuals working within a community, *power* (the modern opposite) is based more on force or is tied into a system of bureaucratic administration; thus its legitimacy is open to serious question and doubt. The opposite of status is specialized classes; the opposite of sacred is secular or utilitarian. Nisbet sees alienation as the opposite of social and moral progress. With the alienation that modernism is thought to bring, man is estranged from himself, from his fellow man, from values and principles.

A Double-Edged Sword. The shift in the form and quality of human relationships as society moved from the small and rural to the large, urban, and industrialized can best be seen in the ideas of de Tocqueville, Weber, Fromm, and Simmel. (This discussion was helped in great measure by the analyses provided in the writings of Nisbet, 1966.) One manner of viewing these great historical shifts is in terms of what I term a double-edged perspective.

On one edge of this sword of modernism we find newly gained individual freedoms that man experienced as the traditional communal social order broke down. Man's place in the *Gemeinschaft* had been integrated and comfortable, but it also had its drawbacks. He was usually so firmly rooted in tradition that his individual efforts and initiative could not remove him. As Fromm (1941) noted, with the modern, industrial era man became mobile in space and in position; no longer was he tied to family-based roles In the mid-nineteenth century a Frenchman, de Tocqueville, visited the United States and returned home to write his classic *Democracy in America* (see 1945 edition; originally published in 1835). He commented on the new freedoms that democracy provided; he saw the emphasis on secularism and equalitarianism as the mark of a bright new future.

Weber, some of whose ideas we have previously examined (p. 309ff.) described modern Western society in terms of the *bureaucratization* and *rationalization* of life. Complex technological and industrial society demanded an equally complex form of social organization to administer to its needs. The bureaucratic structure seemed ideal to meet these demands; Weber's bureaucracy is the ideal-typical model of all social organization of the modern era. According to Weber, the motive force behind bureaucracy and in fact behind the entire era it heralded was rationalization: "the conversion of social values and relationships from the primary, communal and traditional shapes they once held to the larger, impersonal, and bureaucratized shapes of modern life" (Nisbet, 1966, p. 293). A rationalized existence is one guided by the advanced methods of science and technology toward the most organizationally efficient attainment of scientifically selected goals.

Simmel (1950) saw the direction of history as movement toward modernism and what he called *metropolis*, the objectified society of the mind rather than the heart (Nisbet, 1966, p. 308). In metropolis man's mind becomes more calculating, precise, and regimented; his attitude becomes one of protective reserve. He becomes sophisticated and blasé.

On the other edge of this same sword, however, each of these authors—and many other more recent social critics as well—have commented on the disastrous consequences to the individual and to humane relationships that eventually result. Such terms as dehumanization, alienation, fragmentation, inauthenticity, routinization, brutalization, capture a sense of the life that was seen for modern industrial man.

Fromm (1941) talked about man's desperate efforts to escape from this newly won freedom. For de Tocqueville, the power of democracy ". . . does not destroy, but it prevents existence; it does not tyrannize, but it compresses, enervates, extinguishes, and stupefies a people, till each nation is reduced to nothing better than a flock of timid and industrious animals, of which the government is the shepherd" (1945, p. 319).

Weber in one breath praised the high-level efficiency that the impersonal and rationalized system of bureaucracy provides and pointed out the other, inevitable consequences that excessive bureaucratization and rationalization would produce. As Nisbet (1966) states the case for Weber,

"So long as the process of rationalization had something to feed on—that is, the structure of traditional society and culture that was formed during the Middle Ages—it was a generally creative and liberating process. But with the gradual diminution and desiccation of this structure, with man's increasing disenchantment with the values of this structure, rationalization threatens now to become, not creative and liberating, but mechanizing, regimenting, and, ultimately, reason-destroying" (p. 294).

Simmel noted how the fragmentation of one's life in metropolis defies man's natural bent toward a unity and totality of existence, serving only to alienate him even further from himself. His life is no longer a whole; in metropolis man exists as a fragmented collection of roles. Bits and pieces of his character are carved in functional niches, known differently to each role-audience before whom he plays in his daily lives; perhaps known differently even to himself.

Some Modern Spokesmen. De Tocqueville discussed the subtle enervating and tyrannizing influences that the structure of egalitarian democracy eventually produces. In the rhetoric of today the structure is called *corporate liberalism* (see Lynd, 1969); its effect, however, is described in much the same manner de Tocqueville, Weber, and Simmel employed in their analyses. Lynd, a historian and a key figure in the New Left movement says,

"It is an instrument of mystification, which solicits the oppressed to accept their oppression willingly because oppression describes itself as freedom . . . the celebrated New Left revolt against authority is especially a revolt against paternalistic, indirect authority which hides the iron hand of power in the velvet glove of rhetorical idealism" (1969, p. 70).

Quoting from the Port Huron statement of 1962 (in Jacobs & Landau, 1966; Hayden, one of the founders of SDS, was the major author), Lynd notes that

". . . The dominant institutions are complex enough to blunt the minds of their potential critics. . . . The American political system is not the democratic model of which its glorifiers speak. In actuality it frustrates democracy by confusing the individual citizen, paralyzing policy discussion, and consolidating the irresponsible power of military and business interests" (p. 70).

Morgenthau (1967) sees America's crisis in democracy as resulting from three factors: "The shift of effective material power from the people to the government, the shift of the effective power of decision from the people to the government, and the ability of the government to destroy its citizens in the process of defending them" (p. 17).

In what I find to be a most perceptive analysis of contemporary social organization, building on foundations laid down by Weber, among others, Arendt offers an overview of the various forms of government:

". . . as the rule of man over man—of one or the few in monarchy and oligarchy, of the best or the many in aristocracy and democracy, to which today we ought to add the latest and perhaps most formidable form of such dominion, bureaucracy, or the rule by an intricate system of bureaus in which no men, neither one nor the best, neither the few nor the many, can be held responsible, and which could be properly called the rule by Nobody. Indeed, if we identify tyranny as the government that is not held to give account of itself, rule by Nobody is clearly the most tyrannical of all, since there is no one left who could even be asked to answer for what is being done. It is this state of affairs which is among the most potent causes for the current world-wide rebellious unrest" (1969, p. 23).

In an analysis similar in many respects to Arendt's, Galbraith (1967) argues that the locus of power in American society is no longer in one person or office, but rather exists in what he calls a *technostructure*, an interlocking collection of technicians, experts, and organization types who run the bureaucratic show in this "new industrial state."

I would add to this collection Marx and his discussion of the alienating qualities of work, and several contemporary authors, for example, Goodman (1960), Keniston (1965), Mills (1961), and Marcuse (1966). Although I cannot elaborate here on the unique contribution of each of these authors, each carries into today's writing several themes that emerged from the mid-nineteenth to the twentieth century. In the main, each notes how the social structures and institutions that maintain and enhance contemporary industrial society serve to frustrate essential human needs, threaten to extinguish the humane and creative potential that is man's heritage and hope, and provide motive force behind the varieties of protest that mark the American and international landscape.

One significant thrust of these writers is the argument that democracy, corporate liberalism, bureaucracy, rule by Nobody, or whatever term we use, is a form of social organization that *appears* to give each citizen a voice in decision making but in fact sees decisions cranked out by an impersonal entity, the bureaucratic organization, primarily to serve military and industrial economic interests. The argument runs further, as several directly involved in the protest movement have noted (e.g., Mario Savio) that in such a system of social organization one is granted freedoms up to that point at which the underlying economic foundations are threatened. One may *speak* freely, for example, as long as one does not *act* in any way to threaten the economic status quo. Or one may protest just as long as that protest does not interfere with those same economic interests.

Oglesby and Shaull (1967) note specifically the intimate connection between American military activity and what they call a fundamentally expansionist economic system. They argue that the United States does indeed want peace around the world, primarily so that worldwide markets will be safe for American businessmen. To this end, they maintain, the U. S. government supports whatever native governments are most helpful in stabilizing their country for U. S. business interests; or, if that fails, it intrudes its military forces to keep our economic colonies politically secure. The essence of this argument is that the form that political and social organization takes is shaped, in the end, by the basic economic interests it must serve.

Those who are truly wedded to the movement's ideology argue further that participatory democracy, a form of social organization reminiscent of the town-meeting form of government, is a threat to the existing order because the public, if honestly given an opportunity for expression, would not long put up with the economic enhancement of a few at the expense of the needs of many. The few, in this view, include the largest business corporations and conglomerates and the massive national combine of the defense establishment. Their corpo-

rate aspirations, expanding throughout this nation and around the world, are assumed to be the underlying real structure that determines policies; democratic participation is simply superimposed to mask the basically coercive nature of the corporate society. The velvet glove of coercion is revealed in the following passages by Fromm in his introduction to Neill's *Summerhill* (1964):

". . . The concentration of capital led to the formation of giant enterprises managed by hierarchically organized bureaucracies. . . . The individual worker becomes merely a cog in this machine. In such a production organization, the individual is managed and manipulated. . . . And in the sphere of consumption (in which the individual allegedly expresses his free choice) he is likewise managed and manipulated. . . . Our economic system must create men who fit its needs; men who co-operate smoothly; men who *want* to consume more and more. . . . Our system needs men who *feel* free and independent but who are nevertheless willing to do what is expected of them. . . . It is not that authority has disappeared, nor even that it has lost in strength, but that it has been transformed from the overt authority of force to the anonymous authority of persuasion and suggestion. . . . The same artifices are employed in progressive education. The child is forced to swallow the pill, but the pill is given a sugar coating. Parents and teachers have confused true nonauthoritarian education with education by means of persuasion and hidden coercion" (1964, pp. x–xi).

Some Relevant Statistics. Some of the facts and figures are startling, especially in the context of the movement's claims as just outlined. In 1965, for example, 60 U. S. companies reported earnings of at least $1 billion. In 1966 200 corporations, about one tenth of 1 percent of the total number of corporations, controlled nearly 60 percent of the nation's manufacturing wealth (Barber, 1966). Furthermore, the larger companies are getting even larger, becoming highly diversified conglomerates. In 1965 about 1000 companies merged into larger companies; over a decade earlier, by contrast, mergers totaled only about 200 per year.

Business growth of this sort does not occur without government sanction and outright support in the form of special tax benefits and corporate tax relief and expenditures. Oil companies, in particular, benefit from a hefty oil depletion allowance that for many years permitted them to exempt 27½ percent of all income from taxes. In 1968 a U. S. congressman reported that Standard Oil of New Jersey—one case in point—paid only 3.8 percent in taxes on profits of nearly $2 billion (T.R.B., 1968). Compare this corporate tax to that of the average Joe, who shells out a considerably higher proportion of his already beleaguered income to the government each April 15. Startling as it may sound, 2.5 million Americans of low income paid some $100 million in taxes, an average of 14 percent. By contrast, 22 of the largest oil companies with a profit of $5.2 billion paid taxes at a rate of only 4 percent. (*The New Republic*, April 5, 1969.) In like manner, the Federal Government pays millions of dollars each year to farmers—especially large corporate farms—*not* to grow crops, while resisting and resenting suggestions of a negative income tax for the nation's poor and unemployed. In 1968, for example, California farmers received payments totaling over $47 million *not* to raise certain crops; the figure for Arizona was over $28 million (*N.Y. Times Almanac*, 1969). Critics —including U. S. congressmen—have noted that we call the payment to the farmers a *subsidy* and think of it as good for the nation, whereas we view the payment to the poor as *welfare doles* that threaten to undermine individual initiative. Large corporate interests are supported and justified while the common man still awaits his day in the sun.

Critics of the new industrial state (e.g., Galbraith) argue that consumers, who must be taught to want what is made and to consume more and more, are managed carefully through media advertising. As a consequence our national economic priorities often read more like a baby's demand schedule than an adult's reasoned evaluation of national need. The wealth of the nation is channeled into consumer goods rather than into public services:

"We spend as much for chewing gum as for model cities. We spend as much for hair dye as for grants to urban mass transit. We spend as much for pet food as on food stamps for the poor. We spend more for tobacco than government at all levels spends on higher education. We spend $300 million for jewelry, and quarrel over $10 million for the Teachers Corps" (T.R.B., 1968).

Shocked as we may be by those consumer figures, adherents of the campus protest movement—and many others as well—are shocked even more by defense- and military-related spending that takes so much away from community services. During the sixties, when protests on the campus gained their major impetus, spending in Vietnam and in related endeavors took the lion's share of the national budget. For example, it is estimated that of a tax burden of some $2834 per family, the largest chunk, about $1250, goes for national defense (*N.Y. Times Almanac*, 1969). Although there is always some controversy over how profitable a war is, and for whom, at least one analyst of the Vietnam War (Perlo, 1970) noted a steady rise in the net income of the big five Pentagon contractors: $137 million in 1960; $395 million in 1964; and $587 million in 1968.

"The pervasive and insistent disquiet on many campuses throughout the nation indicates that unrest results, not from a conspiracy by a few, but from a shared sense that the nation has no adequate plans for meeting the crises of our society. . . . We do not say that all the problems faced by colleges and universities are a reflection of the malaise of the larger society. That is not true. But we do say that until political leadership addresses itself to the major problems of our society—the huge expenditure of national resources for military purposes, the inequities practiced by the present draft system, the critical needs of America's 23 million poor, the unequal division of our life on racial issues—until this happens, the concern and energy of those who know the need for change will seek outlets for their frustration" (Plimpton, 1969).

Rule by Nobody and a lost faith in the processes of government; rule by Nobody and an economy that gives more to fewer and less to more; rule by Nobody that shapes priorities in ways that abandon those in need while filling the coffers of the military and maintaining the economy with frivolous consumption.

Another View. Before examining the specific conditions of the university that are conducive to the development of the student protest movement, let's listen for a moment to the comments of two important movement critics, Kerr, former president of the University of California and Brzezinski, a professor of political science at Columbia. It is important to keep in mind that both the adherents of a movement and its critics represent a particular value bias; the critics can no more pass themselves off as dispassionate and objective than can the adherents. The adherents, as we've just seen, claim that certain societal conditions create strain that forms the basis and motive force of their movement. The critics typically do not attempt to deny the presence of strain (this would be like telling a hungry person that he's not hungry), but rather place it in a context unlike that in the minds of the movement's supporters. The adherents, for example, see their movement as the wave of the future; the critics usually see the movement as the last gasp of those who are ill suited to move into tomorrow.

For Kerr the movement's theories are naively Utopian; the function of the university—as it presently exists—is to service the needs of a technological society:

"The cry for community, the cry for integration of thought and action, are cries that call backward to a smaller, simpler world. The revolutionary visions of today are of the old, not the new, of ancient Athens and medieval Paris and not of modern New York. It is a sad commentary when the new revolutionary goal is the old past, not the future. . . . The standard model for the university is not the small, unified, autonomous community. Small intellectual communities can exist and serve a purpose, but they run against the logic of the times. . . . The longing for community, for this fantasy, this pie-in-the-sky, can actually impede efforts to make better that which must be. . . . The campus consistent with the society has served as a good introduction to society—to bigness, to specialization, to diffusion of interests; to problems, to possibilities" (1967; see also Kerr, 1963).

There are several key phrases in that passage. One is the "logic of the times," by which he means the university *must* turn out persons who can fit the machinery of this advanced technological age. The communal and antitechnological aims that characterize the protest movement, in Kerr's terms, defy this logic. Another is "that which must be." Again he implies

a condition of society that is inevitable and to which man must learn to adapt himself. Are those who do not fit what *must* be destined to suffer alone with their alienation? As Kerr himself notes, his "analysis should not be confused with approval or [his] description with defense" (1968, p. 13). Furthermore, he deplores the existing conditions of isolation and fragmentation that he describes. He says that "there is no inherent reason why the student must be lost; no inherent reason why a more comprehensive understanding of man and society must be sacrificed" (p. 13).

Brzezinski, talking both about the 1968 uprising at Columbia and the larger picture of student protests, maintains that U.S. society has passed beyond its industrial era; we are now in our *postindustrial* phase. In his terms we have become a *technetronic society*; "a society in which technology, especially electronic communications and computers, is prompting basic social changes" (1968, p. 25). He defines a true revolutionary movement as one that is oriented toward the future rather than to the past; past-oriented movements are counterrevolutionary, like the peasant uprisings in response to the industrial era, or the Luddite movement in England in the early nineteenth century, when workers ran about smashing machinery in the belief that the machines would displace them. Counterrevolutionary movements fail, according to Brzezinski because ". . . they do not provide meaningful programs and leadership for the coming age. . . . Rather they reflect concern that the past may be fading and a belated attempt to impose the values of the past on the present and on the future" (p. 25). For Brzezinski the student protest movement is clearly counterrevolutionary; we hear in them "the death rattle of the historical irrelevants" (p. 25).

The adherents of the movement and at least these two critics have different views of history and of man's role in it. I think I am being fair to Kerr and Brzezinski if I suggest that the key variable in their system is the nature of man; in simplistic terms, both would accept the argument that man is malleable and must fit himself to the changing demands of his society. Kerr does make overtures to changing the form of social organization as well, although he clearly does not like the kinds of revolutionary change the movement's supporters demand; he thinks their vision is out of step with reality and must be changed to fit with modern society. He is especially hostile to the view that links thought (or scholarship) with action. In contrast, the movement subscribes to the idea that man has a certain degree of malleability, but within clear limits; that he can bend only so far in fitting himself to social structures; and these structures and their organization must be reshaped to fit man's needs.

I think there is little need for me to repeat my own position in this matter, but here goes anyway. There are essential human needs and requirements for humane living that will not yield to the demands of a particular social organization. Man's malleability is limited; nor are social structure and social organization infinitely malleable or inevitably fixed. The coordination of large numbers of persons does require a different kind of social organization from that in a tiny village isolated from the rest of the world; but although we are indeed moving into a technetronic or postindustrial age, this does not mean that man must adapt all the way while social organization plods on in what I and many others consider a disastrous direction. Social organization will clearly have to undergo drastic changes if man is to live healthfully and creatively. Furthermore, in my view, the visions of the student protest movement contain seeds of beneficent social change.

The dialectic of history swings between organizational efficiency and humane living. Contemporary society has moved too far toward efficiency, with the personal manipulation and other consequences that follow rapidly on its heels. The pendulum is swinging again toward man. If a golden age has any meaning, it must center on humane living, even at the expense of efficiency. After all, what does it really matter if we get to the moon and the planets, only to return home to the ghetto, despair, hunger, ignorance, overpopulation, disease, pollution, emptiness?

Target of the sixties: Big U

The political protest movement of young America during the sixties, although broad in its over-all aims and responding to strains general in the society, came of age and maintained its vigor on university and college campuses in the United States and around the world. That this should be so is no mere accident. In examining the origins of this social movement, then, the selection of Big U as both the target and the home base reveals many of the structural conditions conducive to this form of collective behavior. This is not to deny that other, even larger targets exist. It is rather intended to indicate that as long as there is a strong partnership between the university and the military-industrial complex the university will continue to be a target. This is more than a matter of convenience, although convenience is a relevant factor; it *is* more convenient to attack a concretely represented local institution than the more abstract institutions in Washington. The university is not seen as an innocent accidentally caught in a war not of its making. In the eyes of the movement's adherents it is a key cog in the structure of the society they wish to change.

Once Big U (really Small C) was the playground for the elite and the home of the classic liberal arts scholar. The advent of the public land-grant college, devoted primarily to applied problems (e.g., in agriculture), drastically changed the nature of the beast. After World War II masses of middle-class youth began to flock in, to be met by technicians and specialists who would help train them for the skilled careers that the technological society required. In the sixties this mass grew and became a significant social category. In 1950 there were about 2.2 million college students; by 1960 this figure had risen to 3.6 million; by 1968 the figure jumped to 6.9 million.

Despite the influx of persons coming to be trained, Big U retained a semblance of its classic system of values. In particular it presented individuals with the challenge of critical questioning and critical thought. To be sure, there was much rote learning and multiple-choice feedback of snippets of often unrelated knowledge. Yet there was also an underlying ethic that called on one to keep an open mind and always to question, doubt, examine, analyze, criticize. All ideas, in theory at least, were there to be examined and discussed. As any good dictator knows, an educated populace, one that questions, thinks critically, and is open to a wide range of ideas, is potentially dangerous. A governor of Virginia (seventeenth century) wrote, "Thank God there are no free schools or printing.... For learning has brought disobedience and heresy into the world, and printing has divulged them.... God keep us from both" (in Griffen, 1969).

The Big U brought together in one setting a large mass of young persons; it helped open their eyes and introduced them to a critical system of values. It was only natural that this group should come to examine critically the very institution that housed them daily for four crucial years of their life. What they saw was another kind of eye-opener.

Is Anyone Responsible? In its structure the Big U (I suppose I could use Kerr's more dignified term, *multiversity*, but I am somehow fond of this more traditional reference) looks like a complex collage of the new plastered hastily and tenuously over the old. The traditional model of a community of scholars and learners with shared intellectual values exists side by side with the modern big-business university of faculty entrepreneurs, administrative managers, and scores of preprofessional students, all of whom often have more conflict of interest than values shared. Above all else, it was the thinking man's bureaucracy. It had red tape in so many shapes, sizes, and even colors that General Motors would be embarrassed by the comparison. Getting into and out of Big U was a feat that did indeed require a college education.

Arendt's rule by Nobody seemed all too keenly descriptive. Never was this more apparent than when students changed the nature of their extracurricular activities from springtime panty raids and fall football blasts to political matters. The man on top—the chancellor or president—could easily delegate his authority to the office of the dean of students when it came to handling apolitical outbursts, but with political activity the chancellor found himself under more pressure than usual from his own superiors (the regents or trustees). He had to take the reins more directly; yet the dean's

office remained fully functioning. The students were not certain with whom they should talk about grievances; if they used normal channels and went to the dean, they would be given some mystical incantation that meant, " I can't make a firm decision about so touchy a matter." The chancellor in turn felt himself increasingly incapable of making decisions until checking with the regents. As campus protest came fully into its own, the regents couldn't act until they checked things out with the legislature, who in turn were tuned in to public opinion, most of which had been shaped by media-borne images of bearded weirdos doing their thing on "our taxpayers' campus."

Down at the bottom of the heap the student wandered about seeking someone in charge who could take responsibility for just long enough to handle his grievance. But at each door, he got the same message: "I'll let you know in a few days after I check it out." He knew all too well what that meant. As Arendt noted, rule by Nobody is tyranny without a tyrant. Not surprising, therefore, that grievance procedures move to the streets and the barricades; not surprising either that symbols of the tyrant are sought in the form of policemen or university property. What I am saying, in essence, is that rule by Nobody—all too characteristic of the modern Big U—creates the very conditions that give rise to more protest and even violent outbursts.

In this connection, I note that the protest movement can be characterized in much the same way; Nobody rules there either. An administrator who wishes to talk has as much difficulty locating a responsible party as the protestors have in locating a fully responsible administrator. Structurally, therefore, this situation is conducive to a continuing cycle of escalation that serves to enlarge the movement through a radicalizing process, and simultaneously to enlarge the pressure against the movement. A concrete example at this point should be helpful in outlining the process. Although I draw on the scene at Berkeley, with which I am most familiar, there is good reason to believe that comparable processes have occurred at other locations as well.

Early in 1969 Berkeley shuddered at what has come to be called the "People's Park" controversy. There are several facets to this problem, but for the present I would like to indicate how the rule by Nobody worked. On vacant, university-owned property a couple of blocks from the main campus, students and local people began to build themselves a park. For several weeks the university ignored this event, which later it would call a "land seizure." When it became apparent that the park people were seriously intending to develop a user-maintained park, the university administration took action; they ordered a chain-link fence to be built. This required more than builders. People threatened to fight for this land they were developing, so several hundred policemen and 2000 National Guardsmen arrived to help build the fence and to guard it. Many battles erupted; one man was killed, another blinded; many were injured; nearly everyone was tear-gassed repeatedly, and over 1000 were arrested.

Although responsibility for building the fence was clearly taken by the chancellor, responsibility for removing it and for settling the state of war in Berkeley was another matter entirely. The chancellor claimed he could not remove the fence or discuss the issues involved. The City Council of Berkeley got into the act when the police and National Guard's indiscriminate use of tear gas had implicated most of the community as victims, but the Council argued that things were out of its hands as well. The regents kept quiet; one of them even maintained that settlement of the issue was up to the chancellor. As a week of occupation passed, and as more Berkeley citizens came into contact with the outside forces, the Berkeley City Council finally had to act. They realized that they had no control over their city, a position unusual for mayor, city manager, and councilmen. The chancellor likewise had no control over his campus. The faculty had no control. The students had no control. The regents had no control. The governor had control, but he claimed that he had ordered troops in at the request of the city and the chancellor.

From the sidelines this looked like a football game being played with a hot potato. Nobody wanted to touch it; nobody wanted to take responsibility; nobody wanted to do anything. Each called on the other parties to do something. If it had not been so tragic and serious a matter, it would have been laughable. As it was, for most of the students involved the People's Park issue simply brought to the surface what they had known for a long time: rule by Nobody, with nobody willing or able to take any responsibility, creates an impossible situation of governance. As it surfaced, this absurd condition of modern social organization helped expand the number of adherents to the movement. For once in its history the campus movement had as its supporters the street people, the left-leaning politicos, the right-leaning politicos, most of the usually silent middle, the athletes, fraternity, sorority, and rah-rah types, and even many ROTC cadets.

In such a structural setting the typical chain of events begins with efforts by students to discuss, moves out into street and campus confrontations, and eventually returns to the discussion table. Initial discussions fail because no one is willing to run the ship. Moving into the streets usually forces several elements out into the open. In particular, the faculty emerge from their studies and try to take on mediating functions. Here is a puzzling fact of too many situations. At Berkeley, at least, the faculty know fully that certain administrative actions are likely to produce a street confrontation. In the People's Park issue this was known to everyone weeks before any fence was put up. Yet the faculty rarely takes any action to mediate a potential conflict *before* it happens. They assume no responsibility until after a serious battle has taken place; at that point, and only at that point, do they attempt to take on the role of Somebody in moderate control. Their refusal or inability to enter beforehand to open channels for discussion forces those with grievances to create conditions of disruption that make them (and others) enter after the fact. Those who decry violent confrontations after they occur usually could have prevented the occurrence if they had acted in advance. The perversity of the situation is that we are not discussing evil men with evil intentions; we are talking about men of good will who are caught up in a structural arrangement that creates the conditions they later will come to condemn. Yet the structures perpetuate themselves, serving thereby as catalysts for continuing disruptions.

So far I have indicated several conditions that favor the development of the protest movement within the university: (1) the congregation of many young persons; (2) a system of values that calls for questioning and critical analysis, thereby permitting examination of the university itself; (3) a structure of rule by Nobody that facilitates angry confrontations. Several other features warrant examination: (4) leadership; (5) the essential hypocrisy and double-bind quality of the university; (6) its key role as a port of entry to society. Although not part of the university, (7) the mass media must be included in any listing of the contemporary conditions conducive to the formation of a social movement.

Leaders. Any social movement requires a leadership corps that provides focus to the frustrated needs that are experienced and helps define the sources of strain and solutions. Part of this leadership must involve itself with the ideological justifications that keep the movement together in the face of an often hostile surround. I will deal later with some of the specifics of the protest ideology; suffice it to note at this point that the university provides a setting in which leadership emerges and intellectual justifications are provided. In fact the intellectual world of academe provides justifications *both* for the established social order and for those who seek its change. Both sets of ideologies often exist in the same department.

Double Bind. By its very nature the Big U is not only the essence of bureaucracy, but also the essence of hypocrisy. A double-bind communication (see p. 61ff.) is one that carries two contradictory messages; it seems that the university specializes in such communiques, and once again the student is the victim. While spending much of their time preparing, getting, and administering research grants or consulting to big business, big labor, or big government, faculty members pause occasionally to teach a class or advanced seminar. They talk about the pleasures of seeking knowledge for its own sake while they personally seek fame,

fortune, and promotion. Their purpose for acquiring what they claim is objective knowledge seems to be to please a publisher or a sponsoring agency, or to be up on the mainstream fad of their particular profession. They deny any value bias, but luxuriate in the professional limelight, count royalties, clip coupons, buy property. They claim that their research is basic and that they have no responsibility for the use to which it is put, yet they help create the weaponry of warfare or the ideologies that support the society's status quo.

Commenting on Bell's essay *The End of Ideology*, Chomsky (1967) argues that the intellectual community shares a general consensus about the basic "goodness" of U. S. society: "they see no further need for a radical transformation of society" (p. 22). However, "this consensus of the intellectuals is self-serving. . . by and large, intellectuals have lost interest in 'transforming the whole of a way of life' [because] they play an increasingly prominent role in running the Welfare State. . ." (p. 22). He concurs with Bell (and others) that the academic of today is offered too much prestige and wealth ever to wish a radical transformation.

Students are not stupid, whatever their final examination scores. They can readily observe the true facts of Professor Fat Cat's life through the obfuscations of rhetoric he erects. "How," they ask, "can he be objective—especially in history, economics, sociology, social psychology, and political science—when his self-interest is involved in the support of a particular political, economic, and sociopsychological system?" They come to doubt his disinterestedness or the disinterestedness of the heavily federally funded Big U. It is my guess that there is less anger at the true facts of his life than there is with the hypocritical way in which he represents himself. In family life the double bind might drive one to neurotic illness; in university interaction it is likely to drive one to soured cynicism or to membership in a social movement of protest.

Port of Entry. The university today is the port of entry through which almost everyone must pass if he is to make it out there in the surrounding society. Once it served the interests of the church; today the university serves the interests of society. Going to college has become an essential phase in the life of a growing body of young Americans. Those who do not gain entry suffer economically for the rest of their lives. The average yearly income of college graduates (1963) was $10,000, compared with an average of $6700 for high-school graduates and $4900 for those with eight years of elementary school (*U.S. Book of Facts*, 1965). One cannot seriously be said to go to college voluntarily; it is a societal requirement. It is not a privilege, it is a necessity.

School attendance occupies an increasingly long period of a person's life. A relatively mature and sophisticated young person enters college and remains often through graduate or professional school. He is not a child anymore, but the institution tends to treat him like a second-class citizen. He must pass through this gate to get into society; but he is told that while passing through he does not possess the rights and privileges he has on the outside. Is it any wonder that the university becomes the target for many students' efforts to regain control over their lives? They are told too often to wait to gain full participation as citizens in their society; their answer increasingly has been to demand participation in the university itself. "How can I wait to participate when I do not like the direction in which either the society or the university is heading?"

Part of the origin of the 1964 Free Speech Movement was the university's denial of facilities to participate in civil rights activities. Students returned to Berkeley from summer activities in the South, hoping to continue organizing on campus, only to be informed that they could not collect funds or sell literature from tables set up in the large Sproul Plaza area. From their perspective the university was denying them rights of expression and political activity on the campus that they were constitutionally guaranteed off campus.

The thrust of ethnic studies programs and admission demands is likewise rooted in the nonvoluntary quality of higher education in the United States. Any group that is systematically denied access to a quality college education in essence is being denied access to the mainstream of the society. All citizens therefore feel it is their right to demand and receive entry into Big U.

The Media. The mass media function in conjunction with university events to facilitate the development of a protest movement. National and international organization is possible through the mass media today as never before. A movement leader in California need not have a wire service or telephone connection with leaders in Tokyo, Paris, Chicago, or New York. He simply appears on television and is thereby hooked into the larger protest movement of youth. Those who see an international conspiracy in the similarity of upheavals at campuses in the United States and around the world have forgotten the power of the mass media to bring uprisings rapidly around for all to see. The media, in fact, serve a dual function. First, they carry the misfortunes of the world into each locale and thus facilitate a sharing of world strains that has never before been possible in the history of mankind. Second, as noted, they permit real communication among separate campus movements. When Paris explodes, Berkeley hears about it and can respond in kind. During the People's Park episode news quickly reached Berkeley that students in Rome had seized their administration building in sympathy. Columbia's problems become Berkeley's; Berkeley's problems become Wisconsin's. Leadership in one area becomes leadership in another. Ideological justifications in one part of the country are rapidly transmitted. Clearly, then, the role of the media cannot be overlooked in any overview of the conditions of contemporary society that are conducive to the development of a social movement.

STRUCTURES OF THE MOVEMENTS

The existence of strain, even under conditions conducive to the formation of a social movement, may set the stage for a variety of expressions of collective behavior; a social movement, however, involves an *organized* effort to produce social change. With organization we can speak of the patterns of relationship and the texture of ideology, the structure of the movement. As noted on p. 361ff. Smelser differentiates between a social movement that is norm-oriented and one that is oriented toward changing society's basic values. In one view Black America is seeking social justice and an equitable share of the material affluence that exists; it is norm-oriented. Campus protestors, on the other hand, seem intent on creating a new *quality* of living. Whether this quality can be attained by adherence to the present values of American society (i.e., by a norm-oriented movement) or whether it will require an entirely new value framework is a question that splits both the movement and its interpreters.

Third World movement for social justice

The jargon of the Cold War gave us the First World of the "free" nations, the Second World of the iron-curtain countries, and the Third World, those largely populated but economically and technologically depressed developing nations. Unaligned politically with either of the first two, these Third World nations provided ready targets for courting by the United States, Russia, and even mainland China.

Fanon in particular (e.g., 1963) described vividly the colonial situation of the Third World nations and plotted their union to overcome their socially down position. Before the emergence of the Third World as independent nations, colonialism pervaded their political, economic, and social relationships. Politically, the colonizers, although numerically in the minority, held all the positions of power, especially military strength, and made the decisions that governed the lives of their colonies. Economically, the colonizers exploited the human and natural resources of the colonies to serve the needs of the "mother country" for their own gain. Social relationships between the colonizer and the colonized took the form of master to slave (see Chapter 17). More often than not the colonized identified with the colonizer, saw himself through the other's eyes as an incompetent, childlike creature, and wished above all else to be "white."

During the late sixties in the United States a relatively small but growing number of militant blacks, joined occasionally by other peoples of color, defined their own situation vis-a-vis white American society in terms of this Third World

colonizer-colonized model. Cleaver (1968) for example, was significantly influenced in his own political thinking by the writings of Fanon. Rather than attempting to document the degree of validity of this model—there are both similarities and differences between the situation of the American Negro and that faced by colonized colored in the Third World nations—suffice it to point out, first, that how a man defines his situation affects the manner by which he relates to that situation and, second, that there are, in fact, several compelling parallels between the situation of blacks in the United States and the colonial situation worldwide.

Increasingly the black ghetto deep in the central city has been and is the colony. Into the ghetto stream white colonials to conduct business in their shops, taking money out, bringing little benefit back to the ghetto community. Out from the ghetto stream black house cleaners, janitors, or manual laborers; black works for white while controlling little or nothing of his own. Skin bleaches, hair straighteners, light skin, and white features define the good and the beautiful. Pride in race, pride in culture, and pride in self wither and die with barely a whimper in this atmosphere.

To break the master-slave or colonizer-colonized cycle in the Third World model requires a sharp move toward political, economic, and social independence. No longer does slave define master's way as good; no longer does slave permit himself to see the world through master's eyes. Black becomes beautiful. Afro culture has a status and dignity of its own; natural hair and Negroid features take on new value; pride in race and pride in self slowly emerge.

The university campus became a special target. Efforts were made to create black studies colleges or departments that were run by blacks for blacks. Pride in self and in race does not come to a person simply because he is allowed to study his own history, sociology, or psychology; pride has its locus in the self-determination of one's life and education. Whites who had been involved in civil rights work suddenly encountered a new movement that demanded their ouster. No whites allowed. "Reverse racism!" went up the cries, "Segregation in black!" Yet in the context of the Third World's model we can understand the basis for distrust of white involvement in black activities. For the black, whenever whites came around, good intentions and all, the relationship of superior to inferior, of master to slave or colonizer to colonized was experienced. And shouting that this is not so or not intended does not remove the deeply etched scars of the experience.

When participation in the mainstream of society has been systematically denied for hundreds of years, when justice has too often been served up with careful reference to skin color, when the human soul has been so degraded that man can hardly face himself each day, the thirst for involvement, equity, justice, and dignity does not easily await the former master's slowly evolving sensitivities. For example, during the San Francisco State College crisis over black studies in 1968–1969, 15 demands were put forth by the Black Student's Union and the Third World Liberation Front, among them: a department of black studies whose chairman, faculty, and staff have the sole power to hire and fire without the interference of the racist administration and the chancellor; all black students who wish to should be admitted to the college beginning in the fall of 1969; the California State College Trustees should not be allowed to dissolve any black programs on or off the San Francisco State campus. Demands off campus had the same ring of immediacy; blacks were to share *now* in everything the society offered to its white citizens but had for so long denied to them. In early 1969, following much the same Third World model, some militant blacks called on churches to pay reparations in sizable sums for the neglect, damage, and crimes against their humanity that had been committed since the time of slavery.

The goals of this Third World-black movement seem to lie within the value framework of U. S. society, but the militant ideology of the colonizer-colonized model has clear revolutionary overtones, for the solution for the colonized lies in overthrowing the power of the oppressing colonizer. Thus in its very structure the black movement has a mixture of reform and revolution. Personally, I think it is an oversimplification to assume that the protest movement of black Americans is entirely norm-oriented or, as Katz (1967) suggested, legitimate in the eyes of white America because it is congruent both with American ideals of justice and with the needs of the military-industrial complex. The question as yet unanswered is the degree to which reform will aocomplish the goals of bringing black America into the nation's mainstream. Even if we maintain that the rhetoric of militant blacks who argue from the Third World model is simply talk, it remains to be seen whether the nation's military and industrial goals are compatible with participation of blacks, the poor, and, for that matter, a growing segment of disaffected whites.

In my view the Third World model is not simply rhetoric, but refers to a definite stage of development that an oppressed group must pass through before it can ever feel sufficient self-esteem and self-confidence to face and overcome an oppressive system. The truly downtrodden and oppressed remain that way until the first glimmer of hope propels them out of apathy and into a fighting posture; as the sit-ins of the early Civil Rights Movement gave way to the stand-up-and-fight posture of the late 1960's we witnessed the passage through a key psychological barrier. The benign view is that we will pass through this fighting stage and someday become a society that has retained its basic values but truly lives up to them for all its citizens.

A less benign perspective is that a more radical upheaval will have to occur. In this view the basic, original values of the United States are rhetoric used to disguise an economic and political system that is not basically just and humane. This way of looking at the situation adds further complexity to the problem of norm-versus value-oriented movements. When values are simply words that conceal a structurally faulted social system, achieving ends congruent with those stated values requires an upheaval in the structure to make it fit the values. This seems to be revolutionary, an extreme change in the political and economic institutions, the institutions of power in the society.

Fourth World movement for quality

Although it appears at first that color of skin

is the sole characteristic that identifies members of the black protest movement, this identity includes attitude and age as well. In like fashion, members of what I term the Fourth World (Sampson, 1970), although white, find their identity in position, age, and attitude. Black militants identify themselves with the Third World; whites of the Fourth World often identify themselves with the blacks. In their own eyes they are society's white niggers.

This Fourth World is one primarily of the young, the affluent, the white, the educated, the middle and upper-middle classes. Theirs is an emerging and still relatively small movement that occurs among the advantaged classes in societies that have reached their proper historical point. Affluence has settled for them the *quantity* questions, but the conditions requisite to producing and maintaining that affluence have brought into focus concerns about life's *quality*. To paraphrase Disraeli, they are responding to a society that has mistaken material comfort for civilization.

The movement is most marked among the affluent classes of societies that are technologically advanced. That it should be in evidence mostly among the young should also come as no surprise. The young and the sensitive are quicker to spot, often intuitively, the key contradictions and sore spots of their society. They fought for civil rights and opposed the war in Vietnam long before these became more generally popular causes. They tend to be more imaginative and more innovative in seeking solutions required to produce social change because they are not caught in worn ruts. Typically, they are more willing or able to take risks, to think the unthinkable, to ask questions. Many also tend to be more optimistic and hopeful than the often cynical post-thirty group. Some even have the audacity to imagine that they can bring about change.

Is this Fourth World a norm-oriented or a value-oriented movement? Keniston (1967) maintains that the activists seek to live in accordance with credal American values such as free speech, participation in decision making, equal opportunity, and justice. Their protest derives from the disparity between the present structure and organization of society and those values.

In his view, then, the campus movement is norm-oriented. A selective examination of Hayden's "Port Huron Statement" of 1962 reveals some of the movement's goals that support this interpretation:

"We are people of this generation, bred in at least modest comfort, housed now in universities, looking uncomfortably to the world we inherit. . . . When we were kids the United States was the wealthiest and strongest country in the world. . . . As we grew . . . our comfort was penetrated by events too troubling to dismiss. First, the permeating and victimizing fact of human degradation, symbolized by the Southern struggle against racial bigotry, compelled most of us from silence to activism. Second, the enclosing fact of the Cold War, symbolized by the presence of the bomb, brought awareness that we ourselves, and our friends, and millions of abstract 'others' we knew more directly because of our common peril, might die at any time. . . . Our work is guided by the sense that we may be the last generation in the experiment with living. . . . Unlike youth in other countries, we are used to moral leadership being exercised and moral dimensions being clarified by our elders. But today, for us, not even the liberal and socialist preachments of the past seem adequate to the forms of the present. . . . Doubt has replaced hopefulness. . . . The decline of utopia and hope is in fact one of the defining features of social life today. . . . A first task of any social movement is to convince people that the search for orienting theories and the creation of human values is complex but worthwhile. . . . Our own social values involve conceptions of human beings, human relationships, and social systems.

We regard *men* as infinitely precious and possessed of unfulfilled capacities for reason, freedom, and love. . . . We oppose the depersonalization that reduces human beings to the status of things. . . . Human relationships should involve fraternity and honesty . . . human brotherhood must be willed . . . as a condition of future survival and as the most appropriate form of social relations. . . . We would replace power rooted in possession, privilege, or circumstance by power and uniqueness rooted in love, reflectiveness, reason, and creativity. As a *social system* we seek the establishment of a democracy of individual participation, governed by two central aims: that the individual share in those social decisions determining the quality and direction of his life; that society be organized to encourage independence in men and provide the media for their common participation . . ." (Hayden, 1966).

Comparable goals emerge in the published

writings of others. Flacks (1966), a founder of SDS and a professor of sociology, lists such movement goals as first-class citizenship for every person in the society and a challenge to the legitimacy of antidemocratic authority, laws, and institutions. Gitlin (1965), a former president of SDS argues that power must be shared among those affected, and resources guaranteed to make this possible; the institutional props of racism must be extirpated; America must put down the big stick and take self-determination seriously.

From even this brief examination it appears, as Keniston suggests, that the movement's stated goals are generally consistent with basic American values. However, before we declare the case closed and append our label of norm-oriented, we must realize that, as with the Third World model, many Fourth World adherents feel that the achievement of such goals requires a revolutionary change of the basic economic and political structures of the society. To create participatory democracy, for example, requires so drastic a reshuffling of the present institutions and power arrangements of U. S. society that only a revolutionary upheaval could possibly achieve this goal. Lynd states the case succinctly:

"...at this writing (August 1968), the sentiment is growing in the movement that participatory democracy, like nonviolence, may have been the product of a naive early stage of protest, before the magnitude of the movement's task was fully recognized. Nonviolence and participatory democracy will exist in the good society created after the revolution, it is increasingly said. But the work of transformation requires tools suited to this age of blood and iron: insurrectionary violence and a Marxist-Leninist Party." (1969, p. 71).

A "revolutionary call" put out in early June 1969 by Hayden and several others in the Berkeley area offers yet another view of the revolutionary nature of the movement. I present only selected parts of their 13-point program to make Berkeley a revolutionary example throughout the world: we will turn the schools into training grounds for liberation; we will destroy the university unless it serves the people; we will struggle for the full liberation of women as a necessary part of the revolutionary process; we will break the power of the landlords and provide beautiful housing for everyone; we will protect and expand our drug culture; we will unite with other movements throughout the world to destroy this racist capitalist imperialist system; we will create a soulful socialism in Berkeley.

Throughout all of these accounts of movement goals runs a theme to which I have alluded: individual freedom versus efficiency of social structure and organization. During the Free Speech Movement the cry was that for the sake of efficient processing the bureaucracy had transformed man into a number. During the Columbia University outbreak it was said that galloping university development threatened to push aside an entire community. During the People's Park controversy individual needs of expression were to be sacrificed by demands for organizational neatness. (See Wolin & Schaar, 1969, for a similar analysis and conclusion.) Somewhere between total anarchy and 1984's system of efficient control there must lie an answer for all mankind.

In attempting to reassert the freedoms of the individual against organizational demands, the campus protest movement, although congruent with the *stated* values of early democracy, runs headlong into the as yet *unstated* values of technological democracy. I am suggesting that America's value system, founded originally in a small, rural system of organization, is undergoing substantial changes in an era of scientific and technological wonderment. A vital disparity exists between values once professed and practiced and values still professed but practiced less. These newer values are unstated formally as such but are encountered in the facts of daily life in the society, where some few have much greater power than many; where decisions are made behind the scenes without meaningful citizen involvement; where big business grows into conglomerates; where science has opened moral problems concerning life and death heretofore unimagined; where military expenditures almost demand war, and economic ventures in foreign nations (over $50 billion in 1966) often provide the reasons. Almost imperceptibly for most, but painfully obviously to a few, the original values have gone by the boards, serving today more as masks that conceal reality than as a codification of reality.

A social movement oriented toward the credal American values by its very nature, then, is revolutionary: it is oriented toward a drastic change in the economic and political institutions of the society. Thus I see both the Third and Fourth World's movements as revolutionary rather than reformist; they are consistent with basic American values that are decreasingly operative in contemporary social structures. In their efforts either to restore justice or to create a better quality of life the movements encounter resistance, quite understandably, from those whose investment is in the present structure of the society regardless of the congruence or dissonance between that structure and basic American values. In what can only be added to our list of perversities, the defenders of the structures and organizations of the status quo call the movement's adherents un-American. Their meaning of un-American is best captured in a high-school guerrilla theater episode; in the scene portrayed the father gave his son a Cadillac, which the son refused flatly. The father, shocked, said, "Why, it's un-American not to want a Cadillac!"

If we examine the nature of the cases taken and the decisions handed down by the U. S. Supreme Court during the 1950's and 1960's, the distinction between societal or organizational efficiency and individual human rights becomes even clearer. In decision after decision the Court found in favor of the individual against what it, too, sensed to be the creeping encroachments of organizational control. Human rights in criminal cases, for example, took precedence over the demands of police and law-enforcement agencies to use constitutionally questionable tactics to apprehend those they felt to be criminals. In the area of civil rights the Court broke open barriers that had existed for years and helped lead the way into the era of individual rights as guaranteed by the Constitution. In its "one-man-one-vote" reapportionment decision the Court likewise sought to return voting representation to segments of the society that were underrepresented. Many of the Court's decisions met heavy criticism as it attempted to move along the delicate line be-

tween the needs of society and the needs of individuals in that society. I think the Court's actions reveal its sensitivity to the balance shifting over the last several decades away from the individual and toward organization.

Revolutionary Goals versus the Reality. I hasten to add that a movement may be revolutionary in its aims, yet not foster a revolution. Too often we think simplistically that if a movement's aims are revolutionary, then a revolution will be the result if that movement is not repressed; so we act to restrict it and often thereby help enlarge its membership and even create a climate more hospitable to its aims.

Moore (1969) outlined three conditions fundamental to the creation of a revolutionary climate in a nation. First, the intellectuals must desert the established order and put forward an alternative to the traditional views of society. Second, there must be clashes and conflicts of interests within the dominant classes of the society. Third, the dominant classes must lose their control over the instruments of force and violence, the military and the police. In a civil war one class gains control over these elements; in a true revolution the police and the army become separate from dominant governmental control. Moore further notes that in an urban society the creation of a *revolutionary mass*—a group predisposed to revolt and seeking a new order—demands a combination of serious hardship and a sudden breakdown in the routines of daily living: getting food, going to work, living life normally. The power blackout in New York City or even that city's garbage strike might have provided this latter kind of disruption. Moore concludes that revolution in the United States is an unlikely prospect as things presently stand. Conditions could change, however, especially the growing independence of the police and the military from civil control. But by themselves, movement aims, however revolutionary, cannot create a revolution unless other conditions are also in effect.

The relationship between the Third and Fourth World movements

The norms and beliefs by which members relate to one another and to nonmembers are part of the structure of any movement. The more militant black organizations have strict and highly disciplined policies concerning member-to-member relationships, whereas campus protest groups tend to be loosely knit both locally and nationally. A cadre builds up of persons who are frequently involved in the day-by-day business of leafleting and informally meeting and talking things over. As with any small group, these persons develop ties to one another. Perhaps the most important bond of relationships among Fourth Worlders across the nation is a sense of camaraderie on arriving in a new and strange community and encountering the "local underground." This may be focused around a newspaper, rock group, radio station, drugs, campus or community project, and so on; whatever its focus, a stranger who is "a brother" finds aid and comfort, a little pot, a pad to crash, some friendly conversation, some good music, and a bit of home. This experience is foreign to the typical traveler, who arrives at the Hilton with his credit cards, lost as one stranger among many.

Relationships between black and white militant groups are another matter entirely. There are both parallels and distinct differences, even conflicts, between the two groups. At times coalitions are formed and cooperative ventures undertaken; at other times one group seeks an ally and finds little interest; there are "brothers" and there are Brothers. One fascinating characteristic of their relationship involves what appears as a reversal in the typical black-white pattern. If we return to the colonial model we note that the colonized usually identifies with the colonizer and wishes to be just as he is. In breaking that pattern the militant blacks have rejected much of white society and things white as models for identification. So have many militant white radicals. Black is beautiful, white is pale and colorless. To be black means to have *soul*. To be white, by contrast, means to be plastic, unreal, and too abstractly mental. It is soul that the Fourth Worlder seeks for himself.

The Fourth Worlder actively strives to break away from both his socially "up" position and the kind of relationship with others that it implies. Although his background and education allow him to become part of the established elite, he wishes to relate more as an equal. That

he can never attain real entry into the black world or is rebuffed in his efforts leaves him even further alienated. He does not wish to relate to others from the one-up stance that his color and privilege allow; but he cannot become black and relate as a true member of that group. A marginal man between two worlds, he casts about in search of a place for himself. Many manifestations of his efforts are seen in his clothing, language, mannerisms, musical tastes, dance forms, and styles of personal expression, in which he attempts to emulate the Third Worlders.

This reversal in identification is apparent as well in the folk heroes of the Fourth World during the late sixties: Malcolm X, Martin Luther King, Huey Newton, Eldridge Cleaver, Che Guevara, Fidel Castro, oppressed Third Worlders engaged in their own struggles for independence, and similarly alienated existential writers and poets. Dylan, whose music in its several phases has captured the spirit of the movement and been one step ahead of it, is another kind of folk hero. Washington, Lincoln, or other traditional political folk figures are not found high (or anywhere) on the list.

Tactical Similarities. Tactically the Fourth World has followed rapidly on the heels of the Third World. For many years the blacks in this country made little noise; they seemed to have passively accepted their status in the society. Then with the beginnings of the Civil Rights Movement, especially in the late 1950's, the blacks began to emerge from their silence into action. White involvement in civil rights marked the beginnings of the Fourth Worlder's own stirrings out of the apathy of the 1950's, when the college generation had earned the name "The Silent Generation." It was but a tiny step from involvement in the black man's civil rights battles to an awareness of the personal relevance of those battles.

As black tactics began to shift from sit-ins and protest marches to greater militancy and eventually to spontaneous outbursts of violence, the campus protest scene likewise changed. Universities across the land experienced this shift; administrators had barely sufficient time to accommodate themselves to free speech, sit-ins, and protest marches when greater disruption became their daily diet. As the militant blacks began to think more politically, they sought to control spontaneous violence and to substitute threats (sometimes realized) of organized hit-and-run guerrilla warfare. It was not long before white campus groups caught the message, likewise beginning a series of episodes of nearly hand-to-hand street fighting, midnight bombings, burnings, and so forth.

I must point out—as I will do again later—that the choice of tactics is more often dictated by society's responses to a movement's appeals for change than it is any self-consciously sought desire to be violent or to use guerrilla tactics. There are few, if any, adherents of either the black or white militant movement who preach these tactics for their own sake. Rather, when efforts to produce change peacefully are met with no success, and when goals are so highly valued that one must persist until his very death, the choice of tactics is stringently limited.

Strain. Often the same sort of strain exists between the Third and Fourth Worlders as exists between each movement and the larger society. In part, the black militant sees the white radical as having great choice in the system, and therefore as like a little kid playing the game of revolution. When it's all over the white radical can shave off his beard, cut his hair, put on a new Brooks Brothers suit, and return to his normal, overprivileged life. The black does not have similar options; for him the game is deadly serious. Often I have heard Berkeley's black militants challenge the whites to become serious; often the challenge is to play the game with guns and bombs rather than the playful flower-power tactics that engage some white radicals' fancy. Strain is created as the white continually has to prove himself to be an honest radical, no easy feat for one brought up in middle- and upper-middle-class America where words and ideas replace the use of physical force as the preferred means for attaining ends. The picture in the late sixties changed somewhat; some nonviolently reared white kids began to act as though they had spent most of their lives in the heart of Harlem or Watts rather than on the upper East Side or Beverly Hills.

An especially informative encounter between the white radicals and the black community occurred in Berkeley in the early summer, 1969. To meet an expected influx of wandering youth, a group of radicals and some concerned business types sought to lease some apartments from the Berkeley Board of Education. They hoped to create a "People's Pad," where kids could find rooms and facilities for their summer's stay in Berkeley. The area they were to lease was part of a series of Navy surplus housing; a few months earlier Negro families had occupied this low-income housing and had been moved out when the Board of Education obtained the land for school construction. So here comes whitey radical to take over for three months, at $1 total cost, housing for white youth in a Negro area from which Negro families had been evicted.

The Black Panthers supported the white radicals, reflecting their split both from middle-class blacks—who were opposed to Panther militancy—and from more separatist black militants who were opposed to cooperation with any whites. The middle- and working-class blacks who lived in the area objected to the influx of hippie whites for exactly the same reasons that the majority of the white community objects: black mothers did not want their kids associating with those dirty, drug-using, lazy good-for-nothings! Separatist blacks and families who had been displaced from the housing objected to giving an already overprivileged group further privilege. Why not lease the property for three months for $1 to the blacks, who more desperately needed housing?

This one incident brought to the surface the underlying tensions that exist within the black community as well as between black and white militants, even while they share somewhat similar beliefs concerning the larger Establishment as "their common enemy." Discrepancies such as white outrage over People's Park, but minimal white effort to fight for a black studies program; white horror over the killings of whites at Kent State, but relatively less horror over the black deaths at Jackson State serve to intensify the tensions and the sense of distrust between members of the Third and Fourth World groups.

Historically, leftist political movements have

experienced great difficulty in getting themselves together and organized. They tend to fragment and waste their time in internal battles. The protest movements of the sixties lived up to this historical truth; not only was there a split between black and white militants, but also splits within each group. Although an outside observer might not have noted any differentiation, in point of fact these movements of the 1960's were highly differentiated as to ideology and structure. Some branches were more revolutionary than others; some were more separatist; some were more traditionally political than others, which in turn were more anarchistic.

Membership and leadership

Any social movement has a variety of leaders and followers; this is as true of the two social movements we have been examining as of movements in general.

Leadership: Black. The black protest movement has been blessed with strong, often charismatic, leaders. In 1914 in Jamaica and in 1917 in New York City Marcus Garvey established the Universal Negro Improvement Association, a Negro separatist movement that preached black nationalism and a return to Africa. In the 1920's Garvey's movement had more than 500,000 followers, mostly urban blacks who had migrated north, enticed by World War I jobs, only to encounter white hostility and riots directed against them. In the 1930's Elijah Muhammad founded the Lost Found Nation of Islam in the Wilderness of North America: the Black Muslims. In the 1960's Malcolm X inspired significant growth of the Muslim movement; in 1964 he broke with Muhammad to begin his own influential black movement.

Martin Luther King, Jr., rose to national prominence as a leader of SCLC and the Montgomery Bus Boycott of the mid-1950's. Until his assassination in 1968 King provided inspirational leadership for a large segment of the black community. Unlike the Muslims, King held the attention of the dominant white political structure and thereby provided a bridge between his movement and the surrounding society. During the late 1960's some young black militants, dissatisfied with King's moderate policies and unable to swallow the full personal and moral strictures of the Black Muslim faith, converted the Student Nonviolent Coordinating Committee into an aggressive organization. Stokely Carmichael became a significant leader, founding the Black Panther political party in 1965 in Alabama; he chose the black panther as a contrast to the white rooster emblem of the Alabama Democratic Party. Rap Brown, even more militant than Carmichael, later emerged as a SNCC leader.

On the West Coast Huey Newton, Bobby Seale, and, later, Eldridge Cleaver joined to form the contemporary version of the Black Panther Party. Their leadership functions were carefully divided into several "ministries," much as in a government in exile waiting to claim its rightful place in its homeland. Cleaver's writings as the Panther minister of information provided an intellectual focus for the movement; Newton's and Seale's leadership talents in organizing and stimulating a movement gained adherents across the country.

Each local community had its own leadership, usually clergymen who held great sway over their flocks. Yet the younger blacks were more militant and sought outlets through the Black Power thrust of the movement. Even a moderate like King was increasingly pushed to militancy, both to retain a hold on his followers and in response to the intransigence of the white community in making significant progress in race relations.

Leadership: White. We do not have a comparable list of the leadership of the campus protest movement; anyone who knows the functioning of the nonorganizations of campus protest will realize the extent to which traditional leadership or leadership like that of the black community is generally missing. Each campus, it seems, develops its own core of leaders, a steering committee. However, the media and many of the public insist that there be a leader, so one figure who is a slightly better speaker, or perhaps more agitated in appearance, appears frequently enough in the media to be thought of as the leader. At Berkeley during the Free Speech Movement Mario Savio became the media's leader. At Columbia the "created" leader was Mark Rudd. In an interesting way, of course, that media-selected personality comes to have certain leadership qualities, even for those he's leading. People waited breathlessly to hear what Savio had to say; he had certain charismatic qualities, a combination of the video image and his own talents in speaking publicly and in capturing the essence of the moment.

The problem of finding clearly identifiable movement leaders was brought home to me in 1969 when I attended a planning session for a large Memorial Day March on People's Park. It was felt that publicity would be helpful, and that television and radio interview shows would be a useful approach to gaining this publicity. Who would appear on those shows? No one was very eager. A woman who had some experience with such matters indicated that one person would have to be chosen as chairman, since the shows always wanted to interview a leader. "But we have no chairman," was the reply. The solution was simple. A committee of four or five decided to call themselves chairmen; each time a show asked to interview the chairman one of them could legitimately say that he or she was the chairman. Anyone keeping track would be confused; yet this free flow of leadership was, in fact, *the* fact.

There is a leadership core, a group of persons associated much of the time with most things that happen on or around a campus. But this is a changing group, losing some persons, gaining some. Few names endure. Even those who are rated high in the public's mind as leaders often play minor roles in setting policy, planning events, and planning tactics. All of this is indeed puzzling to a nonmovement layman who is looking for a single person responsible for the mess. Courts, for example, have tried to fix conspiracy charges against several collections of persons who have had no greater contact with one another as conspirators than any other subset of the total group of planners and hangers-on.

If there is any consistent movement leadership, at least of an intellectual sort, it derives from the collection of academic and literary authors and critics who have captured the ideology of the movement and have provided its justifications for being. Marcuse, Fanon, Goodman, Mills, Chairman Mao (his little Red Book is a big seller) Oglesby, Zinn, and more recently Chomsky have taken on intellectual leadership roles. In a sense they fuel the local talent, who in turn fuel others with the "message."

An analogy may be helpful in gaining a sense of the campus movement's organizational properties. Contrast, if you will, an old-fashioned sandlot baseball game (if you can remember back that far) with today's Little League. In the first, kids in the neighborhood are just around and ready to get up a game when the moment is right. Sure, there are some big guys, known hitters and pitchers, and there are some who seem to be helpful in getting a game going, but mainly it's just a loosely organized group ready to play ball one day and disappearing next. Much of its appeal is its spontaneity, its lack of formal leadership and organization. Now look at the Little League, adult-sponsored, adult-managed, adult-run. Uniforms to delight a kid, equipment fancy enough for a big leaguer; hardly a match for the hastily put together uniforms and shoddy hand-me-down equipment of the sandlotter. Organized by age, by area, by league. Carefully umpired games; records neatly kept of who's hitting what. Victory is a joy; to lose wracks a little body with deep pain. Teams have order, organization, hierarchy; they lack spontaneity.

We tend today to think primarily in Little-League terms, even for our pastimes. Thus we have great difficulty in appreciating the organizational structure and, more importantly, the felt quality of the protest movement. Although it's not a game, its organization has much in common with the sandlot adventure of yesteryear.

Followers: Insurrection in Watts. Formal membership figures for such groups as SNCC or the Black Panthers are not readily available, but the depth and breadth of the movement's appeal is revealed in research conducted after the 1965 Watts uprising. A group of researchers (J. Cohen, 1967; N. Cohen, 1967a, b; Morris & Jefferies, 1967; Murphy & Watson, 1967; Sears & McConahay, 1967), under the direction of N. Cohen of UCLA, surveyed 2070 persons from seven populations: residents in the Negro curfew area; Negro riot arrestees; white residents of the Los Angeles area; white residents of the curfew area; Mexican-American residents of the curfew area; social service workers; and merchants who suffered property damage during the demonstrations. In this discussion I am concerned mainly with the findings on Negro participation in the upheaval.

The careful analysis of actual riot participation by Sears and McConahay (1967) divided the active participants into *gladiators* and *spectators*. The former were involved in breaking windows, throwing Molotov cocktails, shooting at police, and looting stores; the latter were a supportive audience who were involved and sympathetic but did not themselves loot, burn, or shoot. *Inactives* were either "distant spectators" or "saw-nothings."

In terms of self-reported activity, 22 percent of the curfew-zone sample was very or somewhat active. Combining self-reported activity with self-reports of seeing looting, burning, and so on, 15 percent were gladiators, 31 percent were active spectators, 27 percent were distant spectators, and 27 percent "saw nothing." In actual numbers, between 31,000 and 34,000 persons were active participants, a sizable number. In addition, approximately 64,000 persons were involved as active spectators, presumably lending tacit support.

Beyond these figures, which clearly show the widespread support the riot had, separate analyses indicated characteristics of persons most involved. I quote below from the summary report:

"Young people were much more active than older people. Men were more active than women, but young women were more active than middle-aged or older men. . . . Support for the riot was as great among relatively well-educated and economically-advantaged as among poorly educated and economically disadvantaged in the curfew area. . . . Support for the riot was as great among relatively long-time residents of South Central Los Angeles as it was among the more recent migrants from the South. Our data, furthermore, indicate that the majority of people in South Central Los Angeles are long-time residents, thus dispelling the belief that the riot was a product of a recent influx of migrants from the South" (N. Cohen, 1967a, p. 3).

Details about some of the arrested sample are provided in a report (*Los Angeles Times*,

1965) issued by the Los Angeles County Probation Department, pertaining to the 402 youths under 21 who were arrested. The typical juvenile arrestee had no previous contact with the police: 36.2 percent had none at all; 19.6 percent had one previous police contact. A little more than 10 percent had been arrested six times or more before the arrest during the Watts upheaval. Only 27 percent of arrested juveniles came from homes containing both parents; 40 percent came from homes with seven or more persons present; in almost 30 percent of the homes studied both poverty and chronic unemployment existed.

A supplement to the report of the U. S. National Advisory Commission on Civil Disorders (Whitten, 1968) provides further insights into the characteristics of riot participants:

"Contrary to popular belief that only a tiny percentage of riot area dwellers took part in disorders, the average for participants was 18 per cent. The low was 4 per cent in Cincinnati, the high 35 per cent in New Haven. . . . Although many believe rioters were riffraff and outside agitators, in fact, they constituted a good cross section of young Negroes and 95 per cent were residents of the riot city. . . . Women played a big role in the riots, but they were arrested far less often than men. About 40 per cent of the Detroit rioters were women, but only 10 per cent of those arrested were. . . . Three out of four of those arrested during the riots were employed" (p. 7).

Both the Presidential Commission report and the Watts survey indicate that although a majority of the Negroes interviewed deplored the violence and destruction that the riots brought, most also felt that the outcome would be beneficial because it would increase white concern with their plight. In the Watts study itself about 34 percent were in favor of what had happened. Thirty-eight percent felt that the riot would help the Negro cause; 20 percent felt it would hurt the cause. By contrast, 74 percent of the white population of Los Angeles felt the Negro cause would be hurt.

In addition to its specific focus on the insurrection, the Los Angeles Riot Study provides some valuable figures on the black *militant* population of the curfew area. In summarizing the work N. Cohen (1967a) classified the Negro community in three groups: the *traditionalists*, who strive for individual achievement in white America; the *militants*, who feel that only through collective action can the Negro's problem be solved; and the *survivalists*, the direct victims of "disease, desperation, joblessness, and hopelessness" (p. 12). Cohen classified persons as militant if they approved of militant organizations in the area (about 30 percent of the population surveyed); as conservatives if they disapproved (35 percent); and as uninvolved if they were unfamiliar or indifferent to such organizations (35 percent). The one background characteristic that differentiated two of the groups from the third was employment; both militants and conservatives were employed more than the uninvolved. The core of the militant group "is educated, tend to come from educated families, are less religious, and do not identify themselves as lower class. They are making strong efforts to build a sense of pride in their color and to rebuild a sense of ethnicity" (p. 12).

Militants differ from conservatives in several attitudes. They are less favorable to news media, objecting to the portrayal of the Negro. They have less confidence in standard political institutions; they hold a low opinion of political figures, whether local, state, or national. Militants as a whole are action oriented; they were more active in the riot and are more involved in traditional political activity as well. The militants had a heftier list of grievances than the conservatives, including personal encounters with police brutality, victimization by merchants, and discrimination in housing, schools, jobs, and so on. The conservatives tended to view the events in Watts of 1965 as a riot; the militants termed it a revolt. They are committed to disrupting the system as a tactic for gaining political bargaining power. The conservatives still have access to the white establishment; however, as militancy grows they are having greater difficulty in maintaining their leadership in their own communities.

From these several bits and pieces of evidence I think it fair to conclude that the protest movement of black Americans is not a minor happening that involves only a few dissidents. It seems increasingly clear, rather, that a substantial number of blacks who are a part of their community (as opposed to "outside agitators") actively participate in or lend their support to demonstrations. Furthermore, although any community is a differentiated collection, there seems to be an increasing movement toward militancy. Whites who live with their heads buried in the sand are about the only ones remaining who can speak of a small group of agitators and militants who are making trouble in an otherwise progressive racial scene.

Followers: Back on the Campus. It seems those same persons who claim that the black movement is tiny and manned by a handful of outside agitators wrote the script for commentators on the campus protest movement as well. Although precise figures are scarce, there can be little doubt remaining that by 1970 many of the larger universities and colleges in the United States (and around the world) had experienced some form of disruptive student activity. One report (Etzioni, 1969) indicates 221 demonstrations at 101 colleges involving almost 39,000 participants between January and June, 1968. Although usually only a small percentage of students were involved on any one campus —estimates range from 2 to somewhat over 20 percent—on the national scene we are still talking about a large number of persons. But this numbers game misses the point. A social movement would not be a movement if it contained the majority of persons in a democratic society. It is a movement because it seeks to change a society in which it is not in the majority. Those in the lead of social change—as movement adherents like to see themselves—are never very many in number.

Those who enjoy numbers, however, will be interested in a national Gallup Poll reported in May 1969 (Gallup & Davies, 1969). Twenty eight percent of all college students reported participation in a demonstration of some sort; 72 percent reported never having participated. This figures out roughly to 1.8 million persons who participated in some kind of demonstration. Of course, if the socially approved value is to demonstrate, these self-reports may be over-inflated estimates. Nevertheless, this number is not to be ignored or treated as simply a handful of agitators. The same Gallup poll indicates substantial attitude similarity between the 28 percent and the remaining 72 percent on several issues that have been important on many campuses; what is more, there is greater similarity between the actives and the nonactives than between either group and the general public. For example, 81 percent of all students surveyed and 92 percent of the demonstrators, but only 25 percent of the general public felt that students should have a greater say in running their colleges. Pertaining to the treatment of campus rule violators, 82 percent of the general public felt that demonstrators who break laws should be expelled; 54 percent of all students and 31 percent of demonstrators surveyed felt this way. In other words, although only 28 percent were sufficiently active in the campus protest movement to have participated in at least one demonstration, the remainder of the student population was and is a generally sympathetic audience.

Other estimates of participation in the student protest movement tend to range downward from this Gallup figure of 28 percent. A survey by Peterson (1966, 1968) in 1964–1965 and again in 1967–1968 indicates less than 10 percent of any student body involved with protest over any issue. His 1968 data indicate that while more campuses reported protest activity than in 1965, and while more students were involved (as enrollments grew), the *proportion* of activists remained about the same. As Peterson sees it, the New Left amounts to only about 2 percent of national student population (about 134,000); another 8 to 10 percent, however, are sufficiently sympathetic to participate on occasion. It is important to note that Peterson's data came from surveying college and university deans.

Several direct student surveys indicate that relatively *low* political involvement of any sort is the norm. In one study Trent and Ruyle (Trent, 1970) compared college graduates of the 1960's with graduates of the 1920's and 1940's. They report more similarity than disparity in political attitudes and activity across these generations. Few are politically active or even active in community affairs; few even have activist attitudes: 3 percent of the males and 1 percent of the females said they were politically and socially liberal or radical; 25 percent of the males and 30 percent of the females reported themselves as conservative both politically and socially. The graduates of the 1960's are neither

more nor less liberal or conservative. These data, coupled with data reported by Flacks (1967) and Keniston (1967) and a survey reported by Adelson (1970), suggest less of a generation gap than is commonly imagined; most persons, young and old alike, are politically apathetic. Those who are active, however, appear to come from family backgrounds that are likewise activist and involved. Adelson, in fact, finds substantial homogeneity across generations in politics and values; it is indeed the minority of students who are in any significant way unlike the generation of their parents: 80 to 90 percent are similar.

Keep in mind that this numbers game often conceals the true import or force of a social movement. Although this entire chapter is concerned with minorities of black or white, this does not mean that the social movements we are examining are trivial. Although few are vitally active, more are approving spectators; even more, of course, are apathetics, whose inaction gives a social movement a freedom and potential it might not otherwise enjoy. Remember, furthermore, that if we measured impact in terms of majority involvement we might overlook the fact that a nine-man Supreme Court, beginning in 1954, contributed to a radical revolution in the lives of some nearly 200 million Americans. In the right place and at the right time, even small numbers can and have shaped the course of history.

Typology of Members. I think it is clear that not everyone involved in these two social movements is a fanatic or hard-core activist. Killian (1964) described members who hop aboard a movement as the wave of tomorrow, conforming to this future rather than protesting against the present; adventurers and opportunists along for a trip; and those who are part of the cheering section, lending sympathetic support but not much active involvement. There is little doubt in my mind that some persons were involved in the student protest movement both because it was the thing to do at that age and in that location and because that was where the action was for that night. Such persons are involved, at least initially, less out of some depth of ideological commitment than out of a sensitivity to the demands of their group and its norms. Opportunists and adventurers are also in evidence. The media give a public platform to those who would see themselves nightly on the television screens or read about themselves in the next day's paper. Although the group is large, the spectator role is difficult to play in campus demonstrations because nonparticipation often does not have any meaning. When a demonstration is in progress, police make no differentiation between actives and spectators. Everyone is involved equally in their eyes; no innocents exist. A person who thought he was part of the cheering section soon finds himself running with the ball down the middle of the field, pursued by two cops swinging batons.

Another category of supporter I have noticed in almost every large demonstration I call, for want of a better description, the neurotic acting out his favorite fantasy. This type, very few in actual number but very noticeable nevertheless, comes out to alleviate his personal neurosis in the midst of the struggle. He may have a severe problem with authority; the setting of a demonstration gives him the opportunity to act out this problem by taunting the police or university administration. He may have some relatively severe paranoia that is given harsh validity in the context of a demonstration when enemies are clearly defined and seem to be everywhere. At times I have been struck by the resemblance between a demonstration and a mental hospital; students come wandering into this setting to act out their fantasies. It so happens that what they imagine to be real *all* the time comes out to be real *this* time; so they blend in perfectly shouting in unison with those who are not always so plagued.

The cultural revolution

Political activism, as manifested during campus demonstrations, is only one form the student protest movement has taken. It is possible to think of some of young America of the 1960's as involved in a cultural revolution in addition to its political revolution. This cultural revolution involves a youth culture with its own music, language, clothing, hair, and, in particular, its own view regarding both drugs and sex. Although a few students on a select few campuses seem to be leading a sexual revolution—casual

sexual relations, male-female roommates, informal marital ties, etc.—it is generally agreed that any sexual revolution in the United States had its start in the 1920's and has been progressing gradually since, and that most students remain sexual traditionalists (Adelson, 1970).

Another Gallup poll (American Institute of Public Opinion, 1969), examining college students across the nation in a variety of schools, concluded "that students today are indeed a 'new breed'": 20 percent reported trying marijuana, a figure higher in 1969 than in 1968; 73 percent felt that a student caught smoking marijuana should *not* be expelled; 10 percent reported having used LSD. The new breed (to use the pollsters' term) also dress and wear their hair differently than did students of several years ago: 6 percent of the males had beards; 28 percent had long sideburns; 13 percent were rated slovenly (shall *we* say comfortable and casual) in their dress. Career lines and occupational choices likewise shifted: 51 percent reported having done work with underprivileged groups. In fact, and I quote from the survey, "Evidence that demonstrators are willing to do more to try to change society than march and carry placards is seen in the fact that 65 percent of this group have done social work as opposed to 45 percent among nondemonstrators." In response to the question concerning their occupation at age 40, the survey reports that 29 percent expected to be teaching; only 8 percent leaned toward business.

Another fascinating feature of this particular survey is that it demonstrates a link between the cultural and the more directly political aspects of the campus protest movement. For example, 40 percent of the political demonstrators had tried marijuana; only 15 percent of nondemonstrators had.

The depth of the youth movement, especially in its cultural forms, is given some credence by studies conducted in several high schools and junior highs in Northern California (*San Francisco Chronicle*, August 8, 1968). Note that this area is near enough to Berkeley to be unlike the scene we might find in North Dakota or Wyoming; thus these survey results should not be taken as necessarily representative of the national picture—at least as of 1968. In one survey 18 percent of the boys and 12 percent of the girls in the seventh grade in one school had tried marijuana; 9 percent used it regularly. By the twelfth grade 42 percent of all students had smoked pot; 37 percent of the boys and 32 percent of the girls used it regularly. For those who still shudder at these figures, let it be known that this survey found even higher percentages using alcohol and smoking cigarettes regularly. Other surveys in the same geographical area found much the same results. Imagine what things will be like in college when *that* generation begins to arrive.

Aliens and Activists. In outlining some of these last figures I have drawn a distinction between the cultural revolution and the political revolution. Others have made a similar differentiation, particularly between an alienated or hippie pattern and a more political or activist pattern (e.g., Keniston, 1967). Haan, Smith, and Block (1968) make an even finer differentiation. Using a two-dimensional scheme involving degree of involvement with political and social issues and degree to which an individual accepts or rejects traditional values and institutionalized authority, they derive five patterns of youthful involvement:

1. *Politically apathetic* youth have low involvement in political matters and a high acceptance of the status quo.

2. *Alienated* youth have rejected traditional values and authority and are politically uninvolved.

3. *Individualist* youth are involved politically and accept the status quo. They have been described as obedient rebels; Ayn Rand is one of their favorites.

4. *Activist* youth are involved politically but have rejected both traditional values and authority.

5. *Constructivist* youth overlap somewhat with the activists, but do not as severely reject traditional values or authority. These are the youth who enter the Peace Corps, VISTA, and so on.

Any classification scheme, including this one, is at best a helpful tool; at worst it clouds the real issues. The usefulness of such schemes is primarily to remind us of the wide variety of ways in which students today (and, for that matter, through history) have responded to society. We commonly think of the activists as the *real* protest movement members, but, increasingly, I have seen boundaries crumble and fade away.

As we examine the ideologies of the political activists we cannot help noting that many of their social aims are congruent with the life style of the hippies and street people. Although hippie groups may be so disaffected and alienated that they do not wish to play at politics and demonstration, they consistently form a background of involved and sympathetic spectators, dropping in and out of more active participation. In like manner, many of those who are politically active drop in and out both of the movement and the hippie life style. As boundaries blur, categorizations of movement types become less useful.

Individual motives and social movements

It is important not to confuse individual motivation with the social movement itself. Any successful (i.e., enduring) social movement, or, for that matter, any political party or other organization or group, must exist apart from and serve the heterogeneous needs and motives of a variety of persons. People are linked together in a movement not because they all share the same basic motivations, but rather because each finds his own needs best served by this particular collectivity. For this reason a purely psychological analysis of a social movement— one that seeks to uncover the motives and personality of each participant—too often misses the boat when it comes to understanding the movement itself. I am not saying that motivations and personality are irrelevant to understanding a social movement; I am saying that such an analysis gives an incomplete, often erroneous picture of its true dynamics.

A recent example is helpful. Feuer (1969) developed a generational-conflict thesis to explain social movements, both historical and contemporaneous, and in particular the radical student movement of the sixties. Taking a psychoanalytic view of the relations between generations, Feuer argues that the sons are attacking the authority of their fathers. In their irrational rebellion the sons do not identify with their fathers, but exist apart and alienated from all they stand for. Like all good psychoanalytic sons everywhere, however, guilt over their rebellion leads the sons into self-defeating actions; blindly violent, they strike out with little care for the pragmatic, driving themselves into self-destructive failure.

In this view student protests are not founded on economic or political grounds, but are oriented primarily toward a destruction of the father and of all authority that comes to symbolize him. Normally, however, one generation succeeds the next without undergoing this destruction. Rather than asking what there was about society in the 1960's that led the sons to alienation from their fathers rather than to identification, Feuer tends to ignore societal conditions that could lead a reasonable man to rebel. But there are more troubles than this basic oversight with Feuer's analysis of the student protest movement.

In terms of existing data, those most intimately involved in the student protest movement seem to be living out in practice the *ideals* of their fathers (e.g., Adelson, 1970; Flacks, 1967; Keniston, 1967). The sons, then, are *like* their fathers, only more so. If the fathers are generally liberal politically, but tend to be somewhat hypocritical and preach more than they practice, the sons have sought to be liberal or radical as preacher and practitioner. This is hardly a generational conflict. Moreover, if everyone has some Oedipal conflict and seeks to overthrow the father, why are some involved in a social movement while others are not?

This last point raises another question. If a purely psychological theory is not sufficient, then isn't a purely sociological theory also deficient as explanation of a social movement? Yes. Just as a personality or motivational explanation ignores both the reality of social processes that drive a movement, and the variety of individual functions a movement can serve, so, too, does a sociological explanation leave out key qualities of individual socialization and experience that select some for the movement while casting others into society's mainstream. To understand a social movement, therefore, we must examine predisposed per-

sonalities in predisposed societies, both coming together at that ripe moment in historical time when conception is possible and the birth of a movement likely.

CAREERS

Born out of need, a movement ebbs and flows, riding high on the crest one day, plummeting to the depths on the next. Its viability depends on the depth and persistence of its members' dissatisfactions with the general social order, on society's continued inability to offer satisfactory solutions to their needs, and, eventually, on society's manner of relating to the surges of the movement. In this section we examine three related aspects of a movement's career: its relationship to the larger society and to other social movements; its process of gaining and losing members; its consequences for social change.

The movement and society

As we have seen, a social movement arises when a stable society does not meet the needs of a group of its members. The more extensive the movement, the more threatening it is to the existing social order. Reactions to this threat are varied. As noted (p. 362ff.), Killian (1964) suggests three likely types of opposition: the movement is taken as an honorable opponent and is granted the same status as more stable institutions; it is considered relatively safe, but is isolated from the mainstream; it is publicly defined as dangerous to the existence of the society, and efforts are made to extinguish it.

Response to the Blacks. The protest movements of black and young Americans have experienced several different treatments at the hands of mainstream society. Tracing the up-and-down swings of reaction to the black movement in general, or to some of its specific manifestations, we get a mixed picture of societal patience and outrage. Initially the pursuits of civil rights groups in the South were greeted with hostility in the South and either indifference or acceptance by those as yet untouched in the North. Myth-making went its usual round: many Southerners talked about outside agitators and Communists; the movement talked about racists, bigots, rednecks.

While the Negro sought equal rights in public accommodations, the segregation-conscious Southerner talked about each man's right to determine with whom he associates. Thus each side grasped at highly valued American ideals. As the Southern reaction to the black man's efforts became more openly vicious and repressive, the federal government was forced to intervene to protect the Civil Rights Movement. On paper, at least, it appeared that the movement had captured mainstream support and the battle for change was being won.

The scene, however, began to shift northward to the urban ghetto; the focus moved from public accommodations to employment opportunities, housing, and deep-lying racial prejudice, both personal and institutional. The fondness with which the movement had been embraced began to fall apart as the real meaning of civil rights became clear and more basic conflicts of interest between various groups surfaced. Ghetto reaction to increased white resistance and failure to make significant progress for the movement took the form of urban riot or insurrection. These outbursts, plus the push for Black Power and Black Nationalism, cast out many white liberal supporters and convinced those originally most resistant that the black man wanted too much too soon and he had better stand in line "like the rest of us have done."

Morris and Jeffries' (1967) study of white reaction to the Watts riot shows clearly the mainstream's response to this phase of the black protest movement: about one-third of the whites interviewed showed some degree of sympathy for the upheaval; the other two-thirds were either indifferent or generally antagonistic. Twenty-eight percent attributed the riot to unfair treatment of the Negroes, to police brutality, or to a history of injustice; 26 percent felt the cause to lie in agitators, outsiders, or troublemakers in the Negro community. Seventy-three percent felt the riot had increased the gap between the races; only 13 percent felt the gap had been decreased. Most whites felt that police had handled the riot well. Of particular interest is the finding that those who reacted most antagonistically to the riot came from an all-white community of low socioeconomic status

(SES), whereas those who were most sympathetic came from an all-white, high-SES community. The most antagonistic, low-SES community ranked highest in number of people who had thought of using firearms to protect themselves; the high-SES community ranked lowest in this regard.

This reaction by socioeconomic class uncovered in the Watts situation is consistent with most other work relating economic and educational level to anti-Negro attitudes (see p. 305ff.). Evidence from national voting in the presidential election of 1968 and many state and local elections of 1969 and 1970 suggest that the white community, and particularly the community of working men of moderate income, were reacting with increasing hostility to the black protest movement. Even federal civil rights legislation passed in 1968 included some antiriot provisions, indicating a combined carrot-and-stick approach to the movement: passing federal open-housing legislation to meet some of the movement's demands, while passing antiriot legislation to meet the mainstream's demands for law and order, peace and quiet.

It should be noted, and not just casually, that efforts to adopt the Civil Rights Act of 1968 began in earnest in 1966; it was passed finally after the assassination of King. Other evidence of a federal slowdown in responding affirmatively to the demands of the Negro protest movement involves the cool official response received by the Kerner Commission report in 1968. This was the first report by the U. S. National Advisory Commission on Civil Disorders appointed by President Johnson in 1967 to study the urban upheavals that had occurred in 128 American cities in 1967 alone. Little presidential or congressional response to the report was noted; the movement's demands, amply documented and certified by the Kerner Commission, were to be filed away. Indifference ("benign neglect") and hostility seemed to await the movement as it prepared to leave the turbulence of the 1960's and enter the difficult decade of the 1970's.

Response to Students. Tracing the societal response to student protest shows many of the same reactions just noted. In fact, in the public mind of 1969, both movements in their extreme were equally threatening and thereby to be treated similarly. In 1964 the Free Speech Movement at Berkeley brought about significant public outcry and strongly negative feelings; at the same time enlightened public response turned to an examination of the universities that created the turmoil. But as protest spread around the country in succeeding years, public and societal response became louder and increasingly more repressive. There is little doubt that Reagan was elected governor of California in 1966 and 1970 largely on his strong stand against student protests; little doubt either that the public's attitude by 1970 had polarized even more. In 1969 the California State Legislature faced a carload of bills (over 100) dealing with campus protests and what to do to stop them. There were few, if any, politicians who did not feel that this movement was politically hot; to win politically one had to be on the side of law and order, and this usually meant opposition to protests of any sort. Most graduation addresses in June 1969 and 1970 carried the theme of campus protest, vacillating between harsh attitudes toward the protestors and softer views that something positive must be done to change the educational system. The federal government's response in June 1969 was to call for records of students in several large universities who had been arrested for campus disturbances and who also received federal funds.

One of the typical societal responses, usually offered by political figures and later picked up by the general public, built on a divide-and-conquer model. The argument ran as follows: Most students are in college to get an education and care little for rioting or demonstrating. In their pursuit of a quality education, however, these students have encountered a faculty often too busy to teach well and an administration often too slow to respond to their requests for needed change. Thus many of these students have real and legitimate complaints about the university. However, there is a tiny handful of troublemakers and anarchists who only want to destroy the university and to create riots and violence for their own sake. They are committed revolutionaries who care little for building and constructive change; they only want to tear down. On occasion these troublemakers have

been able to sway the majority of good students over to their side by distorting issues and by capitalizing on legitimate complaints. This small band of troublemakers and dissidents must be separated from the university. In the meantime, however, the faculty and the administration must begin to take seriously the complaints of the vast majority of good students who only want to make the university better.

Here are the good guys and the bad guys in the student movement; the bad guys must be eliminated and the good guys must be listened to. Sounds very reasonable. One difficulty, however, concerns the clarity with which, in practice, this neat differentiation can be maintained; in the main, good and bad get lumped together, and get their lumps together, despite the political rhetoric. A related difficulty is the tendency of adherents of this viewpoint to overlook the real grievances in their pursuit of the bad guys. The idea that a small band of conspirators has manipulated the minds of a larger group of good-but-naive followers too often leads one to ignore the basic reasons why that larger group is also out on the streets, is also demonstrating, is also expressing its dissatisfaction. It seems highly improbable to me that a dedicated handful of revolutionaries could generate the support of hundreds, sometimes thousands of students and others in any action unless that larger group shared some basically similar dissatisfactions. If this analysis is correct, elimination of the hard-cores will not solve the problems that gave rise to the movement. It would be like getting rid of a disagreeable odor by perfuming the air rather than by dealing with the garbage dump next door.

Another form of societal response, particularly to the student protest movement, derives from the so-called "liberal intellectual establishment." These critics usually have the grand sweep of history outlined and available for use in interpreting the "true meaning" of the movement. Recall that both Kerr and Brzezinski (p. 378ff.) see much of the movement as an effort by those who cannot cope with the future to try to relive a simplified but irrelevant past. From this perspective the student movement is more an irrelevancy than a basic threat, more to be pitied than feared.

The other main direction of this liberal-intellectual criticism notes the unfortunate parallels between the student movements of today and the Nazi youth movement (or any fascist youth movement) of the 1920's and 1930's. Drucker, for example, comments,

"There is a frightening resemblance between the student 'activists' of today, with their slogans of 'idealism' and 'sincerity,' and the German youth movement just before and just after World War I. The resemblance even extends to externals, to long hair, to folk songs, and to such slogans as 'Make love, not war.' Yet the idealistic, antiauthoritarian *Wandervoegel* of the German youth movement—who also did not trust 'anyone over thirty'—became in short order fanatical, dedicated, unquestioning Nazis and idolators of Hitler. The young want and need faith. And the demagogue is the specialist in 'sincerity' " (1968, p. 245).

Drucker is not alone in outlining these parallels or in suggesting the real threat that the movement thereby implies. In 1966 a writer in the *New York Times* expressed a deep worry over the movement's attacks on the university campus, wherein lies a tradition "that has been a vital instrument working toward a progressive, open society." Movement attacks on the campus, in other words, threaten to destroy what many feel to be the delicate thread of Western civilization. Furthermore, those attacks on academic freedom and intellectual integrity—which during the latter part of the 1960's came as rapidly from the far left as from the far right—threaten the very tenets that have permitted a critical examination of the social order. Movement efforts to silence unpopular professors, or to fire those whose research does not appeal to the movement's goals, lends an unfortunate degree of validity to the arguments of these liberal-intellectual critics.

The rhetoric of some movement adherents lends further credence to those who criticize its tendency to destroy institutions and ideologies that presumably are highly valued even by the movement. Recall the quotation from Lynd (p. 387), who notes that although the good society may be nonviolent and open, to get there will require the use of insurrectionary violence and strong discipline. I am reminded of a line from Brecht: "Alas, we who wished to lay the foundations of kindness could not ourselves be kind" (1947, p. 177). Thus the movement justifies its antidemocratic activities; and thus it provides ample fuel for those who find such activities to be a frightening parallel to the German youth movement.

I should add that thus the movement loses some supporters who refuse to join activities that violate the goals they envision. It is not only critics from outside who fault the movement, but also those inside. Some call for the internal discipline required of an army fighting a guerrilla war; others call for strong-arm tactics; others insist that idealism be maintained even in a society whose response to such idealism is inaction or repression. Some argue that nonviolence is inappropriate to U. S. society; it offers up too many sacrificial lambs for slaughter. Others believe that if nonviolence is to be the goal of the movement, it must be the prime tactic employed. Some argue that since the university serves to justify the status quo it must be eliminated and its professors dealt with harshly. Others feel that, although faulty, the university represents a tradition that must be maintained, but in a changed form. The former would fire professors who do not meet their ideals of "good work"; the latter would increase the number of professors who represent alternative viewpoints but not deny the others a home.

The criticisms cannot be ignored, nor can they be answered directly or simply. In my view, however, the strong core of genuine idealism in the movement, reflected in its multiple philosophies and splits over goals and means, suggests the unlikelihood of fascism sweeping the movement. I think if those critic-professors will reread their history, they will find that Hitler's rise in Germany came less because the students themselves were fascistic than because his programs promised to solve the broader problems of the average citizen, and because the so-called "liberal intelligentsia," through silence or sometimes direct approval, gave support to his ideas. I personally fear the student movement's fascistic tendencies less than I fear those liberal-intellectuals who in the name of democracy and freedom will trumpet the arrival of the mainstream's new Hitler, will write his speeches, and rewrite history so that in the year 2000 we will read about the fascism of the student movement of the 1960's but never will read about the significant role these liberal-intellectuals played.

Some Survey Results. Three surveys are particularly instructive in outlining the public's response to the student movement. In one the Educational Testing Service (1969) examined the attitudes of trustees of the nation's colleges and universities. Approximately 40 percent of the trustees felt that students should share in decision making on matters about housing rules, but only 22 percent felt students should have any role in the selection of a commencement speaker or in policies governing student protests. Forty percent felt the administration should control the content of student newspapers; 50 percent felt that college authorities should discipline students who are punished by police and the courts as well. Finally, 53 percent felt that faculty should sign loyalty oaths. One of the major goals of the movement is to gain a greater role in university governance; this response of the governing boards to this goal looks more like an outline for further upheaval than a view to a peaceful future.

A national Gallup poll (January 1969) indicates somewhat the same picture. In response to a question concerning whether students should have power in academic matters (e.g., courses, examinations)—55 percent said no, 33 percent said yes. A breakdown according to age is also interesting. Whereas 49 percent of those under 30 said yes and 43 percent said no, 56 percent of those from 30 to 49 and 59 percent of those 50 and over said no, 34 percent and 26 percent respectively said yes. Since most trustees are in their fifties, their responses concerning student participation differ only slightly from the responses of their age-mates (22 percent yes for the trustees, 26 percent for their age-mates).

In a survey specific to California, Field (1969) asked a variety of questions and obtained "startling responses." This survey provides results comparing 1967, 1968, and 1969, and thus gives us an opportunity to note trends in public reactions as the movement's politics has pro-duced wider disruption on California campuses. I have selected several results from the Field poll.

1. Students who challenge and defy university and college authorities should be kicked out to make room for those who are willing to obey the rules.

	1969	1968	1967
Agree strongly or somewhat	83%	73%	80%

2. Students should be given more voice in deciding campus rules and regulations.

	1969	1968	1967
Disagree somewhat or strongly	57%	60%	58%

3. Professors who advocate controversial ideas or speak out against official policy have no place in a state-supported college or university.

	1969	1968	1967
Agree strongly or somewhat	57%	52%	50%

Several questions were asked only in 1969:

4. The really serious students don't get involved in campus demonstrations—it's a small minority of misfits who cause the trouble. Eighty-three percent agree strongly or somewhat.

5. The state university and college system should accept many more black students than it now does even if many of them do not meet regular scholastic entrance requirements. Eighty-four percent disagree strongly or somewhat.

6. Having the police on a college campus to maintain order makes matters worse instead of better. Sixty-nine percent disagree strongly or somewhat.

Although the trends over time are not particularly significant, a striking finding clearly indicates that in California, where the campus movement has been especially vigorous since 1964, public opinion is overwhelmingly negative. Much the same negative reaction was true of public response to the demonstrations at the Democratic National Convention in Chicago in 1968. Thus as demonstrations increased in the late 1960's the public's position hardened, setting the stage for approval of strong police reactions.

The issue of legitimacy

In the eyes of the public, after hundreds of years in the socially "down" position, the black protest movement has been granted some degree of legitimacy. Even conservative politicians recognize the need for blacks to be given greater access to the affluence and material advantages of this society. This legitimacy is based on both an understanding that the deprived group should share in the society's general affluence and on fear. The fear factor is part of the folklore of whites, who sense there is a real possibility for a Negro uprising in retaliation for years of deprivation. The threats of the blacks, therefore, are taken seriously; deep down, we all know why they are serious.

The protests of the student movement, however, were met with much puzzlement and growing hostility. In the eyes of most people this movement has little if any true legitimacy. These kids have had the best of everything and a great future awaiting them; what's their complaint? In terms of all the criteria of *quantity* that we use to evaluate how happy a man should be, the campus protestor is overprivileged. It is just these criteria of quantity and material success against which his protest is directed; yet, because others do not easily identify with his kind of frustration, to them his protest lacks legitimacy. These critics seek other reasons, particularly in theories of outside agitation, communist conspiracy, or simply deranged troublemakers.

Myths. When legitimacy is lacking, strong myths develop to help explain the "why" of a movement and justify the repressive treatment it receives. Even when a sense of legitimacy is in evidence but a conflict of interest exists, for example between whites who have just made it up from their own slavery and the threatening blacks who are trying to make it, a system of myths develops to discredit the movement's effort.

Theories of "why" are not difficult to formulate, as I've indicated (p. 214ff.). During the slave period any revolt was explained by reference to outside troublemakers; it was far easier and more beneficial to the status quo to imagine this than to think the unthinkable, that there

was something basically wrong with the institution of slavery. When a movement consistently refuses to fade away, and especially when its presence becomes both more noticeable and more threatening, greater numbers of persons abandon theories of "why" that focus on a troubled social system and turn increasingly to a ready collection of "devil" theories. Campus protestors, in particular, are seen to be in a conspiracy with the devils of anti-Americanism. That they do in fact read Chairman Mao and subscribe to the revolutionary calls of Castro, Guevara, and Fanon, of course, just reaffirms the myth.

Of the public officials who contribute to this myth-making approach to discrediting the movement, FBI Director J. Edgar Hoover must be placed near the top of the list. He finds a Communist conspiracy in almost anything that meets with his personal disapproval. The 1969 report of the President's Commission on Violence (U. S. National Commission on the Causes and Prevention of Violence) singled Hoover out as a figure who contributed significantly to confusing local police, making them feel every act of dissent is an act of Communist subversion.

As a movement is pushed into further despair and hopelessness by societal reaction—I think this adequately describes the morale and condition of both movements at the end of the sixties—it either fades away or resorts to even more disruptive tactics. Disruption, especially as it involved the destruction of property, came to rank high on the movements' tactical chart; such tactics offered mainstream society another handle on which to pin discrediting labels. "They are violent!"

"Violence is an ambiguous term whose meaning is established through political processes. The kinds of acts which become classified as 'violent,' and, equally important, those which do not become so classified, vary according to who provides the definition and who has superior resources for disseminating and enforcing his definitions. . . . Violence . . . is legitimized or illegitimized through political processes and decisions" (Liberation News Service, 1969, p. 1).

This passage is quoted from the Presidential Commission's Report; given our earlier discussion concerning the attribution of causality (see p. 40), we should find it not the least surprising. An act gains meaning in terms of the context within which it occurs.

Violent acts, in particular, are shaped by societal definitions. If a father slaps his son to discipline him for stealing a comic book at the local drugstore, would we call that violent? Perhaps yes, but more likely we would think his act justified in this context. If a person hits a policeman, we'd call that violent and illegitimate. If the policeman hits him, we might not think of that as true violence, but, considering the context and the actors, might see it as justified.

A nation in war clearly commits thousands of acts of violence against property and against persons every day. But that is "war" rather than "violence"; too often we think of such acts as justified. When a demonstrator wars on the society, however, society defines his acts as violent, discredits him and his entire movement, and builds another bomb. The Presidential Commission on the Causes and Prevention of Violence, after examining the history of violence in the United States, concludes that we are now and always have been a "bloody-minded" people. It debunks the myth that violence is a new social phenomenon in the United States, a myth, of course, that emerged at a time when it was most helpful in discrediting the protest movements.

The point is not that all acts in the movement have been nonviolent; rather there are two related aspects to the matter. First, the label "violent" is readily attached to actions the society seeks to discredit. Comparable acts in a different context receive a different label and carry a different psychological meaning. The tendency is to label as violent all those who seek to challenge or change existing institutions, but to refuse to recognize as violent actions by those who seek to uphold the existing social order. Such labeling deflects our attention away from the main efforts of the movement and into the game of name calling.

Second, because the legitimacy of any violent act is determined by societal definers, the movement's use of violent tactics is illegitimate but the mainstream's use of violence is legitimate. The issue is difficult. On one hand, it does not seem possible to legitimize every citizen's use of violence without creating a wild-west battle of each against each. On the other hand, the unchecked use of violence by those who have the legitimate authority to do so (e.g., the police) can be equally disastrous. Naturally, if we are talking about truly revolutionary social movements, it is clear that the society, in its own defense, will legitimize many unchecked forms of violence carried out in its behalf, including that of private citizens (e.g., vigilante groups), while condemning all acts of violence conducted by the revolutionaries.

Lest you imagine that all of the myth-making, discrediting, and inspired labeling are carried on by the society while the movement's personnel sit pristinely on the lofty peaks of pure idealism, let me reassure you that the movement's myth factories are every bit as busy. Police brutality is when he hits me; if I throw a rock at him, it's only because he deserves it. This ethnocentric logic is evidenced when Americans cheer Czech students fighting against Russian intervention—freedom fighters—but refuse to cheer U. S. student protestors; or when Americans cheer North Vietnamese or Russian or Chinese troops who defect to the United States, but call American troops who defect traitors. In like manner, black militants "hate" all whites and think them all oppressors; campus militants think all middle-class citizens are corrupt, stupid, mindless, and plastic. The man in the suit and tie is seen as "uptight": people who watch television each night, get drunk on weekends, or buy a new car each year are felt to be national disasters. Middle-class comes to mean evil. It is as difficult for a movement adherent to imagine a meaningful and self-fulfilling life for this stereotyped, middle-class "straight" going about his eight-hours-a-day ritual as it is for the "straight" to imagine fulfillment in the seemingly hang-loose, do-nothing life of the stereotyped movement follower.

When you get right down to it, the polarization that black and white protest movements produced in the United States by the late 1960's led to a situation in which each side thought so poorly of the other that there was little basis for communication, let alone resolution of problems. It is not unusual to encounter student-movement adherents who think that every white

American is fundamentally an ill-willed, selfish racist. This student has about as much understanding of the life of the establishment man he seeks to discredit as that man has of him. Unfortunately for all concerned, that man occupies a politically more powerful position.

Once extreme polarization has occurred, a kind of neurotic symbiosis develops between the two polar opposites. Although this is usually a relationship reserved for the far left and far right, given the public's reaction to the black and campus movements there remain few middle-ground persons not caught up in a *we* versus *them* game. Once caught in that game, we perceive *them* as the incarnation of evil; we define every encounter in terms of a zero-sum game in which if *they win, we lose*, so we had better win; each move we make fuels their side's ardor, and each move they make fuels our side. You end up with a nation ready for internal war. In the perversity of this symbosis each campus protest (in California and elsewhere) helps maintain conservative politicians in the statehouse. And in turn as each conservative politician moves toward campus repression, he helps add more persons to the movement. There were times when I felt I was a member of Reagan's campaign committee, lacking only public recognition for services performed. There were other times, however, when I thought he must be working for me; he did such a good job of making converts to the campus protest movement that maybe we should hire him.

The police and the movement

When society is challenged by what it feels to be a basically threatening social movement, it calls on all of its resources to keep order and to destroy the movement. At the root of these resources is the power to restrict and repress through police force. In a sense the police are the society's own court of last resort, described by some as a thin blue line between anarchy and law and order. In the normal course of events in a democratic society, where channels to produce change are open and flexible, we would not expect it to be necessary to bring up troops to maintain order at home. Their presence suggests a breakdown in the normal processes of decision making and change; a serious failure in any free society.

In the late 1960's the police became national symbols. For some they represented that thin blue line so essential to the society's welfare; for others, however, they symbolized in concrete form the society and all of its ills. Heroes or pigs, defenders or destroyers; the police became the movement's niggers, targets of its own brand of racism. The circle was complete; every group had its favorite symbolic hate object. For some the object was black; for some it had long hair and a beard and was always waving a placard; for some it wore a badge and a uniform and was seen brandishing a club and tossing tear-gas canisters or squirting mace in every available face.

A *Newsweek* survey in 1969 indicated a shift in Negro attitudes about the police. In 1966 33 percent had felt the police to be harmful to Negro rights; by 1969 the figure was 46 percent. In 1968 the *New York Times* reported results of a study of police operations in the slums of three northern cities that indicated that 27 percent of all the police either were directly observed in some misconduct or admitted such activities as shaking down traffic violators, altering testimony, and so on. Researchers also found that the worst police were assigned to the slums, perpetuating a bad state. The more subtle kinds of police harassment were not reported by the study but form a part of every ghetto dweller's personal history. As almost every protestor or "cultural deviant" will attest, harassment in many forms has become the norm for them as well. They are stopped often on the streets and while driving—that is, if their physical appearance marks them as a part of that new breed.

On their part, the police are called on to do a difficult job, often with groups of people whom they fear and distrust as much as they themselves are feared and distrusted; it is often a toss-up to ascertain during a demonstration which side is more frightened of the other. The 1969 Presidential Commission report indicates a direction in which the police are heading as they are called in to deal with the disruptive aspects of the black and student movements. In response to the harassment they experienced, and out of a concern for the more traditional labor issues of better pay and working conditions, the police organized themselves into associations that operate in some cities and states as potent lobbies that must be taken into account by every legislator. These organizations have given the police a degree of independence from civilian authorities; in part this makes them seem like armies that have taken it on themselves to defend the established order regardless of the costs involved or the individual rights jeopardized. Their lobbying activities in New York City virtually guaranteed that no civilian review board would get approval. In California the police keep careful tabs on all legislation; reportedly, legislation pertaining to campus disorders of the late 1960's was affected more by the demands of police organizations than by the requests of campus officials (personal communication, 1969).

As the movement grew and became more disruptive, the police organizations also grew and became more independent. A police force not under the control of the people of a community through their elected government officials, like a military organization without civilian control, is not beyond the realm of possibility. Under such conditions of virtual independence, the phrase "law and order" would truly come to mean the sacrifice of the basic freedoms on which our nation was founded and that the police presumably defend.

A combination of factors, including the differential administration of police practices by race, by neighborhood, and often by appearance, plus the growth of police organizations that operate like unions lobbying in support of police interests, has drastically altered the image of the police as an impartial agency of the whole society. As long as the policeman was seen as impartial, treating rich and poor, black and white, hip and straight, legal demonstrator and nondemonstrating citizen all alike, there was little basis for questioning the legitimacy of his authority. However, as impartiality has diminished, legitimacy has likewise declined. Illegitimate authority fosters an atmosphere of compliance gained through coercion rather than by shared agreements concerning law and order. A vicious cycle develops; a citizen's response of defiance or disrespect in the face of illegitimate authority increases the partiality and coercive policies of the police, which in turn produces even further illegitimacy. The outcome of such a cycle, unfortunately, is people-hating police and police-hating people.

Conversions and disaffections

A movement that hopes for any endurance and widespread support must encompass diversity of membership. Of course it risks opening its doors so widely that it loses its thrust and soon its members, or later expanding in such a way that it drives out its founding members. A faculty union with which I am familiar comes to mind. For many years it had a membership of only about 40 to 50 members. Then it decided to recruit and build itself up to 300 to 400. Those initial 40 or so were dedicated and action-oriented radicals; the union had appeal for them but not for many others. To expand its membership it had to change its image; it began to deradicalize and deactivate itself on various issues. Nothing was to be done that might alienate the growing cadre of new members. However, in this very process of growth, it began to alienate some of its old members, who began to shop around elsewhere.

Conversions. Converts, particularly to the campus protest movement, according to the movement's favorite myth, are created by radicalizing experiences. And radicalizing experiences, it is further argued, occur in a confrontation in which many spectators who may be sympathetic, although inactive, are driven into conversion by having their heads hit by a police club, by being arrested or gassed, or even by witnessing such atrocities. I call this a myth because it is simply not known for a fact just how many persons are converted to the movement by such experiences or how many are turned off or turned away by these same experiences. The more directly and blatantly violent a movement becomes, the more likely it is to lose members. I suppose that the most ideal circumstance, in this radicalizing theory at least, is to have an entirely peaceful demonstration busted by an angry police or military group.

What is also not clearly known is the depth of

conversion that takes place when a predisposed spectator witnesses or is personally involved in such experiences. For example, how enduring are the changes in those who witnessed the killings at Jackson or Kent State? Do people return to classes and books several days later, when the first blush of confrontation has faded and academics once again hound them? Fully active involvement in the student protest movement is a very time- and energy-consuming matter; full devotion to academics interferes with movement matters. It seems more reasonable to expect that radicalizing experiences will change persons from indifference to sympathizers than they will change many predisposed persons into enduring active converts.

Interestingly enough, one of the key precipitating events that can move a predisposed person into actual conversion may be the college experience itself. Having an encounter with literature and the humanities in particular seems to have had a startling, now-I-see-the-light effect on certain individuals. One group of indicted draft resisters that I had the opportunity to interview, for example, consistently indicated that they had moved toward their position of resistance after they had encountered the college environment (see Chapter 25).

Undoubtedly, from 1965 to the end of the decade key precipitating events driving more and more persons into the movement in one or more of its various forms were the draft and the Vietnam War. Most contemporary writers agree, and no doubt historians of the future will concur, that the Vietnam War and all it brought to light about the functioning of the American system of government created major disaffections of the young from the mainstream of society. The entire Selective Service System, and in particular its concept of "channeling," whereby young men would be directed "voluntarily" (its term) into roles considered essential by society (e.g., science and technology) while others would be impressed into military service brought home very personally to thousands of young men and women their position as society's white or black niggers. I have little doubt that without the draft and the war the disaffection from mainstream society would not have been sufficiently intense to produce the magnitude of

conversion to the campus protest movement that occurred in the late 1960's. Continuing societal problems in dealing with racial matters and the serious shortcomings of bureaucracy, all significant contributors to the protest movement's development, were vastly intensified by the draft and the war. There would still have been a protest movement; but it would not have been nearly as great, run as deep, nor involved such passions.

Disaffections. Disaffections from the movement also occur. A movement's failure to accomplish its collective goals or the personal goals of its individuals drive some persons out. Likewise, getting older, graduating, entering graduate or professional school, getting a job, or raising a family often force some persons out of active involvement and into the generally sympathetic background. Disaffections that produce a full reversal, so that a movement supporter becomes a movement antagonist, seem less evident among younger persons, but is not unusual, at least around Berkeley, among the professorial generation. There are several notable cases of faculty who were at the forefront of the Free Speech Movement, joining nightly with students in planning and doing, who in 1966, 1968, and 1969 turned around and became outspoken against the movement, discrediting every student advance.

Among students some of the disaffections that I have observed—really a move from active participation to barely interested spectator—are amusing. One case in particular stands out, a student who in 1964 had been very active in the FSM, had even been arrested. In 1966, however, when the campus was again caught up in its annual hassle, he was well in the background. I talked with him briefly one day. Smiling, fatherly as a senior, he nodded in the direction of a group of demonstrating freshmen and said, "Well, they should have their day; me, I'm studying to get into medical school." After a brief two years this senior was talking like those of the faculty who had been active in the 1930's, now looking around with fond memories at their demonstrating students. Has the generation of protest dwindled from 30 years to two? Unfortunately, there is little more than anecdotal evidence to indicate what happens to movement personnel when they graduate. What data there are indicate that as a group they are motivated by scholarly pursuits (e.g., Flacks, 1967; Keniston, 1967); many have undoubtedly gone on to graduate and professional work, perhaps to enter the movement again some years later as doctors, lawyers, and college professors.

Conversion and Disaffection: Black. Conversions to and disaffections from the black protest movement do not appear to follow the same course as that of the campus scene. Young blacks, and especially those brought up in non-middle-class urban conditions, are readily predisposed to join a variety of forms of collective behavior, including the militant groups that are the backbone of a social movement. Although precipitating events may be required to bring about a spontaneous outburst, little additional is needed for an individual to adopt the militant stance and style. If anything seems clear, it is that the level of militancy and involvement in protest increased during the 1960's; conversion outran dissaffection. Specific disaffections, as, for example, a move out of the Black Panthers and into some other militant group, did occur with some frequency, but exact figures are not available. It does appear, however, that few blacks dropped out of protest in the way some white student militants did. Undoubtedly it is as the blacks themselves noted regarding their white sometimes-brothers: If you are white and affluent you can drop back into society whenever you please; but if you're black there's nowhere to drop back into.

Outcomes

This is the payoff section. After all, one joins a social movement to produce social change. But what effect, if any, occurs? To answer this difficult question I would like to divide the issue into two related aspects. First, the movements I've been discussing are not simply a vehicle for producing social change, but are an entire way of life, so it is possible to examine the functions the movement serves in providing an alternative way of life for its members. I'll examine this for the student protest movement. Second, what effect have these movements had in producing change in the society? Here,

we must look at positive change and backlash effects as well as short- and long-term effects.

As a Way of Life. The campus protest movement, combining elements of hippiedom, practical education, and radical politics, offers its members alternative careers, a new community, and a different way of life. For many of its adherents its life-style offerings are more personally important and valuable than its political protests or its visions of some distant day creating a radical new society. A sociologist, Berger (1967), has outlined several life-style characteristics that in his view describe Bohemianism of the 1920's and the hippie movement of the mid-1960's: emphasis on self-expression; living for the moment; equality for women; high value on personal liberty—doing one's own thing; a strong love of persons and places that have not been tainted by the inroads of technological civilization; an effort to expand one's consciousness to new levels of reality. Most of these also apply to the student protest movement.

The movement's essence, in particular its free-floating organization, its emphasis on participation, its mass demonstrations, its music, its dancing, its keen sense of humor, its pursuit of fun and things pleasurable, all add significantly to making a new home for the individual. Take a demonstration, especially one that is met with rapid and vigorous police activity, as one key example. The build-up to the demonstration, the demonstration itself, and its often lengthy aftermath offer a variety of *new community experiences* that are generally absent in the larger society. As such the movement's tactics give the individual a satisfaction of needs that are not otherwise being met:

1. *Excitement.* It is apparent to anyone who has planned and participated in demonstrations, and spent endless hours afterward comparing atrocity stories, that these confrontations are exciting. They enliven an otherwise bland existence. Often they give instant truth and instant clarity, highlighting the good and the evil in an otherwise confusing world. I have watched persons picket peacefully with disappointment etched on their faces, bored because no police or campus official has come around to hassle them. But the moment of truth arrives, the police enter; the day has been made.

2. *Fun and games*. The silent majority attend Saturday's football game, mount their stadium seats, and fulfill their silent role; some few may even go so far as to participate in the sport. But for some, America's pastime takes place on the campuses and in the streets, where one tries to outwit his opponent. Unlike football, in this new game of cops and demonstrators the stakes are high. At any moment the opponents, holding greater force of arms, may be driven to use them against the agile, graceful, hit-and-run movements of guerrilla warfare. Partly it's a new ballet and surrealistic drama; a modern version in which lithe demonstrators cavort about in their living theater, while the plodding, heavily equipped, gas-masked blue meanies descend. A tossed flower, a gesture of love or one designed to taunt, is met with a nervous smile, a weak laugh, a fearful thrust of club. It's sheer drama in which everyone participates and tries out his skill.

3. *Camaraderie and sense of community*. Undoubtedly there are few occasions available in technetronic society that bring the individual a vital sense of community, of belonging together with his fellows, of creating living history, other than during a demonstration or a "be-in" or a rock festival. Loomis (1967) has discussed the halo effect, the new sense of community and good will, that is experienced after a natural disaster has hit a town. Strangers approach one another as friends; helpful brotherhood replaces the competitive strangeness and hostility of moments earlier; out of disaster a fund of good will is generated. Much the same experience is offered to the movement's participants, both in and out of demonstrations.

Once again I can wax anecdotal and relate numerous instances in which this feeling of belonging, of community, of brotherhood carried the day. On the streets of Berkeley, just across from the campus, demonstrators lined up against the police. Tear gas had been thrown earlier; masks were still on, canisters were at the ready. Small clusters of people had spent hours running about challenging the police. Here they gathered for a moment's rest, still facing off against the police lines, waiting for the second half to begin. A colleague of mine approached; we smiled and talked briefly. He said, "This is why we're here; this sense of community in the streets that is totally missing over there in the university." I knew exactly what he meant. There is no anarchy in this community; there is camaraderie. One finds help readily available, a friendly, smiling face, a person to talk with. A person who is busy hurling rocks at the police accidentally bumps into you, a member of his community; he smiles and says politely, "Excuse me."

4. *The peak experience*. Religion in modern society, like so many of its institutions, has become meaningless and overintellectualized, trying to compete, and badly at that, with other intellectual institutions. Few young persons find traditional religion meeting their needs, perhaps a basic human need for a peak experience, a vital contact with the unknown, the mystical, the other-worldly. Aspects of the campus protest movement offer the individual these emotional and mystical encounters that feed his questing soul. The music, the lights, the clothing, the drug scene, the encounters, the movement toward nature and toward Eastern religion, the rituals of living, in fact, all combine at the center of the movement to provide unusual experiences and at the same time to legitimize them.

The point is that the movement meets a variety of deeply felt individual life-style needs that otherwise are unmet. The appeal of the movement, then, ranges well beyond its purely political aspects; it embodies deep-lying psychological qualities and offers satisfactions of a unique sort. In terms of its effectiveness, there can be little doubt that the movement *gives* much to its adherents.

Inducing Political Change. The name of this game is power. Those who have little are trying to get more; those who have more are not likely to give any of it up beneficently unless the costs of keeping it are too great. Both the black protest movement and the student movement seek to produce change by grabbing for power, by attempting to gain at minimum a voice in determining their own affairs. Beyond that, movement ideology varies. Some argue for a total upheaval of society; others seem more willing to settle for a better share in determining the manner by which present structures function. For those who see the goal as complete revolution, success as the 1960's closed was more negative than positive. If we think of a revolution as involving a seizure of the reins of power of a society so that its structures may be changed, we are talking about an action that requires a much larger base of public support than either movement had. The backlash effects of the late 1960's, in fact, indicate that rather than bringing a greater number of converts to its cause, the movement drove more of the silent middle into the opposition camp. If a left-oriented revolution in the United States requires a broad base of disaffected mainstreamers, it is unlikely that either movement has successfully produced many disaffections among the majority of the society. To be sure, each movement expanded its appeal to younger members of the society, so that in the long run, over generations, radical change may occur. However, if anything seems likely in the short run it is a right-wing move, a societal response to quell the disorders produced by the left-leaning movements.

For those whose aspirations for the movement are less revolutionary there is evidence of short-term positive success. Student participation in university affairs, for example, is a reality in most universities that have been deluged by demonstrations; and development of black and ethnic studies programs in response to the demands of minorities has occurred across the nation. For those who want a greater voice immediately, undoubtedly these will be seen only as token changes. Considering the power battles involved, however, I think that even token change should be viewed as one positive step on a long road of change.

A positive effect of both social movements, clearly not satisfying to those who want change now, is the educational impact of the movement on society: the unmasking of the American myths. Picture a relatively complacent and self-satisfied society that is suddenly and rudely awakened by shouting and demonstrating throngs. The message comes through loud and clear, even to those who don't wish to hear it: "Wake up America! You've got bad problems!"

The antiwar movement, the antidraft movement, the Civil Rights Movement, the antimilitarism movement, the ecology movement have all, in their own ways, provided a basis for educating the public to some of the key contradictions and problems of the society. The shouting demonstrators in part have cleared the path for politicians at all levels to enter the picture and move the complacent middle a little bit forward.

I remember a comment made by Eldridge Cleaver. He was often criticized by those with a flair for public relations for his loud, obscene, and threatening public performances. They would tell him, "that's no way to win public approval." But I think he knew what he was doing. He was not seeking public approval for himself, except perhaps among the black community, which delighted in a black finally telling off those uptight whites; but rather, as he put it, "I am trying to make it possible for a blackman someday to get elected mayor of this town." What he meant is that his extremism opened the doors for less extreme blacks to gain entry to the council chambers of the society. After all, a Martin Luther King looks increasingly beautiful, even to a white Southerner, when compared with the likes of a Cleaver.

I think that in much the same way the student protest movement has forced America to examine itself and has allowed enlightened legislators to move into areas in which they previously had not dared to tread. For example, it seems clear that the movement's devastating critique of the war in Vietnam has allowed politicians to enter this area and eventually to force a reappraisal of the entire U. S. foreign policy. Likewise, much of the critique of military expenditures that began in the late 1960's under the sharp eyes of congressional committees occurred not coincidentally against a background of sharp movement criticism of military programs. In my view this political intervention is not a sop to the movement, an attempt to buy it off with token gestures; rather, the movement allowed otherwise hesitant public officials to tread on once-sacred cows. It does seem paradoxical. For while the movement's particularly vigorous protests drive most to hostile response, making one imagine that no politician would dare enter except to advocate law and order (and this, of course, does happen), at the same time it opens new territories for examination and change.

All this must in no way suggest that a movement should sit back satisfied at congressional action against the war and military spending and in favor of civil rights, and at local action in favor of increased student involvement in university governance. The squeaky axle does get the grease; or if *it* doesn't, perhaps one very similar to it will. Sometimes the grease is thrown in such amounts as to clog the gears; but there are good moments as well.

Some Critical Questions. There remain several critical questions concerning the relationship between these social movements, especially the student movement, and successful social change. The student movement has been criticized for lacking well-defined programs for the future. Many have asked, "What do you want?" only to receive a foggy reply. How can the movement expect others to join in its venture without known ends? As a gadfly, a thorn in the side of society, the movement fulfills a useful purpose; as a direct agent of social change, however, the absence of a well-defined program makes recruitment difficult, knowledge of progress or regress almost impossible. One senses what the movement is against, and thus intuitively what it might be for. But my intuition and yours may vary drastically, so how can we ever work together?

The mounting of a demonstration of protest is one matter; the skill required to sustain a full-fledged social movement, however, is an entirely different issue. There is serious doubt in many minds, including those of hard-core student-movement adherents, that there is sufficient dedication, political knowhow, and discipline, to do more than mount an occasional confrontation. Time after time throngs of hotly angered students have been caught up in protest, demanding a change in some aspect of their college. But the weekend arrives, and on Monday morning the energy level is down to normal complacency; everybody has gone into the background to await the next big battle; no one keeps involved in the process of organizing a movement. It seems, in fact, that American youth of the 1960's are like their elders; not

sufficiently self-directing or self-sustaining to get up for long. A hard core may be dedicated; but it has not yet figured a way to break the wall of complacency and routine.

As Crews, generally counted among movement sympathizers, commented, there are some nasty questions that one must ask about the student movement, including its questionable devotion to democratic ideals, especially when it "regularly uses minority coercion in the name of 'the people'" (1969, p. 32). Crews is also puzzled over the likelihood that a movement that is so driven by a "generational animus" can ever hope to reach out in cooperation with blue-collar workers and clerical employees who so despise the radical students. He seriously questions how romantic idealism without the discipline and hard work of political organization can ever make a truly effective social movement of change.

I find related critical questions involve the relationship between the romantic ideals of the student movement—e.g., its antiorganizational and antitechnological positions—and the apparent realities of the future of organized society. Neither technology, nor economics, nor complex organization, in my view, will die out or become obsolete in the years that lie ahead. All will grow even more complex and become increasingly life-encompassing. A movement that will feel success only when it has killed off these devils has written itself a program of failure. As I understand the movement's cries, however, they are in response to the dehumanizing impacts of technology-economics-organization. Efforts directed at bringing community (*Gemeinschaft*) back into the society (*Gesellschaft*) need not do away with society. Whether the movement has the willingness and patience to examine the knotty problems that are involved in making society fit for the individual and to come up with proposals that are both revolutionary and related to reality, however, is a serious and as yet unanswerable question.

If we take the goals of the movements seriously, we see that their road ahead is extremely long, filled with many potholes, and undoubtedly will require several steps back or detours to the side just to make it over the next collection of steep hills and carefully erected roadblocks.

Some movements fade out and die at the first roadblock; others do not have sufficient vital energy to get over the first big hill; others look at the road ahead and drop out of the race. No one in his right mind would urge people to take the trip; the route is rugged and tiring, there are few rest stops along the way; you may not make it, or even if you think you do, you'll come to realize that there is no pot of gold waiting there. Some continue, though, hoping to plant the seeds of change along the way, although they may never see them bloom. Others continue driven by the dream of total revolution; others keep moving just out of inertia. I suppose that as long as there's a road ahead, a vision of a better world, however vague, just beyond the next hill, there will always be people making the trip. The vitality of an entire society depends on them. Their insistent refusal to rest assured that this is the best of all possible worlds affirms man's continuing efforts to be master of his destiny. You may not love a social movement; but it is unthinkable to live without them.

Section VII

Developmental change

Chapter 24

The ecological revolution: The effects of technology and population, briefly noted

There are many facts and figures, much speculation, and more controversy. There are few solid foundations of rigorous data, and even fewer answers to what appear to be the enormous questions and problems facing modern man. We suspect, however, that the combined operation of advanced technology and an explosion in population are affecting social organization and individual life style as society and the individual attempt to accommodate themselves to these external realities of contemporary existence. Before we can look meaningfully at the figures or ask more questions, what we need is a helpful heuristic model that will enable us to conceptualize the relationship between the realities of population and technology on one hand and the social and individual transformations of accommodation on the other. For this we turn to Barker's view of psychological ecology.

BARKER'S PSYCHOLOGICAL ECOLOGY

For many years Barker and several co-workers have been involved in a systematic study of the effects of the environment on the individual (Barker, 1960, 1965; Barker & Barker, 1963; Barker & Gump, 1964; Barker & Wright, 1955). In particular, Barker has been interested in charting the variety of encounters an individual has with his natural daily environment. He noted that it was meaningful to discuss the environment in terms of separate units within which sequences of behavior occur; he referred to these units of the environment as *behavior settings*, which might include such things as baseball games, parties, a classroom, a restaurant, and so forth. For Barker behavior settings had a structure and an existence apart from any particular individual who happened to be present: a baseball game, for example, involves patterns of relationship that hold regardless of the characteristics of individual participants. A behavior setting not only includes these normative patterns of relationship that define it, but also contains a variety of objects or paraphernalia: walls, chairs, doors, typewriters.

Behavior settings, furthermore, are thought to be *homeostatic* or *self-regulatory* systems. This quality is a key to Barker's thinking about the relationship between the person and his environment. A self-regulatory setting persists with a relative degree of stability despite a multitude of forces acting to change it. It has a life of its own, so to speak, governed by principles other than those of individual psychology: for example,

". . . availability and the price of food, the season of the year, the prevailing temperatures, the size,

415

lighting, and ventilation of the building, the state laws concerning hygienic practices, the customers, and the employees are all involved [in maintaining a restaurant as a behavior setting] (Barker, 1960, p. 18).

Although persons are interchangeable in the life of a behavior setting, the relationship between people and setting is nevertheless vital. Barker explores several aspects of this relationship.

1. People are the most essential component in the functioning of any behavior setting. A classroom, for example, can get by without a blackboard, but is no longer a classroom without people.

2. Each behavior setting has an optimal population requirement, a given number of people necessary for its structure or organization. Settings, therefore, may be optimally populated, underpopulated, or overpopulated. We shall return to this crucial matter.

3. Barker assumes that "of all the equipment and paraphernalia of a setting, people are among the most immediately malleable and adjustable" (1960, p. 22). Walls do not push out and allow rooms to expand as easily as people "quickly spread out or crowd together, speed up or slow down" (p. 22).

One clear implication of this last point is that behavior settings, in pursuit of their own self-regulation, can effect a change in the behavior of individuals who enter them. We should not imagine behavior settings to be evil monsters intentionally driving their inhabitants around solely for their own survival; but the analogy is not bad. Settings are neither self-conscious nor intentional, but their survival is important to many persons who get satisfactions out of them and therefore strive to maintain them. A restaurant, for example, gives its owners and its customers a variety of satisfactions. Maintaining a setting, however, establishes certain requirements, some of which necessitate a change in the behavior of individuals who are involved with it.

Both Marx and Ellul view the behavior settings of technology in a manner congruent with Barker's view. Marx (1956) puts forth two specific propositions: an individual's location in the productive process determines his outlook on a wide variety of personal, social, and political matters; and there is a *logic* to the forms of production that is independent of the individuals who are involved. These forms change and develop in accordance with their own principles, creating new functions, new roles, and new demands as they live out their own life. In a discussion and analysis of technology Ellul (1964) makes a similar point. For Ellul the technology of a society not only has a logic of its own, but in addition, once begun, follows its own life independent of the intentions of man. In this view man becomes the pawn and technology the master.

Population and setting

Much of the preceding discussion is a preliminary to Barker's main concern, which is to relate the population requirements of behavior settings to effects on individual life. We may picture a setting that is *optimally* populated, with just enough people to maintain it; one that is *underpopulated*, and one that is *overpopulated*. As the population changes relative to requirements of the setting, several consequences are in store for the individual.

Barker lists a variety of consequences that follow when a behavior setting is *underpopulated*. An overpopulated setting simply reverses the direction of these consequences.

1. Greater effort is required by each person in the setting. A restaurant that is optimally staffed by three waitresses is caught understaffed; each waitress now works much harder. We would expect less individual effort demanded of each waitress in an overpopulated setting, say, with five waitresses.

2. Each person must take on more difficult tasks and play more roles. The waitress may have to cook or wash dishes as well. By implication, when a setting gets overpopulated there should be greater specialization of function to allow for a better match between level of skill and job requirement.

3. There is less sensitivity and less evaluation of differences among people. With underpopulation each man becomes important regardless of who he is or what he's like; as long as he can pull his own, he's wanted. The implication is that in overpopulated settings one can afford the luxury of discrimination and sensitization to sex differences, skill differences, race differences, age differences, and so on. In other words, in an underpopulated setting men, women, and children all are called on to help keep things going; in certain overpopulated settings women and children may be asked to remain at home or in school, while men—and at that only some kinds of men—enter the work force.

4. Each person's labors have greater functional importance; each person has greater responsibility. Each man *is* important, as is each job he performs; what he does is essential to the maintenance of the setting.

5. There is a greater functional identity in an underpopulated setting. Barker notes a shift from "Who is he?" to "What can he do?" The evaluations that others make soon become the criteria for self-evaluations as well. Thus in an underpopulated setting a man judges his own worth in terms of what he's done rather than who he is or what personal qualities of charm, wit, intellect, wealth, possessions, and so on, he has. The overpopulated setting, by contrast, shifts the basis of evaluation from performances to qualities. Who one is becomes central; in particular, symbols of identity that are little related to one's work roles take on central self-defining importance.

Big School—Small School. Barker examined several interesting implications of this model. One study (Barker & Gump, 1964) compared consequences to the individual of big schools versus small schools. A big school had relatively many students (a median of 36) per behavior setting; a small school had a median number of around 11. Small schools provided individuals with "... *more* satisfactions related (a) to the development of competence, (b) to being challenged, (c) to engaging in important actions, (d) to being involved in group activities, (e) to being valued, and (f) to gaining moral and cultural values" (Barker 1965, p. 11). As expected, students in small schools experienced greater pressure to participate than their large-school counterparts. Barker noted in particular how group pressure and negative feedback is employed in the small schools to engage students

in performing in those programs established in the setting. For example, teachers were reported to urge students to participate, or students recognized that the school play needed extra girls in the cast so they felt obliged to try out. In the large schools, by contrast, pressure and negative feedback was brought to bear on selected students—those who showed promise —whereas others, more marginal, were allowed not to participate.

Midwest versus Yoredale. In another study Barker (1960, 1965; Barker & Barker, 1963) examined two towns. One he called Midwest, Kansas, U.S.A., the other, Yoredale, Yorkshire, England. Midwest and Yoredale had the same kinds of behavior setting; Barker suggested that in terms of content one could transpose the settings of Kansas to England with minimal disruption. However, the Kansas settings were underpopulated—1.25 persons per setting— whereas those in Yoredale were relatively overpopulated—2.63 persons per setting. Each setting in Midwest, then, had almost half the number of persons to maintain it as did settings in Yoredale. Given this relation of numbers to setting, we would predict that the citizens of Midwest should be busier, more versatile in the number of roles they occupied, more responsible, and so on, than citizens of Yoredale. Results generally confirm the expectations. For example, Midwest citizens participated in the town's behavior settings on the average of 2.5 hours per week more than citizens of Yoredale, and they were more involved in responsible positions.

It was among the adolescent population, however, that the most striking differences were uncovered. The adolescents of Midwest, living in a generally underpopulated community, *had to* participate in running the community. Midwest's adolescents filled 3.5 times as many responsible positions as the adolescents of Yoredale: each "acts in a play, works in a store, teaches a Sunday school class, plays in a basketball league game every three weeks; Yoredale adolescents occupy such positions every eleven weeks, on the average" (Barker 1960, p. 44). Barker maintains that if an adolescent from Yoredale were transported to Midwest, he would quickly take on higher participation and higher responsibility positions; and if a Midwesterner went to live in Yoredale, he would soon drop out of such active community involvement.

Barker's examination of the educational philosophy that characterized these two communities is equally interesting. In Midwest education was thought to prepare a youth for adulthood by involving him at an early age in significant community participation. Without the involvement of the youth, the town could not maintain its variety of behavior settings; thus their participation was essential and encouraged. In Yoredale, by contrast, the school setting was relatively isolated from community participation; children were placed with experts to be trained and excluded from responsible positions in the community where their services, essentially, were not needed.

"It would be extremely difficult to exchange the educational systems of the two towns. Many Midwest community settings which would be crippled by the *removal* of children would in Yoredale be disrupted by their presence. In fact it appears that the towns could not tolerate such a shift without a major transformation in the whole community system" (1960, p. 47).

Barker's insights, I think, reveal the vast system of interdependencies that we too often overlook in our efforts to understand human behavior. Here we have a link among environment, population, and ideological justifications in the form of educational philosophies. We also have a conceptual mapping that helps us gain further insights into the links between ecology and behavior and into the implications of ecological change for transformations in social organization and individual life style.

THE POPULATION EXPLOSION

It will be helpful at this point to look at what facts and what controversies exist concerning both the population explosion and the varieties of technological revolution. I might add, by way of preface, that the implications of these two ecological bombshells range well beyond the kinds of consequence we have so far considered. An overpopulated setting not only has con-

sequences for man's energy expenditure, versatility, identity, and so on, but, in addition, for the broader *quality* of human life, including the air we breathe, the space of free movement we have, the privacy we retain, the individuality we experience and can express, the choices we can make, and our very survival.

The figures are startling, the projections into the future are shocking, and the implications almost beyond belief. Numbers alone hardly communicate the immensity of the issue. What does it mean to know that this world of ours is growing by about 2.2 persons every second, 132 every minute, 190,000 each day and over 1.3 million each week (Associated Press, 1969), or to realize that the *rate* of world population growth is increasingly higher, as shown in Table 24.1?

Table 24.1 World population growth (from Sundermeyer, 1969)

It Took from	for Population to Reach
The beginning of man to the Neolithic Age	10 million
Neolithic to the birth of Christ (10,000 years)	300 million
Christ to Columbus (1500 years)	500 million
Columbus to 1850 (350 years)	1 billion
1850 to 1925 (75 years)	2 billion
1925 to 1962 (37 years)	3 billion
1962 to 1975 (13 years)	4 billion
1975 to 1982 (7 years)	5 billion

Five stages into the future

In an effort to give some meaning to all of these numbers Fremlin (1969), an English physicist, offers us a five-stage view of man's future, if we assume that the world's population doubles every 37 years. In paraphrased form, this is what he has to say.

Stage 1. In 260 years there will be a world population of 400,000 million persons. Existing food technology (as of the 1960's) will allow us up to about four population doublings, "though the complete elimination of all land wild-life, the agricultural use of roofs over cities and roads, the elimination of meat-eating, and the efficient harvesting of sea food, might allow two or three further doublings" (p. 200). In this way, we would have up to 260 years to develop nonconventional food technologies.

Stage 2. In 370 years the world population would be up to 3 million million. To feed them we would have to remove all sea life and harvest special organisms in the sea, the sort that are involved in primary photosynthesis, thereby eliminating the wasteful food chain we normally use. "Since the world's surface (land and sea) is 500 million-million square metres, each person would have a little over 160 square metres for his maintenance—about a thirtieth of an acre—which does not seem unreasonable ... so long as no important human activity other than food production takes place on the surface" (pp. 200–201).

Stage 3. In 450 years the population will be up to 15 million million persons. Thermal efficiency becomes a problem, especially keeping the world well lit day and night so that food production is possible; therefore reflectors put into orbit might be helpful to give extra light to the poles and to the earth's night side. Doing this "would bring the whole Earth to equatorial conditions, melting the polar ice and allowing one further doubling of population" (p. 201).

Stage 4. In 680 years the population will be up to 1000 million million persons. Energy efficiency remains a problem, although within 680 years it should be solvable, especially if we homogenize cadavers and change waste products back into food products. Population density would amount to two persons per square meter, including the total area of lands and seas.

Stage 4a. In 800 years the population will be up to 12,000 million million persons. This Fremlin calls the dead end. "Above two people per square metre, severe refrigeration problems occur. If the oceans were used as a heat sink, their mean temperature would have to rise about 1°C per year. ... Two more doublings would be permitted if the oceans were converted into steam, although that would create an atmospheric pressure comparable with the mean ocean bottom at present" (p. 203).

Stage 5. In 890 years a population of up to 60,000 million million. Rather than using the ocean as a heat sink, Fremlin sees a possibility of roofing it over to stop evaporation and to provide more room for housing. He also suggests hermetically sealing the planet, keeping the atmosphere required for ventilation in tanks

and pumping the rest to the outer seal; this latter operation would help in the planet's cooling, by this time, as in the last couple of stages, a vital necessity. "If heat removal were the sole limitation, then we could manage about 120 persons per square metre" (p. 203).

I should mention that Fremlin rejects the idea of shipping people off to other planets to keep our world's population within reasonable limits. He notes that we would have to begin shipping out about 60 million people each year, *now*! Furthermore, rather pessimistically, he suggests that other planets would soon reach the same troubled condition as the earth.

Fremlin's account focuses primarily on the heat transfer involved in keeping the earth's population growing, fed, and housed. He intentionally ignores the life-style consequences, although these are apparent. In essence, we would have to live a carefully regimented and totally programmed life. Fremlin notes that travel over only a few hundred meters would be possible, but since there would be about 10 million persons in that area we would have many choices for friends!

Population and Food. In getting caught up in these long-range population and life-style projections, we tend to forget the more immediate consequences of population on life today and in our immediate future. One of the most striking consequences of the population explosion is connected with food production and consumption. The highly industrialized countries are less explosive in population and more productive of food than their less industrialized brethren. For example, estimates are that the population will double in 58 years in developed areas of the world, but in only 32 years in the less developed areas of South and East Asia, Africa, and Latin America (Nortman, 1965).

These less developed nations are both agriculturally and economically incapable of supporting such a population increase. A combination of a higher birth rate and the benefits to longevity of advanced medical technology—which are available even in the developing nations—accounts for this increase. A striking example is Ceylon's gain of 16 years in life expectancy in only an eight-year period; the expectancy in 1946 was 44 years; it rose to 60 years in 1954. In essence, these nations have maintained "the combination of a medieval birth rate, 40 to 50 per thousand population, and a twentieth century death rate, less than 10 per thousand population" (Nortman, 1965, p. 10).

In 1967 a presidential advisory committee indicated that the world would face a staggering food crisis by 1985 unless the more advanced nations took it on themselves to provide an extra $12 billion each year both to feed others around the world and to assist them in programs of population control (United Press International, 1967). A special assistant to the Secretary of State (Johanesen, 1967) urged all nations to join in the greatest race in human history—between food and people. The food deficit posited by 1985 is 88 million tons, an amount greater than U. S. capacity even if all acreage were brought back into production and technology were significantly improved (UPI, 1967).

Education. Food is only one consequence, albeit a significant one, of the population explosion. Worldwide education is another area to suffer as population has grown. Some U. N. figures indicate a growth in illiteracy of over 200 million people in the developing nations (Johanesen, 1967). Worldwide figures released in 1967 showed that about 70 percent of school-age children were not in school: too many children for too-meager facilities, teachers, money.

Congregation in Cities. Analysis of the trends in population movement indicates still other human problems that emerge as population grows and congregates. One report, for example, presented in 1966 by Owen, who is a U. N. expert on cities, indicated that whereas the total world population between 1800 and 1965 multiplied five times, the population in cities of over 100,000 multiplied by 20 times. Again much of this urban growth occurred in the underdeveloped nations; Owen estimated that growth of cities in the underdeveloped nations was about 60 percent. Furthermore, "On a very conservative estimate . . . there are likely to be as many people living in large urban complexes by the year 2000 as were living in the entire world in 1950".

U. S. trends

Detailed figures on population trends in the United States are especially revealing. Taeuber (1967) notes several periods in U. S. population growth and dispersion.

1. In 1790 the U. S. population was 3.9 million. It was 95 percent rural, with 85 percent involved in agriculture.

2. 1790 to 1890 was a period of increase and expansion. Population rose to 25 million in 1850 and 75 million in 1900. The problem was sparsity of labor; the nation was underpopulated before millions of immigrants swarmed ashore and land expansion grew.

3. By 1900 40 percent lived in places of 2500 or more; 60 percent were involved in non-agricultural work.

4. In 1900 to 1960 there was a rapid shift in population toward metropolitan areas. Occupationally, workers moved increasingly into professional, technical, and managerial positions.

From 1900 to 1910 the urban population increased almost 40 percent, rising nearly 20 percent each subsequent decade except in the 1930's. Between 1900 and 1910, rural increase was only 10 percent; the figure became negative between 1950 and 1960. In 1910 the urban population was about 30.2 million; in 1960 it was 125.3 million. By contrast, in 1900 the rural population was 46 million, rising only slightly to 54.1 million by 1960. In that year about 7.5 percent of the total U. S. population lived on farms.

In essence, the shifts in U. S. population were away from farms and scattered rural areas into more congested, high-density metropolitan areas. In 1960 70 percent of the population was urban, but occupied only 1 percent of the total land area; the rural 30 percent occupied the remaining 99 percent (Taeuber, 1967).

There are few optimists when it comes to examining the population explosion and its implications for human survival and for the quality of human life. Many see the outcome to be continual unrest because of starvation, overcrowding, and disease; they see the world in a constant state of turmoil, perhaps until the bubble finally bursts in some ghastly holocaust. Many emphasize the directly physical consequences that overpopulation produces; others emphasize the social and psychological outcomes that seem likely. The former group shudders at the way in which man appears to be ruining his environment: polluting water and air, removing parks and green space; inundating land, sea, and air with garbage and waste (over 35 million tons each year in the U. S. alone—five pounds of refuse per person per day!); building high-rises to make dark canyons of the large cities; cluttering the highways with cars; crowding out persons from recreation areas.

On the social-psychological side, available crime statistics indicate man's restive response to his crowded urban life. In 1967, for example, 10 times as many violent crimes were committed in cities as compared with rural areas. The sociologist Angell (1951) computed an index of the *moral integration* of American cities, using crime statistics and welfare figures as the basis of this index. He reports that two factors, population heterogeneity and mobility, account for most of the variation in a city's degree of moral integration. As we have seen, over the years America's population has been mobile, moving from the farms into the cities and from city to city; movement also has been noticeably westward, creating new cities where desert cactus once grew. Likewise, the movement of blacks and others into the cities created a population less stable and less homogeneous than in rural America.

In 1938 Wirth emphasized the consequences of urban living for modern man. Although he may engage in face-to-face meetings with others, urban man nevertheless lives an impersonal, superficial, segmented, and transitory existence. He wanders about anonymously, tied into few enduring social relationships. His behavior is integrated with that of others through formal and contractual arrangements rather than the informal primary-group ties that bound him to his fellows in nonurban days.

THE TECHNOLOGICAL REVOLUTION

Not by bread alone, nor muscle, in fact, but by brains, by tools, and by culture did man survive and so extend his presence even on earth while reaching for the universe beyond. We think it startling that the world's population doubles in 37 years; how striking it is that in the relatively short space of 60 years from the Wright brothers' first flight, man set foot on the moon. With each development and use of a new tool man extended his capacity for dealing with his environment. He became a more efficient hunter or a better farmer, allowing a surplus to gather and the beginnings of a more complex social organization to evolve. With the development of the wheel man became more mobile, as he did when he domesticated animals for his use and when he captured the winds in his sails and set forth to explore his world and expand his horizons. With the development of steam power generated from fossil fuels man began the industrial revolution in earnest, creating machinery run by power that was beyond his own personal physical capacities but within his reach as a sentient being.

The advent of automation, or the *cybernetic* revolution as some like to call it, came into being when technology advanced to a point at which it became self-monitoring and self-regulating. Electronic computers took on functions that formerly had to be overseen by individual workers. Entire assembly lines could be put into the hands of a few trained technicians who monitored the computer that monitored and controlled operations up and down the line. Communications systems, traffic control, rapid transit, guidance systems, filing and retrieval systems, and so on, all became automated.

Automation: The debate

It is not clear precisely when the great debate began; but when a report appeared in 1964 entitled "The Triple Revolution" (Ad Hoc Committee), citing cybernation as one of the key changes confronting our society, the battle lines were drawn. There are several aspects to the debate, and few hard facts. First, there is a combined employment-economy controversy. Does automation, in fact, create vast unemployment and therefore threaten the nation's economic stability? Second, there is a psychological debate concerning the working force. Does automation create dissatisfaction among workers, giving them a sense of impotence and meaninglessness? Third, there is a broader social-psychological debate. Does automation create a society that is overorganized, overplanned, excessively rationalized, and sterile? Related to the entire issue of automation is an issue of continuity versus discontinuity in evaluating the impacts of technology on the individual and on social organization.

Automation and Employment. The economist Lekachman (1966), reviewing a Presidential Commission report of 1964 that examined employment issues involving automation, states,

"During the last five years, 'automation' has indeed displaced workers, and quite probably at the 20,000 per week clip so often cited in alarm, but most of those displaced have secured other jobs. The Commission has a point when it says that 'the basic fact is that technology eliminates jobs, not work,' at least when sensible public policy directs itself to the maintenance of high levels of aggregate demand" (p. 67).

The sensible public policy to which Lekachman refers involves, among other things, a realization of the rising demands that automation does have for urban, white-collar, skilled workers. This means providing greater access to high-skilled training for those who presently are disadvantaged in this regard, especially in the nonwhite community. The Commission's point is that with growing automation, if nonwhites hold the same proportion of jobs in each occupational category in 1975 as in 1964 (when the report was published), their rate of unemployment will have risen to be *five* times that of the entire labor force. In other words, when the technology of an entire society is rising so that highly skilled workers are increasingly required, those who are not trained will be inextricably caught in the vast pit of unemployment.

The over-all national figures are clear, as are the conclusions from several specific case studies of the impact of automation on skill requirements. Nationally, between 1910 and 1960 the percentage of white-collar workers rose from 22 percent of the total to 43 percent; by contrast, the blue-collar percentages remained much the same, 37 percent in 1910 and 36 percent in 1960 (Wolfbein, 1962). Studies of industrial organizations indicate both rising skill and education accompanying introduction of automation (see Wolfbein, 1962, for a summary and discussion).

In his analysis of the changing nature of society Drucker (1968) discusses what he calls the *knowledge society,* noting, "In the last twenty years the base of our economy shifted from manual to knowledge work..." (p. 287). A knowledge worker, according to Drucker, is a man who produces knowledge and ideas rather than goods or services; he is involved in the application of information to society (as a physicist, say, applies his knowledge to help people live better). The knowledge worker will come to replace the unskilled laborer, whom Drucker sees as an *engineering imperfection* who has his job only because "we have not taken the trouble to apply enough knowledge to his work so as to 'program' it for the machine" (p. 299). Knowledge workers will not have to learn specific skills as much as they will have to learn *how to learn* and how to apply knowledge to practical matters.

An examination of chronic unemployment (Wolfbein, 1962) indicated (for 1961) that whereas unskilled workers were 5 percent of the working force, they contributed 13.5 percent to the chronically unemployed. Professional and technical workers were about 11 percent of the total labor force but contributed only 2 percent to the chronically unemployed. In Drucker's view the knowledge worker will not contribute to unemployment statistics; however, his pattern of work will be unlike the traditional patterns to which we are presently accustomed. He will have less rather than more leisure time; he will be motivated by intrinsic challenges on his job rather than its external qualities; he may experience several employment shifts in his lifetime, becoming employment-mobile by adopting a second career rather than retiring at an early age.

Given these figures and speculations, it seems that the nature of the automation-employment debate needs some modification. Automation does indeed replace workers, particularly those who are unskilled. It will provide a continuing threat to employment, especially for those who remain unskilled or unknowledgeable. Any group in the society that is chronically unskilled (e.g., blacks and some other minorities) will experience the effects of an automated technology to a much greater degree than skilled workers.

Automation and the Life of the Worker. Is automation likely to deprive the worker of his sense of personal worth, alienating him both from his work and from himself? Will the worker of tomorrow be like the night watchman of today, simply watching the machine for signs of trouble, checking dials and printouts, lacking any sense of pride or ego-involvement in his work (Ferry, 1968)? If the evidence concerning employment and automated technology is moderately clear, the evidence concerning its psychological consequences is not yet firmly supported by systematic data.

Several studies of the effects of a change-over to automation in a factory are instructive. Walker (1957) studied a steel-tube mill that under automation was able to produce a better quality of pipe four times as fast as conventional mills and with half the number of men. The men in this plant were scattered over a large area, manning several different stations; they experienced some sense of isolation and had few chances to meet and talk together. Over-all working conditions in the automated plant were better than in conventional plants: better lighting, space, ventilation, cleanliness, and so on. After a while workers earned more in the automated plant; however, with small numbers and high skill requirements they knew their chances for advancement were minimal. The men reported that their jobs were physically easier but psychologically more difficult in their demands for alertness and constant attentiveness. They felt themselves to be more responsible; they felt more anxious because tiny errors could create major breakdowns. A fascinating finding and a clear indication of the often impenetrable psychology of the human mind is that fully two-thirds of the men reported that they felt automated mills to be a threat to the working man; this occurred in spite of the fact that their own jobs were secure and those who had been laid off were given other jobs with equal pay.

Mann and Hoffman (1960) studied two power plants, one of which was more highly automated than the other. This plant generated a third more energy with slightly more than half the workers required in the older plant. Various measures indicated that the men were proud of their new plant and were more satisfied with their chances for promotion and with their salaries. Workers felt that they had a great deal to say about how things were run. Those in the new, automated plant tended to be younger, more educated, and newer to the company than workers in the other plant. More workers in the new plant admitted to being nervous and "on edge" about their work. Men in both plants were rotated on shift-work schedules, seven days on and a few off in the new plant; one month on in the old. In general none freely commented that they liked shift work; however almost 2.5 times as many of those in the new plant reported that they did not mind it.

The introduction of technological advances also reshaped aspects of the new plant's social organization. The higher satisfaction of those in the new plant, therefore, is a joint function of the newer technology and the changed organizational structure it brought about. Furthermore, some of the positive effects attributed to the technological improvement appear to be related to the increased prestige, benefits, and interest in how the worker is doing when an organization shifts to a newly automated system. When everyone is automated and no one in management or social-scientific circles much gives a damn any more, I wonder if these side effects will wash out and diminish the apparently positive results that Mann and Hoffman report.

Other findings provide similar difficulties in determining worker satisfaction. The introduction of a small computer into an office, for example, provoked some worker dissatisfaction; but another study indicated little or no impact on worker attitudes when a small computer was introduced (Hardin, 1960a, b). First, the change-over to electronic equipment further "rationalized" the work. Formal rules were substituted for individual decision making, and there was a greater centralization of responsibility. Deadlines were more important. Performance standards were set higher and were more closely supervised and enforced. Any absence or lateness became more disruptive than in the past. Second, risks were far higher, errors were more costly, and it was easier to locate the person who made the error. Third, however, workers directly involved with the computer felt considerable job satisfaction; it was more challenging and interesting. In toto it seemed that the positive benefits of job satisfaction were somewhat dulled by the tight schedule, high risk, performance standards, and formalization of work.

Hoos (1960), reports that automating an office reduced the number of jobs, did not generally raise the skill level for any job, did not prove to be very challenging or interesting. A small group of programmers experienced considerable satisfaction; the rest, however, felt themselves to be part of a "paper-processing factory" involved in dull, routine labor with a greater demand for accuracy and detail than in precomputer days.

It is obvious that the state of our systematic knowledge is such that we do not yet know what to make of apparent inconsistencies in the empirical data relating technological automation to worker attitudes. When we must simply study effects without knowing precisely the host of relevant variables that affect the relationship between technology and attitudes, we do not know whether two studies are inconsistent or whether they reveal different aspects of the total picture. For instance, one of Mann's studies indicated that there were younger workers in the automated plants and that workers in these plants expressed general job satisfaction; we might expect that younger persons would more easily take to new ways of work than old-line workers. How this kind of issue influences the results of other studies is not clear, but data suggest that the relationship between automation and worker attitudes is not simple.

In pulling it all together, Mann (1962) concludes,

1. Automation creates conditions in which office work and plant or factory work are becoming increasingly similar. In both job responsibility is increased, technical know-how imperative, errors more costly. There is some indication that this change toward similarity between white- and blue-collar workers is met with greater satisfaction on the part of the latter than the former.

2. Both office and plant workers under automation realize the degree of uncertainty that is now introduced into their lives. Blue-collar employees are beginning to worry about job displacements and layoffs.

3. The introduction of automation breaks up informal social organizations and cliques in both the office and the plant, forcing a readjustment of social relationships. The new pace and demand for precision cuts down time for free talking and informality of relationships.

4. Promotion opportunities and channels are radically changed by the introduction of automation. There are fewer opportunities for advancement.

5. The introduction of automation proves an exciting challenge for some workers and a disastrous period of turmoil for others. It is fairly obvious, then, that the introduction of automated technology has widespread impacts on the individual and on the entire organization itself.

Leisure. Technology and automation, coupled with growth in the labor force, have in fact created conditions that liberate the man once caught in an endless cycle of labor. In 1900 the estimated average work week was 60 hours; in 1950 the average had dropped to 40 hours (Clawson, 1964). Figures projected for the year 2000 suggest an average of 28 hours. In 1900 about 27 percent of the total national time was available for leisure; in 1950 this figure rose to 34 percent and is projected at 38 percent by 2000.

Leisure based on the age of retirement increased fourfold between 1900 and 1950, and is expected to double again by 2000. Vacation leisure time has doubled since 1900 and is projected at more than five times its present level by 2000. In 1956, as one example, more than 50 percent of all paid vacations were three weeks or more. Weekend leisure time has also increased, from 50 billion hours annually in 1900 to 179 billion in 1950; it is projected to 483 billion hours by the year 2000 as more weekends become three days in length. Daily leisure time, although rising, has become a relatively small fraction of man's total leisure time in the United States. What this means, of course, is that persons have continued to work about the same number of hours each day, but now work fewer days each week, fewer weeks each year, and fewer years of their life before retirement.

This release into leisure has created a host of new problems, most of which we have yet to deal with adequately. Certain kinds of leisure activity have risen dramatically. For example, figures indicate that outdoor use, especially camping, water sports, and other such activities have risen about 10 percent annually for many years (Clawson, 1964); this is a rate more than five times the rate of population growth. Anyone who has tried to get into a national park during summer vacation periods will know the true meaning of these figures. Hiking on a wooded mountain trail only to stumble over beer cans or look out on the view of assorted gum wrappers and a horde of teenagers, kids, and youthful elderlies in hiking boots and canteens captures all too well one consequence of this outdoor leisure boom.

High-Kultur lovers, take heart. Participation in attendance at concerts and at art museums has also risen; even reading is at an all-time high (Clawson, 1964). Travel, of course is up; both extra time and general affluence contribute to the growth of the mobile American. Some estimate (e.g., Revelle, 1964) that the average person soon will double the miles he travels each year, with possibly half of this travel, or around 5000 miles per year, devoted to a *search* for recreation. And if he runs to the beach in search of his place in the sun, the demand for those places will give us an estimated two people per foot. At least we won't need much sun-tan lotion with all those crowding people casting shadows.

Not everyone will experience this increased leisure. The poorly educated or the workers who have been displaced by technological advances may experience more idleness but little real leisure. Highly trained specialists may have little time away from their work. As Drucker (1968) suggests, the knowledge worker will neither have much time for leisure nor retire early. But between these extremes the majority of citizens already have experienced increases in their total leisure, and more time awaits tomorrow's man.

Although time may be liberated, this does not necessarily mean it will be spent in ways that some would evaluate as productive or creative. Some workers are already taking on extra jobs in their leisure time; others wander about lost or glue themselves to their televisions, waiting for time to pass. Some analysts maintain that daily leisure is wasted time; increased *annual* leisure time, however, would allow opportunities for travel, for a return to education, for pure play, and even for some public service (see Clawson, 1964). Given both the present state of affairs and projections into the future, it is imperative to devote serious efforts at this time to examining ways to help people use their leisure in ways they will find productive.

Continuity versus discontinuity

Some people maintain that the future can be predicted by extrapolations of present trends in population and technology; others maintain that a basic discontinuity exists between patterns existing today and those that are likely in the future. The latter group—with which I generally concur—argues that technological developments of an entirely new order make it foolish to rest assured that the forms and patterns known to us today will exist, only in a more complex form, in the years ahead. The development of print, for example, created a qualitative difference in the life of man, a life discontinuous with his previous existence.

Drucker (1968) attacks the continuity position.

". . . it is unlikely that the trends of the last sixty years will dominate the rest of this century, as most predictions about the year 2000 assume. Instead we can expect different and new trends to emerge, and different and new concerns to claim our attention" (p. 381).

In documenting his claim Drucker notes that we are emerging from an *age of continuity*; most of the technological inventions that underlie our industrial society were developed in the late 1800's and early 1900's, so that our present society is founded on a past technology. "An economist of 1913 could, therefore, have forecast the industry structure of the 1960's with reasonable accuracy'' (p. 7). For his major examples Drucker examines "the aging 'modern' industries" of agriculture, steel, and automobiles," noting how each was founded on technological discoveries made years ago.

Advances in the postindustrial knowledge business, however, are entirely new and are already changing the shape of older industries while creating new organizations and occupations. Communications media, for example, have created a global community and a global marketplace that the world never had before. The implications of such technological advances are so broad that clearly they will have a significant impact on all of mankind. Never having experienced this condition of new technology before, how can we assume that the future will merely extend present trends? Never having lived in an era of high-speed computers, how can we really know what life tomorrow will be or how man and society will be changed?

Drucker does not dispute the likelihood that present industries will continue to develop and prosper for some time to come, especially in technologically underdeveloped countries. He suggests, however, that the knowledge industries will create an entirely new, qualitatively different, and thus *discontinuous* fabric for society and for individuals. Governments will change; organizational structures will change; economic policies will change; and so will most aspects of society. These changes will *not* be simply extensions of what exists today.

Dehumanizing or rehumanizing?

Dehumanization: A Definition. That word dehumanization is used in several contexts, especially as an outcome of life in contemporary civilization. But just what does it mean? I call freely on the writings of Bernard, Ottenberg, and Redl (1968) in the psychiatric field, and the religious philosopher Buber (1958) who sensed all too well the potential duality of human relationships. Bernard and her colleagues see dehumanization as a psychological defense mechanism that includes the use of denial, repression, and the isolation of affect. As a de-

fense it helps a person cope with extreme situations by decreasing the sense of his own humanness and the humanness of others. As with most psychological defense mechanisms, there is a beneficial side. During an extreme crisis, for example a violent accident or illness, an individual who is able to be distant from the people in the situation—that is, able to dehumanize them and respond to them without pity or disgust—is better able to help. Certain occupations require a degree of dehumanization or human distancing if they are to function effectively. A surgeon, for example, would do poorly if he were not able to maintain some distance from his patients. Interestingly enough, the military and the police are two other occupations in which dehumanization can be a helpful mechanism.

Lifton (1969) interviewed many survivors of the Hiroshima atomic bombing and noted several interesting things relevant to this discussion. For one, his subjects (a dehumanizing term in itself) reported how after the initial horror they experienced they soon became devoid of all feeling content; they felt nothing, even when confronted by the writhing and blistered bodies of their fellows cut down and burning alive in the streets. Second, he noted a change in himself. Initially he experienced nearly overwhelming emotions during these interviews; later, when he came to view himself as a scientist engaged in data collection, he was no longer so deeply affected.

In each of these cases there is some benefit to be gained by dehumanizing oneself and others. For the victims of a total disaster it permits survival by strength when it is most needed, both to help others and themselves. For the researcher the treatment of victims as the subjects of scientific inquiry permits him, in fact, to conduct the inquiry.

The problem with dehumanization is that the defensive process itself may become overwhelming and determinative in areas well beyond those of its major use. At this point the dehumanizing person no longer sees himself or others as possessing human qualities.

Imagine this use of dehumanization as a daily way of viewing and relating to others. Gone are the shreds of humanity; gone are the feelings of empathy and compassion; gone is the understanding of the plight of others. In their place are points on a map, statistical tables, bomb tonnage figures, routine measures of efficiency, numbered lists of dead and wounded, and so on. People become interchangeable pieces, subjects, targets, roles; the enemy to be destroyed; objects to be viewed dispassionately and at a great distance.

Buber (1958) had another way of stating the case. He spoke of man's *dual nature* that derived from his twofold attitude toward himself and others. Man can relate to others in terms of *I* to *It* or *I* to *Thou*. In the *I-It* form we relate to others as objects out there, apart from ourselves. Our attitude is analytic and objective; we dissect, we divide, we note parts and pieces. The *I-Thou* relationship, however, is subjective, personal, and nonanalytic; we relate to others as persons, as living beings with whom we share much. We relate to the totality of another person and his unique bond with us.

In Buber's view, as one begins to relate to others in the *I-It* form, the *I* itself soon changes, producing an *It-It* relationship between two objects rather than persons. Rollo May captures this in a comment on today's slick magazines such as *Playboy*, which portray two *Its* facing each other; the detached, sex-object-oriented bachelors facing likewise detached, mechanical, vacuous females who "... are not sexy at all. ... *Playboy* has only shifted the fig leaf from the genitals to the face" (1969, p. 29). Bernard, Ottenberg, and Redl make much the same point; dehumanization is a defensive process by which the individual who considers others as nonhuman objects (*It*) soon comes to have that view of himself. Neither Buber nor the psychiatric group denies the presence of this dehumanized form of relationship, nor does either deny the potential value of such forms under certain conditions. Each, however, is disturbed by the consequences for mankind of the apparently growing depersonalization (*It-It*) of the modern age. The psychiatric group in particular is concerned with the dehumanizing impact of military technology; in this regard their worry is shared with many.

Two Sides. Although an occasional voice proclaims the positive impact of technology in liberating man from his toil and giving him leisure and freedom to become creative, by far the loudest cries are heard from those who consider labor and life in technological society as dehumanizing (e.g., Ellul, 1964). It is likely that technological innovation introduces new possibilities for a better life and simultaneously introduces new problems, many of which remain unsolved. The automobile gave us freedom of movement beyond our wildest dreams; it cut distances and created recreational possibilities previously unavailable; and these freedoms were offered to a great number and variety of individuals. Although it displaced blacksmiths and others connected with the horse trade, the automobile opened vast new companies with hundreds of thousands of new jobs. Roads had to be built; fuel had to be produced economically; autos and auto parts had to be built; recreation areas had to be developed; gas stations, restaurants, and accommodations had to be provided for newly mobile man. Yet at the same time it opened the way for air pollution, highway congestion, accidents, business monopolies seeking expanding markets, and a host of other less desirable, often unforseen outcomes.

Galbraith (1967) has much to say about the social consequences of "the imperatives of technology." He argues that the shape of our economic system is determined by the technological demands of time, capital, specialized manpower (which our universities gratefully crank out), and an assurance of stability. He claims our government shapes its policies to meet these demands. Oglesby and Shaull (1967) (see p. 376) argue that the survival of the American system requires an assurance of "fertile frontiers" or markets for its products. They, too, relate the technology of the American economic system to its international policies. Clearly we cannot speak about the possible negative consequences of technology, especially in the United States, without coming headlong into a serious critique of the entire political system.

A related consequence of technology is brought to light whenever the United States engages in a significant leap forward in space or military science while its urban ghettos steam with the poor, the unemployed, and the hungry. Technology seems to demand an ever-increasing investment, both to maintain its given levels and to guarantee continuing expansion. In the matter of national priorities technological demands often win out over human demands.

Careful documentation is not easy to come by, but it is reasonable to hypothesize that modern technology confronts man with a host of psychological problems as well. The worker faces these directly as he must adjust himself to meet the needs of an increasingly automated world. As several of the studies cited suggest, the worker in an automated factory or office feels considerable stress as he realizes how major each error on his part can be and how observable his errors are. His personal time schedule becomes tuned to the time schedule of technology; absences and tardiness are troublesome to the machine world, so pressure increases for him to be punctual, orderly, rational, precise.

The mysteries of technology, especially the awesome abilities of modern computers and modern science, undoubtedly have another kind of effect in diminishing man's faith in his ability to control his life and his world. Although the forces of technology have in fact provided a greater degree of environmental control than ever before, they have created another world, another environment, that is beyond most men's ken; this new world seems to operate by some incalculable set of economic and social forces that have consequences beyond man's personal control, a world that follows its own logic (Ellul, 1964).

Parsons (1968) argued that such technological advances, coupled with advances in the social and behavioral sciences, have had several important psychological consequences. We might imagine that having created so many great things and having achieved so many wondrous feats of science and technology, man would thereby have his sense of uniqueness reinforced. Yet each advance in our knowledge concerning human behavior can communicate a sense of personal powerlessness in the face of the Great God Science. To be known as an atom is known is both frightening and seems to limit our freedom to be unpredictable, variable, and unknown. Man's uniqueness as man, his view of himself as somehow apart from the rest of the universe,

is challenged by his realization that biology has placed him in an evolutionary sequence along with other animals; that chemistry views him as a collection of rather common elements and compounds; that genetics sees him in terms of a bunch of chromosomes and protein molecules that can be messed around with; that medicine sees him as a source of organs for transplants, and finally, that computer science sees him as an interesting model for building bigger and better computers. In a sense the scientific approach to man has had an effect on him much like what Maurois said happens when you seek to analyze wit: like dissecting a frog, analyzing wit leads you to take it apart; you find out what it is made of, but the subject is killed in the process.

For those brought up in an age when it seems that technology can do almost everything, there is less wonderment than for those older generations for whom air travel may still be amazing, let alone travel to the moon. Some children watching the moon landing in 1969 were disappointed while their elders were amazed; the kids had been reared on such miracles, and television space thrillers were really more dramatic. Leaving such differences aside, however, I think it important to note that modern man has come to believe technology is capable of almost anything, given only the will and the cash. Does this not tend to narcotize an individual in much the same way the media are said to (see p. 346)? Many problems of human living are *not* problems of engineering or technology, but believing them to be so may deflect any efforts to apply nontechnological means to their solution. Racial prejudice, for example, is not to be solved simply by advanced techniques of modern science. Yet, narcotized into believing that science can do everything, we withdraw from the arena, hoping that George-the-scientist will do it for us; what a rude awakening we may all have someday.

Technology of Militarism. We have indeed come a long way from the days of the stone, the ax, the spear, the bow and arrow, and even from the war machines of World Wars I and II. A committed and well-known scientist, DuBridge, while extolling the virtues of technology in general, doubts that the technology of warfare "has brought new opportunities, new comforts, new possibilities for better, safer, and less painful living" (1962, p. 28). No one can doubt, however, that military technology has brought much with it, including high budgetary priorities (see p. 377), the creation of weapons that literally can wipe out all of mankind, either with a noisy nuclear blast or a softer aerosol cloud carrying chemical and biological agents. Military technology, in addition, gives a meaning to dehumanization that few who are critical of "benign" forms of the cybernetic revolution would have imagined.

The killing of six million Jews and others in Nazi Germany marked a shocking point in the history of man's relationship with his fellow man. The development of nuclear power and its use on the Japanese in World War II was another such military horror. Although one may find military or national justifications for either of these actions, the very pursuit of such justifications and their continued application in contemporary warfare speaks only too clearly of the dehumanized quality that life has. The technology of modern warfare is such that even grasping the potential of such weapons is a psychological impossibility; so we turn to our statistical charts and map out the maximum acceptable loss of 30 to 60 million citizens in a nuclear attack. As we come to think in these objective terms, we find it increasingly difficult to experience any responsibility for the consequences of our actions. It was not "us," but only our role, our job; it was not individual human beings, but "the enemy"; we were only following orders—perhaps the essence of an *It-It* bond linking mankind.

In our efforts to protect ourselves from being overwhelmed by the uncontrollable forces that appear on the scene we find it convenient to dehumanize the victims and ourselves. We face the world as one machine to another, and thereby divest ourselves of both our feelings and our remaining rationality; for a crucial aspect of man's rationality, in fact, is his unique ability to relate to others and to himself with the sensitivities that feelings permit. When we so objectify everything that those feelings have been eliminated or reduced to flimsy whispers in hoarse throats, we will have finally recreated man in the image of automated technology.

In summary

It is obvious that we are not going to settle the great debates here. It is even more obvious that the technological revolution has both dehumanizing and rehumanizing aspects to it. Perhaps if we begin to direct our attention to more systematic and serious examination of the dual impacts of technology on man and on society we will gain better answers to the questions we ask. In that society seems more interested in churning out more innovations than in examining the implications and meanings of what it's already got, I fear that such systematic study will never be undertaken. The fact of incessant churning may provide an answer in its own right.

MANY QUESTIONS, FEW ANSWERS

The combined impact of growing population and advanced technological wizardry place the United States and much of the world in a situation today for which there are really no historical precedents. What faces us tomorrow offers hopes and horrors that we can only project with doubt and speculation. There are more questions to be asked than answers to be given.

That both technology and population have significant effects on the individual and on social organization we have no doubt. That man will be able to master these effects, however, is not easy to assess. I agree with Michael (1968) and others who reject the notion that the lessons from the past will guide us. As Michael notes (and as discussed on p. 425ff.), first, there is only a slight similarity between the past and our present and future. He offers leisure in ancient Greece as an example: few persons were involved, it lasted only a couple of generations, and, finally, no women participated; it was obviously very different from leisure of the present and future. Second, there is an argument that we've mastered the first Industrial Revolution; Michael suggests this argument is full of flaws, chiefly that we have never really mastered the social consequences of the first Industrial Revolution. The gap between the industrialized nations and the huge number of have-not nations; the creation of poverty, unemployment, and ghetto slums in the industrialized nations; and the instability of values still in transition are residues that still haunt us.

Michael raises a variety of questions as he examines developments in biological technology, cybernation, and social engineering. To mention but a few:

1. The significant advances in chemical and biological warfare raise moral and ecological questions. The use of defoliants in warfare (or in agriculture), for example, can effect a change in the entire ecological life cycle of an area, from its weather to its animal and human population.

2. The advances in psychopharmacology raise important questions concerning the individual's freedom to work with his own mind, expanding or restricting his consciousness as he wishes. To whom do our mind and body owe allegiance? If the answer is "to ourselves," why are drug laws so stringent?

3. Organ transplants and genetic engineering raise another host of problems. It is increasingly possible to maintain human life by technological means. But who shall live? For how long? Who determines who is to survive? If genetic engineering eventually permits sex and other characteristics to be determined (including intelligence), who is to have the say in these matters? With birth control we are already beginning to see the role of government involvement in family planning. When other technologies are likewise advanced, new issues of control and freedom will be raised.

4. We have already examined some of the implications of the cybernetic revolution, but several other consequences have not yet been mentioned. Problems arise in connection both with the young and the old. The length of time spent in school is already extensive; adolescence in the sense of less-than-full participation and responsibility in the society carries many young men and women into their thirties. This in turn creates other problems, ranging from withdrawal and apathy to open protest and demands for increased participation. The elderly are increasingly displaced from centers of social importance, participation, and responsibility. Medical science lengthens man's life span, but when he reaches those older years, he finds little room remaining for him in society. Just as the young have started a youth culture, the more affluent elderly have begun slowly to move into their own adult communities where some semblance of a significant existence remains possible. It is likely that a future decrease in manpower demands will intensify this delay of the young and casting off of the elderly unless efforts are put into maximizing their energies and talents rather than letting them waste away.

5. All of the advanced techniques of social engineering, wherein economic indicators are developed so that a government can manipulate the economy and social indicators are developed so that social life can be similarly assessed and manipulated, raise other serious questions of individual freedom and social control. In the sphere of economics, when the economy is sagging the government's Council of Economic Advisors takes a reading and the government can step in to heat it up; or if the reading shows it to be too hot, efforts can be made to slow it all down. These economic manipulations already affect individuals, who, for example, may wish to get a home loan and find that rates have risen astronomically for national economic reasons they may little understand or appreciate. What will happen when we have a Council on Social Indicators (see Bauer, 1966, for a discussion) that takes a reading of the national index of joy or happiness or political restlessness? Will the government then step in to up the joy level or decrease the restlessness? Who makes these decisions? Who is tomorrow's social architect? In Barker's analysis of the effects of overpopulation on the character and life style of individuals, he notes that the personal qualities that emerge from an underpopulated setting read like a disciplinarian's listing, including effort, difficult tasks, responsibility, and so forth. He goes on to note,

"We have made a nation's ideal of the fact that these are not *imposed* controls in American culture. We sometimes call them self-discipline. In reality they are controls built into the structure and the dynamics of the setting. . . . What happens when the ecological environment changes to one of overpopulated settings without intrinsic controls, with the old ideals lingering on, but no longer true?" (1960, p. 48).

6. A variety of questions can be raised concerning the personality types that live best in a high-density, high-technology society. Socialization practices in the home, in school, in peer groups, and in the media never create a homogeneous population of like personalities who mesh in neatly with the kinds of opportunity that modern society offers; some persons seem to fit in better than others. Given a crowded and dense world with complex technologies controlling almost everything, how will the individual keep himself tuned in to things? Michael (1968) notes that whereas some theorists maintain that technology opens new horizons, the individual may in fact become very selectively involved to preserve his own sanity amid what seem to be overwhelming conditions; he may psychologically reduce the number of options he sees simply to avoid the destructive blast of information overload. Or he may withdraw completely, searching for a simpler life.

7. Shifts in sex and age roles may also be an outcome of movement into this advanced society. As more workers move into service occupations requiring face-to-face human relationships, the traditional masculine role is somewhat altered. The traditional female role likewise undergoes a shift as technology demands a more logical and scientific approach to things and permits her to compete as it replaces muscle power with brain power. Another dilemma already faces highly educated women, who may feel it is a waste of education and talents just to be a housewife. How will people resolve these role shifts in the traditional images of male and female? The unisex movement in the late 1960's, in clothing, hair styles, softer qualities for males and liberated aggressiveness for females suggests a direction.

In terms of the usual age-grading system, in which older means wiser and more experienced, we have already witnessed a societal shift, brought on in great measure by rapid technological advances combined with a rapid rise in the number of young persons. In the first time in recorded history rapid social change has threatened to outdate older persons' knowledge so that many younger persons are more skilled and knowledgeable. This places a special burden on the young while providing even greater insecurity for those of older years, who fear that each passing day they get just that much further behind.

8. In addition to questions concerning the personalities of individuals, serious questions remain concerning values necessary to fit new forms of society. Religious values in particular seem to be targets for change. Ideas that developed in low-density rural population concerning work and, in one case at least, birth control are undergoing transition as man becomes urbanized. How can work continue to be associated with salvation and identity when leisure will become an increasingly potent force in society?

CONCLUSION

There will be those who will attempt to dictate values, personalities, and social policy as the combined effects of population and technology are felt ever more intensely. Some will demand a return to the old past, when small numbers lived in rural settings and technology was a tiny shadow. Others will demand a rapid leap forward, casting out every quality of humanity built up over time in favor of a neatly tailored technetronic man. Governments will intervene. Passions will run high. Errors will be made; occasional progress will occur. If anything should prevail in these times, it is the idea that no voice should be ignored. When we become so dehumanized that we usher in tomorrow as though it were simply another feat of engineering, there may be no one left to appreciate it. Worse yet, those who are around may have lost the humanness that makes it all worthwhile.

It should be obvious that we cannot talk about population and technology with dispassionate unconcern. That we *must* talk about it, study it, and do something, however, should also be obvious. Right now we should be industriously engaged in investigations of the effects of the population-technology revolution on man's personality, his relationships with others, and the quality of his life.

If you saw a man driving toward a bridge that had just been washed away, would you not feel a responsibility to warn him of the danger?

If you were a scientist who had carefully studied the effects of pesticides on man, animals, and the general ecology of an area, would you not likewise feel a responsibility to warn mankind of the peril your research uncovered? And what if you as a social psychologist should uncover negative health consequences of a particular form of social organization, a particular density of population, or a particular technological innovation? Would you not also feel a responsibility to warn the world of this danger?

There are psychotherapists who help individuals deal with the problems they encounter in their lives; there are group therapists who try to deal with more than one person at a time. But where are society's therapists, that hearty group who will take on society as their patient and try to help it work out its problems? I suggest that this is a role appropriate for social psychologists. A role of this sort—uncovering nasty truths—is fraught with difficulties as it cuts its way across politics and planning and through issues dangerously central to the economy of the society and to the lives of every person. This would not be the first time, however, that a person who lit one candle in a darkened room was cursed.

Chapter 25

Moral development

At birth, charming though he may be, the human infant is a bundle of surging drives and impulses, ill equipped for independent survival, let alone for the subtleties of thought and deed that mark man's socialized existence. He has great potential: to learn, to develop skills and knowledges. And he will learn much: the language of his group; its customs and its laws; its games; its habits and routines; its beliefs and ideologies; its compass of values, marking out good on one side and evil on the other.

The essence of socialization is to make a social man out of this raw material. Although *of* society at birth, the human is not yet ready to live *in* society. He lives at the center of his world; what he wants, he wants, and right now. His passions are worn on his shoulder; he has no guile, nothing that is civilized to conceal his feelings, wants, tensions, needs. He is honest. Clearly he is not ready to make his way in a society in which he is not the center, in which control of impulses is necessary, in which sensitivity is more helpful than raw honesty. It is at these points of transition, where the infant meets society preparatory to his entry into it, that he seems to be waging war *against* it.

Those with a practical bent view the infant's war as culminating in a victory for both sides. The society gains a new member ready to take on the various burdens that come from communal (i.e., interdependent) living; the person gains a new array of rewards that would be unavailable to him should he adamantly refuse to yield his passion to self-control. Others, however, view man's encounter, especially with modern society, as resulting in an unfortunate personal loss: he gives up everything, his passions and his unique individuality, and gets little of real value in return. In troubled modern times some even demand a return to the infant in each adult, the anarchy of total individualism: let each do his own thing and society be damned.

It is difficult to imagine a long-enduring society of infants. Can I really be at the center when you too crave that position? Can I really express my every wish while you and millions of others likewise demand that yours and theirs be expressed right now and right here? For a time the strong would win, the weak would be pushed aside. But in their very winning, would they not also lose? A society of infants is no society at all.

The development of the human infant into a socialized adult forces us to examine a variety of questions. Although they rightfully sound ancient and philosophical, they are as immediate and alive as the latest decision of the Supreme

Court. The First Amendment gives me the right to freedom of speech and expression. Is that freedom limitless? Can I shout "Fire!" in a crowded theater? What about obscenity? I am expressing myself when I shout, for all to hear, "Fuck you!" Yet what happens to the rights of persons who are offended by that language to be free of things they find offensive? At what point does the expression of my freedom infringe on their freedoms? And at what point do theirs infringe on me?

I live by the ocean, right on the beach (I wish!). I want to build a tall house. So what if it blocks the view of the person whose house is behind mine? What do I care! It's *my* land; I can do with it what I will. Can't I? The President has decided to send 500,000 troops to a war, and I am drafted to go off and fight. But that's not my war; I won't fight. I say, "Hell no, I won't go." So they send me to jail for two years for following my conscience and doing what I personally want to do. "What kind of free society is this?" I ask. The kid in the adjoining sandbox has a nice new toy. I want it, so I take it from him, leaving him crying in the dust. My whole family is hungry; we haven't eaten anything for three days. I see a bag of groceries in a car. No one is watching, so I steal it. It's evening and I want to play my stereo; you want to study for tomorrow's examination. But I really enjoy listening to loud music, so why don't you go study somewhere else? As for the people down the hall who also want to study, well. . . . Of course tomorrow night I may want to study and you may want to play the stereo.

As even these few examples indicate, man in society cannot simply be as he would be were he somehow living apart from any vital relationship with another human being. Once that union between himself and another occurs, even *one* other in fact, the individual joins an enterprise that requires something from him for the benefits provided to him.

TOWARD INDEPENDENCE

There are two interrelated streams of development we can examine. The first is the trans-

formation of an individual into a social being: from impulsive and egocentric to controlled and sociocentric. The second is the progressive development of the individual from a position of dependence to one of relative independence: his behavior becomes less dependent on his external environment and increasingly self-determined and self-guiding; it becomes *internally controlled*. All theories of development emphasize this progression from external to internal control as the individual becomes socialized. But what does this mean?

We are talking about the locus of control over an individual's behavior. Presumably in the course of development that locus shifts from the external application of sanctions to their self-directed, internal application. The use of rewards or punishments by an external agent (e.g., parents, school officials) comes to be replaced by an internal monitoring system that is said to dispense rewards and punishments in a parallel fashion. But because it is internal the individual carries the voice of control around with him. In Freudian theory this inner voice is termed the *superego*. Out of the satisfactory resolution of the Oedipal situation a child comes to identify with the parent of the same sex and thereby resolves his Oedipal strivings for the other; a superego is born. This newly formed set of functions soon dispenses the reward of pride and the punishment of guilt or inferiority that formerly were dispensed by the parents. Their voice now resides in the individual.

See our discussion of sorcery, sin, the superego, and so on (p. 310ff.), for a brief review of other mechanisms of social control. In each case a system is internalized and functions as a controlling agency. Even in traditional learning theory models development of control involves an internalization process whereby an individual comes to hand out rewards and punishments to himself for actions that are congruent with or deviate from parental and societal demands. I shall examine the cognitive-developmental approach more fully in a moment; suffice it to indicate at this time that a similar inward movement of control is posited.

A view of morality

An individual's movement toward socialization necessitates that he yield certain personal demands to social requirements; but, paradoxically, he is said to be independent and autonomous only when he has internalized these social requirements and has taken them on as his own voice of conscience. Independence, then, does not refer to freedom from all restraints and controls, but rather is a particular *form of restraint,* one that is self-imposed. According to such a view the most independent individual is one who *wants* to do what his society (or group) feels he *must* do. The socialization process is a means whereby the institutions of the society, from parents on up, manage this meshing of individual wants with social musts. It is only one step further to the position that a moral individual is one whose actions both conform to these social oughts or musts and are self-guided.

This latter conception of morality is perhaps the most common. Morality is defined in terms of societal values and demands; moral behavior is behavior that conforms to these demands. But the individual is not said to be moral simply if his behavior *conforms*; rather he is said to be moral insofar as he has sufficiently internalized the society's values and standards so as to want to follow them independently of any threats of punishment or promises of reward. A child who does not steal because he fears punishment may appear to be acting morally and in accordance with a standard of his society; however, unless he carries this value within him we think less of his morality. We may say he has not learned his lesson well, for he still will steal if he can get away with it; a moral man supposedly has learned that one must not steal, period, end of sentence.

A quotation from as far back as 400 B. C. defines morality as *walking like others upon the path.* Throughout history a similar emphasis exists: the moral is equated with the customary, the inoffensive, or the popular. Moral man does not want to engage in any actions his society would deem inappropriate or offensive. Even Freud's notion of the superego has this same sense of morality; the individual's conscience, although self-guiding, is derived from his family's representation of society's standards. The individual who acts immorally and experiences guilt is one who acts in ways that contradict these standards.

If morality is equated with social custom or social standards it is possible to study an individual's morality by (1) testing his knowledge of social standards or moral values; (2) examining his sense of guilt in response to transgressions defined in terms of those standards; or (3) placing him in a situation that tempts him and observing his behavior. All three of these approaches have long been employed in psychological inquiry. Back in the 1920's Hartshorne, May, and several others (Hartshorne & May, 1928; Hartshorne, May, & Maller, 1929; Hartshorne, May, & Shuttleworth, 1930) developed a variety of tests designed to measure an individual's knowledge of moral principles. They described situations and subjects were to select one of several alternative solutions. They obtained several attitude measures, especially those concerned with attitudes toward misconduct. Scores on the series of tests were related to individuals' behavior in a variety of situations of temptation such as chances to steal or to cheat. Interestingly enough, Hartshorne and May found little differentiation in test scores between moral and immoral actors in the temptation situation; behavior in a situation seemed to bear little relationship to knowledge of social standards or attitudes toward misconduct.

In a review of the literature Pittel and Mendelsohn (1966) conclude that no tests of moral values have been found to predict with much success to any behavioral situation. Their examination of the relationship between expressions of guilt and the strength of individual morality also revealed an ambiguous picture. The presence or absence of guilt in projective test protocols did not unequivocally relate either to moral judgment or behavior: "No studies have demonstrated that strength of moral values, resistance to temptation, and proneness to give projective guilt responses all covary" (p. 32). We could take this news as just another indication of the generally low correspondence between test-taking behavior and actual situational behavior. However, we might also feel that the entire conception of morality on which these approaches are based is faulty.

A different conception

It can be argued that principles of morality are not of the same type as general principles of social custom and manner; that is, that moral principles have a quality of the imperative about them that other social customs do not possess. Moreover, although we commonly confuse the moral with the socially acceptable, in another sense morality rises above society and extends to more general principles or ideals of human relationship. In this latter sense the moral is not definable in terms of any given society's standards or customs; it is seen to involve general principles of living or modes of relating that are independent of any given social order.

Kohlberg (1969) suggests that whereas all other standards of conduct are like hypothetical imperatives that vary as a function of a person's particular instrumental aims in a given situation, principles of morality are more like *categorical imperatives*, universally and absolutely binding.

The example Kohlberg cites is tooth-brushing. There are norms about this behavior, and most of us have learned (internalized) the norms so that we no longer need external guidance to brush once or twice a day. However, there is no ideal or principle to which we relate this action; it is simply *instrumental* in keeping decay down, or our teeth bright, and so on. In other words, although we brush our teeth in conformity to a social norm we have internalized, we hardly think of this as falling within the realm of the moral. Moral principles, then, are not necessarily coexistent with other social norms. They are unique and in particular involve ideals concerning human relationships.

Furthermore, morality is defined independently of the content of any given society's standards. When we think of a truly moral person, we tend to think of someone who would follow ideals that had universality across time and culture. Or do we? In this age of relativism, when we assume that everything is merely relative and that *this* value is as good as *that* value, we may find ourselves morally confused. On one hand we think that moral principles should be universal; but on the other hand we believe that principles of one culture or one era are no better or worse than those of another, since such principles are themselves simply relative anyway.

If rules governing human relationships are relative to a given culture, and if morality is defined in terms of these rules, morality must itself be entirely relative, coexistent with social custom—in this case, custom concerning how one relates to others. However, if we still imagine there are general principles and ideals behind specific societal rules, then morality cannot be defined in terms of custom (those rules), but rather must be understood in terms of the underlying universal ideals of human relationship. A person who conforms to a societal rule is not *by that fact alone* moral or immoral. Most of us intuitively accept this point of view. Rarely would we maintain that an individual is behaving morally by automatically following a social custom that he has internalized.

We can imagine conditioning a person to follow the rules of his society: punish him when he deviates and reward him when he conforms. After a while his actions become functionally autonomous from the original external conditions under which they were learned. Soon he becomes a model person, yet we do not feel he is moral or immoral any more than we would feel a machine is moral or immoral; we still do not consider him to behave morally if he is thus automated and without awareness of underlying principles or basic ideals.

There are several ways of stating these last several points. Wilson, Williams, and Sugarman (1967) said, "... we should be able ... to *get outside* the rules, to inspect their point and purpose, and make decisions about them which must of necessity be based on something other than the rules themselves: that is, on the wants, wills, feelings or interests of other people" (p. 66). Their point, like Kohlberg's, is that there is a sphere of the moral beyond the rules by which a given society or social group function. Although we may all agree to act in accordance with our society's standards, and do so for a variety of reasons ranging from the external fear of punishment to the internal whiplashing guilt of our superego, in another realm we examine those rules in terms of underlying universal ideals about human relationships. Moral behavior in this latter sense may mean an individual at times conforms to his society's rules and at other times does not conform.

If we accept this approach to morality, we are faced with an interesting problem. As Kohlberg notes, this universalistic view argues that an individual develops his own internal formulation of a general moral principle and differentiates the rules of his society from the more general rule; we cannot then study morality by examining the correspondence (or lack thereof) between a society's standards and an individual's internalization of them. Rather, we must examine the way in which he himself has formulated principles, regardless of their specific content and regardless of their reference to a particular society's standards. In this view the *structure* rather than the specific content of morality takes center stage. The argument, again, is that morality involves (1) an internal moral principle or universal ideal that (2) has been formulated according to general principles of structural development, and (3) is not simply a copy of external rules internalized but rather is the culmination of a series of transformations or *restructurings*. Perhaps it all will become clearer if we look at Kohlberg's theory of moral development.

KOHLBERG'S THEORY OF MORAL DEVELOPMENT

Kohlberg (1968; 1969), in a manner similar to Piaget's pioneering efforts in this regard, sought to uncover a universal sequence of cognitive development in the sphere of morality. A cognitive-developmental theory posits certain stages of development, at each of which an individual structures the world in a *qualitatively* different manner. That each person passes through a definite sequence of stages suggests that his behavior at no point is a mere copy of the world as externally represented by his parents, his peers, or other social institutions. Rather, unique transformations of the outside are made as he represents the external to himself, and this representation varies qualitatively as he passes through the stages of development. For example, he structures the outside differently at age three than at age ten. His manner of thinking at the earlier age does not permit him to see things in the same way as he is capable of later, when he has progressed far enough to make new differentiations and higher integrations. What better example exists than the young in contemporary society, who are not simply learning adult standards but rather are beginning to carve out their own standards and principles of living? If internalization of parental standards were the entire story of moral development, we would expect the young simply to be undeveloped copies of their elders; this seems to be an especially noticeable oversimplification in our rapidly changing society.

Stages of morality

In moral development, as in other forms of cognitive development, the quality of an individual's morality is a function of the stage at which he is located at a particular age. Each stage represents a different *kind* of moral philosophy or a different *manner* of differentiating and integrating encounters with the environment. Kohlberg (1969) distinguishes three major levels of moral thinking: the premoral; the conventional; the principled. Within each level there are earlier and later substages.

Level I: The Premoral. Sometimes this is referred to as the *preconventional* level. An individual at first does not differentiate between moral value and external sanctions. Power to enforce rules makes rules morally correct; might makes right. There is great concern with avoiding punishment or getting rewarded by those in power. Initially there is minimal differentiation between property or material objects and human values. Hitting another child, for example, or breaking his toy, has no different value from breaking the branch of a tree or hitting a rock.

Later in this level an individual does not differentiate between his own desires or needs and moral value; things are right and proper if they satisfy his own needs. The essence of Level I is a simple relativism; the individual recognizes that others also have needs that they want to satisfy: okay, let them. As Kohlberg notes, at this level life is like the economic marketplace with a minimal conception of reciprocity; there is no sense of justice or fairness in an exchange, rather just a base realization that each has needs and for me to satisfy mine I'll sometimes have to help you satisfy yours.

Level II: The Conventional. At this level moral judgment comes to be rooted in a social order and in the fulfillment of the obligations and responsibilities of one's roles. Reciprocity is involved but, unlike the premoral conception, there is a recognition that each person must conform to conventional social roles and expectations so that all may live harmoniously. Conformity to and justification of the social order is an end in itself. In the early part of this level the individual simply equates moral value with being a good person who is approved by others while helping them. "One seeks approval by being 'nice'" (1968, p. 26). Later he makes a definite commitment to convention and to the existing social order. Morality is defined in terms of the existing social order. Doing one's duty, respecting authority, supporting the system as it exists are all high moral ends in their own right.

Level III: Principled. At this highest level of moral development the individual has formulated general and universal principles of morality or ideals of human conduct that he has made part of himself (his personal system of values) and that are independent of any specific authority, society, or group. He differentiates between social customs and social norms on one hand and moral principles on the other, and recognizes that the latter conform to a higher authority than his society or group and pertain to general conceptions of human justice and equality. The initial stage of this level involves a social-contract notion. The individual is able to understand the arbitrary nature of specific rules and is aware that they can be changed to

better exemplify human values. He sees that a contract of a legalistic sort exists among persons and defines general rights for all; the contract, however, is not seen as frozen, as in Level II thinking, but can be modified as greater social needs demand. The most advanced phases of Level III morality involve adherence to conscience and to general, universal, and abstract principles or ideals across historical eras and cultural or social customs. These principles are categorical imperatives, embodying "universal principles of *justice*, of the reciprocity and *equality* of human rights, and of respect for the dignity of human beings as *individual persons*" (1968, p. 26).

As Kohlberg notes, a key distinction between the conventional and the principled levels is that the former defines morality and social justice in terms of the existing social order; the latter uses principles of justice and equality to define the proper form of social order. That is, the conventionally moral person does not differentiate between what his social order defines as justice and a general concept of social justice. The principled person, on the other hand, differentiates between the general principle and its application in any given society. His own actions are guided by the principle, not the customs or norms of a particular society. Thus, when the social order does not offer justice, the principled person opts for justice over the order; the conventionally moral person opts for the conventional order.

As Turiel has noted (1969), the transition from Level II conventionality to Level III principled morality is a difficult one to make. His argument is that this transition involves both an *increasing* degree of relativism, by which the individual recognizes the arbitrariness of the conventions and norms of each social order, and a *decreasing* relativism, so that he recognizes the validity of universalistic principles of morality. Since progression requires increasingly higher levels of both differentiation and integration, movement to the principled level is especially complicated by these relativistic requirements. The person must see things at once in a more complex light and also be able to integrate this complicated differentiation into a higher order before he can progress. Perhaps it is for this reason that research has shown so few persons at the principled levels (Kohlberg, 1969).

By Way of Summary. Before examining some of that research, let us pause for a moment and review the territory we have just covered. The argument is that morality is best understood by reference to the structure of its development rather than to the specific content or set of societal standards that have been internalized. A person is considered moral not because he has learned to model his behavior in accordance with a set of external standards but rather because he has come to formulate general principles or ideals of human relationship in a certain manner. Each individual, regardless of the society in which he lives, shares with all persons the same structural sequence of cognitive development in morality, defined in terms of a series of levels or stages, each of which involves a transformation and reintegration of its predecessor. At each successive level the individual makes new differentiations and higher-order integrations, thereby transforming the view held in preceding stages. The ordering of the levels is seen to be a logical necessity. One cannot think in terms of principled morality, for example, until he has successfully mastered the differentiations and integrations that characterize conventional morality. Likewise, one cannot achieve Level II functioning until he has passed through Level I. The levels define qualitatively different moral philosophies. "Might makes right" is a theory of morality characteristic of premoral functioning that is qualitatively distinct from "Social convention makes right," which characterizes functioning at the stages of conventional morality.

The research program

To put these ideas to the test, Kohlberg developed a measuring instrument (1958; 1969) consisting of a series of stories that contain classic moral dilemmas. For example,

In Europe, a woman was near death from a special kind of cancer. There was one drug that the doctors thought might save her. It was a form of radium that a druggist in the same town had recently discovered. The drug was expensive to make, but the druggist was charging ten times what the drug cost him to make. He paid $200 for the radium and charged $2,000 for a small dose of the drug. The sick woman's husband, Heinz, went to everyone he knew to borrow the money, but he could only get together about $1,000, which is half of what it cost. He told the druggist that his wife was dying, and asked him to sell it cheaper or let him pay later. But the druggist said, "No, I discovered the drug and I'm going to make money from it." So Heinz got desperate and broke into the man's store to steal the drug for his wife.

The subject is asked several questions about this incident: "Should Heinz have done that?" "Was it wrong or right?" "Would a good husband do that?" "Did the druggist have the right to charge that much?" "Heinz was caught; should the judge send him to jail for stealing or should he be let go?" "Why?"

Typically the subject is presented with 10 such moral dilemmas and interviewed carefully about each incident. It should be obvious that Kohlberg's theoretical perspective requires that one get deeply into the reasons and reasoning of the individual in each case; it is not sufficient to have him state "no he shouldn't have stolen it" or "yes he should have." All interview material is carefully coded according to a system developed by Kohlberg. Each individual yields a profile that includes the dominant stage he is presently thinking at, the stage he is just leaving but still thinks in terms of, and the beginnings of the stage he is beginning to move into. Kohlberg reports that about 50 percent of an individual's moral thinking will fall at one of the stages.

Several important empirical questions need to be answered. First, if there are thought to be universal structures of moral development, cutting across different societies, it should be possible to uncover the same stages and the same ordering in a variety of cultural settings. Studies undertaken in Taiwan, Mexico, and Turkey generally find results comparable to those of studies in the United States (Kohlberg, 1968; 1969). Although the *rate of development* by age varies from culture to culture, the existence of the stages and their order as posited has been supported by Kohlberg's empirical data.

Second, a firm documentation of the sequence of stages and levels is best demonstrated by a longitudinal study that follows the same persons over time to see if they in fact do change their moral judgments in accordance with the sequence that has been posited. Kramer (in Kohlberg, 1968) administered the moral dilemmas to a group of subjects at three-year intervals during a period of 13 years, from age 14 to 27. Kohlberg reports these data from Kramer as confirming the posited stage sequence. For example, at age 13 Richard was asked if a doctor should perform a mercy killing if the patient requests it. He replied, "If she requests it, it's really up to her [if she *wants* it, that's all that matters]. She is in such terrible pain, just the same as people are always putting animals out of their pain." This response placed him as a mixture of Level I and Level II concerning the value of life. A pure Level I would see human life only as instrumental to the satisfaction of the person's needs; a pure Level II response would value human life in terms of the empathy of family members toward its loss.

At age 16 Richard said: "I don't know. In one way, it's murder, it's not a right or privilege of man to decide who shall live and who should die. God put life into everybody on earth and you're taking away something from that person that came directly from God, and you're destroying something that is very sacred, it's in a way part of God and it's almost destroying a part of God when you kill a person. There's something of God in everyone." This response was rated Level II; he saw life as sacred in terms of a religious order, not as valuable for man in and of itself. Its value is dependent on the external authority of God. As Kohlberg comments, if God ordered Richard to destroy a human life, at Level II conventionality he would do so.

At 20 Richard gave a Level III principled response in which life was placed in a human context in terms of community welfare: "There are more and more people in the medical profession who think it is a hardship on everyone, the person, the family, when you know they are going to die. . . . If it's her own choice, I think there are certain rights and privileges that go along with being a human being." Finally, at age

24 Richard achieved advanced Level III thinking: "A human life takes precedence over any other moral or legal value, whoever it is. A human life has inherent value whether or not it is valued by a particular individual. The worth of the individual human being is central where the principles of justice and love are normative for all human relationships." This is taken to be an advanced principled response in that it reflects a sense of universality of the ideals based on general principles rather than to any specific doctrine or social order. Furthermore, the sense of justice implied covers everyone equally.

Another aspect to the longitudinal data reported by Kohlberg concerns the correlations between moral maturity scores at various points in the individual's life history. Some data indicate generally high correlations, upward of .76, between scores at age 13 and scores in the mid-twenties (Kohlberg, 1969). Correlations of this magnitude are not typically obtained in psychological research; thus, although preliminary, they suggest the value of the approach that Kohlberg has taken.

A third implication of the stage model of moral development concerns the impact of training procedures in facilitating progressive development. Turiel (1966) in particular has been concerned with this matter. If persons pass through an invariant sequence of levels, efforts to push them ahead should work best when they introduce a person to an advance *slightly* beyond his present level; presentations that are too advanced for the individual will not facilitate progress. To test this Turiel experimentally presented groups of subjects (seventh-grade boys from public schools in New Haven) samples of moral reasoning that was either one stage below or one or two stages higher than their own. Remeasures of their moral reasoning after these presentations indicated that exposure to the first stage above their own was the most effective in producing progression in moral development. Moral reasoning two stages removed from their initial level was found to be least effective. In a related endeavor Rest, Turiel, and Kohlberg (in press) found that children expressed a preference for the reasoning of stages somewhat above their own level. A study by Le Furgy and Woloshin (1969) offers further confirmatory data.

A fourth line of research has applied Kohlberg's conception of moral development to groups with known characteristics. Three studies in particular are relevant. The first was conducted by Haan, Smith, and Block (1968). They examined the level of moral development of students, particularly those who had been actively involved in the Free Speech Movement at Berkeley. In general their data indicate that politically active students, as compared with a random sample of nonactives, were more generally of principled rather than of conventional morality. They defined moral values beyond those of their institution; their allegiance was to general human values rather than to the form of justice they experienced in their university. Their action, then, was to protest the authority of the institution in support of these general ideals of social justice.

A second study (reported in Kohlberg, 1969) examined those who had participated in Milgram's obedience study (see p. 76ff.). Recall that his study put subjects in a position of either defying authority in the name of higher principles or yielding to the authority of scientific legitimacy and administering presumably painful shocks to another person. Kohlberg reports that 75 percent of advanced Level III subjects quit the study, as compared with only 13 percent of those at lower moral stages. Again we see action following from level of moral development: going against authority required allegiance to a system of values that transcended both social contract ("The other subject and I have made a deal to participate voluntarily") and conventionality ("This is what is expected of subjects in experiments and thus it is legitimate").

Cadets and resisters

I would like to spend a bit more time and offer more details on a third study, first because it is one that I conducted (Sampson, Fisher, Angel, Mulman, & Sullins 1969), so I am familiar with both its reported details and its subtleties, and second because it opens the door to a wider examination of some additional aspects of moral development, especially the antecedent conditions that facilitate progressive development.

The hypothetical moral dilemmas in Kohlberg's test have their counterpart in all our lives, even if not always in the form depicted in the stories. We may not have to decide to steal in order to save our spouse's life; yet in many ways each of us must make decisions of a moral sort. No example is more striking or intensified than a time of national war, whether declared by Congress or enacted by presidential decision. And no more striking example of a moral dilemma has occurred in recent times than in connection with the war in Vietnam. The war was never very popular among young Americans, those who would be drafted to serve. As time wore on and protests grew, the war's popularity diminished even further; yet the draft continued; troops in great numbers remained in Vietnam fighting. During this period the entire issue of military service came into serious question. Society, men, and laws had not been so sorely tested in recent memory.

In recognition of man's dedication to values beyond those of his society, the law allows a person to request the draft status of conscientious objector. Traditionally, this has been based on a belief in a supreme being as part of a recognized religion that prohibits its followers from killing. CO's have been offered alternative service in civilian social agencies or noncombatant work—usually of a medical sort—in the military. What happens, however, to a man who does not see himself as a traditional conscientious objector, but rather feels the war and the draft to be immoral according to the principles of conscience he holds to be true? Should he resist the draft and suffer the penalties of imprisonment and all that it implies for his present and future? Should he serve in spite of his beliefs, to avoid the punishments that will follow if he does not? Should he leave the country? Cut off a toe or a finger? To some extent the Supreme Court has alleviated this problem. Recently it extended the status of CO to individuals who have deeply held moral or philosophic objections to war and killing, even if they are not based on religious beliefs, and at this writing is considering the question of objections to specific wars on moral grounds.

My colleagues and I were interested in studying draft resistance during the late 1960's, however, before such nontraditional appeals were possible. Even more, we were interested in comparing two groups who solved the issue of military service in different ways. The first group, the resisters, refused service, accepting jail if that was necessary, rather than fight in the military during the war in Vietnam. The comparison group, the cadets, were all top-level senior cadet officers in a university Army ROTC program, preparing themselves for an officer's commission in the military on graduation. This cadet sample had been selected for us by other cadets, who described this group as being "real red hots"; presumably they were not in the advanced ROTC program to avoid the draft. The resisters, at the time of our interviews in early 1968, had all been officially indicted and were awaiting their cases in the federal courts. Theirs clearly was not a hollow commitment; it was a clear-cut action choice with extremely serious consequences. The choice and consequences for the cadets were of no less extreme importance in their lives.

We selected small samples of each (11 resisters and 20 cadets), and spent up to seven hours interviewing and testing each person. Data analyses were preliminary and based on a careful in-depth examination of the interview and some projective test material.

We did not present our subjects with any of Kohlberg's hypothetical situations. Rather, we took the living dilemma each man faced and sought to uncover the reasons for his decision, the several alternatives he had thought of and rejected; that is, how he had formulated his situation and reached his decision. Although this interview material was not coded in terms of Kohlberg's system of scoring, it was nevertheless possible to note the levels of moral development that emerged. The general pattern confirms the theoretical prediction: in terms of Kohlberg's theory of moral development, the resisters' choice, somewhat like that of the Free Speech Movement activists, is based on conscience, a reference to laws or ideals or prin-

ciples that transcend their society and its demands. When their society no longer functions in the service of those principles, their morality demands allegiance to the principles rather than to the society; their resistance can be seen as an act of principled morality. The cadets, on the other hand, can be seen to have chosen a route that is either premoral and attuned to the reward-punishment features of the situation (to refuse service is to invite punishment, so the moral choice is to avoid punishment) or conventionally moral (it is one's obligation to serve his society). A sampling of selected quotes from the interviews will reveal this difference clearly. First, the cadets:

"I believe that the moral responsibility for my actions falls upon the government. I can't condemn the Germans. I cannot condemn Hitler because he was crazy and I don't condemn crazy people. If I were a German and they told me to go out and shoot that man, I would do it. If you disobey, you will be killed."

"Moral judgments made by people depend on the context. In the case of the war, it's a legal context. In a war the soldier who shoots and kills another is partly responsible. Like I said, I don't think I'm going to like to shoot anybody; and I'm going to feel responsible for killing him to an extent. On the other hand, this is your job. An evil necessity; it has to be done."

". . . The U. S. Government has decided the moral issue and has chosen to fight. I disagree with this. . . But I don't think resisting the draft is the answer. As a citizen of the U. S. I must go . . . As for me, I will do what the Army tells me to do."

Perhaps the strongest denial of personal responsibility is seen in the following cadet's comment:

"I am not, in that uniform, an agent of myself. I will not walk out in the street and kill someone. If I went to Vietnam, I would not think of myself as killing the people. If one walked into my sights and I pulled the trigger, I would have no moral conscience about it, because I was sent there by the government."

We shall return to the point in a moment; keep in mind the important connection between level of moral development and sense of personal responsibility for one's actions. As several of the passages indicate, in complying with the demands of one's role in a social order one simultaneously denies himself to be an agent responsible for his actions. At times there is a mixture of the premoral fear of punishment and the conventional turn to social obligations; in either case, personal responsibility is denied.

Let us now examine a selection of resisters' comments:

"Things were pretty bad in the U. S.; the war was getting worse. For me to leave the country would be for me to take a little bit of America's conscience with me, and I didn't feel that I really had the right to do that. My responsibility to the people I care about in this country is to provide them with the benefit of life. . . . I couldn't feel any integrity inside of myself with that draft card burning a hole in my pocket knowing that I was cooperating with that whole system. It finally struck me that the most immediate target for me was the selective service and that was where my protest had to begin. I feel that I have some responsibility towards all the people my age who are now in the army and who are in Vietnam being killed because no one spoke out before them. I feel responsibility especially to the people who will come after, for whom the Resistance might really do some good, if we can somehow convince people that the whole thing is all wrong."

"I can think of no situation where the taking of human life is morally justified. I can see no situation in this country where I would fight a war. I can appreciate going to war in certain circumstances and I am not sure that I would be able to maintain my principles under certain circumstances: for example, perhaps when my life or that of someone I loved were threatened. I might better be able to do it [kill another] under that circumstance and still live with myself. But I wouldn't have relinquished my conscience [and responsibility] to the government."

Still another resister, whose comments clearly show the sense of personal responsibility he feels, puts it this way:

"When I went to Africa in 1964–1965, Africans were asking how come you do this [put down peasant uprisings]? How come you hate the Congolese? How come you hate the Vietnamese? They literally hold you responsible. In one sense that isn't right, for you are not responsible for what your government does to them. But yet, you are in some sense if you live there [in the U. S.] and allow your country to be called democratic. If you allow yourself to take benefit of what your country offers, then you also have to take responsibility for what your country does. And I was really blamed for a lot . . . Everyone knows inside that there is no such thing as LBJ's war. The most satisfying thing you can do for yourself is to face squarely your own complicity."

From an examination even of these few examples it is clear that the two groups differ in their level of moral development and in the related sense of personal responsibility. Although not all are pure cases of any given stage, the cadets center more on the conventional level and the resisters' dominant mode of morality is principled.

It follows from a position of principled morality that one is personally responsible unless he takes positive action to remedy a problem: if you are not part of the solution, you are part of the problem. Seeing the situation as the resisters do, action in defiance of the draft and the military becomes essential. Recall our discussion on p. 35ff. of origins versus pawns and the relation of this discussion to the inference of intentionality in person perception. Seeing another person as a pawn acting in accordance with external pressures (recall that a large organization asking him to do something is enough to make him seem more a pawn) leads us to absolve him of having acted with intention. Thus we do not hold him responsible: he has to act that way. Nor does he hold himself responsible. But the more information we have that he is acting as an origin, the more intentionality and thus personal responsibility (or personal causality) we read and he himself reads into his behavior.

A premoral or conventionally moral person is more likely than a man of principled morality to see himself more as a pawn than as an origin; he is more likely to be seen by others in this manner as well. Thereby everyone absolves him of responsibility for his actions. We do hold the man of principled morality responsible, however, for in our minds, as in his, he is an origin, an agent, an actor who affects his environment. A line is drawn and limits set, however, for even Adolf Eichmann was held responsible in spite of his pleas that he had only been following orders; a pawn thus is sometimes held responsible and eliminated.

Mechanisms and antecedents

Most efforts to examine the antecedents of individual moral development look especially at the nature of parental discipline that a child receives. Usually a distinction is drawn between love-oriented or psychological discipline (punishment by withholding love) and physical punishment. Morality taught by punishment and based on fear of external authority does not produce much internalization of values; thus punishment operates against progressive moral development. Child-rearing based on guilt-induction or threats to withhold love seems to be somewhat more positively related to moral development, although even here the picture is equivocal. Psychoanalytic theory and some learning theories emphasize the anxiety that psychological punishment induces and that provides the motive force behind moral development. One argument is that a child's relationship of identification with the parent is intensified by psychological discipline, whereas physical punishment severs the identification.

The picture is muddied, as Hoffman and Saltzstein (1967) suggest, in that psychological discipline itself may be reconceptualized. They argue that this form of discipline might do one of two things: (1) It might arouse empathy, especially if the parent indicates the painful consequences of the child's action for the parent and for others. This they call *induction*. (2) It might involve love withdrawal directly, as when, in anger, a parent literally withdraws his affection from the child. This aspect of psychological discipline does imply, "your action is painful for me," and thus is similar to induction, but it does not arouse as much empathy as an indication of the consequences of the child's misdeeds for others. Hoffman and Saltzstein's research indicates a direct relationship between the use of induction techniques and moral development; more specifically, their results show that physical discipline is associated with weak moral development, whereas induction produces advanced moral development. Love withdrawal is barely related to moral development, suggesting that psychological discipline

may involve more empathy than is considered in the psychoanalytic or learning concepts of anxiety about loss of love.

This notion of empathy, conceptualized in terms of *role-taking opportunities*, forms the key to Kohlberg's view of the antecedents and mechanisms of moral development. Recall our discussion of Mead's idea of symbolic interaction (p. 25ff.). He saw the individual's control over his behavior as derived from his ability to view himself as an object seen through the eyes of others, his ability to take the others' roles and see the consequences of his action as it appears to them. Hoffman and Saltzstein refer to this as empathy; Mead thinks of it as a basic process of human interaction; Kohlberg refers to it as role-taking opportunity, a chance for a child to see things from variant perspectives. In Kohlberg's view, and consistent with Hoffman and Saltzstein's data, the opportunity for role taking provides the basis for progressive moral development. In this connection it is interesting to note that in Pittel and Mendelsohn's (1966) review of the literature on moral development the one paper-and-pencil technique that seemed best at discriminating between persons of high and low moral development involved the socialization scale devised by Gough (1960; Gough & Peterson, 1952) and based on Mead's (1934) notion of role taking. Sarbin (1954) has reported data indicating a relationship between positive psychological adjustment and the number of roles one is able to take on. The circle grows tighter as we pull together these snippets of information; all of them suggest support for the picture Kohlberg offers, that role-taking opportunities are intimately related to level of moral development.

As Kohlberg notes, this view of role-taking as the key ingredient to progressive moral development has some important implications. For one, the family need not be seen as the major locus of the individual's development of morality. For example, Kohlberg (1969) reports that children reared on an Israeli kibbutz have typical moral development even though they have only minimal contact with their parents or other adults; they have a sufficiently stimulating and varied environment that provides ample opportunities to try on a variety of different roles.

Another implication is that the important ingredient of the familial relationship, the peer relationship, or the relationship of an individual to his community and to his society is the degree to which these relationships offer the individual sufficient freedom to participate in a variety of role contexts. The more restrictive any of these settings are, the less the opportunities for role taking (Kohlberg also calls this a *restriction of social stimulation*), and thus the lower the level of moral development.

Let us look for a moment at the nature of the mechanism that may be involved in role taking. The essence of developmental change is conflict between present levels and incoming stimuli. The conflict or disparity must be neither too little nor too great: optimally an individual encounters stimuli (information) that are sufficiently dissonant to create conflict that leads to a search for another perspective, but are sufficiently consonant to fit in somewhat with his present level. Although we do not know the precise degree of incongruity that maximally motivates development, a departure from this optimal position can either pass by unnoticed or in some cases impede development. In his efforts to induce moral development (p. 440) Turiel found movement forward when an individual was presented with a solution one stage above his own. In another study Blatt (in Kohlberg 1969) was able to move a significant number of subjects up one level by presenting them over a period of time with arguments at first one step then two steps removed from their own position.

Both Turiel and Kohlberg suggest that movement from one stage to the next requires that the individual take a critical look at his present stage while at the same time developing the beginning of a new form that makes differentiations that the earlier form did not and integrates the old and the new into a higher-order framework.

"The transition from conventional to principled moral functioning must include: a criticalness of the absolutism and concreteness of [Level II] thinking; an awareness of the relativity of social conventions and their separability from universal principles; an initial intuitive understanding of universal moral principles which feed back on the undifferentiated absolutism

of conventionality; and finally, the beginning of an integration of the conventional system with the moral system" (Turiel, 1969).

Role-taking opportunities offer an individual multiple views and perspectives; this provides the stimulus to moral development by casting his present position in a critical light and by showing him one or more new possibilities. In this view, role taking does not stimulate moral development simply through the empathy it offers—though this may be important—but rather, by opening the doors to alternatives that force one to rethink present frameworks.

Kohlberg suggests that any context has the potential to provide adequate or inadequate opportunities for role taking. As such, moral development, which does not occur suddenly at one moment during the Oedipal period but carries on through many years of the life of the individual, into his mid-twenties, apparently, is stimulated or thwarted by encounters with family, peer group, school system, community, and society in general. In each setting approaches that open the doors to experimentation facilitate moral development; approaches that are restrictive, punitive, nonparticipatory, or even so permissive as to produce apathy and withdrawal, work against moral development.

Kohlberg points to the use of participatory techniques in each of these settings as a groundwork for progressive moral development. He notes, as I have suggested (Chapter 19), that the more an individual is responsible for group decision making—in any context—the more involvement he has in the roles of others, the more social stimulation he experiences, and thus the higher the level of moral development likely. Stunted moral growth derives from settings that deprive an individual of participatory rights and responsibilities. These may occur in any context; a restrictive family, an autocratic school system, a society that deprives people of a role in determining its affairs can all reduce role-taking opportunities and thereby stunt moral development.

Resisters and Cadets Revisited. Although we did not undertake our study of resisters and cadets with Kohlberg's scheme or his theory in mind, the data are strikingly consistent with both the antecedents and mechanisms he outlines. A careful examination of the cadets' and resisters' life histories and life styles uncovers systematic differences congruent with the differential level of moral development they manifest in their decisions concerning the draft and the military. In several ways the cadet's life, in terms both of family experiences and peer-group preferences, suggests a relatively sheltered and restrictive style of living, one that does not seem likely to produce moral development beyond the conventional levels. As a group, the cadets prefer a well-ordered, structured life style as compared with the more adventuresome, hang-loose approach of the resisters. The cadets are more likely to live in fraternities, where they can continue relating to others in terms of power and status rather than equality. The ROTC and the fraternity are contexts in which they are less likely to gain the diverse role-taking opportunities essential to progressive moral development. The resister, by contrast, tends to live in an apartment, perhaps alone, or with a girl, or with a few other men. He is more independent and on his own.

The cadets favor the traditional, institutionalized church, another carefully ordered structure that provides few opportunities for the kinds of stimulating encounter so essential to progressive moral development. The resisters are not basically less religious than the cadets; but theirs tends to be a personal religion, a moral ethic of their own, not one neatly packaged for them. In terms of family structure, the generally stern and restrictive quality of the cadets' homes contrasts with the more open and participatory style that the resisters faced. The last finding is consistent with data from several other studies that relate student activism to more participatory family structure (Flacks, 1967; Keniston, 1967).

Perhaps the most striking indication of how their relatively impoverished encounters with their overly structured environments mark the lives of the cadets, in contrast to the lives of the resisters, is the entire impact of the collegiate experience. One always hopes that the university is an institution that facilitates moral development by opening up vistas only barely imagined by the student. That this is not always the case is an unfortunate testament to what is wrong with multiversities. The cadets show an especially insulated pattern. Test scores on the intellectual disposition of these cadets—all of whom were juniors and seniors—compare with normative data for college freshmen. In other words, as they neared graduation they remained as intellectually disposed as entering freshmen. Apparently their well-routinized and sheltered existence on the campus protected them from the kinds of encounter that would facilitate intellectual growth as well as moral development.

The resisters' reaction to college was twofold and complex. On the positive side, they often reported encountering a new book—say, in philosophy or history—or some new idea in a class that set them to thinking and helped them crystallize some of their ideas. At times, however, college had a negative impact; their experience with this institution threatened to stifle their curiosity unless they dropped out or sought stimulation elsewhere.

One aspect of role taking that is relevant to moral development is the ability to anticipate the consequences of one's actions *before* taking them. The quality that best characterizes the cadets is a pattern I call "sorry-too-late." What happens is that they manage to blunder into situations with other people and do things they later feel sorry about; but it's always too late, after they've handled the matter poorly. One cadet, for example, talked about other persons as being like a rope whose strength you don't know until it breaks. This means essentially that he had no way of anticipating the consequences of his actions on others until they broke down; then he knew, too late, that he had gone too far. He had a reputation, in fact, for driving his men too hard. The resisters, by contrast, seemed very sensitive to others' needs; they were much better able to anticipate the consequences of their actions before acting, and thereby to moderate their behavior in light of these consequences. We might say that they were generally more empathic.

These data offer a nicely consistent picture. Nicely, that is, from the perspective of data that are congruent with a theory. The cadets will still go off to war and the resisters to jail, and *that* I cannot think about nicely. The data, however, paint a portrait of a variety of conditions that operate to stunt moral development in the cadets and to facilitate it in the resisters. Stunting experiences begin in the restrictive home and move out to a variety of other settings that remain so well structured and generally autocratic that the kinds of disconfirming encounters needed to open a person up to a critical self-examination rarely occur. When the cadet arrives at a level of conventional morality he feels that the answers to all dilemmas lie in the hands of the society in which he lives and to which he feels he owes his major allegiance. Resisters, however, undergo a series of awakenings. I picture some of them almost as little boys with wide eyes having continually wondrous encounters with people, books, ideas, things, institutions, and what-have-you. They have opened themselves up to a wide variety of role-taking experiences and eventually arrive at a level of principled morality. When their society calls them to a war that defies the general human values to which they owe their allegiance, they have no real choice other than to resist. At that point, it becomes only a matter of how best to resist. Most of this sample chose jail over leaving the country.

RELATIVITY VERSUS A NEW ABSOLUTISM

In this final chapter I have sought to examine some aspects of moral development, offering a rather nontraditional perspective and approach to the problem. Yet I think it important also to view this perspective in the context of the changing *Zeitgeist* of our modern times, especially as regards moral relativism and personal responsibility. Influenced undoubtedly both by relativity doctrines in the physical sciences and by incoming data from anthropology and sociology, social science in general has taken a relativistic stance. Although there are many arenas in which such a stance is helpful—for example, I have devoted one part of this book to a discussion of the relative and comparative nature of person perception—there are serious questions involved when we apply relativity doctrine to moral values as well. By this reasoning no one set of values is better or worse than

any other, for each is simply relative to a given society at a given point in its history. As suggested, this relativistic notion tends to confuse moral values with social norms, thereby justifying as morally good all things that a given society comes to value. When Nazi Germany chose the way of war, national socialism became an imperative for all to follow. What could be higher than allegiance to the fatherland? "My country right or wrong" is another reflection of moral relativism. It is one tiny step from this kind of relativism to a complete denial of personal responsibility.

If all morality is relative, mine is as good as yours; and we are both right. Of course, God is on my side, even if you think he is on yours. And in God's name and in the name of our respective nations we shall wreak havoc on all who cross our path. I think this kind of reasoning, plus the Eichmann variety, plus the implications of the war in Vietnam, opened the door a crack to a nonrelativistic doctrine, at least for morality. A somewhat similar opening was urged by Etzioni (see p. 367), who was critical of our *over-socialized* view of man that seemed to ignore what he felt to be universal human needs. Interestingly enough, he, too, was moved by contemporary social conditions, including the war in Vietnam and the general quality of urban-technological life, to urge us to re-examine social-science views in which relativity places the weight of explanation on society and the burden of living on the individual.

Perhaps rather than positing a shift in the entire *Zeitgeist*, it would be more accurate if I indicated that the relativity position is itself becoming more highly differentiated, thereby allowing for a new, more sophisticated kind of absolutism to enter certain corridors of social scientific inquiry. Kohlberg's conception of moral development and, for that matter, any conception that builds on a structural-development argument (from Piaget through Werner to Harvey, Hunt, & Schroder) forces us to reexamine our relativistic views. Universalism enters, in this approach, in terms of the *structure* of development rather than in its *content*. Thus, although we will not long argue that specific content is more or less moral, we can argue that certain formulations of morality are more or less highly developed. But content is not entirely read out of a scheme such as Kohlberg's. The basic principles, which are universal and form ideals for all mankind, regardless of society or era or position, are principles of equality and justice. As Kohlberg himself comments, on the principled levels of morality,

". . . Socrates, Lincoln, Thoreau, and Martin Luther King tend to speak without confusion of tongues. . . . This is because the ideal principles of any social structure are basically alike, if only because there simply aren't that many principles which are articulate, comprehensive and integrated enough to be satisfying to the human intellect. And most of these principles have gone by the name of justice" (1968, p. 30).

This sophisticated absolutism that both Kohlberg's and Etzioni's views suggest involves essentially humanistic doctrines. Both place the *person* back into the equation, and see that the basis of morality and justice lies in the manner by which man treats his fellow man. Darwin made man an animal; Freud gave him impulses that made him seem dangerous unless controlled, Rogers and Maslow made man good and potentially healthful and creative; the views of moral development we have been examining make man trustworthy in that the normal course of his development is toward generally beneficent principles of human justice.

It is no mere coincidence that the relativistic *Zeitgeist* is undergoing a change and the glimmer of a new approach is making its first entry. Relativism in physics assumed a framework for assessing movement, even while recognizing its relativity. In the social sciences, however, to avoid the ethnocentric advocacy of one's own values, all reference points were cast aside. The return of reference points or a structured framework for examining moral development, especially a structure centering on humanistic principles, speaks of an era in search of meaning for man in a world whose monolithic scale both dwarfs and upstages the individual. The time has never been more ripe for the perspective we have been examining in this chapter. The methodological demands of this scientific era have been met in Kohlberg's research; increasingly, as noted, the philosophical demands have also been met. The ideas without the methodology would not suffice to move the *Zeitgeist* slowly ahead; nor would the methodology alone suffice. Together, however, they suggest a view of human nature and a manner of assessing it that helps to outline directions for further inquiry.

If *Zeitgeists* are like art, they both respond to strains in the present and point out directions for the future. The return of humanistic doctrines to social science speaks, then, to a need too long abandoned by these fields.

REFERENCES

Abelson, R. P. Computer simulation of "hot" cognition. In S. Tomkins & S. Messick (Eds.), *Computer simulation of personality: Frontier of psychological theory.* New York: Wiley, 1963.

Abelson, R. P., & Carroll, J. D. Computer simulation of individual belief systems. *American Behavioral Scientist,* 1965, **8**, 24–30.

Abrahamson, M. *Interpersonal accomodation.* Princeton, N. J.: Van Nostrand, 1966.

Ad Hoc Committee. The triple revolution. *Liberation,* April 1964, **9**, 9–15.

Adams, D. K., Harvey, O. J., & Heslin, R. E. Variation in flexibility and creativity as a function of hypnotically induced past histories. In O. J. Harvey (Ed.), *Experience, structure and adaptability.* New York: Springer, 1966.

Adams, J. S. Inequity in social exchange. In L. Berkowitz (Ed.), *Advances in experimental social psychology.* Vol. 2. New York: Academic, 1965.

Adams, S. Status congruency as a variable in small group performance. *Social Forces,* 1953, **32**, 16–22.

Adelson, J. What generation gap? *The New York Times Magazine,* January 18, 1970, 10–11, 34–36, 45.

Adorno, T. W. Freudian theory and the pattern of fascist propaganda. In G. Roheim (Ed.), *Psychoanalysis and the social sciences.* Vol. 3. New York: International Universities Press, 1951.

Adorno, T. W., Frenkel-Brunswik, E., Levinson, D. J., & Sanford, R. N. *The authoritarian personality.* New York: Harper, 1950.

Allport, F. H. The influence of the group upon association and thought. *Journal of Experimental Psychology,* 1920, **3**, 159–182.

Allport, F. H. *Social psychology.* Boston: Houghton Mifflin, 1924.

Allport, G. W. The historical background of modern social psychology. In G. Lindzey (Ed.), *Handbook of social psychology.* Vol. 1. Cambridge, Mass.: Addison-Wesley, 1954.

Allport, G. W., & Cantril, H. Judging personality from the voice. *Journal of Social Psychology,* 1934, **5**, 37–55.

Allport, G. W., & Postman, L. J. *The psychology of rumor.* New York: Holt, 1947.

American Institute of Public Opinion. New student breed. *San Francisco Chronicle,* May 26, 1969.

Anderson, L. R., McGuire, W. J. Prior reassurance of group consensus as a factor in producing resistance to persuasion. *Sociometry,* 1965, **28**, 44–56.

Angell, R. C. The moral integration of American cities. *American Journal of Sociology,* 1951, **57**, Part 2, 1–140.

Ardrey, R. *African genesis: A personal investigation into the animal origins and nature of man.* London: Collins, 1961.

Arendt, H. Reflections on violence. *The New York Review of Books,* February 27, 1969, **12**, 19–31.

Argyle, M. *The psychology of interpersonal behavior.* Harmondsworth, Middlesex, England: Penguin Books, 1967.

Argyris, C. *Personality and organization: The conflict between the system and the individual.* New York: Harper, 1957.

Argyris, C. *Interpersonal competence and organizational effectiveness.* Homewood, Ill.: Dorsey Press, 1962.

Argyris, C. *Integrating the individual and the organization.* New York: Wiley, 1964.

Argyris, C. Explorations in interpersonal competence. I. *Journal of Applied Behavioral Science,* 1965a, **1**, 58–83.

Argyris, C. Explorations in interpersonal competence. II. *Journal of Applied Behavioral Science,* 1965b, **1**, 255–269.

Argyris, C. *Organization and innovation,* Homewood, Ill.: Irwin, 1965c.

Aronson, E., & Mills, J. The effect of severity of initiation on liking for a group. *Journal of Abnormal and Social Psychology,* 1959, **59**, 177–181.

Asch, S. E. *Social psychology,* Englewood Cliffs, N. J.: Prentice-Hall, 1952.

Ashley, W. R., Harper, R. S., & Runyon, D. L. The perceived size of coins in normal and hypnotically induced economic states. *American Journal of Psychology,* 1951, **64**, 564–572.

Associated Press. World growing 1.3 million a week. *San Francisco Sunday Examiner and Chronicle,* May 4, 1969.

Atkinson, J. W. Explorations using imaginative thought to assess the strength of human motives. In M. R. Jones (Ed.), *Nebraska Symposium on Motivation.* Lincoln, Neb.: University of Nebraska Press, 1954.

Atkinson, J. W. *Motives in fantasy, action, and society: A method of assessment and study.* Princeton: Van Nostrand, 1958.

Atkinson, J. W. *An introduction to motivation.* Princeton: Van Nostrand, 1964.

Atkinson, J. W., Heyns, R. W., & Veroff, J. The effect of experimental arousal of the affiliation motive on thematic apperception. *Journal of Abnormal and Social Psychology,* 1954, **49**, 405–410.

Atkinson, J. W., & Litwin, G. H. Achievement motive and test anxiety conceived as motive to approach success and motive to avoid failure. *Journal of Abnormal and Social Psychology,* 1960, **60**, 52–63.

Atkinson, J. W., & McClelland, D. C. The projective expression of needs. II. The effect of different intensities of the hunger drive on thematic apperception. *Journal of Experimental Psychology,* 1948, **38**, 643–658.

Aurthur, R. A. TV: The 21″ bore. *The Nation,* September 20, 1965, **201**, 227–231.

Avant, L. L. Vision in the ganzfeld. *Psychological Bulletin,* 1965, **64**, 246–258.

Back, K. W. Influence through social communication. *Journal of Abnormal and Social Psychology,* 1951, **46**, 9–23.

Bales, R. F. *Interaction process analysis: A method for the study of small groups.* Cambridge, Mass.: Addison-Wesley, 1950a.

Bales, R. F. A set of categories for the analysis of small group interaction. *American Sociological Review,* 1950b, **15**, 257–263.

Bales, R. F. Adaptive and integrative changes as sources of strain in social systems. In A. P. Hare, E. F. Borgatta,

& R. F. Bales (Eds.), *Small groups: Studies in social interaction*. New York: Knopf, 1955a.

Bales, R. F. The equilibrium problem in small groups. In A. P. Hare, E. F. Borgatta, & R. F. Bales (Eds.), *Small groups: Studies in social interaction*. New York: Knopf, 1955b.

Bales, R. F. Task roles and social roles in problem-solving groups. In E. E. Maccoby, T. M. Newcomb, & E. L. Hartley (Eds.), *Readings in social psychology*. (3rd ed.) New York: Holt, Rinehart & Winston, 1958.

Bandura, A., Ross, D., & Ross, S. A. Vicarious reinforcement and imitative learning. *Journal of Abnormal and Social Psychology*, 1963, **67**, 601–607.

Bandura, A., & Walters, R. H. *Social learning and personality development*. New York: Holt, Rinehart & Winston, 1963.

Barber, R. J. The new partnership: Big government and big business. *New Republic*, August 13, 1966, **155**, 17–22.

Barker, R. G. Ecology and motivation. Reprinted by permission of the University of Nebraska Press, from M. R. Jones (Ed.), *Nebraska Symposium on Motivation*. Lincoln: University of Nebraska Press, 1960.

Barker, R. G. Explorations in ecological psychology. *American Psychologist*, 1965, **20**, 1–14.

Barker, R. G., & Barker, L. S. Social actions in the behavior streams of American and English children. In R. G. Barker (Ed.), *Stream of behavior: Explorations of its structure and content*. New York: Appleton-Century-Crofts, 1963.

Barker, R. G., & Gump, P. V. *Big school, small school: High school size and student behavior*. Stanford, Calif.: Stanford University Press, 1964.

Barker, R. G., & Wright, H. F. *Midwest and its children: The psychological ecology of an American town*. Evanston, Ill.: Row, Peterson, 1955.

Barnett, H. G. *Innovation: The basis of cultural change*. (1st ed.) New York: McGraw-Hill, 1953.

Baron, R. M. Social reinforcement effects as a function of social reinforcement history. *Psychological Review*, 1966, **73**, 527–539.

Bartlett, F. C. *Remembering: A study in experimental and social psychology*. Cambridge, Engl.: Cambridge University Press, 1932.

Bass, B. M. Authoritarianism or acquiescence? *Journal of Abnormal and Social Psychology*, 1955, **51**, 616–623.

Bass, B. M. Reactions to *Twelve angry men* as a measure of sensitivity training. *Journal of Applied Psychology*, 1962, **46**, 120–124.

Bauer, R. A. (Ed.) *Social indicators*. Cambridge, Mass.: MIT Press, 1966.

Bavelas, A. Communication patterns in task-oriented groups. *Journal of the Acoustical Society of America*, 1950, **22**, 725–730.

Beach, L., & Wertheimer, M. A free response approach to the study of person cognition. *Journal of Abnormal and Social Psychology*, 1961, **62**, 367–374.

Beckett, S. *Waiting for Godot: Tragicomedy in two acts*. New York: Grove Press, 1954.

Bell, D. *The end of ideology: On the exhaustion of political ideas in the fifties*. New York: Free Press of Glencoe, 1960.

Bem, D. J. Self perception: An alternative interpretation of cognitive dissonance phenomena. *Psychological Review*, 1967, **74**, 183–200.

Benedict, R. *Patterns of culture*. Boston: Houghton Mifflin, 1934.

Benedict, R. *The chrysanthemum and the sword: Patterns of Japanese culture*. Boston: Houghton Mifflin, 1946.

Bennett, E. B. Discussion, decision, commitment, and consensus in "group decision." *Human Relations*, 1955, **8**, 251–273.

Bennis, W. G. Leadership theory and administrative behavior: The problem of authority. *Administrative Science Quarterly*, 1959, **4**, 259–301.

Bennis, W. B., & Shepard, H. A. A theory of group development. *Human Relations*, 1956, **9**, 415–438.

Benoit-Smullyan, E. Status, status types, and status interrelations. *American Sociological Review*, 1944, **9**, 151–161.

Berelson, B. R., Lazarsfeld, P. F., & McPhee, W. N. *Voting: A study of opinion formation in a presidential campaign*. Chicago: University of Chicago Press, 1954.

Berger, B. Hippie morality—More old than new. *Transaction*, 1967, **5**, 19–20.

Berkowitz, L. The judgmental process in personality functioning. *Psychological Review*, 1960, **67**, 130–142.

Berkowitz, L. *Aggression: A social psychological analysis*. New York: McGraw-Hill, 1962.

Berkowitz, L. Aggressive cues in aggressive behavior and hostility catharsis. *Psychological Review*, 1964, **71**, 104–122.

Berkowitz, L. Impulse, aggression and the gun. *Psychology Today*, September 1968, **2**, 18–23.

Berkowitz, L., & Friedman, P. Some social class differences in helping behavior. *Journal of Personality and Social Psychology*, 1967, **5**, 217–225.

Berkowitz, L., & Geen, R. G. Film violence and the cue properties of available targets. *Journal of Personality and Social Psychology*, 1966, **3**, 525–530.

Berkowitz, L., & Geen, R. G. Stimulus qualities of the target of aggression: A further study. *Journal of Personality and Social Psychology*, 1967, **5**, 364–368.

Berkowitz, L., & LePage, A. Weapons as aggression-eliciting stimuli. *Journal of Personality and Social Psychology*, 1967, **7**, 202–207.

Berkowitz, L., & Rawlings, E. Effects of film violence on inhibitions against subsequent aggression. *Journal of Abnormal and Social Psychology*, 1963, **66**, 405–412.

Berlyne, D. E. Novelty and curiosity as determinants of exploratory behavior. *British Journal of Psychology*, 1950, **41**, 68–80.

Berlyne, D. E. The arousal and satiation of perceptual curiosity in the rat. *Journal of Comparative and Physiological Psychology*, 1955, **48**, 238–246.

Berlyne, D. E. The present status of research on exploratory and related behavior. *Journal of Individual Psychology*, 1958, **14**, 121–126.

Bernard, L. L. *Instinct: A study in social psychology*. New York: Holt, 1924.

Bernard, V. W., Ottenberg, P., & Redl, F. Dehumanization: A composite psychological defense in relation to modern war. In R. Perrucci & M. Pilisuk (Eds.), *The triple revolution: Social problems in depth*. Boston: Little, Brown, 1968.

Bernstein, B. Some sociological determinants of perception: An enquiry into sub-cultural differences. *British Journal of Sociology*, 1958, **9**, 159–174.

Bettelheim, B. Individual and mass behavior in extreme situations. In E. E. Maccoby, T. M. Newcomb, & E. L. Hartley (Eds.), *Readings in social psychology*. (3rd ed.) New York: Holt, Rinehart & Winston, 1958.

Bettelheim, B., & Janowitz, M. *Dynamics of prejudice: A psychological and sociological study of veterans*. New York: Harper & Row, 1950.

Bettelheim, B., & Janowitz, M. *Social change and prejudice, including the dynamics of prejudice*. New York: Free Press of Glencoe, 1964.

Bevan, W. Subliminal stimulation: A pervasive problem for psychology. *Psychological Bulletin*, 1964, **61**, 81–99.

Bexton, W. H., Heron, W., & Scott, T. H. Effects of decreased variation in the sensory environment. *Canadian Journal of Psychology*, 1954, **8**, 70–76.

Bieri, J. Cognitive complexity-simplicity and predictive behavior. *Journal of Abnormal and Social Psychology*, 1955, **51**, 263–268.

Bion, W. R. *Experiences in groups, and other papers*. New York: Basic Books, 1961.

Birdwhistell, R. *Introduction to kinesics: An annotation system for analysis of body motion and gesture*. Louisville, Ky.: University of Louisville Press, 1952.

Blake, R. R. The other person in the situation. In R. Tagiuri & L. Petrullo (Eds.), *Person perception and interpersonal behavior*. Stanford, Calif.: Stanford University Press, 1958.

Blandford, D., & Sampson, E. E. Induction of prestige suggestion through classical conditioning. *Journal of Abnormal and Social Psychology*, 1964, **69**, 332–336.

Blau, P. M. *Exchange and power in social life*. New York: Wiley, 1964.

Block, J. *The Q-sort method in personality assessment and psychiatric research*. Springfield, Ill.: Charles C. Thomas, 1961.

Block, J., & Block, J. An interpersonal experiment on reactions to authority. *Human Relations*, 1952, **5**, 91–98.

Blum, G. S. An experimental reunion of psychoanalytic theory with perceptual vigilance and defense. *Journal of Abnormal and Social Psychology*, 1954, **49**, 94–98.

Blum, G. S. Perceptual defense revisited. *Journal of Abnormal and Social Psychology*, 1955, **51**, 24–29.

Blumer, H. Collective behavior. In A. M. Lee (Ed.), *New outline of the principles of sociology*. New York: Barnes & Noble, 1951.

Bonarius, J. C. J. Research in the personal construct theory of George A. Kelly: Role construct repertory test and basic theory. In B. A. Maher (Ed.), *Progress in experimental personality research*. Vol. 2. New York: Academic, 1965.

Bootzin, R. R., & Natsoulas, T. Evidence for perceptual defense uncontaminated by response bias. *Journal of Personality and Social Psychology*, 1965, **1**, 461–468.

Borgatta, E. F., Bales, R. F., & Couch, A. S. Some findings relevant to the great man theory of leadership. *American Sociological Review*, 1954, **19**, 755–759.

Bowers, R. V. The direction of intra-societal diffusion. *American Sociological Review*, 1937, **2**, 826–836.

Brackman, J. Onward and upward with the arts: The put-on. Reprinted by permission from *The New Yorker*, June 24, 1967, **43**, 34–73.

Brady, J. V. Ulcers in "executive" monkeys. *Scientific American*, October 1958, **199**, 95–100.

Bramel, D. Selection of a target for defense projection. *Journal of Abnormal and Social Psychology*, 1963, **66**, 318–324.

Brandon, A. C. Status congruence and expectation. *Sociometry*, 1965, **28**, 272–288.

Brandon, A. C., & Sampson, E. E. Demand characteristics versus physiological needs: A methodological critique of the "New Look" school of perception. *Journal of Social Psychology*, 1965, **67**, 343–355.

Brecht, B. *Selected poems*, H. R. Hays translation. New York: Reynal & Hitchcock, 1947.

Breed, W., & Ktsanes, T. Pluralistic ignorance in the process of opinion formation. *Public Opinion Quarterly*, 1961, **25**, 382–392.

Breer, P. E., & Locke, E. A. *Task experiences as a source of attitudes*. Homewood, Ill.: Dorsey Press, 1965. By permission.

Brehm, J. W., & Cohen, A. R. Re-evaluation of choice alternatives as a function of their number and qualitative similarity. *Journal of Abnormal and Social Psychology*, 1959, **58**, 373–378.

Brehm, J. W., & Cohen, A. R. *Explorations in cognitive dissonance*. New York: Wiley, 1962.

Brinton, C. C. *The anatomy of revolution*. New York: Vintage Books, Random House, 1957.

Brown, R. W. Mass phenomena. In G. Lindzey (Ed.), *Handbook of social psychology*. Vol. 2. Cambridge, Mass.: Addison-Wesley, 1954.

Brown, R. W. *Social psychology*. New York: Free Press of Glencoe, 1965.

Brown, R. W., & Ford, M. Address in American English. *Journal of Abnormal and Social Psychology*, 1961, **62**, 375–385.

Brown, R. W., & Gilman, A. The pronouns of power and solidarity. In T. Sebeok (Ed.), *Style in language: Conference on style, Indiana University, 1958*. Cambridge, Mass.: Technology Press of MIT, 1960.

Brown, R. W., & Lenneberg, E. H. A study in language and cognition. *Journal of Abnormal and Social Psychology*, 1954, **49**, 454–462.

Brownfield, C. A. Deterioration and facilitation hypotheses in sensory-deprivation research. *Psychological Bulletin*, 1964, **61**, 304–313.

Brozek, J., Guetzkow, H., & Baldwin, M. V. A quantitative study of perception and association in experimental semistarvation. *Journal of Personality*, 1951, **19**, 245–264.

Bruner, J. S. The cognitive consequences of early sensory deprivation. In P. Solomon, P. E. Kubzansky, H. Leiderman, J. H. Mendelson, R. Trumbull, & D. Wexler (Eds.), *Sensory deprivation: A symposium held at Harvard Medical School*. Cambridge, Mass.: Harvard University Press, 1961.

Bruner, J. S., & Goodman, C. C. Value and need as organizing factors in perception. *Journal of Abnormal and Social Psychology*, 1947, **42**, 33–44.

Bruner, J. S., & Tagiuri, R. The perception of people. In G. Lindzey (Ed.), *Handbook of social psychology*. Vol. 2. Cambridge, Mass.: Addison-Wesley, 1954.

Brzezinski, Z. Revolution and counterrevolution. *New Republic*, June 1, 1968, **158**, 23–25.

Buber, M. *I and thou*. (2nd ed.) New York: Scribner's, 1958.

Buchanan, P. C. Innovative organizations—A study in organization development. In *Applying behavioral science research in industry*. New York: Industrial Relations Counselors, 1964.

Budner, S. Intolerance of ambiguity as a personality variable. *Journal of Personality*, 1962, **30**, 29–50.

Bunker, D. R. Individual applications of laboratory training. *Journal of Applied Behavioral Science*, 1965, **1**, 131–148.

Burden, H. T. *The Nuremberg party rallies: 1923–39*. New York: Praeger, 1967.

Burke, R. L., & Bennis, W. G. Changes in perception of self and others during human relations training. *Human Relations*, 1961, **14**, 165–182.

Burridge, K. *Mambu: A Melanesian millennium*. London: Methuen, 1960.

Butler, R. A. Exploratory and related behavior: A new trend in animal research. *Journal of Individual Psychology*, 1958, **14**, 111–120.

Butler, R. A., & Harlow, H. F. Discrimination learning and learning sets to visual exploration incentives. *Journal of General Psychology*, 1957, **57**, 257–264.

Campbell, A. Civil rights and the vote for president. *Psychology Today*, February 1968, **1**, 26–31, and 70.

Campbell, D. T. Conformity in psychology's theories of acquired behavioral dispositions. In I. A. Berg & B. M. Bass (Eds.), *Conformity and deviation*. New York: Harper, 1961.

Canon, L. K. Self-confidence and selective exposure to information. In L. Festinger (Ed.), *Conflict, decision and dissonance*. Stanford, Calif.: Stanford University Press, 1964.

Cantril, H., Gaudet, H., & Hertzog, H. *The invasion from Mars: A study in the psychology of panic*. Princeton: Princeton University Press, 1940.

Carling, F. *And yet we are human*. London: Chatto & Windus, 1962.

Carlson, E. R. Attitude change through modification of attitude structure. *Journal of Abnormal and Social Psychology*, 1956, **52**, 256–261.

Carmichael, S., & Hamilton, C. V. *Black Power: The politics of liberation in America*. New York: Vintage Books, Random House, 1967.

Carroll, J. B., & Casagrande, J. B. The functions of language classifications in behavior. In E. E. Maccoby, T. M. Newcomb, & E. L. Hartley (Eds.), *Readings in social psychology*. (3rd ed.) New York: Holt, Rinehart & Winston, 1958.

Carson, R. L. *Silent spring*. Boston: Houghton Mifflin, 1962.

Carter, L. F., & Schooler, K. Value, need, and other factors in perception. *Psychological Review*, 1949, **56**, 200–207.

Cartwright, D. Achieving change in people: Some applications of group dynamics theory. *Human Relations*, 1951, **4**, 381–392.

Cartwright, D., & Harary, F. Structural balance: A generalization of Heider's theory. *Psychological Review*, 1956, **63**, 277–293.

Centers, R. An examination of the Riesman social character typology: A metropolitan survey. *Sociometry*, 1962, **25**, 232–240.

Champion, J. M., & Turner, W. W. An experimental investigation of subliminal perception. *Journal of Applied Psychology*, 1959, **43**, 382–384.

Chapin, F. S. *Cultural change*. New York: Century, 1928.

Charters, W. W., Jr., & Newcomb, T. M. Some attitudinal effects of experimentally increased salience of a membership group. In E. E. Maccoby, T. M. Newcomb, & E. L. Hartley (Eds.), *Readings in social psychology*. (3rd ed.) New York: Holt, Rinehart & Winston, 1958.

Chomsky, N. *Aspects of the theory of syntax*. Cambridge, Mass.: MIT Press, 1965.

Chomsky, N. The responsibility of intellectuals. *The New York Review of Books*, February 23, 1967, **8**, 16–26.

Chomsky, N. Language and the mind. *Psychology Today*, February, 1968, **1**, 48–51; 66–68.

Chomsky, N. *American power and the new mandarins*. New York: Pantheon, 1969.

Christie, R., Havel, J., & Seidenberg, B. Is the *F* scale irreversible? *Journal of Abnormal and Social Psychology*, 1958, **56**, 143–159.

Christie, R., & Jahoda, M. (Eds.). *Studies in the scope and method of "The authoritarian personality."* Glencoe, Ill.: Free Press, 1954.

Church, J. *Language and the discovery of reality: A developmental psychology of cognition*. New York: Random House, 1961.

Clark, R. A. The projective measurement of experimentally induced levels of sexual motivation. *Journal of Experimental Psychology*, 1952, **44**, 391–400.

Clawson, M. How much leisure, now and in the future? In J. C. Charlesworth (Ed.), Leisure in America: Blessing or curse? *American Academy of Political and Social Science Monographs*, 1964, Monograph 4.

Cleaver, E. *Soul on ice*. New York: McGraw-Hill, 1968.

Coch, L., & French, J. R. P., Jr. Overcoming resistance to change. *Human Relations*, 1948, **1**, 512–532.

Coffin, T. E. Some conditions of suggestion and suggestibility: A study of certain attitudinal and situational factors influencing the process of suggestion. *Psychological Monographs*, 1941, **53**, (4, Whole No. 241).

Cohen, A. M., Bennis, W. G., & Wolkon, G. H. The effects of changes in communication networks on the behaviors of problem-solving groups. *Sociometry*, 1962, **25**, 177–196.

Cohen, A. R. Cognitive tuning as a factor affecting impression formation. *Journal of Personality*, 1961, **29**, 235–245.

Cohen, A. R. A study in forced-compliance. Reported in J. W. Brehm & A. R. Cohen (Eds.), *Explorations in cognitive dissonance*. New York: Wiley, 1962.

Cohen, J. *A descriptive study of the availability and usability of social services in the South Central area of Los Angeles*. Los Angeles: Institute of Government and Public Affairs, University of California, Los Angeles, June 1, 1967.

Cohen, N. E. The Los Angeles riot study. Mimeographed press release, August 1, 1967a.

Cohen, N. E. *The context of the curfew area*. Los Angeles: Institute of Government and Public Affairs, University of California, Los Angeles, June 1, 1967b.

Cohen, W. Form recognition, spatial orientation, perception of movement in the uniform visual field. In A. Morris & E. P. Horne (Eds.), *Visual search techniques*. Washington D.C.: National Academy of Sciences National Research Council, 1960.

Cole, T. (Ed.) *Acting: A handbook of the Stanislavski method*. New York: Crown, 1955.

Coleman, J. S., Katz, E., & Menzel, H. *Medical innovation: A diffusion study*. Indianapolis, Ind.: Bobbs-Merrill, 1966.

Colombotos, J. Physicians and Medicare: A before-after study of the effects of legislation on attitudes. *American Sociological Review*, 1969, **34**, 318–334.

Cooley, C. H. *Social organization: A study of the larger mind*. New York: Scribner's, 1909.

Coser, L. A. *The functions of social conflict*. Glencoe, Ill.: Free Press, 1956.

Couch, A., & Keniston, K. Yeasayers and naysayers: Agreeing response set as a personality variable. *Journal of Abnormal and Social Psychology*, 1960, **60**, 151–174.

Cowan, P. The link between cognitive structure and social structure in two-child verbal interaction. Symposium presented at the Society for Research on Child Development. Reported in S. Ervin-Tripp, 1969, Sociolinguistics. In L. Berkowitz (Ed.), *Advances in experimental social psychology*, Vol. 4. New York: Academic, 1969.

Crews, F. The radical students. *The New York Review of Books*, April 24, 1969, **12**, 29–34.

Crockett, W. H. Cognitive complexity and impression formation. In B. A. Maher (Ed.), *Progress in personality research*. Vol. 2. New York: Academic, 1965.

Cronbach, L. J. Proposals leading to analytic treatment of social perception scores. In R. Tagiuri & L. Petrullo (Eds.), *Person perception and interpersonal behavior*. Stanford, Calif.: Stanford University Press, 1958.

Crowne, D. P., & Liverant, S. Conformity under varying conditions of personal commitment. *Journal of Abnormal and Social Psychology*, 1963, **66**, 547–555.

Crowne, D. P., & Marlowe, D. *The approval motive: Studies in evaluative dependence*. New York: Wiley, 1964.

Davis, K. E., & Jones, E. E. Changes in interpersonal perception as a means of reducing cognitive dissonance. *Journal of Abnormal and Social Psychology*, 1960, **61**, 402–410.

deCharms, R., Carpenter, V., & Kuperman, A. The "origin-pawn" variable in person perception. *Sociometry*, 1965, **28**, 241–258.

deCharms, R., & Moeller, G. H. Values expressed in American children's readers: 1800–1950. *Journal of Abnormal and Social Psychology*, 1962, **64**, 136–142.

DeFleur, M. L., & Westie, F. R. Verbal attitudes and overt acts: An experiment on the salience of attitudes. *American Sociological Review*, 1958, **23**, 667–673.

De Soto, C. B. Learning a social structure. *Journal of Abnormal and Social Psychology*, 1960, **60**, 417–421.

De Soto, C. B. The predilection for single orderings. *Journal of Abnormal and Social Psychology*, 1961, **62**, 16–23.

De Soto, C. B., & Bosley, J. J. The cognitive structure of a social structure. *Journal of Abnormal and Social Psychology*, 1962, **64**, 303–306.

Dennison, H. S. *Organization engineering*. (1st ed.) New York: McGraw-Hill, 1931.

Deutsch, M. The effects of cooperation and competition upon group processes. In D. Cartwright & A. F. Zander (Eds.), *Group dynamics: Research and theory*. Evanston, Ill.: Row, Peterson, 1953.

Deutsch, M. Trust, trustworthiness, and the *F* scale. *Journal of Abnormal and Social Psychology*, 1960, **61**, 138–140.

Deutsch, M. The interpretation of praise and criticism as a function of their social context. *Journal of Abnormal and Social Psychology*, 1961, **62**, 391–400.

Deutsch, M. Cooperation and trust: Some theoretical notes. In M. R. Jones (Ed.), *Nebraska Symposium on Motivation*. Lincoln: University of Nebraska Press, 1962.

Deutsch, M. Conflicts: Productive and destructive (Kurt Lewin Memorial Address). *Journal of Social Issues*, 1969, **25**, 7–41.

Deutsch, M., & Gerard, H. A study of normative and informational social influences upon individual judgment.

Journal of Abnormal and Social Psychology, 1955, **51**, 629–636.

Deutsch, M., Katz, I., & Jensen, A. R. (Eds.) *Social class, race, and psychological development.* New York: Holt, Rinehart & Winston, 1968.

Deutsch, M., & Krauss, R. M. The effect of threat upon interpersonal bargaining. *Journal of Abnormal and Social Psychology*, 1960, **61**, 181–189.

Deutsch, M., & Krauss, R. M. Studies of interpersonal bargaining. *Journal of Conflict Resolution*, 1962, **6**, 52–76.

Dohrenwend, B. P., & Chin-Shong, E. Social status and attitudes toward psychological disorder: The problem of tolerance of deviance. *American Sociological Review,* 1967, **32**, 417–433.

Dornbusch, S. M., Hastorf, A. H., Richardson, S. A., Muzzy, R. E., & Vreeland, R. S. The perceiver and the perceived: Their relative influence on the categories of interpersonal cognition. *Journal of Personality and Social Psychology*, 1965, **1**, 434–440.

Dornbusch, S. M., & Hickman, L. C. Other-directedness in consumer-goods advertising: A test of Riesman's historical theory. *Social Forces*, 1959, **38**, 99–102.

Dreger, R. M., & Miller, K. S. Comparative psychological studies of Negroes and Whites in the United States: 1959–1965. *Psychological Bulletin Monograph Supplement*, September 1968, **70**, No. 3, Part 2, 1–58.

Drucker, P. F. *The age of discontinuity: Guidelines to our changing society.* New York: Harper & Row, 1968.

DuBridge, L. A. Educational and social consequences. In J. T. Dunlop (Ed.), *Automation and technological change.* Englewood Cliffs, N. J.: Prentice-Hall, 1962.

Duncan, S., Jr., Rosenberg, M. J., & Finkelstein, J. The paralanguage of experimenter bias. *Sociometry*, 1969, **32**, 207–219.

Duncker, K. *Zur Psychologie des produktiven Denkens.* Berlin: Springer, 1935.

Dunnette, M. D., & Campbell, J. P. Laboratory education: Impact on people and organizations. *Industrial Relations*, 1968, **8**, 1–27.

Dunphy, D. C. Social change in self-analytic groups. In P. J. Stone, D. C. Dunphy, M. S. Smith, & D. M. Ogilvie (Eds.), *The General Inquirer: A computer approach to content analysis.* Cambridge, Mass.: MIT Press, 1966.

Durkheim, E. *The division of labor in society.* G. Simpson translation. Glencoe, Ill.: Free Press, 1933.

Durkheim, E. *The rules of the sociological method.* A. Solovay & J. H. Mueller translation. Edited by G. E. G. Catlin. Glencoe: Free Press, 1938.

Durkheim, E. *Suicide, a study in sociology.* J. A. Spaulding & G. Simpson translation. Edited by G. Simpson. Glencoe: Free Press, 1951.

Educational Testing Service. Trustees want to keep reins. *San Francisco Sunday Examiner and Chronicle*, January 12, 1969.

Edwards, L. P. *The natural history of revolutions.* Chicago: University of Chicago Press, 1927.

Egerton, J. Black ratio only 1 in 50. Reported in *San Francisco Sunday Examiner and Chronicle*, May 18, 1969.

Eggan, D. The general problem of Hopi adjustment. In C. Kluckhohn & H. Murray (Eds.), *Personality in nature, society, and culture.* (2nd ed.) New York: Knopf, 1953.

Ehrlich, D., Guttman, I., Schönbach, P., & Mills, J. Postdecision exposure to relevant information. *Journal of Abnormal and Social Psychology*, 1957, **54**, 98–102.

Ehrlich, H. J. Attitudes, behavior, and the intervening variables. *American Sociologist*, 1969, **4**, 29–34.

Ekman, P. The communication of interview stress through body language. Paper presented at the meeting of the Western Psychological Association, San Francisco, April 1962.

Ekman, P. Body position, facial expression and verbal behavior during interviews. *Journal of Abnormal and Social Psychology*, 1964, **68**, 295–301.

Ekman, P. Communication through non-verbal behavior: A source of information about interpersonal relations. In S. S. Tomkins & C. E. Izard (Eds.), *Affect, cognition, and personality: Empirical studies.* New York: Springer, 1965a.

Ekman, P. Differential communication of affect by head and body cues. *Journal of Personality and Social Psychology*, 1965b, **2**, 726–735.

Ekman, P. A lecture on micromomentary gestures. University of California, Berkeley, 1968.

Ekman, P., & Friesen, W. V. Non-verbal leakage and clues to deception. *Psychiatry*, 1969, **32**, 88–106.

Ekman, P., Friesen, W. V., & Taussig, T. VID-R and SCAN: Tools and methods in the analysis of facial expression and body movement. In G. Gerbner, F. R. Holsti, K. Krippendorff, W. J. Paisley, & P. J. Stone (Eds.), *The analysis of communication content: Developments in scientific theories and computer techniques.* New York: Wiley, 1969.

Ellison, R. *Invisible man.* New York: Random House, 1952.

Ellsworth, P. Dissonance reduction from the subject's point of view. *American Psychologist*, 1966, **21**, 694.

Ellul, J. *The technological society.* J. Wilkinson translation. New York: Knopf, 1964.

Emery, F. E. Psychological effects of the Western film: A study in television viewing. *Human Relations*, 1959, **12**, 195–232.

Eriksen, C. W. Subception: Fact or artifact: *Psychological Review*, 1956, **63**, 74–80.

Ervin-Tripp, S. An Issei learns English. *Journal of Social Issues*, 1967, **23**, 78–90.

Ervin-Tripp, S. Sociolinguistics. In L. Berkowitz (Ed.), *Advances in experimental social psychology.* (Vol. 4.) New York: Academic, 1969.

Etzioni, A. Interpersonal and structural factors in the study of mental hospitals. *Psychiatry*, 1960, **23**, 13–22.

Etzioni, A. Basic human needs, alienation and inauthenticity. *American Sociological Review*, 1968, **33**, 870–885.

Etzioni, A. Campus upheaval. In *The New York Times Encyclopedic Almanac*, 1969. New York: *New York Times*, 1969.

Exline, R. V. Explorations in the process of person perception: Visual interaction in relation to competition, sex, and need for affiliation. *Journal of Personality*, 1963, **31**, 1–20.

Exline, R. V., Gray, D., & Schuette, D. Visual behavior in a dyad as affected by interview content and sex of respondent. *Journal of Personality and Social Psychology*, 1965, **1**, 201–209.

Exline, R. V., & Winters, L. C. Affective relations and mutual glances in dyads. In S. S. Tomkins & C. E. Izard (Eds.), *Affect, cognition and personality: Empirical studies.* New York: Springer, 1965.

Exline, R. V., & Ziller, R. C. Status congruency and interpersonal conflict in decision-making groups. *Human Relations*, 1959, **12**, 147–162.

Fanon, F. *Wretched of the earth.* New York: Grove Press, 1963.

Feather, N. T. Cognitive dissonance, sensitivity, and evaluation. *Journal of Abnormal and Social Psychology*, 1963, **66**, 157–163.

Feffer, M. Symptom expression as a form of primitive decentering. *Psychological Review*, 1967, **74**, 16–28.

Feffer, M., & Suchotliff, L. Decentering implications of social interactions. *Journal of Personality and Social Psychology*, 1966, **4**, 415–422.

Feldkamp, R. H. Current crop of freshmen—swingers. *San Francisco Sunday Examiner and Chronicle*, March 5, 1967.

Ferry, W. H. The technophiliacs. *Center Magazine*, 1968, **1**, 45–49.

Feshbach, S., & Feshbach, N. Influence of the stimulus object upon the complementary and supplementary projection of fear. *Journal of Abnormal and Social Psychology,* 1963, **66**, 498–502.

Festinger, L. The role of group belongingness in a voting situation. *Human Relations,* 1947, **1**, 154–180.

Festinger, L. Informal social communication. *Psychological Review,* 1950, **57**, 271–282.

Festinger, L. An analysis of compliant behavior. In M. Sherif & M. O. Wilson (Eds.), *Group relations at the crossroads.* New York: Harper, 1953.

Festinger, L. Motivations leading to social behavior. In M. R. Jones (Ed.), *Nebraska Symposium on Motivation.* Lincoln: University of Nebraska Press, 1954a.

Festinger, L. A theory of social comparison processes. *Human Relations,* 1954b, **7**, 117–140.

Festinger, L. *A theory of cognitive dissonance.* Evanston, Ill.: Row, Peterson, 1957.

Festinger, L. Behavioral support for opinion change. *Public Opinion Quarterly,* 1964, **28**, 404–417.

Festinger, L., & Carlsmith, J. M. Cognitive consequences of forced compliance. *Journal of Abnormal and Social Psychology,* 1959, **58**, 203–210.

Festinger, L., Pepitone, A., & Newcomb, T. M. Some consequences of de-individuation in a group. *Journal of Abnormal and Social Psychology,* 1952, **47**, 382–389.

Festinger, L., Riecken, H., & Schachter, S. *When prophecy fails.* Minneapolis: University of Minnesota Press, 1956.

Festinger, L., Schachter, S., & Back, K. *Social pressures in informal groups: A study of human factors in housing.* New York: Harper, 1950.

Feuer, L. *The conflict of generations: The character and significance of student movements.* New York: Basic Books, 1969.

Fiedler, F. E. A contingency model of leadership effectiveness. In L. Berkowitz (Ed.), *Advances in experimental social psychology.* Vol. 1. New York: Academic, 1964.

Field, M. D. The California poll: Tougher line on students. *San Francisco Chronicle,* March 4, 1969.

Fisher, S., & Lubin, A. Distance as a determinant of influence in a two-person serial interaction situation. *Journal of Abnormal and Social Psychology,* 1958, **56**, 230–238.

Fishman, J. A. A systematization of the Whorfian hypothesis. *Behavioral Science,* 1960, **5**, 323–339.

Fitzgerald, E. T. Measurement of openness to experience: A study of regression in the service of the ego. *Journal of Personality and Social Psychology,* 1966, **4**, 655–663.

Fjeld, S. P., & Landfield, A. W. Personal construct consistency. *Psychological Reports,* 1961, **8**, 127–129.

Flacks, R. Thoughts of young radicals: Is the Great Society just a barbecue? *The New Republic,* January 29, 1966, **154**, 18–23.

Flacks, R. The liberated generation: An exploration of the roots of student protest. *Journal of Social Issues,* 1967, **23**, 52–75.

Flavell, J. H. Repression and the "return of the repressed." *Journal of Consulting Psychology,* 1955, **19**, 441–443.

Flavell, J. H. *The developmental psychology of Jean Piaget.* Princeton, N. J.: Van Nostrand, 1963.

Fodor, J. A. How to learn to talk: Some simple ways. In F. Smith & G. Miller (Eds.), *The genesis of language: A psycholinguistic approach.* Cambridge, Mass.: MIT Press, 1966.

Frankel, M. Morality in psychotherapy. *Psychology Today,* August 1967, **1**, 24–29.

Frederiksen, J. R. Cognitive factors in the recognition of ambiguous auditory and visual stimuli. *Journal of Personality and Social Psychology Monographs,* September 1967, **7**, (1, Whole No. 639), 1–17.

Freedman, J. L. Confidence, utility, and selective exposure: A partial replication. *Journal of Personality and Social Psychology,* 1965, **2**, 778–780.

Freedman, J. L., & Sears, D. O. Voters' preferences among types of information. *American Psychologist,* 1963, **18**, 375.

Freedman, J. L., & Sears, D. O. Selective exposure. In L. Berkowitz (Ed.), *Advances in experimental social psychology.* Vol. 2. New York: Academic, 1965.

Fremlin, J. H. How many people can the world support? In J. R. Landis (Ed.), *Current perspectives on social problems.* (2nd ed.) Belmont, Calif.: Wadsworth, 1969.

French, J. R. P., Jr. The disruption and cohesion of groups. *Journal of Abnormal and Social Psychology,* 1941, **36**, 361–377.

French, J. R. P., Jr., & Raven, B. The bases of social power. In D. Cartwright (Ed.), *Studies in social power.* Ann Arbor: Research Center for Group Dynamics Institute for Social Research, University of Michigan, 1959.

Freud, S. *Group psychology and the analysis of the ego.* J. Strachey translation. New York: Boni & Liveright, 1922.

Freud, S. *Collected papers.* Vol. 1–4. J. Riviere translation. London: Hogarth Press and The Institute of Psycho-Analysis, 1924–1950.

Freud, S. *Psychopathology of everyday life.* New York: New American Library, 1951.

Freud, S. *The interpretation of dreams.* J. Strachey translation. London: Allen & Unwin, 1954.

Freud, S. Construction in analysis. In *Standard edition of complete works of Sigmund Freud.* Vol. 23. J. Strachey translation. London: Hogarth Press and The Institute of Psycho-Analysis, 1964.

Friedenberg, E. Z. *Coming of age in America: Growth and acquiescence.* New York: Random House, 1965.

Fromm, E. *Escape from freedom.* New York: Holt, Rinehart & Winston, 1941.

Fruchter, B. *Introduction to factor analysis.* Princeton, N. J.: Van Nostrand, 1954.

Gage, N. L. & Cronbach, L. J., Conceptual and methodological problems in interpersonal perception. *Psychological Review,* 1955, **62**, 411–422.

Galbraith, J. K. *The new industrial state.* Boston: Houghton Mifflin, 1967.

Gallup, G. Public against student power. *San Francisco Chronicle,* January 8, 1969.

Gallup, G., Jr., & Davies, J. O., III. Student majority favors goals of militant few. *San Francisco Chronicle,* May 26, 1969.

Gamson, W. A. Experimental studies of coalition formation. In L. Berkowitz (Ed.), *Advances in experimental social psychology.* (Vol. 1.) New York: Academic, 1964.

Gamson, W. A. *Power and discontent.* Homewood, Ill.: Dorsey Press, 1968.

Gardner, R. W., & Long, R. I. Control, defense and centration effect: A study of scanning behaviour. *British Journal of Psychology,* 1962a, **53**, 129–140.

Gardner, R. W., & Long, R. I. Cognitive controls of attention and inhibition: A study of individual consistencies. *British Journal of Psychology,* 1962b, **53**, 381–388.

Genet, J. *The Maids, Deathwatch: Two Plays.* B. Frechtman translation. New York: Grove Press, 1954.

Gerson, W. M. Social structure and mass media socialization. Discussed by O. N. Larsen, Social effects of mass communication. In R. E. L. Faris (Ed.), *Handbook of modern sociology.* Chicago: Rand McNally, 1964.

Gilbert, C. M. Stereotype persistence and change among college students. *Journal of Abnormal and Social Psychology,* 1951, **46**, 245–254.

Gilson, C., & Abelson, R. P. The subjective use of inductive evidence. *Journal of Personality and Social Psychology.* 1965, **2**, 301–310.

Gitlin, T. Power and the myth of progress. *New Republic,* December 25, 1965, **153**, 19–21.

Glass, D. C. Changes in liking as a means of reducing cognitive discrepancies between self-esteem and aggression. *Journal of Personality,* 1964, **32**, 531–549.

Goffman, E. *The presentation of self in everyday life.* Garden City, N. Y.: Anchor Books, Doubleday, 1959.

Goffman, E. *Asylums: Essays on the social situation of*

mental patients and other inmates. (1st ed.) Chicago: Aldine, 1961.

Goffman, E. Behavior in public places: Notes on the social organization of gatherings. New York: Free Press of Glencoe, 1963a.

Goffman, E. Stigma: Notes on the management of spoiled identity. Englewood Cliffs, N. J.: Prentice-Hall, 1963b.

Goffman, I. W. Status consistency and preference for change in power distribution. American Sociological Review, 1957, 22, 275–281.

Gold, M., & Slater, C. Family structure and integration setting. Ann Arbor: Institute for Social Research, University of Michigan. Undated mimeographed report.

Goldberg, S. C. Three situational determinants of conformity to social norms. Journal of Abnormal and Social Psychology, 1954, 49, 325–329.

Goldings, H. On the avowal and projection of happiness. Journal of Personality, 1954, 23, 30–47.

Goldstein, K. The organism: A holistic approach to biology derived from pathological data in man. Boston: Beacon Press, 1963.

Goldstein, K. Methodological approach to the study of the schizophrenic thought disorder. In J. S. Kasanin (Ed.), Language and thought in schizophrenia: Collected papers presented at the meeting of the American Psychiatric Association, May 12, 1939. Berkeley and Los Angeles: University of California Press, 1944.

Goldstein, M. J. A test of the response probability theory of perceptual defense. Journal of Experimental Psychology, 1962, 63, 23–28.

Goldstein, M. J., & Barthol, R. P. Fantasy responses to subliminal stimuli. Journal of Abnormal and Social Psychology, 1960, 60, 22–26.

Goodman, P. Growing up absurd: Problems of youth in the organized system. New York: Vintage Books, Random House, 1960.

Gordon, W. J. J. Synectics: The development of creative capacity. (1st ed.) New York: Harper, 1961.

Gore, P. M., & Rotter, J. B. A personality correlate of social action. Journal of Personality, 1963, 31, 58–64.

Gough, H. Theory and measurement of socialization. Journal of Consulting Psychology, 1960, 24, 23–30.

Gough, H. G., & Peterson, D. R. The identification and measurement of predispositional factors in crime and delinquency. Journal of Consulting Psychology, 1952, 16, 207–212.

Gouldner, A. W. The norm of reciprocity: A preliminary statement. American Sociological Review, 1960, 25, 161–178.

Greenblum, J., & Pearlin, L. I. Vertical mobility and prejudice: A sociopsychological analysis. In R. Bendix & S. M. Lipset (Eds.), Class, status and power: A reader in social stratification. Glencoe, Ill.: Free Press, 1953.

Greenspoon, J. The reinforcing effect of two spoken sounds on the frequencies of two responses. American Journal of Psychology, 1955, 68, 409–416.

Greenwald, A. G., & Sakumura, J. S. Attitude and selective learning: Where are the phenomena of yesteryear? Journal of Personality and Social Psychology, 1967, 7, 387–397.

Griffen, W. L. Free and unfree schools. Changing Education, 1969, 4, 17–19.

Guetzkow, H., & Dill, W. R. Factors in the organizational development of task-oriented groups. Sociometry, 1957, 20, 175–204.

Guetzkow, H., & Gyr, J. An analysis of conflict in decision-making groups. Human Relations, 1954, 7, 367–382.

Haan, N., Smith, M. B., & Block, J. Moral reasoning of young adults: Political-social behavior, family background, and personality correlates. Journal of Personality and Social Psychology, 1968, 10, 183–201.

Haber, R. N. Discrepancy from adaptation level as a source of affect. Journal of Experimental Psychology, 1958, 56, 370–375.

Haber, R. N. Nature of the effect of set on perception. Psychological Review, 1966, 73, 335–351.

Haggard, E. A., & Isaacs, K. S. Micro-momentary facial expressions as indicators of ego mechanisms in psychotherapy. In A. Gottschalk & A. H. Auerbach (Eds.), Methods of research in psychotherapy. New York: Appleton-Century-Crofts, 1966.

Haiman, F. S. Effects of training in group processes on open-mindedness. Journal of Communication, 1963, 13, 236–245.

Hall, E. T. The silent language. (1st ed.) Garden City, N. Y.: Doubleday, 1959.

Hall, E. T. Proxemics: The study of man's spatial relations. In I. Galdston (Ed.), Man's image in medicine and anthropology: Arden House Conference on Medicine and Anthropology, 1961. New York: International Universities Press, 1963.

Hardin, E. Computer automation, work environment and employee satisfaction in an insurance company. Industrial and Labor Relations Review, 1960a, 13, 559–567.

Hardin, E. The reactions of employees to office automation. Bureau of United States Labor Statistics: Monthly Labor Review, 1960b, 83, 925–932.

Hardyck, J. A., & Braden, M. Prophecy fails again: A report of a failure to replicate. Journal of Abnormal and Social Psychology, 1962, 65, 136–141.

Hare, A. P., & Bales, R. F. Seating position and small group interaction. Sociometry, 1963, 26, 480–486.

Harlow, H. F., Harlow, M. K., & Meyer, D. R. Learning motivated by a manipulation drive. Journal of Experimental Psychology, 1950, 40, 228–234.

Harman, H. Modern factor analysis. (2nd ed.) Chicago: University of Chicago Press, 1967.

Harrington, M. The other America: Poverty in the United States. New York: Macmillan, 1962.

Harris, L. A health survey—Poor are tense. San Francisco Chronicle, November 16, 1968.

Harrison, R. Impact of the laboratory on perceptions of others by the experimental group. In C. Argyris (Ed.), Interpersonal competence and organizational effectiveness. Homewood, Ill.: Dorsey Press, 1962.

Harrison, R. Group composition models for laboratory design. Journal of Applied Behavioral Science, 1965, 1, 409–432.

Harrison, R., & Lubin, B. Personality style, group composition, and learning. Journal of Applied Behavioral Science, 1965, 1, 286–302.

Hartrey, A. Personal communication to E. E. Sampson, 1966.

Hartshorne, H., & May, M. A. Studies in the nature of character. Vol. 1. Studies in deceit. New York: Macmillan, 1928.

Hartshorne, H., May, M. A., & Maller, J. B. Studies in the nature of character. Vol. 2. Studies in service and self-control. New York: Macmillan, 1929.

Hartshorne, H., May, M. A., & Shuttleworth, F. K. Studies in the nature of character. Vol. 3. Studies in the organization of character. New York: Macmillan, 1930.

Harvey, O. J. System structure, flexibility, and creativity. In O. J. Harvey (Ed.), Experience, structure, and adaptability. New York: Springer, 1966.

Harvey, O. J., Hunt, D. E., & Schroder, H. M. Conceptual systems and personality organization. New York: Wiley, 1961.

Harvey, O. J., & Ware, R. Personality differences in dissonance resolution. Journal of Personality and Social Psychology, 1967, 7, 227–230.

Hastorf, A. H., Kite, W. R., Gross, A. E., & Wolfe, L. J. The perception and evaluation of behavior change. Sociometry, 1965, 28, 400–410.

Hayden, T. The Port Huron Statement. In P. Jacobs & S. Landau (Eds.), The new radicals: A report with documents. New York: Vintage Books, Random House, 1966.

Haythorn, W. The effects of varying combinations of authoritarian and equalitarian leaders and followers. In

E. E. Maccoby, T. M. Newcomb, & E. L. Hartley (Eds.), *Readings in social psychology*. (3rd ed.) New York: Holt, Rinehart & Winston, 1958.

Heider, F. *The psychology of interpersonal relations*. New York: Wiley, 1958.

Heider, F., & Simmel, M. An experimental study of apparent behavior. *American Journal of Psychology*, 1944, **57**, 243–259.

Helson, H. *Adaptation-level theory: An experimental and systematic approach to behavior*. New York: Harper & Row, 1964.

Henley, N. M. Achievement and affiliation imagery in American fiction, 1901–1961. *Journal of Personality and Social Psychology*, 1967, **7**, 208–210.

Henry, A. F., & Short, J. F., Jr. *Suicide and Homicide: Some economic, sociological, and psychological aspects of aggression*. New York: Free Press of Glencoe, 1954.

Henry, J. The formal social structure of a psychiatric hospital. *Psychiatry*, 1954, **17**, 139–151.

Herbart, J. F. Discussed in E. G. Boring, *A history of experimental psychology*. New York: Appleton-Century-Crofts, 1950.

Hernández-Peón, R. Psychiatric implications of neurophysiological research. *Bulletin of the Menninger Clinic*, 1964, **28**, 165–185.

Heron, W. The pathology of boredom. *Scientific American*, 1957, **196**, 52–56.

Heron, W. Cognitive and physiological effects of perceptual isolation. In P. Solomon, P. E. Kubzansky, P. H. Leiderman, J. H. Mendelson, R. Trumbull, & D. Wexler (Eds.), *Sensory deprivation: A symposium held at Harvard Medical School*. Cambridge, Mass.: Harvard University Press, 1961.

Heron, W., Doane, B. K., & Scott, T. H. Visual disturbances after prolonged perceptual isolation. *Canadian Journal of Psychology*, 1956, **10**, 13–18.

Hess, E. H. Attitude and pupil size. *Scientific American*, April 1965, **212**, 46–54.

Hicks, J. D. *A short history of American democracy*. Boston: Houghton Mifflin, 1943.

Hill, H. Racial inequality in employment: The patterns of discrimination. *Annals of the American Academy of Political and Social Science*, 1965, **357**, 30–47.

Hinkle, R. C. Antecedents of the action orientation in American sociology before 1935. *American Sociological Review*, 1963, **28**, 705–715.

Hodge, R. W., & Treiman, D. J. Occupational mobility and attitudes towards Negroes. *American Sociological Review*, 1966, **31**, 93–102.

Hoffer, E. *The true believer: Thoughts on the nature of mass movements*. (1st ed.) New York: Harper, 1951.

Hoffman, L. R., Harburg, E., & Maier, N. R. F. Differences and disagreement as factors in creative group problem solving. *Journal of Abnormal and Social Psychology*, 1962, **64**, 206–214.

Hoebel, E. A. *Anthropology: The study of man*. New York: McGraw-Hill, 1966.

Hoffman, M. L., & Saltzstein, H. D. Parent discipline and the child's moral development. *Journal of Personality and Social Psychology*, 1967, **5**, 45–57.

Hoijer, H. Cultural implications of some Navaho linguistic categories. *Language*, 1951, **27**, 111–120.

Hollander, E. P. Conformity, status, and idiosyncrasy credit. *Psychological Review*, 1958, **65**, 117–127.

Hollander, E. P. Competence and conformity in the acceptance of influence. *Journal of Abnormal and Social Psychology*, 1960, **61**, 365–369.

Hollander, E. P. Some effects of perceived status on responses to innovative behavior. *Journal of Abnormal and Social Psychology*, 1961, **63**, 247–250.

Hollander, E. P., & Willis, R. H. Some current issues in the psychology of conformity and nonconformity. *Psychological Bulletin*, 1967, **68**, 62–76.

Hollingshead, A. B., & Redlich, F. C. *Social class and mental illness: A community study*. New York: Wiley, 1958.

Hoos, I. R. Impact of office automation on workers. *International Labour Review*, 1960, **82**, 363–388.

Horwitz, M. The recall of interrupted group tasks: An experimental study of individual motivation in relation to group goals. *Human Relations*, 1954, **7**, 3–38.

House, R. J. T-group education and leadership effectiveness: A review of the empiric literature and a critical evaluation. *Personnel Psychology*, 1967, **20**, 1–32.

Hovland, E. I. Effects of the mass media of communication. In G. Lindzey (Ed.), *Handbook of social psychology*. Vol. 2. Cambridge, Mass.: Addison-Wesley, 1954.

Hovland, C. I. Reconciling conflicting results derived from experimental and survey studies of attitude change. *American Psychologist*, 1959, **14**, 8–17.

Hovland, C. I., Harvey, O. J., & Sherif, M. Assimilation and contrast effects in reactions to communication and attitude change. *Journal of Abnormal and Social Psychology*, 1957, **55**, 244–252.

Hovland, C. I., & Janis, I. L. (Eds.). *Personality and persuasibility*. New Haven, Conn.: Yale University Press, 1959.

Hovland, C. I., Janis, I. L., & Kelley, H. H. *Communication and persuasion: Psychological studies of opinion change*. New Haven, Conn.: Yale University Press, 1953.

Hovland, C. I., Lumsdaine, A. A., & Sheffield, F. D. *Experiments on mass communications*. Princeton: Princeton University Press, 1949.

Hovland, C. I., & Mandell, W. An experimental comparison of conclusion-drawing by the communicator and by the audience. *Journal of Abnormal and Social Psychology*, 1952, **47**, 581–588.

Hovland, C. I., Mandell, W., Campbell, E. H., Brock, B. T., Luchins, A. S., Cohen, A. R., McGuire, W. J., Janis, I. L., Feierabend, R. L., & Anderson, N. H. *The order of presentation in persuasion*. New Haven: Institute of Human Relations, Yale University, 1957.

Hovland, C. I., & Pritzker, H. A. Extent of opinion change as a function of change advocated. *Journal of Abnormal and Social Psychology*, 1957, **54**, 257–261.

Hovland, C. I., & Weiss, W. The influence of source credibility on communication effectiveness. *Public Opinion Quarterly*, 1951, **15**, 635–650.

Howes, D. H., & Solomon, R. L. A note on McGinnies' "Emotionality and perceptual defense". *Psychological Review*, 1950, **57**, 229–234.

Hull, C. L. *Principles of behavior: An introduction to behavior theory*. New York: Appleton-Century, 1943.

Hyman, H. H. The psychology of status. *Archives of Psychology*, 1942, **38**, No. 269.

Hyman, H. H., & Sheatsley, P. B. Some reasons why information campaigns fail. In E. E. Maccoby, T. M. Newcomb, & E. L. Hartley (Eds.), *Readings in social psychology*. (3rd ed.) New York: Holt, Rinehart & Winston, 1958.

Hymes, D. (Ed.) *Language in culture and society: A reader in linguistics and anthropology*. New York: Harper & Row, 1964.

Iverson, M. A. Personality impressions of punitive stimulus persons of differential status. *Journal of Abnormal and Social Psychology*, 1964, **68**, 617–626.

Iverson, M. A., & Schwab, H. G. Ethnocentric dogmatism and binocular fusion of sexually and racially discrepant stimuli. *Journal of Personality and Social Psychology*, 1967, **7**, 73–81.

Izard, C. E. Personality similarity and friendship. *Journal of Abnormal and Social Psychology*, 1960a, **61**, 47–51.

Izard, C. E. Personality similarity, positive affect, and interpersonal attraction. *Journal of Abnormal and Social Psychology*, 1960b, **61**, 484–485.

Jackson, E. F. Status consistency and symptoms of stress. *American Sociological Review*, 1962, **27**, 469–479.

Jackson, J. M. A space for conceptualizing person-group relationships. *Human Relations*, 1959, **12**, 3–15.

Jackson, J. M., & Saltzstein, H. D. The effect of person-group relationships on conformity processes. *Journal of Abnormal and Social Psychology*, 1958, **57**, 17–24.

Janis, I. L. Personality correlates of susceptibility to persuasion. *Journal of Personality*, 1954, **22**, 504–518.

Janis, I. L., & Feshbach, S. Effects of fear-arousing communications. *Journal of Abnormal and Social Psychology*, 1953, **48**, 78–92.

Janis, I. L., & Gilmore, J. B. The influence of incentive conditions on the success of role playing in modifying attitudes. *Journal of Personality and Social Psychology*, 1965, **1**, 17–27.

Janis, I. L., & King, B. T. The influence of role-playing on opinion change. *Journal of Abnormal and Social Psychology*, 1954, **49**, 211–218.

Jansen, M. J., & Stolurow, L. M. An experimental study in role playing. *Psychological Monographs*, 1962, **76**, (31, Whole No. 550).

Jaspers, K. *Von der Wahrheit*. Berlin: Springer, 1947.

Jaspers, K. *Philosophie*. (2nd ed.) Berlin: Springer, 1948.

Johanesen, H. 88 Million ton food shortage. *San Francisco Sunday Examiner and Chronicle*, February 26, 1967.

Jones, A. Information deprivation in humans. In B. A. Maher (Ed.), *Progress in experimental personality research*. Vol. 3. New York: Academic, 1966.

Jones, E. Mother-right and the sexual ignorance of savages. *International Journal of Psychoanalysis*, 1925, **6**, 2, 109–130.

Jones, E. E. *Ingratiation: A social psychological analysis*. New York: Appleton-Century-Crofts, 1964.

Jones, E. E., & Davis, K. From acts to dispositions: The attribution process in person perception. In L. Berkowitz (Ed.), *Advances in experimental social psychology*. Vol. 2. New York: Academic, 1965.

Jones, E. E., Davis, K., & Gergen, K. J. Role playing variations and their informational value for person perception. *Journal of Abnormal and Social Psychology*, 1961, **63**, 302–310.

Jones, E. E., Gergen, K. J., Gumpert, P., & Thibaut, J. W. Some conditions affecting the use of ingratiation to influence performance evaluation. *Journal of Personality and Social Psychology*, 1965, **1**, 613–625.

Jones, E. E., Gergen, K. J., & Jones, R. G. Tactics of ingratiation among leaders and subordinates in a status hierarchy. *Psychological Monographs*, 1963, **77**, (3, Whole No. 566).

Jones, E. E., Jones, R. G., & Gergen, K. J. Some conditions affecting the evaluation of a conformist. *Journal of Personality*, 1964, **31**, 270–288.

Jones, E. E., & Thibaut, J. W. Interaction goals as bases of inference in interpersonal perception. In R. Tagiuri & L. Petrullo (Eds.), *Person perception and interpersonal behavior*. Stanford, Calif.: Stanford University Press, 1958.

Jordan, N. Behavioral forces that are a functional of attitudes and of cognitive organization. *Human Relations*, 1953, **6**, 273–287.

Jordan, W. D. White over black: *American attitudes toward the Negro 1550–1812*. Chapel Hill: University of North Carolina Press & Institute of Early American History and Culture, 1968.

Jourard, S. M. *Disclosing man to himself*. Princeton, N. J.: Van Nostrand, 1968. Used by permission. Copyright 1968 by Litton Educational Publishing.

Jung, C. G. *Studies in word association: Experiments in the diagnosis of psychopathological conditions carried out at the Psychiatric Clinic of the University of Zurich under the direction of C. G. Jung*. M. D. Eder, translation. London: Heinemann, 1918.

Kahl, J. A. Some measurements of achievement orientation. *American Journal of Sociology*, 1965, **70**, 669–681.

Kahn, H., & Wiener, A. J. *The year 2000: A framework for speculation on the next thirty-three years*. New York: Macmillan, 1967.

Kardiner, A. *The individual and his society: The psychodynamics of primitive social organization*. New York: Columbia University Press, 1939.

Kardush, M. Status congruence and social mobility as determinants of small group behavior. Doctoral dissertation, University of California, Berkeley, 1968.

Kasl, S. V., & Cobb, S. Effects of parental status incongruence and discrepancy on physical and mental health of adult offspring. *Journal of Personality and Social Psychology Monograph*, 1967, **7**, (2, Whole No. 642).

Kasl, S. V., & Mahl, G. F. The relationship of disturbances and hesitations in spontaneous speech to anxiety. *Journal of Personality and Social Psychology*, 1965, **1**, 425–433.

Kassarjian, W. M. A study of Riesman's theory of social character. *Sociometry*, 1962, **25**, 213–230.

Katz, D. The functional approach to the study of attitudes. *Public Opinion Quarterly*, 1960, **24**, 163–204.

Katz, D. Group process and social integration: A system analysis of two movements of social protest. *Journal of Social Issues*, 1967, **23**, 3–22.

Katz, D., & Brady, K. W. Racial stereotypes of 100 college students. *Journal of Abnormal and Social Psychology*, 1933, **28**, 280–290.

Katz, D., & Kahn, R. L. Human organization and worker motivation. In L. R. Tripp (Ed.), *Industrial productivity*. Madison, Wis.: Industrial Relations Research Association, 1951.

Katz, D., Sarnoff, I., & McClintock, C. Ego-defense and attitude change. *Human Relations*, 1956, **9**, 27–45.

Katz, E., Levin, M. L., & Hamilton, H. Traditions of research on the diffusion of innovation. *American Sociological Review*, 1963, **28**, 237–252.

Kelley, H. H. The warm-cold variable in first impressions. *Journal of Personality*, 1950, **18**, 431–439.

Kelly, G. A. *The psychology of personal constructs*. Vol. 1 & 2. (1st ed.) New York: Norton, 1955.

Kelly, G. A. *A theory of personality: The psychology of personal constructs*. New York: Norton, 1963.

Kelman, H. C. Effects of success and failure on "suggestibility" in the auto-kinetic situation. *Journal of Abnormal and Social Psychology*, 1950, **45**, 267–285.

Kelman, H. C. Compliance, identification, and internalization: Three processes of attitude change. *Journal of Conflict Resolution*, 1958, **2**, 51–60.

Kelman, H. C. Processes of opinion change. *Public Opinion Quarterly*, 1961, **25**, 57–78.

Kelman, H. C., & Barclay, J. The F scale as a measure of breadth of perspective. *Journal of Abnormal and Social Psychology*, 1963, **67**, 608–615.

Kelman, H. C., & Hovland, C. I. "Reinstatement" of the communicator in delayed measurement of opinion change. *Journal of Abnormal and Social Psychology*, 1953, **48**, 327–335.

Kendon, A. Some functions of gaze direction in social interaction, *Acta Psychologica*, 1967, **26**, 22–63.

Keniston, K. *The uncommitted: Alienated youth in American society*. (1st ed.) New York: Harcourt, Brace, 1965.

Keniston, K. The sources of student dissent. *Journal of Social Issues*, 1967, **23**, 108–137.

Kerr, C. *The uses of the university*. Cambridge, Mass.: Harvard University Press, 1963.

Kerr, C. The university and utopia. *Daily Californian*, May, 11, 1967.

Kerr, C. Response to Richard Lichtman. *Center Magazine*, 1968, **1**, 13–14.

Key, V. O., Jr. *Public opinion and American democracy*. (1st ed.) New York: Knopf, 1961.

Killian, L. M. Social movements. In R. E. L. Faris (Ed.), *Handbook of modern sociology*. Chicago: Rand McNally, 1964.

Klapper, J. T. *The effects of mass communication*. Glencoe, Ill.: Free Press, 1960.

Klein, G. S., Spence, D. P., Holt, R. R., & Gourevitch, S. Cognition without awareness: Subliminal influences upon conscious thought. *Journal of Abnormal and Social Psychology*, 1958, **57**, 255–266.

Kluckhohn, C. Navaho witchcraft. *Papers of the Peabody Museum of American Archaeology and Ethnology, Harvard University*, 1944, **22**, 2.

Kluckhohn, C., & Murray, H. A. Personality formation: The determinants. In C. Kluckhohn, H. A. Murray, & D. M. Schneider (Eds.), *Personality in nature, society, and culture*. (2nd ed.) New York: Knopf, 1956.

Kogan, N., & Wallach, M. A. Risk taking: A study in cognition and personality as a function of the situation, the person, and the group. *New directions in psychology*. Vol. 3. New York: Holt, Rinehart & Winston, 1967a.

Kogan, N., & Wallach, M. A. The risky-shift phenomenon in small decision-making groups: A test of the information-exchange hypothesis. *Journal of Experimental Social Psychology*, 1967b, **3**, 75–84.

Kohlberg, L. The development of modes of moral thinking in the years ten to sixteen. Unpublished doctoral dissertation, University of Chicago, 1958.

Kohlberg, L. The child as a moral philosopher. Reprinted by permission from *Psychology Today*, September 1968, **2**, 24–31. Copyright Communications/Research/Machines/Inc.

Kohlberg, L. Stage and sequence: The cognitive-developmental approach to socialization. In D. A. Goslin (Ed.), *Handbook of socialization theory and research*. Chicago: Rand McNally, 1969.

Kramer, E. Judgment of personal characteristics and emotions from nonverbal properties of speech. *Psychological Bulletin*, 1963, **60**, 408–420.

Krech, D., & Crutchfield, R. S. *Theory and problems of social psychology*. (1st ed.) New York: McGraw-Hill, 1948.

Kuhn, T. S. *The structure of scientific revolutions*. Chicago: University of Chicago Press, 1962.

Külpe, O. *Versuche uber Abstraktion*. Berlin International Congress of Experimental Psychology, 1904, 56–68.

Kutner, B., & Gordon, N. B. Cognitive functioning and prejudice: A nine-year follow-up study. *Sociometry*, 1964, **27**, 66–74.

Lambert, R. D., (Ed.) Political intelligence for America's future. *Annals of the American Academy of Political and Social Science*, 1970, **388**, 1–132.

Lambert, W. E. A social psychology of bilingualism. *Journal of Social Issues*, 1967, **23**, 91–109.

Lambert, W. W., Solomon, R. L., & Watson, P. D. Reinforcement and extinction as factors in size estimation. *Journal of Experimental Psychology*, 1949, **39**, 637–641.

Lamm, H. Will an observer advise higher risk taking after hearing a discussion of the decision problem? *Journal of Personality and Social Psychology*, 1967, **6**, 467–471.

Lane, R. E. The decline of politics and ideology in a knowledgeable society. *American Sociological Review*, 1966, **31**, 649–662.

Lang, K., & Lang, G. E. *Collective dynamics*. New York: Crowell, 1961.

La Piere, R. T. Attitudes versus action. *Social Forces*, 1934, **13**, 230–237.

Larsen, O. N. Social effects of mass communication. In R. E. L. Faris (Ed.), *Handbook of modern sociology*. Chicago: Rand McNally, 1964.

Larsen, O. N., Gray, L. N., & Fortis, J. G. Goals and goal-achievement methods in television content: Models for anomie? *Sociological Inquiry*, 1963, **33**, 180–196.

Lasswell, H. D. The world revolution of our time: A framework for basic policy research. In H. D. Lasswell & D. Lerner (Eds.), *World revolutionary elites: Studies in coercive ideological movements*. Cambridge, Mass.: MIT Press, 1965.

Lasswell, H. D., & Lerner, D. (Eds.) *World revolutionary elites: studies in coercive ideological movements*. Cambridge: MIT Press, 1965.

Lazarsfeld, P. F., Berelson, B., & Gaudet, H. *The people's choice: How the voter makes up his mind in a presidential campaign*. (2nd ed.) New York: Columbia University Press, 1948.

Lazarsfeld, P. F. & Merton, R. K. Mass communication, popular taste and organized social action. In L. Bryson (Ed.), *The communication of ideas*. New York: Harper, 1948.

Lazarus, R. S., & McCleary, R. A. Autonomic discrimination without awareness: A study of subception. *Psychological Review*, 1951, **58**, 113–122.

Leary, T. F. *Interpersonal diagnosis of personality: A functional theory and methodology for personality evaluation*. New York: Ronald Press, 1957.

Leavitt, H. J. Some effects of certain communication patterns on group performance. In E. E. Maccoby, T. M. Newcomb, & E. L. Hartley (Eds.), *Readings in social psychology*. (3rd ed.) New York: Holt, 1958.

Le Bon, G. *The crowd: A study of the popular mind*. London: Unwin, 1896.

Lefcourt, H. M. Internal versus external control of reinforcement: A review. *Psychological Bulletin*, 1966, **65**, 206–220.

Le Furgy, W. G., & Woloshin, G. W. Immediate and long-term effects of experimentally induced social influence in the modification of adolescents' moral judgments. *Journal of Personality and Social Psychology*, 1969, **12**, 104–110.

Lekachman, R. The automation report. *Commentary*, May 1966, **41**, 65–71.

Lenneberg, E. H. A probabilistic approach to language learning. *Behavioral Science*, 1957, **2**, 1–12.

Lenneberg, E. H. The natural history of language. In F. Smith & G. A. Miller (Eds.), *The genesis of language: A psycholinguistic approach*. Cambridge, Mass.: MIT Press, 1966.

Lenski, G. Status crystallization: A non-vertical dimension of social status. *American Sociological Review*, 1954, **19**, 405–413.

Lenski, G. Social participation and status crystallization. *American Sociological Review*, 1956, **21**, 458–464.

Lenski, G. Status inconsistency and the vote: A four nation test. *American Sociological Review*, 1967, **32**, 288–301.

Lerner, M. J. Evaluation of performance as a function of a performer's reward and attractiveness. *Journal of Personality and Social Psychology*, 1965, **1**, 355–360.

Lerner, M. J., & Matthews, G. Reactions to suffering of others under conditions of indirect responsibility. *Journal of Personality and Social Psychology*, 1967, **5**, 319–325.

Lerner, M. J., & Simmons, C. H. Observer's reaction to the "innocent victim": Compassion or rejection? *Journal of Personality and Social Psychology*, 1966, **4**, 203–210.

Leventhal, H., & Niles, P. A field experiment on fear arousal with data on the validity of questionnaire measures. *Journal of Personality*, 1964, **32**, 459–479.

Leventhal, H., Singer, R. P., & Jones, S. The effects of fear and specificity of recommendation upon attitudes and behaviors. *Journal of Personality and Social Psychology*, 1965, **2**, 20–29.

Leventhal, H., & Watts, J. C. Sources of resistance to fear-arousing communications on smoking and lung cancer. *Journal of Personality*, 1966, **34**, 155–175.

Levine, J. M., & Murphy, G. The learning and forgetting of controversial material. *Journal of Abnormal and Social Psychology*, 1943, **38**, 507–517.

Levine, R., Chein, I., & Murphy, G. The relation of intensity of a need to the amount of perceptual distortion: A preliminary report. *Journal of Psychology*, 1942, **13**, 283–293.

Levinger, G., & Schneider, D. J. Test of the "risk is a value" hypothesis. *Journal of Personality and Social Psychology*, 1969, **11**, 165–169.

Lewin, K. Frontiers in group dynamics: Concept, method and reality in social science; social equilibria and social change. *Human Relations*, 1947a, **1**, 5–41.

Lewin, K. Frontiers in group dynamics, II: Channels of group life; social planning and action research. *Human Relations*, 1947b, **1**, 143–153.

Lewin, K. *Field theory in social science: Selected theoretical papers*. D. Cartwright (Ed.), New York: Harper & Row, 1951.

Lewin, K. Group decision and social change. In E. E. Maccoby, T. M. Newcomb, & E. L. Hartley (Eds.), *Readings in social psychology*. (3rd ed.) New York: Holt, Rinehart & Winston, 1958.

Lewis, H. B. An experimental study of the role of the ego in work: I. The role of the ego in cooperative work. *Journal of Experimental Psychology*, 1944, **34**, 113–126.

Liberation News Service. National violence cited as political phenomenon. *Daily Californian*, January 27, 1969, 1 and 3.

Lieberman, S. The effects of changes in roles on the attitudes of role occupants. *Human Relations*, 1956, **9**, 385–402.

Lieberson, S., & Silverman, A. R. Precipitants and underlying conditions of race riots. *American Sociological Review*, 1965, **30**, 887–898.

Lifton, R. J. *Thought reform and the psychology of totalism: A study of "brainwashing" in China*. (1st ed.) New York: Norton, 1961.

Lifton, R. J. *Death in life: Survivors of Hiroshima*. New York: Vintage Books, Random House, 1969.

Likert, R. *New patterns of management*. New York: McGraw-Hill, 1961.

Lilly, J. C. Mental effects of reduction of ordinary levels of physical stimuli on intact, healthy persons. *Psychiatric Research Reports*, June 1956, No. 5, 1–9.

Lilly, J. C., & Shurley, J. T. Experiments in solitude in maximum achievable physical isolation with water suspension on intact, healthy persons. Symposium, Harvard Medical School, Boston, June 1958.

Lippitt, R., Watson, J., & Westley, B. *The dynamics of planned change: A comparative study of principles and techniques*. New York: Harcourt, Brace, 1958.

Lippitt, R., & White, R. K. An experimental study of leadership and group life. In E. E. Maccoby, T. M. Newcomb, & E. L. Hartley (Eds.), *Readings in social psychology*. (3rd ed.) New York: Holt, Rinehart & Winston, 1958.

Loewe, F., & Lerner, A. J. *My Fair Lady*. Copyright 1956. Reprinted by permission of Chappel & Co., Inc.

Lohman, J. D., & Reitzes, D. C. Note on race relations in mass society. *American Journal of Sociology*, 1952, **58**, 240–246.

Loomis, C. P. In praise of conflict and its resolution. *American Sociological Review*, 1967, **32**, 875–890.

Los Angeles Times. Watts: The typical juvenile in the riot. November 28, 1965.

Luborsky, L., Blinder, B., & Schimek, J. G. Looking, recalling, and GSR as a function of defense. *Journal of Abnormal Psychology*, 1965, **70**, 270–280.

Lundberg, G. A. *Social research: A study in methods of gathering data*. New York: Longmans, Green 1929.

Lynd, S., The New Left. *Annals of the American Academy of Political and Social Science*, 1969, **382**, 64–72.

Maccoby, E. E. The effects of emotional arousal on the retention of film content: A failure to replicate. *Journal of Abnormal and Social Psychology*, 1956, **53**, 373–374.

Maccoby, N., Jecker, J., Brictrose, H., & Rose, E., Sound film recordings in improving classroom communication: Experimental studies in non-verbal communication. Report, Institute for Communications Research, Stanford University, 1964.

Maier, N. R. F., & Hoffman, L. R. Organization and creative problem solving. *Journal of Applied Psychology*, 1961, **45**, 277–280.

Maier, N. R. F. & Solem, A. R. The contribution of a discussion leader to the quality of group thinking: The effective use of minority opinions. *Human Relations*, 1952, **5**, 277–288.

Maine, Sir H. J. S. *Ancient law: Its connection with the early history of society and its relation to modern ideas*. London: Murray, 1861.

Malinowski, B. *Argonauts of the Western Pacific: An account of native enterprise and adventure in the archipelagoes of Melanasian New Guinea*. London: Routledge, 1922.

Mann, F. C. Psychological and organizational impacts. In J. T. Dunlop (Ed.), *Automation and technological change*. Englewood Cliffs, N. J.: Prentice-Hall, 1962.

Mann, F. C., & Hoffman, L. R. *Automation and the worker: A study of social change in power plants*. New York: Holt, 1960.

Mann, F. C., & Williams, L. K. Observations on the dynamics of a change to electronic data-processing equipment. *Administrative Science Quarterly*, 1960, **5**, 217–256.

Mann, F. C., & Williams, L. K. Some effects of the changing work environment in the office. *Journal of Social Issues*, 1962, **18**, 90–101.

Mann, J. A., & Kreyche, G. F. (Eds.) *Reflections on Man: Readings in philosophical psychology from classical philosophy to existialism*. New York: Harcourt, Brace, 1966.

Mannheim, K. *Ideology and Utopia: An introduction to the sociology of knowledge*. L. Wirth & E. Shils translation. New York: Harcourt, Brace, 1936.

Marcuse, H. *One-dimensional man: Studies in the ideology of advanced industrial society*. Boston: Beacon Press, 1966.

Marx, K. *Selected writings in sociology and social philosophy*. T. B. Bottomore & M. Rubel (Eds.) London: Watts, 1956.

Maslow, A. H. *Motivation and Personality*. (1st ed.) New York: Harper, 1954.

Maslow, A. H. *Toward a psychology of being*. Princeton, N. J.: Van Nostrand, 1962.

Maslow, A. H. Further notes on the psychology of being. *Journal of Humanistic Psychology*, 1964, **4**, 45–58.

Maslow, A. H. A theory of metamotivation: The biological rooting of the value-life. *Journal of Humanistic Psychology*, 1967, **7**, 93–127.

Mason, J. G. *How to be a more creative executive*. New York: McGraw-Hill, 1960.

Mason, J. G. Suggestions for brainstorming technical and research problems. In S. J. Parnes & H. F. Harding (Eds.), *A source book for creative thinking*. New York: Scribner's, 1962.

Matthiessen, P. Profiles: Organizer, II: Cesar Chavez. *The New Yorker*, June 28, 1969, 43–71.

Mattson, J. M., & Natsoulas, T. Emotional arousal and stimulus duration as determinants of stimulus selection. *Journal of Abnormal and Social Psychology*, 1962, **65**, 142–144.

May, R. Love and will. *Psychology Today*, May 1969, **3**, 17–64.

Mead, G. H. *Mind, self and society from the standpoint of a social behaviorist*. Chicago: University of Chicago Press, 1934.

Meltzer, L., & Salter, J. Organization structure and the performance and job satisfaction of physiologists. *American Sociological Review*, 1962, **27**, 351–362.

Memmi, A. *The colonizer and the colonized*. H. Greenfeld translation. Boston: Beacon Press, 1967.

Mendelsohn, G. A., & Griswold, B. B. Assessed creative potential, vocabulary level, and sex as predictors of the use of incidental cues in verbal problem solving. *Journal of Personality and Social Psychology*, 1966, **4**, 423–431.

Menzel, H. Innovation, integration and marginality: A survey of physicians. *American Sociological Review*, 1960, **25**, 704–713.

Merton, R. *Social theory and social structure*. Glencoe, Ill.: Free Press, 1957.

Meumann, E. Cited in R. B. Zajonc, *Social psychology: An experimental approach*. Belmont, Calif.: Wadsworth, 1966.

Michael, D. N. Some speculations on the social impact of technology. In R. Perrucci & M. Pilisuk (Eds.), *The triple revolution: Social problems in depth.* Boston: Little, Brown, 1968.

Miles, R. E. Keeping informed: Human relations or human resources? *Harvard Business Review,* July-August 1965, **43,** 148–163.

Milgram, S. Behavioral study of obedience. *Journal of Abnormal and Social Psychology,* 1963, **67,** 371–378.

Milgram, S. Liberating effects of group pressure. *Journal of Personality and Social Psychology,* 1965, **1,** 127–134.

Miller, D. R., & Swanson, G. E. *The changing American parent: A study in the Detroit area.* New York: Wiley, 1958.

Miller, G. A. Professionals in bureaucracy: Alienation among industrial scientists and engineers. *American Sociological Review,* 1967, **32,** 755–768.

Miller, N., & Campbell, D. T. Recency and primacy in persuasion as a function of the timing of speeches and measurement. *Journal of Abnormal and Social Psychology,* 1959, **59,** 1–9.

Mills, C. W. *Letter to the New Left.* New York: Students for a Democratic Society, 1961.

Minard, R. D. Race relations in the Pocahontas Coal Fields. *Journal of Social Issues,* 1952, **8,** 29–44.

Minas, J. S., Scodel, A., Marlowe, D., & Rawson, H. Some descriptive aspects of two-person non-zero-sum games: II. *Journal of Conflict Resolution,* 1960, **4,** 193–197.

Montgomery, P. Poverty on the Lower East Side: 6 live "Heavy life" on $1 a day. *New York Times,* January 10, 1964, p. 17.

Moore, B. J., Jr. Revolution in America? *The New York Review of Books,* January 30, 1969, **12,** 6–12.

Moore, S. *The Stanislavski system: The professional training of an actor.* New York: Viking Press, 1965.

Moreno, J. L. *Who shall survive? A new approach to the problem of human interrelations.* Washington, D.C.: Nervous and Mental Disease Publishing Company, 1934.

Moreno, J. L. *Sociodrama: A method for the analysis of social conflicts.* Beacon, N. Y.: Beacon House, 1944.

Moreno, J. L. *Psychodrama.* Vol. 1. Beacon, N. Y.: Beacon House, 1946.

Moreno, J. L. *The theatre of spontaneity.* Author's translation. Beacon, N. Y.: Beacon House, 1947.

Moreno, J. L. *Psychodrama.* Vol. 2. Foundations of psychotherapy. Beacon, N. Y.: Beacon House, 1959.

Morgan, W. R., & Sawyer, J. Bargaining, expectations, and the preference for equality over equity. *Journal of Personality and Social Psychology,* 1967, **6,** 139–149.

Morgenthau, H. J. What ails America? *New Republic,* October 28, 1967, **157,** 17–21.

Morris, R. T., & Jeffries, V. *The white reaction study.* Los Angeles: Institute of Government and Public Affairs, University of California, June 1, 1967.

Morrissette, J. O. An experimental study of the theory of structural balance. *Human Relations,* 1958, **11,** 239–254.

Morse, N. C., & Reimer, E. The experimental change of a major organizational variable. *Journal of Abnormal and Social Psychology,* 1956, **52,** 120–129.

Moulton, R. W., Raphelson, A. C., Kristofferson, A. B., & Atkinson, J. W. The achievement motives and perceptual sensitivity under two conditions of motive-arousal. In J. W. Atkinson (Ed.), *Motives in fantasy, action, and society: A method of assessment and study.* Princeton, N. J.: Van Nostrand, 1958.

Murphy, R. F. Social distance and the veil. *American Anthropologist,* 1964, **66,** 1257–1274.

Murphy, R. J., & Watson, J. M. *The Structure of discontent: The relationship between social Structure, grievance, and support for the Los Angeles riot.* Los Angeles: Institute of Government and Public Affairs, University of California, June 1, 1967.

Murray, H. A. The effect of fear upon the estimates of the maliciousness of other personalities. *Journal of Social Psychology,* 1933, **4,** 310–329.

Myrdal, G. *An American dilemma: The negro problem and modern democracy.* New York: Harper, 1944.

McClelland, D. C. *Personality.* New York: Sloane, 1951.

McClelland, D. C. Risk taking in children with high and low need for achievement. In J. W. Atkinson (Ed.), *Motives in fantasy, action, and society: A method of assessment and study.* Princeton, N. J.: Van Nostrand, 1958.

McClelland, D. C. *The achieving society.* Princeton: Van Nostrand, 1961.

McClelland, D. C. *N* Achievement and entrepreneurship: A longitudinal study. *Journal of Personality and Social Psychology,* 1965, **1,** 389–391.

McClelland, D. C., & Atkinson, J. W. The projective expression of needs. I: The effect of different intensities of the hunger drive on perception. *Journal of Psychology,* 1948, **25,** 205–222.

McClelland, D. C., Atkinson, J. W., Clark, R. A., & Lowell, E. L. *The achievement motive.* New York: Appleton-Century-Crofts, 1953.

McClelland, D. C., & Liberman, A. M. The effect of need for achievement on recognition of need-related words. *Journal of Personality,* 1949, **18,** 236–251.

McDougall, W. *An introduction to social psychology.* London: Methuen, 1908.

McGinnies, E. Emotionality and perceptual defense. *Psychological Review,* 1949, **56,** 244–251.

McGinniss, J. *The selling of the President, 1968.* New York: Trident, 1969.

McGregor, D. *The human side of enterprise.* New York: McGraw-Hill, 1960.

McGregor, D. *Leadership and motivation: Essays.* W. G. Bennis & E. H. Schein (Eds.), Cambridge, Mass.: MIT Press, 1966.

McGuire, W. J. Cognitive consistency and attitude change. *Journal of Abnormal and Social Psychology,* 1960, **60,** 345–353.

McGuire, W. J. Resistance to persuasion conferred by active and passive prior refutation of the same and alternative counterarguments. *Journal of Abnormal and Social Psychology,* 1961, **63,** 326–332.

McGuire, W. J. Persistence of the resistance to persuasion induced by various types of prior belief defenses. *Journal of Abnormal and Social Psychology,* 1962, **64,** 241–248.

McGuire, W. J. The current status of cognitive consistency theories. In S. Feldman (Ed.), *Cognitive consistency: Motivational antecedents and behavioral consequents.* New York: Academic, 1966.

McGuire, W. J. The nature of attitudes and attitude change. In G. Lindzey & E. Aronson (Eds.), *The handbook of social psychology.* Vol. 3. Reading, Mass.: Addison-Wesley, 1969.

McGuire, W. J., & Papageorgis, D. The relative efficacy of various types of prior belief-defense in producing immunity against persuasion. *Journal of Abnormal and Social Psychology,* 1961, **62,** 327–337.

McGuire, W. J., & Papageorgis, D. Effectiveness of forewarning in developing resistance to persuasion. *Public Opinion Quarterly,* 1962, **26,** 24–34.

McLuhan, H. M. *Understanding media: The extensions of man.* New York: McGraw-Hill, 1964.

McLuhan, H. M. *The Gutenberg galaxy: The making of typographic man.* Toronto: University of Toronto Press, 1965.

McLuhan, H. M., & Fiore, Q. *The medium is the massage.* New York: Bantam, 1967.

McNeill, D. Developmental psycholinguistics. In F. Smith & G. A. Miller (Eds.), *The genesis of language: A psycholinguistic approach.* Cambridge, Mass.: MIT Press, 1966.

Nader, R. *Unsafe at any speed: The designed-in dangers of the American automobile.* New York: Grossman, 1965.

Neill, A. S. *Summerhill: A radical approach to child-rearing.* New York: Hart, 1964. Reprinted by permission.

Newcomb, T. M. *Personality and social change: Attitude formation in a student community.* New York: Dryden, 1943.

Newcomb, T. M. An approach to the study of communicative acts. *Psychological Review*, 1953, **60**, 393–404.

Newcomb, T. M. Attitude development as a function of reference groups: The Bennington study. In E. E. Maccoby, T. M. Newcomb, & E. L. Hartley (Eds.), *Readings in social psychology.* (3rd ed.) New York: Holt, Rinehart & Winston, 1958.

Newcomb, T. M. *The acquaintance process.* New York: Holt, Rinehart & Winston, 1961.

Newcomb, T. M., Koenig, K. E., Flacks, R., & Warwick, D. P. *Persistence and change: Bennington College and its students after twenty-five years.* New York: Wiley, 1967.

Newsweek editors. Report from Black America. *Newsweek,* June 30, 1969, 16–35.

New York Times, Harsh report of police conduct. In *San Francisco Chronicle,* July 5, 1968.

New York Times Encyclopedic Almanac, 1969. New York: *New York Times,* © 1969.

Nisbet, R. A., *The sociological tradition.* New York: Basic Books, 1966.

Nord, W. R. Social exchange theory: An integrative approach to social conformity. *Psychological Bulletin,* 1969, **71,** 174–208.

Norman, W. T. Toward an adequate taxonomy of personality attributes: Replicated factor structure in peer nomination personality ratings. *Journal of Abnormal and Social Psychology,* 1963, **66**, 574–583.

Nortman, D. L. *The population problem.* New York: National Educational Television, 1965.

Ogburn, W. F. *Social change with respect to culture and original nature.* New York: Huebsch, 1922.

Oglesby, C., & Shaull, R. *Containment and change.* New York: Macmillan, 1967.

Olds, J., & Milner, P. Positive reinforcement produced by electrical stimulation of septal area and other regions of rat brain. *Journal of Comparative and Physiological Psychology,* 1954, **47**, 419–427.

Orne, M. T. On the social psychology of the psychological experiment: With particular reference to demand characteristics and their implications. *American Psychologist,* 1962, **17**, 776–783.

Orne, M. T., & Evans, F. J. Social control in the psychological experiment: Antisocial behavior and hypnosis. *Journal of Personality and Social Psychology,* 1965, **1**, 189–200.

Orne, M. T., & Scheibe, K. E. The contribution of nondeprivation factors in the production of sensory deprivation effects: The psychology of the "panic button." *Journal of Abnormal and Social Psychology,* 1964, **68**, 3–12.

Osborn, A. F. *Applied imagination: Principles and procedures of creative thinking.* New York: Scribner's, 1957.

Osgood, C. E., Suci, G. J., & Tannenbaum, P. H. *The measurement of meaning.* Urbana, Ill.: University of Illinois Press, 1957.

Osgood, C. E., & Tannenbaum, P. H. The principle of congruity in the prediction of attitude change. *Psychological Review,* 1955, **62**, 42–55.

Osmond, H. Function as the basis of psychiatric ward design. *Mental Hospitals,* 1957, 23–29.

Owen, D. Reported by J. R. Bruckner. Expert on cities sees grave population peril. *Los Angeles Times,* April 14, 1966.

Papageorgis, D., & McGuire, W. J. The generality of immunity to persuasion produced by pre-exposure to weakened counterarguments. *Journal of Abnormal and Social Psychology,* 1961, **62**, 475–581.

Parsons, T. The position of identity in the general theory of action. In C. Gordon & K. J. Gergen (Eds.), *The self in social interaction.* Vol. 1. *Classic and contemporary perspectives.* New York: Wiley, 1968.

Parsons, T., Bales, R. F., & Shils, E. A. *Working papers in the theory of action.* Glencoe, Ill.: Free Press, 1953.

Parsons, T., & Shils, E. A. (Eds.). *Towards a general theory of action.* Cambridge, Mass.: Harvard University Press, 1951.

Passini, F. T., & Norman, W. T. A universal conception of personality structure? *Journal of Personality and Social Psychology,* 1966, **4**, 44–49.

Pavlov, I. P. *Conditioned reflexes: An investigation of the physiological activity of the cerebral cortex.* G. V. Anrep, translator and editor. New York: Dover, 1960.

Pavlov, I. P. *Lectures on conditioned reflexes.* Vols. 1 & 2. W. H. Grant translation. New York: International Publishers, 1963.

Payne, D. E. Role constructs versus part constructs and interpersonal understanding. Reported by J. C. J. Bonarius, Research in the personal construct theory of George A. Kelly: Role construct repertory test and basic theory. In B. A. Maher (Ed.), *Progress in experimental personality research.* Vol. 2. New York: Academic, 1965.

Pear, T. H. *Voice and personality.* London: Chapman & Hall, 1931.

Perlo, V. Arms profiteering: It's not a myth. *New Republic,* February 7, 1970, 23–25.

Personal communication to E. E. Sampson from a legislative aide working in Sacramento on campus-protest legislation, 1969.

Peters, R. S. (Ed.). *Brett's history of psychology.* London: Allen & Unwin, 1962.

Peters, R. S. *The concept of motivation.* New York: Humanities Press, 1958.

Peterson, R. E. Organized student protest in 1964–1965. Symposium report presented at the meeting of the American Psychological Association, September 1966.

Peterson, R. E. *The scope of organized student protest 1967–1968.* Princeton, N. J.: Educational Testing Service, 1968.

Pettigrew, T. F. Social psychology and desegregation research. *American Psychologist,* 1961, **16**, 105–112.

Pettigrew, T. F. *A profile of the Negro American.* Princeton: Van Nostrand, 1964.

Pettigrew, T. F., Allport, G. W., & Barnett, E. O. Binocular resolution and perception of race in South Africa. *British Journal of Psychology,* 1958, **49**, 265–278.

Piaget, J. *The psychology of intelligence.* M. Percy & D. E. Berlyne translation. New York: Harcourt, Brace, 1950.

Piaget, J. *The origins of intelligence in children.* M. Cook translation. New York: International Universities Press, 1952.

Piaget, J. *The construction of reality in the child.* M. Cook translation. New York: Basic Books, 1954.

Pine, F. Incidental stimulation: A study of preconscious transformations. *Journal of Abnormal and Social Psychology,* 1960, **60**, 68–75.

Pinter, H. From an interview reported in *The San Francisco Actor's Workshop Playbill,* November, 1963.

Pittel, S. M., & Mendelsohn, G. A. Measurement of moral values: A review and critique. *Psychological Bulletin,* 1966, **66**, 22–35.

Plimpton, C. H. The Amherst College statement. *New Republic,* May 17, 1969, **160**, 7.

Pollack, H. B. Change in homogeneous and heterogeneous sensitivity training groups. Unpublished doctoral dissertation, University of California, Berkeley, 1967.

Pope, L. *Millhands and preachers: A study of Gastonia.* New Haven, Conn.: Yale University Press, 1958.

Porter, L. W., & Lawler, E. E. The effects of "Tall" versus "Flat" organization structures on managerial job satisfaction. *Personnel Psychology,* 1964, **17**, 135–148.

Postman, L. J., Bronson, W. C., & Gropper, G. L. Is there a mechanism of perceptual defense? *Journal of Abnormal and Social Psychology,* 1953, **48**, 215–224.

Postman, L. J., Bruner, J., & McGinnies, E. Personal values as selective factors in perception. *Journal of Abnormal and Social Psychology,* 1948, **43**, 142–154.

Pytkowicz, A. R., Wagner, N. N., & Sarason, I. G. An experimental study of the reduction of hostility through fantasy. *Journal of Personality and Social Psychology,* 1967, **5**, 295–303.

Rabow, J., Fowler, F. J., Jr., Bradford, D. L., Hofeller, M. A., & Shibuya, Y. The role of social norms and leadership in risk-taking. *Sociometry,* 1966, **29**, 16–27.
Rapaport, D. *Diagnostic psychological testing: The theory, statistical evaluation and diagnostic application of a battery of tests.* Vol. 1. Chicago, Ill.: Year Book, 1945.
Rapoport, A., & Chammah, A. M. *Prisoner's dilemma: A study in conflict and cooperation.* Ann Arbor: University of Michigan Press, 1965.
Redfield, R. The folk society. *American Journal of Sociology,* 1947, **52**, 293–308.
Redl, F. Group emotion and leadership. In A. P. Hare, E. F. Borgatta, & R. F. Bales (Eds.), *Small groups: Studies in social interaction.* New York: Knopf, 1955.
Rest, J., Turiel, E., & Kohlberg, L. Relations between level of moral judgment and preference and comprehension of the moral judgment of others. *Journal of Personality,* in press.
Rettig, S., & Turoff, S. J. Exposure to group discussion and predicted ethical risk taking. *Journal of Personality and Social Psychology,* 1967, **7**, 177–180.
Revelle, R. Environment: Land, air, water. *New Republic,* November 7, 1964, **151**, 25–32.
Riesman, D. *The lonely crowd: A study of the changing American character.* New Haven, Conn.: Yale University Press, 1950.
Riesman, D. *Faces in the crowd: Individual studies in character and politics.* New Haven: Yale University Press, 1952.
Ringer, B., & Sills, D. L. Political extremists in Iran: A secondary analysis of communication data. *Public Opinion Quarterly,* 1952, **16**, 689–701.
Rivers, W. L. *The opinionmakers.* Boston: Beacon Press, 1965.
Robinson, D., & Rhode, S. Two experiments with an anti-Semitism poll. *Journal of Abnormal and Social Psychology,* 1946, **41**, 136–144.
Roethlisberger, F. J., Dickson, W. J., & Wright, H. A. *Management and the worker: An account of a research program conducted by the Western Electric Company, Hawthtorne Works, Chicago.* Cambridge, Mass.: Harvard University Press, 1939.
Rogers, C. R. *Counseling and psychotherapy: Newer concepts in practice.* Boston: Houghton Mifflin, 1942.
Rogers, C. R. *Client-centered therapy: Its current practice, implications and theory.* Boston: Houghton Mifflin, 1951.
Rogers, C. R. *Freedom to learn: A view of what education might become.* Columbus, Ohio: Merrill, 1969a.
Rogers, C. R. The group comes of age. *Psychology Today,* December 1969b, **3**, 27–31, 58–61.
Roheim, G. *Psychoanalysis and anthropology: Culture, personality and the unconscious.* New York: International Universities Press, 1950.
Rokeach, M. Political and religious dogmatism: An alternative to the authoritarian personality. *Psychological Monographs,* 1956, **70**, (18, Whole No. 425).
Rokeach, M. *The open and closed mind: Investigations into the nature of belief systems and personality systems.* New York: Basic Books, 1960.
Rokeach, M. Attitude change and behavioral change. *Public Opinion Quarterly,* 1966, **30**, 529–550.
Rosenberg, M. J. A structural theory of attitude dynamics. *Public Opinion Quarterly,* 1960, **24**, 319–340.
Rosenberg, M. J. When dissonance fails: On eliminating evaluation apprehension from attitude measurement. *Journal of Personality and Social Psychology,* 1965, **1**, 28–42.
Rosenthal, R. Experimenter outcome-orientation and the results of the psychological experiment. *Psychological Bulletin,* 1964a, **61**, 405–412.

Rosenthal, R. The effect of the experimenter on the results of psychological research. In B. A. Maher (Ed.), *Progress in experimental personality research.* Vol. 1. New York: Academic, 1964b.
Rosenthal, R. *Experimenter effects in behavioral research.* New York: Appleton-Century-Crofts, 1966.
Rosenthal, R. Covert communication in the psychological experiment. *Psychological Bulletin,* 1967, **67**, 356–367.
Rosenthal, R., Persinger, G. W., Vikan-Kline, L., & Fode, K. L. The effect of early data returns on data subsequently obtained by outcome-biased experimenters. *Sociometry,* 1963, **26**, 487–498.
Rosenzweig, S. An experimental study of "repression" with special reference to need-persistive and ego-defensive reactions to frustration. *Journal of Experimental Psychology,* 1943, **32**, 64–74.
Rotter, J. B., Seeman, M., & Liverant, S. Internal versus external control of reinforcements: A major variable in behavior theory. In N. F. Washburne (Ed.), *Decisions, values, and groups.* Vol. 2. London: Pergamon, 1962.
Rowland, L. W. Will hypnotized persons try to harm themselves or others? *Journal of Abnormal and Social Psychology,* 1939, **34**, 114–117.
Rubin, I. M. Increased self-acceptance: A means of reducing prejudice. *Journal of Personality and Social Psychology,* 1967, **5**, 233–238.
Rudin, S. A. The psychology of nations. *Discovery,* June 1965, **26**, 22–28.
Ruesch, J., & Kees, W. *Nonverbal communication: Notes on the visual perception of human relations.* Berkeley: University of California Press, 1956.
Rusk, H. A. A profile of poverty. *San Francisco Sunday Examiner and Chronicle,* December 11, 1966.
Ryder, N. B. The cohort as a concept in the study of social change. *American Sociological Review,* 1965, **30**, 843–861.

Saenger, G., & Gilbert, E. Customer reactions to the integration of Negro sales personnel. *International Journal of Opinion and Attitude Research,* 1950, **4**, 57–76.
Sampson, E. E. An experiment on active and passive resistance to social power. Unpublished doctoral dissertation, University of Michigan, 1960.
Sampson, E. E. Status congruence and cognitive consistency. *Sociometry,* 1963, **26**, 146–162.
Sampson, E. E. The study of ordinal position: Antecedents and outcomes. In B. A. Maher (Ed.), *Progress in experimental personality research.* Vol. 2. New York: Academic, 1965.
Sampson, E. E. Studies of status congruence. In L. Berkowitz (Ed.), *Advances in experimental social psychology.* Vol. 4. New York: Academic, 1969.
Sampson, E. E. Two revolutions. In E. E. Sampson & H. Korn (Eds.), *Student activism and protest: Alternatives for social change.* San Francisco: Jossey-Bass, 1970.
Sampson, E. E., & Brandon, A. C. The effects of role and opinion deviation on small group behavior. *Sociometry,* 1964, **27**, 261–281.
Sampson, E. E., Fisher, L., Angel, A., Mulman, A., & Sullins, C. Two profiles: The draft resister and the ROTC cadet. Unpublished report, University of California, Berkeley, 1969.
Sampson, E. E., & Hancock, F. T. An examination of the relationship between ordinal position, personality, and conformity: An extension, replication, and partial verification. *Journal of Personality and Social Psychology,* 1967, **5**, 398–407.
Sampson, E. E., & Insko, C. A. Cognitive consistency and performance in the autokinetic situation. *Journal of Abnormal and Social Psychology,* 1964, **68**, 184–192.
Sampson, E. E., & Kardush, M. Age, sex, class and race differences in response to a two-person non-zero sum game. *Journal of Conflict Resolution,* 1965, **9**, 212–220.
Sampson, E. E., & Levine, N. The prediction of individual behavior within a T-group from a test of interpersonal

needs. Unpublished report, University of California, Berkeley, 1963.

San Francisco Chronicle. Drug use by San Mateo students. August 8, 1968.

Sanford, R. N. The effects of abstinence from food upon imaginal processes: A further experiment. *Journal of Psychology,* 1937, **3,** 145–159.

Sapir, E. *Culture, language and personality: Selected essays.* D. G. Mandelbaum (Ed.). Berkeley: University of California Press, 1956.

Sarbin, T. R. Role theory. In G. Lindzey (Ed.), *Handbook of social psychology.* Vol. 1. Cambridge, Mass.: Addison-Wesley, 1954.

Sarbin, T. R., & Allen, V. L. Role theory. In G. Lindzey & E. Aronson (Eds.), *Handbook of social psychology.* Vol. 1. (2nd ed.) Reading, Mass.: Addison-Wesley, 1968.

Sartre, J. P. *Existential psychoanalysis.* H. E. Barnes translation. New York: Philosophical Library, 1953.

Sartre, J. P. *No exit* (Huis clos), *a play in one act, and The flies (Les mouches), a play in three acts.* S. Gilbert translation. New York: Knopf, 1954.

Sartre, J. P. *Being and nothingness: An essay on phenomenological ontology.* H. E. Barnes translation. New York: Philosophical Library, 1956.

Saugstad, P. Effect of food deprivation on perception-cognition. *Psychological Bulletin,* 1966, **65,** 80–90.

Scanzoni, J. Socialization, N achievement and achievement values. *American Sociological Review,* 1967, **32,** 449–456.

Schachtel, E. G. *Metamorphosis: On the development of affect, perception, attention, and memory.* New York: Basic Books, 1959.

Schachter, S. Deviation, rejection, and communication. *Journal of Abnormal and Social Psychology,* 1951, **46,** 190–207.

Schachter, S. *The psychology of affiliation: Experimental studies of the sources of gregariousness.* Stanford, Calif.: Stanford University Press, 1959.

Schachter, S., & Burdick, H. A field experiment on rumor transmission and distortion. *Journal of Abnormal and Social Psychology,* 1955, **50,** 363–371.

Schachter, S., & Singer, J. S. Cognitive, social, and physiological determinants of emotional state. *Psychological Review,* 1962, **69,** 379–399.

Schanck, R. L. A study of a community and its groups and institutions conceived of as behaviours of individuals. *Psychological Monographs,* 1932, **43,** (2, Whole No. 195).

Schatzman, L., & Strauss, A. Social class and modes of communication. *American Journal of Sociology,* 1955, **60,** 329–338.

Scheerer, M. Cognitive theory. In G. Lindzey (Ed.), *Handbook of social psychology.* Vol. 1. Cambridge, Mass.: Addison-Wesley, 1954.

Schein, E. H. The Chinese indoctrination program for prisoners of war: A study of attempted "brainwashing." In E. E. Maccoby, T. M. Newcomb, & E. L. Hartley (Eds.), *Readings in social psychology.* (3rd ed.) New York: Holt, Rinehart & Winston, 1958.

Schmid, C. F., & Nobbe, C. E. Socioeconomic differentials among nonwhite races. *American Sociological Review,* 1965, **30,** 909–922.

Schroder, H. M., Driver, M. J., & Streufert, S. *Human information processing: Individuals and groups functioning in complex social situations.* New York: Holt, Rinehart & Winston, 1967.

Schutz, W. C. *FIRO: A three-dimensional theory of interpersonal behavior.* New York: Holt, Rinehart & Winston, 1960.

Schutz, W. C. On group composition. *Journal of Abnormal and Social Psychology,* 1961, **62,** 275–281.

Scodel, A., Minas, J. S., Ratoosh, P., & Lipetz, M. Some descriptive aspects of two-person non-zero-sum games. *Journal of Conflict Resolution,* 1959, **3,** 114–119.

Scott, T. H., Bexton, W. H., Heron, W., & Doane, B. K. Cognitive effects of perceptual isolation. *Canadian Journal of Psychology,* 1959, **13,** 200–209.

Scott, W. A. Attitude change through reward of verbal behavior. *Journal of Abnormal and Social Psychology,* 1957, **55,** 72–75.

Scott, W. A. Cognitive complexity and cognitive balance. *Sociometry,* 1963, **26,** 66–74.

Sears, D. O., & McConahay, F. B. *Los Angeles riot study: Riot participation.* Los Angeles: Institute of Government and Public Affairs, University of California, June 1, 1967.

Secord, P. F., & Backman, C. W. Interpersonal congruency, perceived similarity and friendship. *Sociometry,* 1964, **27,** 115–127.

Secord, P. F., & Backman, C. W. An interpersonal approach to personality. In B. A. Maher (Ed.), *Progress in experimental personality research.* Vol. 2. New York: Academic, 1965.

Segall, M. H., Campbell, D. T., & Herskovits, M. J. *The influence of culture on visual perception.* Indianapolis: Bobbs-Merrill, 1966.

Selznick, P. Foundations of the theory of organization. *American Sociological Review,* 1948, **13,** 25–35.

Seward, G. H. *Sex and the social order.* (1st ed.) New York: McGraw-Hill, 1946.

Shakespeare, W. *The complete works of William Shakespeare.* W. G. Clark & W. A. Wright (Eds.) New York: Hearst's International Library, 1914.

Shapiro, A. K. A contribution to a history of the placebo effect. *Behavioral Science,* 1960, **5,** 109–135.

Shaw, M. E., & Blum, J. M. Effects of leadership style upon group performance as a function of task structure. *Journal of Personality and Social Psychology,* 1966, **3,** 238–241.

Sheldon, O. *The philosophy of management.* London: Pitman, 1923.

Sherif, M. A study of some social factors in perception. *Archives of Psychology,* 1935, **27,** Number 187.

Sherif, M., & Sherif, C. W. *Groups in harmony and tension: An integration of studies on intergroup relations.* New York: Harper, 1953.

Shils, E. A. Authoritarianism: "Right" and "Left." In R. Christie & M. Jahoda (Eds.), *Studies in the scope and method of "The Authoritarian Personality."* New York: Free Press, 1954.

Shipley, T. E., & Veroff, J. A projective measure of need for affiliation. *Journal of Experimental Psychology,* 1952, **43,** 349–356.

Shoemaker, D. J. The relation between personal constructs and observed behavior. Reported by J. C. J. Bonarius. Research in the personal construct theory of George A. Kelly: Role construct repertory test and basic theory. In B. A. Maher (Ed.), *Progress in experimental personality research.* Vol. 2. New York: Academic, 1965.

Shomer, R. W., Davis, A. H., & Kelley, H. H. Threats and the development of coordination: Further studies of the Deutsch and Krauss trucking game. *Journal of Personality and Social Psychology,* 1966, **4,** 119–126.

Silberstein, F. B., & Seeman, M. Social mobility and prejudice. *American Journal of Sociology,* 1959, **65,** 258–264.

Simmel, G. Sociology of the senses: Visual interaction. In R. E. Park & E. W. Burgess (Eds.), *Introduction to the science of sociology.* Chicago: University of Chicago Press, 1921.

Simmel, G. *The sociology of Georg Simmel.* K. H. Wolff, translator and editor. Glencoe, Ill.: Free Press, 1950.

Simmel, G. Conflict as sociation. In L. A. Coser & B. Rosenberg (Eds.), *Sociological theory: A book of readings.* New York: Macmillan, 1957.

Skolnick, J. H. *The politics of protest.* New York: Simon & Schuster, 1969.

Slobin, D. I. Some aspects of the use of pronouns of address in Yiddish. *Word,* 1963, **19,** 193–202.

Slobin, D. I., Miller, S. H., & Porter, L. W. Forms of address and social relations in a business organization. *Journal of Personality and Social Psychology,* 1968, **8,** 289–293.

Smelser, N. J. *Theory of collective behavior.* New York: Free Press of Glencoe, 1963.

Smith, E. E. The power of dissonance techniques to change attitudes. *Public Opinion Quarterly*, 1961, **25**, 626–639.

Smith, G. J. W., Spence, D. P., & Klein, G. S. Subliminal effects of verbal stimuli. *Journal of Abnormal and Social Psychology*, 1959, **59**, 167–176.

Smith, M. B. An analysis of two measures of "authoritarianism" among Peace Corps teachers. *Journal of Personality*, 1965, **33**, 513–535.

Smith, M. B., Bruner, J. S., & White, R. W. *Opinions and personality.* New York: Wiley, 1956.

Solomon, R. L., & Howes, D. H. A note on McGinnies' "Emotionality and perceptual defense." *Psychological Review*, 1950, **57**, 229–234.

Sommer, R. The distance for comfortable conversation: A further study. *Sociometry*, 1962, **25**, 111–116.

Sommer, R. Further studies of small group ecology. *Sociometry*, 1965, **28**, 337–348.

Sommer, R. Man's proximate environment. *Journal of Social Issues*, 1966, **22**, 59–70.

Sommer, R. Sociofugal space. *American Journal of Sociology*, 1967, **72**, 654–660.

Spence, D. P., & Ehrenberg, B. Effects of oral deprivation on responses to subliminal and supraliminal verbal food stimuli. *Journal of Abnormal and Social Psychology*, 1964, **69**, 10–18.

Staats, A., & Staats, C. Attitudes established by classical conditioning. *Journal of Abnormal and Social Psychology*, 1958, **57**, 37–40.

Stager, P. Conceptual level as a composition variable in small-group decision making. *Journal of Personality and Social Psychology*, 1967, **5**, 152–161.

Stampp, K. M. *The peculiar institution: Slavery in the antebellum South.* New York: Vintage Books, Random House, 1964.

Stanton, A. H., & Schwartz, M. S. *The mental hospital: A study of institutional participation in psychiatric illness and treatment.* New York: Basic Books, 1954.

Star, S. A. The public's ideas about mental illness. Mimeographed report. Reprinted by permission of National Opinion Research Center, Study NORC 272. Chicago: University of Chicago, 1955.

Steiner, I. D., & Field, W. L. Role assignment and interpersonal influence. *Journal of Abnormal and Social Psychology*, 1960, **61**, 239–245.

Steinzor, B. The spatial factor in face to face discussion groups. *Journal of Abnormal and Social Psychology*, 1950, **45**, 552–555.

Stevenson, B. (Ed.) *The home book of proverbs, maxims, and familiar phrases.* New York: Macmillan, 1948.

Stock, D. A survey of research on T-Groups. In L. P. Bradford, J. R. Gibb, & K. D. Benne (Eds.), *T-group theory and laboratory method: Innovation in re-education.* New York: Wiley, 1964.

Stoller, F. H. The use of focused feedback via video tape in small groups. In *Explorations in human relations training and research, No. 1.* National Training Laboratories, National Educational Association, 1966.

Stoller, F. H. Group psychotherapy on television: An innovation with hospitalized patients. *American Psychologist*, 1967a, **22**, 158–162.

Stoller, F. H. The long weekend. *Psychology Today*, December 1967b, **1**, 28–33.

Stone, P. J., Dunphy, D. C., Smith, M. S., & Ogilvie, D. M. *The General Inquirer: A computer approach to content analysis.* Cambridge, Mass.: MIT Press, 1966.

Stotland, E., Katz, D., & Patchen, M. The reduction of prejudice through the arousal of self-insight. *Journal of Personality*, 1959, **27**, 507–531.

Stouffer, S. A. *Communism, conformity, and civil liberties: A cross-section of the nation speaks its mind.* (1st ed.) Garden City, N. Y.: Doubleday, 1955.

Stouffer, S. A., Suchman, E. A., De Vinney, L. C., Star, S. A., & Williams, R. M., Jr. *The American soldier.* Vol. 1. *Adjustment during army life.* Princeton, N. J.: Princeton University Press, 1949a.

Stouffer, S. A., Lumsdaine, A. A., Lumsdaine, M. H., Williams, R. M., Jr., Smith, M. B., Janis, I. L., Star, S. A., & Cottrell, L. S., Jr. *The American soldier.* Vol. 2, *Combat and its aftermath.* Princeton: Princeton University Press, 1949b.

Strauss, M. A., & Houghton, L. J. Achievement, affiliation, and co-operation values as clues to trends in American rural society, 1924–1958. *Rural Sociology*, 1960, **25**, 394–403.

Strodtbeck, F. L. Family interaction, values and achievement. In D. C. McClelland (Ed.), *Talent and society.* Princeton, N. J.: Van Nostrand, 1958.

Strodtbeck, F. L., & Hook, L. H. The social dimensions of a twelve-man jury table. *Sociometry*, 1961, **24**, 397–415.

Suedfeld, P. Conceptual and environmental complexity as factors in attitude change. Doctoral dissertation, Princeton University, 1963.

Sullivan, H. S. *Conceptions of modern psychiatry.* Washington, D. C.: William Alanson White Psychiatric Foundation, 1947.

Sullivan, H. S. *The interpersonal theory of psychiatry.* H. S. Perry & M. L. Gawel (Eds.) New York: Norton, 1953.

Sullivan, H. S. *The psychiatric interview.* H. S. Perry & M. L. Gawel (Eds.) New York: Norton, 1954.

Sundermeyer, N. Take a look at tomorrow: "No vacancy" says Mother Earth. In "California living," *San Francisco Sunday Examiner and Chronicle*, April 7, 1968, 16–17.

Swanberg, W. A. *Citizen Hearst: A biography of William Randolph Hearst.* New York: Bantam, 1963.

Taeuber, I. B. Demographic transitions and population problems in the United States. *Annals of the American Academy of Political and Social Science*, 1967, **369**, 131–140.

Taft, R. Selective recall and memory distortion of favorable and unfavorable material. *Journal of Abnormal and Social Psychology*, 1954, **49**, 23–28.

Tagiuri, R., Bruner, J. S., & Blake, R. R. On the relation between feelings and perception of feelings among members of small groups. In E. E. Maccoby, T. M. Newcomb, & E. L. Hartley (Eds.), *Readings in social psychology.* (3rd ed.) New York: Holt, Rinehart & Winston, 1958.

Taylor, D. W., Berry, P. C., & Block, C. H. Does group participation when using brainstorming facilitate or inhibit creative thinking? *Administrative Science Quarterly*, 1958, **3**, 23–47.

Taylor, F. W. *The principles of scientific management.* New York: Harper, 1911.

Terhune, K. W. Motives, situation, and interpersonal conflict within prisoner's dilemma. *Journal of Personality and Social Psychology Monograph Supplement*, March 1968, **8**, 3, Part 2, 1–24.

Thelen, H. A. *Methods for studying work and emotionality in group operation.* Chicago: Human Dynamics Laboratory, University of Chicago, 1954.

Thelen, H. A. Work-emotionality theory of the group as organism. In S. Koch (Ed.), *Psychology: A study of a science.* Vol. 3. New York: McGraw-Hill, 1959.

Theobald, R. The implications of American physical abundance: With questions and answers. *Annals of the American Academy of Political and Social Science*, 1968, **378**, 11–21.

Thibaut, J. W., & Kelley, H. H. *The social psychology of groups.* New York: Wiley, 1959.

Thomas, W. I., & Znaniecki, F. *The Polish peasant in Europe and America: Monograph of an immigrant group.* Boston: R. G. Badger, 1918–1920.

Thompson, D. F., & Meltzer, L. Communication of emotional intent by facial expression. *Journal of Abnormal and Social Psychology*, 1964, **68**, 129–135.

Thurstone, L. L., & Chave, E. J. *The measurement of attitude: A psychophysical method and some experiments with a scale for measuring attitudes toward the church.* Chicago: University of Chicago Press, 1929.

Tiryakian, E. A. Existential phenomenology and the socio-logical tradition. *American Sociological Review*, 1965, **30**, 674–688.

Toch, H. *The social psychology of social movements*. Indianapolis, Ind.: Bobbs-Merrill, 1965.

Tocqueville, A., de. *Democracy in America*. H. Reeve translation. New York: Knopf, 1945.

Tönnies, F. *Fundamental concepts of sociology*. C. P. Loomis translation. New York: American Book, 1940.

Torrance, E. P. Some consequences of power differences on decision making in permanent and temporary three-man groups. *Research studies, Washington State College*, 1954, **22**, 130–140.

T.R.B. From Washington: The rich always with us. *New Republic*, May 11, 1968, **158**, 4.

T.R.B. From Washington: The Big Issue: *New Republic*, May 18, 1968, **158**, 4.

T.R.B. From Washington: To them that have. *New Republic*, July 13, 1968, **159**, 4.

T.R.B. From Washington: The noose. *New Republic*, May 31, 1969, **160**, 4.

Trent, J. W. Revolution, reformation, and re-evaluation. In E. E. Sampson & H. A. Korn (Eds.), *Student activism and protest*. San Francisco: Jossey-Bass, 1970.

Trent, J. W., & Craise, J. L. Commitment and conformity in the American college. *Journal of Social Issues*, 1967, **23**, 34–51.

Triandis, H. C., Loh, W. D., & Levin, L. A. Race, status, quality of spoken English, and opinions about civil rights as determinants of interpersonal attitudes. *Journal of Personality and Social Psychology*, 1966, **3**, 468–471.

Tupes, E. C., & Christal, R. E. Recurrent personality factors based on trait ratings. U.S.A.F. A.S.D. *Technical Report*, 1961, Numbers 61–67.

Turiel, E. An experimental test of the sequentiality of developmental stages in the child's moral judgments. *Journal of Personality and Social Psychology*, 1966, **3**, 611–618.

Turiel, E. Progressive and regressive aspects of moral development. Mimeographed report. University of California, Berkeley, July, 1969.

Turner, R. H., & Killian, L. M. *Collective behavior*. Englewood Cliffs, N. J.: Prentice-Hall, 1957.

Tymieniecka, A. *Phenomenology and science in contemporary European thought*. New York: Noonday Press, 1962.

Underwood, W. J. Evaluation of laboratory method training. *Journal of the American Society of Training Directors*, 1965, **19**, 34–40.

United Press International. A warning on staggering food crisis facing world. Reported in *San Francisco Sunday Examiner and Chronicle*, June 18, 1967.

The United States Book of Facts, Statistics, and Information, 1966. New York: Pocket Books, 1966.

The United States National (President's) Advisory Commission on Civil Disorders. O. Kerner, chairman. New York: Bantam, 1968.

United States National Commission on the Causes and Prevention of Violence. M. Eisenhower, chairman. Final Report. *To establish justice, to insure domestic tranquility*. Washington, D.C.: United States Government Printing Office, 1969.
Task Force Reports:
Assassination and political violence. J. F. Kirkham, S. G. Levy, & W. J. Crotty, directors.
Crimes of violence. D. J. Mulvihill, M. M. Tumin, & L. A. Curtis, directors.
Firearms and violence in American life. G. D. Newton, Jr., & F. E. Zimring, directors.
Law and order re-considered. J. S. Campbell, J. R. Sahid, & D. P. Stang, directors.
Mass media and violence. R. K. Baker & S. J. Ball, directors.
The politics of protest. J. H. Skolnick, director.

Violence in America: Historical and comparative perspectives. H. D. Graham & T. Gurr, directors.
Investigative Reports:
Miami report. L. J. Hector & P. L. E. Helliwell, directors.
Rights in concord. J. R. Sahid, director.
Rights in conflict. D. Walker, director.
Shoot-out in Cleveland. L. H. Masotti & J. R. Corsi, directors.
Shut it down! A college in crisis. W. H. Orrick, Jr., director.

Urwick, L. W. *The elements of administration*. New York: Harper, 1944.

van den Berghe, P. L. *Race and racism: A comparative perspective*. New York: Wiley, 1967.

Verinis, J. S., Brandsma, J. M., & Cofer, C. N. Discrepancy from expectation in relation to affect and motivation: Tests of McClelland's hypothesis. *Journal of Personality and Social Psychology*, 1968, **9**, 47–58.

Vernon, J. A., & Hoffman, J. Effects of sensory deprivation on learning rate in human beings. *Science*, 1956, **123**, 1074–1075.

Vernon, J. A., & McGill, T. E. The effect of sensory deprivation upon rote learning. *American Journal of Psychology*, 1957, **70**, 637–639.

Verplanck, W. S. The control of the content of conversation: Reinforcement of statements of opinion. *Journal of Abnormal and Social Psychology*, 1955, **51**, 668–676.

Volkart, E. H. (Ed.). *Social behavior and personality: Contributions of W. I. Thomas to theory and social research*. New York: Social Science Research Council, 1951.

Wachtel, P. L. Conceptions of broad and narrow attention. *Psychological Bulletin*, 1967, **68**, 417–429.

Walker, C. R. *Toward the automatic factory: A case study of men and machines*. New Haven, Conn.: Yale University Press, 1957.

Walker, E. L., & Heyns, R. W. *An anatomy for conformity*. Belmont Calif.: Brooks/Cole, 1967. ©1962, 1967 by Wadsworth Publishing Co., Inc. Reprinted by permission.

Wallach, M. A., Kogan, N., & Bem, D. J. Group influence on individual risk taking. *Journal of Abnormal and Social Psychology*, 1962, **65**, 75–86.

Wallach, M. A., Kogan, M., & Bem, D. J. Diffusion of responsibility and level of risk taking in groups. *Journal of Abnormal and Social Psychology*, 1964, **68**, 263–274.

Wallach, M. A., & Wing, C. W., Jr. Is risk a value? *Journal of Personality and Social Psychology*, 1968, **9**, 101–106.

Walster, E. Assignment of responsibility for an accident. *Journal of Personality and Social Psychology*, 1966, **3**, 73–79.

Waly, P., & Cook, S. W. Attitude as a determinant of learning and memory: A failure to confirm. *Journal of Personality and Social Psychology*, 1966, **4**, 280–288.

Warner, L. G., & DeFleur, M. L. Attitude as an interactional concept: Social constraint and social distance as intervening variables between attitudes and action. *American Sociological Review*, 1969, **34**, 153–169.

Watson, J. B. *Behaviorism*. New York: Norton, 1925.

Watts, W. A., & McGuire, W. J. Persistence of induced opinion change and retention of inducing message content. *Journal of Abnormal and Social Psychology*, 1964, **68**, 233–241.

Weber, M. *The Protestant Ethic and the spirit of capitalism*. T. Parsons translation. New York: Scribner's, 1930.

Weber, M. Class, status, party. In H. H. Gerth & C. W. Mills (translators editors), *From Max Weber: Essays in sociology*. New York: Oxford University Press, 1946.

Weber, M. *The theory of social and economic organization*. T. Parsons & A. M. Henderson translation. New York: Oxford University Press, 1947.

Wellman, D. Lecture given October 31, 1968 at University of California, Berkeley.

Westie, F. R. The American dilemma: An empirical test. *American Sociological Review*, 1965, **30**, 527–538.

White, B. J., & Harvey, O. J. Effects of personality and own stand on judgment and production of statements about a central issue. *Journal of Experimental Social Psychology*, 1965, **1**, 334–347.

White, R. K. Misperception and the Vietnam War. *Journal of Social Issues*, 1966, **22**, (Whole issue).

White, R. W. Motivation reconsidered: The concept of competence. *Psychological Review*, 1959, **66**, 297–333.

Whiteman, M., & Deutsch, M. Social disadvantage as related to intellective and language development. In M. Deutsch, I. Katz, & A. R. Jensen (Eds.), *Social class, race, and psychological development*. New York: Holt, Rinehart & Winston, 1968.

Whiting, J. W. M. Sorcery, sin, and the superego: A cross-cultural study of some mechanisms of social control. In M. R. Jones (Ed.), *Nebraska Symposium on Motivation*. Lincoln: University of Nebraska Press, 1959.

Whitten, L. H. 15-city study of Negroes. *San Francisco Sunday Examiner and Chronicle*, July 28, 1968.

Whorf, B. L. *Language, thought and reality: Selected writings*. J. B. Carroll (Ed.). Cambridge, Mass.: Technology Press of MIT, 1956.

Wiest, W. M. A quantitative extension of Heider's theory of cognitive balance applied to interpersonal perception and self-esteem. *Psychological Monographs*, 1965, **79**, (14, Whole No. 607).

Wild, C. Creativity and adaptive regression. *Journal of Personality and Social Psychology*, 1965, **2**, 161–169.

Will, R. E., & Vatter, H. G. (Eds.). *Poverty in affluence: The social, political and economic dimensions of poverty in the United States*. New York: Harcourt, Brace, 1965.

Wilson, J., Williams, N., & Sugarman, B. *Introduction to moral education*. Baltimore, Md.: Penguin Books, 1967.

Winch, R. F. *Mate selection: A study of complementary needs*. New York: Harper, 1958.

Wirth, L. Urbanism as a way of life. *American Journal of Sociology*, 1938, **44**, 1–24.

Wishner, J. Reanalysis of "Impressions of Personality." *Psychological Review*, 1960, **67**, 96–112.

Witkin, H. A., Dyk, R. B., Fattuson, H. F., Goodenough, D. R., & Karp, S. A. *Psychological differentiation: Studies of development*. New York: Wiley, 1962.

Witkin, H. A., Goodenough, D. R., & Karp, S. A. Stability of cognitive style from childhood to young adulthood. *Journal of Personality and Social Psychology*, 1967, **7**, 291–300.

Witkin, H. A., Lewis, H. B., Hertzman, M., Machover, K., Meissner, P. B., & Wapner, S. *Personality through perception: An experimental and clinical study*. New York: Harper, 1954.

Wolfbein, S. L. Automation and skill. *Annals of the American Academy of Political and Social Science*, 1962, **340**, 53–59.

Wolfe, T. *The kandy-kolored tangerine-flake streamline baby*. New York: Pocket Books, 1965.

Wolin, S., & Schaar, J. Berkeley: The battle of People's Park. *The New York Review of Books*, June 19, 1969, **12**, 24–31.

Worsley, P. *The trumpet shall sound: A study of "cargo" cults in Melanesia*. London: MacGibbon & Kee, 1957.

Worthy, J. C. Organizational structure and employee morale. *American Sociological Review*, 1950, **15**, 169–179.

Wrench, D., Endicott, K. Denial of affect and conformity. *Journal of Personality and Social Psychology*, 1965, **1**, 484–486.

Wrightsman, L. S. Personality and attitudinal correlates of trusting and trustworthy behaviors in a two-person game. *Journal of Personality and Social Psychology*. 1966, **4**, 328–332.

Yinger, J. M. *Toward a field theory of behavior: Personality and social structure*. New York: McGraw-Hill, 1965.

Young, P. C. Antisocial uses of hypnosis. In L. M. Le Cron (Ed.), *Experimental hypnosis*. New York: Macmillan, 1952.

Zajonc, R. B. The concepts of balance, congruity, and dissonance. *Public Opinion Quarterly*, 1960a, **24**, 280–296.

Zajonc, R. B. The process of cognitive tuning in communication. *Journal of Abnormal and Social Psychology*, 1960b, **61**, 159–168.

Zajonc, R. B. *Social psychology: An experimental approach*. Belmont, Calif.: Wadsworth, 1966.

Zajonc, R. B. Attitudinal effects of mere exposure. *Journal of Personality and Social Psychology Monograph Supplement*, June 1968, **9**, 2, Part 2, 1–27.

Zajonc, R. B., & Burnstein, E. The learning of balanced and unbalanced social structures. *Journal of Personality*, 1965, **33**, 153–163.

Zeitlin, M. Economic insecurity and the political attitudes of Cuban workers. *American Sociological Review*, 1966, **31**, 35–51.

Zeller, A. F. An experimental analogue of repression, II: The effect of individual failure and success on memory measured by relearning. *Journal of Experimental Psychology*, 1950, **40**, 411–422.

Zinn, H. Marxism and the New Left. In A. L. Young (Ed.), *Dissent: Explorations in the history of American radicalism*. DeKalb, Ill.: Northern Illinois University Press, 1968.

Zipf, S. G. Resistance and conformity under reward and punishment. *Journal of Abnormal and Social Psychology*, 1960, **61**, 102–109.

Zuckerman, M. The effects of subliminal suggestion on verbal productivity. *Journal of Abnormal and Social Psychology*, 1960, **60**, 404–441.

Zuckerman, M., & Cohen, N. Sources of reports of visual and auditory sensations in perceptual isolation experiments. *Psychological Bulletin*, 1964, **62**, 1–20.

NAME INDEX

SUBJECT INDEX

473

campus protest (unrest) *(cont.)*
　also civil rights protest movement; student protest movement
capitalism, 2, 139, 203, 207, 330, 387
career of a social movement, 359, 362–363; *see also* civil rights protest movement; social movement; student protest movement
cargo cult, 348
caste relationship, 290–291
castration anxiety, 158
catharsis, & mass media, 341
causal models & causality, external, 37–40; *see also* origin of action vs. pawn laws, 22
　personal, 206–208, 323–324, 443
　phenomenal, 35
　social, 207–208
censorship, 184, 353
change agent, 230, 232–235, 236, 237, 241, 243, 245, 250–251, 253, 257, 272, 274, 276, 294, 302, 347
　& cooperative orientation, 272
　ethics & responsibility of, 233–234, 241, 319
　independence of change from, 299, 302
　motivation of, 232, 233, 236
　role of social movement as, 361–362, 364
　training of, 280
change in response to social influence, degree of voluntarism in, 302
　dependence of on influence agent, 298, 300
　permanence of, 300, 302, 307–308
　public vs. private, 298–299
　rewards vs. punishments in, 299
change, developmental, *see* developmental change
　toward health in groups, 287
　planned, *see* planned change
　process of, 240–243, 250–251
　types of, 223
　unplanned, 223, 226
channel factors in the influence process, 235
character, social, 308–309
　of inner-directedness, 208
　of other-directedness, 208
　& security orientation, 208
character disorder, 209–210
charisma, 372, 391, 392
　& authority, 309–310
　& social movements, 361
cheating, 435
Chicago-8 conspiracy trial, 366
Chicano Power, 336
child rearing, 131, 204, 206, 444
choice, 23, 419
　existential view of, 279
　freedom of, 40, 109, 132
city, *see* urban society; urbanization
CIA, 230
civil liberties, 208
civil rights, 220, 384, 385
　demonstrations, 333–334, 384–385
　legislation, 143, 332, 165, 388, 399, 411
　see also civil rights protest movement
civil rights protest movement, 127, 143, 215, 220, 260, 332, 357, 361, 362, 363, 365–366, 367, 383, 385, 389
　career of, 398–412

legitimacy of, 363
origins of, 367–373
personality factors in, 325
societal response to, 398–400
structures of, 384, 385, 382–398
values of vs. societal values, 363
class consciousness, 198
clergymen, ideology of, 194
Clever Hans, 79–80
client system of change, 230–232, 233, 235, 236, 237, 245
cliques, 106, 424
codifiability of languages, 51–53
coercion, 337, 376, 406, 411
cognitive approach to development, 434, 437
　& group composition, 262
　& group performance, 262
cognitive complexity-simplicity, 179–180
　& cognitive balance, 182
　& impression formation, 181–182
cognitive consistency & balance, 33, 38, 100–108, 114–117, 120, 121, 125–128, 131–132, 143, 319–320, 323, 327
　actual vs. perceived differences in, 105–106, 107
　& attitude structure, 114–116
　& behavior change, 104
　& cognitive complexity-simplicity, 181
　& communication, 103, 106–107, 127
　functional bases of, 121, 126, 129–130, 133, 174
　& the influence process, 103, 106
　& learning, 105
　& selective exposure, 174; *see also* perceptual-cognitive selectivity; selective exposure
　similarity vs. complementarity in, 107
cognitive function of attitudes, 315 31–35
cognitive principles of organization,
cognitive process (model, theory), 8, 20, 22, 24, 28, 31–32, 48, 49, 56, 86, 105–106, 107–109, 225, 331, 358
cognitive sensitivity in T-groups, 277
cognitive states in groups, 283–284
cognitive style, *see* perceptual-cognitive style
cognitive system, 101, 114, 174
　complexity vs. simplicity of, 181–182
　differentiation of, 172–173, 177, 178, 179, 180, 181, 262
　organization & integration of, 172–173, 178–179, 180, 181
cognitive tuning, 172–173
cohesiveness, 64, 128, 241, 249, 259, 260, 286, 292
　community, 373–374
　& conflict, 260
　society, 134, 260
collective behavior, 18–19, 123–124, 357–362, 371–372, 379, 383
　role of rumor in, 172
　theories of, 358–359
　see also social movement
collectivism vs. individualism, 201–204
colonialism, 384
　colonizer-colonized relationship, 213–222, 384–385
　ideology of colonizer, 216–219
　modern forms of, 375–377
　Third World model of revolution, 384–385

commitment, 279
　behavioral, 303
　in collective behavior, 358
　to convention, & moral development, 438
　decision-making, 242, 243, 244, 261–262
　to draft resistance, 442
　to a group, 287, 289, 345
　public, 243, 318
　to a social movement, 361, 395, 406, 411
　to values in a society, 308
common sense, 102
　personality theory, 5–8
commune, 140–141
communication, 28, 80, 81, 82, 103, 136, 169, 232, 247–248, 250, 259, 269, 270, 271, 272, 273, 275, 281, 292, 347, 404
　in attitude-change research, 230; *see also* attitude change
　covert, 81–82
　defensive & nondefensive, 276
　& development of social movements, 371–372
　& deviation, 126–127
　& diffusion, 348–350
　double-bind, *see* double-bind communication
　kinesic, 61, 65–69
　nonverbal, 32, 61–71
　paralinguistic, 61, 69–71, 82
　persuasive, 50, 58, 297, 300–302, 312–314, 330, 339; *see also* influence process
　proxemic, 61, 62–65
　tactile, 61–62
　& trust, 271–272
　two-step flow of, & role of mass media, 347
communications media, 338–356, 426; *see also* mass media
　hot vs. cool, 344
communications model of change, 235–236
communication network, 64, 168, 172–173, 247–248, 339
communicator factors in influence process, 235–236, 300, 312–313, 322–324
Communists (Communism), 184, 194, 202, 208, 215–216, 254, 398, 306–307, 398, 403
community, 210, 225, 226, 230–231, 232–233, 246, 248, 275, 276, 280, 321, 328, 336, 339, 351, 394, 406, 417–418, 430, 440, 445
　new sense of in student protest movement, 408–409, 411
　traditional sense of, 373, 378
community organization, 230, 232, 237, 371
comparison level, see interaction
compatibility, 42, 286
　of interpersonal orientations, 286–287
competence, development of sense of 417
　motivation, 44–46, 276
competition, 194, 203–205, 409
　as ideology, 201–202
competitive orientation, 269–273
　development of distrust, 271

income, of defense contractors, **377**
    differentials in & development of a
        social movement, 368–369
    distribution of in U.S., 368
    & educational level, 368, 383
    of farm workers, 368
    level of & attitudes toward Negroes,
        399
    of nonwhites vs. whites, 368
    & social class, 134
independence, 240, 242, 388, 389, 433,
    446
    of change from change agent, 250,
        268
    in communication networks, 248; *see
        also* autonomy
    as direction of human development,
        434
    as interpersonal orientation, 282, 286,
        323
    as a value, 322
indeterminacy principle in psychological
    research, 83
Indians, American, 202, 221, 369–371
    ideological justifications about, 216
    life conditions of, 369–370
    treatment of, 216
indifference point in judgments, 95–97;
    see also adaptation level
individualism vs. collectivism, 19, 201,
    202
industrial psychology, 251–253
industrialization, 374, 419, 430
    manpower needed for, 363
    & the new industrial state, 375, 377
    & technostructure as a source of
        power, 375
inference process in person perception,
    7, 34–45, 443
influence agent (source), 35, 36, 37
    act of, 296–297
    characteristics of, 302, 322
    see also communicator factors in the
        influence process
influence process, 204, 242, 289, 296–337
    & cognitive consistency, 103, 106
    & communication, 103
    & group conformity pressures, 241
    & the mass media, 346, 351
    nature (form) of influence, 296, 298,
        301, 322
    personality factors in, 297
    public vs. private change in, 298–308
    relation of influence agent to target,
        296–297, 302
    risky-shift effect, 265–266
    & sharing of influence, 272
    as social exchange, 139, 320, 321, 323,
        324–326, 333, 334, 337
    in traditional society, 373
    see also resistance to influence &
        change
information, deprivation of, *see* sensory
    deprivation
    processing, 262, 263
    seeking, 85, 88
ingratiation, 42–46, 221, 312
    & conformity behavior, 320, 322
inhibitions and restraints, vs. expression
    of emotions, 341
    of behavior open to public scrutiny,
        328
    in a society, 280

initiation, & cognitive dissonance,
    110–111
innate forms of behavior, 225
inner-directed social character, 41, 208,
    308–309, 311
innovation, 318
    & creativity, 254
    diffusion of, 348, 349
    in problem-solving groups, 254, 261,
        262, 320
    technological, 197, 225, 230, 349, 425,
        426, 427, 432
insight, 282
    & attitude change, 317
instincts, 16, 17, 18, 19, 20, 367
institutionalization process, & collective
    behavior, 359
    & career of a social movement, 364
integration, 326, 328–329, 365
    & black separatism, 365
    protests over, 366; *see also* civil rights
        protest movement
    of public facilities, 302, 332
    of schools, 315, 331, 332
integrity, 175, 199, 219
intellectual disposition, 212, 446
intellectualization as defense mecha-
    nism, 284
intelligence (intellect), 331, 417
    & attitude change, 312
    effects of social deprivation on, 217–
        218
    genetic determination of, 430
    ideology about differences between
        blacks & whites, 215
    & resistance to influence, 318
intention, 35, 39, 40, 42, 43, 44, 45, 54,
    55, 66, 416, 443
    of communication source, 235
    see also accidental vs. intentional ac-
        tion; motivation; purpose
interaction, 34, 49, 58, 62–63, 75, 107,
    207, 247, 275, 286
    analysis of, 289
    changes in, technological innovation,
        226
    coding of, 126, 157, 249
    distortions in, 283
    exchange model of, 140, 324, 333
    & eye contact, 67
    freedom of in communication net-
        works, 247–248
    individual rates of, 249
    & interdependence, 129–130
    as orientation of individual, 283–288
    rewards, costs, & outcomes in, 97–99,
        138, 139, 322–323
    & seating arrangement, 63, 64, 65
    shared assumptions of, 121
    standards for evaluation of, 97
interdependence, 108, 129–130, 179, 231,
    247, 269, 270, 418, 433
    of attitude components, 327
    & coordination of interaction, 129–130
    & Zeigarnik effect, 166
internal locus of behavior control, 36,
    308, 336
    vs. external locus, 324–325
internal system of a group, 248–250; *see
    also* socioemotional system
internalization, in the influence process,
    299–303, 307–311
    & moral development, 437

    of norms, 436
    of parental standards, 437
    & social control, 434
    of values, & type of discipline used,
        444
interpersonal orientation, 283–288
    changes of, 291
    & group performance, 262
intersubjective meaning, 25
intimacy, 58, 239, 245, 277, 280, 286, 288,
    352, 373
    as dimension of interpersonal relation-
        ships, 288, 289, 291
    in groups, 284, 288
    individual orientations to, 282, 283, 289
    nonverbal cues in, 62, 63, 64, 65
    problems with, 282, 283
irrationality, 16, 315, 358, 359, 364, 398

Jackson State College (Miss.), 366, 390,
    407
judgmental process model, 93–99
    & social judgments, 93–97
justice, 38, 235, 260, 448
    & cognitive consistency, 138
    as equity vs. equality, 139–141
    in exchange theory, 138–139
    as goal of contemporary protest move-
        ments, 384–385, 388
    & injustice, 355, 372, 373, 385, 399
    & moral development, 438, 440, 441
    for Negroes, 362
    & resource distribution, 135
    & social-comparison processes, 137–
        139
    & status consistency, 143–137
    as a value, 367
justification, 196
    & the American dilemma, 331, 333
    & collective behavior, 259
    of colonialism, 216–217
    & ideology, 204, 213
    of inconsistency between attitudes and
        behavior, 328
    & moral development, 438, 443
    of slavery, 213–214, 215
    & social movements, 361–363, 382, 403
    society's makers of, 363
    of status differences between groups,
        216–217
    of treatment of American Indians, 216
    & violence, 341, 403
    see also ideology; legitimacy

Kent State College (Ohio), 366, 390, 407
knowledge, of action's consequences,
    35, 39, 40, 45
    evaluation of, 195
    as function of attitudes, 316
    legitimacy of, 202; *see also* legitimacy
    process, 2, 4, 5, 8, 11, 22, 27, 28
    relational quality of, 196
    social & historical factors in, 193–195,
        198–199, 202–203, 205
    styles of, 196–197, 198
    system of, 2
knowledge society, 422
    & end of ideology, 199–200
Kwakiutl, 201–202

labor, manual, 249, 167, 183
    sparsity of, 420
labor force, 422

validity (*cont.*)
   of societal model of reality, 132
   of thought & knowledge, 195, 200
value, 3, 27, 101, 103, 106, 115–116, 132,
      156, 185, 193, 195, 197, 205, 241,
      246, 308, 316, 332, 348, 367, 374,
      386, 394, 433, 435, 436, 437, 438,
      440, 441, 447
   acceptance of, 397
   of American creed, 214, 331, 332, 362,
      367, 386, 387, 388, 389
   & bias, 240, 378, 382
   & change agent's role, 235; *see also*
      change agent
   conflicts over, 359, 379
   of democracy vs. technological
      society, 387
   internalization of, 435, 444
   in modern, technological society, 375,
      435
   & moral development, 440
   & perceptual vigilance & defense, 156
   & the risky-shift effect, 265
   & selectivity of diffusion, 350
   & social movements, 359, 363, 378
   in T-groups, 283
   universal or societal, 441
value change, 233, 331
   in brainwashing, 307
value-expressive function of attitudes,
    316
value-oriented social movement, 384,
    385, 386
   vs. norm-oriented social movement,
     361–362
value system, 207, 325, 362
   as factor limiting diffusion, 350
   of social movement, 363
vested interest, 193, 195, 199, 200, 238,
    268
victim, 38–39, 45, 217, 244, 331, 336, 426
   dehumanization of, 429
   devaluation of, 38–39
   of double-bind communication, 382;
    see also double-bind communication
Vietnam & Vietnam War, 36, 47, 165, 170,
    337, 351, 377, 404, 407, 441–443, 447
   distortions in perception of, 175–176
   perceptual-cognitive selectivity in,
    175–176
   protest over, 363–364, 386, 410–411;
    see also student protest movement
videotape, feedback of self by, 69
violence, 170, 217, 337, 381, 388, 389–
    390, 393, 398, 400, 401, 421, 426;
    see also aggression
   & career of a social movement, 363
   & fantasy behavior, 340
   legitimization of, 341, 342, 403–404
   & mass media, 339, 340–342
   & radicalization process, 406
   social & political definitions of, 403–
    404
   as society's response to protest move-
    ments, 366
   types & frequence of, in protest move-
    ments, 366
voice quality, 278
   & impression formation, 70–71, 353
   & nonverbal communication, 61, 69–71
voting behavior, 173–175, 236, 399
   cross-pressure in, 135

   & mass media, 343–344, 346–347, 350

war, 238, 239, 306–307, 326, 338, 341,
    356, 363–334, 366, 377, 387, 401,
    404, 405, 410, 430, 433, 434, 441–
    442, 443, 446, 447; *see also* Vietnam
Watts, insurrection (riot) in, 70, 365, 372,
    390, 392–393
   reaction of whites to, 399
Weltanschauung, 50, 53
wishful thinking & perceptual-cognitive
    selectivity, 116, 151–152
withdrawal as psychological defense,
    103, 325
women, & role playing, 221
   word association, 52, 188, 189
work, 38, 44–46, 373
   alienation from, 376; *see also* aliena-
    tion
   attitudes toward, 350, 431
   in exchange theory, 138
   in Protestant Ethic, 139
worker, 203
   & automated technology, 423–424, 428
   skill level & employment opportuni-
    ties, 368
   white- vs. blue collar, 203, 422–423

youth culture, 396–397, 430
   clothing of, 280, 297, 349, 382, 389,
    396, 409
   & hair length, 297, 349, 390, 396, 405
   music of, 349, 350, 389, 397, 408, 409

Zeitgeist, 16, 17, 18, 19, 198, 199, 277,
    358, 447–448
Zeigarnik effect, 166–167; *see also*
    memory & recall
zero-sum game, 270–271, 405
zuñi, 18, 201–202